HELLENISTIC
CIVILIZATION

HELLENISTIC CIVILIZATION

FRANÇOIS CHAMOUX

Translated by Michel Roussel
(in cooperation with Margaret Roussel)

Blackwell Publishing

350 Main Street, Malden, MA 02148-5018, USA
108 Cowley Road, Oxford OX4 1JF, UK
550 Swanston Street, Carlton South, Melbourne, Victoria 3053, Australia
Kurfürstendamm 57, 10707 Berlin, Germany

First published 1981 in French by Arthand as *La civilisation hellénistique*
First published 2003 in English by Blackwell Publishers Ltd, a Blackwell Publishing
company

Transferred to digital print 2006

Library of Congress Cataloging-in-Publication Data

Chamoux, François.
   [Civilisation hellénistique. English]
   Hellenistic civilization / François Chamoux ; translated by Michel
Roussel.
      p. cm.
   The present translation has benefitted from a revision of the original
by the author.
   Includes bibliographical references and index.
   ISBN 0–631–22241–3 — ISBN 0–631–22242–1 (pbk)
   1. Hellenism.   2. Greece—Civilization—To 146 B.C. I. Title.
DF77 .C4613 2001
931′.08—dc21

                       2002000877

A catalogue record for this title is available from the British Library.

For further information on
Blackwell Publishing, visit our website:
http://www.blackwellpublishing.com

CONTENTS

PLATES

FIGURES

MAPS

FOREWORD TO THE 1981 EDITION

This book is a sequel to an earlier work on the civilization of Archaic and Classical Greece. It begins with a review of the main historical events, followed by a number of chapters aimed at defining the themes of the period. The broad geographical framework of this period, the abundance and diversity of the supporting documents, the crucial role played by individuals – all mean that it is more difficult than for earlier periods of Greek history to gain an overall view. The pace and tempo of the narrator's account will accordingly vary in keeping with the uneven quality of available data. It will be for the reader to judge if any loss of clarity as a result is balanced by a greater awareness of the complex nature of reality.

This is an essay in personal assessment, in which, after years of reading, travel, and critical reflection on texts and monuments, the author has tried to express the viewpoints suggested to him over the years by many different pieces of work. Exhaustiveness has not been his aim, but candor. As he mistrusts ideological stances and systematization, he prefers to indicate the contours of various pieces of work by the study of concrete examples. He has no wish to speak of sites he has never seen, texts he has not translated, or archaeological monuments he has not had the time to examine with his own eyes. Indeed, dealing with such a vast subject, who can boast of not often relying on others? Even so, one should whenever possible go straight to first-hand documentation, with specialized help when it is needed. This can be a humbling effort, but it is a reassuring one in the final analysis.

It remains for me to acknowledge my debt to those without whom this work would not have seen the light of day. I have in mind first and foremost those scholars from a variety of nationalities, belonging to numerous scientific disciplines, whose immense and unremitting effort gathers the scattered data of history, makes them accessible to those with an interest in them, and gradually brings to light their meaning. Little is known to the wider public of the amount of cheerful sacrifice entailed in the relentless labor of scholars who devote a lifetime to peering into manuscripts, classifying shards, getting stones to make sense. Beyond doctrinal disagreement or personal strife, from which the republic of historians, philologists, and archaeologists is no more immune than any other human group, a common faith unites them – a constant quest, sometimes awkward and flawed, but always a passionate one, for a vanished reality. Every scholar brings his or her own ray of light, and the contours of Truth emerge slowly with the passing years from a number of studies devoted to particular points. Whoever tries at one time or another to take stock of progress to date, as I have tried to do, feels indebted to all his colleagues.

FOREWORD TO THE 2002 ENGLISH TRANSLATION

A book that I presented for the first time to the French public in 1981 is now available to a new readership in its English version. For this I am indebted to the friendship and initiative of Professor Michel Roussel of the University of Ottawa. With Margaret Roussel's constant help, he undertook the arduous task of making the content of this volume accessible to English-speaking readers, giving it renewed youth and vigor. I am very grateful to them both, as well as to Anne-Marie Georgi-Roussel and Dominique Roussel, whose assistance in their parents' endeavor proved invaluable.

After a twenty-year interval, an essay in synthesis like the present one demands careful revision in the light of recent scholarly production. The guiding thought to which I gave expression at the time does not appear to have lost its relevance. In the work of revision I received the valued help of Professor Claude Vial, of the University of Montpellier, who also provided me with a number of additions to the bibliography. I should not have been able to give the book an indispensable updating without her assistance. I am very much in her debt.

I wish also to tender thanks to Professor Arthur Eckstein, of the University of Maryland, for his extremely helpful critical evaluation of the book; and to Professors Waldemar Heckel, of the University of Calgary, and John Yardley, of the University of Ottawa, whose advice guided Michel Roussel in the inception and execution of his project. Special thanks are due to Professor Heckel for the finishing touches he brought to the bibliography. My colleagues Edmund Bloedow and Symphorien Van de Maele showed interest in the project, and gave assistance whenever this was needed. To them and to those I have mentioned I wish to express my heartfelt appreciation.

Finally a tribute is due to Blackwell Publishers for promptly responding to Professor Roussel's approach. To them and their courteous, helpful, and efficient staff my friend Michel and myself are very grateful.

FRANÇOIS CHAMOUX
Paris, January 2001

A Note on the 2002 English Translation

The present translation has benefited from a revision of the 1985 paperback edition by the author. Thanks are due to Blackwell Publishers' reviewer, Professor Waldemar Heckel, of the University of Calgary, for his perceptive and constructive appraisal; and to Professor Arthur Eckstein, of the University of Maryland, who revised parts of the translation, notably where Roman history was concerned, and provided a number of historical complements. New features of the book are chronological tables, a lexicon of terms, an index, illustrations and additional maps borrowed from the 1981 (hardback) edition, and the use of cross-referencing. The bibliography has been enlarged and updated. The number of town plans has been reduced. Greek proper and place names have been Latinized (which for the most part means that the endings -*os* and -*oi* have become -*us* and -*i*, and -*ai* as an ending or a diphthong has become -*ae*).

INTRODUCTION

Here is my shield, Ares, god of war. Take as well the trappings of my horses – they
  glow and sparkle!
This staue of Victory, so Eupolemus proclaims, shall be King Magas' noble share.
  Under her wing, may your dominions, your cities, your people remain safe.
                              Epigram in the style of Callimachus, *c.*280 BC; the inscription carved
                                    on a block of gray marble found in the harbor of Cyrene on 1954:
                                        see pp. 218–19, and *Bulletin de correspondance hellénique,*
                                                            82, 1958, pp. 571–87.

■ *Definition of the term* Hellenistic ■ *Our sources: the insufficiency
of literary texts, the overabundance of inscriptions and papyri, the
uncertainty of archaeological data*

The term *Hellenistic* was first used as a qualifying adjective for the Greek language, tinged with Hebraisms, which was used by the Hellenized Jews – for
example, those who, in the reign of Ptolemy Philadelphus, translated the Bible
into the Septuagint as it is called (for more about this term, see the lexicon).
Much later, in the mid-nineteenth century, the German scholar J. G. Droysen
started the widespread use of the word *Hellenismus* to designate the period in
ancient history that stretches from the beginning of Alexander's reign (336 BC)
to the battle of Actium (31 BC) which established Octavian (the emperor Augustus)
as master of the Roman world. It has no exact equivalent in English or French.
Since that time it has been customary to call this three-century period Hellenistic, as well as the civilization that took shape during that time in the Greek world.
The term thus provides a convenient demarcation from the previous ages of
Archaic and Classical Greece, and the civilizations that characterize them. Alexander's venture and its aftermath brought about a deep change in the mind-set
of the Greeks. The broadening effect on their culture, the seminal character of
the discoveries made in that period by their scholars, their thinkers, their engineers, and their artists in every area of their activity, deserve to be studied in their

own right. In attempting such a study, we shall aim to throw light on the originality and historical importance of a period too often rated in the public imagination, even in our own day, as merely one of transition between the brilliance of Classical Athens and the majesty of Imperial Rome.

We are faced with a difficult task. This is because, for those three centuries, we no longer have at our disposal synthetic surveys of the essential facts, with ordered perspectives, provided in the earlier period by the *Histories* of Herodotus, Thucydides, or Xenophon. This does not mean that the period in question aroused no interest in the ancient world. On the contrary, the rich content and varied nature of its events, the fascination exercised by individual actors, its geographical diversity aroused widespread interest. There was no dearth of learned writers, followed in the course of time by numerous compilers, who were at pains to respond to such an appetite for knowledge. Their writings were sometimes the history of one individual city or another, sometimes ambitious universal histories in which the changing fate of nations and the unsteady fortunes of kings were shown in a light that would urge the reader to meditation. But these works are all lost, or nearly so. In spite of the aura of Alexander's reign, those who study it are left with nothing but a sadly incomplete indirect tradition.

In the following period there is a dearth of literary sources. Of the numerous memoirs written by actors in the political drama or by contemporaries there remains nothing but rare quotations – brief, garbled ones – or passing references to them. Nothing is left of the great history of the Western Greeks written by the Sicilian Timaeus in the first half of the third century, which stopped at the year 264 BC. There is nothing either of the Athenian Phylarchus, whom a taste for anecdotal writing and an appetite for moralizing predisposed to a dramatization of history, and who recounted in his work those events of the third century which he himself had witnessed. In the next century, Polybius belongs to a different class of observer. But out of the forty books of his work, which told of the events leading to the submission to Rome of the Mediterranean world between 220 and 144 BC, we have only the first five. After an introduction dealing with the first Punic War, they recount the events of the years 220–216. Of the other books nothing remains but more or less extensive fragments. Polybius is an essential source of information for us, though a sadly mutilated one. Diodorus Siculus, who lived under Caesar and Augustus, had compiled in his *Historical Library*, also divided into forty books, a universal history planned as a book of annals – that is, recounting the events year by year – endeavoring, not without some difficulty, to reconcile the Roman and Greek chronologies. For our period, unfortunately, there remain only books XVII to XX, dealing with the years 336–301, those of the reign of Alexander and the first rivalries of the Diadochi (or Successors) of Alexander. All the rest, which gave a continuous and detailed account of Hellenistic history down to the years of the Gallic wars with which the work ended, has disappeared, apart from some quotations preserved in Byzantine compilations. The Gaul Pompeius Trogus, a contemporary of Augustus, had written in Latin his *Philippic Histories*, a sort of universal history, in which the emphasis was put on nations other than the Roman conqueror. What we have left is a wretched muddled summary, made in the third century AD by a certain Justin. The dryness and the clumsy composition of this text do not allow us to draw much benefit from it. This may be the result of Justin having a rhetorical rather than a historical viewpoint (see Yardley and Heckel's commentary on Justin's *Epitome*, 1997: details of it are in the bibliography).

For want of a systematic and unbroken account of the facts, the modern historian feels obliged to attempt to fit into a coherent picture, in spite of intervening gaps, various items of partial evidence that chance has preserved. Such is the case with Plutarch's *Lives*, among which the heroes of the Hellenistic period occupy a choice position. Demetrius Poliorcetes, Eumenes, Pyrrhus, Agis and Cleomenes, Aratus, Philopoemen have won the right to a place beside Alexander the Great in this array of outstanding men, and live before our mind's eye with extraordinary intensity. Certainly Plutarch has no pretensions to historiography, but wants his readers to reflect on human conduct and human destiny. He therefore selects in his hero's biography only those elements that will bring to light his objective, giving precedence to colorful or revealing anecdote over a detailed account of a political or military event. Had we nothing but the *Life* of Alexander to tell us about the conqueror's endeavors, we would remain ignorant of many essential elements of his fantastic venture. But, once this limitation is recognized, Plutarch must be credited with firmly grounded and extensive documentation, which a marvellous sense of drama and an exceptional power of evocation have used with admirable effect. There is no comparison between the powerful pen-pictures of the *Lives* and the pallid historical summaries which Pausanias, a half-century after Plutarch, inserted in his *Description of Greece*. The latter are nevertheless useful in that, for various aspects of the Hellenistic period, they convey reminiscences of lost works which dealt with them.

Contrasting with this dearth of literary sources, the overabundance of raw documents is a cause of just as much difficulty for the historian. Inscriptions are coming to light in extremely large numbers. In spite of the efforts of epigraphists to bring together in handy collections all inscriptions found on the same site or all those relating to the same category of documents, as a rule they remain hard to consult and interpret. This is due not only to the incomplete or mutilated state in which they have reached us; it is also because they raise numerous problems of language, vocabulary, or style. Every city, every sanctuary had its own customs, its institutions, its administrative turns of phrase, sometimes its own dialect. Each text, composed and engraved in a manner conforming with local requirements, was intended for a public who understood easily the language in which they were addressed, the allusions, the formulaic expressions. Today all these demand annotation and explanatory comparison – to put it briefly, scholarly commentary. No inscription can be thoroughly understood without being placed within a series of parallel documents; such a degree of professional insight is acquired only through long years of practice. Thanks to this work historians, while unable to secure an overall view or new insights into events of major importance, to which epigraphic texts refer only rarely, gather by way of compensation a harvest of chance information. This bears on events and institutions of local interest, and revives in infinite variety humanity's daily concerns in its restricted environment. Such is the reality which history writ large tends to neglect. Epigraphy restores it for us, thanks to the raw documents it puts at our disposal, though their multiplicity defies synthesis.

There is another category of raw documents, which first appeared at the outset of the Hellenistic period and proliferated thereafter: the Greek papyri from Egypt. The dry climate of that land allowed the preservation amid garbage heaps or within mummy wrappings of a large number of texts written on papyrus. The Egyptians had mastered its preparation in much earlier times, starting from a plant growing plentifully in the damp soil of the Nile valley. Outside Egypt, in lands where papyrus was in no less common use, a less propitious climate has caused such documents to disappear. The number of Greek papyri from Egypt runs into tens of thousands: they provide nothing but minor evidence, preserved by accident, concerning daily life. None is derived from the royal archives of the Ptolemies, the Greek rulers of Egypt (also called the Lagids, i.e. descendants of Lagus, father of the first Ptolemy). None relates to diplomatic negotiations. They are fragments from the archives of villages or rural domains – remnants of private correspondence, petitions to magistrates or to civil servants in charge of provincial administration, rough drafts or personal ledger accounts, transcriptions of literary texts, even school exercises. Such is their variety, their often puzzling content, the difficulty they present in any attempt at interpretation or commentary. Just like inscriptions, these require a specialized type of scholarship, which is the domain of the papyrologist. Historians need to handle cautiously the abundant indications provided by papyrology of the economic, social, religious, and intellectual life of the Egyptian countryside under Greek sovereignty. They must beware of extrapolation, of extending to the Hellenistic world evidence valid for Egypt alone and explained by this country's particular situation. But, for this privileged area, papyri are a rich source of information, which history must take into account.

In the last source of documentation on our list, interpretation is no less difficult: this is archaeology, which is concerned with architectural and representational monuments, as well as furniture and other equipment. Paradoxically, an archaeologist's chronological criteria are least certain in the Hellenistic period. We shall see later the reasons for such uncertainty. It is a fact that the complex nature of the evolution of styles often puzzles the best-informed specialists in ancient sculpture. This is so true that they hesitate, even in the case of major documents with well-defined characteristics, to assign a probable date – and, if they hazard a guess, the dates they arrive at can be two or three centuries divergent from each other. Even pottery, so useful for chronological purposes until that historical divide, becomes henceforth much less clearly characterized, and is largely bereft of its role as the "guide fossil" in the archaeologist's quest for information. Only numismatics (the study of coins), though as a rule of less value for quality and diversity, remains a precious source of historical information. In the realm of architecture, the domestic habitat is relatively well known, thanks to excavations on Delos and at Priene. But we are in total ignorance (or nearly so) regarding the palaces in which the rulers lived. The architecture of the great urban ensembles can be better grasped, thanks to fine public buildings such as the Stoa of Attalus in the Athenian Agora. Yet one must admit that the main monuments of the Hellenistic period, its temples or public buildings, have not yet aroused an interest leading to studies and publications as numerous as those that proliferate on the least significant remains of monuments in the Archaic or Classical period. Here too our research options remain subordinated to fashion and the passing whims of contemporary taste.

■ *The chronological limits: Alexander's accession to the throne (336 BC) and the battle of Actium (31 BC)*

The information at the historian's disposal is therefore characterized either by an abundance that causes bewilderment (for want of well-established criteria of classification) or by lamentable inadequacy (resulting from the ravages of time). We have to put them to work in the task of restoring to the Hellenistic period its own defining personality in the age-old adventure of Western civilization. Regarding the chronological boundaries within which our account must be confined, there is some divergence – of no essential importance, after all – among scholars. Some believe that the distinguishing features of the Hellenistic world are already perceptible in the middle, or even the beginning, of the fourth century before our era. The year 360 (or thereabouts) has been chosen as a point of departure by scholars who rank as authorities on the subject. In conformity with a more traditional point of view, others prefer to place the start of the Hellenistic period at the death of Alexander on June 13, 323 BC. This has the advantage of using a precise marker linked with an event of major importance. Still another group places the end of the Classical age at the battle of Chaeronea in 338, which spelled the collapse of the Greece of the city-states, faced with the increasing power of the Macedonian monarchy.

Each of these solutions is founded on serious arguments, and there may be reason to hesitate in choosing among them. But debate on this point is really nothing but an academic exercise, for the problem is an artificial one. The evolution of a civilization, and of its customs and mores, however profound it may be, never happens in a sudden, brutal way – barring a cataclysm of universal proportions – but makes its appearance by degrees over the years. It is by retrospective analysis that one can grasp, amid the complex mass of facts – those that prepare, or allow one to perceive in them, the advent of later developments. The choice of a specific chronological limit therefore provides a convenient method of exposition, without in any way claiming to give a full explanation of actual facts. This is why we have chosen as a starting point of our study Alexander the Great's accession to the throne in the summer of 336 BC, after his father's assassination. Earlier attempts and projects of a similar nature had paved the way for his enterprise of conquest; and the new world he brought into being was already in a certain measure sketched before him in the Greek society whose leadership he inherited. The choice of this date, however, underscores the prominent part played by this great man in a major historical phenomenon.

As for the later limit, we shall conform to widely established usage, which places it at the battle of Actium: September 2, 31 BC. On that day, as it did at Marathon, the clash of arms chose between two styles of civilization, one turned toward the Egypt of the Ptolemies and Hellenized Asia, the other dominated by Rome and the Latin tradition. The latter prevailed, and, applying the political system of the Principate, organized the Mediterranean world within a unitary framework, annexing the Hellenistic heritage and taking over Alexander's ambition for a universal monarchy. Until that date, despite Rome's continual and spectacular advances in the east, Roman historiography shares with its Greek counterpart the burden of unfolding the course of events, but each keeping its own perspective: a twofold approach that complicates in no small way the narrator's task. After Actium, on the contrary, history recovers its unity. Rome becomes the hub of the world, and while the eastern half of the Mediterranean goes on speaking Greek and living its daily life in the framework of the *polis*, henceforth it is with reference to Rome that politics, economics, and even culture evolve and undergo transformation. The change is clear-cut, and one can see that it served as a starting point for a new era, as demonstrated by the dating of inscriptions in certain provinces. The fact remains that, from more than one point of view, the kind of life that developed in the Hellenistic period did not disappear entirely after the beginning of the Empire. Sometimes we shall refer to documents which postdate Actium, when they are particularly illustrative of Hellenistic taste, customs, or mores which, considered as an organized whole, were in no way repudiated by the Imperial age. The time has now come to deal with the facts of history.

1/ALEXANDER:
A UNIVERSAL MONARCHY

■ *The young king: his education* ■ *Campaigns in the Balkans*
■ *Thebes revolts and is destroyed* ■ *Preparation for war*
against the Achaemenid Empire

Alexander, the third of that name in the Macedonian dynasty of the Argeads, was hardly 20 years old when, in the summer of 336, the murder of his father Philip was the unexpected cause of his accession to supreme power. In recent times the father–son relationship had grown tense, Philip having abandoned his queen Olympias, mother of Alexander, for the sake of a new marriage with a young Macedonian woman, Cleopatra, who gave him a daughter. But soon after the king's death, the resolute character of the young prince, benefiting from the advice and support of Antipater, one of his father's foremost friends, secured his unchallenged succession. Introduced by Antipater to the assembly of the Macedonian people, he was soon acclaimed and acknowledged as king. At the same time, a series of state-ordered murders brought about the disappearance of (actual or suspected) claimants and adversaries: a first cousin of Alexander's, whom Philip had ousted from power in order to take his place; the child born to Philip by Cleopatra; Cleopatra herself; her uncle Attalus. Such merciless rivalries, such settlements of accounts by bloodshed, were to be a permanent feature during the entire history of Hellenistic monarchies. The Greeks soon invested the new sovereign of Macedon with the same authority as that granted to Philip after his victory over the city-states in 338. The Amphictyonic Council, as well as the Council of the League of Corinth (the puppet alliance of Greek states set up by Philip after that victory), acknowledged his paramount position and confirmed him as head of the federal army which, in compliance with decisions made in 337, was to lead an expedition into Asia against the king of Persia. Alexander took up without any hesitation or delay the grand project devised by his father.

In spite of his youth, he was well prepared for such an endeavor, both at the psychological level and from the point of view of ability. How could the heir to the dynasty of the Argeads, which traced its ancestry to Heracles son of Zeus, not have a sense of his mission? Philip had taken pleasure in commemorating such an illustrious origin by striking, in the very year of Alexander's birth (356), gold coins bearing Heracles' effigy. On the side of his mother Olympias, daughter of Neoptolemus king of Epirus, Alexander's ancestry had its roots in the ancient dynasty of the Aeacids (see the lexicon), descended from Achilles (on the importance for the Greeks of such connections with the heroes of mythology, see pp. 210–11). The twin memory of the achiever of the Twelve Labours and the youthful hero of the *Iliad* was to haunt the mind of the young king, eager to equal their feats. Such a glorious ancestry was in the eyes of the Greeks the hallmark of the Hellenic *persona* of the king of Macedon, who could, on the other hand, rely on the fidelity of the people from which he had sprung. The Greek cities did not feel that they were allying with a barbarian, since for generations the Macedonian dynasty had been allowed, as Greeks, to take part in the Olympic Games, where they won prizes. In conformity with tradition, the education of the young prince had been entrusted to Greek masters, one of them (it appears) being the rhetor Anaximenes of Lampsacus (see p. 11). Then, for three years, from his thirteenth to his sixteenth year, Alexander's tutor was the greatest mind of the time, Aristotle of Stagira, whose teaching of philosophy and imparting of his encyclopedic knowledge were to leave an enduring impression on him. Later the king felt able to say that, while he had received from Philip the gift of life, his debt to his master Aristotle was to have learned how to live nobly. Nurtured on Greek literature, he would quote from Homer's poems or Euripides' tragedies, which haunted his imagination. In the course of his long adventure in Asia he was to show his scientific curiosity regarding those exotic lands, their indigenous peoples, and their beliefs and mores. This reflected the Hellenes' eager interest in geography and ethnography since the days of Hecataeus of Miletus in the fifth century BC, and Herodotus, who continued his work: a trend kept alive by historians like Xenophon, and developed into a system by the researches of Aristotle and his school. Alexander was, of course, bilingual. He would address his subjects and his devoted soldiers in Macedonian, a language distantly related to Greek. But it was in Attic Greek, already the most widespread dialect in the Greek-speaking world as a result of Athens' prestige in the political and economic fields, its cultural aura, that he would converse with his usual companions (his Hetairoi) and with foreigners.

His faith in his nation's greatness, his belief in his own destiny, the sterling qualities of his mind and character – all these the young prince had already been able to demonstrate by his father's side. At the age of 16, in 340/39, while Philip was leading an expedition against Byzantium, Alexander, who directed the business of the Macedonian state in the king's absence, founded the first city to bear his name, Thracian Alexandropolis, which has kept this name up to our own time. This was a significant foundation, to be followed by many others. Two years later, at the battle of Chaeronea in 338, Philip did not hesitate to put his son in direct command of the heavy cavalry, whose charge, on the left wing of the Macedonian formation, was to carry the day. The young man's ardor, a spirit in combat that carried his troops along by the power of example, was in evidence at every moment of his career as a warrior, often turning the tide of battle in his favor.

In conformity with his father's policy, Alexander had no wish to make war in Asia without having solidly reinforced his battle lines in Europe. Before making for the bridgeheads set up beyond the Straits by the Macedonian general Parmenio, he had to ward off the threat that hung on his northern and western borders from the age-old unruliness of barbarian tribes. This was the goal of short and brilliant northward campaigns in the spring of 335, when he subdued certain Thracian tribes, headed back to the Danube, and crushed beyond the river the nomadic Getae who sometimes dared to cross it. The Greek colonies on the western shore of the Black Sea (Apollonia on the Pontus, Odessus, Istrus), whose confidence had thus been restored, rallied to the Macedonian side. In the west he had to bring to heel the pillaging Illyrians among the Balkan Mountains. While Alexander was engrossed in the task of chastising those barbarians and strengthening his hold on the Macedonian army by means of such forays into the hinterland, the experienced politician Antipater filled the position of Regent at Pella, showing that his loyalty could be counted upon without any reservation.

In Greece proper nevertheless, there remained a number of people like Demosthenes, who had in no way renounced their hatred of Macedon. They did not lack the means to take action: the new king of Persia, Darius III Codomannus, whose reign started in 336, anxious to ward off the threat of a Macedonian invasion, liberally distributed among the Greeks funds that were to buy consciences and cover the expenses of war against Alexander. When an unfounded rumour emanating from faraway Albania reported Alexander's death in combat with the Illyrians, the opportunity seemed to have arisen to erase the memory of Chaeronea. Thebes, the great loser in that battle, rose in revolt in response to the city's democrats, who besieged the Macedonian garrison placed by Philip in the citadel of the Cadmea. The Athenians, roused by Demosthenes, were very much tempted to join the revolt. In the Peloponnese, Arcadia and Elis were less sure. Was the Macedonian hegemony established by Philip to be put in question again?

The counterblast was shattering. In the autumn of 335 Alexander took just thirteen days to come back from Illyria by mountain tracks, gather around him contingents from other Boeotian cities which were jealous of Thebes, and, with the help of the Phocians, crush the Theban troops and occupy their city. Mindful of the institutions put in place by his father, he adroitly left it to the Council of

the Corinthian League, the supposedly united voice of the Greek cities, to determine the punishment to be meted out to those guilty of having broken a sworn
alliance with Philip. The Council's sentence was terrible: the city of Thebes was
to be razed to the ground and its entire population driven into slavery. Alexander enforced this severe punishment, which was not, be it said, contrary to the
traditional right of war among the Greeks, but which had seldom happened to
such an important and venerable city. His object was to strike terror into the
opposition by the power of example – a goal that was attained in full. Out of a
whole city destroyed to its foundations, the king spared only one house, the one
that had been the residence of the poet Pindar – testimony to his admiration for
the culture on which he had been nurtured by contact with his Greek teachers.
The Athenians, spared by Alexander as they had been by Philip after Chaeronea,
made a show of attentive subservience. Any risk of an uprising against Macedonian authority was henceforth removed. Indeed, no serious sign of it appeared
until the end of Alexander's reign, with one serious exception: Agis of Sparta
went to war in 332/1 against Macedonian control in the Peloponnese, but was
crushed by Antipater (see pp. 16 and 32).

Peace having been restored in mainland Greece, the Corinthian League, in
agreement with the king of Macedon, whom it had acknowledged as head of
an expeditionary force, decided that war on the Achaemenid empire was to
start the following spring (334). The contingents from the Greek cities gathered at Amphipolis. Numerically they were unimportant – scarcely 7,000 infantry and 600 cavalry, a derisory contribution in comparison with the Greek
mercenary troops, numbering over 50,000, under the command of the Great
King. Athens, the most populous of Greek cities, had provided no more than
700 soldiers and twenty warships (it may be noted in passing that naval power
was not destined to play any more than a back-up role in later operations).
The bulk of Alexander's army was made up of Macedonians, Thessalian cavalry, and barbarians enrolled in Thrace and Illyria. More than the hoplites of
the League it was those hardy troops, bonded to the king by personal allegiance, who were to conquer Asia. For that was very much Alexander's goal.
As he set foot for the first time on the Asian bank of the Dardanelles, he
drove his spear into the ground, symbolically taking possession of it, thus
renewing the gesture attributed by epic tradition since the *Cyprian Songs* to
Protesilaus, the first Greek to land on the shores of Troy. The epithet *doriktetos*,
"conquered by the spear," was henceforth to designate, throughout the Hellenistic period, territory occupied by right of conquest and administered by
virtue of that right. At the moment of embarking on a great adventure that
would end with his life, Alexander was implicitly laying the foundation of a
new order legitimizing the use of force beneficial to the privileged one, the
favorite of the gods, who granted him victory. The consequences of that
gesture were to be felt for a long time.

■ *The sources of Alexander's history: Diodorus, Plutarch,
Arrian*

How do we know the history of those ten years or so which, from 334 to 323, so radically transformed the destiny of the western world? Surprisingly, no contemporary account, nor even one from someone chronogically close to the events, has been preserved. Yet there had been no lack of such narratives, whether in the form of an official history (like the one written by the philosopher Callisthenes, Aristotle's nephew, until his tragic death in 327 – see pp. 26–7) or as memoirs left by many of the king's companions. Among such writings were those of Ptolemy, the general who was to rule Egypt, of Nearchus, the admiral who led the fleet from the Indus to the Persian Gulf, and of the engineer Aristobulus, whose work, written with some benefit of hindsight, won widespread fame. The royal archives or *Ephemerides*, carefully kept by a Greek, the chancellor Eumenes, were a sort of daybook, with a wealth of documents, to which was added the king's correspondence, an abundant one (our texts mention seventy-two letters by him), though the allegedly preserved ones appear in some cases to be of doubtful authenticity. Contemporaries who wished to preserve the memory of the Conqueror's exploits without themselves having any claim to personal involvement made more or less direct use of these documents, as well as of accounts by participants in the events. Included among them are Alexander's former tutor Anaximenes of Lampsacus (see p. 8), but especially the historian Clitarchus, an intimate of Ptolemy, anxious to show in a favorable light the part (an important one by all accounts) played by an officer who gave promise of a royal future. Parallel with these serious works, a pamphlet literature – some pieces hostile, the rest favorable to the Conqueror – reflected the interest of public opinion in a historical figure of exceptional stature.

Yet, from such an abundant body of writing, nothing, or almost nothing, has come down to us by direct transmission. We know of it only through much more recent adaptations or compilations, the most ancient in the latter category being that of Diodorus (second half of the first century BC). Book XVII of his *Historical Library* presents the first uninterrupted narrative of the history of Alexander at our disposal. It rests on a combination of many sources, among which Clitarchus appears to have received preferential treatment. A lively and document-based account, it makes agreeable reading, filled with anecdotes meant to underscore the king's heroic qualities and his generosity. Quintus Curtius, Justin, and especially Plutarch derive from the same composite tradition, with Clitarchus the dominant contributor, which we call the *Vulgate* (not to be confused with Jerome's Latin version of the Bible). Arrian's case is different. He combined with extensive scholarship a first-hand acquaintance with public affairs (he administered Cappadocia under the emperor Hadrian in the second century AD). In his work called *The Anabasis*, intentionally adopting the title once chosen by Xenophon for his narrative of the expedition of the Ten Thousand through the Achaemenid empire, he tries to offer a critical account of Alexander's expedition. Another work of Arrian's, the *Indica*, recounted Nearchus' sea voyage from the Indus delta to the Persian Gulf. Arrian grants privileged status to the evidence of Ptolemy and Aristobulus: hence the amount of divergence, sometimes striking, from the *Vulgate*. We need not take into account the fanciful embellishments which have over the centuries gone into the making of the *Romance of Alexander*, attributed to an apocryphal Callisthenes, and its numerous medieval versions in various languages (including French). Our knowledge of the Conqueror and his exploits therefore rests ultimately on a dual tradition: the *Vulgate* and Arrian. A few interesting inscriptions and a number of numismatic data add little to what these texts have to say. While the sequence of events and their chronology are well enough established, factual details sometimes remain obscure; nor is their proper interpretation certain. But the mere listing of Alexander's victories and the magnitude of his successive endeavors, viewed in the context of the territorial dimensions of his conquests and the challenge they presented, are eloquent enough on their own, as will soon be demonstrated.

■ *The landing in Asia* ■ *Battle of the Granicus* ■ *Conquest of Ionia, then of southern Asia Minor* ■ *Alexander in Phrygia: the Gordian knot* ■ *Departure for Syria* ■ *The battle of Issus and its consequences* ■ *Capture of Tyre* ■ *Alexander's rejection of Darius' peace proposal* ■ *Conquest of Egypt* ■ *Foundation of Alexandria* ■ *Submission of Cyrene* ■ *Alexander's visit to the Oasis of Ammon*

The army that had landed in Asia, in the region of Abydos on the strait of the Dardanelles, was none too impressive in its size: about 30,000 infantry, 5,000 cavalry. It was to face the much larger force of the Great King, Darius III Codomannus, whose reign, like Alexander's, had begun in 336, and who owed his accession to the throne to a palace revolution. He certainly was no equal to his adversary in leadership. Yet his authority over his subjects, nurtured in a centuries-old tradition of obedience, his resources of manpower and hoarded wealth, the sound organization (marked by smoothness and efficiency) of his empire, presented him as a formidable foe to an invader from abroad – and rightly so.

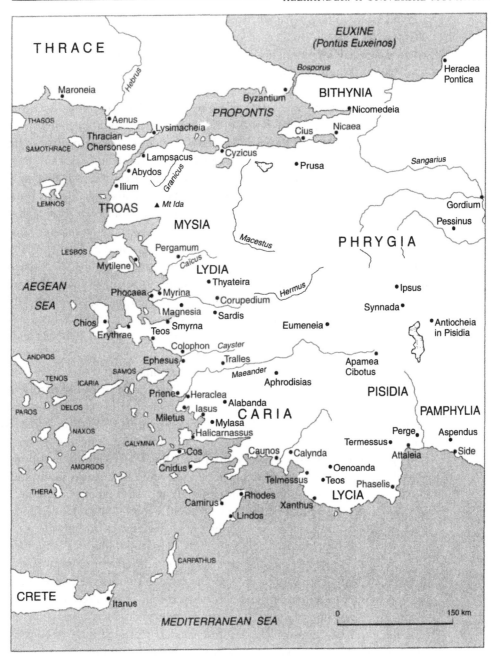

Map 1 Western Anatolia.

Trusting in his superiority, apparently based on such solid foundations, he found it unnecessary to take personal charge. He left the conduct of operations in Asia Minor to his generals – his Persian satraps in command of the provinces of Anatolia, and the Rhodian Memnon, head of an important contingent of Greek mercenaries. Memnon would have liked to resort to a scorched-earth policy, allowing the invading army to move into a land stripped of its resources in order to be more certain to crush it. But the satrap of Hellespontine Phrygia refused to allow his province to be ravaged, and it was decided that battle would be joined without delay. After a pilgrimage to the site of Troy in memory of his ancestor Achilles, Alexander came back to his troops in Abydos and, proceeding eastward, met the enemy waiting on the bank of the Granicus, a minor coastal river flowing into the sea of Marmara. A spirited charge by the Macedonian cavalry, led by the king himself, threw the Persian squadrons into disarray after a violent clash and won the day. Alexander himself joined the fray without restraint. If one of his companions, Clitus the Black, had failed to intervene, he would have fallen victim to a Persian horseman. His flair and boldness foiled the enemy's plan. The Greek mercenary force, the mainstay of the Great King's infantry, was hacked to pieces after the rout of the cavalry left its flanks exposed. In that very first encounter Alexander had shone in his adversary's eyes as a star in the ascendant, while confirming his prestige as a leader and a warrior among his generals and his troops.

The fallout from the battle of the Granicus was immense; and Alexander showed as much clearheadedness as resolution in making the most of his victory. Not only Hellespontine Phrygia, but also the rich province of Lydia, the heartland of western Anatolia, with its capital Sardis, the centre of Persian power in Asia Minor, followed by the Greek cities of Ionia, surrendered or rallied under his authority. In the provinces he brought under his sway, Alexander appointed Macedonian officers as satraps to replace Achaemenid officials, without modifying the existing system of local administration. In the Greek cities Priene, Ephesus, Miletus (the only one that had to be won over by force), he pretended to reinstate autonomy and independence, inherent characteristics of the *polis*. As Persian power had been accustomed to seek its support among local tyrannies or oligarchies, the sequel to its collapse was as a rule the advent of democratic regimes, the Great King's supporters stepping aside in favor of the opposite party. In contrast, in Greece proper the Macedonian throne more often supported oligarchical, even tyrannical, rule. There was no question of ideological preference, but rather a choice imposed by circumstances. It mattered little to Alexander whether the administration of Greek cities complied with one style of government in preference to another, provided it showed some regard for his own views. His one concern in Asia was to substitute his authority for that of the Great King, making the best possible use of local conditions. The diversity of these he left untouched, since it suited his purpose. He therefore took care to demarcate the Greek cities' own territory, exempt from payment of tribute, in contrast with the rest of the land, which was royal property. Conscious of such a privilege and grateful for being freed from the Achaemenid yoke, the Greeks of Asia were the first to grant divine honors to Alexander in his lifetime, and to celebrate these with the foundation of a special cult. Adulation of that kind, of which Agesilaus had until then been the sole beneficiary, was to have an extraordinary history.

Leaving Ionia, Alexander made for the south. Without delay he set about the conquest of the southern coast of Asia Minor. Caria rallied under his authority, with encouragement from the aged princess Ada, sister of the late Mausolus. Her other brother, Pixodarus, had in times past thrust her aside from power: the young king treated her with honor and respect, even consenting to be adopted as her son. He thus applied for the first time a novel policy of personal understanding with native princes, a practice he often went on to use in the future. Nevertheless the coastal city of Halicarnassus, the principal port of Caria, to which Memnon had retreated, backed by a still untouched and powerful Persian fleet, warded off his first assaults. He subdued the city after a long siege, and Memnon managed to escape by sea. Though the season of rough weather was starting, Alexander worked his way along the coastal regions of Lycia and Pamphylia, subduing each in turn. He then marched inland in a northerly direction, through Pisidia and Phrygia, where, in the very heartland of Anatolia, at Gordion, the ancient capital of King Midas, he joined up with the expeditionary force he had sent from Caria under Parmenio's command. There it was that in the winter of 334/3 he saw in a sanctuary the chariot that had belonged to the founder of the Phrygian dynasty, Gordius. An ancient tradition promised the empire of Asia to the one who managed to undo the intricate knot that bound the yoke to the beam of the waggon. If we are to believe some of his historians (whose version modern critics are not inclined to endorse), he cut the famous Gordian knot with one stroke of his sword. True or false, this story is a perfect illustration of the Conqueror's eagerness to impress the popular imagination, his respect for the premonitory meaning of oracles, his disinclination to put off action. For this reason its celebrity is well deserved.

Meanwhile Darius and his generals were reorganizing their armies, a process not without drama. Memnon, making good use of his fleet, had occupied Chios and landed on Lesbos, but he died on the latter island while besieging Mytilene. Thus did the Great King lose the best strategist he had: the Persian fleet was to play no more than a minor role in future, carrying out a few raids in the Aegean. Darius was concentrating his troops in Syria, where he had summoned Memnon's Greek mercenaries. The Athenian Charidemus advised him to rely on these men, if he wanted to confront the Macedonian army with a tough, seasoned, and homogeneous force. But the Iranian nobles' jealousy toward that Greek caused the rejection of a piece of advice that would have been salutary, and Charidemus, who had not accepted such a verdict with good grace, earned the Great King's wrath and died at the hands of the executioner. Thus it was that a sizable army, but a heterogeneous one, awaited Alexander's assault. The mercenaries made up the battle formation, with the Asiatic light troops and the Iranian cavalry on the wings.

Alexander did not allow his attention to be distracted by the Black Sea coast, but entrusted one of his best generals, Antigonus, with the task of watching over Phrygia and guarding the Halys river, the eastern frontier of his Anatolian conquests, against any hostile attempt. Antigonus was to show himself worthy of his king's trust till the end of his reign. Free from worry in that direction, Alexander left for Syria, clearly demonstrating his purpose not to limit his ambition to the conquest of Asia Minor. Detained for a while by sickness at Tarsus in Cilicia, he was treated by Philip, a doctor from Acarnania. As Philip was in the act of handing him a potion, Alexander received a letter from Parmenio warning him that Philip had been bribed by Darius' agents and intended to poison him. The fearless king handed the letter to the physician and drained the cup. The trust that bound him to his friends proved stronger than a slanderous accusation. His conduct on that occasion indicates the degree of devotion he was capable of instilling in those close to him.

When Alexander had recovered, he crossed the mountain passes leading to Syria and descended into the coastal plain of Alexandretta in the autumn of 333. As he advanced to the south he suddenly learned that Darius, moving in the opposite direction by chance (though not by design), had in his turn crossed the mountains and occupied Issus behind the invader's lines. The Macedonian army thus found itself cut off from Asia Minor. Doubling back immediately, Alexander confronted Darius' army, a larger one, on the opposite bank of the Pinarus, a minor coastal river that flows into the inner part of the gulf of Alexandretta, near Issus. The two armies confronted each other in positions that were reversed – Alexander facing north, the Persians south. A cavalry charge personally led by the king, on his right wing, determined the outcome of the battle after a keen fight. Darius turned round and fled in his chariot, starting his army's rout. Most of his Greek mercenaries, who had put up a courageous fight, escaped in good order. Many of them made their way back to Greece, where they enlisted in the service of Agis the Spartan king (see pp. 10 and 32). In Darius' baggage-train, abandoned in Damascus, the Macedonians found his splendid tent, his luxurious furniture. Most important, they captured the Great King's mother, his wife, his two daughters, and his son. Far from treating the captive women as slaves, which the laws of warfare allowed, Alexander showed them – especially the queen mother – great respect, and reassured them about the fate of Darius, whom they believed dead. Such compassion made a deep impression: the king's restraint and generosity won great praise.

Even more than the battle of the Granicus, that of Issus brought prestige, glory, and benefit to Alexander. Cut off from his rearguard, he turned a dangerous position to his advantage, using the narrowness of the field to prevent his adversary from deploying greater numbers of troops. Leading the decisive charge in person, he got the better of Darius himself, who, terrified, sought safety in flight. The dramatic face-to-face encounter between the Macedonian and Persian kings, between a spirited horseman and a distraught figure turning to flee in his chariot, was a scene that struck the popular imagination and inspired artists. The famous mosaic that was discovered in a wealthy house in Pompeii (now in the National Museum of Naples: see pp. 386, 389 and p. 428 in the bibliography) is a faithful reproduction of a painting dating back to a few decades after the event, but drawing upon eyewitness accounts. Only a few figurative documents are so rich in historical significance. Now he was in possession of the treasures left behind in the Persian camp, Alexander was rich enough to pay for the pursuit of the war without appealing for finance to the none-too-willing cities of Greece. In that one day in the month of October 333, almost the whole western portion of the Achaemenid empire was handed over to Macedonia.

Darius, seeking refuge beyond the Euphrates, launched his troops in vain against the centre of Asia Minor: Antigonus firmly warded off every assault on the new frontier of the Halys river. Meanwhile, Alexander subdued Syria and Phoenicia, where only the city of Tyre, trusting in what appeared to be an impregnable position, rejected the Conqueror's demands. It took eight months to subdue, at the cost of heavy losses. Its population was slaughtered or sold into slavery. Deprived of its last base, Darius' fleet, which the Persian general Pharnabazus had at some point tried to bring together with a view to operating in the Aegean Sea, had dispersed or surrendered. Cyprus and Rhodes, first adopting a wait-and-see attitude, eventually joined the stronger antagonist. The whole of the eastern Mediterranean, with the lands bordering it, Egypt excepted, was henceforth subservient to Alexander.

Darius could gauge the immensity of his defeat. Not only had he lost his Asian dependencies bordering the Mediterranean, but even some regions untouched by Alexander's campaign were breaking loose from the Achaemenid empire. This was the case with the provinces of Northern Anatolia, Bithynia or Paphlagonia, for example, while the loyalty of Cappadocia or Armenia was far from sure. The Great King decided to safeguard his future and cut his losses. He sent a letter to Alexander that reached him during the siege of Tyre. In that message he offered, beside an enormous ransom for the liberation of the captive women of royal blood, to give up all the conquered territories and their dependencies, in other words, Asia Minor up to the Halys, and Syria and Palestine up to the Euphrates. As a pledge of his good faith he offered one of his daughters in marriage to the Macedonian conqueror.

The offer was seductive: it amounted to much more than the dream of Isocrates, who had seemed a visionary to many when he incited the Greeks and Philip to conquer Asia Minor. There now appeared the prospect of an extensive Macedonian empire, astride the Aegean sea and the Straits, stretching from Illyria to Jerusalem. It would bring together under one rule a diversity of wealthy countries, encircling the Greek cities now reduced for good to the status of allies, if not of subjects, and forming a more powerful state than had ever been seen in the Mediterranean from time immemorial. Alexander had the terms of the proposed arrangement read out before his council. Parmenio, a seasoned warrior with a wealth of experience and honor, immediately shouted, "I would say 'yes' if I were Alexander." "So would I," was the king's reply, "were I Parmenio." This rejoinder, reported by Plutarch, is perhaps apocryphal, but illustrates very well the huge gap between the young king's grand ambition and the cold calculations with which his closest subordinates buttressed their hopes. We shall see later the consequences of such a difference in outlook.

Rejecting Darius' proposal, Alexander, intent on pursuing his career of conquest, decided to win control of Egypt, the only one of the western provinces of the Achaemenid empire which still eluded his grasp, before seeking another encounter with the Great King, who was regrouping his army in Mesopotamia. Delayed for two months by the siege of Gaza, where he was seriously injured, he next appeared at Pelusium, on the eastern edge of the Nile delta. The satrap who governed Egypt in Darius' name decided not to fight and, negotiating with the Macedonian conqueror, turned the country over to him. Conscious of the special character and the richness of that part of the empire, Alexander did not entrust it to an officer, but kept it under his direct control, content with putting a Greek native of the land, Cleomenes of Naucratis, in charge of local finance. He spent the winter of 332/1 in Egypt. It was then that, acting on advice received in a dream, the king founded a city which he called Alexandria, after his own name. It faced the coastal island of Pharos already known to Homer, at the borders of the Delta and Marmarica. The new city was provided with the traditional institutions of Hellenic states. It was soon populated with citizens from every quarter of the Greek world. Its large and safe harbors were to encourage the exchange of local agricultural produce, brought there from one generation to another by the channels of the Nile, for goods from all parts of the Mediterranean world. Its foundation meant the definitive opening to the outside world of the richest region of Antiquity.

It is not known what circumstances prompted Alexander to venture far away to the west to visit the Oasis of Ammon, in the midst of the Libyan desert. This was the seat of an Egyptian oracle, which the Greeks had long known and consulted, fully aware of its foreign character. A mental process of assimilation often illustrated in their religious history urged them to find in the Egyptian god revered in the oasis of Siwah none other than Zeus. They would therefore depict him with the features of their supreme god – decked in a strange head-dress, a ram's horns framing his bearded face. As Alexander believed in his own direct descent from Zeus through his ancestor Heracles, it was normal that he would plan to consult that god's oracle. Ammon's oasis, which had agreed to submit to the Great King's authority, welcomed the arrival of the Conqueror, to whom the Greek city of Cyrene had sent gifts as a token of allegiance. Thus did the trip to Siwah, halfway toward the rich province of Cyrenaica, allow him to extend his authority to the whole of Hellenized Libya, without the need to go there in person.

From Paraitonion (Marsa-Matruh), where Cyrenaean envoys had come to meet him, the king and his companions moved on into the utter bleakness of the desert to reach Siwah, following a track on which many a caravan had gone astray. There is a tradition that when their passage encountered difficulties, sacred animals, birds or snakes, appeared and put them on the right track. When Alexander reached the far-flung oasis, the priests of Ammon hailed him by the title which by tradition they gave to the Pharaoh, "Son of Râ" the Sun-god, synonymous with Ammon. Such a term, taken literally, later appeared to the Greeks to guarantee the king's direct descent from divinity. Alexander did not reveal what answers he had received from his "divine" father's oracle. But popular imagination, struck by the strangeness and the remoteness of its location, welcomed the fables that were soon prompted by that visit. The importance of the Siwah venture for the later development of the royal cult should not be discounted.

Once back in Egypt, Alexander decided it was time for him to resume the conquest of Asia. The more remote areas in the western part of his dominions were now stable. That was a result of the submission of Cyrene, the dispersion of Pharnabazus' fleet, deprived of any base for its operations, and the firm administration of Macedon and Greece by Antipater, who a few months later managed to check an armed revolt by Agis III, king of Sparta. Leaving Memphis in the spring of 331, Alexander reached Tyre, where he took various political and administrative measures. He ordered, for instance, the liberation of Athenian prisoners, which won gratitude in their city, and entrusted Harpalus with responsibility for the war chest that was later to finance the army's expenses. Then, warned that Darius was gathering in Babylon an army of considerable size, he marched on Mesopotamia, leaving those Mediterranean shores that he was destined never to see again.

■ *Alexander's return to Asia* ■ *Battle of Arbela* ■ *Capture of Babylon and Susa* ■ *Destruction of Persepolis by fire* ■ *Discharge granted to soldiers at Ecbatana* ■ *Murder of Darius* ■ *Philotas' supposed plot: the execution of Parmenio* ■ *Conquest of Afghanistan* ■ *Campaigns in Bactria and Sogdiana* ■ *Chastisement of Bessus* ■ *Clitus put to death* ■ *The marriage of Alexander and Roxane* ■ *The* proskynesis *incident* ■ *The march to the Indus river* ■ *Occupation of Taxila* ■ *Operations against Porus* ■ *The army reaches the Hyphasis* ■ *The retreat towards the Indus* ■ *The descent to the coast* ■ *The return*

That was the beginning of an amazing venture lasting nearly seven years, inspired by a truly Oriental mirage. Alexander, having definitely disposed of Darius, had replaced him as sovereign of the Persian section of Asia. With a handful of men, Macedonians and Greeks, reinforced according to circumstances by allies recruited locally, he was to march through the Middle East, crossing mountains and deserts, well beyond Mesopotamia and Persia, the heartland of the Achaemenid empire. He would skirt the Caspian Sea, cross and subdue Afghanistan, strike northward over the plains of central Asia, beyond Samarkand up to the Syr Daria, clear the formidable barrier of the Hindu Kush twice, eventually emerge by the upper reaches of the Indus river near Kashmir, and conquer the Punjab. That long march was punctuated by violent clashes with warlike tribes, as the army confronted hostile Nature and followed scarcely cleared tracks, far away from regular sources of help. It took four years, from 330 to 326. It was interrupted by pauses of a few months in various places, to allow the army to recuperate and the king himself to organize the process of conquest. When he had reached India and once again been a victor, his troops' reluctance to go any further compelled Alexander to decide to march back, by another route, which he covered in a little more than a year. It is worth retracing briefly the stages of that stupendous expedition, in which one man's dynamism overcame every obstacle and dazzled his contemporaries and posterity.

In the summer of 331 Alexander left Syria for Mesopotamia, leading an army of 40,000 infantry and 7,000 cavalry. He crossed the Euphrates at Thapsacus, on the high road from Sardis to Susa, then the upper Tigris, without meeting any serious opposition. Darius III, who had gathered far greater forces from all the eastern provinces of his empire, planned to choose his own field of battle so as to crush the invader in one encounter through the larger numbers at his disposal,

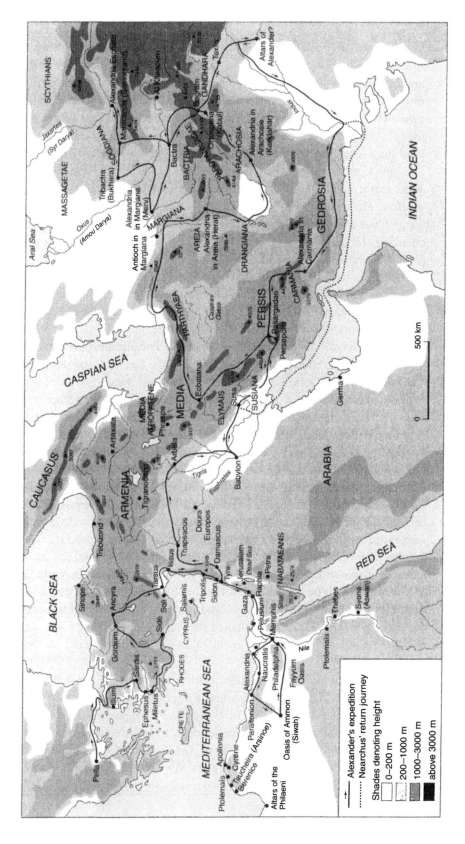

Map 2 Alexander's conquests (drawn by P. Goukowsky).

especially of cavalry. Besides, he had a weapon by which he set much store: a massive group of chariots armed with scythes fixed on the front part of the beam and on the wheel-hubs, which were intended to throw the Macedonian phalanx into disarray under their impact. To use these to their greatest advantage he awaited his enemy in the plain of Gaugamela, northeast of ancient Nineveh (Mosul today). As he had previously stopped at Arbela, the name of this place was wrongly used for a long time as the designation of the decisive battle that took place at Gaugamela on October 1, 331. Confronted by a much larger enemy force, Alexander extracted every possible advantage from a tactic marked by foresight and subtlety. He arranged his troops in a formation like the Greek letter *pi*, both wings tilted along the uprights like the rungs of a ladder so as to avoid being encircled. In the central position of his arrangement he placed in front the phalanx, light troops that riddled with missiles Darius' scythed chariots. Alexander himself took his station on the right wing, with the elite of his cavalry.

There ensued a violent clash, the Macedonian left wing being hard-pressed by the massive force of the enemy cavalry. But in the centre the charge from the scythed chariots, thrown into disarray by the shafts that mowed down horses and charioteers, did not deliver the impact expected. The phalanx opened its ranks to make way for the last chariots, which were soon forced to surrender. Finally Alexander led in person his Companions' assault on the enemy's centre, where Darius had placed himself. As he had done at Issus, Darius lost his nerve, turned round his state chariot, and fled. On that occasion too the Great King's flight determined the outcome of the battle. While Darius was taking shelter in Ecbatana in Media, Alexander, having taken possession of the field at Gaugamela after a last, and very bloody, encounter with the Persian cavalry, was hot in pursuit of the defeated army as far as Arbela, thus confirming his victory.

He soon entered Babylon, where one of Darius' best generals, Mazaeus, a brilliant fighter at Gaugamela, came over to Alexander's side and was rewarded with the satrapy of Babylonia – accompanied, however, by a general and a treasurer both of whom were Macedonians. Alexander was demonstrating his wish to make accessible to Darius' erstwhile servants the top posts of the new administration with which he was replacing the former one in his capacity as "King of Asia," an appellation to which he judged himself entitled henceforth. Then, in the ensuing weeks, Susa, the capital of the Achaemenid rulers, surrendered to the Conqueror, who confirmed in his office the Persian satrap who had just handed the city over to him.

The capture of Susa not only bore glaring testimony to the collapse of the Persian monarchy, but put at Alexander's disposal the fabulous hoards of precious metals which the ancestors of Darius had brought together in that city. The king was going to use them without delay to finance his further endeavors, not forgetting to send a share of them to Antipater, thus helping him maintain his authority over Greece and the Aegean. Aware of the resources now commanded by the Macedonian sovereign, mercenaries did not hesitate to offer their services. They were a source of recruitment indispensable to Hellenistic armies, and turned out to be valuable help for Alexander in his lengthy eastern expedition.

From Susa the king made for Persepolis, a city of magnificent palaces built by the Achaemenids. Entrusting Parmenio with the bulk of the army, which was to follow the direct road to that city, he put himself at the head of a light column. In the dead of winter, at the cost of great hardship and hard-won encounters with the Uxians, a barbarian tribe, he crossed the mountains and forced the passes called the Persian Gates, breaking down a valiant defence. The capture of Persepolis crowned that winter campaign, in which the Conqueror had shown that, for all the glory of his previous victories, he would still choose for himself the hardest task in the pursuit of his designs. Under his orders the great palace of Persepolis was set on fire, not (as was claimed by a romantic tradition) in a fit of drunken folly or transported by Dionysiac frenzy, but to avenge by some spectacular deed Xerxes' acts of destruction in Greece during the second Persian war. Nothing could better demonstrate to the Greeks that their acknowledged leader had fully accomplished the task for which they had acclaimed him as their commander, and that Philip's promises had been kept. Furthermore, the destruction of Persepolis by fire, which followed the capture of Susa, proclaimed to Asia the end of the Achaemenid empire, and the replacement by a new authority of the one that had belonged to Cyrus the Great's descendants. From Ecbatana Darius had sought refuge in Hyrcania, southeast of the Caspian Sea, beyond the passes east of Teheran which are called the Caspian Gates. He was accompanied by the satraps of the eastern provinces of the empire, among them Bessus, satrap of Bactria, who had commanded the left wing of the Persian army at Gaugamela. Alexander, having put in order the affairs of the recently conquered regions, had gone in pursuit of the Great King in the spring of 330. When he in turn had reached Ecbatana, he did not wish to proceed further without being assured of his troops' loyalty. That prompted him to dismiss the contingents from the Greek cities, which had accompanied him as leader of the League of Corinth since his crossing into Asia. Such a decision was meant to mark an official end to the Greeks' common endeavor, for it had been crowned with success by Alexander's victory at Gaugamela and the downfall of the capitals of what had been Persia. Henceforth the grand design that was to sweep the army along toward a faraway and mysterious East would belong to Alexander alone, and to those bound to him by personal allegiance. Greek soldiers who decided to stay with him would do so individually as mercenaries, not as members of contingents provided by the cities. Many of them were tempted to do so, attracted by the Conqueror's prestige and the prospect of conquest.

Leaving half the army under Parmenio's orders at Ecbatana, Alexander made for Hyrcania by forced marches, with troops that were far from numerous. On the way there, he learned that Bessus and the other satraps had deposed Darius and intended to take over in their own name the responsibility for resisting the invader. Soon afterwards his scouts found Darius' corpse, which the satraps, after murdering him, had abandoned in the course of their retreat. Alexander ordered royal honors to be paid to the dead monarch, and proclaimed himself his heir and avenger. After this, in contrast with the plain etiquette, devoid of pomp, of the Macedonian monarchy, in the presence of his newly won Asian subjects, the king adopted the sumptuous ceremonies and the intricate protocol of the Persian court. He looked upon himself as both the sovereign of Macedonia and the Great King's successor. The Asian people bowed before such demands more readily than the Macedonians or the Greeks, who were shocked by such ambivalence. We shall soon see the outcome of that situation.

Bessus meanwhile, having found shelter in his own satrapy of Bactria, had taken the title of Great King under the name of Artaxerxes. As Alexander marched on his enemy, the defection of the satrap of Areia (a region of western Afghanistan), who had pretended to be his ally, forced him to modify his plans. Putting off for a while the conquest of Bactria, he turned southward and occupied Drangiana, near the river Helmund and its lakes. He then made a momentous decision, which must have seemed necessary for the conduct of future operations. Parmenio, the seasoned elderly general who had long enjoyed his full confidence, was hardly showing any diligence, from Ecbatana where he was still in command of one half of the army, in backing the advance of an expedition that had penetrated so deep into the heartland of Asia. The king decided to get rid of him and to use him as a warning. He seized the occasion of an imprudent act on the part of Philotas, Parmenio's son, who accompanied Alexander as leader of the elite corps of the *hetairoi*. A plot, real or imaginary, against the king was disclosed. Proof was given that Philotas, though informed of it, had failed to warn the king. Charged before the army, which, in accordance with Macedonian custom, had gathered as an assembly, he was declared guilty, tortured, and put to death. A confession had been wrung from him, implicating his father. Alexander forthwith sent orders to Ecbatana for Parmenio to be executed. The command of Parmenio's former troops, when they had joined up with Alexander in Drangiana, was handed over to the Macedonian Craterus. Two close friends of the king's, Hephaestion and Clitus the Black, shared the command of the *hetairoi* after Philotas' death. Among the officers appointed to major positions after that crisis are the names of Ptolemy and Perdiccas, who were to play important parts in future events.

Having thus reorganized and reinforced his army, Alexander, in spite of the winter, resumed his march on the east and penetrated into Arachosia (the central region of Afghanistan), where he founded a city, Alexandria in Arachosia (Kandahar). He had already founded another city in Drangiana, and was to multiply similar foundations in central Asia as landmarks of his progress. In each of them, once the plan had been marked out and the religious ritual performed, he would leave a contingent of Greeks or Macedonians, who were to be settlers as well as soldiers, and of traders. As he pursued his northward journey, he spent the balance of the winter at Kabul. In the spring of 329, he advanced to the foot of the lofty chain of the Hindu Kush and there founded Alexandria "under the Caucasus," the latter name being mistakenly extended to those mountains in the Himalayas. Wherever he went he would appoint Macedonian or Persian governors, strengthening to his advantage the Achaemenid administration in the Oriental provinces of the empire, as they were subdued one after another.

His main objective remained the northern provinces beyond the Hindu Kush: Bactria and Sogdiana. Bactria, a rich agricultural plain, extended to the river Oxus (Amu Darya), not far from which was the city of Bactra (Balkh), its capital. Sogdiana, beyond the Oxus, had as its northern boundary the river Jaxartes (Syr Darya), which, like the Oxus, flows west and northwest until it joins the Aral Sea. Its two principal centers were Maracanda (Samarkand) and Buchara. Further on was the unexplored land of the Scythian nomads, the Massagetae (toward the northwest and the Aral Sea) for example, or the Sacae of central Asia. It took three years, from the spring of 329 to that of 326, to reduce those northern provinces to submission. That was at the cost of fierce battles in which Alexander again put his own life at risk, received many injuries, and had to use an extremely flexible strategy and constantly renewed tactical invention. There is nothing more fascinating than a blow-by-blow account of that major episode of his grand venture, with its constant reversals of fortune, its moments of brutal drama, its triumphs. He was isolated, with far fewer men, a long way from any help from the motherland. Yet he had to subdue a region as vast as Asia Minor, fringed by an inhuman wilderness and impregnable mountains, inhabited by fierce tribes as well used to guerrilla warfare on horseback as to ambushes on rugged terrain. At each step in that great operation one is made aware of Alexander's genius.

First he eluded Bessus, who was awaiting him at the foot of the passes of the Hindu Kush. That formidable barrier he cleared by a pass situated further east, in a circuitous movement that handed over to him the whole of Bactria, which Bessus had to abandon, taking cover in Sogdiana. In his turn Alexander crossed the Oxus. The lords of Sogdiana, to earn his goodwill, handed over Bessus, betrayed by his own as he had betrayed Darius. Alexander had him tried and tortured, as a betrayer of his sovereign: in accordance with Oriental custom his nose and ears were cut off, then he was sent to Ecbatana, there to undergo the ultimate penalty and be nailed to a cross. Meanwhile the king had advanced up to the Jaxartes, after occupying Samarkand, and had founded on the river's edge the most northerly city to bear his name, Alexandria the Farthest (*Eskhaté*), on the present site of Khodjend. He had even crossed to the northern bank, in spite of the Saca cavalry, thanks to cover afforded by catapults massed on the south bank to back up the operation: that was the first ever tactical use made of a concentration of machines against cavalry. An agreement reached with the Sacae, as a result of that show of force, allowed Alexander to retrace his steps to Sogdiana to fight a rebellion that had broken out behind his advancing force. He wintered at Bactra, and started on a systematic reinforcement of his Asian contingents.

The year 328 was taken up with a variety of policing operations, directed either at incursions on the part of nomads from the steppes, or against smoldering embers of resistance which had to be put out in various parts of Sogdiana. In the intervals between those expeditions, Alexander found relaxation in hunting parties, and was faithful to the Greek custom of prolonged banquets every night, with conversations marked by familiarity. On the occasion of one of those drinking bouts, one of his dearest companions, Clitus the Black, his spirits heated by wine, went to the length of repeatedly provoking the king with hurtful remarks, blaming him for having introduced novelties that would not have been to his father's liking. Alexander at first kept calm, but ended up by giving vent to his anger: he seized a guard's spear, and as Clitus, overcoming the efforts of those present, returned to scoff at him, he transfixed him at one stroke. Such a violent reaction, whatever the excuse put forward, seriously disturbed the king, who gave way to a deep-seated melancholy, declining food for many days and pleading guilty to having killed the friend who had saved his life at the Granicus. He took many weeks to recover from that moral crisis.

Yet the demands imposed by conquest helped him at that time, claiming action on his part to ward off new threats or reduce to submission the last centers of rebellion. Alexander had already stormed some mountain strongholds in Sogdiana. In January of 327 he began a new operation against one of those fortresses, situated on an almost inaccessible rock, held by the troops of a local prince, Oxyartes, who used it as a safe refuge for his family. The Macedonian troops scaled that mountain amid snow, and the stronghold had to give in. Oxyartes' daughter, Roxane, was among the prisoners. Politics, if not love, impelled Alexander to marry her. The rebel lords came on side as a result of that marriage, demonstrating as it did a will to hold an even balance between Macedonians and Asians both in service to the kingdom and in royal favor. This became evident when Alexander appointed as satrap of the important province of Media the Persian Atropates, who had held the same office under Darius.

Such appointments must have aroused jealousy among the Macedonians. Nor were they favorably impressed by innovations in protocol like the practice of *proskynesis* (prostration) customary at the Achaemenid court, which Alexander wished to preserve as a sign of respect for his own person. Some Greeks at the king's court, the philosopher Anaxarchus for instance, expressed support for the adoption of that custom. Nevertheless, it was sharply at odds with Macedonian tradition and Greek mores, in which prostration could only be considered the homage due to divinity. Aristotle's nephew, Callisthenes, who composed the annals of Alexander's reign and had so far been a dedicated servant of his prestige, did not conceal his hostility to *proskynesis*, a position openly supported by a large number of Macedonians. Faced with such widespread feeling among his compatriots, the king decided not to impose a ritual that they disliked. But he bore Callisthenes a grudge. Not long after, an inept plot was uncovered on the part of a few young men of the royal escort (what is called the Pages' Conspiracy). Callisthenes had imprudently uttered condemnatory remarks about tyranny, likely to cause offense to the king. He was accused of being implicated in that plot and put to death with those responsible for it. The Aristotelian philosophical school, the Peripatos, never forgave Alexander for having struck down one of its representatives, and showed toward him a hostility which Plutarch, many centuries later, still thought it necessary to counter.

It took three years of strenuous effort to subdue the northern provinces. If he was to complete his annexation of all territories that had once been under Achaemenid overlordship, Alexander now had to forge ahead eastward, toward India. Greek historians, from Hecataeus to Ctesias, mentioned the conquest by Darius the Great of the Indus basin, which had in later times cut loose from his successors' authority. Alexander planned a reconquest. Therefore in the summer of 327, leaving one of his lieutenants in Bactria with adequate occupation forces, he crossed the Hindu Kush in the reverse direction to go back to the Kabul area, and again advanced eastward. While he was still in Afghanistan, it was announced to him that the Indian kingdom of Taxila, on the left bank of the Indus, had come on side. It thus became possible to gather in that kingdom, along the banks of the Indus, enough troops to control the whole of that imperfectly known region, and advance beyond Taxila, further than the Achaemenids had ever dared to lead an army. He decided to march without haste and find time to bring over those troops. Among them were counted a substantial number of Greek, Phoenician, Egyptian, and Cypriot sailors needed to man the vessels that were to sail down the Indus, after being built *in situ*. Leaving Hephaestion to lead the bulk of the army to Taxila, he took command of another column, which advanced further north into the mountains, though forced to do battle on many occasions with warlike tribes. In the spring of 326 his march led him through the town of Nysa, whose inhabitants worshipped a local god whom the Greeks, in accordance with their age-old custom of assimilating their own divinities to those of foreign lands, judged to be Dionysus. That was the origin of the myth of Dionysus' travels in India, which was to gain much popularity in Hellenistic mythology. Soon after, Alexander crossed the Indus on a bridge of boats and joined Hephaestion at Taxila. A considerable army, more than 100,000 men strong, had gathered there. The native king was at war with his eastern neighbor, Porus, whose kingdom extended beyond the Hydaspes, a sub-tributary of the Indus, and hoped for decisive help from the Conqueror in that conflict. The operations that followed constitute Alexander's last major military exploit and set the extreme limit of his eastward advance. They took place in the summer of 326.

Porus led a strong army. Its most powerful component was a massive force of 120 war elephants. It was the first time Alexander's troops had faced such enemies. They posed much too serious a threat for him to try to cross the river while they awaited him on the opposite bank. But he managed to elude the enemy's watch by dividing his own forces, and eventually managed to cross the river upstream from the spot where Porus was waiting for him. The two leaders met in a pitched battle on the left bank of the Hydaspes. Once more Alexander's tactical superiority won the day. By a skillful maneuver, he put out of action the enemy's cavalry before his own infantry joined battle with the elephants. The latter, after a prolonged and bloody encounter, were at last defeated, and Porus, who fought mounted on one of them, was injured and taken prisoner. As a tribute to his courage, Alexander treated him as a king and had him cared for by his own physicians. An agreement made with the Indian prince left him in possession of his kingdom, restored peace with the neighboring kingdom of Taxila, and granted him military assistance to help him overcome a number of local tribes. In those far-flung areas, Alexander chose, as Darius had done, a protectorate regime in preference to direct governance. Nevertheless, a Macedonian satrap, Philip brother of Harpalus, was to represent the king's authority over the whole area, supervising in his name the native princes.

The victory over Porus, won at such a high price, dazzled everyone. It was later commemorated by an issue of coinage displaying a degree of documentary precision of truly exceptional quality in the tradition of numismatics. On the reverse it showed Alexander on horseback pursuing in person Porus' war elephant. The king founded two cities in the area: Nicaea, on the site of the battlefield, celebrated his victory (*niké*); the other, Bucephala, was so named in memory of Bucephalus, the famous horse he had ridden since his early youth and which had just died. Next, after offering sacrifices of thanksgiving, he decided on Porus' suggestion to push even further east, while Craterus brought to completion the building of the ships which were to be used later for the journey down the Indus. While fighting the tribes that still held that eastern part of the Punjab, Alexander reached the bank of the Hyphasis. He prepared to cross that river to explore the unknown lands that stretched far away toward the Orient, in the basin of the Ganges, where the almost fabulous kingdom of the Gangaridae was supposed to be found. Then, in an army sorely tried by losses incurred in recent battles and by unceasing monsoon rains, a mutiny broke out against which the Conqueror's prestige proved powerless. The exhausted soldiers were convinced that going any further would mean the loss of all hope of return, and obstinately refused to follow their king beyond the Hyphasis. When he realized that it was impossible to bend his soldiers' resolve, Alexander, as a realistic statesman, gave in to them. As a signpost of the outermost limit of his conquests he caused to be erected close to his camp, on the right bank of the Hyphasis, twelve monumental altars, each in honor of one of the twelve major Olympian divinities. Then, after solemn sacrifices, he gave the order for the return journey to start, hailed by an army whose confidence in its leader had been renewed.

Back on the Hydaspes, Alexander, having thus subdued thePunjab and part of Kashmir, completed his preparation for the journey south. When the fleet of a thousand ships was ready, it was placed under the command of the Cretan Nearchus, an excellent choice. The signal was given early in November 326, and the army started on its march in two main columns. One moved, under Craterus' command, along the Hydaspes, then the Indus on the right bank; the other, under Alexander and Hephaestion, on the left bank. Thus they enclosed Nearchus' fleet as it sailed down river. Only the eastern column had to fight, in the first part of its progress, between the Hydaspes and the Hyphasis. Opposition was put down without mercy. It was then that the king, during an assault on a citadel, came close to losing his life. He had been the first to climb a ladder on to the surrounding wall. There he remained alone with two or three companions, and with them jumped inside the fort. Seriously wounded in the chest by an arrow, he fainted, but his soldiers came to his rescue in the nick of time. This episode filled with high drama throws light on what remained to the end a defining trait of Alexander's character, an urge to be personally involved in combat. In his eyes, as traditionally for the Greeks, physical courage, *areté*, was the foremost quality of a hero.

These operations occupied the army until the spring of 325. Near the confluence of the Indus and the Hydaspes, a new Alexandria was founded. Dividing up his troops for the return journey, Alexander had sent Craterus in the direction of Kandahar, over the mountains by the Mulla Pass, with part of the phalanx and the heavy components of the army (the elephants and the engines of war). He was instructed to meet up with the king in Carmania, north of the opening on the Persian Gulf. Alexander himself was to accompany the fleet, and undertook to push on to the Indus delta and the Ocean river. He had a harbor built at Pattala, on the northern tip of the delta, subduing the surrounding area. On reaching the sea he offered a sacrifice to Poseidon; throwing a gold cup into the waves, he prayed to the god to extend his protection to Nearchus' fleet. The ships were to reach the Persian Gulf by hugging the inhospitable coast of Baluchistan, gathering on their way every piece of information that would allow the establishment of a regular sea route between Mesopotamia and the mouths of the Indus. To ensure the safety of such a difficult passage, Alexander meant to follow the same itinerary as Nearchus, skirting the seaboard. Combined operations of this kind, a column moving on land and a fleet hugging the coast, each affording support to the other, were familiar to ancient armies.

The plan was foiled by geographical and climatic factors. Nearchus was delayed by the monsoon, yet, without heavy losses, he overcame a number of difficulties and reached the Straits of Hormuz at the entrance to the Persian Gulf. The broken coastline prevented Alexander from marching close to the sea.

He had to entrust himself to the inland deserts, in Gedrosia, where the army, hard-pressed by hunger and thirst, lost men and beasts. The latter end of his progress was less difficult. In December 325 he reached Carmania, where Nearchus and Craterus met up with him. Another Alexandria was founded, and great religious celebrations, accompanied by sacrifices and athletic competitions, marked the end of those lengthy trials for the reunited forces and their king.

■ *The empire reorganized* ■ *Punishment meted out to unfaithful satraps* ■ *Harpalus' treason* ■ *Athens' prudent policy under Lycurgus and Phocion* ■ *Agis III's failure and death* ■ *Conclusion of the Harpalus case: Demosthenes' exile* ■ *The edict on the return of the banished* ■ *The grant of divine honors to Alexander* ■ *The nuptials at Susa* ■ *The Macedonian veterans' mutiny: reconciliation at Opis* ■ *The death of Hephaestion* ■ *New plans of conquest* ■ *The death of Alexander*

Soon after his return Alexander had to take stern measures to put an end to the liberties taken by a number of powerful men, encouraged as they had been by his prolonged absence. Many satraps had failed to send supplies to the army during its difficult crossing of Gedrosia. For such culpable negligence they paid with their lives. The same penalty was meted out to Cleander, who had submitted Media to periodical extortion: the king could not allow his native subjects to be robbed. All satraps were ordered to dismiss any mercenaries recruited for their personal service: the king reserved for himself exclusive control of the armed forces. Even his friend Harpalus, the confidential agent to whom Alexander had handed over the management in Babylon of the royal treasury, had taken for granted the rumored death of the king, injured in battle while in India, and been guilty of embezzlement. He had lived the sumptuous life of a sovereign, demanding for his mistresses a deference due to queens. Learning of Alexander's return, he left Babylon for Cilicia, taking from the royal treasury the considerable sum of 5,000 talents, which he spent on the recruitment of mercenaries. When he saw that the king's authority was reasserting itself unchallenged, he thought he would find refuge in Athens, where a powerful party still harbored enmity toward the Macedonian monarchy.

Since their defeat at Chaeronea in 338 and the destruction of Thebes in 335, which had left Greece proper terror-stricken, the Athenians had maintained an attitude of cautious reserve. No doubt Demosthenes and Hyperides, champions of the struggle with Philip, were no less resolved to fight Alexander. Nor had they lost all credit with the people. That had been demonstrated by the famous lawsuit involving Ctesiphon in 330, in which Aeschines, Demosthenes' old enemy, had indicted Ctesiphon for having – illegally, according to him – placed before the Council a proposal to bestow a crown of gold on Demosthenes, as a mark of honor. In that lawsuit, the occasion on which the famous orator delivered in his friend's defense the celebrated speech *On the Crown*, the real matter at issue was the policy of hostility toward Macedonia. The outcome of the case, Ctesiphon's acquittal by a large majority and Aeschines' exile to Rhodes, was evidence of the state of public opinion. Far from being hostile to Demosthenes for having placed the city in the ranks of the vanquished, the Athenians were grateful to him for having so eloquently championed the glorious tradition of national independence. Yet Athens, conscious of reality, was wary of a premature break with the dominant power, whose resources far exceeded her own. She followed the wise advice given by the patriot and competent administrator Lycurgus. He urged that finances be set in order and that morale be restored by the punishment of cowards and traitors (his speech *Against Leocrates*, delivered in 330 against an Athenian who had fled his city at the time of Chaeronea, illustrates his feelings on the subject). Finally, he wanted the city to be endowed with a new land army and a new fleet. The influence he exerted on his fellow-citizens for twelve years, from 338 to 326, had made them heal their city's wounds. They built an arsenal, fitted out the military harbor of the Piraeus, and renewed their fleet, adding to the traditional triremes, quadriremes, and quinqueremes, larger and more powerful vessels that carried more oarsmen. Furthermore, with a view to reviving among the people a feeling for age-old tradition, a variety of measures reorganized the celebration of cults, the moral bonding agent of the city. Shrines were beautified, for example that of Dionysus, where the theater, formerly a wooden structure, was given stone tiers of seats. Out of faithfulness to the past a *ne varietas* (that is, a standard edition) of the tragedies of Aeschylus, Sophocles, and Euripides, glories of Athens since the previous century, was established. Sculpted portraits of those tragedians were erected at public expense. The ancient institution of the *ephebeia*, which introduced Athenian youths between the ages of 18 and 20 to military service, was reorganized in a style that aimed to revive an ancestral practice. Athletic installations, the stadium where the Panathenaic competitions were held, gymnasia and palaestrae were improved or rebuilt to allow young men to train in physical fitness. To oversee the reestablishment of the armed forces, the citizens elected many times in succession Phocion, a veteran of former struggles with Philip. He was widely respected for his military talent and integrity, and was endowed with qualities that embodied the ancient ideal of manhood. The picture of him that Plutarch has painted has remained legendary. To the renowned austerity of his virtue was added a sound appraisal of the existing balance of power. With his conservative turn of mind guided by clarity of vision, he prepared for war while advising peace.

Alexander tactfully flattered Athenian susceptibility by gracious gestures, sending to the city some of the spoils from the battle of the Granicus or freeing Athenian prisoners who had been mercenaries in the service of the Great King. The Athenians were quite willing to follow Lycurgus' or Phocion's advice. They thanked the king for freeing the prisoners by bestowing on him a gold crown. The Spartan king, Agis III (see pp. 10, 16), appealed to them to take part in the war that his city, which was not a member of the League of Corinth, waged in 331 against Antipater, with an army reinforced by mercenaries who had escaped from the battle of Issus. But they abstained. Marching on his Arcadian neighbors, Agis laid siege to the federal city cf Megalopolis, founded in 369 by Epaminondas as a rallying point for the Arcadian tribes and a counterweight to Sparta in the Peloponnese. Soon Antipater and the Macedonian army came to the help of the city, which put up a victorious resistance. In a pitched battle which took place nearby, Agis was defeated and killed. The Macedonian hold on Greece proper was thus confirmed until the end of Alexander's reign.

In the Aegean Sea the economy had fallen on hard times, but that was a contributing factor to an undisturbed peace. From 330 to 326 a series of bad harvests brought about a serious shortage of cereals in the whole of the peninsula, especially in large populated areas like that of Athens, where supplies depended on imports by sea. An inscription from Cyrene demonstrates how in those years of hardship Hellenic solidarity came into play and helped weather the crisis. The African colony, whose territory was one of the granaries of the Greek world, quotes figures in an inscription about cereal supplies that it sent at that time to a number of cities, large and small. These amounted to 805,000 medimni (more than 40,000 tonnes), 100,000 to Athens alone. When the problem of daily bread became serious to such a degree, no one could be tempted into making war.

Thus it was that when Harpalus appeared before the harbor of the Piraeus in the spring of 324 with a squadron and a few thousand mercenaries, the Athenians refused to receive him. Sending his troops to Cape Taenarus, the large mercenary market, he begged to be admitted into Athens as a suppliant. His request granted, he strove, by distributing financial aid around him, to win the city over to his cause. When Alexander sent a request for his unscrupulous treasurer to be extradited, Harpalus was jailed. He soon escaped and joined his mercenaries, first at Cape Taenarus, next in Crete, another important mercenary market, where the Lacedemonian Thibron, one of his lieutenants, caused him to be murdered. But his stay in Athens had serious repercussions. Demosthenes, who had been involved in Harpalus' arrest and the confiscation of various sums of money in his possession, was accused before the Areopagus of having been bribed. He was found guilty and had to seek exile in Troezen.

Meanwhile Alexander, back in the heart of his Asian empire, was taking important measures aimed at ensuring internal security in the complex world he was governing. It was right for component states to be pacified and prosperous before he started on new ventures. At Susa, at the end of the winter of 324, he promulgated an edict (*diagramma*) addressed to the Greek cities, instructing them to recall their exiled citizens and return their belongings to them. Indeed, there was hardly a single city where political discord had not caused proscription, sometimes on a massive scale. Alexander's goal was to put an end to a situation harmful to the internal peace of states, by restoring a fatherland to thousands of banished people. No doubt such a measure meant interfering with the domestic concerns of member cities of the League of Corinth, an eventuality which was not provided for by the pact agreed between them and the king of Macedon. But in actual fact what Greek state, when it exercised hegemony, had ever shrunk from such interference? The blanket measures prescribed by Alexander could be put forward as an act of generosity and magnanimity. To give it greater resonance, the king had it proclaimed by Nicanor of Stagira, Aristotle's adopted son, at the celebrations taking place at the Olympic Games in the summer of 324. An inscription from Tegea and another from Mytilene show how that return from banishment was translated into fact, not always without harmful effects.

To consolidate his moral authority among the Greek cities, Alexander asked them, through the agency of local friends and supporters, to acknowledge his own personal divinity, which had seemed evident to him since he consulted Ammon's oracle. Such an acknowledgment was to be enshrined in the institution of a cult honoring him as an "invincible god," *theos anikétos*. In itself the apotheosis of a mortal appeared in no way objectionable to the ordinary Greek, who found in current myths, like those of Heracles or Asclepios, more than one well-established example of authenticity. Besides, recent history supplied precedents like that of Lysander, a memorable one. No doubt scruples or skepticism in certain minds balked at such attempts. Agesilaus had received with derision the wish of some to honor him like a god. But Hellenic polytheism, favorable as it was to the most varied beliefs provided they fitted in with the ritual forms in customary usage, did not reprove such novelties if they were supported by the authority of an oracle and, obviously, by power and success. The Greek cities of Asia had shown the way after their liberation from the Persian yoke. It was the turn of the cities of Greece proper to follow the same path, without apparent eagerness. Alexander's choice for the reverse of a silver coin, a tetradrachm struck in 324 to 323 by the royal mint in Babylon, in which care had evidently been taken to make him look like a god, shows how earnest he was to have his own cult established.

At variance with general willingness in Greece, Macedonians as a whole, and Antipater in particular, did not follow that initiative. As long as Alexander was alive, no cult was dedicated to him in his native country. Fidelity to the ancient forms of monarchy was very much alive and popular feeling was mistrustful of innovations. Yet Alexander had just inaugurated one of these, in a striking fashion. At Susa in the spring of 324 he celebrated with great solemnity his marriage with two Persian princesses of the Achaemenid family, one the daughter of Darius III, the other of his predecessor, Artaxerxes III Ochus. He already had for a wife Roxane, daughter of Oxyartes, who had married him in Bactria and was to bear him a posthumous son. Polygamy had no place in Greek custom but corresponded to Oriental usage. Its adoption by Alexander was understood to imply acceptance of such a custom by the master of the immense Asian empire. Already the king had sometimes appeared in public in Persian dress. People could not forget what concessions he had made to the etiquette of the Achaemenid court. The wish to bring about a welding of the diverse components of his states – in the first place the union of the Macedonian and the Iranian ones, the foremost among them – was made even more evident by other marriages, those of his principal lieutenants with Iranian women. Hephaestion, his closest friend, married another daughter of Darius. In a similar fashion Craterus, the Greek Eumenes, and Seleucus (founder-to-be of the Seleucid dynasty) set an example by choosing a wife from the noble families of Persia – an example that was followed by 10,000 Macedonian soldiers. All these marriages, known as the "Susa Nuptials," were celebrated at the same time as the king's, an occasion of festive rejoicing that made a widespread impression.

It was not without some misgiving that quite a few veterans saw the descendant of the Argeads embarking on a policy of fusion between the Greek world, to which they felt they belonged, and the barbarian world against which they had carried on a hard fight. Many of them did not contemplate ending their lives in Asia, even beside their sovereign. Thus it was that when Alexander proposed that they should return to Macedonia if they so wished, the vast majority of them agreed, with an enthusiasm that soon degenerated into open mutiny. The boldest among them did not hesitate to give vent to harsh criticism of the king. Disturbed at the sight of a rebellion in which some of his most senior veterans took part, Alexander's reaction was marked by both severity and an appeal to their better feelings. The ringleaders were arrested on his orders by loyal troops and handed over to the executioner. Simultaneously, by a passionate harangue, he won over the hearts of the mutineers. A sacrifice ensued, at Opis on the Tigris, accompanied by solemn prayers for the restoration of concord. The banquet that followed brought together Macedonians and Persians in brotherly union; 10,000 veterans then took their leave of Alexander, before returning to Macedonia under the leadership of Craterus and Polyperchon. On the king's instructions, rich farewell presents had been given to them. For other veterans who agreed to stay in the Orient a district was set apart in a new city, Alexandria on the Persian Gulf. It was given the name of the capital of Macedonia, Pella.

Another trial, which left him sorely afflicted, was awaiting Alexander in the autumn of 324, in the course of his stay in Media, at Ecbatana. This was the death of his friend Hephaestion. Of all his companions this one was dearest to the king, who had bestowed on him the foremost dignity in the realm by appointing him as *chiliarch*, a Greek title given in the Achaemenid empire to one holding the position of prime minister. His death in the full bloom of youth filled the sovereign with grief. After consulting the oracle of Ammon, Alexander decided to hold a sumptuous funeral in honor of his friend. The catafalque that was built for him in Babylon, described in great detail by Diodorus, was one of unheard-of lavishness, wrought in the most precious materials and adorned with priceless statues. If anything was to move the king, it had to be above the common measure.

When he had overcome his grief, Alexander threw himself into the planning of his next endeavors with his usual eagerness. His plan was, on the one hand, to exploit the resources of his Asian realm by the development of river transport and sea trade, using to advantage the discoveries Nearchus had made on his return journey from India. On the other hand, he wished to extend the frontiers of the empire. He led a brief winter campaign against the Cosseans in the Zagros. He contemplated northern expeditions toward the Caspian Sea, southern ones toward the Red Sea, and in the immediate future the conquest of Arabia, the coast of which his vessels were beginning to reconnoitre, starting both from the Persian Gulf and from the Gulf of Suez. Early in the spring of 323, while he was making these preparations, numerous delegations arrived from Greek cities, asking for help in meeting difficulties caused by the return of the banished. The envoys approached him with crowns, as they would a god. Others kept coming from far-off regions of the western Mediterranean, from southern Italy, from Etruria or Carthage, paying their respects to a sovereign whose fame and power were exalted far beyond the boundaries of the Greek world. Among these barbarian embassies, tradition also lists Ethiopians, Iberians, and Celts from the Danube area. The whole universe known to the Ancients appeared to bow in reverence before Alexander.

The manifold activities described above had no doubt weakened his tough constitution, already put to a severe test by injuries sustained in battle and the strain of his travels. In early June 323, when the Arabian expedition was about to start, Alexander was brought down by a bout of fever, which in a few days drained him of all strength. On June 13, 323, he died in the palace of Babylon. Sickness had deprived him of the time to provide for his succession. He was not yet quite 33.

- *Alexander's denigrators* ■ *The originality of his grand design*
■ *Its aftermath in world history*

While Alexander's glory has survived through the ages, securing for him the leading place among conquerors within human memory, conflicting judgments have been passed on the man and his achievements. The hatred felt by the adversaries of the Macedonian monarchy never laid down arms, even faced with the young prince's generous acts of forgiveness or his benefactions. Their role was taken over after Callisthenes' death by the hostility of some philosophers of the Peripatetic school, who never forgot the capital punishment meted out to their founder's nephew. The age-old mistrust harbored by intellectuals toward war leaders, even those endowed with the highest degree of culture, reinforced such an attitude of denigration with the passage of centuries. For how could one's contempt for the powerful that the world admires be better expressed than by passing a severe judgment on the most illustrious among them? This is the drift of the famous anecdote about Diogenes the Cynic replying to Alexander, who had asked what he could do for him, "Get out of my light." The fame of great men has always clouded the judgment of many who find some sort of revenge for their own humble position by belittling achievements too dazzling for them. Paul-Louis Courier, writing to the Hellenist Guilhem de Ste Croix, who took a special interest in Alexander, put in stark terms that state of mind:

> Please do not extol your hero [he wrote]. He owed his glory to the times in which he lived. Otherwise, what more did he possess than such men as Genghis Khan, as Tamerlane? No doubt he was a good soldier, a good captain. But those are common virtues. In any army you will find a hundred officers capable of commanding it with success . . . As for him, he achieved nothing that could not have happened without him. Long before his birth, it was written that Greece was to take possession of Asia . . . Fate handed over the world to him. What did he do to it? Please do not reply, *Would that he had lived on!* For day by day he had turned fiercer and more of a drunkard.

Here a brilliant pamphleteer betrays the bitterness of an ordnance officer to whom circumstances, and no doubt his lack of drive and his pride, had denied the promotion he expected. He thus carried back to Alexander the critical judgment, devoid of any allowances, that he had often passed on Napoleon and his marshals. The historian's duty, however, is to steer clear of summary preconceptions, but first and foremost to look at the facts. These speak for themselves in the case of Alexander.

It is true that many Greeks in the fourth century, following the example of Isocrates, were in favor of a war of conquest against the Achaemenid monarchy that would allow the restoration among Greek cities of the moral unity they had known at the time of the Persian wars. Yet no one imagined that an operation of that nature could go beyond the liberation of the Aegean seaboard. Had Philip lived to undertake it, there is reason to believe that his realism would have imposed limits on his ambition, and that in response to Darius' offer he would have behaved like Parmenio (see p. 18), not like Alexander. Never in the course of his stupendous venture did the Conqueror stop being its conscious (and sole) originator, despite the resistance and apprehension of his associates. His aim was not only to bring under his authority the Great King's former possessions, but to reach in the east the furthest confines of the world down to the Ocean river, before exploring south and north, as is made clear by the preparations made in the year 323. His ambition was obviously to bring under unified control the whole extent of the inhabited world, the *Oikoumené*, to use the Greek term. That was a dream taken over from the great Achaemenid sovereigns, Darius or Xerxes, but enlivened by an original view of the complex nature of the world and the mutual relationship of nations. As the undertaking unfolded, one can see, at every step, the plan that was meant to be translated into reality. A great distance separates the conflagration at Persepolis, an act of atonement for a past that it was to expunge, from the Susa Nuptials. These were meant to create the climate of a brand-new future – a universal monarchy, gathering under the same stewardship Macedonians, Greeks, and barbarians, inspired by the same loyalty toward their sovereign and professing for each other a feeling of mutual esteem, as happened at the banquet at Opis. Institutions marked by flexibility, with their components of Greek and barbarian custom, were to ensure coexistence, if not a perfect blend. There was nothing Utopian in such a scheme, provided its author had at his disposal the time needed for its execution. The sovereign's authority, which imposed itself on everyone and (as was shown in many instances) knew how to assert itself, was the one bond able to keep united in a vast empire of that size such a diversity of peoples. This Alexander had understood. He alone was capable of bringing to completion the enterprise that he had thought out with a clear vision and on which he made a beginning in such a masterly fashion. That his death meant the rapid collapse of the system he had initiated does not prove its lack of viability. It shows that a man of Alexander's calibre was needed to put it in place and be its guarantor. His successors, aware of their shortcomings, were soon to scale down their aims to a level that they thought suited such men as they were. Yet even these often had to be reduced further!

The demonstration of a universal monarchy was, however, not wasted. It was later to be put to use by Augustus, in a manner adapted to the changed times. The Roman empire was in large part the realization of Alexander's dream. That was certainly the thought of the artist inspired to create the Great Cameo of France, now in the Cabinet des Médailles in Paris. Above the enthroned couple of Tiberius and Rome, a deified Alexander hovers in the empyrean, at the side of Augustus in apotheosis, and handing over the government of the world to his far-off successor.

Plate 1 The (so-called) Sarcophagus of Alexander: detail (Istanbul Museum; photo Hirmer Fotoarchiv).

The Sarcophagus, built for a local dynast in the late fourth century, was found in the necropolis of the princes of Sidon in Phoenicia. The features, reminiscent of the Conqueror's, of a horseman wearing a helmet shaped like a lion's head on one of the four upright faces, have led to the monument being given that name. Lively reliefs adorn its four sides. The side shown here portrays scenes of lion and deer hunting, in which Greeks (in heroic nudity) and Orientals in Persian dress take part. The ornamentation is made up (in vertical order) of meanders (or Greek braids), ova, beads and reels, hearts-and-darts (see p. 286).

2/THE DIADOCHI AND THE DREAM OF UNITY

■ *The succession problem: the child Alexander IV and his uncle Philip Arrhidaeus* ■ *Perdiccas appointed regent* ■ *First sharing of the empire* ■ *The period of the Diadochi*

The illness that killed Alexander in the bloom of youth had been so sudden and so brief that he had not had time to provide for his succession. In the last four days of his life, as the end was in sight, he had lost the power of speech. The Macedonians around him were of course loyal to the dynastic tradition. But it combined succession to the kingship by right of blood with acclamation by the Macedonian assembly, which would be represented in the existing circumstances, on foreign soil, by the army. Alexander had no direct offspring. One of his wives, Roxane, princess of Sogdiana, was pregnant, and in the month of August was to give birth to a son called Alexander IV. In the period before the latter's expected birth, the royal blood of the Argeads had no better representative than an illegitimate son of Philip II, Arrhidaeus, a feeble-minded epileptic. The companions and soldiers of Alexander, hesitating to choose between such a pitiable candidate and the heir-to-be, agreed on a provisional compromise that would safeguard their respective rights. It was based on a notional dual monarchy; the states were to be administered in the immediate future by the principal collaborators of the late king.

The chiliarch Perdiccas, who had succeeded Hephaestion in that position of major importance, was to act as a sort of regent by virtue of it. Craterus had often held the highest military commands under Alexander. He was entrusted with the task of being the personal representative of the king (or of both kings). As for the aged Antipater, he would continue in his capacity as *strategos*, as he had done for eleven years, to hold Europe firmly under his control. Thrace, because of its challenging position and its importance in holding the key to the Straits, was given a special status under Lysimachus' authority. In Asia, the agreement reached among the generals became a blueprint for sharing the provinces. Ptolemy obtained Egypt, where he soon got rid, by murder, of the Greek

Cleomenes of Naucratis, whom Alexander had placed at the head of the local administration. Antigonus the One-eyed (Monophthalmus) kept responsibility for Phrygia and Western Anatolia, which had been under his guardianship since the first days of conquest. The Greek Eumenes of Cardia, who, as custodian of the royal archives, had been one of Alexander's closest associates, was put at the head of Cappadocia and Paphlagonia, in Central and Northern Anatolia. Seleucus did not receive a territorial command, but was placed at the head of the cavalry, the elite of the armed forces. These Macedonian leaders, among whom Eumenes appears as an incongruous figure, are Alexander's real successors, the heirs or *Diadochi*, as history calls them. Between them and between their sons, the *Epigoni* (a name given in the Archaic period to the sons of the Seven Chiefs who marched on Thebes), was enacted during the next forty years a bloodstained saga of rival ambitions. Each tried to restore to his personal advantage the unity of an immense empire. Their successive failures were to lead to a newly found balance of power in the world of the Hellenistic monarchies.

In a first phase, from 323 to 316, the myth of the unity of the empire was upheld, at least in principle, to the advantage of two kings: Arrhidaeus, the feeble-minded one, who had taken the name of Philip, his father; and the child Alexander IV. Next, after a series of political murders perpetrated in cold blood had erased the dynasty of the Argeads, the Diadochi, each in turn, attempted to restore the empire under one man's authority, each endeavor thwarted by a coalition of the other Diadochi. Antigonus the One-eyed, supported by his son Demetrius, looked for a long time like succeeding, until the battle of Ipsus in 301 put an end to his hopes and his life. After his death Demetrius, the eponymous "City Besieger" (Poliorcetes), a surprising individual with outstanding military skill but uncertain political convictions, acted on the stage of history with constant and muddle-headed attempts ending in victory or defeat, until his definitive fall in 285. But already Lysimachus, after long years of adopting a policy of caution with limited objectives, in his turn indulged in a dream of domination over Europe and Asia from his central base on the Straits. His ambition was shattered at the battle of Corupedium, where he met defeat and death. Seleucus, his victor, was the last to embark on the unitary adventure – a short-lived illusion, brought to an end a few months later, in 280, by his murder at the hands of a treacherous friend. With the passing of the last of the Diadochi, and the advent of a new order, came the end of a chaotic and tortured period, of which we shall now evoke the main episodes, the principal actors.

■ *Revolt in mainland Greece: the Lamian War* ■ *The battle of*
Crannon ■ *The humiliation of Athens* ■ *Death of Demosthenes*
and Hyperides ■ *Perdiccas invades Egypt* ■ *His murder* ■ *Defeat*
and death of Craterus ■ *The Triparadisus agreements*
■ *Antipater and the kings return to Macedonia* ■ *Death of*
Antipater ■ *Polyperchon as Regent* ■ *Death of Phocion*
■ *Cassander's success* ■ *Athens governed by Demetrius of Phalerum*
■ *Death of Philip Arrhidaeus* ■ *Eumenes' battles and final*
defeat ■ *Antigonus Monophthalmus master of Asia*

The news of Alexander's death caused no disturbance among the indigenous peoples of Asia, long accustomed to a life of bondage. The Greeks, on the other hand, never having fully renounced their old ideal of a jealously guarded autonomy, rose in rebellion on the furthest edges of the empire. In the outer satrapies, in Bactria and Sogdiana, toward the north of the Hindu Kush barrier, the colonies of veterans, who had agitated for two years without success for their return to Europe, regained hope and gathered in a combat force under the leadership of a Greek satrap. Thus was fathered the Greek state of Bactria, which in the second half of the third century was to become an independent kingdom with a glorious future.

At the opposite end of Alexander's dominion, the Greek cities of Europe, or some at least, were ill at ease under the Macedonian yoke and decided that the time had come for them to shake it off. Athens, whose forces had been reconstructed thanks to Lycurgus' wise stewardship and Phocion's military experience, allowed herself to be tempted by such a venture. Lycurgus had just died. The eloquence of Hyperides, violently hostile as before toward Macedonia, caused Phocion's warnings to be treated with contempt. Demosthenes was recalled from exile. Leosthenes, who had won fame as the leader of a mercenary force, was chosen as commander of the army. In the work of the historian Pausanias (*Periegesis* I, 25), who was writing 500 years later, there is an echo of the enthusiasm aroused by that endeavor. What was left of Harpalus' treasure allowed mercenaries to be recruited, the fleet was put on a war footing, alliances were made. Sparta, Corinth, and the Boeotians shied away, but Argolis, Elis, Messenia in the Peloponnese, and in continental Greece the Phocians, the Locrians, the Aetolians, and finally Thessaly sent contingents. Leosthenes led the coalition's army to battle and, after occupying Thermopylae, forced Antipater and the Macedonian forces to shut themselves up in Lamia – hence the name of the Lamian War given to the Greek cities' final burst of energy against Macedon. The siege of Lamia went on through the winter of 323 to 322. But Leosthenes died in a skirmish within sight of the besieged city. The disappearance of such an able and respected leader proved fatal to the coalition, which began to break up. Though defeated on open ground, Antipater managed to retreat into Macedonia and await the reinforcements that Craterus was bringing from Asia. The Athenian fleet was guarding the Straits so as to hamper their passage. It was thwarted by the squadron that backed up Antipater. Engagements in the Aegean Sea culminated in a decisive encounter near the island of Amorgos, south of the Cyclades. That was a disaster from which the Athenian navy never recovered.

Forsaken by her allies, who had lost all hope, Athens was forced to negotiate peace with Antipater and submit to the heavy terms imposed on her. A Macedonian garrison was to take up a permanent position in the citadel of Munychia in the Piraeus. Oropus, a market town of disputed ownership on the frontier with Boeotia, was severed from Attica. The Athenian cleruchs in Samos were to leave for good that large island, now restored to its inhabitants. A heavy war indemnity would have to be paid. As well as that, the city's internal system of government was to be given new foundations. As Macedon's adversaries had come from the supporters of democracy, an oligarchic and census-based regime was henceforth to replace the traditional institutions, thus removing their political rights from about 12,000 citizens whose financial position was below the census rating. Phocion, who had fought valiantly in recent operations and whose personal prestige had dissuaded Antipater from a military invasion of Attica after the battle of Crannon, was to administer the State in the aftermath of defeat, together with the orator Demades, a long-time supporter of Macedonian interests. As for the instigators of the war, Athens agreed to hand them over. Hyperides had fled but was arrested and put to death. Demosthenes had taken refuge in Calauria; as he was about to be taken prisoner he poisoned himself. His death marked the end of any policy of independence for his fatherland. His boldness, his constancy, his genius had failed to restore its greatness and its freedom.

It seemed fitting to dwell in some detail on that last episode of a long and memorable history. But as soon as Athens had disappeared from the political scene, the game of rivalries and intrigues was transferred again to Asia. The chiliarch Perdiccas, after helping Eumenes to take possession of Cappadocia, which Alexander had not subdued, insisted on asserting, in the name of the two kings, an authority which the other Diadochi were in no way willing to acknowledge. The aged queen Olympias, mother of Alexander the Great, who had retired to her native Epirus, was possessed by an unremitting desire to play a political role equal to her ambition. She decided to offer to Perdiccas, in the hope of winning his agreement to her plans, the hand of Cleopatra, sister to Alexander and now a widow. Accession through such a marriage to the royal family of the Argeads appeared to Perdiccas to be the path to supreme power. He allowed himself to be tempted. But his rivals were not deceived, all the more mistrustful of him

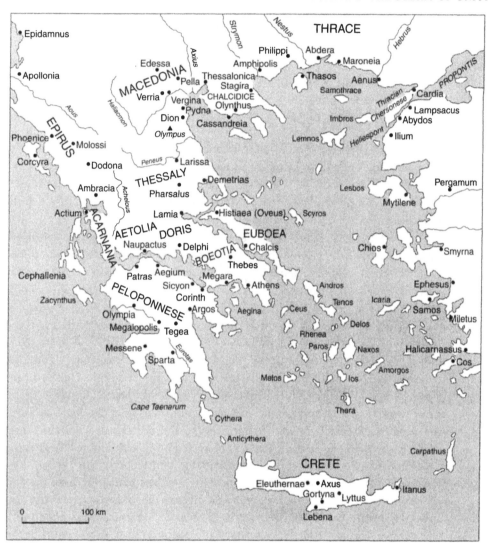

Map 3 Greece and the Aegean Sea.

because, in order to marry Cleopatra, Perdiccas would have to renounce another match that was in the offing, one with Antipater's daughter. It is obvious to what degree such personal ties, turning into dynastic connections, were henceforth to count in political relationships between princes.

Perdiccas, conscious of increasing hostility toward him, made a preemptive attack. Taking advantage of the fact that his adversaries were dispersed on the frontiers of his empire, he decided to march first on the most isolated one. That was Ptolemy, son of Lagus (hence the occasional references to him as "the Lagid," and to members of the dynasty he created as "the Lagids," the descendants of Lagus). Remember that Ptolemy had obtained sovereignty over Egypt. There he had established his rule on a solid foundation, seconded by a large number of Macedonians who had for a long time appreciated his qualities as a clear-headed and generous leader. He had shown decisiveness and political flair by extending his authority in 322 to the rich colony of Cyrene, which he had conquered, thanks to the city's internal disagreements, by the despatch of the strategist Ophellas. Finally, in an adroit move, he had obtained approval for Alexander's embalmed corpse to be routed toward the oasis of Ammon, meaning toward Egypt, instead of being taken to Macedonia to be interred in the royal necropolis at Aegae by the side of his father Philip. In the course of its progress Ptolemy gave it provisional burial at Memphis until the mausoleum in which the Conqueror was to rest was completed in Alexandria, in the very city he had founded. The transfer of the illustrious remains on a ceremonial coach of unheard-of luxury, which Diodorus (*Historical Library*, XVIII, 26–8: see p. 386) describes in great detail, appealed to the popular imagination. The keeper of such a talisman would be expected to use that privilege in furthering his imperial ambitions.

Such was the adversary whom Perdiccas most wanted to eliminate. Leaving the faithful Eumenes to cover his rear lines in Asia Minor, he led a strong army into Egypt and advanced until he faced Memphis. There he failed in his attempt to cross the Nile with his troops. His unsuccessful operation caused heavy losses. A mutiny broke out, led by Perdiccas' generals, Seleucus among them. They went in person to his tent and murdered their chief. Ptolemy declined the position of regent offered to him by the murderers, thus showing that, unlike the other Diadochi, he was not interested in universal monarchy, for the now undisputed possession of Egypt appeared to him a more secure proposition. Meanwhile the armies of Antipater and Craterus had landed in Anatolia and clashed with Eumenes' forces. Revealing a military talent unsuspected in an archivist, Eumenes had defeated Craterus, who had died in battle. A period of a few weeks in the year 321 thus witnessed the disappearance of two actors in the drama that was unfolding. A new distribution of the main parts seemed to be in order.

The exercise took place in that very year (321) at a meeting of the Diadochi in a market town of northern Syria, Triparadisus. The army chose as *epimeletes* of the kings (that is, for the position of regent) the aged Antipater, whose years and proven loyalty made him a fairly obvious choice for the post. The satrapies were redistributed. Ptolemy of course kept Egypt, which his victory over Perdiccas henceforth designated as a "conquest by the spear" in the same category as the territories conquered by Alexander. Seleucus had Babylonia, another rich and prosperous region, in the very center of the Empire. Antigonus kept Phrygia and Lycia. He was moreover appointed *strategos* of Asia, as he was to command the royal army in the war it was to wage on Eumenes, guilty of having supported Perdiccas and slain Craterus. The widow of Craterus, Phila, one of Antipater's daughters, was given in marriage to Antigonus' son, Demetrius, a 15-year-old youth – she was to be the mother of Antigonus Gonatas, future king of Macedon. The incumbents of the other Asian satrapies were appointed or confirmed in their appointments, right down to and including the king of Taxila and Porus in India. That was the last settlement in which Alexander's empire appeared as a whole, albeit a precarious one. Thereafter Antipater made his way back to Macedonia, taking with him the two kings who, for the first time since Alexander crossed the Straits in 334, were to set foot in Europe, in the land of their fathers.

Antipater's return to Macedonia, accompanied by the two kings, had a symbolic value. It demonstrated how dear the Argeads' old tradition, with its close links to the Macedonian fatherland and its people, remained to the hearts of the Diadochi. These were obsessed, one after the other, with an urge to be the recipients of that inheritance and to become in their turn kings of Macedon, the only title invested with legitimacy in their eyes. All of them – with the exception of Ptolemy, a realist and a clear-headed man – were to be distracted by a venerable but derisory temptation from more obvious and safer heights. The Macedonian mirage was one of the most powerful motive agents of the Diadochi, and the main cause of their failures. By forgoing such a vision their successors, the Epigoni, were able to establish securely their dominion over their respective States and found new dynasties. In addition, by transferring to Macedonia the permanent seat of royal power, Antipater was actually renouncing in the name of the two kings, whose representative he was in the eyes of his peers, Alexander's universal monarchy, for that monarchy could not have its seat anywhere else than in the very heart of the empire, in Asia. From such a point of view the Triparadisus agreement was a major turning point in history. It marked the abandonment of Alexander's dream by those who had the closest blood-ties with him.

Antigonus, whose task was to head in Anatolia the struggle with Eumenes, satrap of Cappadocia, proscribed by the other satraps for his attachment to Perdiccas, had taken advantage of his position to extend his authority to the greater part of Anatolia. He was besieging Eumenes in a Cappadocian fortress when in the summer of 319 Antipater died at a great age. He had an ambitious son, Cassander, a dynamic and unscrupulous man. But, no doubt finding him too young, Antipater had appointed as his successor in the post of *epimeletes* of the two kings, which he himself had held since Triparadisus, an old Macedonian officer of great experience, a former companion of Philip and Alexander, Polyperchon. The very act of appointment constituted an abuse. What authority did Antipater have to choose the kingdom's regent on his own? Though the army approved his decision by acclamation, the choice provoked a most hostile reaction among the other Diadochi. Against Polyperchon, who was taking charge of the kings and of the government of Macedon, a coalition was soon formed, as one had been two years earlier against Perdiccas. In addition to Lysimachus it brought together Antigonus, Cassander, and Ptolemy. Antigonus had abandoned the plan of bringing Eumenes to heel, and restored to him his freedom of action and his territories. Cassander was embittered by his father's preference for a successor other than himself. Finally, Ptolemy saw in the operation the chance to round off his Egyptian realm by attempting to conquer Phoenicia, the traditional glacis of Pharaonic Egypt.

To thwart so many enemies, in particular Cassander, who was trying to gain a foothold in Greece and Macedonia, Polyperchon attempted to win the favor of the Greek cities. He restored the rights they had enjoyed in the days of Philip and Alexander, and which they had lost as a result of the Lamian War. The text of the edict (*diagramma*) written in the name of Philip Arrhidaeus has been preserved for us by Diodorus (XVIII, 56). It plainly demonstrates that the Macedonian sovereigns and their advisors were basically uninterested in the political and social rivalries that divided the citizens of Greek cities. They cared for them only so far as that was to their personal advantage. The terms "democrats" or "oligarchs" meant little to them per se. The essential point for them was to use those men as pawns on a chessboard.

As it happened, Polyperchon's endeavor produced hardly any result. The military reverses of the man who had prompted the promulgation of the edict cut short its application. Yet it provoked a tragedy that, relayed by Diodorus and Plutarch, has reverberated through the ages. That was the death, at a great age and after a glorious career, of Phocion, the *strategos* who had obtained leniency from Macedon for his fatherland in the hour of defeat. Forgetful of his services, Polyperchon had him handed over to the Athenian democrats, dazzled by the unexpected rebound of their fortunes and eager to make him expiate their exclusion from power or their exile. At a stormy meeting of the Assembly, where a delirious populace broke every constitutional rule, Phocion was charged with treason and denied a chance to defend himself by the jeers of his adversaries. He was condemned with his friends to drink hemlock. Their bodies, deprived of burial, were cast outside the boundaries of Attica. Such was the end of a man of integrity whose life was totally devoted to his fatherland, and whom Plutarch compares to Cato of Utica. He fell with many others in May 318, a victim of the multitude's blind passion. A few months later, faced with Cassander's military successes and Polyperchon's repeated failures, Athens was forced to bow again before a foreign victor. She agreed to continued occupation of the citadel of Munychia by a Macedonian garrison, submitted to a census-based regime alien to her democratic tradition, and entrusted its implementation to an *epimeletes* chosen in agreement with Cassander. For ten years, until 307, the Peripatetic philosopher Demetrius of Phalerum provided a competent and moderate administration of the city's internal affairs.

Meanwhile, events were happening at a great pace, both in Asia and Macedo-

nia, sealing in a dramatic fashion the fate of the Argead kings and their supporters. While Polyperchon was warring in vain in the Peloponnese, where he kept by
his side the child-king Alexander IV, the other king, Arrhidaeus, in total bondage to the intrigues of his wife Eurydice, herself a princess of royal blood, had
thrown in his lot with Cassander. To counter them, Polyperchon encouraged
the return to Macedonia of Alexander the Great's aged mother, Olympias. Relegated to her native Epirus, she still dreamed of power. She arrived, supported
by Epirot troops, and was met by Polyperchon, who brought the little king back
to his grandmother. The old queen's prestige impressed the Macedonians, who
abandoned Philip Arrhidaeus' party and surrendered him and his wife Eurydice,
the instigator of his policy. Pitiless, Olympias had them thrown into jail, before
leaving Philip to the mercies of his executioners, who did away with him, and
forcing Eurydice to commit suicide, which she did with courage and dignity.
Thus did one of the two kings disappear from the scene in an atmosphere of
Shakespearean drama, leaving in a heart-to-heart encounter a bloodthirsty ancestor and the 6-year-old prince. The old woman gave free vent to her spite and
had quite a few of the foremost Macedonians slaughtered. She thus brought
upon herself feelings of hatred that deprived her entirely of support. Cassander
took advantage of the situation and blockaded her in the town of Pydna, where
hunger forced her to surrender. At Cassander's request, her fate was decided by
the army, who condemned her to death. Her victims' families took charge of her
execution, which she bore with no sign of weakness, no complaint, true to the
end to an unbending nature. Cassander, for whom Polyperchon, forsaken by his
supporters, was now no obstacle, had Alexander IV and his mother Roxane placed
securely under armed guard, and held solemn obsequies, with funerary games, in
honor of Philip Arrhidaeus and Eurydice. They were buried in the royal necropolis of Aegae. He then married one of Philip II's illegitimate daughters,
Thessalonice, thus revealing his claim to the traditional kingship of Macedon.
Taking up a custom started by Philip and Alexander, he founded a port at the
head of the Thermaic Gulf, east of the mouth of the river Axius (now the Vardar),
and gave it the name of his new spouse. That was Thessalonica, a city promised
a long and brilliant future. Not far off, on the site of the former Greek colony of
Potidaea in Chalcidice, he placed his capital, which he called Cassandreia. He
had no hesitation in asserting his possession of power, and was bold enough to
restore in 316, with the help of other Greek cities, the city of Thebes, which
Alexander had destroyed and razed to the ground in 335. Clearly a new page
had been turned in the great book of history.

The situation was no different in Asia, where the last defender of Argead legitimacy had just disappeared from the scene. It was one of the paradoxes so frequent in those tumultuous times, and on which Hellenistic historians lay so much
stress, that Macedonian legitimacy was proclaimed to the very end against the
Macedonian Diadochi by a Greek, Eumenes of Cardia. To hold in check the

coalition of his adversaries in Asia, Polyperchon had turned to Eumenes, whom he had appointed, in the name of the two kings, *strategos* of Asia, a title formerly given by Antipater to Antigonus. Taking advantage of the position entrusted to him, Eumenes had in two years (318/17) brought under his authority the greater part of Alexander's former empire. He had obtained the support of the elite corps of Macedonian veterans, 3,000 heavy infantry, who had for thirty years taken part in all campaigns under Philip and Alexander, and because of their gleaming armor were called the "Silver Shields," *Argyraspids.* No other army unit could vie with those fighters laden with glorious wounds. Eumenes also held the royal treasury, which was entrusted to his custody by letters from the sovereigns. With such military and financial means, he displayed a talent for politics and strategy unexpected in a man used to a life of cloistered study. An expert both in arranging the order of battle and in deciding on maneuvers in the midst of combat, he knew how to employ ruses while impressing his soldiers with a physical courage unaltered by his occasionally faltering health. His countryman Jerome (Hieronymus) of Cardia, who had been his fellow-worker and friend, later wrote the history of those troubled years. His account is now lost, but Diodorus, who declares that he obtained direct information from it, relates in detail Eumenes' extraordinary adventure. Braving opposition from Antigonus and Seleucus, he traveled the length and breadth of Mesopotamia and Persia, obtaining from the major satrapies contingents that included barbarian troops and elephants. Preserving unity among such heterogeneous forces, he managed for a long time to counter Antigonus, old and experienced general that he was. One can see why Plutarch found it necessary to include him in his gallery of famous men.

Such constancy and talent – and unswerving fidelity to the memory of Alexander – did not suffice to obtain victory for him. At the start of the year 316 an indecisive battle between his troops and those of Antigonus shook the confidence of the Argyraspids. They decided to go over to Antigonus' camp. Handed over by them, Eumenes was put to death, while his victor added to his own troops those they had recently been fighting. There are many instances in these wars of troops moving from one camp to the other. These were wars in which Macedonians were opposed to each other, while Greek or barbarian mercenaries were a source of manpower ready to sell itself to the highest bidder. Thus reinforced with sizable contingents, and now the custodian of the royal treasury secured from Eumenes, Antigonus henceforth appeared as the true master of Asia, which he governed as such, just as Cassander held sway in Europe. The eruption of a conflict between these two could not be long in coming.

■ Formation of a coalition against Antigonus ■ First exploits of Demetrius Poliorcetes ■ Battle of Gaza ■ Capture of Babylon by Seleucus ■ The agreements of 311 ■ Slaughter of Alexander IV and Roxane ■ Operations in Greece ■ Fall and exile of Demetrius of Phalerum ■ Demetrius Poliorcetes in Cyprus ■ The Diadochi proclaim their kingship ■ Siege of Rhodes ■ Poliorcetes in Athens ■ His occupation of Acrocorinth ■ Battle of Ipsus

Another coalition was formed. Lysimachus and Ptolemy joined Cassander, as well as Seleucus, who, expelled from Babylonia, had found shelter in Egypt. Antigonus rejected their ultimatum in the winter of 315/14. A series of intricate and widely scattered operations were soon started. While Antigonus was subduing the Syrian and Phoenician seaboard and building the fleet he lacked, he had himself proclaimed by his assembled Macedonian soldiers *epimeletes* of the young Alexander IV, still sequestered by Cassander, whose betrayal was stigmatized. Moreover, to create difficulties between the same Cassander and the Greek cities, Antigonus, reviving the policy lately adopted by Polyperchon, proclaimed them free, immune from occupation by any foreign garrison, and politically autonomous. Ptolemy responded by publishing an identical proclamation. Such mutual outbidding shows just how sincere the Diadochi's interest was in the freedom of the Greek cities. Polyperchon, who was still at war with Cassander in the Peloponnese, allied himself, as might be expected, with Antigonus, who gave him renewed encouragement by confirming his authority over that area.

Concerning hostilities in the eastern Mediterranean during those years, we shall mention only a few important events. Since he had to deal with adversaries surrounding his territories, Antigonus assigned to his son Demetrius, who was still very young, the task of safeguarding his southern frontier in Syria and Palestine. He busied himself with putting together in Anatolia an army with which to attack Lysimachus and Cassander beyond the Straits. Simultaneously he used his fleet to confront Ptolemy's squadrons in Cyprus, in Caria, and in the Cyclades, with some success: for it was no doubt then that Delos detached itself (around 314) from Athens and recovered a long-lost independence. At the same time a League of Islanders (*Nesiotai*) united under Antigonus' sponsorship the Cycladic islands and cities. In 312, however, Ptolemy, after putting down a revolt in Cyrene and carrying out various operations of harassment around Cyprus, launched an offensive in Palestine, where, in the neighborhood

49

of Gaza, Demetrius had no hesitation in confronting him in a pitched battle. The young man's valor did not save him from defeat, and he retreated, leaving Syria exposed to invasion. Warned of this reverse, Antigonus came to his aid from Anatolia. Ptolemy, satisfied with having devastated the land and won considerable booty, decided to return to Egypt. Yet he had in the meantime given to Seleucus, who accompanied him, a small troop to carry out a project of astonishing boldness. Leading scarcely a thousand men, Seleucus, with complete confidence in his destiny, marched on Mesopotamia, recruiting on his way the local populations under his banner. He thus reached Babylon, from which he had been expelled by Antigonus, and regained power after storming the citadel. He asserted that the oracle of Apollo, which he had consulted in the sanctuary of the Branchidae near Miletus, had called him *King Seleucus.* That explains how, later, the years of the reign of the Seleucid dynasty, which he founded (see p. 52), were counted from his return to Babylon in the spring of 311. For many centuries the Seleucid era was to be used in the whole of that region as an agreed point of chronological reference.

The defeat at Gaza and Seleucus' successful endeavor were two severe blows for Antigonus the One-eyed. It is true that he had succeeded, by coming to his son's help, in recapturing Syria and Palestine. But an expedition led by Demetrius against the Nabataean Arabs occupying the hinterland extending to the Dead Sea (then called the Asphaltite Lake) had ended in failure. Nor had Demetrius succeeded, in spite of an expedition to Mesopotamia, in expelling from that land Seleucus, whose authority henceforth extended to Media and Susiana and was already being confirmed like that of a sovereign. Antigonus resigned himself to negotiating with his main adversaries, Cassander, Lysimachus, and Ptolemy. The agreements reached between them in 311 acknowledged each one's authority over the states in which he had established his rule. That confirmation of the status quo was subject to two restrictions that were of no more than stylistic importance. The Greek cities' autonomy was proclaimed again, and the rights of Alexander IV appeared to be preserved in principle, since Cassander was given responsibility for Macedonian and Greek affairs only so far as he was *strategos* of Europe and until the young king, then 12 years old, came of age. Cassander was unwilling to continue running the risk of being ousted by the legitimate heir, and in 310 had the little prince and his mother Roxane, whom he kept in captivity, assassinated. This was the death blow of the Argead lineage. To quote Diodorus' very apt remark (XIX, 105): "Since there was henceforth no other heir for the empire, each one of those who commanded nations or cities could cherish the hope of becoming a king, and considered that the lands placed under his authority constituted for him a kingdom won by the spear."

These agreements were soon to be put in question. Seleucus, engrossed in bringing the upper satrapies in eastern Iran under his authority, was not a party to them. Antigonus, who had subdued those areas after Eumenes' defeat, would have liked to regain possession of them but fell short of his goal, and after a grievous military reverse had to negotiate an arrangement with his more successful adversary. Seleucus agreed to this, as he had his own difficulties in eastern Iran. That region had been threatened ever since an Indian sovereign, Sandracottus (Chandragupta), founder of the dynasty of the Mauryas, had evinced a desire to occupy not only the valley of the Indus, but also the mountainous provinces that overlooked it on the west. Seleucus campaigned against him for a few years, until the turn of events in the west recalled him in that direction. He found it expedient to yield to Sandracottus the possession of territories that now lay defenceless – the region of Ghandara in the north, part of Arachosia with Kandahar in the center, part of Gedrosia in the south. He obtained in exchange war elephants, which proved a decisive asset in later campaigns.

Antigonus, having settled the situation in Mesopotamia and Iran by withdrawing before Seleucus, turned toward the west, where his partners in the agreements of 311 were taking advantage of his difficulties in Asia to further their designs. The most active among them was Ptolemy, who had at his disposal seasoned naval squadrons, with solid bases in Cyprus, and the support of the wealthy city of Rhodes, which had been quick to recover from catastrophic flooding in 316. Antigonus was the protector of the League of the Islanders in the Cyclades. Ptolemy, in order to keep a watch on him and with a view to an eventual intervention among the Greek cities of Asia, established his headquarters on the island of Cos in the Dodecanese, fairly close to the Anatolian coast. His future heir, Ptolemy II Philadelphus, was born there in 309. Meanwhile the situation changed in Greece, where Cassander and Polyperchon, after years of war, had become reconciled. This gave Cassander a free hand. Ptolemy and Antigonus, eager to arouse hostility against their dangerous rival among the Greek cities, put a temporary halt to their differences in favor of an intervention in Greece proper. Ptolemy sent an expedition into the Peloponnese, Antigonus entrusted his son Demetrius with the task of freeing Athens from Cassander's tutelage. Ptolemy's expedition was of short duration. Demetrius, by contrast, landed in the Piraeus in 307, captured by force the harbor fortifications and the citadel of Munychia held by Cassander's garrison, and compelled Demetrius of Phalerum, still in power in Athens, to hand the city over to him before leaving for exile. Restoring traditional democracy to the Athenians (at least in principle), Demetrius concluded an alliance with them. They showered unheard-of honors on their liberator and on Antigonus. Golden statues of them were erected on a chariot in the Agora, side by side with those of Harmodius and Aristogeiton, the Tyrant-slayers (*Tyrannoktonoi*). An altar was dedicated to them as Saviors. Finally two new tribes were added to the ten traditional ones bearing the names of revered heroes. These were to be the eponymous tribes, Antigonis and Demetrias, of which they were to remain the protectors. Never during his lifetime had any man received such exaltation from the Athenian people.

Demetrius, having also subdued Megara, was recalled by his father to lead an expedition against Cyprus, still in the hands of Ptolemy, whose designs Antigonus intended to oppose once more. That was the young captain's most brilliant campaign: he showed equal mastery in all his pitched battles, in the siege of the Greek city of Salamis (on the eastern coast of Cyprus) and in naval encounters. His success was complete. He forced Ptolemy himself, who had come in person from Egypt with a squadron to the rescue of his forces, to retreat toward Alexandria (summer of 306). The whole of the island of Cyprus was in the hands of Antigonus and Demetrius, and for ten years was to escape Ptolemy's grasp. Intoxicated by triumph, father and son no longer hesitated to fulfill the grand ambition that had haunted the minds of the Diadochi since Alexander's death. They officially took the royal title and put on the diadem that symbolized it. For the sake of saving his prestige, Ptolemy did the same. So did Seleucus, Lysimachus, and Cassander. There was now not one single Argead monarch, but six kings sharing the title, no longer with any thought of dynastic legitimacy. That was the consummation of the official break-up of Alexander's monarchy.

In the autumn of 306 Antigonus wished to crown his victory in Cyprus with a march on Egypt, where Ptolemy still appeared to him to be a redoubtable foe. But the military and naval expedition led by Antigonus and Demetrius (the latter leading the fleet) was put to a severe test by the unfavorable weather and by storms. It sustained heavy losses, and once arrived in the Nile Delta failed to force the defenses set up by Ptolemy's troops. They had no choice but a pitiable retreat to Syria. Ptolemy seemed invulnerable in his Egyptian bastion.

To erase that failure, Antigonus wished to bring over to his side Rhodes, once allied to the Lagid king. The Rhodians' rejection of his ultimatum provoked war. Demetrius came and laid siege to the great maritime city, which put up a valiant defense. Its siege lasted a year (305/4), with a great deployment of military devices which earned Demetrius a title that history has retained, Poliorcetes (Besieger). Diodorus has related in detail the stages of a successful resistance that was helped by the arrival of supplies from Ptolemy, but also from Lysimachus and Cassander. Finally, unable to capture the city, Demetrius preferred to negotiate. The Rhodians were to stay free, without any foreign garrison, and agreed to an alliance with Antigonus provided they would never have to fight Ptolemy. By way of demonstrating that their autonomy was in no way diminished by the agreement, once peace had been restored they raised statues to Lysimachus and Cassander. And, on the advice of the oracle of Ammon, they instituted, in a sanctuary built for that purpose, a cult honoring Ptolemy as a god. As a result of the Rhodian measure, Ptolemy received the title *Sôter*, Savior, an appellation that was given to major divinities like Athena or even Zeus. Deification of kings in their lifetime, at Rhodes or Athens, was becoming part of Greek mores.

Soon after the Rhodian episode, Demetrius was sent to the rescue of Athens, besieged by Cassander. Since the city had shaken off Macedonian domination in 307, it had never stopped fighting Cassander, who was attempting to preserve his authority over continental Greece. After various ups and downs the Macedonians had regained the upper hand, had invaded Attica, and were now again attacking the beleaguered city. Demetrius, landing at Aulis behind Cassander's troops, forced him to raise the siege and leave Attica. He thus for a second time appeared to the Athenians as their liberator, and spent the winter of 304/3 in their city. But by then the 30-year-old king had allowed his successes and the adulation that surrounded him to go to his head, and yielded to a propensity for sensuality and debauchery. Taking up residence in the Parthenon, with a suite of courtesans, he turned the temple of the virgin goddess into a brothel: since he was a god himself, he would say, why not be a guest in his sister's home? He caused a cult to be instituted in honor of his mistress Lamia, who thus became another Aphrodite. An incredible privilege, which ran counter to a tradition jealously preserved until then by the guardians of the cult of Demeter, allowed him to be initiated at Eleusis outside the dates assigned by the calendar for the celebration of the mysteries there. Meanwhile he was constantly interfering in the internal affairs of the city, whose magistrates would anticipate his wishes. Athens had never fallen so low.

After months of folly and debauchery, Demetrius made a new start in his campaign in the spring of 303, and wrested from Cassander's generals the greater part of the Peloponnese. It was then that, in circumstances unknown to us, Polyperchon, now a very aged man (he belonged to the generation of Antigonus the One-eyed), disappeared from the political scene. The next year Demetrius, in a political maneuver of the kind used by his father in 315, attempted to win the Greek cities over to his side. He provided them with an apparent guarantee of political independence, under the formula of a confederate organization that might turn out to be, for Antigonus and Demetrius, a convenient and effective means of controlling the aggregate of States in Greece proper. Many inscriptions have preserved a record of that attempt to group the cities in a league, on the occasion of a convention gathering their envoys at the Isthmus. This was a throwback to the famous League of Corinth set up in 338/7 on Philip II's initiative. Examining these documents, one notices the action of a Greek, Adeimantus of Lampsacus, who served as a go-between for Demetrius in negotiations aimed at realizing the project. Once again, that attempt to set up a confederacy of Greek States and harmonize their policies had no lasting success, for its instigator's sole objective was none other than to continue his struggle with Cassander and conquer Macedonia. Demetrius did in effect secure his own election as supreme military leader, just as Philip, then Alexander, had once done. He obtained from the Corinthians the authorization to place a garrison in the fortress of Acrocorinth, a strategic position commanding the passage from continental Greece to the Peloponnese. But the occupation of that site, the main consequence of a short-lived league, was to last sixty years.

The other Diadochi were bound to react to the twofold menace represented by Demetrius' activity in Greece and Antigonus' preparation for war in Anatolia. Cassander in Macedonia and Lysimachus in Thrace were the obvious targets of a projected offensive, coming in a pincer movement from the south under Demetrius' leadership and from the east across the Straits under that of Antigonus. They decided to forestall such actions and prepared a bold, detailed plan of campaign, with the cooperation of Seleucus and Ptolemy, who were justifiably worried by the success already achieved by Antigonus and his son. Their object was to take the initiative and bring war into Anatolia by a joint attack coming from Europe and Babylonia. This would be at the risk of eroding the defenses of Macedonia, already under direct threat from Demetrius, who had in the spring of 302 penetrated into Thessaly with considerable forces. While Cassander was left to deal with such a threat, Lysimachus, at the head of a powerful force provided by Cassander, landed in Asia Minor and was soon rewarded with some success. Seleucus, leaving Babylon at the same time, was marching west with substantial forces, including 500 elephants given by Sandracottus, the Indian monarch to whom he had relinquished the eastern provinces of the empire. Antigonus soon recalled Demetrius, who came back to Asia, carrying out in Ionia and on the Straits operations that were successful but of secondary importance. Meanwhile Lysimachus and Antigonus were confronting each other in Phrygia and Bithynia, with indecisive results.

In the spring of 301, after the winter truce, the armies regrouped. The decisive encounter took place in the very center of Anatolia, near the Phrygian city of Synnada, at Ipsus. That was the "battle of the Kings." Lysimachus and Cassander aligned forces more or less equal to those of the enemy, about 80,000 men. But the elephants of Seleucus, far more numerous than those of the enemy, tilted the odds in his favor. Antigonus perished in defeat. Demetrius, whose brilliant cavalry charges had failed to save his father, fled toward Ephesus, where he could rely on the support of his fleet, which had the mastery of the seas, and help from the maritime cities. The battle of Ipsus signified not only the end of Antigonus' reign, with the violent death of the octogenarian Diadoch, but also the failure of the final serious attempt to reconstruct into one political unit, firmly rooted on both sides of the Aegean Sea, a kingdom inherited from Alexander's dream. The agreement reached by the Diadochi, after Antigonus' life ended in disaster, confirmed for good the sharing of the empire, even though the myth of unity was to kindle ambition in the hearts of some of them, with no palpable result.

■ *The Greek West* ■ *The failed expedition of Alexander the
Molossian* ■ *Agathocles seizes power in Syracuse* ■ *His operations
in Sicily* ■ *His expedition to Africa against Carthage, with
support from Ophellas of Cyrene* ■ *Ophellas' violent death*
■ *Agathocles' return to Syracuse*

While the Greek world in the East was experiencing these rivalries and struggles, the Greek West had just as large a share of internal quarrels or external threats. Since Timoleon of Corinth had laid down in 337 the power entrusted to him by the Syracusans, of which he had made exemplary use, the great city of Syracuse had been faced with renewed turmoil. She had not been concerned with an expedition to southern Italy led by Alexander the Molossian, a brother of Queen Olympias and an uncle of Alexander the Great, which lasted from 334 to 330. The city of Tarentum had applied for his help in fighting the native tribes, Lucanians and Messapians, who had for a long time pressed them hard. A short time afterwards, the Syracusans had helped Croton, threatened in its turn by the mountaineers from Bruttium. Their intervention was marked by the distinguished role played for the first time by a Syracusan officer of modest origin (he had been a potter by trade), but a brilliant warrior. His name was Agathocles. Diodorus has given us a vigorous portrait of that unique personality, a counterpart to the series of exceptional characters appearing among the Diadochi, his contemporaries. After having played *condottiere* in southern Italy, in the service of Tarentum, then of Rhegium, and finally in Sicily (in the violent clashes between rival factions that tore apart his own country), he had been elected *strategos*. It was then, in 317/16, that (in keeping with the tradition of Greek tyrannies) he gained the support of the democratic faction and seized power in Syracuse. He handed over for plunder the property of the oligarchy's real or imagined supporters, these being massacred (4,000 of them, according to Diodorus), while their families were left to suffer the worst forms of violence for two days and two nights. Then, after a farce performed with consummate art, where, in the presence of the popular assembly, he feigned resignation of all public office, he was acclaimed sole *strategos* with full powers, thus becoming master of the State for an indefinite period. Indeed, he declined the royal title for a long time and never wished to wear the badge of kingship, the diadem. But the powers at his disposal made him a political and military chief comparable in every way to the Diadochi of the Greek Orient. Actually, the very name of *dynast* that Diodorus gives him is often used by that historian when speaking of Hellenistic sovereigns.

Agathocles first devoted his efforts to the task of bringing under his authority the greater part of Greek Sicily, with a view to confronting subsequently the Carthaginians who occupied the western part of the island. After lengthy operations that were often crowned with success, he was nevertheless beaten near Gela, and managed with great difficulty to retreat to Syracuse (June 310). But he had by now formed a bold plan: to transfer the battlefield to Africa, in the very territory of Carthage. Leaving his brother behind to keep watch on the city, he departed from Syracuse in August 310 and reached Tunisia after a six-day crossing. A year of campaigning went by and he had not yet managed to force a victorious decision. Ophellas governed Cyrenaica in the name of Ptolemy, some 1,200 kilometers east of Tunisia: Agathocles appealed to him for help. Despite the long distance and the Saharan waste surrounding the Gulf of Syrtis, Carthage and the Greek cities of Libya had nevertheless shared for half a century a frontier at the Altars of the Philaeni, near the southernmost point of the Great Syrtis. The Carthaginians had repulsed all attempts made by the Greeks to expand westward. Ophellas had at his disposal the considerable resources of Cyrene and neighboring cities, whose inhabitants were used to grappling with the African tribes. One could reasonably expect him to be tempted by an adventure toward the land of the Cinyps river (the region of Leptis Magna) and Carthaginian Africa. He embarked on it in 308, after elaborate preparation, and, in a difficult two months' march along the Syrtis sandbanks, led all the way to Tunisia an expeditionary force that included a hundred combat chariots, the elite unit of the Cyrenaean army. The operation had obviously been approved by Ptolemy, who counted on the growth of his realm were his lieutenant to meet with success. But Agathocles, yielding to a sudden feeling of mistrust toward an ally whose military deployment appeared to steal the spotlight from him, laid an ambush and had him slain, then enrolled in his own army Ophellas' leaderless soldiers. For another year he carried out operations in Tunisia, taking

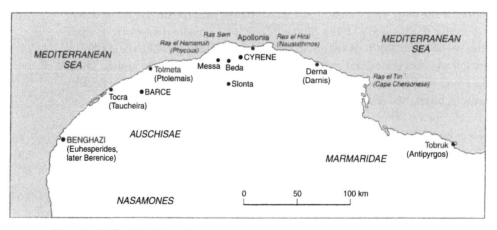

Map 4 Hellenistic Cyrenaica.

and sacking many cities, but failing to occupy Carthage. Finally in October 307, after heavy reverses and a trip to Sicily, where his affairs were not going well in his absence, he had to leave Africa for good. He abandoned the remnants of his army and his two sons, whom his soldiers, angry at his departure and thirsting for revenge, put to death. His great ambition to conquer Africa thus ended in disaster.

After Ophellas' death Cyrene revolted against Ptolemy, who was soon forced to send his son-in-law Magas to reconquer the province. Agathocles, however, had received news from the East after his return to Sicily. Judging himself in no way inferior to the Diadochi, who had recently proclaimed their kingship, he in turn took the royal title. But he still refused to wear the diadem, preferring to Oriental usage the wearing of a crown, a traditional priestly emblem. But it was rumored, as happened later in Caesar's case, that what he actually preferred was to conceal his baldness. Taking Sicilian affairs in hand, he at last managed to come to an agreement with Carthage, on the basis of a territorial status quo, and an indemnity in gold and cereals which the Carthaginians agreed to pay him. Having then crushed the opponents who wanted to oust him from Syracuse, he restored his power, and was thus able to direct his political aims toward Italy and the Adriatic.

■ *The Greek East after Ipsus* ■ *Princely marriages among the Diadochi* ■ *Demetrius Poliorcetes' endeavors in Greece* ■ *First exploits of Pyrrhus* ■ *Poliorcetes becomes king of the Macedonians* ■ *Foundation of Demetrias* ■ *Pyrrhus and Lysimachus expel Demetrius from Macedonia* ■ *Poliorcetes in Anatolia* ■ *His captivity and death*

In the eastern Mediterranean the battle of Ipsus eliminated Antigonus and allowed his victors to share the old king's territories. Ptolemy, who had sent an expedition to Syria without pushing further the advantage he had won there, kept in his power the southern part of that region to serve as a bulwark for Egypt. Lysimachus and Seleucus reaped the greatest benefit from that joint victory. Lysimachus took for himself the west and center of Asia Minor, with the exception of Cilicia, which was given to a brother of Cassander's, and some coastal strongholds that were already under Ptolemy's control. Seleucus obtained access to the sea with northern Syria, but he did not abandon the wish to recover Palestine from Ptolemy. Cassander remained content with his European possessions, where he fully expected to have a free hand both in Macedonia and in

Greece. There remained a spoiler in the person of Demetrius Poliorcetes. He had his all-powerful fleet, supported by bases in the Aegean (thanks to the League of the Islanders), in Asia Minor (though Lysimachus was soon going to capture these), in Cyprus, at Tyre and Sidon on the Syrian coast, and finally in mainland Greece, especially at Corinth. Athens, however, shook herself free of her irksome protector, sending back to him the squadron he had left moored in the Piraeus. The Hellenic League had hardly been put in place (in 302: see p. 53) when Antigonus' defeat at Ipsus sealed its fate. But its founder, urged on by a fiery temperament, had in no way given up the thought of being an actor in the ongoing drama. He was to enliven the political scene for fifteen years.

In their wish to create personal links over and above (and reinforcing) their political agreements, the Diadochi were quite willing to arrange princely marriages between their families – a practice that demonstrates how the personal exercise of power had developed into a system in the organization of major States. After Ipsus Ptolemy made Lysimachus his son-in-law, bestowing on him the hand of his daughter Arsinoe, an absolutely remarkable woman who was for thirty years to exert a determining influence on events in Thrace, then in Egypt. Seleucus married Demetrius Poliorcetes' own daughter, Stratonice, to incorporate in his master plan a fiery and still young father-in-law. These marriages, dictated solely by self-interest, took no account of the respective ages of the parties involved. That fact was brought to light when the young Stratonice aroused in her husband's son from a previous marriage, the future Antiochus I, a passion that the young man did not dare to avow to her. So violent was his love that he fell prey to a sickly spell of listlessness that put his life in danger. When the physician Erasistratus discovered the cause of the disease, Seleucus, to save his son, parted with Stratonice and gave her in marriage to the young prince. This romantic love story, an inverted form of the tale of Phaedra, but crowned with a happy ending, was later brilliantly recounted by Plutarch and became a recurrent theme in literature and art until modern times (see further p. 357). Thanks to his accord with Seleucus, Demetrius managed to recapture Cilicia from Cassander's brother, who had not governed it for long. But that was not enough to satisfy his ambition, which was soon revived by a favorable circumstance, the death in 298/ 7 of Cassander, who left as successors in Macedonia sons too young to make good their claim. Demetrius first aimed at reconquering Athens, which had been prey to serious civic discord since his departure in 302. That situation had led to the seizure of power by a de facto tyranny, that of the *strategos* Leochares, with the covert support of Cassander. A violent and unscrupulous man, Leochares had not hesitated to deprive Phidias' Athena Parthenos of its gold covering, and obtain pay for his mercenaries by having it melted down. Pausanias and Plutarch enshrined in their writings the horror-stricken memory of that odious deed perpetrated on the goddess's treasury. Demetrius' first assault was repulsed in 296. He went off to wage a war in the Peloponnese, in which he met with some success. On his return he laid siege to Athens and captured it in 294, while Leochares took flight. Ptolemy sent a squadron, which failed to break Demetrius' blockade. He was, however, taking advantage elsewhere of his opponent's absence. He captured Cyprus, from which he had been expelled ten years earlier. Lysimachus brought under his control the major cities of Ionia, Ephesus and Miletus. Seleucus acquired Cilicia. While gaining anew a footing in Greece, Demetrius had lost his Asian possessions.

The already complex interplay of these rival ambitions was made still more intricate by the arrival on the scene of a new competitor, younger and with an even greater appetite for glory than Demetrius: his own brother-in-law Pyrrhus, prince of Epirus. Having lost his kingdom through the actions of Cassander, Pyrrhus had joined up with Demetrius and fought beside him at Ipsus. But shortly afterwards he had been sent as a hostage to Ptolemy when Seleucus and Demetrius, before Cassander's death, tried to ally themselves with that king. The death in 298 of Pyrrhus' sister, Demetrius' second wife, had loosened the personal tie existing between the brothers-in-law. With Ptolemy's help, Pyrrhus returned to Epirus, where he managed to regain his throne. He soon married a daughter of Agathocles' (see p. 55–7), Lanassa. She brought him as a dowry the island of Corcyra (Corfu), recently conquered by Agathocles, who, from his base in Syracuse, was reviving Dionysius' former designs on the Adriatic. Pyrrhus was thus strengthening his Epirot territories toward the sea. His ambition was soon to find means for a grand political endeavor, supported by an exceptional military skill that occasionally won him comparison with Alexander.

His first move was to interfere with the internal affairs of Macedon by taking sides in the dispute between Cassander's two surviving sons. Pyrrhus supported the elder son, obtaining territorial concessions in payment. But that same son had also appealed to Demetrius, who was then campaigning in the Peloponnese. Giving up an operation against a Spartan city that he was about to take by storm, Demetrius hastened to Macedonia, got rid of Cassander's elder son by having him murdered, and had himself proclaimed king in the autumn of 294. He had thus become ruler of a monarchy with an age-old tradition, and was now in possession of the vast territories of Macedonia and Thessaly, rich in manpower. Furthermore he controlled a large portion of mainland Greece, thanks to garrisons which he had been allowed to place in the foremost strategic locations – Acrocorinth, Chalcis in Euboea on the narrow passage of the Euripus, Munychia in the Piraeus – and to the League of the Islanders. What a change in his destiny, so few years after the disaster he had suffered at Ipsus! The former fugitive, now master of the ancestral kingdom of the Macedonians, decided to underline his triumph in the way others had adopted before him – Alexander the Great, Cassander, Lysimachus, Antigonus the One-eyed: just what Seleucus was soon to do. He founded in Thessaly a new capital named after him, near present-day Volos, at the inner edge of the Gulf of Pagasae, not far from the spot from which, according to tradition, Jason had departed, leading the expedition of the Argonauts. That town was Demetrias. There, in a carefully chosen location, between well-protected harbors, the king had a surrounding wall built, eight kilometers long. Its present remains are impressive, and it was destined to be, until the end of the Macedonian monarchy, along with Chalcis and Acrocorinth, one of those strongholds of first-rate strategic importance that were called "the Fetters of Greece."

Demetrius had put his affairs in order brilliantly. But then he yielded to his love of luxury, of sumptuous ceremonies, of court procedures borrowed from Oriental monarchies, far removed from the simplicity and austerity, the direct relationship between king and subjects traditional in the Argead dynasty. His popularity was damaged as a result, while the heavy expenses incurred by his plans for the future aroused a hostile reaction in Macedonia and the Greek cities. Two successive revolts in Boeotia, encouraged by the Aetolians and by Pyrrhus, had forced him to exercise once more in 291 his talent as the "Besieger of Cities," this time on Thebes, restored from its ruins in the recent past by Cassander. To avenge himself on Pyrrhus, he seized Corcyra, to which he was called by Lanassa, the Epirot monarch's forsaken wife and daughter of Agathocles. He was thinking of marrying her. He then led an expedition against Aetolia, while Pyrrhus ravaged part of Macedonia in his absence (289).

Ptolemy, quick as usual to seize any opportunity for extending his power, took advantage of Demetrius' difficult situation by naval action in the Cyclades. He took the place of Demetrius as protector of the League of the Islanders, just as a few years earlier he had deprived him of Cyprus. That did not stop Poliorcetes from putting together, in his strongholds and in the Piraeus, considerable numbers of troops and a fleet of 500 ships, according to Plutarch. Such preparation for war, obviously aiming at a reconquest of Asia, worried Pyrrhus and Lysimachus, Macedon's western and eastern neighbors. They agreed to forestall Demetrius by joint action, and in 288 simultaneously invaded Macedonian territory. Caught in a pincer movement, Demetrius was unable to resist a double attack. Near Beroea, he was trying to stop Pyrrhus' advance when a large number of his soldiers abandoned him. He was forced to flee for safety, in no very glorious way – by concealing his princely outfit under a plain black cloak. He rejoined his wife Phila, daughter of Antipater (see p. 45), in Chalcidice. In an act of despair she took poison, while her husband went back to Greece, and mustering some more troops, tried to regain his position at Athens. The city that had greeted him with adulation three years earlier, after his Aetolian campaign, closed its gates to him and appealed to Pyrrhus for help. Demetrius had to come to terms in 287, and acknowledged the loss of Athens after that of Macedonia, which Pyrrhus and Lysimachus had shared. His son Antigonus, surnamed Gonatas, whom Phila had borne him, was already of an age to take command, and kept control of the other strongholds which his father had retained, notably his capital Demetrias.

Poliorcetes, though a defeated and despoiled man, was again prey to his Asian dreams. Gathering a few thousand mercenaries and what was left of his fleet, he crossed to Anatolia, captured a few coastal towns that had acknowledged Lysimachus' authority, then forged ahead into the interior, where he occupied Sardis. But in 286, while advancing further east, with a plan marked by daring and folly, to create a new kingdom for himself among the upper satrapies, he was sorely tried physically while crossing an unhealthy and desolate land. With the reduced forces at his disposal, he had to change his objective and turn south across the Taurus Mountains in the direction of Tarsus. There he found Seleucus' army facing him, while behind him Lysimachus' son Agathocles held the passes over the Taurus and cut off his retreat. For a number of months longer, he struggled desperately on the southern slopes of the mountain range, performing many isolated exploits against an adversary who was certain to wear him down. Finally, at the beginning of the year 285, he was forced into a surrender which Seleucus, mindful of Poliorcetes being his father-in-law, received generously. Poliorcetes received royal treatment and was taken to a princely residence on the banks of the Orontes, where in the midst of opulence he led an idle life of dissipation, under armed guard.

Such a lifestyle soon got the better of his health, shaken as it was by the trials of war. He died in 283, after a tumultuous half-century filled with Fortune's spectacular reversals. He had been extreme in every imaginable way, with his natural gifts, his insatiable desires, his endeavors that were as grand as they were unpredictable, a strange inability to pursue lucidly a grand design until it became reality. In a period so rich in extraordinary destinies and exceptional personalities, no figure prompts more wonder than Demetrius Poliorcetes. Seleucus had his remains conveyed with honor to Antigonus Gonatas, who celebrated his father's funeral in great pomp at Corinth, before his interment at Demetrias, the city he had founded.

■ *Lysimachus' endeavors and successes* ■ *His undivided possession of the kingdom of Macedon* ■ *His conflict with Seleucus* ■ *Battle of Corupedium* ■ *Murder of Seleucus by Ptolemy Ceraunus* ■ *The Celtic invasion* ■ *Death of Ceraunus.*

While, in the mountains of Anatolia and on the banks of the Orontes, the last episode in a drama with multiple developments took place with Poliorcetes as the central figure, another Diadoch, Lysimachus king of Thrace, was asserting in his turn his claim to the foremost role. Since the first round of power sharing at Alexander's death, that energetic and cunning Macedonian, a capable warrior prudent in his designs and resolute in carrying them out, had slowly consolidated his position in Thrace. This was a harsh region where barbarian tribes lived alongside some prosperous Greek cities on the coast of the Aegean Sea, the Straits, and the Euxine: Thracians east of the chain of Mount Haemus, and the Getae in the north, between Mount Haemus and the Danube (then called the Ister). The river Strymon in the west and the Black Sea in the east were the boundaries of a vast territory, where Greek influence was ancient and deep-rooted, but which the Macedonian kings had brought under political submission only with great difficulty. Lysimachus had had to fight a long and difficult war to keep the native principalities or bring them back under his authority. The Greek cities, the most important of which was Byzantium on the Bosporus, remained free in principle, but had an alliance with the sovereign that, as was the case elsewhere, bordered on a subject–master relationship. Kept busy for a long time by his arduous task in mountainous country and on the northern limits of his kingdom, Lysimachus had taken part only at a late stage in the conflicts between the Diadochi. But his role had been a decisive one in the downfall of Antigonus and in the operations culminating in the battle of Ipsus. As a result he had made large territorial gains in Asia Minor, the western half of which was henceforth under his rule, so that he had authority over the Anatolian coast of the Aegean Sea on both sides of the Straits. He exercised close supervision over the nominally autonomous Greek cities of that region, and his very heavy fiscal demands pressed hard upon the rural areas of Anatolia, so much so that the Phrygian peasants looked back with yearning to the days when Antigonus was their ruler. In his turn he had founded in 309 his own capital on the site of Cardia, named after himself: Lysimacheia. After his successful war with Demetrius and the addition to his kingdom of part of Macedonia, he felt capable of aiming higher.

In 288, when Pyrrhus defeated Demetrius, his soldiers, joined by his adversary's army, hailed him as king of Macedon. He retained that title, though master of only part of the land, since Lysimachus had annexed the rest. He could after all claim it as he was an Aeacid. Olympias, mother of Alexander, was a sister of Pyrrhus' grandfather: he thus happened to be a second cousin of the Conqueror. Like Alexander, he was descended from Achilles, ancestor of the family of the Aeacids, whom he himself had taken as a model. Filled with an insatiable thirst for conquest, Pyrrhus took advantage of Demetrius' departure and annexed Thessaly, in which he took a special interest because his mother Phthia, whom he revered, belonged to an illustrious Thessalian family. That annexation was a major addition to the states ruled by the king of Epirus. It prompted Lysimachus to intervene and quell such a dangerous neighbor. Appealing to the Macedonian patriotism of his adversary's troops, as though they were duty-bound to come over to his side away from an Epirot prince, he caused them to change their allegiance, just as Pyrrhus had enticed Poliorcetes' soldiers in a not too distant past. Watching his troops melting away as a result of these desertions, Pyrrhus withdrew to Epirus, leaving Lysimachus in possession of Macedonia and Thessaly: Demetrias excepted, where Antigonus Gonatas, son of Demetrius, was still holding out firmly. Thus, in addition to the States belonging strictly to his kingdom, the king of Thrace was henceforth ruling in Europe the entire Argead inheritance, and in Asia the larger part of Anatolia. In these later days of his life, his power was at its peak.

He did not enjoy that situation for long. A family tragedy contributed to his downfall. From his first marriage to Antipater's daughter a son was born, Agathocles, who had reached an age to be a leader, and had played his part with efficiency in the final operations against Demetrius Poliorcetes. Lysimachus' second wife was Arsinoe, daughter of Ptolemy Sôter and sister of Ptolemy II, who since 285 had been an associate in royal power in Egypt and was to succeed his father in 283. She was the cause of Lysimachus' resentment against Agathocles, to the point where the old king, urged by suspicion, had his son executed. Such cruelty appeared scandalous. Faced with mistrust and criticism, Lysimachus became more tyrannical. Seleucus, begged by the widow of the deceased prince to intervene, allowed himself (in 281) to be persuaded, and started a campaign against Lysimachus north of the Taurus. On the plain of Corupedium west of Sardis Lysimachus was defeated and, like Antigonus before him, perished in the encounter. Many of those in the service of the king of Thrace had betrayed him in favor of Seleucus. The State that Lysimachus had built with perseverance and patience, half in Europe and half in Asia astride the Straits, had lasted but a brief moment in history. After Alexander's dream with its grandiose vision, it was the turn of Philip's, one that seemed closer to reality, to be shattered a short time after coming true.

Seleucus was the last of the great Diadochi to have served under Alexander. He now dominated the whole of Asia, with the exception of the northern area, where Bithynia, Paphlagonia, and the Pontus, at the edge of the Black Sea, had always been independent. To such an extensive Asian empire he wished to join Macedon, for in his turn he had yielded to the temptation of succeeding the Argeads. With Macedon under his rule, Seleucus would have reassembled all of Alexander's empire except Egypt. Though he was 80 years old, there is no reason to doubt what would have happened next.

But Seleucus' apogee was – as often in this period – followed by a sudden and unexpected reversal. Crossing the Hellespont, he was approaching Lysimacheia, capital of his fallen adversary, when a close associate of his, Ptolemy Ceraunus (*Keraunos*, transliterated from Greek, "the Thunderbolt"), murdered him in late summer 281. The murderer was a son of Ptolemy Sôter by his first marriage. He had been dispossessed of his inheritance by his father, in favor of Ptolemy II, born like Arsinoe of a second marriage with the beautiful Berenice. The young man had first found shelter at Lysimachus' court, and seems to have had a share in the intrigue that had led to the old king's bitter feelings toward his son Agathocles. He had then gone to the court of Seleucus, who had received him with favor. He had now repaid his benefactor with treachery, under the pretext of avenging Lysimachus. But the ambitious, unscrupulous youth obtained in his place the acclamation of Seleucus' army as king of Macedon. His misdeed was well calculated, for the son of Seleucus, Antiochus I, was kept back in the depths of Asia, where his father, giving him a share of kingly power, had entrusted him with the rule of the eastern provinces, and was soon engrossed in taking possession of that part of his legacy. Antigonus Gonatas, still occupying his strongholds in mainland Greece, did not have the means to intervene effectively. Pyrrhus, who had been called on for help by Tarentum in southern Italy, was busy preparing a faraway expedition to the west. Ptolemy Ceraunus therefore had reason to hope that he could establish himself firmly in Macedonia and make up for the disgrace his father had inflicted on him. To strengthen his hold on Lysimachus' inheritance, he did not hesitate to marry his widow Arsinoe, his own half-sister and also the king of Egypt's sister by blood. But, showing typical mistrust and cruelty, he caused two of Arsinoe's sons by Lysimachus to be murdered. She immediately left her bloodthirsty spouse and, thinking of nothing but revenge, made for Alexandria, where she was soon to marry her own brother, Ptolemy II, henceforth called "His Sister's Lover," *Philadelphus*. Ceraunus, however, seemed likely to establish his authority on his newly acquired kingdom. An invasion by the Gauls prevented him from doing so.

Armed bands of Celts had already threatened for many years the northern frontiers of Thrace and Macedonia. Coming from the Danube to the Balkans, they surged toward the southeast. The Greeks and Macedonians dreaded these barbarian warriors, whose ways appeared strange to them, as can be seen from the long digression Pausanias devoted to their attempt to pillage the sanctuary at Delphi (*Periegesis* X, 19ff.). With the incautious recklessness that had won him the title of Thunderbolt (*Keraunos*: see above), Ptolemy Ceraunus attacked the invaders in open country, was crushed by them, and perished on the battlefield (early in 279). Macedon was once again without a king, a situation that proved favorable to Poliorcetes' son, Antigonus Gonatas. In an operation undertaken in Thrace, he met a band of Gauls head-on near Lysimacheia and wiped them out in a well-executed maneuver (277). The glory of victory over barbarian invaders who had hitherto stayed unvanquished helped him to earn Macedon's respect. By the next year he was the country's master and leader. The kingdom was now in capable hands. Like the Seleucid monarchy in Asia with Antiochus I, and the Ptolemaic kingdom of Egypt with Ptolemy II Philadelphus, Macedon had now found in Antigonus Gonatas a dynamic and clear-headed sovereign, yet a cautious one with limited goals, able to safeguard its integrity and put it on a sound footing. Around the year 280, after the insane adventures that left their mark on the era of the Diadochi, the world of the Hellenistic kingdoms finally followed a pattern that was to last.

Alexander's dream of a universal empire had not become reality. The Mediterranean and the Near East were now shared by a number of strong powers, among which Rome was ultimately to assert her supremacy.

3/THE HELLENISTIC MONARCHIES: THEIR YEARS OF GLORY

■ *Importance of the third century* BC: *the great monarchies, the dynasts, the cities*

The history of the Diadochi, so rich in unforeseen developments and spectacular reversals, deserved to be recounted in some detail because of the major part played in it by certain exceptional personalities, for their ambitions, their passions, even their whims were determining factors in the unfolding of events. By contrast, for the period after 280, when the monarchical states born of Alexander's empire had found a certain degree of equilibrium, we need no longer trace their development in such detail. In future, it was to comply with certain simple laws that can easily be deduced from the complex mass of events. It will therefore be enough to survey the major aspects of the history of the three principal Hellenistic kingdoms in the third century when, under the first sovereigns of each dynasty, each kingdom underwent its greatest development and shone most brightly. Around the Ptolemaic, Seleucid, and Antigonid monarchies, some less powerful states, linked by a close relationship with them and sometimes playing a part in their rivalries, enjoyed prosperity for a more or less long period. Examples are the monarchies of Magas at Cyrene (see the epigraph of this book, p. 1), of the Attalids at Pergamum, of Hiero II at Syracuse, or the kingdoms of the Anatolian coastland on the Black Sea. There were also innumerable Greek cities great or small, famous or obscure, sometimes federated in leagues that enhanced their military power or political influence. Each of them lived its particular life. Some, like Athens or Sparta, dreamed of their brilliant past. Others, like Delos or Rhodes, took advantage of the new economic or political situation. They all honored their gods, took care of their own affairs, attended to local problems that arose unceasingly day after day. For the vast majority of Greeks this was the social framework in which everybody's human adventure took place. Behind the stage on which was enacted the clash of dynastic conflicts, wars of independence or conquest arising in endless succession over the years, the profound and enduring reality of the Greek city was a continuation of the pattern of the Classical age, without any fundamental change. This is a fact that should always be kept in mind.

■ *The Ptolemaic kingdom* ■ *Its policy in Syria and Cyprus*
■ *The problem of Cyrene: Magas' government* ■ *The management of Egypt under Ptolemy Sôter's reign* ■ *Ptolemy II Philadelphus*
■ *His quarrel with King Magas* ■ *The first and second Syrian Wars* ■ *Ptolemaic endeavors in the Aegean Sea* ■ *Egypt's wealth and prosperity* ■ *The role of Arsinoe II Philadelphus* ■ *Ptolemy III Euergetes* ■ *His marriage with Berenice, daughter of Magas* ■ *Cyrenaica becomes a Ptolemaic possession again*
■ *The third Syrian War* ■ *Euergetes' Greek policy*

The kingdom founded in Egypt by Ptolemy, later called Sôter, was chronologically the first of the great States of the Hellenistic world to emerge from the post-Alexandrian chaos. Its founder, an intelligent and realistic man, seems to have had from the start the idea of a prudent and safe policy which would establish for good his dynasty's rule in the Nile valley, rich as a result of its own resources. Outside that central bastion, which proved impregnable with the passage of time, the dynasty was to extend its reach by means of strategic territorial gains, useful alliances, and judiciously chosen support bases. We have seen how Ptolemy managed, each time a threat loomed in the treasured area of the Delta, to counter it with necessary military measures: something that Perdiccas (in 321), Antigonus and Demetrius (in 306) learned at their expense. Outside Egypt, on the other hand, he did not allow himself to be lured by inordinate ambition into rash projects. In this he stands in stark contrast to the other Diadochs. Alone among them, he never desired to restore a universal monarchy to his advantage. He was content to secure his share in Alexander's legacy by schemes of limited scope, but efficiently pursued.

In the first place, his plan was to subdue or at least control southern Syria and Palestine, a natural ramp and bulwark on the only land frontier through which an invader could threaten Egypt. This had been the policy of the great pharaohs of the New Kingdom. Ptolemy was obviously complying with a constant feature of Egyptian tradition imposed by geography. Furthermore, these regions supplied Egyptian shipyards with timber, which was lacking in the Nile valley. Ptolemy thus made renewed forays into Palestine and Syria, retreating when forced to do so, but going on the offensive once more at the first opportunity, until the battle of Ipsus (see p. 54) allowed him to occupy that area permanently. Many years later he put the finishing touch on that conquest, on the occasion of Demetrius Poliorcetes' disastrous defeat, by occupying the Antigonid ports of Tyre and Sidon. In spite of Seleucus' pressing demands, neither Ptolemy Sôter nor his son Philadelphus ever contemplated ceding southern Syria, however close it was to the vital center of the Seleucid empire. This proved a constantly recurring cause of conflict between the two kingdoms, provoking a succession of "Syrian Wars."

The Ptolemaic policy toward Cyprus should be seen in the same perspective. This large island was shared by a number of small kingdoms, with some of which Ptolemy seems to have made alliances after his accession to power in Egypt. He soon secured his influence in that outpost, which he obviously thought essential to his purposes. For this reason Antigonus badly wanted to take it away from him, by sending Demetrius in 306: it would serve as a formidable base of operations for a naval invasion of Egypt. Ptolemy suffered a heavy defeat, but that did not dissuade him from wishing to recover a base of such major importance. He was successful ten years later. Cyprus was to stay a Ptolemaic possession until the Roman conquest.

Relations were more difficult with Cyrenaica, a Greek settlement of great antiquity in Libya, separated from the Nile valley by a thousand kilometers across the desert and a coast hardly accessible to ships. Ancient and prosperous Greek cities situated there had shown deference to Alexander. Starting in 322, Ptolemy had forced them to submit to his personal authority by taking advantage of internal discord among the Cyreneans. But the spirit of independence was not dead in Cyrene. Many revolts broke out against Ptolemaic rule, in 312, then in 306/5. After a reconquest by Magas, the whole region experienced under that prince's government a de facto then a de jure autonomy that lasted half a century. A princely marriage accompanied by another military campaign proved necessary to renew Cyrenaica's union with the Ptolemaic monarchy. While that union lasted until annexation by Rome, it nevertheless had a chequered history, caused by dynastic conflicts, illustrating the unusual character of this external possession of the Ptolemies. Actually, all through the Hellenistic period the Greeks of Libya continued with their own lifestyle, administering their own local affairs without worrying about the larger picture of Ptolemaic policy.

While southern Syria, Cyprus, and Cyrenaica were for the Ptolemies essential bases of power outside Egypt, they occasionally eyed much more remote regions: the Aegean Sea as far as Thrace, as well as Greece proper. For them it was less a matter of permanent settlement in those areas than of an occasional expedition, of bases for their fleet or alliances with a military or commercial objective. Their aim was to ensure some balance of power among the major states of the eastern Mediterranean, so that Egypt's safety and the health of the royal finances could be preserved, linked as they were with the freedom of maritime trading. Such a policy, with flexible and limited objectives, was put in practice during the reigns of the first three kings of the dynasty. Later it suffered rapid degradation because of the sovereigns' indolence and fratricidal quarrels.

We shall not say much more about Ptolemy I Sôter. The various steps of his prudent policy have been noted at every stage in our account of the history of the Diadochi. The part he played in setting up the internal administration of Egypt is not known in any detail. We have every reason to believe that the structures shown by the papyri as having existed under his successors were given a definite shape by him between 323 and 283. In that crucial period of forty years, Ptolemy endowed the new monarchy with external prestige and internal stability. Both of these rested on an economy firmly taken over by the governing power. Cleomenes of Naucratis (see p. 18) had already ensured substantial benefit by bringing under his exclusive control the export of cereals produced by the rich soil of the rural areas fertilized by the Nile. Such a source of income for the royal treasury did not escape Ptolemy Sôter's notice. Apart from the use made of that income for military expenses, he did not neglect the country's infrastructure. Under his rule the port of Alexandria was fully developed with the building of the Pharos in 287 (see pp. 279–81). Finally, on the advice of the philosopher Demetrius of Phalerum (see pp. 46, 361), who had taken shelter in Egypt after the capture of Athens by Poliorcetes (see p. 51), he invited scholars and men of letters to his court, thus laying the foundation for Alexandria's fame as the intellectual metropolis of Hellenism. This Macedonian soldier, whose heavy features concealed a penetrating intellect, clear-headed judgment, and a generous temperament, was a real builder of the monarchy. In his old age (in 286), anxious to ensure the future of his dynasty, he took as his associate his son Ptolemy. That son was born of his beautiful mistress Berenice, who became his second wife. She was elevated with him to divine rank. They were known as the Savior Deities.

Ptolemy II, born in 308, was 23 at his father's death. In addition to a characteristic roving eye for women, he had inherited from Ptolemy Sôter a lively interest in literature and intellectual matters. His special interest in the principles of government allowed him to preserve the power of the Ptolemaic State while he put the final touches to its organization. The portraits we have of him reveal a more nonchalant temperament, and a less striking personality, than those that appear to have belonged to the dynasty's founder, if one can judge from Sôter's authoritarian features. But his long reign, from 283 to 246, represents the peak of the Ptolemaic empire.

Outside Egypt he was faithful to his father's policies, with varied fortunes but on the whole not without success. Certainly he was unable to prevent the secession of Cyrene and the Greek colonies in Libya, where his half-brother, Magas, his senior by many years, refused to acknowledge his authority. But Magas' only attempt to conquer Egypt and appropriate Sôter's estate ended in failure without any battle. Indeed, a revolt of the Marmarica Libyans behind his rear lines forced the king of Cyrene to hasten back to his base (about 275). A modus vivendi was afterwards reached between Berenice's two sons (for Magas was a son of hers by Philip, a Macedonian), who, separated by immense expanses of desert that were hard to cross, refrained from interfering with each other. Furthermore, toward the end of their respective reigns, the two sovereigns' reconciliation was sealed in a dynastic betrothal between Magas' daughter, called Berenice after her grandmother, and Ptolemy II's son, who was to succeed his father. The marriage, celebrated after Magas' demise, brought about the return of Cyrene to the Ptolemaic monarchy.

To the northeast, Ptolemy II was often embroiled in serious conflict with his powerful neighbors the Seleucid kings. Soon after Seleucus' death, Ptolemy took advantage of Antiochus I's preoccupation with the eastern areas of his empire. He devoted his efforts to reinforcing and developing bases already established by Sôter on the southern and western coasts of Asia Minor – in Cilicia, Pamphylia, Caria, on the island of Samos, and, it appears, at Miletus. The Seleucid monarch overlooked the matter at first. A short time later, when he had concluded an alliance with Magas, who had married his daughter Apamé, Antiochus contemplated military action against Egypt. But as the threat from Magas had been of short duration, as noted above, Ptolemy was ready to make a counterattack. The First Syrian War (about 274–271) ended with recognition of the status quo in Syria and elsewhere. A new conflict broke out ten years later, when Antiochus II had just succeeded his father. The sequence of the operations is not known, but they lasted many years (till 253, apparently) and cost Ptolemy territorial losses among sites that he controlled on the coasts of Ionia, Pamphylia and Cilicia. When peace came, Antiochus II married a daughter of Ptolemy II's named Berenice, like her cousin the daughter of Magas and in memory of their common grandmother. That marriage, far from ensuring peaceful relations between the two dynasties, was to be the cause of a bloody rift soon after Ptolemy II's death.

Toward the north Ptolemy II had inherited from his father a favorable situation in the Aegean, where the Ptolemaic naval squadron had supporting bases at their disposal. The League of the Islanders (*Nesiotai*) had been founded to unite the cities of the Cyclades under the patronage of Antigonus the One-eyed, but had now been brought under Ptolemy Sôter's control. All the ports of the Anatolian coast in Ionia, supported by Rhodes' friendship, served as bases from which the activity of Ptolemy's admirals spread in the archipelago. After the First Syrian War they intervened in Crete, where a permanent post was set up at Itanus, at the eastern end of the island. The anxiety to keep control of the Aegean Sea was no doubt motivated by economic considerations, as Egypt's export trade, particularly in cereals (the sale of which was essential to the Ptolemaic treasury), was above all directed at Greek cities all over that region. But the aim was also to prevent the growth of any other navy that might eventually be a military threat on the Egyptian coast. The coast of the Delta had suffered in times past from attacks by pirates coming from the north: the memory of raids by the "Peoples from the Sea," so often mentioned in Pharaonic texts, was still alive. As in Coele-Syria, the Ptolemies' anxiety was a throwback, by force of circumstances, to the days of the Rameses dynasty. So when the Macedonian sovereign, Antigonus Gonatas, revived in the Aegean Sea the policy of his father Demetrius Poliorcetes and in his turn created a powerful fleet, Ptolemy II gathered a coalition against him in mainland Greece, where Macedon's old enemies found themselves united again. As will be seen later, the Chremonidean War (as it is called) took a bad turn for Antigonus' adversaries. In any case it inflicted on Ptolemy the heaviest military failure of his reign: the naval battle of uncertain date (perhaps 262) that his fleet, facing a Macedonian squadron, lost near the island of Cos. Nevertheless, though weakened by that defeat, Ptolemaic influence did not disappear from the Cyclades as a result.

Solidly protected by its warships and by the territorial glacis situated on its frontiers, Ptolemy II's Egypt enjoyed outstanding prosperity, as vouchsafed by every ancient testimony. Thus the poet Theocritus, shortly before 270, appeals to the king's generosity, flattering him:

> His ships are always victorious at sea . . . How many horsemen, how many infantry bearing sparkling bronze shields congregate in his armies . . . His peoples attend to their tasks, feeling completely secure. No! Never has an enemy troop crossed the Nile haunted by its monstrous beasts, never invaded the villages, uttering full-throated shouts; never has a battleship landed on Egypt's shore armed plunderers, intent on raiding the cattle herds.

The peaceful occupations of the fellahin tilling the fertile plains of the Nile Valley filled the coffers of the sovereign who watched over their safety: "What a stream of riches flows each day from the whole land toward his luxurious palace!"

Ptolemy II gave the administrative machinery set up by his father its most remarkable development, as papyri demonstrate in great detail. An improved fiscal system allowed the monarch, assisted by his ministers, access to large financial resources, the use of which was not confined to war. The great projects that were carried out demonstrated the monarchy's opulence. These included building a number of royal palaces in Alexandria and sanctuaries for the gods; organizing the harbors and the urban area of the capital; enriching the famous Library and systematically developing the Mouseion as a center of higher teaching and research. With his lively interest in intellectual matters, the king attracted (and paid) learned men and poets, who, following the example of the Syracusan Theocritus and the Cyrenean Callimachus, pompously extolled his glory.

A man practiced in war and government, the king had experienced passions of another kind. After a first marriage with a daughter of Lysimachus, Arsinoe I, who had given him a son, the future Ptolemy III, he conceived a violent passion for his own sister Arsinoe II, his senior by quite a margin. She had in the first place married Lysimachus, then taken refuge in Egypt after her husband's death. Arsinoe II was a strong-willed woman who exerted great influence on her younger brother. A captive to her charms, he repudiated Arsinoe I and married her. This was evidently an incestuous union in the eyes of the Greeks, but that Pharaonic tradition had become acceptable in Egypt, as it had been under the Achaemenid monarchs. The new queen's profile, with its sharp features, soon appeared on coins struck by Ptolemy. In her honor he took the title Philadelphus, "His Sister's Lover." Together they celebrated with exceptional brilliance in 271 the festival of the *Ptolemaea*, instituted a few years earlier to render divine honors to Ptolemy I Sôter and Berenice I. Arsinoe did not live long after that triumphal ceremony. She died in the same year 271, leaving behind an inconsolable brother–spouse. She had already been granted apotheosis, in which Ptolemy rejoined her not long after, while he was still alive, forming with her the couple of the "Brother–Sister Deities." Thus it was that under the second Ptolemaic monarch, royal majesty was promoted to the highest of all dignities, earning divine status for those who were invested with it.

Ptolemy III, on succeeding his father in 246, had to settle two difficult questions without delay: the return of Cyrene to the empire, and a new crisis in relations with the Seleucid monarchy. It did not prove an easy task to reinstate Ptolemaic control over Cyrenaica. Magas' young daughter Berenice, called Berenice II, showed really outstanding strength of character in these circumstances. Though she had been betrothed by her father to the heir to the Egyptian kingdom, her mother Apamé, a Seleucid princess (daughter of Antiochus I: see p. 70), wished to break the promised marriage in favor of a brother of Antigonus Gonatas, Demetrius the Fair. That would mean handing over Cyrenaica to a family that was, like the Syrian monarchy, an enemy of the Ptolemies. But Berenice was unwilling to go back on her father's pledge. As Demetrius, who owed his surname to his character as a seducer, had imprudently seduced Apamé, the young princess had her mother's lover killed in her bed. That was one of those Hellenistic incidents, romantic and yet bloody, in which passionate and vindictive royal women played a determining role: a tradition among Macedonian princesses (so different from their Greek sisters) that has been noted on other occasions.

Berenice at last married the young Ptolemy III, to whom she brought her father's kingdom of Cyrenaica as a dowry. But while the people of Cyrene, in their loyalty to Magas' daughter, seem to have agreed without too much resistance to return to Ptolemaic rule, the other cities of Libya refused to submit, and Ptolemy's armies had to go to war and reconquer the whole of western Cyrenaica. After defeating the rebels, the Egyptian king took stern measures to chastise them. Barce was deprived of its port, which became an independent city under the significant name of Ptolemais. The new city was soon to eclipse its metropolis. Taucheira, losing its traditional name, was refounded under the name of Arsinoe, one of the brother–sister divine couple. Finally Euhesperides, conquered by Ptolemy's mercenaries, was replaced by a new city built on the coast a short distance away. It was named Berenice. Ptolemais, Arsinoe, Berenice: all the important cities of Libya, Cyrene excepted, received in their very names the imprint of the Ptolemaic seal, which they were to bear until the Roman conquest (see p. 253).

A third Syrian War broke out at about the same time in 246. It forced Ptolemy to leave his bride while they were honeymooning. A poem by Callimachus, preserved in a Latin translation by Catullus (poem LXVI), evokes the trial that their separation imposed on Berenice II. But it was impossible for the young king to shirk a duty prescribed by family links as well as strategic opportunity. It will be recalled that after the Second Syrian War Antiochus II had married the daughter of Ptolemy II Philadelphus, also called Berenice. For the sake of that marriage, enshrined in a treaty, he had repudiated his former wife Laodice, who had retired to Ephesus with the two sons she had borne him. When Antiochus died in 246, a few months after Philadelphus, it turned out that Laodice's elder son Seleucus, in conformity with his father's wish, was chosen to ascend the throne: not the son, who was still a child, born to Berenice, the titled queen, a few years earlier. She, however, supported by some parts of the Seleucid Empire, claimed the diadem for her son, appealing to her brother Ptolemy III for help in her demand. Ptolemy hastened to Antioch, but too late. The queen had just been murdered, together with the royal child, by Laodice's emissaries (hence the name "Laodicean" War given by contemporaries to this new dynastic conflict). It was still possible to avenge the double murder by making the most of the wave of sympathy felt across the Seleucid empire for the deceased queen. That thought prompted Ptolemy's action, in its first stages a successful one, as he dashed into the depths of Mesopotamia, after crossing the Euphrates, until he reached Babylon. There he believed he had obtained the support of the satraps governing the Iranian and eastern provinces of the empire, all the way to Bactria. This is at least suggested by a triumphal inscription composed in the pompous style common to announcements of Pharaonic victories, found at Adulis, an African port on the Red Sea. But Ptolemy did not have the means to keep such vast territories under lasting control. The threat of internal problems in Egypt forced him to retrace his steps, and persuaded him to adopt the prudent political goals of his ancestor Sôter. Without great effort, Seleucus II recovered the essential part of those short-lived conquests. However, after five years of war, he left in Ptolemy's hands a substantial part of the Anatolian coast in Ionia, Caria, Lycia, Pamphylia, and Cilicia; and, apart from Coele-Syria (crucial to Egypt's defense), the port of Seleucia, which served Antioch. In addition there was a Ptolemaic presence in the far north of the Aegean Sea, at Samothrace, on the Thracian coast around

Aenus in the Chersonese, and even in the Hellespont. The Ptolemaic empire had never extended so far. By the year 240 Ptolemy III could legitimately pride himself on such an achievement. He had brought back from Asia, with enormous booty, a number of statues of Egyptian gods, once taken away by Cambyses after his conquest of Egypt in 525. They were restored to their original shrines. In gratitude for such benefits, the Egyptians hailed their monarch by the title of Benefactor, in Greek *Euergetes*, which remained attached to his name. Henceforth the divine couple of the *Euergetai* Ptolemy III and Berenice II joined that of the Brother and Sister Deities (*Philadelphoi*) in the cult officially dedicated to Egypt's sovereigns.

The Laodicean War seems to have exhausted Euergetes' appetite for fighting. After that he did not undertake any important operations abroad. His Seleucid neighbor and rival had to face serious difficulties in the eastern provinces of his empire and in Anatolia. But Ptolemy did not take advantage of this. In Greece proper, where conflicts and rivalries were always springing up and seemed to invite intervention from outside, he limited himself to diplomatic action of the kind chosen by his father toward the end of his reign, when he granted subsidies to the Achaean League. Euergetes continued for a long time the annual financial grant promised to Aratus by Philadelphus: this gained the Ptolemaic king the title of General (*strategos*) of the League. He also maintained a policy of generous gifts to Athens. These contributed to the liberation of the city when in 229 it bought for money the departure of the Macedonian garrison which had occupied the Piraeus since the Chremonidean War (see p. 71; also p. 297 on the gymnasium named after Diogenes, the departing Macedonian commander). The Athenians acknowledged his generosity by granting him an exceptional honor: they created in their civic community a thirteenth tribe, Ptolemais, as they had already done eighty years earlier in honor of Antigonus the One-eyed and his son Poliorcetes (see pp. 51–2). In the final years of his life, Ptolemy believed that he would secure a valuable ally in mainland Greece by granting financial support to Cleomenes, king of Sparta – abandoning in favor of that king his former policy of accord with the Achaean League. But when after his initial successes Cleomenes met with reverses, Euergetes put an end to his subsidy and advised the Spartan to make peace. Yet after Cleomenes' defeat at Sellasia he received the vanquished king, who had sought refuge at Alexandria. That was the last political act of Euergetes, who died soon after (February 221). With his death the third reign of the Lagid dynasty came to an end, as well as the brilliant period of the Ptolemaic empire, the ultimate model for a Hellenistic monarchy. Henceforth the weaknesses or the vices of the Ptolemaic sovereigns prevented them from finding lasting solutions for the internal Egyptian difficulties that were soon to emerge, or preserving the empire's cohesion against external threats. A long period of decadence was beginning, which was to end two centuries later, after the battle of Actium.

■ The Seleucid monarchy ■ Abandonment of provinces bordering on India ■ Difficulties in Asia Minor ■ The birth of the Bithynian kingdom ■ The Galatians in Anatolia ■ Foundation of the kingdom of Pontus ■ Philetaerus and the beginnings of the Pergamene State ■ Antiochus II ■ Secession of Cappadocia ■ Seleucus II Callinicus and Antiochus Hierax ■ Success of Attalus I against the Galatians ■ The Greek kingdom of Bactria ■ The Arsacid Parthians come onto the scene ■ Death of Seleucus II ■ Seleucus III

The Ptolemies' main rivals had been, and were to remain, the Seleucids, who had inherited the major territorial share of Alexander's legacy in Asia. We saw earlier how Seleucus I, founder of his dynasty, had used moderation combined with boldness to win over, by an attitude favorable to local authorities, the immense territories of the Near and Middle East. The success of his efforts proved lasting enough (his descendants reigned until 64/3 BC), for the Seleucid era, reckoned from the date of Seleucus' coming to power (312/11), became the common point of reference in the generality of Asiatic states, whether or not they depended on the Seleucid monarch. This fact reveals the importance of his empire in the history of Greek civilization in the east. Seleucus safeguarded the essence of Alexander's legacy in a vast area of great diversity.

It is true that, starting from Seleucus' time, part of Alexander's conquests had to be given up. The provinces of the Indus, Gedrosia (Baluchistan), and Arachosia (southern Afghanistan) were ceded in 303 to Sandracottus (Chandragupta), the Hindu prince who founded the dynasty of the Mauryas. But enduring traces of Greek influence can still be recognized in those remote areas, thanks to the evidence provided by epigraphy and representational artifacts that archaeology has unearthed (see pp. 321–2). In the other eastern provinces of the empire, Antiochus, who had been joint ruler with his father since 294/3 with the title of king, was given his own capital, Seleucia on the Tigris. That city, founded by his father north of Babylon, shared with Antioch in later years the status of capital of the monarchy. In line with a policy started by Alexander, both sovereigns were very active in creating cities or refounding others (under new names) on the routes that were essential to the political and commercial life of the empire. Numerous cities bore the same name. Examples were Antioch (from the one on the Orontes to Antioch of Margiana in Turkmenistan); Seleucia (from that on the Tigris to the one in Pieria on the Syrian coast of the Mediterranean); Apamea (after the name of Seleucus' Iranian wife, the mother of Antiochus I); later came

Laodicea, named after Antiochus II's wife. Surely included in those foundations was the wish to safeguard peripheral satrapies by establishing or reinforcing military colonies. However, after Antiochus I's accession to the throne, Anatolian and Syrian affairs became a priority for Seleucid sovereigns: they had no choice but to neglect their possessions in Iran and the eastern satrapies. A number of cases of disaffection resulted, which will be mentioned in due course.

Indeed, soon after his father's death, Antiochus was confronted by a rebellion in Syria, Ptolemaic attempts on the coasts of Anatolia, and serious difficulties in Asia Minor. The history of these goes back to the time of Alexander, who concentrated his efforts on other tasks and thus missed the opportunity to put his authority on a sure footing in the northern regions of the Anatolian peninsula. Adjoining the Greek colonies of ancient origin, independent and prosperous entities, were native principalities whose Hellenized leaders had no wish to submit to external authority. Toward the west, along the Black Sea starting from the Bosporus, a Thracian population, traditionally warlike, inhabited Bithynia. The local prince took the royal title at the start of the third century. His son Nicomedes, who succeeded him in 280 or thereabouts, enlisted in his service Gallic tribes from among those then surging forward over Thrace, Macedon, and northern Greece. Those barbarians (Galatians, as the Greeks called them) then spread in large numbers among the western provinces of Asia Minor, resorting to merciless plunder, as their ethnic brethren were doing in the same period in Europe. Antiochus I had to fight them. He defeated them in 275/4, thus winning the title of Sôter ("Saviour"), and ended up assigning them a region in Asia Minor where they were allowed to settle. For a long time they were a menace to neighboring populations.

It was in this period that a young Hellenized prince of Persian descent, named Mithridates, founded at the eastern end of the Asian coast of the Black Sea, on both sides of the Greek city of Trapezus (Trebizond), the kingdom of Pontus. It was to be a power for two centuries. Between Pontus and Bithynia was a wild stretch of country, Paphlagonia, encircling the city of Sinope. Seleucid authority did not extend to that area, with the result that the whole of the Black Sea coast and its hinterland were exempt from domination by Antiochus.

It was otherwise in the western part of Asia Minor. There Antiochus and his successors were linked with the numerous and prosperous Greek cities by a "friendship" to which many epigraphic texts bear witness – a term which did not preclude a relative degree of submission. A number of those cities, as we have seen, also sought (or preferred) an alliance with the Ptolemaic sovereign, thus playing a game of seesaw between the two great empires. But the Seleucid monarchs never managed to put together in the Aegean Sea a fleet of warships capable of rivaling the Ptolemaic squadrons. One of the Greek cities in the area became at that time the cradle of an independent state, owing to a particular set of circumstances. North of the lower Caicus river, Lysimachus had chosen the fortress of Pergamum to be the repository of treasure that he left in the safekeeping of one of his officers, Philetaerus.

That man betrayed him and joined Seleucus in 281, and then, when Ptolemy Ceraunus murdered Seleucus, was cunning enough to redeem his corpse and donate it to Antiochus I, thus winning the sovereign's goodwill.

Philetaerus, having won de facto independence, used it gradually to increase his power. He had at his disposal enough trained troops to oppose any Galatian attempt at pillaging. A monument raised in his honor after his death commemorated his victorious resistance, with an emphasis common to dedicatory epigrams of the time:

> Happy Philetaerus! Your personality, prince, provides a theme both to poets whom the gods favor, and to sculptors gifted with skillful hands. They proclaim your power and glory, the poets in their hymns, the sculptors as they draw on the utmost resources of their art. For one day, against the hardy Galatian warriors, you roused impetuous Ares and drove them from the frontiers of your realm. In your honor Sosicrates has consecrated, in wave-encircled Delos, these statues by Niceratus, works of exquisite art, a memorial worthy of being extolled in song by generations to come. Even Hephaestus, were he to see them, could not better such works.

In his own lifetime, Philetaerus made numerous dedications in cities and shrines. The Greek city of Cyzicus on the Propontis, which, like Miletus, Priene, or Erythrae, had suffered from Galatian raids and benefited from the help of the Pergamene dynast, founded in his honor, about the year 276, a festival called after him the *Philetaereia*. This policy of prestige proved fruitful. When his nephew Eumenes (Philetaerus had no children, being, it is said, a eunuch) succeeded him at Pergamum in 263, he felt strong enough to face Antiochus I himself in combat. Eumenes defeated Antiochus near Sardis, and could then, in a territory framing the valley of the Caicus from Mount Ida in the north to the neighborhood of the Hermus river in the south, behave like an independent sovereign. On his coins Seleucus' traditional effigy was replaced by Philetaerus' likeness, characterized by a powerful ugliness: an eloquent symbol of a new dynasty's birth.

Antiochus I, who had meanwhile been fighting Ptolemy II in the First Syrian War, had shared royal power with his elder son before having him executed on the charge of plotting against him. He then shared power with his younger son, who succeeded him in 261 as Antiochus II. The new king reigned for fifteen years, until 246. He had his trials, like his father. The Second Syrian War lasted until 253, and there were operations in the Propontis against Byzantium. He had to allow Cappadocia, in the east of Asia Minor, to become an independent kingdom. The Iranian princes governing it took the royal title in 255. They were to reign for a century and a half over a vast mountainous region with no access to the sea. Hellenism nevertheless gradually penetrated into the interior, in the footsteps of travelers and traders.

His son Seleucus II had to conquer his kingdom as soon as his father died, although the latter had designated him as his heir. This was the Laodicean or Third Syrian War. When Ptolemy III was forced to give up his conquests (of

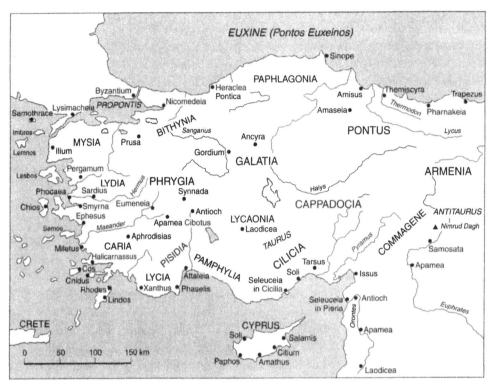

Map 5 Asia Minor.

short duration, as they turned out to be) in Mesopotamia, Seleucus had himself acknowledged as ruler in those areas, but failed to penetrate into Coele-Syria. He had contracted dynastic alliances by arranging marriages for two of his sisters, with Mithridates II, king of Pontus, and Ariarathes, king of Cappadocia. But he was to meet his worst foe in his own family, at the very time when the final, successful outcome of his struggle with Ptolemy III had just obtained for him the glorious title of *Callinicus* ("Brilliant Victor"). During that war he had had to call upon his younger brother Antiochus, surnamed *Hierax*, "The Hawk," whom he had left in control of Seleucid possessions in Asia Minor. When peace was made, a conflict broke out between the brothers, Hierax refusing to submit to Seleucus' authority. The fratricidal war that ensued, the details of which are not well known, took a bad turn for Callinicus, who was beaten near Ancyra (Ankara). He had to acknowledge his brother, who had made an alliance with the Galatians, as possessor of the Anatolian region of the empire. To make use of those troublesome Gallic mercenaries, Hierax trained them for an attack on Pergamum, where Attalus, a great-nephew of Philetaerus, had been dynast since 241 in succession to Eumenes I. That was his undoing: Attalus defeated him in

Plate 2 The Ludovisi Gaul (Museo Nazionale Romano; photo SCALA).

This famous marble group shows a Galatian stabbing himself with his sword after killing his wife to spare her from falling captive to the enemy. It is a second century AD copy of one of the bronze ex-votos that Attalus I had erected at Pergamum in the late third century BC to celebrate his victories over the Galatians. Another element of the same ex-voto is the Dying Gaul (Rome, Capitoline Museum), typically wearing a torque (a rigid collar) round his neck (see pp. 305–6). As usual in Hellenistic sculpture, such compositions convey their full meaning only when the different elements are seen as part of a whole.

many battles and occupied the whole of Seleucid Asia Minor, from the Propontis to the Taurus. Hierax fled, tried in vain to capture Mesopotamia while Seleucus was busy in Iran, and, again defeated, met with a miserable death by being assassinated in Thrace (226). Attalus, however, who had repeated his great-uncle Philetaerus' previous victories over the Galatians, allowed himself to be proclaimed *Sôter* ("Saviour") and took the title of king. The kingdom of Pergamum became one of the foremost monarchies of the Hellenic world. Attalus' magnificent offerings to Athena at Pergamum, and those he made on the Athenian Acropolis, brilliantly celebrated that event.

Meanwhile Seleucus II, who had been forced to cede Asia Minor to his brother, had to face a serious turn of events in the upper satrapies of the empire. In remote Bactria there had been a multiplicity of Greek military colonies since Alexander (Justin, with evident exaggeration, speaks of "the thousand cities" of Bactria). There the Greek satrap Diodotus, after observing the situation for a time, proclaimed his independence from the Seleucids and took the royal title, demonstrated by the coinage he ordered to be struck, bearing his effigy. There too a new dynasty was born, with its own particular destiny, its very own place in the world of Antiquity. Further west, between Bactria and the eastern shore of the Caspian Sea, Parthyaea, a vast region corresponding to the northeast of Iran, was invaded by a nomadic population under a chief named Arsaces. They came from central Asia, beyond the river Oxus (Amu Darya). Settling in Parthyaea, they adopted the name of Parthians under which they are known, and set up their kingdom – the royal era of the Arsacid dynasty, successors of Arsaces, beginning in 248/7. The barbarian state completely cut off the new kingdom of Bactria from all direct communication with the Greek world. Seleucus II attempted to react to those successive secessions. In about the year 230 (the chronology is not well established) he led an expedition into Iran and pushed up to Parthyaea, from which for a while he expelled the Parthians, who surged northward across the steppes toward the Aral Sea. Then, without marching on Bactria, where Diodotus' son had succeeded him under the name of Diodotus II, he returned to Syria, where his aunt Stratonice was plotting against him. Having had the rebel queen executed, he died in an accident in 226. His son Seleucus III reigned for only three years. He was trying to recapture Anatolia from Attalus I of Pergamum when, in the spring of 223, he was murdered by one of his officers. Heavily amputated in the east and in the west, the Seleucid empire was to be inherited by the dead king's younger brother, Antiochus III – whose activity and energy were to restore for a while the Syrian monarchy's power and greatness.

■ *Antigonus Gonatas, king of Macedon* ■ *His policy toward the Greek cities: the "Fetters of Greece"* ■ *Pyrrhus' expedition to Italy: his first victories, his definitive failure* ■ *His unfortunate endeavors in Macedonia, then against Sparta* ■ *His death at Argos* ■ *The role of the Aetolian League: its influence at Delphi, its good relations with Antigonus* ■ *Antigonus' firm hold on mainland Greece* ■ *The Chremonidean War* ■ *Naval battle at Cos* ■ *The Achaean League* ■ *Sicyon joins it* ■ *Aratus' occupation of Corinth and its citadel* ■ *Agis III's reforms and ultimate failure at Sparta* ■ *Death of Antigonus Gonatas: portrait of that prince* ■ *Demetrius II: his break with the Aetolians, and his death* ■ *Antigonus Doson* ■ *Cleomenes III's reforms at Sparta* ■ *His endeavors in the Peloponnese* ■ *Battle of Sellasia*

The third of the great Hellenistic monarchies took over the Argead legacy and gave it continuity in the state in which Cassander had preserved it. The Macedonian kingdom had exerted, like a mirage that reappeared again and again, a sort of fascination on the minds of the great Diadochi (Ptolemy excepted, see p. 44), and led them one after another to their ruin. But after Ceraunus' death and a brief two-year interval, during which the throne seemed vacant, there appeared on the scene a dynamic and capable prince: Demetrius Poliorcetes' son, called Antigonus like his grandfather Monophthalmus, became king. Antigonus Gonatas was thoroughly trained in the techniques of war and politics, the workings of which he had learned while taking part in his father's ventures. But he was a stranger to the insatiable lust for power and debauchery that had been Poliorcetes' undoing. He had instead received in Athens an education bearing the stamp of intellectual refinement, in the company of poets and philosophers, the most notable among these being Zeno of Citium, the founder of Stoicism, whose moral prestige and lessons were never lost on him. In a long reign that lasted from 277 to 239, Antigonus was confronted by many obstacles, but always faced them with constancy, insight, and moderation. We know the history of his reign in a very imperfect manner. Yet, while his personality is as it were veiled in mist (even his physical appearance is unknown to us), we can divine in him a richly endowed and attractive nature. He was the real founder of the Antigonid dynasty, with which his name is deservedly linked. The Ptolemies and Seleucids expended their energy on saving in Asia and Africa what was left of Alexander's conquests. Meanwhile the Antigonids, settled in the ancestral realm of Macedon, assigned to themselves the exclusive role of preserving and guaranteeing its integrity, while exerting on the states of Greece proper the control they had inherited from Philip II's policy. This is why, in the long century extending from the start of Antigonus' reign to the fall of his last descendant at the battle of Pydna (168), their history is intimately linked with that of the Greek States, whose autonomy disappeared, as a matter of fact, simultaneously with the kingdom of Macedon.

Antigonus Gonatas owed to his success against a band of Galatians at Lysimacheia the military prestige that was seen in those days as the indispensable complement to royal dignity. In around 270 he made an agreement with Antiochus I that brought peace and mutual friendship between their two dynasties for many years. Furthermore, he had no ambition in the direction of Asia. In Europe, he respected in the east the frontier of the river Nestus, beyond which Thracian tribes and Greek cities had to deal with Seleucid or Ptolemaic incursions, while at the same time making room for a Celtic principality that eventually proved short-lived. Antigonus' sole interest in that principality was the recruitment of Galatian mercenaries, which he often used. He had to keep watch in the north and west, as his predecessors had done, on the mountainous frontiers where barbarian tribes took advantage of every opportunity to demonstrate their independence. That was a permanent feature of Macedonian policy. In the south he kept under his control the rich Thessalian plain, the fate of which had long been linked with Macedon's, and where his father Demetrius had founded, in the recess of the Gulf of Volos, his capital, Demetrias, a port providing shelter for his naval squadrons. With Chalcis holding a commanding position on the Strait of the Euripus between Euboea and Boeotia, and Corinth with the impregnable fortress of Acrocorinth, it made up the triad of the "Fetters of Greece." Their possession gave the Macedonian sovereign a dominant strategic position in Greece, for they allowed the swift transport of Macedonian troops both to central Greece and into the Peloponnese. He wished to give his fatherland, sorely tried by political unrest, invasion, and war, a breathing space in which to restore domestic prosperity; to keep Thessaly, and if possible central Greece, under close control; finally, to prevent any hostile coalition from taking shape in the Peloponnese. The policies of Gonatas were to be based on these broad principles. He managed to be faithful to them, unswervingly and successfully.

Yet difficulties were not wanting. He had hardly taken his kingdom in hand when a famous and fearful adversary loomed on the horizon: Pyrrhus king of Epirus, in whom Demetrius Poliorcetes had found a fierce rival. A strange adventure had kept him far from his country between 280 and 275. The powerful city of Tarentum, which dominated the whole of Magna Graecia, had been worried by the progress made by Roman influence in southern Italy. It appealed to Pyrrhus for cooperation. An adventure in southern Italy was a gratifying prospect for his hitherto disappointed ambition. He perceived in it the starting point for a large-scale plan that would allow him, as he proceeded from conquest to conquest, to build an empire comparable to Alexander's: to such an extent did the example set by Asia's conqueror haunt the minds of princes all over the Greek world! Pyrrhus' famous conversation with his advisor Cineas, as reported by Plutarch, is an apt illustration of that delirious imagination to which everything seems possible. In 280 he crossed into Italy with the mercenaries and elephants acquired with the help of his princely rivals, Ceraunus and Antiochus (only too happy to be rid of his presence while pursuing their own designs). At Heraclea on the Gulf of Tarentum he had no difficulty in winning a great victory over the Roman legions. An offering in Zeus' shrine at Dodona, the dedication of which has come down to us, recalled that victory "won by king Pyrrhus, the Epirots, and Tarentines over the Romans and their allies." Yet Rome did not give up, in spite of another defeat at Ausculum in Apulia in the summer of 279. Carthage, however, worried by Pyrrhus' ambition and coordinating her actions with those of Rome, had invaded the Greek portion of Sicily and laid siege to Syracuse, a city left divided and weakened by Agathocles' death ten years earlier. A joint appeal from Syracuse, Agrigentum, and Leontini led Pyrrhus to abandon the Italian adventure and intervene in Sicily in 278. His response was brilliant, as he forced the Carthaginians to retreat the moment he arrived. Hailed "Leader and King" by a convention of Sicilian Greeks, he undertook the conquest of the western part of the island, which had long been a Carthaginian possession. He succeeded in the attempt, except for the stronghold of Lilybaeum on the west coast, which repulsed all assaults. This failure, preventing him from achieving the total liberation of Sicily, and the weariness of the Greek cities, lacking in readiness to shoulder the heavy burden of war – along with fears of their possible treachery – persuaded Pyrrhus to go back to Italy, where Tarentum was requesting help against a resurgent Roman menace (276). The following summer he faced the Roman army again, near Maleventum, at the heart of the Samnite region of the Apennines. On that occasion the Romans, no longer impressed by Pyrrhus' elephants, had the upper hand and inflicted a decisive defeat on him. In memory of a victory that was soon to allow them to conquer the whole of southern Italy, they changed the name Maleventum to one of good omen, Beneventum: a name borne to this day by the town of Benevento. Pyrrhus, conscious of having no future in Magna Graecia (Greater Greece), left a garrison at Tarentum: a measure that did not save the city from succumbing to Roman power in 272. Pyrrhus himself returned to Epirus in the autumn of 275. It was then that he decided to confront Gonatas by attacking Macedonia.

Antigonus' authority was not yet firmly established in the western provinces of his kingdom. They shared a common frontier with Epirus and rallied to Pyrrhus' banner. He penetrated into the very heart of Macedonia, at Aegae, the ancient Argead capital. There he was imprudent enough to allow his Gallic mercenaries to pillage the royal necropolis, where Philip II was buried. A sacrilege of such enormity would certainly not win over any Macedonian sympathy for the king of Epirus. It enabled Gonatas, who had withdrawn to Thessalonica, to recover his kingdom, apparently not an easy task, some time before 272. That was the year when Pyrrhus, begged by a Spartan prince ousted from the throne in favor of a nephew, allowed himself to be enticed into a new adventure: he landed in the Peloponnese to conquer Sparta in the name of the prince whose cause he was taking up. But the ancient Lacedaemonian city, mindful of its warlike tradition and its fierce spirit of independence, successfully resisted the invader. Even the women, Plutarch tells us, fought heroically in defence of their hearths. Pyrrhus retreated toward the Argolid, hoping to go into winter quarters in Argos. But the Argives, though some among them were favorable to Pyrrhus, refused to open their gates to him. He was forced to launch an assault on the city. During a confused melee in a street the king of Epirus met his death, killed (so Plutarch states) by a roof-tile, thrown out of a window by an old woman. That was an inglorious death for a hero whose turbulent activity had known so many trials and been inspired by such varied plans. Far from proving to be Alexander's peer, which had no doubt been his dream, he remains in human memory as a symbol of measureless ambition, of a succession of frustrated hopes.

Pyrrhus' death gave freedom of action to Antigonus Gonatas both in Greece and in Macedonia, but he had to reckon with a new power that had appeared on the Greek political scene. This was the Aetolian Confederacy, destined to play an important role through all of the third century. Aetolia is a mountainous region of northwestern Greece, situated between Epirus in the north and the Gulf of Corinth in the south. In the west the mighty river Achelous, flowing down from the highlands of Epirus, separates it from Acarnania. A dialect closely related to Dorian was spoken there, as in the major part of continental Greece. Though very ancient traditions, that of the Boar of Calydon for example, demonstrate a close association, dating from primitive times, between the Aetolians and the other peoples of Greece, they had not till then participated actively in the development of the Hellenic world. The life they led was devoid of refinement, confined as they were by their mountains and organized into a number of small lackluster cities whose center of gravity was a common shrine of Apollo situated at Thermus in the middle of the country. At the end of the fourth century their cities formed a league, a true federal state, with twice-yearly assemblies, a federal council, federal magistrates, and an army made up of contingents provided by the cities. In 279 an army of Gauls, following a leader named Brennus, marched into central Greece up to the neighborhood of Delphi, which they intended to plunder. This was part of the Gallic avalanche that had destroyed Ptolemy Ceraunus in Macedon. The shrine, however, was spared: a divine miracle by popular agreement, but certainly with the aid of Aetolian troops, who had joined the other communities of central Greece in an attempt to ward off the invader. Hardy mountaineers, they moved easily over the Phocian passes, amid the first snowfalls – a trial for the Celtic warriors. Their contribution to the safeguarding of the illustrious shrine of Pythô brought the Aetolians great prestige, which was demonstrated by the Delphic Amphictyony's decision to institute the feast of the *Sôteria*, in commemoration of the miraculous salvation of the shrine. In memory of their victory Gallic shields, the characteristic shape of which has been preserved in stone, were hung as an offering on the entablature of the great temple of Apollo at Delphi. The Aetolians were also admitted to the Amphictyony, in which they very soon became members of exceptional standing, as recorded in epigraphic documents. At that time many Amphictyonic communities joined the Aetolian Confederacy, which thus had their votes at its disposal in the Council of the Amphictyony. In a few years, therefore, the influence of the Aetolian federal state, almost nonexistent until then, had extended, thanks to events at Delphi, over the whole breadth of central Greece up to the valley of the Spercheus and the Malian Gulf, which gave it an outlet on the Aegean Sea. It will be seen later that the Aetolians managed to turn this to great advantage.

Pyrrhus' death freed Antigonus Gonatas from a dangerous rival. He wisely maintained friendly relations with the neighboring Aetolians. Happy that he had reasserted his authority over Macedonia and Thessaly, he was content to keep control of the rest of Greece by means of bases held by the strong garrisons which his father and he himself had placed in three locations. The whole history of third-century Greece illustrates the effectiveness of those "Fetters" – Demetrias, Chalcis, and Corinth (see above, p. 82) – that gave Macedonian power mastery over the whole country. The system was perfected by the complex interplay of diplomatic relationships, and by direct or indirect intervention in the affairs of a number of cities, notably in the Peloponnese, aimed at setting up or maintaining political regimes favorable to Macedon. There was nothing new in that approach: Cassander had made successful use of it. Antigonus Gonatas practiced it in his turn, in a persistent and subtle way.

His supremacy was a source of anxiety for many Greek states, where an old mistrust, even open hostility toward Macedon, was still alive. On the other hand, the Ptolemaic monarchy, whose squadrons had controlled the Cyclades for twenty years, looked askance at Demetrius Poliorcetes' son being in a position once more to gather a fleet that could, as in his father's time, play an important role in the Aegean Sea. Prejudice and apprehension combined led to the formation of an ill-assorted coalition. Athens was part of it; Sparta as well, where King Areus I, though Gonatas had helped save his city from Pyrrhus' attack, had an ambition to restore to his own advantage against Macedon the former Lacedaemonian leadership in the Peloponnese. With the Athenians and Spartans were some cities of Arcadia which had a traditional link with Sparta, such as Tegea or Mantinea, the Eleans, and the Achaean cities. Ptolemy Philadelphus was ready to give support to the coalition in case of need. The Athenian Chremonides, the instigator in his city of the anti-Macedonian policy, persuaded the assembly (in the summer of 268) to vote a decree, the text of which has been preserved, approving the alliance: hence the name of the Chremonidean   given in Antiquity to the operations that followed.

Although the details of that war are little known, what is memorable about it is that it demonstrated the firmness of the Macedonian hold on Greece proper. Areus the Spartan king, leading the Peloponnesian forces north toward Attica, failed in 264 to force the Isthmus passage, held by the Macedonian garrison at Corinth. He perished in that battle: the Peloponnesian contingents immediately went back home. Athens was left to defend itself alone, and surrendered (263/2) after a two-year siege. Ptolemy's fleet, commanded by his admiral Patroclus (whose name still belongs to an islet close to Cape Sunium, along the Attic coast), had been unable to raise the blockade. It was no doubt in the same period that Ptolemy's navy suffered a heavy defeat inflicted by Gonatas' vessels near the island of Cos. Gonatas, however, did not try to exclude Ptolemaic influence completely from the Cyclades. But he was able in future to offer a counterpoise to it, as is shown by epigraphic texts that record gifts of public monuments and buildings (sometimes important ones, on Delos, for example: see p. 246) or political interventions by Antigonus on these islands. In the Peloponnese the situation remained stable, as Areus' death meant that the leader of a movement hostile to Macedon had disappeared from the scene. Finally, Athens had to submit again to military occupation, with Macedonian garrisons in the Piraeus and on the Museum, a hill facing the Acropolis. In addition, various administrative measures allowed Gonatas to keep the city's main governing bodies under close watch. A hard blow had been dealt to Athenian independence. However, liberalizing measures taken a few years later, in 256/5, contributed in some measure to a reawakening of public spirit. With financial help from various sources (including Ptolemy III), Athens freed the Piraeus of its Macedonian garrison in 229 (see pp. 74 and 297). She thereafter played a careful and profitable game of neutrality (see again p. 91) until 200, then profited from an informal alliance with Rome against Macedon and later Antiochus III, a friendly relationship that lasted until 88 BC. (On Athenian civic pride, and the prestige enjoyed by the Athenian heritage in the second century BC, see p. 93, notably on the Amphictyonic decree of 125).

Macedonian supremacy in Greece proper thus seemed after the Chremonidean War firmly grounded on the foundation that Antigonus' clear-headed and firm policy had devised for it. It gave ten years of peace to a region sorely tried by wars and internal dissension. However, toward the middle of the century, a particular set of events conspired to shake the structure he had built. The last years of Antigonus' reign brought him a number of serious worries. The first of these, not the least considering its consequences, came from within his own family. It will be remembered that the major stronghold of Macedon in central Greece, the military base of Corinth, was entrusted to the king's own brother, Craterus. His loyalty and vigilance had secured extensive responsibilities for him, putting under his jurisdiction, in addition to the garrison in Corinth, that of Chalcis, together with control of Euboea. At Craterus' death his son Alexander inherited those powers. His ambition, however, was not satisfied with them. In about 253/2 he broke off relations with his uncle Antigonus and took the title of king, as evidenced by an inscription from Eretria in Euboea. A new monarchy thus took shape in the very heart of the Greek world, centered on those two "Fetters" of Chalcis and Corinth of which Gonatas was now deprived.

Soon afterwards a new actor appeared on the scene, destined to play a part of prime importance: Aratus of Sicyon. That Peloponnesian city in the neighborhood of Corinth had been under his father's tyranny till 264. When the tyrant died, overthrown and killed by political foes, the child Aratus was exiled at Argos, where he grew up. In 271, having reached the age of manhood, he organized a raid on his native city. Though this raid was marked by wild boldness, it managed to free the city from the ruling tyrant. To safeguard Sicyon from external interference, he ensured the city's admission to a political body that had till then attracted very limited attention. This was the League of Achaean cities, a confederacy which had been reorganized thirty years earlier and brought together ten small cities sharing the same ethnic origin and situated in the northwest of the Peloponnese, on the south shore of the Gulf of Corinth and its westward outlet. Like Aetolia facing it across the sea, it was a region with an ancient Hellenic tradition, but had so far hardly had a role in Greek politics. The League agreed to admit Sicyon, since the city shared a frontier with Achaea. At the same time it enlisted in Aratus a political leader whose activities were to place it on the international scene.

Aratus' first move was to obtain subsidies with which to bail out the finances of Sicyon, since it was endangered by domestic unrest. He received this help from Ptolemy Philadelphus, eager as usual to win sympathies in Greece by judicious handouts. The Achaean League, on its part, entered into a friendly relationship with its turbulent neighbor, Alexander, son of Craterus, who, using this to his advantage, attacked Argos and Athens. Both cities had to buy peace, while Megalopolis, the great Arcadian city, freed itself from a tyrant favorable to Macedon, who had long ruled over it. Gonatas' influence in the Peloponnese was thus breached. Yet the king does not seem to have resisted this move, whether because of the weariness of old age, or because of other threats keeping him in the Balkans on his northern frontier. He did not intervene either when in 245 a brief war broke out between the Aetolians and Boeotia. Prevailing in battle at Chaeronea, the Aetolians won the prize of that conflict: a new region in central Greece, eastern Locris, called Opuntian Locris from the name of its capital Opus. That gave them an opening, north of Chalcis, on the Strait of Euboea. Aratus, elected *strategos* by the Achaean League, had tried in vain to help the Boeotians. The rift between the two leagues, the Aetolian and the Achaean, was to widen in the following years.

Meanwhile Alexander, son of Craterus, died in circumstances unknown to us. Gonatas seized this opportunity to regain his hold on Corinth by arranging the marriage of his own son, Demetrius, to his rebellious nephew's widow. At the marriage ceremony, resorting to a farious trick, he was able to seize the Acrocorinth fortress by a coup. But the recaptured stronghold was not to remain in his possession for long. For Aratus, again made *strategos* of the League in 243 and concerned about the Aetolians' intervention in an Elean-Arcadian dispute, decided to strike a strong blow to secure control of the Isthmus, essential as it was to Achaea's safety. In a repetition, on a larger scale, of the bold coup by which he had brought freedom to Sicyon, he took Corinth and its citadel by surprise one night in the summer of 243. Plutarch gives a blow-by-blow account, based on Aratus' autobiography, of an operation that was a complete success. At one stroke the Achaean forces became masters of a strategic location of crucial importance, and secured an opening on the Saronic Gulf and the Aegean Sea. The Achaean League was immediately joined by two cities in the Argolid, Epidaurus and Troezen. Like the Aetolian League in central Greece, it now occupied from east to west an uninterrupted zone between one sea and another, leaving the Peloponnese in complete isolation from Macedon. Worried by that development, the Aetolians concluded a treaty of alliance with Gonatas, the goal of which was the dismemberment of Achaea and the sharing of its territory between them.

Sparta, whose role in past history had been so great, was at this time confronted by a serious crisis. For more than a century Lacedaemonian power had been declining, profoundly shaken by Epaminondas and the Thebans: a consequence of its social system, as Aristotle's lucid analysis in his *Politics* had already convincingly demonstrated. There existed an ever-widening gap between the small minority class of the Equals, by then reduced to a few hundred, and the rest of the Lacedaemonians. These were relegated to an inferior rank as a result of the gradual concentration of wealth, especially land ownership, in a few hands. Most of them were laden with debt. In such circumstances, how could the city recruit an army of citizens faithful to its age-old military tradition? Agis IV, a young king imbued with a rather naive brand of idealism, embarked on a program of reform meant to reinstate equality of resources among Spartans, and to rebuild a body politic that had been drained of its life-blood by the massive enlistment of new elements. His program was started in 242 but stopped in midstream, owing to the opposition of the well-to-do. Agis forced into exile his fellow-king Leonidas – an agent of the wealthy. But only the abolition of debt became effective; land sharing, though promised, did not become a reality. He thus disappointed his supporters. In the meantime an Aetolian army was preparing in 241 to invade the Peloponnese. In order to repel it Aratus appealed to the Lacedaemonian forces for cooperation. Agis led them north toward the Achaeans, but at the moment of joining them had to suffer the insult of rejection. For

Aratus was apprehensive of the example that association with a body of young Spartans motivated by revolutionary idealism would set for his own people's social order. The Lacedaemonian army had to make its way back to Sparta without having fought. Meanwhile King Leonidas, back from exile, had recaptured power, supported by the wealthy class. Agis was arrested and executed. His supporters were banished: his attempt at reform had failed. Aratus and the Achaean troops, however, allowing the Aetolian forces to move into the Peloponnese, took them by surprise while they were plundering the small town of Pellene and slaughtered them. The two antagonistic Leagues then made peace. A provisional balance of power had thus been reached, yet the loss of Corinth certainly meant a weakening of Macedon's military power.

At the end of his long reign Antigonus Gonatas, who died in the winter of 240/239, had therefore failed to keep his hold on Greece to the end. He had at least managed, at the cost of unremitting diplomatic and military effort, to preserve his kingdom's territory, safeguard its Thessalian appendage, and rebuild the Macedonian people's forces. Macedon had been sorely tried by the far-off military ventures of Alexander and the Diadochi, by conflicts between pretenders to Cassander's succession, and by the Gallic barbarians' invasions. Such a task of national reconstruction demanded the firm and clear-sighted will of a man commanding the time necessary for its accomplishment. Contrary to his contemporaries the Seleucid and Ptolemaic monarchs, Antigonus' mind never harbored any grand project of war or conquest. In his capital of Pella, in the heart of Macedonia, he gathered round himself a small, unpretentious retinue of carefully chosen minds. Among these were the poet and historian Euphantus of Olynthus, who wrote for him a treatise *On kingship*; the philosopher Menedemus of Eretria; the poet Aratus of Soli, author of the *Phaenomena*, whose learned poetry was bound to please Zeno's former pupil. Antigonus would now and then receive Bion of Borysthenes, a Cynic philosopher, whose jovial candor was congenial to the king's taste, as he had little enthusiasm for placing himself in a category apart from the common run of humanity. He considered kingship "a glorious state of slavery," to quote his own words addressed to his son. He had been a brilliant warrior (during the battle of Cos he personally commanded his fleet from its flagship), but also behaved humanely toward the vanquished. He treated his enemy Pyrrhus' body with honor, ordering it to be brought back to Epirus with an escort worthy of a king. To Pyrrhus' son, Helenus, who had surrendered to him, he restored his freedom. Those traits of generosity constitute an impressive royal portrait – a strategist, a politician, and a philosopher all in one, approachable yet firm, fearless yet generous – deserving a place in the foremost rank of Hellenistic princes. Most important: despite setbacks late in his reign, his almost forty years of relatively peaceful rule had allowed the Macedonian people to recover demographically from the heavy toll exacted by the campaigns of Alexander and the Diadochi.

His son Demetrius II (thus designated to distinguish him from his grandfather, Demetrius Poliorcetes) had been made an associate ruler by Antigonus many years before his death. He was certainly conscious of the strategic interests of Macedon, those at least for which Antigonus had fought. On one essential point, however, he modified his father's policy. He gave up Macedon's alliance with the Aetolian League, which Gonatas had consistently maintained. His reason for that change was the constant growth of Aetolian power. It had become a threat for Macedon, both in the east with its piratical operations in the Aegean Sea, and in the west with its progress in Acarnania, a source of concern for Epirus. Piracy on the high seas and on the coast had been a profitable activity since the beginnings of Greek history. Both the *Iliad* and the *Odyssey* recount many raids, distinct from open warfare, made by Greek heroes in foreign lands. As soon as the Aetolians had secured an opening on the Euboean channel, they started practicing piracy in the Aegean Sea. From the middle of the third century, many cities on the islands or on the Asia Minor coast, anxious to maintain safety for their trade and peace along their seaboard, made treaties with the Aetolian League. These safeguarded their territories and their possessions: this guarantee against any violent seizure by a state or individuals was called *asylia*. This was the case at Tenos, Naxos, Delos, to quote some examples. The Delphic Amphictyony, totally dominated by the Aetolians, occasionally provided a juridical frame for setting up these privileged relationships: such was the case for Smyrna or Chios. All this was a cause of concern for the Macedonian sovereign, whose ships plied the Aegean seaways. The kingdom of Epirus on the other hand, on his western land frontier, had been weakened under the regency of a widowed queen, and appealed to Demetrius for protection. He was to marry an Epirot princess, Epirus thus becoming an informal protectorate of Macedon.

These circumstances led to a conflict that, from the year 239/8, pitted the Macedonian armies against those of the Aetolian and Achaean Leagues, reconciled against their common enemy. This was the complex "Demetrian" War, the details of which are not well known. Both sides won victories and suffered reverses. Demetrius freed Boeotia from the Aetolian yoke and wrested the Megarid from Achaea. In the Peloponnese, on the other hand, he lost the alliance of Megalopolis, which joined the Achaean League. Yet from 236/5 a new threat required all his attention: the invasion of northern Macedonia, in the Balkan Mountains, by a barbarian tribe, the Dardanians. Demetrius died in 229, fighting these invaders. His 10-year-old son inherited a particularly difficult situation.

Salvation came from a first cousin of the late king, who took up the regency until a time when the youth was of an age to reign. The regent was a son of Demetrius the Fair, younger brother of Gonatas, who, sent to Cyrene after Magas' death, had died there in an episode worthy of the high drama of a storybook (see p. 72). His name was Antigonus, called *Doson*, which means "who will hand over." That was a well-deserved surname, for while exercising his royal powers to the full and bearing the title that went with them, he never sought to supplant young Philip. At his death he left him as inheritance an intact and indeed greatly strengthened kingdom, which he had faithfully cared for.

Doson's first task was apparently to cope with the Dardanian barbarians' menace, which he may have done by giving up some frontier districts in their favor. Then he turned toward the Aetolians, who had taken advantage of a revolt against Macedon in Thessaly. He inflicted a serious defeat on them in 228 or thereabouts. Meanwhile Athens had bought the Macedonian garrison's departure in 229 (see p. 74), in exchange for a considerable sum obtained partly by raising loans, partly by receiving gifts from abroad. However, free once again, the city refused, in spite of pressure from Aratus, to join the Achaean League. It was a recipient of open-handed generosity from Ptolemy Euergetes (see p. 74 again), who founded in Athens a gymnasium named after him (see p. 297). In recognition of his benefactions, the Athenians created a thirteenth tribe, Ptolemais, without abolishing the tribes Antigonis and Demetrias, which they had created in the days of Poliorcetes (see p. 51): they were determined to stay neutral in future.

Having failed to enlist Athens as a member, the Achaean League had recaptured Megara and received in its midst Aegina, Argos, and many other cities of the Peloponnese. This could not have been a source of much worry for Doson, as he managed in 227 to lead a naval expedition all the way to Caria, in the southeast of Asia Minor, where he established a relationship with a local dynast, who placed himself under his protection (on this expedition see p. 209: the Xanthus inscription concerning Cytenium). That was the first attempt – a brief one – by an Antigonid to revive the ancient Asiatic dream of Antigonus the One-eyed and Demetrius. But as soon as he was back in Europe, Peloponnesian affairs claimed his attention. The situation there had reached a crisis, as a result of the policy of Cleomenes III, king of Sparta. In 235 he had succeeded his father Leonidas, colleague of Agis IV and his victor. That did not prevent him, after a few years on the throne, from promoting the reform program that his father had caused to be rejected. According to Plutarch, the new king, under the influence of his wife, once the widow of Agis, had been won over to his predecessor's revolutionary ideas. This is perhaps a figment of romantic imagination, perhaps not. Whatever we think of it, the story was widely accepted, and once again throws light on the part played by women in Hellenistic politics. Anxious to forge the tool he needed in order to restore Lacedaemonian greatness, Cleomenes found himself driven, as Agis had been, to a fundamental reform of Sparta's social system. But, being less naive than Agis, he first of all brought about circumstances favorable to change, in a real coup that got rid of potential opponents. With the help of the Eleans, he had attacked the Arcadian city of Megalopolis, a member of the Achaean League. The Achaeans intervened, and the Cleomenic War began. It had lasted more than a year when Cleomenes returned to Sparta in 2?? ⸳ ⸳hw head of a corps of mercenaries. He soon had the ephors arrested and ⸳⸳⸳ uted, did not bother to replace them, and exiled the main adversaries of his policy. Cleomenes thus had a free hand and was now, as Polybius notes, in the position ⸳ a G⸳ ⸳ rant (rather than that of a constitutional Spartan monarch). Under the ⸳ ⸳ce of a re⸳ ⸳ to the ancestral institutions of Lycurgus, he raised to 4,00⸳ ⸳umber of ⸳ ⸳als by the addition of new members, who received plots of la⸳⸳⸳ made availab⸳⸳ by the redistribution of the extensive holdings of the rich. He reinstated the strict education of earlier times: the repeated military exercises, the meals in common. Finally he brought up to date, on the Macedonian model, the equipment of the Spartan hoplites. His army, comprising as might be expected allied contingents and bands of mercenaries, included from that time a corps of elite soldiers, of equal calibre to those who had made Lacedaemon's troops invincible in the past.

Thus prepared, Cleomenes started again his operations in Arcadia, where he captured Mantinea, and in Elis, from which he advanced further into Achaea and defeated an Achaean army. His victories were troublesome enough for Aratus and the Achaean League to encourage them, after preliminary negotiations, into a complete reversal of alliances. Ptolemy III, who followed Greek affairs through his emissaries, decided to withdraw the financial support the Achaeans had received from him for a long time, and to help Cleomenes' plans with those grants in future: with Cleomenes' fortunes improving, Ptolemy saw him as a more effective agent of Lagid influence in southern Greece. Meanwhile Cleomenes was pushing an offensive toward the Gulf of Corinth up to Pellene in Achaea, and took Argos and other cities of the Argolid, finally occupying Corinth, where the inhabitants opened their gates to him. Only the fortress of Acrocorinth was still held by Achaean troops. Faced with such a serious menace, and with their League on the verge of dissolution, the Achaeans made Aratus *strategos* with full powers. While Cleomenes was besieging Sicyon itself, Aratus' own city, Aratus sent envoys to Antigonus Doson, offering to hand over Acrocorinth to him in exchange for help in defeating the Spartan king. Necessity was thus forcing the man who had once deprived the Macedonians of their main "Fetter of Greece" to return it to them, in order to save the very existence of the Achaean federal state, which Cleomenes' attacks were about to tear to pieces. He was also urged to do so by his aversion to the Spartan ideal of community-wide austerity, and was anxious to ward off the risk of a social revolution that the reforming king's example would bring to the cities, ruled by conservative elites, that made up the League. Plutarch, basing his work on Aratus' own *Memoirs*, brings out this double motivation.

Doson, agreeing to Aratus' proposal, arrived with a strong army in the spring of 241, recaptured the city of Corinth, and placed a Macedonian garrison in the citadel, where they took over from the Achaean one. He then occupied Argos, forced Cleomenes to retreat to Laconia, and in late summer made for Achaea, where the federal Council of the Achaean League was meeting at Aegium. There he was proclaimed "head of the aggregate of allied contingents": this amounted to the reconstruction, to Doson's advantage and against Cleomenes, of the equivalent of a Hellenic League, on the model of the one Philip II led after his victory at Chaeronea. The Achaeans, Epirus, Acarnania, the Boeotians, Phocis, the Locrians, and Euboea, according to Polybius' list, were thus regrouped side by side under Doson's command. In other words, this ensemble was no longer made up of cities, but of groups of cities – geographical entities or federal states. Sparta did not stand a chance against such a strong coalition; furthermore, from the Macedonian point of view, the new alliance would serve as a counterweight to the Aetolian League, which did not belong to it. To Aratus and the Achaeans it brought the hope of regaining influence in the Peloponnese; while Antigonus, again master of Corinth and the Isthmus, now had less to fear from the Aetolians. By that dual success Macedonian authority was brought back beyond the height to which Gonatas had raised it in the middle of his reign.

With the considerable forces at his disposal, Doson was again on the offensive in the Peloponnese in the summer of 223, and recaptured many important cities, like Mantinea and Tegea, from which he posed a direct threat to Laconia. Cleomenes, eager to recruit new troops, freed 6,000 Helots and enrolled them in the army. He made use of them for an attack on Megalopolis, the main city of Arcadia, which belonged to the Achaean League and had so far repulsed all his assaults. On this occasion, however, he captured the city and completely ravaged it. That was his last victory, for his sponsor Ptolemy Euergetes had lost faith in his ability to serve as a counterweight to Macedonian power, and, deciding to cut his supply of funds, advised him to give up the fight. Cleomenes was not resigned to this. He waited for Doson's army at Sellasia, north of Sparta. In July 222 a hard-fought battle ended in the extermination of the Lacedaemonians. With a few faithful followers Cleomenes managed to reach the sea and made a short stop at Anticythera. There he debated his choices: suicide or pursuit of his struggle in exile. After a call at Cyrene, which had a tradition of friendly relations with Sparta, he took shelter at Ptolemy's court in Alexandria. He was to die a few months later, murdered on orders from the new sovereign, Ptolemy IV, reneging on Euergetes' commitments – and fearing (rightly) Cleomenes' ambition to seize Egypt itself.

The battle at Sellasia signaled both the ultimate humiliation of Sparta, suffering foreign occupation for the first time in its history, and the Antigonid monarchy's greatest triumph. The "ancestral order of things" was reinstated in Lacedaemon (with one exception, the monarchy), while Doson celebrated his victory by dedications of thanksgiving in various sanctuaries. The dedication of his offering to Apollo at Delos has been preserved. But Doson, suffering from acute consumption, sensed that his end was near. Nevertheless he left for Macedonia's northern frontier, where barbarian pressure was again making itself felt.

He died early in 221, after taking the necessary measures for his young successor, aged only 17, to benefit from the advice of a Council he had taken care to put together, and from Aratus' friendship and goodwill. After eight years of a vigorous reign he bequeathed to Philip a kingdom that had been restored to the peak of its power and prestige, and once again dominated Greece.

Yet a menace from the west was soon to show its precise shape, a more serious one than all others for Greece and Macedon – although those at the helm had not yet measured its full dimensions. For Rome was beginning to intervene east of the Adriatic, after subduing to its authority the main centers of Hellenism in Italy and Sicily. Now is the time for a brief survey of these events.

■ *First contacts between Rome and the Hellenistic world*
■ *Hiero II of Syracuse: his long reign* ■ *Capture of Syracuse by Marcellus* ■ *Illyrian affairs* ■ *The risk of a conflict between Rome and Macedon*

Pyrrhus' failure and his departure from Tarentum in 275 had been fatal to the cities of Magna Graecia. The Roman armies, having already taken Locri and Croton, forced Tarentum to surrender in 272. Rhegium, the last important city in southern Italy, submitted in 270. The relationship that was established between the Greek cities and their conquerors was generally in the shape of an alliance, obviously not one between equals, but based in principle on good faith. The case of the Locrians bears witness to that: they had a new coin struck on which the allegory of Good Faith, *Pistis,* is seen crowning Rome personified.

This conquest was to have momentous consequences for Rome. The shipyards of Greater Greece contributed to the building of the Roman fleets, which were to play a decisive role in the First Punic War. At a cultural level, contacts multiplied between Hellenic civilization, continuing to flourish as before in the cities of southern Italy, and the still uncouth and fierce Latin peoples. It is not by chance that the first Latin writer, who translated Homer in the second half of the third century, was a Greek from Tarentum, Livius Andronicus. Another consequence was the establishment of formal relations between Rome and the Hellenistic sovereigns. Ptolemy II Philadelphus took the initiative by sending in 273 an embassy with a message of friendship to the Senate, which in its turn despatched ambassadors to Alexandria the year after. The precise content of the "friendship" entered into as a result of these visits is not known. But it is a fact that from this time the existence of Rome was no longer unknown to cultivated minds in the Greek East. Rome had its niche in their erudite curiosity, being mentioned by

Map 6 The western Mediterranean in the Hellenistic age.

Callimachus in one of his works, and by the poet Lycophron in his esoteric poem *Alexandra*. Bonds were thus gradually being created at the level of civilized life between two worlds which had remained for a long time in ignorance of each other.

After a brief reprieve, the Hellenic world in Sicily met with a similar fate to that of the Greek cities in southern Italy. Following Pyrrhus' retreat, Syracuse was for a few years a prey to anarchy. Then, around the year 270/69, a Syracusan leader, Hiero, backed by mercenaries, took up the responsibilities of power, with the title of *strategos*: a revival of the experience the city had had of Dionysius the

Elder or Agathocles. But Hiero took the royal title, something Agathocles had not done. He is called Hiero II, to distinguish him from the illustrious Syracusan tyrant, a friend of Pindar's, who ruled two centuries earlier. By 274, though still a private citizen, Hiero had already been enjoying great prestige, as is witnessed by Theocritus' *Idyll XVI*, addressed by the poet to Hiero in that year, asking (without success) for his patronage. Hiero married the daughter of a distinguished Syracusan family, Philistis, whose profile he had engraved on beautiful silver coins. During his long reign (he died in 215) he looked after the city's affairs skillfully. When Rome intervened in Sicily at the start of the First Punic War (264 BC), Hiero, who was then leading an operation against Messana in conjunction with the Carthaginians, was quick to grasp where the interest of Syracuse lay. In 263 he concluded a treaty of friendship with Rome, which he renewed in 248. Though he supported the Romans with supplies, he stayed clear of the fortunes of that war. The two adversaries were meanwhile battling in the east of Sicily and in Africa (where Rome sent Regulus in 256/5 in a fruitless attempt at invasion), especially at sea, where the Roman fleet ended up winning in 241 the great victory of the Aegates Islands. Syracusan farmers cultivated a territory rich in wheat, and Syracuse was Rome's supplier, often making a profit out of it (but often too, in moments of crisis, giving the grain as a gift, thus cementing good ties with Rome). Hiero took a personal interest in agriculture, on which he wrote a treatise that was later much appreciated in Rome. He organized his deliveries of cereals with efficiency, taking as his model the monopolistic system that was then applied in Ptolemaic Egypt, as well as the collection of land tax. Following a practice usual among Hellenistic kings, he lavished his abundant income on public buildings that enhanced his prestige. The great altar erected in Syracuse on his orders was colossal: 200 meters long, 10 meters high. Using the services of the scientist Archimedes and the naval engineer Archias of Corinth, he had a warship of exceptional size built, which he sent as a gift to Ptolemy – for only the harbour of Alexandria was large enough to accommodate this monster of a vessel (see p. 309). He extended generous help to the Rhodians when a terrible earthquake destroyed their city in 227 (see pp. 247–8). While his fame spread to the eastern basin of the Mediterranean, his sound administration, his benevolence, his mildness toward his subjects won the esteem and personal attachment of the Syracusans. He died aged 90 in 215. "His funeral," says Livy, "was truly a royal one. It was a ceremony that his family had prepared with the greatest attention to detail. But above all it revealed his fellow-citizens' warm affection for him."

Few Hellenistic sovereigns ever aroused such feelings. Yet in 214, immediately after his death, the government of Syracuse under his grandson, beguiled by Hannibal's victories, made the mistake of abandoning Rome in the Second Punic War. The Romans took fierce revenge on what they saw as a friend's treachery. Syracuse fell after a long siege by Marcellus. It was the first time the famous city had been captured by a foreign assault. It was given over to plunder; its territory was annexed to the Roman province of Sicily. Archimedes had been killed by a drunken trooper (see pp. 355–6). Only one important Greek city in the western Mediterranean remained free. That was Marseille.

The Romans, engrossed in their struggles in the west, still showed only an occasional and limited interest in Greece proper. The circumstances of Illyrian affairs, however, made them concentrate their attention more and more on that area. Neither in Rome nor in continental Greece did contemporaries fully gauge the importance of those first contacts, which took place during Antigonus Doson's reign.

The name Illyria was given to the whole Dalmatian coast with its hinterland, as well as Albania. Barbarian tribes occupied this land, though some Greek colonies had obtained a footing either on the coast, for example, Apollonia, Epidamnus, or Lissus, or on the islands with towns such as Pharos or Issa. These barbarians practiced piracy on light vessels (called *lemboi*, plural of *lembos*), with crews of fifty. After some fighting with the Epirots, the Illyrians made an alliance on favorable terms with Epirus and Acarnania toward the end of Demetrius II's reign. It allowed their flotillas to carry out piratical activities down to the Ionian Sea, at the very opening of the Gulf of Corinth. The main sea-route between the Greek world and Italy was thus in danger. Roman and Italian traders suffered from the situation, and when an embassy was sent by the Senate to the Illyrians to call them to account, one of its members was murdered. At the same time an Illyrian corps attacked Corcyra (Corfu) and took its important naval base: Corcyra came under the command of a Greek from the Adriatic, Demetrius of Pharos, who was a henchman of the Illyrians. All in all, Illyrian power was growing rapidly and (from the point of view of both Rome and the Greeks) dangerously. Rome responded in 229/8 with a large naval expedition that quickly defeated the Illyrians and forced Queen Teuta, their leader, to give up two important regions. Part of the Dalmatian islands, with the towns of Issa and Pharos and the opposite coast, became an independent principality to be ruled by Demetrius of Pharos, who had rallied to the Roman side by surrendering Corcyra to them. Further south, a strip of territory along the Albanian coast, from Lissus to north of Corcyra, also became independent, with two Illyrian tribes occupying it. The Greek cities on the Adriatic, Epidamnus and Apollonia, as well as Corcyra, became (like Demetrius of Pharos and the two Albanian tribes) "friends of the Roman people." In other words, they were placed under the protection of Rome, which fully expected to safeguard shipping in that area by such measures.

After this victorious campaign, a Roman embassy came and explained to the Aetolians and Achaeans the reasons for the Romans' military intervention and the results it had obtained. That was Rome's first official contact with the peoples of Greece proper. Soon after, other embassies went to Athens and Corinth and (so Polybius tells us) the Romans were admitted to the Isthmian Games, a privilege that distinguished them from foreign barbarians and granted them a place on an equal footing with the community of Hellenes. Notice that no embassy was sent to the king of Macedon. As a counterpart to this, we learn from Polybius that Antigonus Doson contracted an alliance with Demetrius of Pharos, the friend of Rome, the dynast who ruled the islands of the Dalmatian archipelago. To satisfy his own ambition, Demetrius was trying, by extending his possessions on the coast and in the hinterland, to put together a new great Illyrian state, which was potentially a cause of concern to the Roman Senate. Implicit in Demetrius' friendship with Macedon was the risk of a conflict between Rome and the Antigonids in Illyria.

4/THE EAST TORN APART,
THEN CONQUERED

The years 223–221, a whole century after Alexander's death, form a turning
point in Hellenistic history. New sovereigns ascended the throne in the three
great monarchies. All three were very young. All three in various ways broke with
their respective dynasties' traditions. All three, either because of their own nature's faults and inadequacies, or in spite of their good qualities and laudable
intentions, started their kingdoms on a process of decadence, which more or less
quickly brought their successors to yield to Roman power. From that moment
too, the armies of Rome initiated in the Balkans a series of operations, which, in
an inescapable sequence, resulted in open conflict with Macedon. That was the
first step toward the conquest by Rome of the whole eastern basin of the Mediterranean. The causes of that gradually intensifying Roman involvement in the
East are complex. The following account will try to unravel them.

In Macedon Philip V, almost immediately after his accession to the throne,
had to face a crisis provoked by the Aetolians. They were concerned that the
Peloponnese had by and large come under the new Hellenic League's control,
and sent an expedition to Messenia. The Achaean League and Aratus tried to
counter it, but were beaten in Arcadian territory. They applied for help to their
allies and Philip. A meeting of the League was held in Corinth under the young
king's chairmanship. It decided to go to war against the Aetolians, emphasizing
that its aim was to restore freedom to the peoples forced by the Aetolian League
to join it. Its intention was also to rid the Delphic Amphictyony of the League's

influence. The three years that followed were a series of complex and confusing operations, often bloody ones, both in the Peloponnese and in continental Greece, where the Aetolians plundered the sanctuary of Dodona in Epirus. Philip wrested from them Thebes in Phthiotis, not far from Demetrias. In 217, no doubt worried about what was happening in Illyria, he made peace at Naupactus, on terms that had some effect in lessening Aetolian power. Thus ended what was called the Social War, or the War of the Allies (Latin *Socii*).

In the meantime Rome had been obliged to intervene again in Illyria against Demetrius of Pharos, its former ally. His territorial progress in southern Illyria, and his piratical activities as far away as the Cyclades, understandably aroused concern on the Roman side. A new expedition by their fleet put Demetrius to flight. He was received at Philip V's court, where he schemed to secure the means of recovering his Dalmatian principality. He was aware of the first defeats Hannibal had inflicted on Rome in the Second Punic War, which had just started (in 218), and tried to entice Philip toward the Adriatic. He persuaded him to lead a Macedonian squadron against Apollonia in Illyria, a city enjoying Rome's protection. The arrival of Roman vessels forced Philip to retreat. The king nevertheless had taken a position against Roman expansion in the Adriatic, which led him to take sides with Hannibal, now encamped in Italy, and to conclude with him a treaty of alliance, the terms of which have been preserved for us by Livy. These guaranteed protection against Roman attacks on the Greek colonies in the Adriatic, Apollonia, Epidamnus, Pharos, Corcyra, and on the lower valley of the river Aous (Thessaly and Macedonia's outlet on the Albanian coast); and finally, the restoration of his territories to Demetrius of Pharos. It was thus the situation in Illyria that was the king of Macedon's prime concern. But, ironically, as the Macedonian operations were starting in Illyria, Demetrius of Pharos lost his life in a treacherous attack (authorized by Philip) on Philip's own ally Messene in the southwestern Peloponnese. Philip wanted full possession of this city.

Philip then went to war in the Adriatic: there he was defeated by a Roman squadron within sight of Apollonia, but in his next campaigns he made conquests in the interior of Illyria as far as Lissus. At that juncture Rome concluded, in 212/11, an alliance with the Aetolian League. Adherence to that treaty was open to allies of the League, that is, to Sparta, Elis, Attalus I of Pergamum. In the same year Aratus died. A new *strategos* took his place in the Achaean League, who was one day to be called "the last of the Greeks": he was Philopoemen. This "First Macedonian War" lasted years and cost the Greek cities dearly, for the Roman fleet and armies were relentless in quest of booty. Philip countered his opponents with untiring action, in the diplomatic field as well as his military operations. He got Prusias, king of Bithynia, to attack Attalus of Pergamum, who had been chosen as *strategos* of the Aetolians in 209. He ended up penetrating into Aetolia until he reached Thermus, the federal capital, as he had in the Social War. That led the Aetolians to conclude a separate peace in 206: they agreed to give up the western provinces of Thessaly, which they had held for many years, and the possessions that were still theirs on the Malian Gulf and in Phocis. Rome had recalled her troops in 207, and, as a result of the Aetolian defection, made peace in 205. The disputed Illyrian territories were shared between Philip and Rome, Philip keeping the Aous valley, the main object of his interest.

Apart from the two principal adversaries, the treaty signed at Phoenice in Epirus mentioned (according to Livy) parties interested in that text (*foederi adscripti*, literally, "inserted as adjuncts to the treaty"). These included on one side Philip's allies, those belonging to the Hellenic League as well as Prusias of Bithynia. On the other side were Attalus of Pergamum and Rome's allies: an Illyrian prince, Nabis, tyrant of Sparta, the Eleans, Messene, and two cities that had stayed neutral, Athens and Ilium. The insertion of adjunct parties was made at Rome's request (though many historians, without giving compelling reasons, consider these apocryphal). Roman policy did not yet have a precise project in the East, because of the preparation in Africa of a campaign aimed at bringing to an end the war against Carthage. Philip had fought well in the war against Rome (a war he had started); but those adjunct insertions show that Rome was none the less anxious to preserve her relationships as far as the Aegean Sea, and was no longer uninterested in Greek affairs.

While the Social War and the First Macedonian War were taking place, the Ptolemaic and Seleucid monarchies experienced years of unrest. Antiochus III was not yet 20 when in 223 his brother, Seleucus III, was murdered. Antiochus had as his right-hand man a Greek, Hermias, who had been one of Seleucus' ministers and was for some time to have a strong influence on the young sovereign. They soon had to face rebellion on the part of the satrap of Media, Molon, to whom Antiochus had just entrusted the overall government of the upper satrapies, that is, the eastern regions of the empire, for which the king had had responsibility before his brother's death. The generals sent to deal with Molon were defeated. Molon, advancing into Mesopotamia, captured Seleucia on the Tigris, capital of that region, and had his own coinage struck, usurping the title of king. Antiochus then took personal command of his army, a measure that brought about defections among Molon's troops. Defeated, the rebel killed himself. His body was crucified. Having reorganized the administration of these provinces, the king returned to Antioch in 220: he had got rid of the unwelcome presence of the unpopular Hermias by having him murdered. It is clear that Antiochus could be ruthless with his allies, as Philip was with his; but, like Philip, he lived in a very tough world. Back in Antioch he was faced with another rebellion. One of his distant relations, Achaeus, who had been given the task of governing Seleucid possessions in Asia Minor and had succeeded in recapturing territories which Attalus of Pergamum had occupied, had in his turn proclaimed himself king. But before quelling that new revolt, Antiochus had to devote his energies to waging war on his Egyptian neighbor. That was the Fourth Syrian War.

Since Antiochus' accession to kingship, his ministers (including Hermias) had been bent on persuading him to undertake the conquest of Coele-Syria. Ptolemy III Euergetes' death had improved the prospects of such a venture. His successor, Ptolemy IV Philopator, had little inclination for serious business, as he was strongly attracted by a life of voluptuous luxury. During the whole of his reign he virtually handed over responsibility to his minister Sosibius, an important figure who had served for a long time under Euergetes. A number of dynastic murders heralded the young king's reign. He ordered the death of Lysimachus, Euergetes' younger brother; of his own brother Magas (bearing the name of their maternal grandfather); and of Berenice II, mother to both of them (Sosibius apparently dreaded her haughtiness and audacity). These murders formed a typical episode in the history of bloody settlements of accounts, so frequent in Hellenistic royal families. Ptolemy IV (cf. p. 93) also ordered the death of Cleomenes, the former king of Sparta, who had taken refuge in Alexandria. Harassment by security officers had driven him to despair and revolt.

The climate of suspicion and murder in which the Ptolemaic court was steeped was bound to incite Antiochus to take advantage of the opportunity to reach his goal in Coele-Syria. In 219 the Seleucid army attacked and captured Seleucia in Pieria, the harbor of Antioch, conquered by Ptolemy Euergetes during the Laodicean War (see pp. 73–4), and kept since then in Egyptian possession. The mercenary leader who was to defend southern Syria for Ptolemy IV betrayed his master and handed over the port of Tyre to the invading army. Antiochus' troops arrived at the Egyptian frontier. The Delta was hastily put in a state of defense by an age-old method of halting an invader: flooding the Pelusian region, on the eastern branch of the Nile, by breaching the dams. The operation allowed the Egyptian side to have a reprieve in the winter, and, the year after, to resort to delaying tactics in Palestine. Sosibius used that respite to reorganize the Ptolemaic army, by enlisting in it for the first time – a momentous innovation – 20,000 native Egyptians. These fellahin were hastily recruited and equipped in the manner of the Greeks. They made up a phalanx distinct from the Macedonian troops and the mercenaries. His army thus reinforced, Ptolemy IV met Antiochus at Raphia in 217 and won a convincing victory. Antiochus retreated, leaving behind the whole of Coele-Syria, which he had conquered. Ptolemy then made peace, leaving Seleucia in Pieria in his enemy's possession but keeping Egypt's Syrian bulwark.

The victory at Raphia saved Egypt from invasion, and it was celebrated with great magnificence. Ptolemy IV sacrificed four elephants to Helios, the sun god, the equivalent in the Greek pantheon of Amon-Râ, the great Egyptian solar god. He had bronze statues of the sacrificed elephants erected to perpetuate the memory of such an exceptional offering. But beyond the rejoicing, however well founded it was, that victory had quite harmful results for the future of the Ptolemaic monarchy. The part played in the battle by an important corps of native soldiers helped to make the Egyptian peasantry conscious of its strength vis-à-vis the royal administrators and the Greek and Macedonian colonists. In the last years of Euergetes' reign the finances and economy of Egypt, for reasons that are not very clear to us, went through a crisis that resulted in heavier fiscal pressure (that is, larger taxes). The fellahin reacted to this with undisciplined behavior, disobedience, even local armed revolt, in which the former soldiers at Raphia were now able to play a part. Such events, which cannot be followed in detail, soon became chronic, and, with various symptoms, never ceased in Ptolemaic Egypt. Polybius explicitly remarks that the enlistment of natives in the royal troops at Raphia was useful at the time, but had heavily mortgaged the future. Ten years after that victory, in 207/6, Upper Egypt, traditionally mistrustful toward the central power headquartered in the Delta, resorted to secession and placed at its head a prince of Nubian origin. Its independence was to last until 186, twenty whole years, depriving the government at Alexandria of resources drawn from the southern territories, and trade with Nubia and the regions of the Upper Nile valley. These disturbances could only aggravate the financial and economic difficulties of the country, already suffering, as it did to a certain degree, from the negative impact of the Second Punic War on its western trade. An indication of this situation is given by the diminishing use of silver currency, starting in about 210. It is a sign of the growing rarity of that metal, while the domestic use of copper coinage became widespread. It is clear that, from the reign of Ptolemy IV onward, the abundance of resources which had fostered the endeavors of the first three Ptolemies did not remain at the same level. This decrease in available financial means was to have a serious effect on future Ptolemaic policies.

Raphia had another important consequence. In order to have, within a now restless population, some well-disposed people to negotiate with, Ptolemy IV showed an increasing interest in native sanctuaries and their clergy. A curious document, the "Stele of Pithom" as it is called, has preserved in three versions, Greek, hieroglyphic, and demotic, the text of a royal decree convening at Memphis a synod of Egyptian priests, to organize festivities in memory of the victory at Raphia. These meetings were an opportunity for the king to bestow various benefits, land donations or fiscal privileges, on representatives of native cults to ensure the goodwill of the priestly caste. The custom started in this period for the Greek sovereign to adopt on these occasions the titular persona of a Pharaoh and to be portrayed in traditional Pharaonic fashion. This move did not indeed alter the basic Greek character of the Ptolemaic court and the sovereigns' manner of thinking or their lifestyle, but was one of the formal concessions made, under the pressure of necessity, to the traditions of ancient Egypt.

While Philopator and his minister Sosibius had to come to grips with these internal problems, Antiochus, in spite of his defeat, felt he had a free hand to reassert his authority in the various regions of his empire that still eluded his grasp. Making an alliance with Attalus I, who had not stopped fighting Achaeus in Asia Minor, he made a start by recapturing from his kinsman Seleucid possessions beyond the Taurus. After operations that lasted four years, Achaeus, who had shut himself up in the citadel of Sardis, was finally captured in 213. He had to suffer the barbarous penalty that Achaemenid tradition prescribed for rebels. Though Attalus took advantage of the venture to rebuild his kingdom, Antiochus had reason to believe that his essential objectives in Anatolia had been attained. He therefore turned to the eastern provinces, where he planned to reinstate Seleucid power, a goal that had eluded Seleucus II, his father.

In 212 Antiochus started on that long expedition toward the eastern satrapies that is called the "Anabasis," meaning the expedition toward the interior of the continent. He began by marching on the kingdom of Armenia, a tributary of the Seleucid empire, where he exacted payment from the local dynasts of arrears of their tribute, which they had neglected to settle. He then made for Media, where he assembled a considerable force at Ecbatana. To pay for that force's upkeep, he did not scruple to lay hands on the treasures of a local divinity's sanctuary: that was a high-handed and perilous decision, which tradition later said was to prove fatal to him. In 209 the sovereign marched beyond the Caspian Gates toward the land of the Parthians, where he persuaded King Arsaces II to enter into an alliance with him. Pushing further east, he attempted to reconquer Bactria, where Diodotus II had been replaced by another Greek dynast, Euthydemus, who had extended his realm to the south by adding to it the province of Areia, south of the mountains. Euthydemus seems to have given the young Bactrian state a solid base, judging from the fine silver coinage that he had struck, bearing his effigy. Symbiosis between native and Greek and Macedonian colonists had become a reality, to a degree unknown elsewhere. To give an example, Euthydemus had at his disposal a large force of cavalry, numbering 10,000, the majority evidently being Asiatic. He waited for Antiochus on the banks of the Areius River, then had to retreat and shut himself up in his capital, Bactra. A two-year siege could not force the city to surrender, while the threat of nomads from central Asia put the rear lines of the besiegers at risk. Antiochus therefore compromised with Euthydemus, allowed him to bear the title of king, and concluded a treaty of alliance with him. Thus was the Greek State of Bactria officially recognized. Antiochus then pursued his expedition eastward beyond the Hindu Kush toward the furthermost provinces of Alexander's former empire, where an Indian prince then reigned. He received Antiochus in a friendly manner, giving him 150 war elephants and a sizable sum of money. Happy with such results, the king started on his return journey via Arachosia, Drangiana, and Carmania, where he spent the winter of 206/5. From Carmania he sailed on the Persian Gulf to visit Gerrha, a port on the coast of Arabia, behind the island of Bahrain. There he received considerable quantities of silver, incense, and myrrh, then, laden with these presents, went back to Mesopotamia and its capital, Seleucia on the Tigris.

This "armed tour of inspection" into the depths of Asia appealed to the popular imagination. On his return, Antiochus had earned the right to be called *The Great*. He had put down attempts at revolt and, in the far-off territories of Parthyaea and Bactria, restored his nominal authority by means of treaties of alliance. He had confirmed his presence in Eastern Arachosia, given up by Seleucus nearly a century earlier. As Craterus had once done on his return from India, he had traveled over the eastern marches of his empire, Drangiana, Gedrosia, Carmania, thus tightening their links with the center of power. Like Alexander, he had sailed on the Indus and the Persian Gulf. In these endeavors he had displayed boldness, a continuity of ideas, an awareness of what was possible. The Seleucid empire had not had such a leader since the foundation of the dynasty.

■ *Crisis in the Egyptian kingdom under Ptolemy V Epiphanes*
■ *The Fifth Syrian War* ■ *Intervention by Rome* ■ *The Second Macedonian War* ■ *Flamininus* ■ *Battle of Cynoscephalae*
■ *The Isthmian Games of 196* ■ *The Romans' first plunder from Greece*

Antiochus had just returned to Syria, enjoying the aura of his "Anabasis," while the Peace of Phoenice relieved Philip V of his conflict with Rome. It was at that moment that the Ptolemaic monarchy, weakened since its victory at Raphia, fell into the grip of a serious crisis caused by Ptolemy IV Philopator's early death in 204. His successor, Ptolemy V surnamed Epiphanes, was only 5 years old. His mother was Arsinoe, sister and wife of Philopator (as in the case of Philadelphus, a brother–sister marriage). Ptolemy IV, acting under the influence of his minister Sosibius, had repudiated her a few years earlier. To avoid her becoming regent for such a long time until her son came of age, Sosibius and his accomplices caused her to be murdered, and concealed Philopator's death for some time. Meantime the aged Sosibius died as well, and the government of the kingdom became the object of factional disputes. Such a chaotic situation offered Antiochus an opportunity for action that he could not afford to miss. Did he not have to avenge his defeat at Raphia? As Philip V, on the other hand, was interested in playing his part in the Aegean Sea once more, the two sovereigns, in conformity with the tradition of accord linking their dynasties, reached an agreement in 203/2, providing for a sharing of Ptolemaic possessions. Antiochus was to have Coele-Syria and Cyprus, Philip the Cyclades, Ionia, Samos, Caria, and Cyrene. Our sources do not let us know for certain who was to have Egypt. Polybius calls that plan, aimed at dismembering an empire whose monarch was a child, an act of felony. In any case, it throws light on the designs and the ruthless character of the two accomplices.

Antiochus probably started his Syrian War, the fifth to be so called, in 202. After a period of indecisive fighting, his victory at Panium, won in 200 near the source of the river Jordan, allowed him to occupy the whole of Coele-Syria, extending to the Egyptian frontier. He soon included it in the administrative system of his empire by placing it under the authority of a *strategos*. Philip V, on his part, started by attacking various Greek cities in the Propontis and on the Straits: these operations worried the Rhodians, who traded in that area, and Attalus I, of course. Then in 201, having built a powerful fleet, he occupied many islands in the Cyclades, and besieged Samos, which was under Ptolemaic protection. That prompted Rhodes to intervene and send a squadron, which Philip defeated at Lade, a small island close to Miletus. His success allowed him to occupy Miletus itself, another Ptolemaic dependency. Then Rhodes, with Byzantium and Chios as well as Attalus I, formed a coalition against him. He managed to ravage Pergamum's territory, but failed to take the city and suffered a naval defeat within sight of Chios. He then moved to Caria, where he set up his winter quarters in late 201.

It was at this point that Rome intervened at the request of Attalus and Rhodes, both anxious to stop the progress of an ambitious sovereign who was a serious menace to their respective interests. The Second Punic War had just ended with the triumph of Roman arms. The Republic's resources were thus available for other plans. Because of Philip V's conclusion, in 215 after Cannae, of a treaty of alliance with Hannibal, the Senate still harbored a grudge against him. Some time earlier, the government of Ptolemaic Egypt had also sent an embassy to Rome, warning of serious developments in the East. In response to these appeals and to keep watch on events in the East, the Senate despatched three envoys to that area in 200. They stopped at Athens, which had just declared war on Philip because of his local aggression against the city (he was back from Caria). The Athenians' anger with Philip was demonstrated in the removal from their administrative map of the two "Macedonian" tribes, Antigonis and Demetrias, which had been created a century earlier (see pp. 51–2). Having benefited from the support of Attalus I against Macedon, they created a tribe, Attalis, in his honor. They also received help from the Rhodian fleet.

While at Athens, the Roman envoys formally asked Philip "not to make war on any Greek people" and to agree to arbitration on the grievances that the king of Pergamum had aired against him. Philip took no account of these demands and started another operation in Thrace and on the Straits, particularly against Abydus on the Asiatic bank of the Hellespont, which he besieged. At that point one of the Roman envoys (who were now at Rhodes) came back and reminded him of the content of the Romans' message to him, adding new demands. These were that he should not harm Ptolemaic interests on the north coast of the Aegean, and make good any damage done to the Rhodians. The Roman popular assembly had already voted in favor of war against Philip, and two legions had landed in Apollonia in Illyria, while the roving embassy that had been sent to the east visited Antiochus, fresh from his victory in Syria, asking him to spare Egypt. This he did.

Livy, writing two centuries after these events, portrays this Second Macedonian War as a direct continuation of the first, which had been interrupted by the demands of Rome's struggle with Hannibal. Even if such an a posteriori view derives from too much simplification, it is clear that the Republic, at least in the minds of some members of the ruling class at Rome, considered itself empowered from this point to intervene directly in eastern affairs and maintain a balance among Hellenic states. The armies and the fleet that had vanquished Carthage found in such a policy of intervention (if not of imperialism) some justification for the continued recourse to their services. Veterans from the Punic War and politicians eager for positions of military command were equally interested in these new projects. Henceforth, Rome was to play a determining role in the Greek world.

In this Second Macedonian War, Philip, no longer supported by Antiochus, was almost alone against his adversaries. The Hellenic League was gone for good. The Achaeans, who had formed its centerpiece, after a short spell of waiting and seeing, rallied in large part to the side of his adversaries, partly out of hostility toward Nabis, the Spartan tyrant, with whom Philip was on good terms. Rome reckoned on support from the Rhodians and Attalus – already at war with Philip since 201, of course. Their squadrons had the Aegean Sea under control in conjunction with the Roman fleet. On land the Aetolians were none too eager to help, but the barbarian peoples of Illyria and the Balkans were ready to take advantage of the opportunity given them to attack Macedonia. Philip successfully resisted this heterogeneous coalition for two years; the Roman generals failed to advance beyond the barrier of the Pindus. Everything changed in 198, when a young man of 30, Titus Quinctius Flamininus, was elected consul and sent as commander-in-chief to Illyria. Ambitious, intelligent, and hard-working, he had a sincere empathy for Greek culture, which did not prevent him from waging war ruthlessly in Greece. He brought with him a new series of demands from the Senate, much harsher ones than those which had been conveyed to Philip at Abydus in 200. The Macedonian king was now required to remove his troops from all Greek cities in which he had garrisons; he was also to give up Thessaly, which had become, over a century and a half, almost an integral part of Macedon. Such a message rekindled among the Greeks their old passion for independence and their deep-seated dislike of Macedonian authority. For Philip it was out of question to give in to these demands. Roman operations were renewed, led by Flamininus with a vigor not seen before. He overwhelmed the defenses barring the upper valley of the Aous, invaded Thessaly, and, though defeated by Philip there, reached the Isthmus and rejoined his fleet: commanded by his brother Lucius, it was moored at Cenchreae, Corinth's harbor on the Saronic Gulf. The brothers' combined pressure now led the Achaean League to ally itself overtly with Rome. Flamininus was given as proconsul an extension of his command for the next year, in the course of which he managed to detach from Philip his last allies, the Boeotians and Nabis the Spartan tyrant. He then went on the offensive in Thessaly. There in June 197, south of Larissa, Roman legions clashed with a Macedonian phalanx for the first time, at the foot of the hills of Cynoscephalae ("Dogs' Heads"). Polybius says that the superior maneuvering ability of the Roman infantry won the day. At about the same time the Achaeans took Corinth, and the Rhodians recaptured in Caria the continental territories that Doson and Philip V had taken from them. These reverses, in addition to his defeat at Cynoscephalae, forced the monarch to negotiate peace. As Antiochus III's advances in Asia Minor were now a cause of concern for Flamininus, he did not attempt to push further his military gains, but decided to treat with Philip.

He imposed harsh conditions of peace on the king of Macedon, who had to agree to what he had already turned down as unacceptable. This consisted in abandoning all his possessions and strongholds in Greece, comprising Thessaly and the "Fetters" (see p. 82), and in Asia Minor; payment of 1,000 talent war indemnity; the handing over of his war fleet. The Macedonian State was to survive, with the right to keep an army so as to hold back aggression from the northern barbarians. To Aetolian demands for territorial gains (that is, the return to the Aetolian League of cities that formerly belonged to it but had been occupied by Philip) Flamininus responded that the Senate would decide. The senatorial commission sent for that purpose in 196 was instructed to "ensure freedom for the Greeks," in Asia as well as in Europe. The Isthmian Games, as usual the venue for a great Panhellenic gathering, took place in 196. Flamininus took advantage of the presence of such a vast audience and solemnly proclaimed that the Roman Senate and himself allowed the nations hitherto placed under Macedonian control to be "free, exempt from military occupation or payment of tribute, governed by the laws of their ancestors." Delirious enthusiasm seized the crowd, which hailed Flamininus as its liberator. Several cities granted him honors and raised statues of him. Many inscriptions that have come down to us bear testimony to this. An impressive gold coinage struck in Greece (it is not known precisely in what city) commemorated his victory. One of the faces of the *stater*, the one usually representing a prince or a god, reproduced his likeness. That was an unprecedented honor for a Roman citizen.

As for the application of the Isthmian Declaration, liberty for the Greeks did not become a reality everywhere. King Eumenes II of Pergamum, who had just succeeded his father (he died in 197), continued to hold Aegina, which the Aetolians had sold him after receiving it from the Romans in the First Macedonian War. No one dared claim back from the Rhodians, in order to make them free, the Greek cities they had recaptured in Caria. For another two years Roman troops remained stationed in Greece. They took part in a brief but fierce war in 195 between the Achaean League, which was supported by many allied contingents from the coalition against Philip, and Nabis, tyrant of Sparta, who refused to leave Argos (Philip had put him in control of that city). Nabis had reinforced his army by Helot emancipation on a massive scale, but was finally forced to yield. Thus freed, the city of Argos rejoined the Achaean League and showed its gratitude to Titus Flamininus by founding games called the *Titeia* ("Games in honor of Titus"). Finally, in the summer of 194, the Romans left for Italy after Flamininus had convened one last Hellenic Congress at Corinth, advising the Greeks to use their freedom well. In the proconsul's triumphal procession on his return to Rome, paintings, statues, treasures that were his soldiers' booty were carried aloft in full public view. Such an act of collective plunder was to occur again very often over the next two centuries and made Rome a city of museums crammed with spoils from Greece. There was after all nothing in this practice that was contrary to the law of war in Antiquity. What was new was the destination of these works of art, these sumptuous furnishings. They were removed from the Greek world to enrich the civilization of another people.

■ *Antiochus III's plans* ■ *The welcome he gave to Hannibal*
■ *Eumenes II's intrigues at Rome* ■ *The Aetolians' appeal to Antiochus for help* ■ *Antiochus pushed back into Asia* ■ *Battle of Magnesia on the Sipylus* ■ *Treaty of Apamea* ■ *Its consequences* ■ *Rome the arbiter of the Orient*

Flamininus might well have thought, when he left Greece in 194, that he was leaving behind a free and pacified country. This was to prove a short-lived illusion. Antiochus III, having safeguarded his rear lines by conquering Coele-Syria, decided to carry on with his plan of restoring his ancestor Seleucus I's empire to its full extent. That meant recapturing, and enlarging if necessary, Seleucid possessions in Anatolia and even in Europe – in Thrace (which Seleucus had reached when he crossed the Straits after the death of Lysimachus). Such a plan would lead to conflict with the king of Pergamum: he had annexed Seleucid territory at the time of Achaeus' revolt. It also clashed with Rhodian ambitions: the continental possessions they held facing their island (what was called the Rhodian *Peraea* or outreach) had been in large part occupied by Philip V. Rhodes had every intention of recovering them, and not leaving them in Antiochus' possession. Finally, it was to disturb the more or less independent Greek cities of the Aegean coast and the Propontis. Antiochus' forces were composed of an experienced army, well supported by cavalry and elephants, and a fleet that had recently been refitted. They allowed him to face these adversaries under favorable conditions. The prestige he had earned by his "Anabasis," and his victory over Ptolemaic Egypt at Panium, made him appear as one who was, in Polybius' words, "worthy of holding command not only in Asia, but in Europe as well."

In 197 he was already making his way northward across Asia Minor, while his fleet, advancing along the south coast, was taking possession of Ptolemaic strategic positions in that area, before turning north alongside Ionia (where Ephesus entered into alliance with the king) until it reached the Straits. In 196, Antiochus was busy recommissioning the stronghold at Lysimacheia, in the Thracian Chersonese. On the Asiatic coast of the Dardanelles, Abydus, recently freed from Macedonian occupation, fell again under Seleucid dominance. But the neighboring city of Lampsacus, like Smyrna in Ionia, refused to submit. It appealed to Rome, making use of the connections in the Senate of its sister-city Marseille, far away in the West: the common origin of the two cities, both founded by Phocaea, was enough for Lampsacus to resort to the good offices of the Greek colony in Provence. Rome's reaction was to instruct Antiochus not to cross into Europe with an army and to respect the freedom of the cities of Asia. The king took no notice of this attempt at intervention. He was busy making peace with Ptolemy V Epiphanes, who had recently come of age, and who married Antiochus' daughter, Cleopatra. The Ptolemaic Empire was by then reduced, beyond Egypt, to Cyrenaica and Cyprus, with strategic positions at Thera (Santorini) and in eastern Crete. The Ptolemaic kingdom's naval dominance in the Aegean Sea, having lasted a century, was over by now. Its political import in the eastern Mediterranean was henceforth to be secondary.

At about the same time, Antiochus received at his court Hannibal, exiled from Carthage. He was to become to a certain extent his advisor (though the king did not always follow his advice). Eumenes II, on his part, was making move after move to caution the Romans against the Seleucid's designs. In Greece, finally, the Aetolian League, unhappy with the meager returns of its action in the Second Macedonian War, was scheming to bring together a coalition of Greek states against Rome. It failed to obtain Philip V's cooperation: he remained loyal, prompted of course by his own interests. But Nabis, the tyrant of Sparta, allowed himself to be persuaded, to his own detriment as it turned out, for the Aetolians, who mistrusted him, had him murdered. The coalition then called upon Antiochus to be at their head, with the title of *strategos* "with full powers" (*autokrator*). The king agreed, and landed at Demetrias, which the Aetolians had only just conquered (in October 192). He brought a force of limited strength with him: 10,000 men and six elephants. That was not much for war on a large scale, for the Achaean League and Philip V were on the Roman side, while the Aetolians had with them only the Eleans and Boeotians. When in 191 the Roman army went on the offensive, it soon pushed Antiochus (though he had by then been reinforced by more of his troops) back to Thermopylae, which he failed to hold: he was forced to sail back to Chalcis with the remnants of his army. After his departure the Aetolians eventually had to sue for peace, while the Achaeans took advantage of the situation to force the rest of the Peloponnese into their League; and Philip recaptured many positions, among them Demetrias, and some townships on the Thessalian frontier. Then, while operations were at an end in Greece, they started afresh in the Aegean, where the squadrons of Rome, Rhodes, and Pergamum, working in concert, had defeated the Seleucid fleet by the end of the next year. Antiochus was forced to leave Thrace and tried to negotiate. But by that time Rome's demands were such that he could not bring himself to agree to them. He therefore waited in Anatolia for the assault of the legions. The consul Lucius Cornelius Scipio commanded them. His elder brother accompanied and advised him: he was Hannibal's illustrious conqueror, Publius Scipio. Scythed chariots, elephants, the Seleucid cavalry (these with a two-to-one superiority in numbers) failed to move the legionaries, ably supported by Eumenes' cavalry, from their position at Magnesia. Roman tradition, as reported by Livy, makes a massacre of that victory: 400 dead among the Romans, in comparison with 50,000 on Antiochus' side. This is hard to believe, but it was certainly a decisive encounter. The king sued for peace. An armistice was agreed upon at Sardis, and a treaty signed in 188 at Apamea in Phrygia. Meanwhile the successor of the Scipio brothers, Cnaeus Manlius Vulso, had led his legions into parts of southwest Asia Minor, then against the Galatians in their Phrygian territory, which was cruelly ravaged in punishment for the numerous raids these restless tribes had made on neighboring lands. Nothing did more than that operation of revenge to earn for the Romans the gratitude of the Anatolian and Ionian populations. But Livy charges Manlius with having served the king of Pergamum's interest like a mercenary. The booty brought back to Rome as a result of that campaign was enormous. It made a major contribution to the spread of an appetite for luxury in Roman society.

In Greece, the fate of the Aetolian League was settled in 189 by a treaty imposing harsh terms on it. The Amphictyonic League was henceforth to be freed for good from its control. Rome was to occupy the Ionian Islands, Cephallenia (now Cephallonia), and Zacynthus (now Zante), which, like Corfu, were to serve as a base for its fleet while it monitored the western coast of Greece and the opening on the Adriatic. As for Asia Minor, the Peace of Apamea determined its fate. The text of this treaty, in all its details, has come down to us. Eumenes II of Pergamum benefited most from the Roman victory. He obtained the essential part of Seleucid possessions in the Anatolian interior north of the Taurus, as well as the Thracian Chersonese and the adjacent coast on the Propontis. Rhodes obtained Lycia and Caria up to the banks of the Maeander. Most of the important Greek cities were declared free, except Ephesus, which was to be a dependency of Eumenes. Antiochus lost all his possessions in Europe, in the Aegean Sea, in Anatolia beyond the Taurus and west of the Halys. He surrendered his war elephants and his fleet, keeping only ten vessels, which were not to sail westward beyond the waters of Cilicia. He undertook not to conclude any alliance west of his kingdom, to hand over Rome's enemies (but Hannibal managed to escape), and to pay a crushing indemnity of 15,000 talents. The Seleucid monarchy was indeed not annihilated. But it was in future excluded from the larger part of Asia Minor, shut out of the Aegean Sea, thrown back into its Syrian realm and its immense Mesopotamian and Iranian territories. Prospects for its expansion in international politics were as a result radically curtailed. Finally, decisions concerning the future of areas removed from Seleucid control were reserved for Rome alone, which declared them free or bestowed them on whoever it wished.

As a result of this war, a war started by Antiochus himself in pursuit of his ambitions, the Roman Republic emerged indisputably as the supreme arbiter of Asian affairs: in those of Greece, events had already bestowed that position on it. Within a decade the new power that had loomed on the horizon of the eastern Mediterranean had taken on major responsibilities and imposed its sovereign verdict on differences between kings and between cities. It was to Rome, in far-off Italy, in barbarian territory, that envoys from the Greek states, occasionally princes like Eumenes, went courting the Senate's goodwill, after pandering to commissioners sent by that body to enquire on the spot. It must be acknowledged that after the Peace of Apamea Rome recalled its legions, retaining as so many outposts only its naval bases in the Ionian Islands. Its presence remained nevertheless, in the guise of treaties it had concluded or imposed, guarantees it had granted to some, or threats it had uttered against those who proved unruly. By a fundamental but rapid change, Hellenistic history now becomes in essence the history of the states' relationship with Rome, and the gradual extension of Roman conquest in the Orient.

■ *Death of Antiochus III* ■ *Death of Philopoemen* ■ *Philip V's last years* ■ *Roman intervention in Bithynia and Pontus* ■ *Eumenes II of Pergamum's prosperity* ■ *Perseus and his political endeavors* ■ *New intrigues by Eumenes* ■ *The Third Macedonian War* ■ *Aemilius Paullus* ■ *Battle of Pydna* ■ *The end of the Antigonids* ■ *Macedon's imposed status* ■ *Advantages granted to Athens. Delos an Athenian colony* ■ *The weakening of Rhodes*

The main actors in the twofold drama that unfolded in the first decade of the second century soon disappeared. After his mission of the year 192, Flamininus returned to Greece only once, in 183, on a minor assignment (see Philip V, below). The Scipios were recalled to Italy at the end of the consulate of Lucius, the younger of the two, in 189. Antiochus met a tragic death in 187, the year after the peace of Apamea. So as to fill his coffers depleted by war, defeat, and above all the heavy indemnity demanded by the Romans (1,000 talents a year, till the full 15,000 talents had been paid), he went and looked for money wherever there was any to be found. As he had once done at Ecbatana in Media (see p. 104), he tried to seize the treasury of a native shrine – in Elymais (a province of Persia, south of Susa). In the process he was murdered by an angry population: a sad end for a great king. His elder son Antiochus having died a few years earlier, the younger one, Seleucus IV, succeeded him with the title of Philopator. He had first and foremost to find some means of settling his war debt.

Philopoemen, who had for a long time been the driving force behind the Achaean League's policies, was faced with Sparta's revolt against the League to which it now belonged. He quelled that revolt harshly in 188, capturing the city, razing its walls to the ground, and abolishing the social reforms that had earlier earned support from the Helots and the dispossessed for the tyrant Nabis. Not long after, Messenia in its turn attempted to secede. Philopoemen tried to prevent that from happening. But, taken prisoner by the Messenians, he was put to death in his prison in 183. Thus died "the last of the Greeks." A warrior and city-state imperialist of the old style, he left the Achaean League (in large part through his own efforts, as well as under the aegis of Rome) in control of the entire Peloponnese.

Philip V, the loser at Cynoscephalae, had with clear-headed tenacity spared no effort in preparing for eventual revenge, at least restoring Macedon's strength. We have seen him taking advantage of the war on Antiochus to recapture (as an ally of Rome) a number of Thessalian positions. He had in addition reorganized his kingdom's finances by creating new taxes, and vigorously developing the exploitation of the mines that were a source of precious metal for his coinage. He had also attempted to make up for Macedon's losses in manpower by bringing in measures aimed at stimulating the birth rate. But the repeated denunciations, prompted by jealousy, of the Thessalians and Eumenes of Pergamum were enough to arouse senatorial suspicion against him. The result was an embassy led by Flamininus, which came to him in 183 and forced him to leave two cities on the Thracian coast, Maroneia and Aenus, that he had seized in the course of the conflict with Antiochus. By contrast, Philip was given a free hand when in 184–181 he launched a number of (successful) expeditions against restless Thracian tribes in that area, who were a threat to Byzantium as well as Macedonia. The last years of his life were clouded by discord between his two sons. The elder one, Perseus, had been designated from the outset to succeed his father. But Demetrius, his younger brother, now emerged as a likely rival, supported as he was by relations he had entered into while a hostage in Rome after Cynoscephalae, and later on the occasion of an embassy that his father had entrusted to him. To avoid the evil consequences of a rivalry that would split the Macedonian nation after his death, Philip resigned himself to the loss of Demetrius: with typical ruthlessness he had him executed. That family tragedy stirred widespread emotion: in ancient historiography there are many echoes of that episode. Soon after, Philip himself died, aged 59, in the summer of 179. He had been the primary catalyst of Rome's increasing involvement with Greece – by attacking in the first place Roman Illyria during the Second Punic War as an ally of Hannibal, then the southern Aegean in 201/200, which led the potential victims to appeal for Roman intervention. He had vigorously sought to make Macedon the supreme power in mainland Greece and the Aegean, but had succeeded only in leaving Rome as the patron of a restored balance of power.

Eumenes II, king of Pergamum, who had benefited greatly from his friendship with Rome, had become as a result the most powerful king in Asia Minor. Yet he got involved in a dispute with his neighbor Prusias I of Bithynia. At stake was a piece of territory north of Phrygia, which he claimed with Rome's support and which the Bithynian king refused to make over to him. Prusias had given shelter to Hannibal when he was fleeing from Syria. After some indecisive skirmishes, the two parties agreed to put their dispute before Rome, which decided in favor of Eumenes, and in addition required Prusias to hand over Hannibal. The latter committed suicide (in 183). Eumenes had another conflict, this time with Pharnaces I, king of Pontus, who wished to extend his realm to Cappadocia, while attacking Greek cities on the Black Sea. These were Sinope, which was encircled by his states; Mesembria (part of modern Bulgaria) on the western coast of the Black Sea; Chersonesus on the south coast of the Crimea. From that point in time, Pharnaces nurtured imperial designs on the Greek colonies of the Tauric Chersonese, to which his kingdom, under Mithridates Eupator, was later to extend its dominion. However, he was forced to abandon his plan by another intervention on the part of Rome, which supervised the conclusion of a peace. He was to keep only Sinope: that was after all a momentous conquest for a barbarian state that had until then possessed no city of any importance. He made it his capital – a victory for Hellenization.

At that time, in 180 or thereabouts, the prosperity of the kingdom of Pergamum was at its peak. Eumenes had emerged, as a result of his great conquests and a relationship of mutual understanding with Rome, as the arbiter of Anatolia. Such a position was evidenced by his intervention against Pharnaces, as that conflict was of no direct concern to him, except in so far as he was bound by an alliance with the king of Cappadocia. He reigned supreme in the area of the Straits, on the Ionian coast of the Aegean (save for the free cities), and in the whole of central Asia Minor, with an opening on the south coast of Pamphylia. Such vast territories adjoining each other represented a source of wealth that Eumenes used to embellish his capital. The construction of the famous Altar of Zeus was started at this time, to commemorate another victorious campaign against the

Galatians. Its sumptuous ornament was testimony to the prosperity of his kingdom, just as in Pericles' time the building of the Parthenon had proclaimed the greatness of Athens.

When Perseus took command of Macedon, at his father's death in 179, he was just turning 32. He bore the glorious name of an ancestor of Heracles, from whom the Macedonian royal family claimed to be descended. He was far from devoid of intelligence, personal charm, or steadfastness, but he may have lacked an adequate measure of physical and emotional endurance at moments of crisis. The handsome coins that enshrined his physical portrait illustrate his sensitive features, reminiscent of his father's – but marked by a less self-assertive personality, not as well endowed with natural authority: a high degree of elegance at the expense of forcefulness. From the moment of his accession to the throne, he toned down his father's internal policy on a number of points, granting an amnesty to exiles and abolishing debt. He tried, with some success, to reestablish a friendly relationship with some of the Greek states (still alienated from Macedon by his father's imperialistic policies); regained influence within the Delphic Amphictyony; and did not hesitate, on the occasion of the Pythian Games of 174, to come in person to Delphi with a military escort. In the matter of internal conflicts, which had torn many Greek cities for a long time, he remained faithful to his father's policy: favoring, when the opportunity arose, the proponents of bold social measures detrimental to a conservative, wealthy class. Nothing illustrates better the rule that the policies of princes are dictated by interest, not by ideological choices. Outside Greece, he sought dynastic alliances by marrying Laodice, daughter of Seleucus IV, and bestowing his own sister as a spouse on Prusias II, king of Bithynia. He also tried to have friendly relations with Rhodes. A network of political and personal links was thus being woven between Macedon, restored to health by Philip V's strenuous efforts in the years after his defeat by Rome, and a number of monarchical states or Greek cities.

Rome was aware of Perseus' wide-ranging activity, which sometimes looked like provocation, as on the occasion of his trip to Delphi. For his own part, Eumenes of Pergamum, an old adversary of Macedon's, feared for his possessions in Thrace and on the Straits, and was jealous of Perseus' growing popularity in mainland Greece. He came in person to Rome in 172, and delivered a long speech to the Senate, accusing the Macedonian king of reneging on the obligations imposed by the treaty that Philip had signed and Perseus had renewed in 178. Giving plenty of detailed information, he drew an alarming picture of Macedon's military power – hinting at a covert design to invade Italy, which the actions he recounted appeared to indicate. Livy, who gives an account of that speech, notes the profound impression it made on the Senators, who once more feared the growing power of Macedon. An untoward incident made that forceful accusation even more potent. Eumenes was returning to Pergamum by way of

Delphi: there he narrowly escaped being murdered. The Macedonian king was perceived as being responsible for this failed attempt on his life, the alleged motive being a wish to get rid of Rome's most faithful friend in the East. That was too much for Rome. It was resolved in principle that another war had to be waged, this time on Perseus.

After fruitless negotiations, the Third Macedonian War started in the spring of 171. For two years Roman generals fought in Thessaly without obtaining any worthwhile results. In 169 the consul Quintus Marcius Philippus managed to cross the Olympus; but as his rearguard was being threatened by an Illyrian chief's intervention, he had to defeat this new enemy before pursuing his Macedonian campaign. Perseus held a very strong position on the banks of the Enipeus, a small coastal river. While the Rhodians, whose trade was suffering from the events of this conflict, tried in vain to get the two parties to accept them as mediators, Rome entrusted the leadership of the war to a new consul, Lucius Aemilius Paullus. Livy (Books 44–5) has drawn a vivid portrait of that extraordinary man by showing him in action: he is one of the finest and noblest figures brought back to life by the historian's powerful pen. He had character and a thoughtful, cultured mind. An energetic and experienced war leader, his very presence was enough to put a new face on the situation. He restored discipline and won the soldiers' trust. When he explained how an eclipse they had witnessed was due to natural causes, he put an end to some mistaken beliefs that were rampant among them. On the field he showed consummate technical ability by outflanking the Macedonian fortified positions in the countryside (on the Enipeus river), forcing Perseus to retreat northward. South of Pydna, as a result of a purely accidental skirmish caused by a runaway horse, battle was joined, very soon turning into disaster for the Macedonian army. The lunar eclipse just mentioned allows us to determine the exact date of that decisive encounter: June 22, 168. By the evening of the same day the legions had inflicted total destruction on their enemy, who had lost 20,000 men as against barely a hundred in the Roman ranks. Aemilius Paullus, a Philhellene, commemorated his victory by placing in the Delphic shrine his own statue, raised on a monumental pillar bearing bas-reliefs depicting with precision identifiable scenes of the battle. Perseus fled as far as the Strymon, to Amphipolis, whence he took shelter on the island of Samothrace. That was where, despairing of escape, he ended up surrendering to Aemilius Paullus. He was to appear with his son, also a prisoner, in his victor's triumphal procession before meeting an ignominious death in an Italian prison. With his departure from the scene, the Antigonid dynasty ended in slaughter and shame: the first among the Hellenistic monarchies to disappear.

Macedon, completely occupied by the legions, underwent a wholesale reorganization at the hands of a senatorial ten-member commission based in Amphipolis. It was not turned into a Roman province, which is significant in terms of our understanding of Roman aims in the East at the time. Instead Macedonian power was split into independent pieces. The land was divided into four autonomous republics, called sectors (*merides*), with four capitals. These were Pella for the ancient plain of Macedonia, from the Olympus to the Axius (Vardar) river; Pelagonia for the northern mountainous regions; Thessalonica for the sector between the Axius and the Strymon; Amphipolis for the one stretching from the Strymon to the Nestus. Each *meris* had its own separate and independent type of administration, with annually appointed magistrates. The monarchy was abolished; no federal link existed between these parts of the same nation. The *merides* had no right to trade with each other; nor could their respective citizens enter into marriage links with citizens of other sectors. There was no common currency, but autonomous coinage for each *meris*. Production from the gold and silver mines of the Pangaeum region was forbidden, as was the felling of trees for naval construction. The importation of salt was also forbidden, probably because there were salt mines on the Macedonian plain and the sale of their production might restore economic links with the other sectors. In short, every measure was taken to ensure that the Macedonian people, whose main strength had been its ethnic unity and monarchical tradition, would, with the loss of both, forever be deprived of the chance to become once again a powerful player in the political field of the Greek-speaking East.

The few territories or fortified places that Perseus had owned outside Macedonia were, of course, either proclaimed independent (for example, Magnesia, with the town of Demetrias; as well as the cities of the Thracian coast of the Aegean – Abdera, Maroneia, Aenus), or restored to their previous masters. In certain states, Aetolia and Achaea, for example, settlements of accounts took place between supporters and adversaries of a Roman alliance. A thousand Achaeans were exiled to Italy, under suspicion of hostility to Rome. Among them were the historian Polybius and his father, a high-profile personality at Megalopolis, the famous city of Arcadia, who had been general of the Achaean League. Polybius was then slightly over 30. He owed it to the friendship of Aemilius Paullus and his son Scipio Aemilianus to spend the time of his exile at Rome, in close contact with the Republic's decision-making circles, and thus to gather the information and the experience that were to nurture his reflections on history.

The most severe treatment was meted out to Epirus, which (in part at least) had sided with Perseus. The Roman army plundered and ravaged seventy towns or townships, whose inhabitants, about 150,000 in all, were sold into slavery. Athens, by contrast, gained some expansion of her territory: she obtained the "return" of the islands of Scyros, Lesbos and Imbros in the northern Aegean, on the grounds that she had once settled military colonies (*cleruchies*) on them. She also received the territory of Haliartus in Boeotia, and the island of Delos, which she had lost a century before. Delos was at the same time proclaimed a duty-free port: that status was to bring wealth to it by attracting an important fraction of Aegean Sea trade. Was such a measure meant to harm the prosperity of the port

Map 7   Greece in the Hellenistic period.

of Rhodes, until then the main commercial port of the eastern Mediterranean? It is not certain that this was the purpose intended, but the fact remains that the competition it created was a blow to the Rhodians. According to Polybius the income of their harbor dues went down from one million drachmas to 150,000. Having always sided with Rome in past conflicts, they had been slow to make up their minds during the last one and had done their utmost to play a mediating role (see p. 116). Bearing them a grudge for this, the Senate forced them to give up the territories that the peace of Apamea had given them in Caria and Lycia:

only then were they granted the privilege of Roman friendship. The Rhodian example amply demonstrated that this kind of friendship could mean a subordination of sorts for Greek cities.

■ *Consequences of Rome's triumph for the Seleucid and Ptolemaic monarchies* ■ *Antiochus IV Epiphanes* ■ *The Sixth Syrian War* ■ *"Popilius' Circle"* ■ *Antiochus and the Jews: revolt of Maccabeus* ■ *The feasts of Daphne* ■ *Death of Antiochus IV* ■ *Demetrius I and Alexander Balas* ■ *Demetrius II* ■ *The Parthian advance* ■ *Loss of Seleucid Asia up to the Euphrates* ■ *Constant dynastic quarrels*

In thirty years, the Second and Third Macedonian Wars had dramatically changed the situation in the eastern Mediterranean basin. A non-Greek state, with which the Hellenistic monarchs and cities had until then had nothing more than occasional contact, and belonging to an entirely different geographical area, had burst upon their political scene. Thanks to its military might, aided no doubt by the Greek world's internal divisions, which gave it many Greek allies, it was now laying down the law for them. It had destroyed the most ancient of the three great kingdoms ruled by Greeks, and the dynasty that could boast with more right than any other of upholding the tradition bequeathed by Philip and Alexander. The half-century following the battle of Pydna was to witness the full impact of this novel factor in Mediterranean politics. While the Seleucid and Ptolemaic monarchies entered a rapid process of decay, the Roman grasp on the rest of the Hellenistic world became stronger and stronger, culminating in direct administration with the transformation of Macedon, Greece, and the Pergamene kingdom into Roman provinces. The final phase of this process can be placed in the year 116 BC. This was the year of the disappearance of the last sovereign in the two great surviving dynasties who possessed some of the attributes of a statesman: Ptolemy VIII Euergetes II, commonly named Physcon. The struggle was over after his demise. There followed only the prolonged spasms of agonizing states, and the last stages of the Roman conquest.

In the course of the Third Macedonian War, the Seleucid king had kept out of the conflict, in spite of family ties with Perseus, whose wife Laodice was a Syrian princess. Seleucus IV met with a violent death in 175. His own minister Heliodorus murdered him, soon after being chased from the Temple of Jerusalem while on a mission from the king to seize the Temple treasures – under the lashes, as the Jews said (*Maccabees* II, 3, 26), of the angels of the Lord. The new king, Antiochus

IV, brother of Seleucus, had been a hostage in Rome, and had afterwards taken up residence in Athens. He reached Antioch by way of Asia Minor, helped on his journey by Eumenes of Pergamum. He was on good terms with the Romans, who after all held hostage his nephew Demetrius, son of Seleucus IV, a potential rival. He was aware of the need to maintain the cohesion of an empire certainly reduced in size since the treaty of Apamea, but remaining nevertheless a vast and diverse one. With that aim in mind, he was eager to strengthen the reverence accorded to his own person as a symbol of Seleucid unity. He therefore took the title of Epiphanes, meaning "the god who manifests himself to the faithful." Three problems of unequal gravity confronted him: the Sixth Syrian War with Egypt, the disturbances in Judaea, and the difficulties caused by the upper satrapies and Iran.

The Sixth Syrian War arose from the complicated situation of the Lagid monarchy. Ptolemy V Epiphanes had died in 180, poisoned (so the story goes) after a lack-luster reign that had nevertheless managed to end Upper Egypt's secession. Domestic problems, however, continued to weaken the authority of the throne. As the late king's eldest son, Ptolemy VI Philometor, was still too young to reign, his mother, Cleopatra I, daughter of Antiochus III, became Regent and kept up a friendly relationship with the Syrian kingdom which her brother ruled. But after she died in 176, Ptolemy VI allowed himself to be led by his ministers, who appear to have contemplated a reconquest of Coele-Syria. Informed of these plans, Antiochus IV prepared his defense. War broke out in 170, acclaimed by an assembly of the people of Alexandria. To bolster royal authority, a three-sovereign condominium was placed at the head of the Ptolemaic kingdom. It was made up of Ptolemy VI Philometor, his sister Cleopatra II (whom he had married in the Lagid tradition of brother–sister unions), and his brother Ptolemy the Younger, who was later to reign under the name of Ptolemy VIII Euergetes II. The war went on until 168, and soon turned to Antiochus' advantage. Seleucid forces occupied Cyprus, while the king took Pelusium, thus obtaining access to the Delta, and, after various turns of events, reached and besieged Alexandria. The Ptolemies appealed to Rome, which sent an embassy headed by a former consul, Gaius Popilius Laenas. Popilius met Antiochus during his siege of Alexandria in a suburb of the city that bore the name of Eleusis. There he handed the king the text of the motion passed by the Senate, requiring him, under threat, to leave Egypt. Antiochus expressed the wish to discuss the matter with his council. But Popilius, tracing a circle round the king with his stick, declared that he would not allow him to move out of it before he gave his response. Antiochus yielded, and he withdrew his troops from Egypt and Cyprus. "Popilius' Circle" appealed to the popular imagination, and remained a symbol of the fear instilled by Rome in the minds of Oriental monarchs after its victory at Pydna and the collapse of Macedon. The head of the most powerful among the monarchies still in existence had bowed before the haughty ultimatum of an envoy of the Senate, at the very moment when he looked like winning a decisive victory and achieving the entire conquest of Egypt. The Senate had acted, as in 200, to maintain some balance of power among the major Greek states.

Abandoning his project of conquering Egypt, Antiochus, on his way back to Syria, had to put down a Jewish uprising. The Jews of Jerusalem had been split for many years between two leading factions. On one side were those who had been won over by the Greek way of life, though without forsaking their ancestral faith. Greek habits included frequenting the gymnasia, the very symbol of Hellenic culture (see p. 298). On the opposite side were the hard-core traditionalists, who looked upon such novelties as impious: they were the *hasidim*, the "pious ones." The rift had been deepened when the conquest of Coele-Syria by Antiochus III in 200 brought Palestine under Seleucid control. In 169 Antiochus IV, crossing Jerusalem, laid hands on the Temple treasures, without incurring punishment by the angels (see p. 119, about Heliodorus). The next year, coming back from Alexandria and his humiliation by Popilius, Antiochus found a Jewish population that had risen against the High Priest, accusing him of being a Philhellene. His reaction was a harsh one. He placed a military colony in the citadel, and the Temple was reorganized to accommodate, side by side with the cult of Jehovah, other cults with followers in the mixed population of the city: that of Olympian Zeus for the Greeks, that of Baal for non-Jewish Orientals. The raising of Baal's altar in Jehovah's temple, on the very altar of the sacrifices to God, was in the eyes of the *hasidim* an unbearable scandal, which they called, after a phrase in the Book of Daniel, "the abomination of desolation." There was a feeling of insurrection in the air all through the countryside: that incident brought it out into the open. The king responded with an edict that instructed Jews to forsake their creed and ritual, adopt the cult of Olympian Zeus, and render prescribed honors to the reigning sovereign, whose statue stood in the temple beside that of Zeus. The guiding principle of this edict was what contemporary judgment perceived in it: a wish to realize the unity of the empire by making its various populations "belong to one people, each community giving up its own, particular law" (*Maccabees* I, 1, 41). But violence was the method employed to put the royal edict into operation, and orthodox Jews were subject to cruel persecution. Resistance, led in the lowlands by the family of the Maccabees, met with some success. Antiochus Epiphanes proclaimed an amnesty, a short time before his death in 164, and put an end to persecution. This did not prevent Judas Maccabaeus, head of the rebels, from retaking Jerusalem (except the citadel), purifying the Temple, and rebuilding the altar of the sacrifices (164). The next year an edict was promulgated (by Lysias, who governed in the king's stead because of his tender years) in the name of Antiochus V, the new king: it restored to the Jews the right to celebrate their cult in conformity with their tradition. There ensued a lull in the conflict, until it started again two years later with Demetrius I's accession to the throne.

At the time of these events, Epiphanes, thinking of following his father's example, planned to appear in person in the eastern areas of his empire, where over the past twenty years Seleucid authority had obviously suffered. In Bactria, succeeding Euthydemus on the throne after his death at the start of the century, his son Demetrius had enlarged his realm considerably, pushing southward beyond the Hindu Kush into the Paropanisadae and Arachosia, perhaps as far as the Indus, possibly even the Ganges. It is true that we lack texts that would allow us to determine the precise extent and date of these conquests, which remain quite uncertain. Yet numismatic evidence, the detailed interpretation of which presents difficulties, is ample testimony to the vitality of the Bactrian State at the time. That vitality was not altered as a result of action by a usurper, Eucratides, who at some date in 170–160 overthrew the reigning dynasty in Bactria and ruled in its place. In the same period, the Parthian kingdom was headed by a dynamic and enterprising prince, Mithridates I, who was beginning to pose a threat to northern Iran, while in the southeast Persia had secured autonomy under the leadership of local princes. Epiphanes' father, Antiochus III, had once taken remedial steps in a similarly deteriorating situation: reason enough for him to contemplate in his turn a wide-ranging "armed tour of inspection" in the eastern provinces. In 166 he started gathering considerable forces, and, before leaving Antioch, conducted magnificent celebrations centered around Apollo's shrine in the capital's suburban quarter of Daphne, displaying the loot taken from Egypt. The exceptional pomp of these ceremonies impressed his contemporaries to such an extent that they had doubts about the mental stability of a seemingly megalomaniac sovereign. In the same year other festivals, called feasts of thanksgiving in an inscription, were held at Babylon. There Antiochus IV was hailed as "the saviour of Asia, founder of the city," where he had built, in Greek fashion, a theatre and a gymnasium. In 165 the king left with his troops for Armenia. He crossed into Mesopotamia, then into Elymais, where he made a fruitless attempt to gain possession of the treasures belonging to a native temple. It was then (in 164/3) that he was stricken with a horrible disease, which *Maccabees* II (9, 9ff) describes with relish, presenting it as a heaven-sent punishment.

His son Antiochus V was not yet of age. Lysias, the minister in charge of affairs in his name, called a temporary halt to the Jewish rebellion by means of a liberal edict. But Seleucus IV's son, Demetrius, who was held hostage in Rome, laid claim to his father's throne, on the grounds that it was no longer held by his uncle Antiochus IV. He escaped from Rome with no great difficulty and reached Antioch, where he received a sovereign's welcome. The child-king Antiochus V and Lysias his minister were soon put to death. The new king, Demetrius I, was recognized by Rome after he had put down a rebellion headed by Timarchus, a dignitary of high rank under the previous reign, who had taken the royal title and had his own coinage struck in Babylonia. As soon as he was rid of his rivals, Demetrius had to face a rebirth of Jewish militancy. After a series of violent clashes, in which Judas Maccabaeus died in 160, the Seleucid forces pacified the land.

Meanwhile Demetrius had become involved, unsuccessfully, in a conflict that had broken out in Cappadocia, an independent kingdom in eastern Anatolia. Of the two rivals for the throne, Pergamum supported one, Antioch the other. Pergamum's nominee prevailed. That failure did no good to the cause of the Seleucid monarch, whose brusque and haughty approach, and immoderate appetite for drink, met with widespread disapproval. On the initiative of Pergamum's sovereign Attalus II, a rival to Demetrius came forward: Alexander Balas, who claimed to be Antiochus Epiphanes' illegitimate son. With the help of Timarchus' brother, eager to avenge the rebel leader's death, Balas went to Rome and obtained the Senate's support. He then landed in Phoenicia and fought the troops of Demetrius, who was defeated (*c*.151/150) and died in combat. The Jews had taken advantage of the conflict and obtained various privileges in return for their support of the winning faction (which needed all the help it could get). Balas eventually ratified these, and appointed as High Priest Judas Maccabaeus' brother, Jonathan, entrusting him as well with the official roles of *strategos* and administrator of the land. That seems to have been the only positive measure that Balas took. He appears to have had only one objective: to obtain personal benefits and enjoyment from the royal dignity. To secure external support he married Cleopatra, titled *Thea* ("the goddess"), daughter of Ptolemy VI Philometor, who planned to gain from that marriage a pretext for reoccupying Coele-Syria. That pretext came his way in 147. Demetrius' young son, who bore the same name as his father, dealt Balas a blow similar to the one the elder Demetrius had inflicted on Antiochus V in earlier times. Gaining a foothold in Cilicia, Demetrius reached Antioch, where he was greeted with favor by the population. Philometor hurried to help his son-in-law. He occupied Coele-Syria, then quarreled with Balas when he realized that Demetrius was getting the better of him. He offered Cleopatra's hand to Demetrius: she was soon to become a widow when Balas was defeated, then murdered. It was Demetrius' extra luck that Philometor, injured in the battle with Balas, died soon after: otherwise an Egyptian conquest of Syria might have been seen in the 140s (unless Rome prevented it), just as a Syrian conquest almost happened in the 160s (which Rome did prevent). The Seleucid kingdom kept Coele-Syria, and (in 145) had a new sovereign, Demetrius II.

He reigned for twenty years, from 145 to 125. The length of his reign, however, should not create any illusions. For half of it he remained a captive; the other half he spent fighting usurping rivals. No circumstance can better illustrate the incurable ills that now beset the Seleucid monarchy. Demetrius had first and foremost to negotiate with the Jews. He confirmed and extended the privileges granted by his predecessors to Jonathan. But, as early as 144, one of his officers, Diodotus, rose against him and had a child, the son of Balas, acclaimed under the name of Antiochus VI. Rallying round his own person a large part of Syria, Diodotus soon had young Antiochus murdered, and proclaimed himself king under the name of Tryphon. He was to remain on the scene for many years, negotiating with Jonathan before having him seized and spiriting him away. He even struck his own coinage, on which he called himself a sovereign "invested with full powers" (*autokrator*). Demetrius did not have the leisure personally to mete out his penalty to the usurper. His presence was needed in the east of the empire, where Mithridates, the Arsacid monarch who had reigned over the Parthians since 171, was continually extending his conquests. In 150 or thereabouts, after the death of Eucratides, king of Bactria, the Parthians had taken advantage of the ensuing chaos and occupied all his states, except for the capital itself, Bactra. They had then moved into Iran, taking Media before entering Mesopotamia. Mithridates, resurrecting Achaemenid protocol, had taken the title of "King of Kings," and began to strike coinage in his new empire. The Seleucid king was bound to react to such increasing pressure. This he did, starting in 141, but after some initial success he was beaten and taken prisoner. Mithridates, though, treated him with generosity and high regard. The victor died soon after. He had founded a state of first-rate importance and dealt the Seleucid empire blows from which it could not recover. Mesopotamia, once the heart of Alexander's realm, and of Seleucus Nicator's kingdom, was now a Parthian province. The second capital of the Seleucids, Seleucia on the Tigris, was now lost to them. The new masters of the land, however, made no attempt to erase the Greco-Macedonian culture. Mithridates proved to be liberal-minded and a Philhellene, adding to his Persian name Hellenic epithets that appear on his coinage. But it was clear that Parthian expansion had not yet run its full course, and that what was left of the Seleucid State, pushed back into Syria, would now have to be on the defensive against a constant eastern menace. Even the Romans were to experience that reality, at a heavy price.

As soon as Demetrius II's younger brother learned of his captivity, he came as quickly as possible to Antioch, called by Cleopatra, his sister-in-law, whom he married, taking the royal title under the name of Antiochus VII. His first task was to defeat Tryphon, who committed suicide after being taken prisoner in 137. Antiochus had to deal with the Jews as well. Simon, brother of Jonathan, had rallied to the side of the legitimate Seleucid monarchy as a result of his brother's execution by Tryphon. Yet he preserved the traditional autonomy of the Hasmoneans, thus named after the original habitat of the Maccabees. Proclamation of chronological dating by the Hasmonean era, starting in 143/2, is testimony to their wish to create an independent political entity. When Simon was murdered in a family quarrel, his son John Hyrcanus became High Priest. Antiochus, taking advantage of that dramatic turn of events, came and laid siege in 131 to Jerusalem, but was content to claim tribute and a number of hostages, without resorting to religious persecution. He then left to fight the Parthians, and recaptured part of Iran, but was defeated in that country in 129, his slain body left on the field of battle. A collapse might now be feared, as the Parthians pushed at what was left of the Seleucid Empire. But Mithridates' successor, Phraates II, had in his turn to defend his own kingdom against attack from Scythian barbarians, the Tokhars (who had recently overwhelmed Bactria) and the Sacae. The barbarian assault cost Phraates his life and proved the salvation of Greek Syria. Hellenism had nevertheless lost for good the whole of inner Asia, from Sogdiana to the Persian Gulf and from the Indus to the Euphrates. After two centuries, Alexander's conquest was nothing more than a memory. An "Indo-Greek" sovereign, bearing the Hellenic name of Menander, remained isolated in the Punjab amid Indian principalities: living testimony to the Macedonian epic venture, but now separated from the rest of the Greek world by a revived Iran.

At the time of Antiochus VII's expedition, Phraates had released Demetrius II, who returned to Syria after ten years' absence. His brother's death allowed him to regain his kingdom, a maimed one, weakened by a trend to local autonomy then making itself felt in the Syrian cities, and by the definitive assertion of the Jews' independence under their leader John Hyrcanus, who extended further the boundaries of his new state. Spurned by his wife Cleopatra Thea, Demetrius allowed himself to be enticed by the urgent appeals of his mother-in-law Cleopatra II, queen of Egypt, whose husband and brother Ptolemy VIII was besieging her in Alexandria. But he was unable to raise the siege. Resentful of his attempts at intervention, Ptolemy favored the cause of another usurper, Alexander II Zabinas, who claimed to be Antiochus VII's adoptive son. The people of Antioch in their fickleness welcomed the newcomer, while Demetrius wandered across Syria, and was in the end made a prisoner in the neighborhood of Tyre and put to death in 126/5. Thus ended, in a miserable adventure, the reign of the last of the Seleucids to make a conscientious attempt to preserve his kingdom and fulfill his vocation as a sovereign. He had been crushed under a triple load: dynastic quarrels, the unruliness of cities and ethnic groups, and the growing Parthian menace. After his death these same factors continued to prevail with increasing gravity, and later Seleucid history is no more than a wearisome sequence of quarrels, disasters, and crimes.

■ *The last days of the Pergamene kingdom* ■ *End of Eumenes II's reign* ■ *Attalus II* ■ *Attalus III bequeaths his kingdom to Rome* ■ *Terms of the testament* ■ *Aristonicus' revolt* ■ *Institution of the Roman province of Asia*

In a parallel course of events, but in a less dramatic, less sinister atmosphere, the destiny of the prestigious and powerful but short-lived kingdom of Pergamum had reached its final stage. Under Roman hegemony, the realm of Eumenes II had become the arbiter of Asia Minor. It had gathered the spoils of the Seleucid monarchy after the peace of Apamea. Yet after Pydna its relationship with Rome had lost some of its warmth. Rome had no doubt considered Pergamum's aid insufficient; on the other hand, the Senate was somewhat mistrustful of the growth of its power. Other Anatolian monarchs obtained better treatment, the price of which, it is true, was humiliating flexibility. Prusias II of Bithynia, for example, according to Polybius' story, coming to Rome in 166, arrived at the Curia, where the Senate was meeting, and stooped before the door of the building, kissing its threshold. Eumenes II showed less servility, and was better at keeping his distance. He did not hesitate, when he judged it appropriate, to intervene without asking for Rome's leave and repress new Galatian forays from the Anatolian plateau down into Ionia, particularly in the year 166. His action won the gratitude of the Greeks of Asia, whom he had saved from a dreadful peril. The festival of Athena *Nikephoros* ("she who brings victory"), held in the shrine at Pergamum of the goddess who was patron of the city, had for years provided material for the Attalid dynasty's propaganda. Eumenes made ample use of it, and, like his predecessors, bestowed generous offerings on the great shrines of the Greek world, from which a large quantity of epigraphic evidence has come down to us.

When he died in 159, his brother Attalus, who had long shared with Eumenes the management of Pergamene affairs, succeeded him in a smooth transition and maintained his policies. In spite of his advanced age (he was then over 60), he reigned for twenty years, keeping the kingdom on its prosperous path. He preserved good relations with Rome, and thus prevailed in a conflict with Prusias II that ended in 154. A short time after, a sharp disagreement arose between Prusias and his son Nicodemus: Attalus sided with the son, who in 149 replaced his murdered father on the Bithynian throne. Like Eumenes, Attalus kept watch on the turbulent Galatian tribes of Anatolia, but his vigilance did not involve him in any large-scale operations. He went to war against the Thracians, thus slightly extending his possessions in Europe beyond the Straits. He died, very old, in 139/8. His successor Attalus III (his nephew, son of Eumenes II) inherited a thriving state: one that was wealthy, the most powerful in Asia Minor, having good relations with the other kingdoms in the area, feared by the Galatians, respected by the free Greek cities, and enjoying Roman friendship.

Yet that state, the only one in the contemporary Hellenistic world that seemed to be solidly based, was to disappear at a stroke by the will of one man, the king himself, who bequeathed it to the Roman people. This disconcerting decision had a highly significant result: it ensured for the first time Rome's permanent presence in Asia. Such a legacy was not unprecedented. Twenty years earlier Ptolemy VIII, called the Younger, king of Cyrene (see p. 134) had published his will, bequeathing his Libyan territories to the Romans in case he died leaving no heir. This was a decision that remained without effect, given the ensuing course of events. Was Attalus III influenced by that document, which had been displayed for public viewing at Cyrene, and which its author, with his own interest in mind, had wished to be divulged? The fact remains that the Pergamene sovereign took measures analogous to those taken by the king of Cyrene. Rome reaped the benefit, immediately after his unexpected death, which occurred in 133, five years into his reign.

Attalus left to the Romans, together with his movable goods, all territories belonging to him *in proprio*, that is, what was called the royal domain, or "the king's land." However, the city of Pergamum proper and the citizens' landed property coming under its jurisdiction were explicitly excluded from the bequest. Pergamum became a free city, with the same status as the independent Greek states that were, with their civic territory, under Attalid hegemony. When the news reached Rome, the Republic was in the throes of a serious crisis arising from Tiberius Gracchus' proposed agrarian law. The intent of this law was to redistribute among the Roman poor a large amount of public land (*ager publicus*) and to reduce the privileges that, with the passage of time, the owners of large holdings had secured for themselves over this land. The gift, by Attalus' bequest, of the royal territories to the Roman people created an administrative opportunity that was evident to Tiberius Gracchus: the Pergamene land, if sold, could defray the administrative costs of his program of land redistribution. But Tiberius was then killed in a riot. The senatorial commission that came to study the situation found Asia prey to an immense upheaval. On the death of Attalus, Aristonicus, an illegitimate son of Eumenes II, had immediately laid claim to power under the name of Eumenes III. To rally round his person the less well-endowed strata of the population – foreigners, slaves, native peasants – he granted them civic privileges. He also wished to appear as the champion of a struggle against Roman interference in Asia. The philosopher Blossius of Cumae, the guiding light of Gracchus' policy of reform, came and joined Aristonicus, which might prompt the assumption (no doubt unfounded) that the latter had reforming concerns similar to his in social matters. The citizens of Pergamum, however, were glad to be proclaimed free by Attalus' will. They were opposed to Aristonicus' claim to the throne, while championing in their own name some of his social reforms. Nor were the free cities eager to follow him. A serious civil war ensued, in which Aristonicus, supported by the rural areas, the native citizens, and the slaves, won a number of victories, even over the first troops Rome sent against him. He set up his quarters in the upper valley of the Caicus, and for four years had coinage struck in the name of Eumenes. But he was finally defeated, and the consul Manius Aquilius took possession of the land. Some parts of the Attalid states were allotted to the sovereigns of the Pontus and Bithynia as a reward for their help in the rebel's defeat. The Attalid possessions in Thrace and the island of Aegina were joined to the province of Macedon set up fifteen years earlier (see p. 129). The remainder of Attalus' territories was transformed into the Roman province of Asia, the principal regions of which are listed by Cicero: Phrygia, Mysia, Caria, and Lydia. The Roman administration would in future have to manage these vast and wealthy dominions in the very heart of Asia Minor. It was now solidly established in Europe as well as in Asia, on both sides of the Straits.

■ *Macedon and Greece after Pydna* ■ *An economic and demographic crisis* ■ *Andriscus' insurrection* ■ *Macedon reduced to the status of a Roman province* ■ *Rome the arbiter of Greek cities* ■ *The Achaean League rebels* ■ *Corinth is captured and sacked* ■ *The new order established in Greece*

On the situation in Macedon and in mainland Greece after Pydna, Polybius' evidence is that of a contemporary, though not of an eyewitness (since he spent the years 168–150 in Rome). Whatever remains of his *History* provides us with an overall picture at least, concerning a period on which our information is incomplete. He shows a Macedonian people unsuited to the "democratic" regime that Aemilius Paullus had put in the place of their traditional monarchy, and correspondingly destabilized by internal disagreements. He depicts contemporary Greece as suffering from a demographic crisis, resulting from the disinclination of the wealthy to have more than one or two children to avoid fragmenting their estates. The inevitable outcome, due to disease and early death, was a decrease of the population and economic regress, with land lying fallow for want of hands to make it productive. We shall come back later to the validity of that assessment. But depopulation is an undoubted phenomenon of the period: war losses, factional struggles, denunciation to the Romans, exile or political murder, the harmful effect of growing piracy fostered by unsafe sea-ways, converged, in the context of a change in mores, toward a decrease in the numbers of the citizenry.

In Macedon the major event of these joyless years was the appearance of a pretender who claimed to be a son of Perseus. His real name was Andriscus. He has his place in a line of usurpers with whom various states were afflicted in this period of instability, like Balas and Tryphon in Syria, or Aristonicus in Pergamum. He was handed over to the Romans after an abortive first attempt, but escaped from Italy. Finding in Thrace companions ready to share a new venture, he managed in 149 to reunite all of Macedon under his command, and even occupied Thessaly after defeating a Roman force sent against him. This was a short-lived success, for soon a new army led by the praetor Quintus Caecilius Metellus was to inflict a crushing defeat on him. The episode prompted a thoroughgoing change in the organization of Macedon. The country was reduced to the status of a Roman province. It was governed by a proconsul residing in Thessalonica, with authority not only over the four districts set up after Pydna, but also over Illyria toward the west, and after 129 (cf. Attalus III's will, pp. 126–7) on the Pergamene kingdom's Thracian holdings. A new road, the *Via Egnatia*, was built from Epidamnus and Apollonia on the Adriatic to Thessalonica, across the Balkan Mountains, through the towns of Edessa and Pella. It was later extended to Thrace until it reached the river Hebrus. Thus was demonstrated Rome's purpose: to bring together in a cohesive whole that northern region of the peninsula. The year 148 inaugurated in Macedon what is called the provincial era. Metellus was entrusted with the task of governing the province, the first in time to be set up by the Republic in the eastern basin of the Mediterranean. Note how reluctant the Romans were to take direct control: first they had tried to treat the Antigonid kings as allies, then set up the system of four districts (*merides*).

The Greek cities were in principle entitled to the freedom that Flamininus had proclaimed. But that did not mean that the consequences of the battle of Pydna made themselves felt to any lesser degree. Inter-city rivalries had not disappeared, of course: later on they led to references to the Senate's authority for adjudication. Thus Athens, having occupied the district of Oropus on the Strait of Euboea, on its frontier with Boeotia, was first condemned to a fine of 500 talents by the referee appointed by Rome to settle the dispute – that arbitrator being the Achaean city of Sicyon. The Athenians then sent (in 155) an embassy to Rome, made up of three philosophers: Carneades of Cyrene, Critolaus of Phaselis, Diogenes of Seleucia on the Tigris (a century later, Cicero was to express surprise that none of the three envoys was of Athenian descent). The embassy obtained a reduction of the fine to 100 talents. Obviously the Senate was the supreme authority to which, as to a court of appeal, were referred disputes arising in the land of Greece which was nominally free. When Rhodes, in her anxiety to put an end to Cretan piracy, took a different course and appealed to the Achaean League for support, she met with a refusal, on the plea that the League was reluctant to be involved in the dispute without Rome's approval. In the end a senatorial commission came and examined the Cretan problem. On the other hand, the whole of mainland Greece paid a heavy price for the Achaean League's departure from caution in a case opposing it to Sparta.

In 150 Polybius secured through his Roman friends, Scipio Aemilianus' influential circle, the return to their homeland of the survivors among the thousand Achaeans exiled to Italy after Pydna (as he himself had been). After eighteen years' exile, only 300 were left, and one might expect that their old age and their trials would have made them cautious. Yet it is possible that their return caused a rebirth of opposition to Rome within the Achaean League. It will be remembered that Sparta had belonged to the League since 192. The Lacedaemonians, however, found it difficult to be resigned to such a state of things. Philopoemen had had to quell by the use of force an attempt at secession on their part. Their discontent was aggravated by frontier disputes with the great city of Megalopolis, another member of the League. Finally, Sparta and the Achaeans put their disagreements before the Senate. The latter, after a long delay, decided in 147 in favor of Sparta, allowing it to secede, and demanded besides the surrender by the League of Corinth, Argos, an Arcadian town, and Heraclea Trachinia, a small isolated city in the southern part of the Spercheus valley. The Achaeans were roused against such mutilation of the League and prepared for war with Sparta, and for an eventual conflict with Rome. As Andriscus had done in Macedon (following Perseus' earlier example), and Aristonicus (see p. 127) was to do later at Pergamum, they had recourse to exceptional measures. These consisted in the deferment or abolition of debt, the emancipation of slaves to be enlisted in the army, and a special tax levied on wealthy citizens. Many communities of central Greece, those of Boeotia, Phocis, Locris, and Euboea, agreed to join the Achaean alliance. But after a first defeat inflicted by Metellus, governor of Macedon, on the League's troops, near Scarphea in eastern Locris, the coalition broke up. In 146 the consul Lucius Mummius, heading operations in Greece, inflicted another defeat on the Achaean army at the Isthmus and laid siege to Corinth which the Achaeans left without a fight. The Senate, intent on setting an example and deterring those who might in future feel tempted by rebellion, ordered the city to be razed to the ground. Its citizens were slaughtered or sold, its buildings set on fire after systematic pillage. "I was there," says Polybius. "I saw paintings trodden underfoot; the soldiers used them when playing dice." Such wholesale destruction, comparable to Alexander's sack of Thebes in 335 (see p. 10), produced the expected result: political independence and social renewal did not exert any further attraction until the time of the Mithridatic Wars. The annihilation of Corinth, the site which remained deserted until Caesar refounded the city in 44, was to linger in human memory as a symbol of Roman domination in the east, just as the destruction of Carthage in the same year confirmed the triumph of Rome in the west. There was a total imbalance between the charge levelled at Corinth (maltreatment of Roman envoys in their city on the occasion of one of the Achaean League's meetings about Sparta) and the cold ruthlessness of its punishment. It gives an exact picture of the actual intent behind such conduct: to show in an unequivocal manner who was master now. Nobody failed to understand.

Even so, Greece, which had not taken a unanimous stand on that conflict, was not reduced to the status of a Roman province. Such a transformation, with the appellation of "Province of Achaea" given to the land, finally happened in the time of Augustus – a full century later. A distinction was made for the immediate future between those cities that had taken part in the rebellion and those that had adopted an attitude of reserve, or, like Sparta, had struggled with the Achaeans. The rebellious group were punished in various ways, first and foremost by the confiscation and sale of property belonging to those of their citizens who were notorious for their hostility to Rome – a large number of these disappeared, as a result of execution or suicide. These particular cities were now to be under the direct control of the proconsul of Macedon, who was empowered to intervene in their internal affairs. Thus, as we know from a famous inscription, when in 115 the Achaean city of Dyme was threatened with social unrest, the proconsul made sure that the existing system was left untouched. Part of the territory of Corinth was proclaimed *ager publicus*, a possession of the Roman people. Existing laws were on the whole preserved. Polybius, who was in the retinue of his friend Scipio Aemilianus at the time of the fall of Carthage, had returned to Greece at the news of the war in which the Achaean League had got involved. He managed to persuade the Roman authorities to alleviate the repressive measures taken against his fellow-citizens. The senatorial commission entrusted with the task of settling the affairs of Greece showed great confidence in him, and in large measure took his views into account. Inscriptions show that Polybius was later honored in Greece for his often successful diplomatic efforts with the Romans.

As for those who kept their autonomy in principle – Athens and Sparta, the cities of Thessaly, Magnesia, Aetolia, and Acarnania – they now avoided any move likely to run counter to the plans of the Republic, whose friendship they were anxious to preserve. In the city of Athens, which still had great intellectual prestige, the possession since 167 of the tax-free city of Delos had given a new impetus to trade. The Piraeus certainly benefited from the destruction of the city of Corinth, where its harbors had always competed with the Attic port in times past. Incidents could indeed still occur, for instance, two slave revolts, one that broke out in 134/3, the other in the last years of the century. They did not imperil the social order, because they were put down by force. Economic, administrative, and cultural life continued, with its religious and civic festivals, without interference from Roman power, which now received thanks graciously showered on it by Greek cities, whether free or subject ones, for its benefactions. The generosity of the Roman people as a whole was praised, its magistrates were honored in their own right. This was the consequence of the political rifts that enfeebled Greek resistance to Rome. Athens prospered (indeed, its territory expanded), since it was one of the many city-states that had sided with Rome against its local enemies. The hard fact is that in almost every war Rome fought in Greece she had many Greek allies. Polybius summed it all up with admirable lucidity and in a masterly fashion: "This is the way of Rome's everyday policy. She makes use of the mistakes of other nations to extend and strengthen her dominion. This she does, however, with such adroitness that she appears to be the benefactress of those misguided souls, winning in addition their gratitude."

Given that Rome did bring overall peace, where all that existed before was constant warfare among the Greek states, there was much to be said for that gratitude. But then efficient peace-keeping is one of the major justifications of successful imperialism.

■ *Ptolemaic resources in the middle of the second century*
■ *Family quarrels* ■ *The three main actors: Ptolemy VI*
Philometor, Cleopatra II, Ptolemy the Younger ■ *Sharing the*
kingdom ■ *Ptolemy the Younger at Cyrene* ■ *His testament*
Death of Philometor ■ *A strange royal trio* ■ *Scipio*
Aemilianus' visit ■ *The rift between Cleopatra II and Ptolemy*
VIII Euergetes II Physcon ■ *Their reconciliation* ■ *The sad*
state of Egypt in 116

It now remains to follow, for half a century after Pydna, the destiny of the only Hellenistic kingdom to have preserved at that date the essential territorial bases of its power: the Lagid monarchy. It suffered many a reverse, losing its Syrian bulwark and its strongholds in the Aegean. Yet it kept, in addition to Egypt with its peerless resources, the two external possessions on which Ptolemy Sôter, at the birth of the dynasty, had founded Egyptian security: Cyrenaica and the island of Cyprus. True, since the end of the third century, Egypt had suffered from internal disturbances caused by economic difficulties and the growing consciousness among the native population of its own distinctive character. A symbiotic relationship between the Greco-Macedonian community and Egyptians of the old stock was becoming more difficult: that had an adverse effect on the country's development. The overabundance of resources that had been available to the king in the third century had decreased by then, which meant less flexibility of action. The Ptolemaic sovereign was forced to set limits to his ambitions in the international sphere, as had been demonstrated in the major conflicts of recent times, in which he had refrained from intervening. Yet he remained the most opulent of Hellenistic princes. Visitors were struck by the lavishness of Alexandria's palaces and its celebrations. It appeared scandalous to some, as it did to the companions of Scipio Aemilianus visiting Egypt in 140/39 (see p. 135). According to Diodorus, they judged such a display of luxury to be "a decay of body and soul." Having that abundance of resources at his disposal, and leading a country that was wealthier and more thickly populated than any other in the eastern Mediterranean, the king found it easy to win respect, if not to inspire fear. Even the Romans felt this to be the case. On many occasions they showed anxiety to safeguard Egypt's interest, as happened when Popilius, their envoy, met the invader Antiochus Epiphanes (see pp. 120–1). Yet that kingdom was to put an end to its role in international affairs, without being weakened by any external threat. The cause of this lay simply in dissension among those in a position of leadership, and their weakness. Rarely have family quarrels, dynastic rivalries, or murderous hatred between children of the same blood weighed so heavily, and for such a long time, on a nation's fate. Among the four protagonists (two men and two women), the clash of ambitions, and the animosity they nursed against each other, were to continue unabated over more than half a century, during two parallel reigns from 170 to 116. It left Egypt in a deathly state. Yet both kings could have been great sovereigns. Let us try to disentangle that knot of vipers.

It will be remembered that the Lagid kingdom found itself in a strange situation in 170, when the plan of ill-inspired advisors was put into execution, placing Ptolemy Epiphanes' two sons in joint command of the state. The elder one, Ptolemy VI Philometor, was about to come of age and had married his sister Cleopatra II a few years earlier, conforming to dynastic usage. The mother they had in common, Cleopatra I, who had taken up the regency at Epiphanes' death, died in her turn just before their marriage: the couple took the title of "Divinities who love their Mother" (which is what Philometor means). But at that point, their younger brother was made an associate in their reign, sharing the royal title: he too was called Ptolemy, surnamed the Younger. That was tantamount to creating a climate of crisis, should the members of the trio have any appetite or desire for personal rule. Unfortunately, that turned out to be the case. Philometor was proud of his rights as the elder brother: he was not lacking in judgment or character. His wife and sister Cleopatra had a lust for power and an inclination to make decisions characterized by their lack of control. Ptolemy the Younger was undoubtedly the most gifted of the three. Intelligent and well versed in literature, he had an enterprising spirit; but he was also lustful, cruel, and unscrupulous. These were the three principal actors at the start of the drama. Another woman, Cleopatra III, was to join them later.

The three Lagids were very young and largely dependent on their ministers and advisors in exercising their joint rule. The events of the sixth Syrian War and the invasion of Egypt by Antiochus IV presented them with their first challenge. An untoward initiative by Philometor, who had tried to negotiate with Epiphanes, was a cause of discord within the trio, but their common interest reconciled them for a time, until Popilius' intervention (see above) had repelled the Seleucid peril from Alexandria. Ptolemy the Younger was jealous of his brother, who was trying to govern, in a manner not undeserving of praise, a country that was prey to disturbance. He was forever intriguing against him. In 163, after five years of an experiment in power-sharing that he had found less than comfortable, Philometor went to Rome and asked for help against his troublesome brother. After negotiating with each other, the two agreed on sharing their possessions: Philometor was to keep Egypt, with Cyprus; Ptolemy the Younger was to have Cyrenaica, where Magas had once (as nobody had forgotten) been an independent sovereign (see p. 69). But the younger brother was unsatisfied with a solution that in his view was not to his advantage, and in his turn went to Rome, asking for Cyprus to be added to his share. Both princes were thus turning to the

Senate for arbitration in their disagreement. The Senate granted Ptolemy the Younger's request, but specified that the cession of Cyprus was to be obtained by a peaceful method. Philometor refused to give up the island, and Ptolemy the Younger continued to press his request, all to no avail. Tired of his demands and threats, Philometor took drastic measures in 156/5: he caused an attempt to be made on his brother's life. This was a failure: Ptolemy the Younger was injured, but survived and went to the Senate, exhibiting his scars. At the same time, both to make any further attempt on his life pointless and to win the Republic's favor, he wrote a will, the first of its kind to be recorded in Hellenistic history. He bequeathed his kingdom of Cyrenaica to the Romans, in case he died without leaving an heir. The testament was to be posted up on the Capitol in Rome, as well as at Cyrene in Apollo's shrine, where the stele that bore a document of such importance has been found intact with its date (spring of 155). That move soon prompted the Senate to authorize the king of Cyrene to claim Cyprus by force of arms. Ptolemy the Younger attempted to do this in 153: but he failed. His brother made him a prisoner, but freed him. He was deterred from seeking revenge by the prospect of the will being executed. Ptolemy the Younger thereafter stayed quiet in Cyrene, where he lived a life of lazy luxury, reaching a girth that earned him the nickname of *Physcon* ("Pot-bellied"). Evidence of his public generosity can be found *in situ*. It is likely that Cyrene's great gymnasium, called the *Ptolemaion*, was built during his reign.

Everything changed in 145, when Philometor died in the course of a military campaign for the reconquest of Syria. He had a very young son, whom his mother caused to be proclaimed king under the name of Ptolemy VII *Neos Philopator* (the adjective *neos*, "new," was meant to distinguish him from his grandfather Ptolemy IV Philopator). But Physcon was on the alert. While a popular movement erupted in Alexandria, clamoring for his return, he moved from Cyrene to Cyprus, occupied that island, then arrived in Egypt, where Cleopatra felt compelled to receive him. She also agreed to marry him, hoping that a royal three-some could be made up again, in which her young son would take his dead father's place, and reign with his uncle turned stepfather. Physcon, who had no intention of sharing power, had his nephew murdered on the very day on which he married the young prince's mother. Soon after, captivated by the daughter his wife and sister had borne to Philometor, he seduced her, then made her his second legitimate wife: she is called Cleopatra III. A bizarre and scandalous trio was thus constituted, made up of the king and his two spouses. Ptolemy VIII also took the name of Euergetes, as Ptolemy III had done (hence his usual designation as Ptolemy VIII Euergetes II Physcon). One of his spouses was Cleopatra II, his sister, once his elder brother Philometor's wife; the other was Cleopatra III, daughter of Cleopatra II and Philometor. Their joint husband had recently ordered the murder of one spouse's son, who was the other spouse's brother. None of the crimes that soiled the house of Atreus had been more odious.

Bitter hostility soon arose between the two queens. For ten years, however, the pretence of concord was kept alive, a mask for palace intrigues. It was in that context that Egypt received in 140/39 a mission led by Scipio Aemilianus. He was shocked by the unimaginable display of pomp with which he was greeted, but visited with interest the interior of the Delta. The report given by Diodorus a century later echoes the Romans' feeling of amazement as they viewed, from the barges that transported them, the branches of the Nile and the irrigation channels. They sailed across a countryside of prodigious fertility with a countless labor force – a land capable of easy defense and exploitation. Let us quote Diodorus (*Historical Library*, XXXIII, frag. 28b): "Struck by the immense numbers of the population and the natural endowments of the land, they concluded that the kingdom could be the cradle of a very great State, were it to find masters that deserved to own it." Fifty years later the fashion of "Nilotic" landscapes spread to Italy, with their depiction of the Nile's canals, of its fields, reeds, villages, hippopotami, fishermen, and crocodiles. Not unrelated to that new vogue were the memories that the companions of Scipio Aemilianus treasured of the tour organized in their honor.

Discord between the royal spouses led to a public break in 132/1, when Physcon and Cleopatra III were forced by popular demonstrations to flee to Cyprus for shelter. Cleopatra II seems to have stirred up these riots against her husband. She asked the population of Alexandria to acknowledge as king the child she had borne to Physcon and who was only 12 years old. But the boy was not in Egypt, his father having, as a precautionary measure, caused him to be sent to Cyrene, whence he recalled him to Cyprus. That prompted Cleopatra to seize power for herself alone. She abandoned the title of Euergetes, which she had hitherto shared with her husband, and resumed that of Philometor, which had jointly belonged to her and her first husband, Ptolemy VI, adding to it *Sôteira*, modeled on the title of Ptolemy Sôter ("Saviour"), founder of the dynasty. She seems to have won the support of the Alexandrians, within both the community of Greco-Macedonians and that of the Jews, who had settled in large numbers in the city after leaving Palestine in the days of Antiochus IV's persecution. Thirsting for revenge, Physcon had his son killed and sent the boy's quartered limbs to his mother. Such unbridled cruelty reveals the nature of the bloody struggle between two dynastic factions that raged over Egypt for many years, in an orgy of pillage and murder, a wave of wild anarchy. The memory of that episode has survived in contemporary documents that coined a word to portray it – *amixia*, "savagery." Physcon seems to have secured help from certain native groups against Cleopatra II's supporters. He even appointed an Egyptian of the old stock as *strategos* of Thebaid in Upper Egypt. Within two years the king succeeded in keeping the country firmly in his clasp, while Cleopatra found herself locked up in Alexandria. The idea then occurred to her of calling to her aid Demetrius II, the Seleucid king who had recently regained possession of his Syrian kingdom after being held for ten years in captivity by the Parthians (see pp. 123–5). Demetrius was her son-in-law: he had married

Cleopatra Thea, her daughter by Philometor, to whom the return of her royal husband was unwelcome. Enticed by the prospect of being crowned king of Egypt, Demetrius attempted that new venture, but failed to break down the gates of the Delta. Cleopatra II then escaped from Alexandria, taking her treasures with her. The besieged city surrendered many months after the queen's flight. Ptolemy VIII treated the rebels with great severity. He meted out a heavy penalty to the Greek population who had supported Cleopatra, abolishing the numerous associations in which Greeks congregated, confiscating their belongings, or forcing them to put their property up for sale. Besides, the king displayed toward learned people and scholars a mistrust that led many of them to leave the country and settle elsewhere in the Greek world. Such hostility toward them had started at the very beginning of his reign in 145. It is indeed astonishing to find an intelligent and cultured sovereign, with an enquiring mind on questions pertaining to the human spirit, an author of *Memoirs* in his own right (see p. 248) rich in thought and substance, yet evincing an inclination to persecute intellectuals. His main concern at that juncture was of a political nature, as his goal was to get all his opponents out of the way. The exercise earned him the appellation of *Kakergetes*, "The Malefactor," a playful perversion of his official title of *Euergetes*, "The Benefactor."

Ptolemy VIII had meanwhile managed to get rid of the troublesome Seleucid, the resurrected Demetrius II, by inciting the usurper Zabinas against him. As soon as Demetrius died (in 126/5), Physcon renewed his marital link with Cleopatra II, whom he welcomed on her return to Alexandria. He allowed Zabinas, now useless for his purposes, to be defeated by Demetrius II's son, Antiochus VIII, nicknamed Grypus ("Hook-nosed"), who married a daughter of Physcon and Cleopatra III. That was a subtle and cynical game that bore fruit. Ptolemy was now secure on Egypt's only vulnerable frontier. He had no worries regarding Cyprus. He was certain of loyalty in Cyrenaica. He had been there more than fifteen years, and the memory of his benefactions had earned him a network of dependable supporters. He could now devote his energies to Egypt, where he was to reinstate civic peace. That meant first of all erasing, at least on the surface

Plate 3 Nilotic landscape (Archaeological Museum, Palestrina; Photographie Alinari Anderson-Giraudon).

From the large mosaic in Fortune's shrine at Palestrina (dating from the time of Sulla, the first quarter of the first century BC). The mosaic shows life in the Nile Delta in the Ptolemaic period. Mounds of earth emerge here and there from the flooded plain. One of them (in the upper quarter) is topped with buildings: houses fitted with towers, a Greek shrine with a crenellated surround. The middle section shows peasants in front of a reed hut on which ibises are perched. A cowherd looks after an animal that is drinking, a fisherman seated in the shade holds a trident-shaped harpoon. Others are sailing in canoes on the floodwater. At the front of the picture, framed by a bower of foliage and vines, joyous carousers stretched on long couches drink, chat, or sing to the accompaniment of a harpist (right) and a flautist (left). It is a picture of the pleasures so much relished by the Greek landowners of Psenemphaia (see pp. 262–3) and other townships of the Delta.

and in spite of past horrors, the hatred that had divided the members of the newly reunited royal trio. Even the two odious murders perpetrated on children were moved into the penumbra of voluntary oblivion by the apotheosis of the hapless young victims, Ptolemy VII Neos Philopator and Ptolemy son of Physcon, and their insertion in the dynastic cult. Restoration of internal peace, under the banner of a pretended reconciliation, now became possible. A number of measures were taken with that end in view. They peaked in 118 with a decree of amnesty, with which a papyrus has acquainted us. It was a general amnesty, applicable to everyone who took part in the disturbances we have described. The fellahin were urged to return to their villages and lands, which unsafe conditions had persuaded them to leave. The social phenomenon of peasants deserting the countryside, because they dreaded fiscal imposition or were tempted by highway robbery, had now become widespread and was in years to come to devastate the Nile valley. This is called the trend to "desertion" or "retirement," *anachoresis* in Greek: those who took part in it were *anachoretai*, "anchorites" (the term was later to apply exclusively to those who live a life of retirement in the desert). Apart from amnesty, various privileges were granted or made available to Greeks living in the countryside, where the number of landowners of Greek origin, especially former soldiers, seems to have increased considerably. Other categories in the population who benefited from the attention of royal power were native soldiers and the Egyptian clergy. The latter group had been courted by the Ptolemies since Philopator's reign, and retained the benefit of special patronage. A last measure, meant to give satisfaction to widespread complaints concerning the catastrophic state of agriculture and the pitiable situation of the peasantry, was the cancellation of all arrears of debt, so that work could start again on a sound basis. From royal decisions of that kind, on which light is thrown by petitions and prayers sent to the center of power, one realizes how heavy-handed local administration was, how unbearable, in extreme cases, for the Egyptian peasants. That was the downside of the magnificent setting that had so favorably impressed Scipio Aemilianus' companions some years earlier.

Ptolemy VIII therefore endeavored to apply such remedies to the malady afflicting Egypt. They would have had enduring results only if monarchical authority – restored (and at what cost!) by the aging Lagid sovereign – had managed to preserve its effectiveness, its clarity of vision, its prestige for a long enough period. But whatever essentially political qualities belonged to Ptolemy Physcon, the poison of dynastic quarrels, seriously aggravated by his vices, pursued its nefarious actions, after a short and deceptive respite. Ptolemy VIII Euergetes II Physcon died in 116 after fifty-four years of a reign fertile in breath-taking reversals of fortune. He had the makings of a great king (if his sadistic cruelty is discounted), but he left behind an anemic land of Egypt and a tottering monarchy. These did not recover until the Roman conquest.

5/THE AGONY OF THE HELLENISTIC WORLD

■ *The death of the last great Ptolemy, and Mithridates'*
challenge to Roman power ■

The accession of Mithridates Eupator to the throne of Pontus, in 121/0, almost coincided with the death in 116 of the last great Lagid sovereign, Ptolemy VIII Euergetes II Physcon. Chance had arranged things well in that conjunction of events, since the king of Pontus' personality and unceasing activity were to dominate the history of the Greek East between the end of the second century and the year 64/3. That year witnessed Mithridates' death, and the disappearance of the Seleucid empire with the creation of the Roman province of Syria. By their definitive dismemberment of the political structures, born in Asia, of Alexander's inheritance, Mithridates' actions form a series of successive and rapid stages in the agony of an entire world. To cope with these, Rome was to feel the need to widen the field of her direct and indirect responsibilities in that area, in spite of the difficulties and disturbances that the Republic was experiencing in the West. Next, in a final stage, the only great Hellenistic kingdom remaining, that of the Ptolemies, was to disappear in its turn, and the Roman order was firmly established afterwards in the whole of the eastern Mediterranean. That turn of events happened at the very moment when, in 31 BC, the battle of Actium confirmed Octavius' triumph, which was to allow the establishment of the Principate, the equivalent of a universal monarchy. That signaled the end of an epoch, and the beginning of a new era.

■ *The last Seleucids: their blood-stained rivalries* ■ *The apogee of Tigranes, king of Armenia* ■ *Dynastic quarrels among the Ptolemies* ■ *Ptolemy Apion at Cyrene: his bequest to Rome* ■ *Cyrenaica becomes a Roman province*

The Seleucid dynasty destroyed itself as a result of family quarrels which between 114/13 and 83, a period of thirty years, continued to tear up what was left of the Syrian kingdom. It would be pointless as well as wearisome to attempt to follow the course of these quarrels in every detail. At the start they pitted Antiochus VIII (who in 123 had defeated the usurper Zabinas, with help from the Ptolemaic king) against his half-brother Antiochus IX, son of the same mother, Cleopatra Thea (see p. 123), and of Antiochus VII. The conflict broke out in 114–13 and lasted until the murder of Antiochus VIII in 96. Antiochus IX was to die the next year at the hands of a son of Antiochus VIII, Seleucus VI, himself fated soon to be ousted by his victim's son, Antiochus X. In his turn, Antiochus X had to struggle for power with Antiochus VIII's four surviving sons. Three of these met violent deaths. Only one died a natural death. He left a son, Philip II, who was kept away from the throne by the inhabitants of Antioch, weary of these never-ending family conflicts. They looked elsewhere for someone to be their protector, with a better prospect of permanence. They found him in Armenia, in the person of king Tigranes, who since his accession in 95 had extended considerably his states in Upper Mesopotamia, at the expense of the Parthians: so much so that by then the latter were sharing a frontier with Syria. Antioch chose him as a ruler in 83. His rule secured relative peace for the region over a space of fifteen years, a period full of localized incidents in which various communities played a part. There were in the first place the Jews, who had set up an independent kingdom in 103, ruled by Alexander Iannaeus, son of John Hyrcanus (see p. 124): and the Nabataean Arabs, who in the second century had organized themselves into a monarchical State with its capital at Petra. There were also a number of local dynasts of whom little is known; and, finally, some Greek cities, Seleucia in Pieria, Ptolemais-Aké, or Tripolis, for example, that tried to assert their autonomy in various ways, especially by striking their own coinage. The extreme complexity of the matters in dispute, extensions of those that had been at the root of earlier anarchy, reveals the internal decay of the Seleucid State.

The Ptolemaic kingdom was in no better health. There also family quarrels, an endemic evil of the dynasty, continued relentlessly, not without repercussions on those afflicting the Seleucids: a consequence of marriages between the daughters of Ptolemy VIII (all three were called Cleopatra, each with a distinguishing title) and Syrian princes. One of them, Cleopatra Selene ("The Moon"), after marrying her elder brother Ptolemy IX, married successively three ephemeral monarchs of Syria, before she was captured by Tigranes and sent to Mesopotamia, where she was murdered. At Ptolemy Physcon's death in 116, his wife and niece Cleopatra III and her two sons, Ptolemy IX Soter II and Ptolemy X Alexander, vied for power, the mother favoring the younger son, which did not prevent him from having her murdered in 101. The two brothers governed Egypt and Cyprus respectively. They exchanged realms many times, a reflection of changes in their comparative strength, until Ptolemy IX remained as sole master in 88, having defeated his brother, who lost his life on the same occasion. But Ptolemy Apion, an illegitimate son of Physcon, who had received Cyrenaica as a legacy from his father, had in the meantime taken the royal title. He died in 96, bequeathing (thereby following his father's example: see p. 134) his domains to the Roman people, while the cities of Cyrenaica were proclaimed free, keeping their individual territories. The Ptolemaic monarchy thus lost Libya. That wealthy and prosperous land had, since its conquest by Ptolemy I Sôter, regained its independence on more than one occasion: for fifty years under Magas' leadership, later in the course of Physcon's reign, finally in that of Apion. Even as a part of the Ptolemaic kingdom it had always enjoyed its own special status. Once informed of the situation, the Senate confirmed the freedom of the Greek cities of Libya – Cyrene, Ptolemais, Arsinoe (previously Taucheira), and Berenice (formerly Euhesperides); agreed to collect income from the royal domains; but did not immediately put direct administration in place. The result was that, when in 87/6 the Cyrenaeans needed help for the restoration of their institutions, which internal disturbances had seriously altered, they had to appeal not to a permanent representative of Rome, but to one of Sulla's lieutenants, Lucullus, who was on a provisional mission in the area. He gave assistance, inspired by the Platonic model. The particular turn that the course of political affairs had taken thus impelled the most traditional Greek cities to apply to the authority of Rome as the obvious arbiter of their destinies. In 74, in circumstances that are imperfectly known, the Senate resolved to create a Roman province of Cyrenaica and to appoint a magistrate of no exalted rank, a mere quaestor, to govern it.

■ *The growth of the kingdom of Pontus* ■ *Mithridates VI Eupator's accession to the throne* ■ *His conquests in the Black Sea* ■ *His ambitions regarding Asia Minor*

The dynasty of the kings of Pontus, though of Persian origin, had become profoundly Hellenized. It had annexed Greek cities, like Amisus, "fair daughter of

Athens," and Sinope, which served as its capital. Pontic kings would willingly adopt for their titles Greek epithets similar to those of other Hellenistic sovereigns. In the middle of the second century Mithridates IV proclaimed himself Philopator Philadelphus; Mithridates V was to be Euergetes. These princes had organized their domains, armed forces, and navy with help from their Greek subjects. When Mithridates fell victim in 121/0 to an attempt on his life, his son and successor Mithridates VI was only 11. Proud of his descent, he took the title of *Eupator*, "born of a noble father." Ambitious and (as most contemporary princes were) unscrupulous, he pushed aside as soon as he could those who stood in his way: his mother, then his brother Chrestus. By the year 111, aged 21, he was ruling alone. Hellenistic historiography, if we can rely on the accounts of Pompeius Trogus (as summed up by Justin) and Plutarch, took pleasure in garnering various reports handed down by tradition (apocryphal it would seem, but meaningful nevertheless), relating to the circumstances of his birth. According to them, the personality of the young king bore the stamp of an exceptional destiny. Various celestial phenomena, they said, had greeted his birth, among others, the apparition in heaven of a new star. Mention of those prodigies has been conjectured by some to be a reference to ancient Iranian beliefs. One need not look so far back: for the urge to record prodigious signs, harbingers, as it were, of a prince's extraordinary career, is a constant feature of the history of Hellenistic monarchies, from Alexander the Great to Caesar and Augustus. Such was the imagination of the Greeks that their interest in manifestations of divine attention to the fate of grandees and monarchs could dispense with the backing of Oriental tradition. Oracles were said to have foretold the first-class role Mithridates was to play in the Greek East. That serves only to prove that his contemporaries became conscious of his role, and looked upon Mithridates as the last of the great Hellenistic monarchs (which he turned out to be).

His state of Pontus bordered the Black Sea in the eastern part of the Anatolian coast, with Armenia to the east, Cappadocia to the south, Paphlagonia to the west, and (between the two last-named countries) a shared frontier with the Galatians. Mithridates thus had a base that was reliable enough for the projects he had in mind. It was a region of difficult access, except by sea, not devoid of age-old links with the Greek world, thanks to the Ionian colonies founded in the area centuries earlier. It was indeed a land of legend, since a very ancient tradition placed the battle that opposed the Greek heroes led by Heracles to the Amazons and their queen Antiope, on the banks of a small coastal river, the Thermodon, and on the site of the town of Themiscyra. Colchis too, Aeetes' kingdom made famous by the myth of the Golden Fleece, was quite close to Pontus at the far end of the Black Sea. It was also a land linked with more recent history, since in 400, just to the east of the kingdom of Pontus, near Trebizond, Xenophon and the surviving members of the Ten Thousand had reached the sea (*Thalassa! Thalassa!*), at the end of a long march across the valley of the Tigris and over the Armenian mountains. We have seen how Mithridates Eupator's ancestors, Pharnaces I and Mithridates V in particular, had already played a role in the political and military conflicts that had torn Anatolia in the second century. Pontus had established friendly relations with Cappadocia, whose king had married a daughter of Mithridates V, and with Paphlagonia. On the other hand, Pharnaces I had tried to lay hands beyond the Black Sea on some Greek colonies situated either in the Crimea, like Chersonesus, or on the Thracian coast (in present-day Bulgaria), like Mesembria. He had failed, but had entered into a relationship with those far-off cities, which is attested by Polybius and supported by documentary evidence. That offered Mithridates his first opportunity to extend his empire to areas where he ran no risk of conflict with Rome's interests. Furthermore, if one can rely on the inscription from Chersonesus that gives the text of that town's treaty with Pharnaces, Rome had agreed to stand surety for their agreement and their friendship.

The Greek cities north of the Black Sea now gave him the chance to move in that direction. They were then faced with intense pressure from the Scythian and Sarmatian populations occupying the interior. Already the important colony of Olbia, which had existed for centuries on the estuary of the river Hypanis (modern Bug), close to that of the Borysthenes (Dnieper), had been forced to submit to a Scythian prince from the Crimea in its neighborhood. He in his turn owed support to Sarmatian tribes. The same native potentate threatened the city of

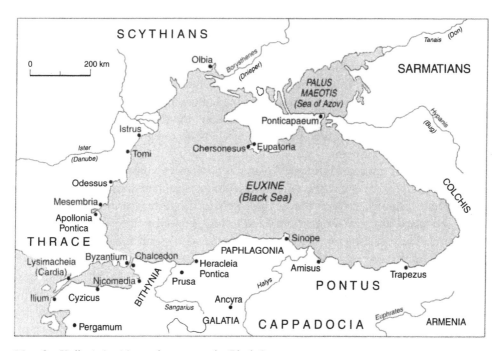

Map 8 Hellenistic cities and states on the Black Sea.

Chersonesus south of the Crimea (not far from Sebastopol), and the ancient Greek state on the edge of the Cimmerian Bosporus (Strait of Kertch), with its capital Panticapaeum (Kertch). Chersonesus and the dynast of the Cimmerian Bosporus therefore turned to Mithridates, invoking the ancient alliance that bound them together, and the attention paid by his ancestors to their part of the world. Responding to their appeal, the king of Pontus sent an expeditionary force of 6,000 Greek mercenaries, led by a *strategos* originating from Sinope, Diophantes. The latter obtained signal success in a few campaigns (from 110 to 107, probably), relieving the threatened cities, occupying the major part of the Crimea (including the State of the Cimmerian Bosporus), and advancing into the continent as far as Olbia. He thus brought the whole of the region under Mithridates' authority. Pontus found itself endowed with a new province on the opposite side of the Black Sea, its administrative center being Panticapaeum, in the region the Greeks called the Tauric Chersonese (the Crimea). It produced wheat in great abundance, thanks to the black earth of the nearby Ukrainian plain, silver, and, no less important for Mithridates, soldiers. The young king's first conquest meant a notable increase in his means of action. He tried to add more to them in the Black Sea area, eastward as well as westward. In the east he extended his dominion to Trebizond and beyond as far as Colchis. Westward, mindful of Pharnaces' designs on the Greek towns of the Thracian coast, threatened as these were by the barbarians of the Danubian plain, he seems to have established a sort of protectorate over Apollonia in Pontus. That city feared that it would suffer the same fate as its northern neighbor Istrus (in Dobroudja, south of the mouths of the Danube), which had fallen victim to attack from nearby populations. In the last years of the second century Mithridates emerged, all round the Black Sea, as the Hellenic world's ultimate recourse against danger coming from the interior of the continent. A sovereign with an Iranian name, he was nevertheless clearly considered a Greek king, which explains how, in years to come, the Greeks of Asia Minor and mainland Greece were to look up to him as their liberator from the Roman conqueror.

The next stage in Mithridates' plan was obviously to prepare for his inevitable clash with Rome by securing in Anatolia points of vantage surrounding the kingdom of Pontus. A secret trip of the king's to the Roman province of Asia had convinced him that Roman domination had aroused universal hostility in the land. This could be translated into revolt if a bold assailant came forward. The truth of the matter is that the Republic had set up in that province a fiscal system that was perceived as crushingly oppressive. The levying of tax (a tithe imposed on the whole territory, including land belonging *in proprio* to Greek cities, hitherto tax-exempt under the Attalids) was farmed out to companies owned by Roman financiers. These tax collectors exploited the population with the complicity of governors motivated by their appetite for personal gain. It might happen that upright magistrates, like the proconsul Quintus Mucius Scaevola and his legate Publius Rutilius Rufus in 93, would attempt to intervene. A lawsuit could then conveniently be entered against them at Rome, before tribunals notorious for their favorable attitude to financiers battening on the provinces, and get them out of the way. Mithridates, aware of such an explosive situation, strove to make the most of it. A series of intricate operations brought him new territories as he shared Paphlagonia with the king of Bithynia, Nicomedes III, and concluded an alliance with Tigranes, king of Armenia, by bestowing on him his daughter in marriage. In Cappadocia, however, he encountered great difficulty, as his own daughter Laodice refused to cooperate. His many attempts to win that kingdom's allegiance were foiled by Roman intervention (entrusted on one occasion to Sulla, then on his first eastern trip). Similarly, on Nicomedes III's death, Mithridates tried without success to win acceptance for his own candidate for the Bithynian throne. The new sovereign, Nicomedes IV, was persuaded by Rome (through her envoy, Manius Aquilius – see below) to invade Pontic Paphlagonia. His attack brought on war in the spring of 88.

■ *The First Mithridatic War* ■ *The massacre of Romans in Asia* ■ *Increased piratical activity in the Mediterranean* ■ *Mithridates' successes in Greece* ■ *Sulla's arrival and victory* ■ *Athens besieged and captured* ■ *Mithridates' Asian difficulties* ■ *He negotiates with Sulla*

Mithridates had prepared carefully for that war. It is believed that he had at his disposal 300,000 men, 130 chariots, and a fleet of 300 vessels. He soon defeated Nicomedes IV's troops, and then two Roman forces in succession, led against him by the governor of the province of Asia and Manius Aquilius, who had been sent by the Senate to settle Anatolian conflicts. The first of these two Roman leaders took refuge in Rhodes, the other on the island of Lesbos, where he was captured and put to death after being tortured. Bithynia and the province of Asia were thus entirely occupied by Mithridates, who was welcomed by nearly all Greek cities as the savior of Asia. To make clear his break with Rome in a decisive manner, the king, who had taken up his quarters at Ephesus in Ionia, decided to strike a mighty blow. After careful preparation, in one night he had all the Italian residents of Asia, 80,000 souls, slaughtered. Such a massacre, in which the entire population played a part, sealed between Mithridates and his newly found dependants a complicity in crime that forbade any compromise with Rome. In addition, the disappearance of these foreign traders or financiers and the ensuing plunder provided the king with rich booty that allowed him to grant the province a five-year exemption from any sort of levy. Social measures were taken to rally the most poverty-stricken elements of the population round their new master: emancipation of slaves and forgiveness of debt in particular. In the organization of his immense realm, Mithridates, like Alexander before him, instituted the administrative system of satrapies. The material prosperity of the new empire was expressed by the issue of superb gold coinage displaying the image of the sovereign as a hero: it obviously drew its inspiration from ancient tetradrachms bearing Alexander's effigy. In the new capital, placed on the site of Pergamum, he tried (following the example set by Hellenistic sovereigns) to keep around him a Greek circle made up of writers and artists. His enterprising spirit and his prestigious leadership make one believe in the rebirth in Asia of the Greek State of the Attalids.

At sea the Pontic fleet had forced the Straits and made its way into the Aegean. Only Rhodes, well defended by its strong walls and its navy, opposed it with a victorious resistance. Mithridates entered into alliances with the pirate fleets that had known considerable development in the late second century. They were mainly based in Crete and, especially, on the south coast of Anatolia, in the well-sheltered bays, difficult to reach by land, that were to be found in Cilicia, north of Cyprus. These squadrons roved the Aegean Sea and the coasts of Greece. They went as far as Libya, even attacking coastal cities like Berenice (Benghazi) in Cyrenaica, where an inscription was discovered not long ago, mentioning the ravages the pirates had inflicted soon after Ptolemy Apion's death (in 96). Such rapine provided, together with other booty, an abundant supply of slaves for markets like the one in Delos. Rome had indeed tried in 102 to repress an activity that did so much damage to sea-trade: but without any enduring success. Her recommendation a few years later to the Ptolemaic and Seleucid monarchs to take their share of repressive measures – an engraved text of which was shown at Delphi – proved fruitless in the end. In addition, the Aegean islands were made to suffer from the Pontic fleet's raids: Delos was plundered, while its numerous Italian population suffered wholesale slaughter. By contrast, the isle of Cos surrendered without resistance. It was there that Mithridates captured three Lagid princes, including those who were one day to become Ptolemy XI and Ptolemy XIII. He welcomed them to his court, and betrothed them to princesses belonging to his family, demonstrating his ambition to make of the kingdom of Pontus the equal of the greatest Hellenistic monarchies.

In that same year 88, Mithridates' troops crossed the Straits on their way to Europe. They occupied in succession Thrace, the Roman province of Macedon, and Thessaly; Athens, roused by the philosopher Athenion, took sides with them, together with Boeotia, Achaea, and Lacedaemon. There also Mithridates was looked upon as the savior of the Hellenic world, its deliverer from Roman oppression. Both sides of the Aegean Sea were, it appeared, witnessing the rebirth of a state comparable to what was once Lysimachus' empire, in control of Asia Minor as well as Thrace, Macedonia, and Greece.

Rome was taken by surprise, as Mithridates' victories happened in such quick succession. The Republic was just emerging from the crisis of the Social War: it had been in conflict with some of its Italian neighbors, and had not yet put an end to the last convulsions of that episode. Besides, strife between the popular party, which was led by Marius and his friends, and the senatorial party did nothing to ease the process of government. News coming from Asia brought on financial panic. Sulla, the consul, took a number of internal measures, with support from the Senate, then left for the East: he was to conduct the war against Mithridates. In 87 he landed in Epirus with five legions, defeated Archelaus, the *strategos* who led the Pontic troops, and laid siege to Athens. The city resisted for months before it was taken by storm on March 1, 86. Sulla proclaimed that he was "granting as a favor to the dead the mercy shown to the living": in other words, that he was sparing Athens after her revolt for the sake of her glorious past. Still he treated the Athenians with a severity that is still evoked with shock by Pausanias two and a half centuries later. The Piraeus was set on fire, a large number of public buildings and private houses were pillaged. Two armies that Archelaus, escaping from Athens before the fall of the city, had raised in Macedonia and Thrace were defeated in Boeotia one after the other. European Greece was thus again, in late 86, under Roman authority. Meanwhile, a lieutenant of Sulla, the famous Lucullus, was making the rounds in the eastern Mediterranean, from Cyrenaica to Cyprus via Egypt and Syria, trying to put together a war fleet. In the course of that tour he helped Cyrene to reform her institutions. But he obtained no help from the Lagid king Ptolemy IX, fearful as he was for his sons, who were Mithridates' prisoners. Yet he secured from other sources enough ships to make up a squadron. With help from Rhodian vessels, it started operations in the Aegean.

In Asia, where he had remained, leaving to Archelaus the conduct of war in Europe, Mithridates was encountering difficulties. His demands – for the purposes of war – for money, soldiers, and ships, appeared heavy to the Greek cities: their dealings with successive holders of power had accustomed them to greater deference. The inhabitants of Chios were not obedient enough and were deported in the direction of Colchis (which they did not reach, as they stopped at Heraclea Pontica on their way). Those of Ephesus rose in revolt, and were cruelly put down. Even the Galatians rebelled against the oppression they had to suffer. Sensing that Anatolia was about to slip from his grasp, Mithridates, while applying stern methods of compulsion, decided to negotiate. For a second Roman army, commanded by one of Sulla's political enemies, had already crossed Macedonia and Thrace, and was, in early 85, advancing beyond the Straits on Bithynia. Nicomedia, capital of Bithynia, then Pergamum fell. Having to choose an interlocutor from his two adversaries, the king of Pontus, who had narrowly missed being made a prisoner near the mouth of the Caicus, made peace with Sulla at Dardanus in the Troad – a peace that looked very much like a surrender.

He gave up his recent conquests, the province of Asia, Bithynia, Cappadocia, paid a very heavy war indemnity, and handed over seventy vessels. Sulla promised to spare the Greek cities that had welcomed Mithridates. The peace put its seal on his triumph: though he was less interested in the return of the East to order than in the Italian political situation. His main objective had been to extract financial resources from the territories he had regained. He meted out heavy penalties to Ephesus. The few cities that had stayed loyal, Rhodes, for example, were rewarded. Contrary to his promise, he punished the others by taking away their independence. The inhabitants of Chios, now back on their island, were spared, their deportation being taken into account. Asia was to bear an enormous levy: 20,000 talents. In 84 Sulla returned to Greece, where he stayed for a few months, gathering booty that included manuscripts (in particular, those of Aristotle) and works of art. Accompanied by his treasures and an army trained in warfare, totally devoted to him, he returned to Italy and Rome. There a new task was awaiting him, one that his victories in the East would enable him to perform.

■ *Second Mithridatic War* ■ *The struggle with the pirates:*
Cilicia becomes a Roman province ■ *Delos sacked in 69*
■ *Bithynia becomes a Roman province* ■ *Third Mithridatic War*
■ *Lucullus' successes* ■ *Pontus becomes a Roman province*
■ *Lucullus' operations against Tigranes* ■ *The principality of*
Commagene ■ *Mithridates reconquers Pontus*

Mithridates, who had withdrawn to his kingdom of Pontus, started rebuilding his forces. The new governor of the province of Asia, Lucius Licinius Murena, accompanied by his son (in whose favor Cicero was later to write a famous speech), launched an offensive against Pontus on three different occasions between 83 and 81. The pretext for these campaigns (under the global appellation of the Second Mithridatic War) was that Mithridates had not completely evacuated Cappadocia. Sulla appeased the conflict, and Roman concern turned to the struggle with the pirates: that was evidently an absolute necessity. Two conditions had to be fulfilled if they were to be beaten on the high seas and tracked down to their bases. Rome was to occupy and effectively control the coastal regions where these bases lay, and place the struggle at sea under a single command with authority to intervene wherever necessary. These were the goals of two sets of measures, which were not immediately successful. Various operations were undertaken in the hinterland of Southern Anatolia in connection with the creation of the Roman province of Cilicia (the date of which is uncertain, some placing it around 80, others as early as 100). The other decision was to create in 74 an unusual command, in fact the first of its kind in the history of Rome. It was an *imperium infinitum*, a command whose terms of reference were not limited. It was to be held in the Mediterranean by one leader, who was empowered to take action on all provincial coasts. The first holder of that position was a man of mediocre ability, Marcus Antonius, the father of the future triumvir Mark Antony, and son of a distinguished orator who had led a naval campaign against the pirates in 102. Marcus Antonius was defeated and made a prisoner by Cretan privateers: he died soon after, in 71. His defeat further emboldened the pirates: they attacked and pillaged in the year 69 the island of Delos, which Sulla had restored to Athens. Coming less than twenty years after a similar action by Mithridates in 88, this event was fatal to a merchant port that for more than a century had been the commercial center of the Cyclades. It never really rose from its ruins. The Roman legate Triarius tried in vain to restore the small city, and provide it with the means to defend itself, by hastily raising a makeshift fortification, traces of which can still be identified. A sparse population eked out a living amid remnants of a vanished prosperity and ravaged shrines. A favorite exercise of poets would henceforth be to sing of the sad destiny of the Cyclades' ancient glory, of Apollo's island now deserted after receiving so many festal assemblies, of illustrious Delos now *adèlos* ("invisible" or "obscure"), a play on words following the Greeks' traditional taste for etymological puns. The decay of one of the most august seats of Greek religion, which had simultaneously become one of the foremost marts of the Hellenistic world, is an apt illustration of that world's agony.

Rid of the presence of Murena, who had been recalled to Rome, Mithridates was in no mood to give up his designs. He had established contact, at the opposite end of the Mediterranean, with the rebel chief Sertorius, who had, since 82, roused the various populations of Spain against Rome and opposed a victorious resistance to the forces sent against him. It is supposed that Sertorius had guaranteed him possession of Bithynia and Cappadocia in the case of his own victory. A policy embracing the whole of the known world was thus being delineated, as had been the case in 215, when Philip V planned an alliance with Hannibal. But, exactly as happened in the case of Philip's effort, no concrete result followed. War in Asia flared up again because of Bithynia. Nicomedes IV died in 74, bequeathing his kingdom to the Roman Republic. The Senate decided to make it the province of Bithynia. But Mithridates soon invaded it, welcomed by a population dreading exploitation by tax collectors. Rome, contrary to custom, had sent both consuls to Asia – luckily for her: one of these proved unequal to his task, but the other was Lucullus, Sulla's former lieutenant, a man of experience and decision. With the help of the Cilician legions, who had fought the pirates, he retrieved his colleagues' losses, forced Mithridates to raise his siege of Cyzicus on the Asiatic coast of the Propontis (Sea of Marmara), then expelled him from

Bithynia. He knew, from experience acquired while leading a squadron under Sulla, how essential naval superiority was in the conflict in which he was engaged. He therefore put all the necessary effort into assembling a fleet. In 72 he won a naval victory over Mithridates at Lemnos, forcing him to clear the Aegean and return to the Black Sea. Taking the offensive, he went straight for Pontus, where he undertook challenging operations, finally (in 71) occupying the whole of the kingdom. Mithridates took refuge at the court of Tigranes, his ally and son-in-law. In 70 the two principal Pontic cities, Sinope on the coast and Amasea inland, fell into the hands of Lucullus, who recommended to the Senate that the land should become a Roman province. North of the Euxine, Mithridates was also to lose his possessions in the Crimea, which he had entrusted to one of his sons. In his desire to have his governing position at Panticapaeum confirmed, that son entered into direct negotiations with Lucullus. The Third Mithridatic War ended in complete victory for Rome, thanks to Lucullus' military ability. He then found himself provisionally invested with authority in the four Roman provinces of Asia Minor, Pontus, Bithynia, Asia and Cilicia. There his humane and benevolent administration, anxious to shield the population from the lust of Roman financiers, earned him widespread sympathy. Meanwhile his brother, who governed the province of Macedon, was conducting campaigns against the Thracians across the Bulgarian plains up to the Danube, which Roman troops reached for the first time. He advanced as far as Dobroudja, on the western coast of the Black Sea, where he placed under Roman protection the Greek cities of the area, with which the kings of Pontus had earlier established a privileged relationship. No doubt these ancient colonies remained free in theory, just as after Lucullus' victory the cities of the Pontus wrested from Mithridates, Sinope and Amisus, had been proclaimed free. But, as in the case of the cities of Asia Minor allowed to be theoretically independent, such freedom amounted to a pretence of autonomy: its value stayed within the limits imposed by the Republic's interest.

Eager to deal a final blow to Mithridates' attempts, Lucullus asked Tigranes to surrender his father-in-law. The Armenian king refused. Lucullus started hostilities against him in 69, and defeated him at the very heart of his states, in Upper Mesopotamia, not far from his capital, Tigranocerta, which fell to Roman troops. Their victory inflicted a fatal injury on the political structure Tigranes had recently established. He had spent fifteen years absorbing the remains of the Seleucid empire. He lost Syria, which was returned to a surviving Seleucid, Antiochus XIII. The short-lived reign of Antiochus XIII was to be the last of his dynasty (Pompey deposed him in 64, see pp. 152–3). A small kingdom, Commagene, whose capital was Samosata on the upper Euphrates, was among the principalities whose sovereigns were eager to show goodwill toward Rome. Its king, Antiochus I, who had chosen for titles the twin epithets of Romanophile (*Philoromaios*) and Philhellene, came and paid his respects to Lucullus. On Mount Nimrud Dagh, in the Anti-Taurus chain, he left an amazing set of monuments in a shrine where colossal statues were erected of the Greek gods and of the king himself. They give impressive evidence of the deep-rooted Hellenization of a small state lost in the hinterland between the mountains and the upper reaches of the Euphrates.

In the following year (68), Lucullus brought his war against Tigranes right into Armenia, but was forced after further victories to return to base. His legions were showing signs of weariness: they had been sorely tried by the campaign. Mithridates meanwhile returned to his kingdom of Pontus with a number of faithful followers, and rallied his supporters, expelling the Roman forces of occupation from the land. By 67 he had regained his kingdom, while Lucullus found himself relieved of his command: his political foes, and the financiers whose lucrative operations he had hindered, had long sought his downfall. Mithridates was saved, again . . .

■ *Pompey's extirpation of piracy* ■ *The Fourth Mithridatic War* ■ *The old king in Tauric Chersonesus* ■ *His final plan for struggle with Rome* ■ *His death* ■ *Pompey master of Asia* ■ *His reorganization of Anatolia* ■ *Reduction of Syria to the status of a Roman province* ■ *Pompey's triumph*

. . . Not for long, however. The man chosen to succeed Lucullus had made his name by winning a brilliant victory over the pirates. This was Pompey. A law, passed at the instigation of Lucullus' adversaries, had entrusted him with an extraordinary command analogous to the one created in 74 for Marcus Antonius (see p. 149), though Pompey was to put his to a very different use. The whole of the Mediterranean, from Spain to Syria, was his venue, with a right to supervision within fifty miles inland. He divided the sea into sections, each entrusted to a squadron provided with competent leadership. He then scoured the Mediterranean from west to east until he eventually cornered the pirates in their main haunts in Cilicia, and crushed them. Cleverly, he offered the survivors of these bands an opportunity to adapt themselves to an honest life by repopulating a number of cities, especially in Cilicia, which had been left desolate by recent misfortunes. The *Lex Manilia*, supported by a speech of Cicero's and passed at a time when Pompey was holding a naval command in the East, now put him in addition in charge of affairs in Asia Minor, from the year 66. In that same year, Pompey, starting from Cilicia in a northern direction, recaptured Cappadocia, penetrated into Pontus, and expelled from his kingdom Mithridates, who in a first move withdrew to Colchis. The king, now over 65, made for the Tauric

Chersonese (the Crimea), where he reasserted his authority, driving to suicide the ungrateful son who had betrayed him five years earlier. There he thought out a bold plan, modeled on Hannibal's campaigns, aimed at bringing war straight into Italy from southern Russia. His purpose was to enlist the populations of central Europe against Rome, in the course of a fantastic expedition on horseback up the Danube valley to Pannonia, to emerge finally into the plain of the Po in Cisalpine Gaul. This was a grandiose project which was never realized, the daydream of an old man refusing to the bitter end to concede defeat: a dream nevertheless that has held human imagination captive by its very extravagance – witness the reports of a variety of historians: Florus, Plutarch, Appian, Dio Cassius. The aged monarch's world was crumbling all around him. His son Pharnaces proclaimed himself king in his stead, and was confirmed by Pompey in possession of the Cimmerian Bosporus. Nothing was left for Mithridates but death. Poisons, to which he had made himself immune by constant absorption over the years, were ineffective. On his own orders, he died by the sword of one of his soldiers, the Gaul Bituit. As Racine described it in his tragedy *Mithridate* (Act I, scene i, 9–13),

> And thus this king who, through full forty years
> Wearied alone the whole leadership of Rome,
> Who in the East held Fortune's scales in balance,
> Avenging the common cause of every king,
> Dies . . .
>
> (trans. Samuel Solomon, *Jean Racine:*
> *Complete Plays*, New York, 1969)

No doubt his death marked the disappearance of the last Hellenistic sovereign, when "that tireless heart, that seemed to grow firmer when burdened with over-whelming challenge" stopped beating. At long last, he allowed Rome's arrogant fortunes to pursue their course.

Pompey had not deigned to follow Mithridates as far as Colchis. The reconquest of Pontus was enough for the Fourth Mithridatic War to be won. He reached an agreement with the Parthians, with whom Lucullus had already concluded a treaty; made peace with Tigranes, henceforth kept within the bounds of Arme-nia; and reorganized Asia Minor, accounted for in the main by the four Roman provinces of Pontus, Bithynia, Asia, and Cilicia. Cappadocia, under a sovereign allied to Rome, occupied the center of the eastern section, with an extension beyond the upper Euphrates. A Galatian kingdom included the principal tribal chiefs of that people. Hellenistic Anatolia was in future to have an administrative structure that it would keep under the Roman Empire.

Pompey completed his work by settling Syrian affairs. Antiochus XIII, in whose favor Lucullus had restored the Seleucid monarchy in 69, had been unable to escape the fatal poison of dynastic quarrels. His cousin Philip II, set aside in 83 in favor of the Armenian Tigranes, claimed the kingdom. The two pretenders were locked in a dispute, backed by Arab chiefs who took advantage of Tigranes' departure to extend their holdings in Syria. Philip perished in a riot, and Antiochus won. Pompey went to Syria in 64, with the design of strengthening the country's safety, as it shared a frontier on the Euphrates with the Parthian kingdom. He judged that Antiochus XIII was unable to keep order in a region where anarchy was endemic, and refused to confirm his position as sovereign. Antiochus took shelter with his Arab protector, who got rid of him by having him murdered. The dynasty thus died in an inglorious episode. In the same year 64, Pompey reduced Syria to the status of a Roman province. That decision spelled the end of the Seleucid monarchy's history, as a similar one had done for the kingdom of the Antigonids and for those of Pergamum, Bithynia, and Pontus. Reduction to provincial status under Roman administration appeared to be the terminal point decreed by fate for these Hellenistic states.

By creating the province of Syria, Pompey did not necessarily give uniformity to the administration of the territory. The Greek cities, whose autonomy had been strengthened step by step, kept their privileges, as confirmed by their coinage. The Jews, split by a dynastic dispute, forced Pompey to military intervention in Jerusalem. He suppressed the independent Jewish kingdom, while allowing the governance of the Jewish community by an ethnarch – he was the former king. The Nabataean Arabs in Petra had to make a financial contribution for their independent status to continue. Pompey penetrated the Temple of Jerusalem, where he was surprised not to find any divine effigy. It was then that he learned of Mithridates' death. Leaving Syrian affairs in the care of the governor of the new province, he returned to Pontus, where he wished to give a final touch to the reorganization of the conquered territories. There he received Mithridates' remains, sent to him by Pharnaces. They were interred at Sinope with royal pomp. Returning to Italy at the end of the year 62, he was honored with a triumph, one endowed with an exceptional citation: the triumph was said to celebrate a victory "over the whole Universe," *de orbe terrarum universo*. Pompey had certainly earned the title of "the Great" – *Pompeius Magnus*, by which he is known in history. He had indeed benefited from favorable circumstances. These included Lucullus' previous victories, and the support he had received from Roman financiers eager to regain a setting for their profit-making activities. Still, he was not solely motivated by an ambition for glory. He was no less driven by a desire for power and the attraction of material profit. He had nevertheless displayed a superior talent for organization in his struggle with the pirates, as well as in the pursuit of his campaigns and the use made of his victories. The Orient to which he had given shape was certainly not the Universe incautiously flaunted by his triumphal citation. Yet that was to be the Orient of the future till the final days of Rome: dependent on Rome, yet Greek-speaking and preserving the essence of the Hellenistic heritage within the framework of Latin sovereignty. It would be an Orient keeping its links with the

Mediterranean world and a privileged relationship with it at the threefold level of political organization, economy, and culture. Pompey's achievement was primarily to make permanent the features of that western Asia which, since the time of Alexander, had lived in close contact with Greece, multiplying exchanges with her, playing the role of intermediary between the Hellenic world and the populations of the Middle East. The frontier of the Euphrates, acknowledged by Lucullus and confirmed by Pompey, became the eastern boundary of the Classical world, which constituted a distinct entity from Spain to Syria and Cappadocia. This was the Greco-Roman cultural universe, the various components of which gradually developed a notion of their common destiny, whether they liked it or not. From this point of view, the episode of Pompey's exploits putting an end to the woeful tale of the Mithridatic Wars appears as a decisive moment in the history of civilization.

■ *The last Ptolemaic sovereigns* ■ *Ptolemy IX Lathyros*
■ *Ptolemy XII Auletes* ■ *Internal disturbances in Egypt*
■ *Ptolemy XIII and Cleopatra VII* ■ *Character portrait of that princess* ■ *Battle of Pharsalus and death of Pompey* ■ *Caesar and Cleopatra* ■ *The Alexandrian War* ■ *Defeat and death of Pharnaces* ■ *The murder of Caesar* ■ *Cleopatra governs Egypt* ■ *Battle of Philippi* ■ *Mark Antony meets Cleopatra at Tarsus* ■ *"The Inimitable Life"* ■ *Antony reorganizes the East* ■ *His campaigns in Asia* ■ *The break with Octavian* ■ *The Donations of Alexandria* ■ *Battle of Actium* ■ *The end of Antony and Cleopatra* ■ *Egypt becomes a Roman province* ■ *Submission of the entire Hellenistic world to Rome*

Only one area of the Hellenistic world was still exempt from Roman control. That was the Ptolemaic kingdom, weakened by dynastic quarrels and internal conflicts, but still rich in the resources of the fertile Nile valley. Its incorporation in the Roman world happened at the same time as the struggles that opposed ambitious Roman generals to each other, and led to the downfall of the Republic. Rivalry between such leaders became the main motive force of history. The men at the helm, belonging to the Greek tradition, played a role only through the agency of a woman: an illustrious one indeed, the great Cleopatra, a historical figure who is very much alive, linking the final episodes of the Roman conquest.

Ptolemy IX Sôter II, who had stayed on as sole sovereign of Egypt in 88, bore the odd nickname of *Lathyros* ("Chick-pea"). The end of his reign in 80 was inglorious, if not free of worry. He had to put down a native revolt, following numerous popular uprisings of this kind in Upper Egypt. On that occasion, in one of the bitterest confrontations to occur in this country, a result of cohabitation between Greeks and fellahin, he destroyed Thebes, the ancient Pharaonic city. His successor, Ptolemy XI Alexander II, reigned for only a few weeks before falling victim to a riot. It is believed that in his will he designated the Roman people as heir to his kingdom of Egypt and Cyprus. Rome chose temporarily not to act on the bequest. The only ones who were in a position to reign were Ptolemy IX's two sons. Once captives of Mithridates, they had eventually been freed. The elder one, Ptolemy XII surnamed Auletes ("the Flute-Player"), had the kingdom of Egypt, the younger that of Cyprus: they shared their father's inheritance in an arrangement that had often been made between previous sovereigns. But Clodius (P. Clodius Pulcher), a demagogic Roman politician, had a law passed in 58 making Cyprus a Roman province, paired with the province of Cilicia. The king of Cyprus committed suicide. As for Auletes, after generous handouts to people in positions of influence, he managed to be recognized in principle by Rome as sovereign of Egypt. But the people of Alexandria rose in revolt and drove away the king. He made for Rhodes, then Rome. A lieutenant of Pompey's, who governed Syria, finally reinstated him (in 55). A troop of auxiliaries made up of Gauls and Germans, and commanded by a Roman officer, served as his bodyguard: Egypt was becoming a Roman protectorate. These political and military interventions were costly, leading to increasing levies from the Lagid sovereign and the usual consequences of such fiscal methods: tax evasion; desertion of the land, left by the peasantry to lie fallow; insubordination and highway robbery. The Egyptian economic system was quickly disintegrating. It was hoped that the native clergy could be won over by being granted favors. It received ever-increasing exemptions and privileges, which further reduced the area of productive territory subject to State control. At his wits' end, Ptolemy Auletes eventually found a Roman financier to manage his treasury: he made him his minister. The collaboration ended badly, and the Roman had to flee home after a period of imprisonment. That long reign, lasting until 51, was a dismal period for Egypt. The people did not mourn the death of the Flute-Player, in spite of the high-sounding epithets in which he took delight as adornments of his name: "god," "reborn Dionysus," Philopator, Philadelphus.

At his death he left his kingdom to his young son, Ptolemy XIII, who was only 10 years old, together with instructions for him to marry his elder sister, Cleopatra VII, a young lady of 17. Cleopatra has become a legendary figure, as few women have been in history. Octavian's propaganda depicted her as a monster of debauchery and perversity, using her bewitching beauty in pursuit of her dark designs, an Oriental woman enveloped in heady perfume, luring away from the path of duty Romans unable to resist her spell. That simplistic, romantic scenario has abused a credulous posterity. Let us rather study texts and portraits, in particular, the fine Cherchell head that belonged to the statue erected by her daughter, Cleopatra Selene, who married Juba II, king of Mauretania. We see noble features, stamped with stern authority and a somewhat cold majesty, with a long aquiline nose enhancing a natural dignity of expression, which is shown to advantage by her profile as it appears on coinage. We find here none of the seductive charm of a courtesan queen, *regina meretrix*, an expression often used by Latin writers. Neither Oriental nor Egyptian, she is of Greek origin, an intelligent and shrewd woman, speaking many languages (Egyptian included). Her power of seduction, which her successive amours reveal in an indisputable manner, owed less to the attraction of an appealing physique, ornamented with luxurious refinement, than to her bright and vivacious glance, and her intellectual endowments. There is no doubt that she made the most of a woman's natural attributes when approaching those whom she was to ask for help and protection. She achieved her purpose with both Caesar and Antony: the one a cool-headed man, with a sensuality prone to every kind of debauchery, but a heart full of passionate dreams; the other a naive soul and a great soldier, who was easily seduced, quickly aroused. This provides evidence that she was the sort of woman to inspire intense passion. To resist her charm, one had to be like Octavian, a sedate young man, wily and heartless. On her part she was far from devoid of emotion, as is shown by Plutarch's account. In her dealings with Caesar she bowed to the power of fame and genius. With Antony, both lover and spouse, she shared (with less infatuation, however) a deep and sincere passion, to which their self-inflicted death bears witness in its tragic simplicity. The Ptolemaic dynasty, never short of women endowed with feeling and intelligence, met an end worthy of its illustrious destiny, in the person of its last figure Cleopatra.

A few years before Auletes' death, an event of the utmost gravity had occurred in 53 in the Middle East. Crassus, a member with Pompey and Caesar of the triumvirate heading the Republic at the time, had arrived in Syria to be its proconsul. Using that province as his base, he had rashly engaged in a war against the Parthians. Their sovereign was the great Orodes. Having crossed the Euphrates, Crassus suffered a disastrous defeat at his hands, at Carrhae in Mesopotamia, dying in the encounter. The Romans were brought back to the frontier of the Euphrates, beyond which they were now to renounce any further expansion. The balance of the opposing forces that Pompey had already conceded was thus confirmed. But Crassus' death deprived the triumvirate of one of its members. That was to lead, among other results, to a confrontation between Pompey and Caesar that culminated a few years later, in the summer of 48, in the battle of Pharsalus in Thessaly, with Caesar the victor. Turning to flee, Pompey remembered that Lagid Egypt had provided him with vessels prior to his defeat, and that in 55 Auletes had been reinstated by one of his legates. That gave him hope

Plate 4 Cleopatra VII (Cherchell Museum, Algeria; photo, Ancient Art and Architecture Collection).

Jean Charbonneaux identified this fine marble piece, now known as the Cherchell Cleopatra, basing his identification on coinage from Antioch, where the queen's effigy displays well-known characteristics – the majestic features, a powerful aquiline nose (which made Pascal remark, "Had her nose been shorter, the face of the whole earth might have changed"), the elaborate coiffure, the loose ribbons of the royal diadem hanging down her neck. Cleopatra wears a veil, as many Ptolemaic queens had done before her. One can understand that her daughter, who became queen of Mauretania and married a native king of Greek culture, wished the statue of her illustrious mother to grace her city.

that he would find shelter at the Egyptian court, and help in putting an end to his difficulties. He went to Pelusium, on the Delta's eastern frontier, where young Ptolemy XIII was at the time, flanked by his advisors Pothinus and Achillas: Cleopatra, at odds with her brother and spouse, had fled to Coele-Syria, where she was raising an army. On his ministers' advice, Ptolemy, anxious to secure goodwill from the victor of Pharsalus, decided that it was to his advantage to have Pompey murdered after deceiving him with a promise of safety.

Reaching Alexandria a few days later, Caesar was pained and angry at Ptolemy's strange gift. It was then that he received another gift, brought to him concealed in a carpet. This was the young queen in person, who had thought up the scheme, which (one might believe) had come straight out of a novel, to approach Caesar without running the gauntlet of her brother's police or the Roman leader's bodyguard. From that moment Cleopatra appears to have prevailed against Ptolemy, since Caesar supported her in her quarrel with him. Yet, canvassed by the king's men, the Alexandrian populace rioted and blockaded the royal palace. War raged in Alexandria until the month of March 47, and ended when an army arrived from Syria to relieve Caesar. Ptolemy XIII died in that episode. Cleopatra soon married her other brother, Ptolemy XIV.

The Alexandrian uprising inflicted an irretrievable loss on ancient culture: the destruction by fire of the renowned Library, a unique repository of the works of Greek literature and science. As for Caesar and Cleopatra, emerging unharmed from these stirring events, they sailed together on the Nile to Upper Egypt, a trip that allowed the Roman statesman, as Scipio Aemilianus had done earlier, to see for himself the vastness of the country and its resources. On their return, Cleopatra and her new husband, Ptolemy XIV, were confirmed as sovereigns. Before leaving, Caesar posted in Egypt an occupying force consisting of many legions: he thus made sure, under the pretext of safeguarding the Ptolemaic monarchy, that Egypt would remain his personal possession. Soon after his departure Cleopatra gave birth to a son, Ptolemy Caesar, commonly called Caesarion, whom his father legitimized in Rome in the Senate's presence. The birth of that son was to give the queen, as long as Caesar was alive, some assurance of closeness to the dictator.

Caesar had by now reached Asia Minor, where Pharnaces, Mithridates' rascally son, having left the Cimmerian Bosporus, was trying to regain Pontus and revive his father's realm. In June 47 Caesar arrived in great haste and in a single battle put an end to the rebel prince's wild hopes. At the end of that campaign he uttered the famous sentence, *Veni, vidi, vici* ("I came, I saw, I conquered"). He returned to Rome in October, and was joined by Cleopatra, who was to stay in one of his villas, until he was murdered. There she held court in the true sense of the term – receiving adulation from all those who feared and flattered Caesar. Meanwhile, between his African and Spanish campaigns, Caesar was accomplishing a political and administrative reorganization, in preparation for a change from a republican to a monarchical system. The successful attempt on his life, headed by Brutus and Cassius, on the Ides (15) of March 44, was to abort that process. Rome was in upheaval, and was soon to be prey to civil war. Cleopatra returned to Egypt, where she caused her lackluster spouse and brother to disappear, associating her son Caesarion with her in sovereignty. Under the name of Ptolemy XV Caesar, he was to be officially the last of the Ptolemies. Yet, no more than any of his uncles was he to play any effective role in the government of Egypt, for which his mother, in point of fact, was to remain entirely responsible. She appears to have had as much success in that task as circumstances would allow. There were two periods of serious penury, caused by inadequate Nile floods, between 50 and 48 and in the year 42. The local administration had its deficiencies; and monetary inflation was rampant, as is made clear by numismatic evidence bearing on Cleopatra's reign. The queen, however, preserved internal order. Egypt's rural areas were not afflicted with the disturbance of earlier years. Such peace and quiet must have been due to the attention that the sovereign – the first among the Ptolemies to speak the native tongue – paid to the wellbeing of her Egyptian subjects. She had her own personal grievance against the Greek population of Alexandria (see p. 158), given as it was to questioning authority: she made sure that she was perceived as the queen of the fellahin. She made a point of sharing (at least nominally, but in compliance with the tradition of the ancient Pharaohs) in purely Egyptian religious ceremonies. In the presence of priests and the faithful, she adopted certain Pharaonic rites presupposing the sovereign's assimilation to the great local divinities. To quote an example, Caesarion was identified at his birth with Horus, and introduced as the son of Caesar-Amon and Cleopatra-Isis. A desire to appear as the sovereign of Egypt in its entirety is more noticeable in Cleopatra than in any of the previous Lagids. The fact is no doubt explained by the monarchy's withdrawal into its Egyptian realm, after the loss of all its external possessions. At any rate, its origin can be traced back directly to a tradition bequeathed by Alexander the Great, acting as the Achaemenids' successor.

The months following Caesar's murder brought to light the importance of the Greek Orient in the Mediterranean world. Brutus and Cassius, the leaders of the conspiracy, took shelter in Macedonia and Syria respectively. They raised funds and troops in Asia, crushing the provinces, the free cities, and the allied princes under their impositions. The decisive encounter between Caesar's killers and his avengers took place in October 42, on the plain of Philippi by the *Via Egnatia*. The poet Horace, who fought on the losing side, recalls dropping his shield to save his life, coward that he was, *relicta non bene parmula* (*Odes*, II, 7, 10: "shamelessly leaving behind my little shield"). He aptly borrows Archilochus' wording, six centuries after the Parian poet: in that very land of Thrace, necessity had forced the same humiliation on his predecessor. One of the two victors at Philippi, Mark Antony, Caesar's former lieutenant, undertook in turn to levy in the East the financial contributions that the new triumvirs needed. Simultaneously, he surveyed the situation in the extensive area unsettled by the recent turmoil. He was at Tarsus in Cilicia in the summer of 41, when he asked Cleopatra to come and discuss matters with him. She arrived, sailing on the river Cydnus in a luxuriously ornamented galley, amid a sumptuous display of pomp calculated to dazzle her Roman host. Yet Antony was not unacquainted with the splendor of an Oriental welcome, for the Ephesians, not so long before, had greeted him as the New Dionysus. She obtained without delay the desired result: yielding to her seductiveness as a woman, subjugated by the queen in her, he was willing to grant her every wish. He spent the next winter in Alexandria, where together, in the midst of diverse pleasures, celebrations, and banquets, they lived what was called "the Inimitable Life": the life led by the divinities with whom they were identified, he being Dionysus-Osiris, she Aphrodite-Isis. Cleopatra, however, did not depart from a true Ptolemy's merciless vigilance. At Tarsus Antony had agreed, at her request, that her sister Arsinoe was to die. At Ephesus, in contempt of her right to asylum, Arsinoe was taken by force out of Artemis' shrine. Political scheming certainly held first place in Cleopatra's conduct, in the very midst of a life of love with its attendant follies.

The enchantment of the "Inimitable Life" lasted only a few months. The demands of Roman politics and the threat of a Parthian invasion of Syria forced Antony to leave Alexandria and return to Italy: he had to sort out his relationship with Octavian and demand troops for war against the Parthians. At his request, his colleagues in the triumvirate entrusted him with affairs in the East. After marrying Octavia, the sister of Octavian, he left for Athens, where he was to spend the winter of 39/8. One of his lieutenants undertook to drive the Parthian invaders out of Syria. In 37, wishing to prepare for the great expedition he was contemplating in the Middle East, Antony took up his quarters in Antioch. He had by then sent his wife back to Italy; invited by him, Cleopatra was now at his side. She had brought with her the twins she had borne him in the year 40. They did not yet know their father, since they were born after his departure. One was a son, Alexander-Helios; the other was a daughter, Cleopatra-Selene. Their names put them under the patronage of two cosmic divinities, the Sun and the Moon, as though they were destined to reign over a universal empire. In the following year Mark Antony was to start on an expedition beyond the Euphrates that was obviously modeled on the precedent set by Alexander. Caesar seems to have had the idea for that journey and planned it.

Before embarking on such a venture and in the same year 37, Antony modified the administrative map of the Greek Orient under Roman power in the light of recent experience. In Asia Minor the province of Pontus was considered too remote to qualify any longer for direct administration: it became a kingdom, bestowed upon a prince who was to be a client of Rome. The provincial status of Bithynia and Asia was left untouched. The province of Cilicia, having proved difficult to administer, was in future to be divided into two parts. The eastern section was paired with its neighbor, the province of Syria. The western one, Cilicia Trachea, a mountainous region (as implied by the epithet *Trachea*, "rugged"), a former haunt of pirates, was turned into a principality that was entrusted to an erudite poet-king, Polemo. Galatia and Cappadocia remained protected kingdoms. The autonomous cities and a few principalities of secondary importance completed the picture of Roman Anatolia, as revised by Mark Antony. Served by his political flair, he had preserved the essence of Pompey's system. But in certain respects he had brought in changes that seemed necessary. These included the abolition of the two provinces of Pontus and Cilicia, but above all, in a region of such vast size and diversity, a number of arrangements aimed at lightening the burden of direct administration and making more flexible the mechanics of political and fiscal control. In the south of the province of Syria, to which had been added the plain of eastern Cilicia, Antony left in place the state of the Nabataean Arabs and the Jewish state of Judaea. After the Parthian invasion, the latter had been remodeled into a kingdom to the benefit of a client of Rome, Herod the Great: thirty years later, during his reign, Christ was born.

On the other hand, the greater part of southern Syria, including Damascus, Chalcis in Lebanon, and the Phoenician coast, was restored to Egypt, which thus unexpectedly reasserted its presence in Coele-Syria. Cyprus was once again annexed to the Lagid kingdom, together with part of eastern Cilicia. These territorial transfers were not simply a lover's gifts to his mistress. Their purpose was also to provide Egypt with the supply of timber necessary for rebuilding a war-fleet that Antony felt he might need soon. An added consideration was the expedition to Asia, due to start soon. It would need a solid backup, in which Egyptian resources would play a prominent part.

In 36 Antony embarked on his Asian venture. Starting from Commagene at the head of considerable forces, he crossed Armenia and reached Media Atropatene, southwest of the Caspian Sea. But his siege-engines having failed to keep up with his advance, he was prevented from taking the town of Phraaspa. Caught in the season of bad weather, he was forced to retreat in very difficult circumstances. Plutarch gives a vivid description of the hardships encountered by the army in the course of that campaign. Antony displayed his attributes as a leader: a never-failing physical courage and endurance, the gift he had for relating to his soldiers. All the same, the outcome was a failure. In 34 a second campaign allowed him to occupy Armenia. He turned it into a province as a punishment for its king, who had proved a faithless ally.

Meanwhile Antony had broken relations with Octavia. He forbade his wife to rejoin him in the Orient: that amounted to repudiation. From that moment onward, Octavian prepared in the west for the inevitable confrontation, already engineering a moral assault on Antony as a traitor to the Roman cause. The latter was, by the very nature of things, led to forge a closer and closer link between his fate and that of Cleopatra and the Ptolemaic kingdom. Beside the queen, who had by now borne him a third child, he appeared to be the virtual king of the eastern Mediterranean, the heir to the Hellenistic world, brought together for the last time in a cohesive whole under one person's authority. He took up his quarters at Alexandria, which for a few short years became the de facto capital of the eastern political world in its entirety: an honor the illustrious city had never attained in earlier days. An amazing and significant celebration took place in the autumn of 34 in the gymnasium of Alexandria, in the presence of the assembled people. Antony solemnly proclaimed Cleopatra "Queen of kings," and Caesarion, who shared Ptolemaic kingship with her, "King of Kings". The three young children born to Antony and Cleopatra were made rulers of kingdoms set up for them among Roman conquests, present and future. Of the three, Alexander-Helios was to have Armenia and the territories beyond the Euphrates; Cleopatra-Selene was to rule Libya – Cyrenaica essentially; Ptolemy Philadelphus, the youngest, born of the reunion of his parents in 37, was to reign over Syria and Cilicia. A sort of Dionysiac triumph had preceded the proclamation. In it Antony, as the New Dionysus, had played the foremost part, with Cleopatra, the New Isis, at his side. The Roman leader was thus adopting the beliefs and customs of Hellenistic monarchies and populations, and abolishing the Roman provinces of Syria, Cyrenaica, and Armenia, turning them into kingdoms for his children's benefit. Alexandria became the center of the world that took shape as a result of these decisions. After one and a half centuries in which Rome had pulled down one after another the political structures of Alexander's empire and substituted for them her own undivided authority, a revolution was now occurring by Antony's will – perhaps implementing Caesar's designs, in part. The ancient dream of the Macedonian conqueror and of the Diadochi seemed to be resurrected from age-old oblivion. This was an opportunity for the Ptolemies' female descendant to be endowed, in the company of her newly chosen spouse (the valiant triumvir) and her children, with a quasi-universal monarchy framed within the boundaries of the eastern Mediterranean.

The dream was soon shattered. The Alexandrian entitlements became fodder for Octavian's propaganda, which raged against the unfaithful Roman deserting his country and his gods for a foreign woman. The formal repudiation of Octavia, which allowed him, by his marriage to Cleopatra, to legitimize the children she had borne him, provided a ready-made argument against Antony. Others were to be found in his will, deposited with the Vestals, which Octavian unscrupulously ordered to be opened. There he read that Antony viewed Caesarion as Caesar's sole heir, even though he, Octavian, claimed the inheritance of Caesar, his great-uncle. The fated outcome of that personal conflict was the passage, in the Senate, of a declaration of war against Cleopatra, in reality against Antony.

After two years' preparation on each side, the armies clashed at the frontier of the Greek and Latin worlds, at the edge of the Ionian Sea, near the Gulf of Ambracia dividing Acarnania from Epirus. Octavian, well advised by Agrippa, occupied Corcyra in the north and Patras in the south. Antony's camp at the head of the Gulf and his fleet (joined by the ships of Cleopatra, who was present in person) had great difficulty obtaining supplies. Battle was joined at sea, near the promontory of Actium, on the second day of September 31. The outcome was still in doubt when Cleopatra decided to flee, taking her ships with her. Noticing this, Antony turned round and followed her to Alexandria. He left behind his army and squadron. He thus conceded to Octavian a victory that had not been a foregone conclusion, but was to seal for centuries the fate of the ancient world. The date of the battle was, with good reason, chosen in many regions of the Roman empire as the starting point of a new era: it was the day of "Caesar's victory." Indeed it consecrated Octavian's triumph, the beginning of a new order. Concurrently, it signaled the collapse of the Oriental dream of Cleopatra and Antony, the end of what we call the Hellenistic age.

Let us consider briefly the defeated couple's last months. Plutarch's moving account, in his *Life of Antony*, is well worth reading. Octavian went back to Italy to deal with a revolt among his soldiers, and allowed the defeated enemy a year's reprieve. Deprived of the greater part of his troops – who, remaining near Actium, rallied to the victor's side – Antony was aware that, in the last analysis, he was personally responsible for the disaster that had befallen him. He fell into a melancholy state that might be called "romantic." He would sometimes remain alone, cloistered in a lodge within the royal palace: he called it the *Timonion*, after Timon of Athens, a famous misanthrope whom he wished to emulate by shunning human company. At other times he would try to drown his sorrow in a frantic round of pleasures, no longer those of the "Inimitable Life," but the diversion, in the strongest sense of the term, of "those who are to die together," as the two lovers now designated themselves. In the summer of 30 Octavian, coming from Syria, where he had landed at Ptolemais-Aké (St John of Acre), reached the neighborhood of Alexandria. Antony engaged in a hopeless encounter; he then committed suicide. Cleopatra, in her abiding anxiety to save at all costs her dynasty's last chance, for her own sake and her children's, tried to cajole Octavian. But her allure was powerless when faced with his cold ambition. As soon as she became aware of this, her only thought was to escape by self-inflicted death the humiliation of appearing in her victor's triumphal train. Her love affair with Caesar had started with the novelettish ruse of the rolled carpet in which she was concealed. In a similar vein, the queen's fatal liaison with Antony ended, when she was 38, in the stratagem of a basket of figs hiding a venomous asp. Some modern interpreters have chosen to find in her suicide by a serpent's bite a choice inspired by an Egyptian religious belief. According to that belief, whoever fell victim to the Naja – a serpent sacred to the god Amon-Ra, which appears on the Pharaoh's crown in the shape of the *uraeus* – became immortal and was admitted to divine rank. But the asp is not the divine cobra; and Cleopatra, already a goddess in the eyes of the Greeks owing to her royal position, had no need of such a contrivance to secure her apotheosis in the afterlife. From a simpler standpoint, more in tune with her nature, Plutarch describes her preparing for death with clear-headed attention to detail, faithful to her royal dignity, her thoughts turning in her last moments toward the man who had died before her, after having shared her fate to the bitter end.

Her death marked the disappearance of the last great Hellenistic monarchy. Her children met diverse fates. Caesarion died on orders from Octavian, to whose ambition he was an obstacle, being Caesar's son. Whatever happened to Alexander-Helios and Ptolemy Philadelphus, her two other sons, is unknown. Her daughter Cleopatra-Selene later married a Moorish prince, an erudite and learned man, Juba II of Mauretania: this explains the discovery, in his capital Caesarea (Cherchell in Algeria: see above), of the only authenticated effigy of Selene's mother. Egypt, stripped again of its external possessions, became in its turn a Roman province, but it received a special status. Octavian was specifically mentioned in it as the Ptolemies' successor. He was not to govern Egypt in virtue of his proconsular *imperium*, as was the case for the other provinces – the Senate entrusted him in 27 with responsibility for these (exercised through legates). His deputy in Egypt was a prefect, who administered the country in his name, as a viceroy would. Egypt was to be the *princeps'* personal realm, directly dependent on him. Apart from that exception, the global organization of the Roman East was in essence to keep under Octavian (on whom the name Augustus was to be conferred) the structures that Pompey had thought out, modified later by Antony's special arrangements (see pp. 160–1). Hellenistic life was to be prolonged within that institutional framework, under Rome's tutelage, throughout the centuries of the empire.

6/THE SURVIVAL OF THE CITY

The earlier chapters have shown the history of the three centuries before the Hellenistic period unfolding like a play in five acts. It opens with Alexander the Great's dazzling and short-lived venture. The plot thickens with the Diadochi's aborted attempts to preserve or revive the idea of a universal empire. It climaxes in the parallel, although varied, successes of the Ptolemies, Seleucids, and Antigonids, and of their less powerful imitators, like the Attalids or king Magas. A momentous turn of fortune is the arrival on the scene of a new actor, the Roman Republic, which deals repeated and decisive blows to the stability of the existing system. Finally, aided by internal factors speeding up the decay of the major states, comes the definitive victory of Rome. Amid the spasms of agony of an entire world, she erects a new order, heir to the old and destined to last many centuries. No doubt, when it comes down to details, the facts are extremely complex. The perspicacity and patience of scholars find in them an immense area of research, where discoveries are continually being made, allowing innumerable modifications of detail to be brought to the broad picture that has emerged. Yet we can stand back and see the essential web of events, and we may judge the major threads as definitive. The fundamental novelty of the age was of a political nature. The Greek world centered on the Aegean Sea and the Hellenic peninsula had hitherto lived in a political system organized around a cell of small dimensions, the city, many copies of which were engaged in constant rivalry. But then a totally different type of state imposed its presence: the monarchy. Its existence was based on the allegiance of vast territories to one man's authority; its *raison d'être* was to keep together and preserve in the same cohesive unit a number of communities with varied characteristics. The relatively short life of the majority of Hellenistic kingdoms, in a period of history singularly fertile in upheaval, should not obscure the strong impact that such a phenomenon had on contemporary mentality, the influence it exerted on ancient civilization, to a degree that we shall try to determine. We should realize that Athenian democracy lasted only one and a half centuries, from Marathon to Chaeronea: no more than the Antigonid or the Pergamene dynasty, far less than those of the Seleucids or the Ptolemies. In the development of the ancient world, the Hellenistic monarchy found ample time to play the capital role that present-day historians are right to acknowledge. Nevertheless, before we look at its mechanism and try to pinpoint its main characteristics, we should bring to light a fact that is too often disregarded, the survival of the Greek city within Hellenistic society.

It is a commonplace to insist, in describing that society, on the increasing importance of the individual relative to the civic community, as though the latter, having suffered deep-seated decay, stayed on as an empty shell. The history of that period does indeed exhibit a wide range of exceptional personalities – sovereigns, military leaders, adventurers, explorers, philosophers, writers, artists – whose glorious destiny or tragic fate seems to have taken place outside the aging limits of city life. Such individual independence was a novel phenomenon in the Greek world: we need to weigh its importance and its significance. But we would be wrong to draw the conclusion that the civic reality had been reduced to the dimension of a mere memory. The political game was indeed no longer dominated by cities, but by kingdoms. As a general rule cities, even when they were grouped in confederacies, would submit to the law of the mightiest, that is, of the states in possession of power. However, the novel phenomenon we have mentioned was verified in events of major importance, and in those turns of fortune that occupied the forefront of the world stage and are given pride of place in historical accounts. Yet, in the background, as far as the daily life of the immense majority of Greeks was concerned, the city remained and went on playing its part. It provided the environment in which ordinary Greeks lived their own lives, with their share of joys and sorrows, closely linked to the town's destiny, sharing its misfortunes and its prosperity, venerating the memory of ancestors, and finding in the civic community the means to realize their own ambitions. In this respect epigraphy has an important contribution to make. Thanks to the multitude of inscriptions at our disposal, and especially of honor-granting decrees that have reached us in such large numbers, we are allowed a direct and immediate insight into the daily life of Greek cities, large and small. Thanks to them, we can see magistrates, notables, and members of commissions and councils doing their work. We can grasp the way in which their civic institutions functioned, gauge the effort that went into coping with internal or external difficulties, with the threat of war or penury, with internal dissension or interference from outside. Such an enormous mass of documentary evidence provides us with the means of putting the record straight whenever the surviving accounts of events on the international stage are skeletal or too summary. It makes us understand what once prompted a respected interpreter of this period to employ an apparently odd expression when he pronounced the Hellenistic period to have been "the Golden Age of the Greek City." It is excessive to speak of a Golden Age, since in that period, in contrast to the Classical Age, the cities did not make history. But they appear no less in history, as they remained after that period the basic element of the social structure, the community-wide cell that was the life of a whole civilization. For this reason, before we approach more specific aspects of Hellenistic life, we should first note the preservation, even the extension, of that asset of fundamental worth that is embodied in the Greek city.

■ *The Greek city in the Hellenistic age* ■ *Autonomy: an ever-living ideal, difficult of realization* ■ *Local problems: the example of Apollonia in Pontus* ■ *Honor-granting decrees: their value as documents*

The Hellenistic city preserved the main features of a city belonging to the Classical age. It was the organized shape of a human community bound together by a shared history, common myths and cults. Its center was a large or small town, to which a territory was attached, usually of modest dimensions. Institutions and laws governed it, and applied specifically to it. It had at its disposal means of defense that ensured its survival. Finally, it was recognized as a state by other states or communities.

The cities of mainland Greece and the islands continued to live with these characteristics bequeathed by the previous age, while rivalries between great powers subjected them to ill effects, from which they could not protect themselves. Such a situation certainly limited seriously their freedom of choice in positioning themselves in matters of foreign policy. It dictated, with no less harmful results, the management of their internal affairs, when a man's or a party's primacy was imposed from outside. It is true to say that there was nothing new in this. At the time of the struggles between Athens and Sparta, or between Sparta and Thebes, the allies of one or other of these dominant States were not free to decide on war or peace. Very often they had to agree in their internal affairs to the choice of the party or mode of government imposed by the state holding power over them. Total autonomy was then no more than an ideal, honored with difficulty the moment a crisis arose. The situation was not at all different in the Hellenistic period. Very few cities could afford to manage their affairs with only their own interests in mind. Most were usually obliged to submit to a more or less discreet form of control, if not of tutelage, even of subordination, by a major or minor power with authority in the area. That was often a sovereign whose states or network of alliances hemmed in the city's territory. It might also be, in Greece proper, the confederacy or league that tried to extend or preserve its hold on a geographical sector, and would not tolerate any secession or even a show of independence. In peripheral areas of Hellenism, it might be a barbarian monarch to whom an occasional tribute (even a regular one) had to be paid, earning his goodwill and protection. Finally, and more and more with the passage of time, Roman friendship had to be treated with special consideration. From one end to the other of the Hellenistic world, a whole system of highly complex relationships was built. These were known by the names of alliance (*symmachia*) or friendship (*philia*), ingredients of which are feelings (at least in words) like those of goodwill (*eunoia*), gratitude (*eucharistia*), zeal (*prothymia*), corresponding to a sort of code of honor and good conduct that governed interstate relationships. Of course such terms, such diplomatic phraseology disguised a mutual assessment of relative strength. But their common use by diverse partnerships in the political game conveyed a widespread preoccupation to acknowledge or assert a city's theoretical independence, even if the reality was of considerably reduced dimensions.

The problems facing a Hellenistic city – provided its interest did not clash with that of one of the major states – were not fundamentally different from those with which a city of Classical times used to be confronted. One example, taken from the history of Apollonia on the Pontus, will suffice to demonstrate the point. It was a city of modest size, fully representative of those urban communities that flourished from one end to the other of the Hellenistic world. It bore a name that was very common among cities. Its divine patron, Apollo, had played an essential role in colonization during the Archaic period, so that a number of colonies were placed under the god's patronage: so much so that it became customary, to differentiate between them, to add their geographical area to the name Apollonia. The one on the Black Sea had been founded by the Milesians at the end of the seventh century, on the Thracian coast (in present-day Bulgaria). It was one of a series of trading settlements that the great commercial center of Miletus had dotted along the coast all the way to the Danube delta. Istrus, in Dobroudja, was one, not too far distant from the mouths of the mighty river; Tomi (Constantza) was another, a little further south (there Ovid was exiled under Augustus and wrote the *Tristia* and the *Pontica*); yet another was Odessus (Varna) in Bulgaria. Apollonia was the southernmost of these Milesian cities. It was on the south side of the Gulf of Bourgas, and had in its turn founded on the opposite (northern) side of the gulf the small town of Anchialus, defended by a fortification. Megara had also founded colonies besides these Milesian settlements, on the western coast of the Black Sea. The most important of these was Mesembria, founded at the end of the sixth century somewhat north of Anchialus, by citizens of the Megarian cities on the Bosporus, Byzantium and Chalcedon. These cities, strung over 250 kilometers on a generally hostile coast, were exposed to the threatening proximity, even the exactions, of the barbarian principalities of the hinterland: the Getae in the north near the Danube, the Thracians or Celts in the more southerly region. Trading relationships and alliances had been formed between them: rivalries as well, in the unhappy tradition of Greek cities, which were a source of frontier disputes like those that the history of Hellenism displays everywhere. One of those conflicts is recalled on a graven stele, discovered about forty years ago. It has preserved for us the text of an honor-granting decree that the citizens of Apollonia passed in favor of a citizen of Istrus, who had put them in his debt when they were faced with very stressful circumstances. The recall of that episode, about which we possess no other source of information, allows us to realize in precise terms the mode of existence and the concerns of that small Greek town in the middle portion of the Hellenistic period. For the textual content and the style of engraving allow us to date the decree with some measure of probability – some time in the first half of the second century BC. Though one line was omitted at the time of engraving, and the account of the measures taken, originally appearing at the end, has been obliterated, we have here a document that on the whole can be read and translated without difficulty:

> The Council and the People have passed the following resolution, on the proposal of the Commissioners [*synedroi* in Greek]. The facts are as follows. The flat country beyond the Gulf [and the fort of Anchialus have been occupied by the Mesembrians], who, having opened against us undeclared hostilities, have perpetrated serious acts of sacrilege on Apollo's shrine and exposed our city to extreme risk. The Istrians, on the strength of a relationship of common descent, of friendship, and of devotion to our people, sent to our help a fleet of warships and troops, led by their admiral and commander-in-chief Hegesagoras, son of Monimus. That man of outstanding merit arrived in the war zone and saved the city, its territories and harbors, with our assistance and that of our allies. Again with our help and that of our allies, he regained by force of arms Anchialus, which the enemy had seized and occupied, and which he now caused to be razed to the ground. Furthermore, in the course of the naval operation against Anchialus, when the enemy attacked his fleet, Hegesagoras fought their superior numbers, gained the upper hand, and seized a ship with its crew – once more with our help and that of our allies. Similarly, during landing operations, he put his life at risk with more boldness than ever, and in all other actions he threw himself into the fight with no thought given to personal risk. He always met with success, and in these operations never failed to instill in his soldiers a high-spirited conduct that secured the desired result.
>
> WHEREFORE, so that the people may show its gratitude and pay tribute to great-hearted combatants: with Good Fortune's blessing, may it please the Council and the People to bestow praise on the people of Istrus, our friend, relative, and ally, for services rendered as recounted above, and first and foremost for having sent as their admiral Hegesagoras, son of Monimus; to restore the honors earlier passed in favor of the Istrians; furthermore, to award a gold crown at the Dionysia to Hegesagoras, son of Monimus; to raise in his honor a bronze statue standing fully armed on a ship's ram, and dedicate that statue in the shrine of Apollo the Healer, inscribing the present decree on the pedestal; to proclaim these honors as well in favor of Istrus, on the occasion of the games celebrated in that city.

Apollonia had thus been attacked, without a prior declaration of war, by its northern neighbor Mesembria: the attacking party had laid hands on Anchialus, which shared a frontier with its territory, while the whole breadth of the Gulf separated Apollonia from that town. The Mesembrians, taking their unsuspecting neighbors by surprise, had occupied Anchialus' small fort. With that initial advantage, they went on to ravage Apollonia's territory, desecrating Apollo's shrine, situated (according to Strabo) on an island in the Gulf. The Apolloniates were obviously on the verge of ruin as a result of that invasion. Indeed, the city felt secure behind its walls, for a siege was a sizable undertaking, demanding considerable forces, equipment manned by experienced personnel, and time. It was nevertheless cut off from resources essential to its survival. These came from its territory and from the fisheries and salt-works of the Anchialus area. Nor could it draw any longer on the economic advantage stemming from control of the Gulf of Bourgas, where it could levy taxes on commercial transactions with the hinterland, involving, for example, the produce of the Thracian mines (iron, lead, copper) and various types of timber. We find here an illustration of the vital importance for these small Greek communities of a continental territory that was a dependency providing them with sustenance. Hence the fierce rivalries that pitted against each other cities sharing a frontier, in their eagerness to extend their small territory at the expense of their immediate neighborhood.

The citizens of Apollonia, whose forces were inadequate to the task of warding off the invasion, appealed for help in their dire circumstances to another city, Istrus. The bond between the two cities went back to their shared origin, as both had been foundations of Ionian Miletus. That meant a common participation in cults inherited from their mother city, like the one in honor of Apollo the Healer, coming from Apollo's great shrine at Didyma, near Miletus. It meant a common language as well, as both cities used the Ionian-Attic dialect, the mode of communication most in favor at the time: while Mesembria, a colony of Megara, used a dialect which included surviving Doric forms. Finally, evidence of their shared history has come down to us from the despatch, more than a century earlier, of a relief force from Istrus in the direction of Apollonia. We should be wary of finding a banal use of set verbal forms in the reference made by our text to the two cities' links of friendship (for these are attested by concrete facts), and of kinship. The latter ties were often kept alive by the memory of mythical genealogies, which in the eyes of the Greeks were the stuff, not of legend, but of history. The sense of a community of origin dating from a distant past was to them a heritage that they were not allowed to forgo.

Istrus, therefore, gave a favorable response to the appeal it received. As the territory of their common adversary, Mesembria, stretched along the coast between the two cities, and because of the distance from Istrus to Apollonia, help had to come by sea, under the protection of war-ships. An Istrian officer, Hegesagoras, was chosen, receiving the title of *nauarchos autokrator* ("Admiral and Commander-in-chief"), to lead the combined land and sea operations. Apollonia's forces (obviously less considerable than the expeditionary corps) were placed under the same Hegesagoras, as well as those of the other allies – contingents from Ionian cities in the area, or auxiliary troops provided by neighboring barbarian tribes. Operations on the periphery of the Gulf of Bourgas met with total success. They warded off any threat that hung over the territory of Apollonia and Apollo's shrine, recaptured from the enemy the area surrounding Anchialus, and chased them from the actual fort. It was deemed more prudent to destroy that stronghold, thus avoiding the eventuality of another Mesembrian invasion that would use it as a base of operations. Parallel to his action on land, Hegesagoras inflicted losses on the enemy fleet, confronting it in the Gulf. For Apollonia on the south side of the Gulf and Anchialus on the north side could more conveniently communicate by sea from the two harbors framing the peninsula of Sozobol, on which Apollonia was situated. The precise and detailed account of Hegesagoras' services, as given in our document, provides a clear picture of a localized conflict between two Greek cities on a vital frontier issue. It presents no radical innovation in comparison with the Archaic and Classical periods. Then as now, a similar conflict of interest would lead to similar physical clashes, in case arbitration failed to resolve the dispute. The policies of ancient cities were dominated by concern for the need to cope with a threat of that kind. They had to maintain armed forces manned by citizens, and especially (as we shall see) by mercenaries, keep their walls in good condition, build forts to keep watch over low ground, and provide them with permanent garrisons. They needed in addition to establish and preserve with neighboring cities, with monarchs, even with barbarian states, an active network of alliances that would discourage covetousness and ward off any hostile attempts. Mesembria's attack on Apollonia's territory amply illustrates a state of affairs that was common in the Hellenistic world.

The document is no less valuable as providing an example of the procedure that was followed, informing us as it does on the manner in which state institutions worked. As in all Greek cities, the Council and the People proclaimed the decree. These two institutions, the Assembly of Citizens and the Council (whatever the method of its recruitment), set up to draft and apply the Assembly's resolutions, continued, as they had done in the past, to manage the city's affairs. The text of the decree had been drawn up and prepared by a board, obviously less numerous than the Council, the Commission of the *Synedroi*, "those who deliberate together," a term that does not define its function. It may have been a board of magistrates, or an offshoot of the Council, a sort of permanent executive, as the *Prytaneis* were in Athens. The decree presents itself in the original as one long complex sentence, with parentheses (occasionally lapsing into *anakolouthon*) to bring out neatly, by an explicit syntactic link, the cause-and-effect relationship between services rendered and honors granted as a reward.

The first part, the more elaborate one, lists the grounds for the decision. It refers to the circumstances in which the person to be honored has benefited the city; and it might amount, as it does here, to a historical account, in a series of coordinate clauses all prefaced by a "Whereas." To the listing of concrete instances is added as a rule the record in general terms of the said person's merit – in fact such a record is in quite a few cases judged sufficient, without a need to add further particulars. After the grounds listed a clause is often found, introduced by "So that," expressing the people's wish to show gratitude to its benefactors, with a view to encouraging further such acts of devotion in the future. Hence the name of a *hortatory* formula, given to that part of the decree. Then, after an appeal to Good Fortune for her protection (a superstitious precaution which is certainly not a purely verbal habit), comes the equivalent of "Be it resolved." That is expressed as a wish, "May it please the Council and the People," the preamble to an enumeration of the decisions proposed to the Assembly by the movers of the decree. In the present case, these decisions are of two kinds. One refers to the people of Istrus: the Apolloniates bestow praise on them, that is, give them public thanks for their benefactions, especially for having put at their disposal the services of their admiral, Hegesagoras. This is used as an opportunity to reinstate undefined privileges that the city of Apollonia once granted the Istrians, privileges that had grown obsolete with the passage of time. The other set of decisions concerns Hegesagoras in person. A gold crown is bestowed on him, an exceptional honor in Classical times, which had then gradually become widespread, replacing the ancient crown of leaves. The Hellenistic age made more common use of precious metals, which were then in greater supply. Hegesagoras was to receive his crown at the feast of the Dionysia. The feast was at that time celebrated in all Greek cities. It was an obvious choice as the occasion for the proclamation of official honors, for the people gathered in the theatre to watch the essential element of the celebrations, their dramatic performances. Besides, a statue was to be erected in honor of the hero, showing him dressed as a warrior, on a base shaped like a prow. This was one fine example, among very many, of those statues that Hellenistic cities erected in their public squares and shrines to honor famous individuals in their lifetime. The shape of this particular pedestal, a ship's ram, is a reminder of Hegesagoras' naval victory. Many other similar instances are known, from various sites in the Hellenistic world – Thasos, Epidaurus, Cyrene: especially Samothrace with its famous Victory, which perhaps also dates from the first half of the second century. In much earlier times, the famous cenotaph that was erected in Babylon, on orders from Alexander the Great after his friend Hephaestion's death, bore, among other ornaments, prows on which stood statues of archers and hoplites. That motif spread, as can be seen from Africa to the Black Sea, via the Peloponnese and the islands. Hegesagoras' statue was to be erected, not in Apollonia's agora, but in the city's main shrine, that of Apollo the Healer. The temple already sheltered valuable works of art.

Among them was the cultic statue, the work of the famous sculptor Calamis, who flourished at the time of Phidias' youth. It was later (c.70 BC) to be removed by the Roman governor of Macedon, Marcus Terentius Varro Lucullus (brother of the consul who had defeated Mithridates), who dedicated it on the Capitol. No area of the Hellenistic world, however remote, was exempt from such looting of works of art – for the benefit of Rome!

Such were the honors that a grateful city bestowed on the Istrian admiral who had saved it from disaster. The end of the text, in the state in which it has come down to us, gives indications to the effect that those honors were to be proclaimed in his city of Istrus also, at the games which, as in all Greek cities, were an annual event. That was the usual arrangement whenever a citizen of one Greek state was honored in another: the latter made a point – something that the beneficiary himself no doubt took to heart – of seeing that his own city was made aware of the fame he had achieved. The custom therefore was for the proclamation of the honors, and the posting of the relevant decree, to take place in both cities – the awarding city and the recipient's. The duplication was a felicitous one in this particular case. No trace has survived of the monument raised in Apollonia in honor of Hegesagoras, but the stele raised at Istrus has been preserved.

■ *The city as the normal environment of human life* ■ *The world of Hellenistic cities: mainland Greece and the islands* ■ *The Anatolian cities* ■ *Syria; Cyprus; Cyrenaica* ■ *The western cities*

The case we have examined illustrates the importance of honorary decrees in providing information about the life of Hellenistic cities. Their proliferation in that age (contrasting with the previous one) can in part be explained, as will be seen, by the need felt by cities to appeal in a systematic manner for selfless devotion on the part of individuals. The cause of this was a decrease in public resources and a certain decadence of traditional institutions, which as a result worked less efficiently. Yet the abundance of these documents is evidence in itself, as would later be the case in the Roman Empire, of the vitality of these civic communities, which continued to be the normal environment for the daily life of the vast majority of Greeks.

This goes without saying for Greece proper, where life went on as in the past, provided we take new factors into account. These are the rise of Macedonian power and the emergence of the Aetolian and Achaean Leagues. These changes in the distribution of the centers of power affected the foreign policy of the traditionally great cities, Athens, Sparta, Argos, Corinth, Thebes, or Chalcis. Nevertheless their buoyant, sometimes prosperous, mode of existence continued (as witnessed by their monuments) within the framework of their ancestral laws. These might be in abeyance during a period of tyranny, but were never challenged. The cities we have mentioned never again occupied an outstanding position in the field of international politics. But they still had their say, and the very hardships that war brought on them are evidence of their willingness to play a part in the great conflicts of the time. While these former front-rank entities had been divested of their power (though still keeping the aura of their days of glory), other cities that had been less illustrious, if not totally devoid of luster, came to the fore and achieved prominence. This was the case with Sicyon, Aratus' city; of Megalopolis, Arcadia's great city; of Messene, where construction programs were regularly carried out in the area round the agora. Elis increasingly won prestige for its conscientious and loyal discharge of its responsibility for the shrine and the games of Olympia. Two cities of Achaea deserve special mention. One was Aegium, the seat of the federal shrine, which replaced Helice, destroyed in 373 by an earthquake. The other was Patras, a town of modest size, soon promoted to the rank of a major port, the main city in the Peloponnese, owing to the increasing importance of connections with Italy and the western seas.

In continental Greece, Megara, with Nisaea, its harbor on the Saronic Gulf, and its two links with the Gulf of Corinth, Pagae and Aegosthenes, benefited from the destruction of Corinth in 146 (see p. 130) and made the most of its friendship with Macedon. In Boeotia a number of cities flourished besides Thebes, whose dominant situation remained undisputed. Among them was Tanagra, reputed to be the most welcoming of cities to foreign visitors, and Thespiae, which prided itself on the possession of Praxiteles' and Lysippus' famous works, and the presence on its territory of the very ancient shrine of the Muses, in a valley on Mount Helicon. There was also Chaeronea – Sulla spared it after his victory over Mithridates; Lebadeia (now Livadia) as well, where the very special oracle of Trophonius was quite famous in those days. In Phocis, Apollo's shrine at Delphi was still amazingly prosperous in the third century, under the Aetolian League's control. Never before had its pious foundations and celebratory monuments been so numerous or so richly endowed. Even the Roman authorities were pleased to honor and protect the Delphic god, until Sulla's troops ravaged the city in 86: a blow from which it was never to recover. West of Phocis, the small towns of western Locris, isolated in the midst of their mountains, felt rich enough in the Hellenistic period to surround themselves with elaborate – and costly – fortifications, about which recent research has yielded more information. From Chaleion (modern Galaxidi) to Naupactus they rose here and there over an undeveloped area which previously had hardly figured in Greek history. The same applies to the vast mountainous districts of Aetolia and Acarnania, stretching north of the

Gulf of Patras over the basin of the mighty Achelous, rightly considered preeminent among rivers because of its abundant water. This is a land of ancient legends (like that of the Calydonian boar), which other Greeks hardly ever visited in the Classical period, save for a few expeditions, devoid of enduring results, aimed at Acarnanian centers of population. We have seen how that population of mountain-dwellers, hated and despised "for their inborn perverseness and insatiable cupidity" (to quote Polybius' phrase), organized itself into a powerful confederacy. Not only did it dominate the whole of central Greece and the Delphic shrine, but it intervened militarily in the Peloponnese and even in the Aegean Sea, so that the Antigonids, the Achaeans, and finally Rome had to take it very seriously into account. Its smaller cities have left no trace of their existence, but the stately ruins (with the remains of powerful fortifications) of Thermus, the Aetolians' federal capital, can still be seen. The same applies to Pleuron, not far from ancient Calydon, and to Acarnania's main city, Stratus – both strongly fortified. Further north, in the land of Epirus, which until then had stayed on the fringe of Greek life, Pyrrhus had transformed the humble rural town of Ambracia, on the river Arachthus, into his wealthy and well-designed capital. Near the seaboard, Ephyra raised in the third century a most curious oracular shrine, where questions were asked of the dead. In the very center of that same land, Dodona's ancient sanctuary found its heyday under Pyrrhus. On the Adriatic, the colonies of Apollonia in Illyria (the starting point of the *Via Egnatia*) and Epidamnus (later called Dyrrachium, modern Durazzo) led a peaceful life, in spite of the Illyrian Wars, until Imperial times: they had agreed to Roman domination, but their Greek way of life remained untouched. In what is now Corfu, the ancient city of Corcyra preserved its traditions as well as its pride, on which a popular saying quoted by Strabo remarks with Aristophanic verve, "Free Corcyra! You do your thing, wherever it pleases you."

In northeastern Greece, Macedonian predominance did not in any way prevent the ancient cities of Thessaly, like Larissa or Pharsalus, from staying prosperous, thanks to that region's agricultural strength, and retaining the kind of provincial flavor inherent in the ancestral beliefs of that cradle of Hellenic mythology. In neighboring Magnesia by contrast, Demetrias, founded by Poliorcetes, was not only a stronghold and a military harbor of extraordinary importance, but also a great cosmopolitan city. An abundant series of painted funerary *stelai*, unique in the Greek world, allows one to grasp the amazing diversity of its ethnic components. In Macedonia proper, at the heart of the kingdom, sovereigns favored the development of cities on the pattern of Greek ones: like Dion, Pydna, or Pella the capital, where luxurious houses have been brought to light by excavation in the last half-century. Better still, they founded new cities, following the example of Philip II's establishment of Philippi near Mount Pangaeus. Instances of these are Thessalonica, whose site was Cassander's inspired choice; or the town of Cassandreia, which the same king settled in Chalcidice, on the isthmus leading to the peninsula of Pallene, on the site of ancient Potidaea. Amphipolis on the Strymon, endowed with ramparts which are now being studied, remained the metropolis of the Thracian part of the Pangaeus, and was home to workshops where the splendid coinage of Philip V's reign was minted. Among adjacent islands, Thasos has a wealth of memorials of the Hellenistic period; and in Samothrace, the shrine of the Cabeiri reached the peak of its fame.

Further south the large island of Euboea, controlled by the Antigonids from the stronghold of Chalcis, had two thriving cities: Eretria, whose ruins are now being cleared by Swiss archaeologists, and in the north Oreus, which kept watch on the northern access to the Euboean channel. Among the Cyclades, united for a time (see p. 49) in a League of Islanders (*Nesiotai*), Delos, after being independent until 167/6, became an Athenian colony. It then knew the most distinguished period of its history, outshining even the brilliance it had derived from its sanctuary in Archaic times. There was a wave of public and private building over the northern part of the island. Large numbers of offerings filled the temples, the free port was alive with a busy sea-trade. Paros, Melos, and Thera (Santorini) have preserved eloquent traces of their prosperity in the Hellenistic period. The two large Anatolian islands of Chios and Samos enjoyed in those days a well-deserved reputation as enchanting holiday resorts. Their wines were famous, their cultural life was never dormant. Further south Cos, the island where Ptolemy Philadelphus was born, was the seat of the most famous medical school in Antiquity, with Asclepius' famous shrine, built essentially between the late fourth and the late second centuries. Rhodes, with its satellite cities of Camirus and Lindos, was one of the liveliest centers of the Hellenistic world. Its prestige was a counterweight to that of the artistic and intellectual capitals of the time – Athens, Alexandria, Antioch, Pergamum. Closing the Aegean Sea in the south, the large island of Crete, a breeding-ground for mercenaries and pirates, kept up a close relationship with powers anxious to make use of its archers or to establish bases for their fleets on its coast. Its numerous small cities, sometimes grouped in modest regional confederacies, had a very buoyant civic life, attested by a great variety of coinage and an abundance of inscriptions.

This brief review of the geographical layout of traditional Hellenism shows that Greek cities in the Hellenistic period showed no signs of belonging to a decadent society. They preserved an undying vitality in spite of the trials inflicted on occasion by war or the demands of the powerful: which shows that the civic framework had lost neither the advantages associated with it, nor its moral integrity. This statement proves even more true when the areas to which Hellenism had spread are considered. It had been implanted in days long past, or had been imported by Alexander and his successors, as happened in the Seleucid and Lagid empires, or was a further expansion of the Greek model, as in the continental provinces of Anatolia. In all cases the ancient cities almost invariably seem to survive, and often to prosper. Cyzicus on the Propontis (Sea of Marmara) is one

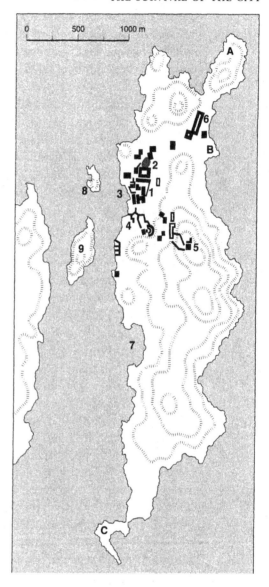

Map 9(a)   Delos, focal point of the Cyclades.

This map illustrates the central position of Delos, which had fostered since Archaic times its role as the Ionian islanders' common sanctuary (and ca. 314 won for the island the leadership of the League of the Islanders). Hellenistic trade gave the island prominence in the warehousing and redistribution of goods. Its position answered the need for shipping to avoid the high seas and find shelter in case of a sudden storm (see Map 9b).

Map 9(b)   Delos.

1. Apollo's shrine. 2. Sacred Lake. 3. Commercial harbor. 4. Theater district. 5. Summit of Mount Cynthus. 6. Stadium area. 7. Bay of Phourni. 8. Lesser Rheumatiari. 9. Greater Rheumatiari. A, B, C. Supposed lighthouse locations.

Between the eastern peninsula of Rhenea island and the western coast of Delos, the north-south channel separating the two islands affords mooring sheltered from northern blasts by the two Rheumatiari islands.

example. Another is Byzantium on the Bosporus, one of the rare cities to have succeeded in staying totally independent of the great kingdoms, and later to have preserved its neutrality vis-à-vis Rome. Round the Black Sea, we may add three colonies, situated on the north coast, to the ones already mentioned on the Thracian coast and in the neighborhood of the mouths of the Danube. Archaeologists have extracted from them an abundance of documentary evidence dating from the Hellenistic period. These are Olbia, better known as a result of recent studies; Chersonesus, which gave itself a constitution imitating Athenian democracy; and Panticapaeum, capital of the kingdom of the Cimmerian Bosporus, in the Tauric Chersonese (the Crimea), with its annexe Myrmecium, recently explored. On the south coast was the important port of Heraclea Pontica, a center of tuna fishing and an independent city within the kingdom of Bithynia. There were also Sinope in Paphlagonia, which was one of the capitals of the kingdom of Pontus and where the philosopher Diogenes and king Mithridates Eupator were born; finally, lovely Amisus, and Trapezus with its proverbial wealth. These were the principal outlets on the sea at the disposal of the Anatolian states. The latter were not short of new towns inland. Nicomedia, founded in the second quarter of the third century by king Nicomedes I (see p. 76), was reputedly one of the finest cities of the Hellenistic world, whose monumental beauty was second only to that of Athens. Nicaea, founded by Antigonus the One-eyed and renamed by Lysimachus after his wife's name, was to preserve its fame until the Byzantine era. The geographer Strabo describes with enthusiasm Amasea, the principal town of the Pontus, where he was born. Important remains of that city have survived.

The western coast of Anatolia was an ancient Greek territory that Alexander freed from the Achaemenid yoke. Antique Ilium, reduced by that time to a minuscule rural community, was set up as an independent city by the Conqueror, who had stopped there to pay his respects to Achilles' tomb and Athena's local sanctuary. Following his example, right down to the end of Antiquity, there was no end of tourists and pilgrims, all participants in Homer's cult, processing in the Greek town that had been rebuilt on the very site of Troy (see p. 316). Pergamum, in the Caicus valley, owed its splendour and prestige to its status as the capital of the Attalid dynasty. But it was also a Greek city, with its institutions and its magistrates, acting as relays in the exercise of the sovereign's authority. How far Hellenism penetrated is attested in the hinterland, on the road to Sardis, by the city of Thyateira. On the Aeolid coast, Myrina was prosperous enough to develop the most important terracotta workshop known as belonging to that period. Dominating the rich Hermus valley, at the foot of Mount Sipylus, the town of Magnesia under Sipylus, founded by Alexander, developed brilliantly up to Roman Imperial times. Further east Sardis, once the capital of the Lydian kings and the Achaemenid satraps, became a Greek city in those days, famous for its shrine of Artemis. The great cities of Ionia, which had languished under Persian domination, regained, from the third century onward, the brilliance and prestige that had been theirs in the Archaic period, before they were conquered. Smyrna and Ephesus were refounded by Lysimachus, and again became splendid, wealthy, and dynamic cities, in spite of being affected by the varied turns of the great powers' political fortunes. Erythrae had a close relationship with the neighboring island of Chios. Colophon's prosperity resulted in the development of Apollo's oracle at Clarus, situated on its territory, as excavations have proved. Near the mouth of the Maeander above the plain was the terraced city of Priene, a typical Hellenistic town, built on a rational plan (see pp. 265–6) and generously endowed with freshwater fountains. On the opposite side of the gulf, the rebuilding of antique Miletus had started in the middle of the fifth century, on plans drawn up by Hippodamus, and proceeded in accordance with them (see pp. 264–6). She was at the same time a major trading port, with marketplaces close to the quays of her two main harbors, and a city rich in magnificent monuments. Adjoining these at some distance in the same neighborhood were those of the great shrine of Didyma, with its oracle of Apollo. Inland up the Maeander valley, Magnesia on the Maeander and Tralles, renamed Seleucia on the Maeander by Antiochus I, formed the most lively centers of Hellenic influence in that age.

In the south of Ionia, Caria was a land where for ages Greek cities had lived in contact with an indigenous population speaking a very ancient Asianic tongue, which remained in use until the first century BC. Halicarnassus, a prestigious principality under the dynast Mausolus, was in the fourth century an early model of a distinct type of Hellenistic State. Alexander's conquest quickened the process of Hellenization in that land. Numerous towns took shape: inland, Alabanda, Mylasa, Stratonicea in Caria (with its famous shrine of Hecate at Lagina), later Aphrodisias; on the coast, Iasus, Halicarnassus, Cnidus, Caunus. Because of its geographical position, this area had a close relationship with the neighboring islands of Cos and (especially) Rhodes.

The situation of Lycia was somewhat analogous. It too was mountainous, and inhabited by a native population with its own language and civilization. There too the Hellenizing process spread fast: a federation of twenty-three cities, headed by the most important of them, Xanthus, managed to keep its independence almost without interruption, all through the Hellenistic period. Calynda, Tlos, Telmessus, Oenoanda, Phaselis were the main settlements. Xanthus was clearly preeminent among them in the Greek world because of its shrine of Leto, mother of Apollo and Artemis, who, according to a certain legend, were born there and not, as generally agreed, on the island of Delos. Excavations have been in progress for half a century, bringing to light its cultic monuments. Further east, on the Pamphylian coastal plain, Attalus II founded in a distinctly favorable location the port of Attaleia, destined to become in modern times the most important town of the area – Adalia. Inland, Termissus, Perge, Aspendos have left impressive remains; likewise Side on the coast. In neighboring Cilicia, where Alexander, and then the Seleucids, zealously founded cities in large numbers, Tarsus, on a small coastal river (the Cydnus), shone brightest among them. Antony summoned Cleopatra to that city; there he succumbed to her charms. On the coast the port of Soli, namesake of another city in Cyprus, produced two famous philosophers, the Stoic Chrysippus (see pp. 346, 371) and the Peripatetician Clearchus (see p. 322), as well as the poet Aratus (see p. 89). Tigranes destroyed it, but Pompey resettled it under the new name of Pompeiopolis. He brought ex-pirates there, who were to start a normal life in new surroundings.

All the coastal regions of Anatolia, on the Black Sea in the north, on the Aegean in the west, facing the Cyprus channel and the eastern Mediterranean in the south, were thickly scattered with Greek cities. Some were ancient ones, but the foundation of others was of a more recent date; all were lively and buoyant communities, and they made Asia Minor in the Hellenistic age, and later in the Roman period, a privileged area of Greek civilization. Even the interior – Phrygia, Pisidia, Lycaonia, Galatia, Cappadocia – regions difficult of access, peopled with indigenous barbarians or invaders like the Galatians, though less well endowed by nature, became gradual recipients of Hellenic influence. Still more cities were planted in these territories: from them the Greek language and way of life spread abroad. Some of these cities were foundations of the Seleucids or Attalids, from whom their names were derived: examples were Antioch or Seleucia in Pisidia, Apamea *Kibôtos* ("The Casket"), Laodicea in Lycaonia, Eumeneia in Phrygia. Others owed their development to local dynasts: Ancyra (Ankara), for example, capital of the Tectosages, a Gallic tribe; or the Cappadocian towns founded by the thoroughly Hellenized kings of the Iranian dynasty, who reigned in that mountainous and remote area.

At the heart of the Seleucid empire, in northern Syria, important cities were growing fast around the capital, Antioch on the Orontes, adjoining which was Apollo's magnificent shrine at Daphne. On the coast were Seleucia in Pieria, serving as the capital's maritime outlet, and Laodicea. Inland was Apamea on the Orontes; on the Euphrates were another Seleucia and another Apamea, as well as the Macedonian colony of Doura-Europus, founded in the reign of Seleucus I, the development of which took place for the most part in later times. In Phoenicia and Coele-Syria, the ancient Phoenician cities of Byblos, Berytus (Beirut), Sidon, Tyre (rebuilt with Carthaginian aid after its destruction by Alexander) became Hellenized. Such was the case, in the interior, of the caravan city of Damascus, and, further south, of Gadara, birthplace of the Cynic philosopher Menippus, Diogenes' peer, and the epigrammatic poets Meleager and Philodemus. We have already seen how the Jews of Jerusalem, for all their anxiety to keep their traditional religion and ethnic heritage, had been influenced by Hellenism.

No further mention will be made here of Alexander's numerous foundations. Those of the Seleucids in Mesopotamia and beyond are directly connected with that dynasty's policy, and will be considered when we deal with it. Similarly, the three Greek cities of Egypt will find their place within our treatment of the Ptolemaic empire. It is appropriate, on the other hand, in the course of the present brief review of Hellenistic cities, to speak of the Ptolemies' external possessions in Cyprus and Libya. On the island of Cyprus, where the Phoenician and Greek populations remained closely intermingled, the various cities were grouped in a league, which was no hindrance, however, to the exercise of Ptolemaic authority. The region bore the clear imprint of Hellenism, both in towns with a Greek tradition, like Salamis or Paphos, and in those where the Phoenician element was still visible, like Amathus or Citium. From the latter city came the founder of Stoicism, Zeno (see p. 89), a man of Phoenician origin: a notable example, among many others, of Hellenism's power of assimilation. Cyrenaica, in principle under Ptolemaic domination, still remained divided into four, later five, Greek cities. These were Cyrene, whose port became an independent city, but only in the first century before our era, under the name of Apollonia; Ptolemais, which replaced Barce under Ptolemy III and prospered; Taucheira, renamed Arsinoe; and, finally, Berenice, built close to ancient Euhesperides. In the third and second centuries all of them were blessed with a prosperity of which monuments and inscriptions provide abundant evidence, an extension without a break of the splendor of earlier days, dating from the time when colonies were founded in the area. Recurring attacks by pirates, in the first half of the first century BC, eventually disturbed for a while what had hitherto been for the Greek cities of Libya a faultless record of success. Rome took advantage of that circumstance.

Hellenism was less fortunate in the West than in Asia or Africa. The relentless growth of Roman power quickly put an end to internal disputes that brought division among the cities of Magna Graecia: after Pyrrhus' failure, the fall of Tarentum in 272 marked the end of their independence. That city's fortunes again attained some vitality in the third century. But after falling again under the blows of Rome in 209, during the second Punic War, it never recovered. Yet the Greek tradition lived on in Campania, around Neapolis (Naples), bound since 327 in fealty to Rome: it manifested itself especially in architecture, in the decoration and furniture of the neighboring towns of Pompeii and Herculaneum, borrowing, with hardly any obvious changes, from the Hellenistic heritage. In Sicily, Syracuse was indebted to the tyrant Agathocles, then to king Hiero II and his prudent policies, for retaining its prestige and wealth in spite of the twofold menace of Carthage, then Rome. But, after its sack by Marcellus in 212, the city no longer played any notable role. Agrigentum suffered a similar fate: rebuilt in the fourth century by Timoleon after its destruction by Carthage, it preserved its Greek institutions until 210, when it fell to Roman troops. However, in the Roman province of Sicily, Greek culture was very much alive in the first century BC, when Diodorus, hailing from the small town of Agyrium, right in the middle of the island, wrote in Greek the forty books of his *Historical Library*.

At the terminal point of this review of Hellenistic cities, attention should be drawn to the importance of Marseille, which managed, until its conflict with Caesar in 49, to retain Rome's friendship. It exercised an enduring influence in the western Mediterranean, with its colonies on the coast of Gaul and Spain, from Nicaea (Nice) and Antipolis (Antibes) to Emporium (Ampurias). That great city, whose aristocratic constitution was famous and survived unbroken through the centuries, kept a constant relationship with the eastern Greek world, priding itself on its Phocaean origin. In spite of its distant location, by its contacts with Liguria, Gaul, and Iberia, it ensured the continuity of Hellenism throughout the Hellenistic period.

■ *The city's social fabric* ■ *Slaves: their living conditions* ■ *The procedure of emancipation*

All these cities, both in Greece proper and within the extensive realm of colonial Hellenism, stayed faithful in essentials to the traditional principles of a political system which had, through the centuries-old experience of generations, gradually molded the inherently Greek shape of a State. The reality of civic life, as it had manifested itself in so many communities of various kinds, had provided an object of reflection to philosophers. Most important, at the dawn of the Hellenistic age, it had been the raw material from which Aristotle (using the prodigious documentary evidence put together by his pupils in 158 monographs on the history and constitution of Greek cities: see p. 354) wrote his *Politics.* Insight and clarity of thought are the hallmarks of this work. Written in the time of Alexander, it studies the characteristics and effects of the various regimes that may belong to a city: for Aristotle has no idea of any other form of state, at least for a Greek. His analysis is a priori relevant to all those civic communities that, in the Hellenistic era, prolonged the life of the city format or resurrected it. Such permanence and continuity find a signal illustration in a work that was written at the turning point between the Classical age and its successor.

Before as well as after Alexander the social fabric, in each of these small states, was made up of three traditional components: citizens, resident aliens, and slaves. On the slaves rested a major part of the burden of the irksome tasks on which the economic survival of the city depended. These included the exploitation of the soil (a task with demands exceeding the capabilities of the freeborn owners of smallholdings) and the mines (where slave labor was by far predominant); and the running of workshops and factories (where free artisans rarely managed without slave help). Let us state a caveat that will often apply: in economic or demographic matters, the dearth of statistical data in the study of Antiquity means that any evaluation must be largely subjective. The historian is forced to extrapolate from rare and sometimes hardly relevant texts or epigraphic evidence (accounts, contracts, schedules of conditions), which constitute heterogeneous and widely dispersed material. These fleeting glimpses may encourage the hope of having discerned a trend, or having established an order of magnitude. Such conclusions, nevertheless, should always be looked on as tentative and subject to revision. It would appear that, with the exception of the Seleucid and Attalid mines and royal domains, there was nowhere any large concentration of slaves. Yet the total number of such workers probably increased from the second century onward: a result, on the one hand, of events connected with war, and of piracy on the other. It is known that from the earliest times it was invariably the custom in the Greek world to sell into slavery the survivors of a town conquered after a bitter struggle. Prisoners of war, fighters or not, belonged to the victor, unless an agreement before defeat guaranteed them safe passage and freedom. Yet that cruel law of war, while it never disappeared, had in practice undergone some alleviation: wholesale executions, like the one perpetrated in 335 in Thebes by Alexander (see pp. 9–10), stand out as exceptional. Roman expeditions in Greece proper led to more than one case of a similar penalty. Instances include the auctioning of Epirotes from seventy rural settlements in 167, on Aemilius Paullus' way back to Italy, or that of Corinthians by Mummius in 146; or, again, many reprisals by Sulla's troops in Greece proper during the war against Mithridates. As a matter of fact, Aratus' Achaeans were no less ruthless toward Mantinea in 222, and the Athenians behaved no better in Oropus. It would be wrong to attribute exclusively to Roman inhumanity conduct basically consonant with the most ancient Hellenic tradition. Whatever may be the case, these huge auction sales, joined with the progress of piracy from early in the second century onward, provided slave markets, like those of Delos or Side in Pamphylia, with an abundance of chattels. There one could find slaves of Hellenic origin, side by side with barbarian slaves (formerly the most common kind), put up for sale in increasing numbers.

Besides providing hard labour, slaves were indispensable if all domestic tasks were to be performed. A household without slaves could hardly be imagined. Without their help it would have been almost impossible to cope with those tiresome tasks that required manual work, given the rudimentary state of existing techniques. One had to go out for one's daily water supply, to obtain and prepare necessary food, to weave most of the clothes and household linen, to watch and look after the children. These added up to more than the ordinary housewife could handle. From that point of view, slavery was a necessity of social life. Servants, male and female, belonged to the family cell, which could not survive without them. No doubt their tasks were often unpleasant: pounding grain in the mortar, turning the millstone, even spinning a fixed amount of wool were elements of a laborious day. Other duties nevertheless were more varied and imposed fewer constraints. These included going out with the master or mistress, taking the boys to school, baby-sitting, shopping, delivering messages. On occasion a slave, if qualified for the job, could also act as a secretary, keep accounts, read aloud, even play a musical instrument. Such duties might offer an opportunity, for those able to grasp it, to create a master–servant relationship marked not only by command and obedience, but also involving cordiality, trust, even esteem and affection. We find ample evidence of such occurrences in the New Comedy of Menander and his fellow-writers, as well as in the plays of Plautus and Terence – these translating into the Latin tongue the inspiration they had derived from it. The behavior of slaves follows diverse patterns: some are cowardly, lazy, and deceitful; others are keen-minded, resourceful, and devoted to their master; similarly we meet with the zealous maidservant or the faithful nurse. They fore-shadow the cunning chambermaid and manservant of classical French comedy.

The fact remains that the life of a slave had an element of bondage, which a trend toward a more humane attitude never managed to eradicate. Corporal punishment was deemed necessary, because loss of freedom resulted in a lower-ing of moral integrity. Shackles were the penalty of serious misdemeanors; tor-ture was used on slaves asked to bear witness. Legal provision might reinforce the constraint of mores in the prevention of abuse, and as a means of protecting the slave population from excessive or unwarranted harshness. Yet the norm was the master's will: that was especially the case in the treatment of women slaves, who were hostages to their buyer's whim. The New Comedy highlights a situa-tion typical of this age. In a frequent scenario, a trafficker, who plans to use her for prostitution, has bought a freeborn young woman exposed by her parents or taken captive by bandits, pirates, or a victorious enemy. A freeborn young man, seduced by her charm, wishes to have her as his own. A dramatic turn of events is needed, a moment of recognition imagined as a last resort by the writer, to save the hapless maid from a lamentable fate.

By an accelerated recourse to emancipation, the Hellenistic period appears to have found its own solution to the problem of slavery. Buying back a slave with liberation in mind had always been an available course. That had been, as is well known, Plato's case in 388, thanks to the intervention of Anniceris of Cyrene. We have many instances of such generous conduct in the Hellenistic cities, where the redemption of prisoners of war by a fellow-citizen or a wealthy stranger is some-times mentioned in honorary decrees. Besides, a slave-owner might no doubt grant freedom, in his own lifetime or by his will, to a servant who had won that reward by his devotion and loyalty. In exceptional circumstances global emancipation took place, for example, when slaves enlisted to serve in the army side by side with free men, at a time when troops were in short supply, had given a good account of themselves in battle. The people would on that occasion grant them freedom by passing a decree listing the names of the beneficiaries. It sometimes seemed desir-able, as a protection for the freedman against a frivolous challenge, to transcribe for public viewing on a stele the actual document that had been drawn up. An-

The political organization of cities underwent no radical change after Alexander. As described above from the example of Apollonia on the Pontus, the popular Assembly and the Council (whatever the diverse designations of those two institutions) remained everywhere the two basic instruments of the State's authority, with the magistrates constituting the executive. We find Aristotle noting that individual constitutions hardly ever conformed to a typical regime in an undiluted form, say democracy or aristocracy (which, based on inherited nobility, was then hardly distinct from oligarchy, founded on the power of money: in actual practice they were indistinguishable). Most cities had a mixed regime. Depending on circumstances, that regime tilted one way or another. It might lean toward popular power exercised by the leaders of the "populace" (ancient historians are prone to employ in their designation of the masses a terminology with pejorative implications); or toward the authority of the well-heeled, who bestowed on themselves flattering appellations, like the "Good" or the "Honorable Ones." Within the extreme diversity of this sector of constitutional history, and in spite of the inadequacy of our sources, we may see, in a very limited manner, a trend of sorts. It would appear that in most cities, Athens included, a traditional order had usually been prevalent, based on respect for the "ancestral" laws, these essentially preserving the privileges of the wealthy class. Such a situation, naturally, did not preclude a number of popular outbursts, which could turn to rioting if a leader emerged who was able to channel them in such a direction. It was thus that Agathocles, who held the position of *strategos* in Syracuse, managed to seize power in 317/16 by fomenting against the ruling oligarchy of the Six Hundred a revolt of the lower classes, supported by the army, which soon turned to pillage and slaughter. External interference sometimes sharpened such domestic antagonism. This was the case, for example, at Cyrene in 322/1 during the Cyrenaeans' conflict with the *condottiere* Thibron, which ended, after a varied history, in the Lagid seizure of the land. Both the democrats and the party of the wealthy had tried to secure support from that adventurer, who was eager to conquer Libya. A good number of aristocrats then found shelter and protection from Ptolemy, whose general Ophellas, with help from those exiles, finally managed to beat Thibron and submit Cyrene to the authority of the satrap of Alexandria. The constitution that Ptolemy afterwards granted Cyrene, described in an inscription – a document of exceptional interest, incidentally – contained a remarkable provision. It did not limit itself to reinstating the exiles in their rights, and confirming for the future Ptolemy's control of the city's affairs, while granting him for life the title of supernumerary *strategos*. The main arrangements of public administration were indeed restored, in conformity with past usage. But the new constitution modified them in one important respect, by increasing tenfold the numerical strength of the body politic, which passed from 1,000 to 10,000 with full civic rights. The obvious purpose of that major concession to the people of Cyrene was Ptolemy's wish to respond to democratic demands and bring peace to the city. Such concern is not surprising, coming from a ruler endowed with his political skill. But it also illustrates an attitude toward the cities that was shared by Alexander and the Diadochi. It was dictated by no underlying sympathy with any political trend in constitutional matters, but only by circumstances and the monarch's immediate interest. We thus see Monophthalmus and his son Demetrius favoring the "freedom of cities" in official proclamations, and destroying in Athens the conservative regime of Demetrius of Phalerum, thus countering Cassander: while their successor in line, Antigonus Gonatas, willingly gave his support to local tyrannies suspending the practice of democracy. In a game of such complexity, where there were frequent clashes between factions which had no qualms about appealing for foreign help, princes made their calculated moves, directly or through the agency of their henchmen, with no thought of matters of principle. Their tranquil cynicism was a predominant feature of the times. But the varying directions their input could take prevented it from steering the constitutional evolution of cities in a systematic manner. For these on the whole responded to other forces, resulting from the slow transformation that society and the economy were undergoing.

No doubt the most important of these forces (at any rate the most evident) was linked with the question of balance in income distribution. The Greek world had always been composed of citizens who were wealthy, and those of modest means: that distinction depended on the size of landed property, the essential component of any fortune. Trade or a craft were the main source of income only in the case of a small number of people. They supplied only a supplementary income to most of those engaged in them. In the Hellenistic age, however, taking into account the strict limitations within which its economic phenomena are clearly visible in our day, one may say that profit from movable goods enjoyed considerable growth. It was, it seems, spurred on by the sudden expansion of trade in the direction of the Near and Middle East, fostered as well by increasing urbanization, both in Greece proper and in the new countries. Archaeological data and textual evidence demonstrate a spread of luxury; expensive food items were in greater demand, precious metals were more widely used than before. Such a trend to greater wealth is especially discernible in the third century, while in the second and first centuries the unrest and the wars attendant on the Roman conquest impoverished many cities. But even at that period one cannot speak of generalized economic decay. It happened nevertheless that such wealth gradually became concentrated in the hands of a small number of people. Landed property, the solid foundation of any personal fortune, seems to have evolved toward the format of large holdings. That was the result of the indebtedness of small landowners who mortgaged their property – and were deprived of it when they defaulted. In many cities in those days we find, rearing its head, an age-old agitation for the abolition of debt, which came with a demand for a new distribution of available land. Such was the case in Sparta in the third century, under king Agis IV. It was the same under Cleomenes III: the threat of such measures, even though this monarch did not implement them outside Sparta, prompted conservative forces in the rest of the Peloponnese to unite against him. A similar situation arose in Asia Minor. The usurper Aristonicus in his kingdom of Heliopolis or Sun-state (after the death of Attalus III of Pergamum in 133), then Mithridates (after the massacre in 88 of the Romans in Asia), proclaimed the abolition of debts, in response, obviously, to the wishes of a substantial part of the population. These events indicate a social tension between rich and poor, which after all rarely led to any open conflict or attempted revolution. We also find traces of it in the speculations of philosophers, notably among the authors of Utopias like Iambulus. The same can be said of certain literary works like the *Meliambi* of the poet Cercidas of Megalopolis. He was indeed in no way a revolutionary: he was his city's ambassador at the court of Antigonus Doson, and served as an officer at the battle of Sellasia. But, as a moralist influenced by Cynic thought, he lashed out at avarice and ostentatious wealth, and urged a generous sharing of unneeded possessions.

The imbalance of income between classes of citizens was to have an impact on the manner in which institutions worked, and on the very life of the city. It led more and more to the body politic shouldering the task of ensuring the survival of an increasing number of destitute citizens. This translated in concrete terms into State control of an essential food commodity, like cereals. There had been instances of that in the Classical age, notably in Athens. Now documents (in greater numbers indeed than before) disclose the presence of "Wheat Commissioners" in various cities. These magistrates had the duty of ensuring the supply to the community of that vital basic food. The arable lands of the community concerned, or its dependencies, would normally provide the necessary supplies. Thus for island cities like Samos or Rhodes: their possessions on the continent across the ocean – what came under the designation of the *peraea* – played the role of a granary and were consequently of vital interest to them. Others, whose territory was hardly fertile or too small, were dependent on imports, coming from producing countries like Egypt or Cyrenaica, often being moved through a redistribution market. Delos played the role of such a market, after the island had regained its independence (*c*.314: see p. 49). That became the source of its prosperity in the Hellenistic age. An honorary decree dating from *c*.230–220 gives a vivid picture of these commercial relationships. In this decree the city of Histiaea in the north of Euboea honors a Rhodian banker who has advanced interest-free money to the Histiaean Wheat Commissioners sent to Delos to buy cereals: the loan has allowed them to carry out their mission most expeditiously. The stele on which the decree has been transcribed, listing the honors bestowed on the generous Rhodian (public praise, a crown of leaves and the right of residence in Histiaea), was erected in Delos, thanks to an authorization granted by the Delians. We thus obtain a picture of exchange over a wide area, weaving relations of mutual interest and interpersonal ties between the cities concerned. That vast area extended from north to south of the Aegean, from the northern promontory of Euboea, then controlled de facto by the kingdom of Macedon, down to Rhodes, a powerful independent city, via Delos and the Cyclades, where Ptolemaic influence was predominant.

A city purchasing wheat must as a matter of necessity sell it to individuals, being careful not to allow free play to speculation, particularly in periods of penury. That was the case in Classical Athens, where *sitophylakes* (Wheat Commissioners) kept a close watch on the dealings of importers and retailers. In the Hellenistic age, states did not limit themselves to controlling the market, but were led by circumstances to make a free distribution of wheat to citizens, after acquiring it with public funds. A legal text from Samos in the second century BC sets out in every detail the machinery of such an operation. Thus did the solidarity of the members of the body politic assert itself, through a complex system of rules and guarantees. This did not lead to a relaxation of the civic bond, which on the contrary acquired a new strength. It now demonstrated its existence not only in the areas of religion and politics, but on the economic plane as well, at the level of daily life and through the supply of basic resources to the most disadvantaged.

The same concern for the public interest led cities to recruit public physicians from abroad, providing them with a salary. They would stay for a shorter or longer period in the host city, and give medical care to citizens and other residents. It would be wrong to compare what was a widespread custom in those days to modern social-security systems. The public physician could very well attend to the destitute and to war casualties without seeking payment; otherwise he would usually claim an honorarium from his patients. The wage that he received from the city's public funds was meant to make him a member of its establishment. It secured for its citizens the availability of a practitioner of the medical profession, at a time when doctors, save in a privileged city like Athens, were not so easily found. They came from the areas where they usually obtained their training, Cos or Cnidus, for example, close to the medical schools that were annexed to shrines of Asclepius. Whenever the public physician chose to return to the place he came from, the city that had benefited from his services made a point of thanking him by means of official honors, a copy of which was handed over to the doctor's city. A large number of these texts, transcribed on stone, have been found, giving us information about the activity of these specialists, whose services were in such demand, and who, in addition to the practice of their profession, gave lectures and demonstrations to share their knowledge with the public at large.

Their recruitment meant a considerable addition to the civic community's financial burden. The expenses that were traditionally incurred by a Greek city included the cost of cultic and civic ceremonies, of public and religious buildings and their maintenance. There was finally the military budget, made more and more onerous by an increasing recourse to mercenaries and the developing use of techniques of warfare. The state could rely on a certain range of resources to cope with such expenditure, among them levies and taxes, usually collected through a farming system, a convenient procedure alleviating the magistrates' workload, though the results were mediocre. These were as a rule indirect levies, raised on transfers of goods or funds or on certain activities. There was also a variety of tolls. We obtain a good idea of those sources of income from the case of Delos. In the period of its independence (between 314 and 166) the accounts preserved in inscriptions are numerous enough for that purpose, and record these categories of revenue. There we find taxes of 2 percent (*one-fiftieth*) on incoming or outgoing food produce, of 10 percent (*one-tenth*) on rents, wheat, fish – particularly the purple-fish caught around the islands – of 5 percent (*one-twentieth*) on sales. Tolls were raised on movements within the harbor, or across the straits separating the islands, or overland across the isthmuses on the islands. Some of those dues were raised for the benefit of the shrine, the others went to the city. All Greek cities used analogous methods to fill the state coffers. By contrast, direct taxation was not customary: as in the Classical age, it was used in exceptional circumstances, when citizens were asked for a monetary contribution. The wealthier citizens made an advance payment, and recovered it later from other taxpayers. That way of appealing in the first place to the affluent was akin to another procedure that was widely used to defray state expenses. That was the system of *liturgies*. It was still employed, as it had been in Classical Athens. It consisted, as is known, in entrusting an individual with the task of taking care, at his own cost, of a statutory public event. The distribution of such duties, the financial implications of which could be very heavy, was made among the wealthier citizens, charges being prorated on an individual's fortune. They dealt with a variety of interests. Defense was one of them: thus the liturgy called *trierarchy* consisted in fitting out a war vessel and maintaining it in fighting order during a campaign. The daily life of citizens was another: a *gymnasiarchy*, for example, consisted in administering the gymnasium where adult and younger men trained, providing them with certain necessities, for instance the oil needed for athletes' massages. Most important of all were the cults, an essential part of city life, also a cause of heavy expenses, entailed by religious ceremonies, sacrifices, games, theatrical performances. For all of these a request for aid from the wealthy, in the shape of *liturgies*, was common.

The three centuries preceding the Christian era witnessed an ever-sharpening distinction between the rich, on whom the major part of the State's financial burden rested, and the remainder of the population, unable to contribute other than collectively and in an anonymous fashion. The result in the long run was that the wealthy took over the magistracies as well, wherever these entailed heavy expenses on their holders – so much so that the difference between a magistracy and a liturgy tended to disappear, and that the working of civic institutions under any regime (those belonging to the democratic tradition included), depended in actual fact on devotion to the common cause among the foremost citizens. To balance its finances the Hellenistic city had regularly to appeal for generosity on the part of benefactors or *euergetai*, whether citizens or foreigners. They were rewarded with a variety of honors and privileges, a satisfaction for the donors' sense of their own dignity and that of their families – since these rewards could be passed on to their descendants. Discharging public duties, contributing to their fellow-citizens' wellbeing and to the beautification of the city: such was the chosen vocation, in each of these close-knit communities, of a few families having adequate means for such a purpose and enjoying widespread respect. They found an incentive in social pressure; honor-awarding decrees often included a turn of phrase that recalled how the praiseworthy deeds of the person honored conformed to his family's tradition, how his devotion to the State was the heirloom handed down by his forebears.

We are thus dealing with a society endowed with notables, where civic solidarity, which is real and manifests itself again and again most concretely through services rendered, gives a remarkable stability to the social order. The Hellenistic age, in spite of frequent wars and economic jolts, experienced on the whole less social struggle within cities than the Archaic and Classical ages. A distribution of tasks that in practice reserved public duties for the affluent, without depriving other citizens of their political rights and a voice in the assemblies, resulted in the disappearance of indemnities (*misthoi*). Democratic cities had instituted these to facilitate access by the popular classes to political or judicial responsibility. But, as it turned out, such heavy expense by the State seemed to serve no useful purpose when individual citizens were found to have the financial means to devote their time to public duties. That change of outlook was especially noticeable in the city of Athens, where, in the fourth century, democracy had put in place an elaborate system of remuneration to encourage citizens to take a hand in the workings of the administrative machinery provided by the constitution. Proponents of political philosophy looked upon the abolition of *misthoi* as a show of mistrust toward democracy, a step on the way to a conservative regime. It is not certain that the ordinary Athenian shared that feeling. It was evident to everybody that the institutions were still alive. The city was governed as before by its Council, the members of which were chosen from the traditional tribes, whose number had been increased by the creation of new ones: the Antigonis, Demetrias, Ptolemais, and Attalis. The addition of these tribes had resulted from new turns (in some cases short-lived) in international politics; it did not bring any essential modification of the system once set up by Cleisthenes. The magistrates kept their ancient appellations and prerogatives, account being taken of changes in matters of detail – those, for example, brought to the responsibilities of the *strategoi*, which were now clearly demarcated, while in the past they had been looked on as equal and interchangeable. Such alterations were hardly visible, and did not prevent Athenian citizens from considering themselves true heirs of their glorious ancestors.

They were no doubt aware that their city no longer possessed the political and military power that it had lost at the battle of Chaeronea, then in the Lamian and, finally, the Chremonidean Wars. But that same city retained its prestige as a

focal point of culture, the Greek world's intellectual center: witness an Amphictyonic decree dated 125 BC. In it the Amphictyons proclaim that: "The people of Athens has been at the very origin of the greatest benefits reaped by humanity, which it has led from a life of savagery to civilization." This it has done by acquainting humanity with the mysteries of Eleusis, which teach us the preeminent value of peaceful relations and mutual trust. The text goes on to say that Athens has handed down to mankind righteous laws inspired by the gods, and the principles of education. It has brought prosperity to Greece by revealing to her the science of agriculture, Demeter's bounty; it was the first to institute dramatic contests in honor of Dionysus. In composing its decree the Amphictyonic League, in which Athens was entitled to only one seat out of twenty-four, borrowed all these themes from the Attic orators' literary tradition: in part from Isocrates, who had expounded them with vigor in his *Panegyricus*. Their reappearance in a historical environment where Athens' political influence had become negligible reveals the persistence beyond its frontiers of a myth carefully nursed by the Athenians themselves, according to which Athens had been the school of Hellas, a model that all other cities should follow. It is no surprise to come across the same thesis in the next century, at the time of Caesar, in the historian Diodorus Siculus (XIII, 26–7), on the lips of a Syracusan. He attempts (in vain, as it happened) to urge his fellow-citizens not to treat the Athenian prisoners with excessive harshness, after their disastrous defeat before Syracuse. That was evidently a common rhetorical theme, a *topos* that had become familiar to all Greeks. Some, however, tried to balance praise and blame, by way of bringing some corrective to its perfunctory aspect as an academic exercise. So does Plutarch, in his *Life of Dio* (58, 1). "It would seem appropriate," he writes, "to say that Athens counts among her sons good men who practice virtue at its highest and evildoers actuated by the worst kind of perversity: just as her land produces the most exquisite honey, and the species of hemlock that brings on death most quickly." No doubt a balanced judgment, which expresses, at any rate, the admiration that an exceptional city still commanded.

■ *The evolution of political* mores, *hand in hand with the survival of institutions* ■ *Increasing role of women in public life* ■ *The sale of priestly offices* ■ *Citizenship rights for sale* ■ *Divine eponymous titles* ■ *The evolution of magistracies*

Very gradually indeed did the feeling of continuity that apparently had stayed unbroken amid the actions of Alexander, the Diadochi and their successors, and finally of Rome, give way to the consciousness of a serious change of direction in the course of history. Polybius contributed a great deal to this happening. We cannot know, on the other hand, if Diodorus was fully aware of such a change, given the almost complete disappearance of books XXI to XL of the *Historical Library*, dealing with the post-301 period up to the Gallic War. But in the second century of our era, Plutarch, then Pausanias, are fully conscious of it. It is true that by that time Greece proper was exhibiting a picture of decay in many areas, though not in Athens, Olympia, and Patras. Above all, these writers, conscious as they were of the events of war and their consequences, could not but take stock of Rome's total triumph.

A modern historian, by contrast, will try, using epigraphical evidence, to sense, beneath the formal survival of institutions, the signs of an evolution in political and social mores. New elements thus come to light, for example, the accession of women to public life, which would have been an object of scandal in the previous age, anxious as it had been to keep spouses in their *gynaeceum*, sheltered from the indiscreet glances of strangers. That was a consequence of the financial difficulties we have mentioned. A city did not hesitate to appeal to wealthy women, as it had done to well-to-do male citizens. It would of course entrust them, as it had done in the past, with positions in the cult of female divinities, as priestesses or *neocoroi* (responsible for maintenance of the shrine, for keeping the buildings and sacred appointments in good order). But as such duties entailed an ever-increasing contribution to the expenses that went with cult practice, they became open to none but wealthy women. When these had drawn generously on their personal funds in the discharge of their duties, it seemed normal for their city to show recognition by bestowing honors and distinctions on them. It was then that statues of draped women began to be erected in public squares and in shrines. Large numbers of these have been found, which archaeologists have great difficulty in dating, especially when (as often happens) their heads have been removed. It would appear that this participation by wealthy women in public life increased notably under the Roman empire. They would even take on actual magistracies, something unthinkable in the Classical age. One case, among others, is found at Cyzicus on the Asiatic coast of the Propontis, where a woman is mentioned as an eponymous magistrate, as a *hipparchus*. As this term's proper meaning is "cavalry commander," the situation would be paradoxical, unless the title borne by the eponymous magistrate had in that case lost its original sense and designated no more than a civil magistracy.

Another case of a woman her city wished to honor for services rendered is that of the Thasian Epié, in the first century BC. She had agreed to take up in Thasos all positions of *neocoros*, among others those of Artemis, of Aphrodite, of Athena, "even though, because of the cost to the holder of such a liturgy, women agreed only with reluctance to be *neocoroi*." She was later to build at her own expense a porch with marble columns to serve as an entrance to Artemis' shrine. She had accepted the position of priestess to Demeter and to Zeus *Eubouleus* ("Of Good Counsel") that no woman took up, "as it brought no income while entailing a heavy outlay" in ornaments and sumptuous raiment for the divine statues. She had consecrated rich offerings in these shrines. Finally, she had been able to help individuals in many ways. To thank her for having thus on every occasion "shown her zeal toward the gods and her fellow-citizens," the Council and People unanimously passed four decrees granting her various honors. These included a public eulogy and the right to inscribe a dedication in her own name on the porch and on the offerings the cost of which she had defrayed. Besides, she was granted the privilege of dressing in white, as a personal distinction, in religious ceremonies. Finally, she was designated as Athena's perpetual *neocoros*, whenever there was no other candidate for the office. The wording and the formulaic style of that decree are very similar to those of honor-granting decrees in favor of male citizens. It evokes her piety, her merit, her wisdom, her devotion, her zeal, her goodwill toward the people, her generosity toward individuals, "a conduct worthy of her ancestors' nobleness and the dignities" which they had earned for themselves: all terms that are found in epigraphic texts honoring *euergetai*. Toward the end of the Hellenistic age the city of Thasos, faced with difficult times, was eager to welcome spontaneous contributions coming from women as well as men, provided they gave the best of themselves and shared their material possessions with the state. Citizens of either gender could thus be counted as foremost members of the community.

Another method of bringing funds into the public treasury was to put up priestly offices for sale to the highest bidder. A number of contracts relating to these sales have survived. The sum paid could be high: one talent or two (6.000 to 12,000 drachmae) at Priene in 150–130 BC to become a priest for life of Dionysos *Phloios* (or *Phleôn*: "God of the Flow" of sap in plants and juice in fruit). The new priest was to receive various honors and privileges in exchange. These included reserved parts from every sacrificial victim (the animal's skin was ordinarily his), free board at State cost, a *proedria* (a place of honor in the theater) with a suit and wreath of a prescribed type, various exemptions from city charges (liturgies notably). The exemptions were graded according to the agreed price of the priesthood. This amounted, in a few words, to a candid recognition of the power of wealth in the State, especially in the realm of cults on which its cohesiveness depended.

An eagerness to make money out of everything sometimes led to auctioning what in Greek eyes was the most precious of possessions: the right to citizenship. In the Classical age that fundamental privilege had been jealously guarded, and had always been granted, as an exalted favor, on an individual basis only – except in very exceptional circumstances. In the Hellenistic period cities would sometimes agree, albeit rarely, to sell that right, so as to fill the public coffers in periods of financial distress, perhaps also to strengthen the body politic by selecting candidates in good standing. In the third century BC Thasos provides an apt illustration of that novel practice, with a decree conferring the title of citizen on a number of people and their descendants, against payment of a rather large sum (100 *staters* for each candidate). The formality stipulated as essential is their registration within a *patré* (an administrative and religious subdivision of the body of citizens); juridical guarantees are provided to forestall any future challenge to that decision. Analogous cases are known: their number increased substantially under the Empire. Even Athens resorted to that inglorious procedure to bail out its financial situation. An epigram dating from the first century of our era has a jibe at the ease with which one can obtain citizenship for the price of a piglet or a small quantity of firewood (*Palatine Anthology*, XI, 319). So much so that Augustus, who had his own grudge against Athens and wished to penalize her, forbade the city to have recourse to that ruse to shore up her resources (Dio Cassius LIV, 7). The debasement of a right that was the very foundation of the ancient city was felt to be scandalous: a self-evident proof that the traditional form of the State had lost none of its prestige in the first days of the Empire.

It was also in periods of financial distress that cities used a subterfuge of a rather surprising nature, divine eponymy. It sometimes happened that no candidate came forward for the highest magistracy, the holder of which was *eponymous* (meaning that he gave his name to the year in which he held that office). The expenses connected with holding that magistracy were sometimes a deterrent for even the wealthiest among those who could aspire to it. In such a case (a rare one, be it said), the major divinity of the city was looked upon as accepting the eponymous magistracy, and the expenses connected with it were borne by the sacred treasury. Thus at Miletus, where the supreme magistrate was called the *Stephanophoros* ("Crown-bearer"), and Apollo of Didyma was the major divinity, the god held the *stephanophoria* for the two consecutive years of 276/5 and 275/4. Indeed, a list of offerings found in the shrine at Didyma is dated by the phrase, "Under the *stephanophoria* of the god succeeding the god. . ." By contrast, as indicated by what follows in the text, citizens of the town held that public office in 277/6 and 274/3, in conformity with custom. On other occasions, a benevolent king was found to accept the costly honor of an eponymous magistracy.

Other innovations happened concerning magistracies, though these kept their old names. We are better informed about them in the city of Athens, where more factual details have survived than elsewhere. For instance, at the start of the Hellenistic period, election (usually by show of hands) to public office replaced designation by lot. The latter method had traditionally been held to be more "democratic," in any case more egalitarian, every candidate (so it was said) being given an opportunity to win, as no interference, pressure, or canvassing could happen then. Indeed, the elective procedure had always been in use for the appointment of *strategoi*, whose heavy responsibilities would not allow their choice to be left to chance. Greater use of elections is perhaps explained by the urge to entrust public duties to the most qualified persons, in conformity with views held by philosophers. It has been seen above (p. 192) that already in Athens a change was evident in the manner in which *strategoi* discharged their duties: a permanent distribution was established among those duties, and, as a result, a form of hierarchy replaced equality in principle. Some magistracies became important in response to new needs. *Nomophylakes* (guardians of the laws) had the duty to see that respect was paid to traditional rules, a duty formerly entrusted to the popular court. The role of *gynaeconomoi* was to keep watch on women's conduct and preserve the moral order. Here too we see the influence of philosophers, particularly that of Plato. Other offices imposed increasing expenses on their holders, since the city henceforth left these matters in their hands, instead of itself providing funds. Thus the *agonothete* or organizer of competitions was not only responsible for the games being held properly, as well as the religious ceremonies accompanying them. He also provided the prizes awarded to winners, and even sometimes, like the poet Philippides, whom an Athenian decree honored in 287, set up a new competition, at his own expense of course. The *gymnasiarch* had not only to supervise the manner in which the gymnasium was run (see pp. 293–8), to see that order and discipline reigned, and to arrange sacrifices in honor of its tutelary divinities. He also had to provide, at his own cost (see p. 191), the oil needed for massaging the athletes; this was expensive. It is quite understandable that some notables were reluctant to embrace such obligations, and sometimes actually declined to do so.

■ *Foreigners in the city* ■ *Travelers* ■ *Resident foreigners* ■ *Legal protection of foreigners* ■ *The two aspects of* Proxenia ■ *Bilateral conventions, or* symbola. *Foreign judges*

Apart from citizens and slaves, all Greek cities of any importance counted among their population a more or less large proportion of foreigners, Greek and non-Greek. That external element probably increased in the Hellenistic age, owing to easier ways of traveling, fostered by a more active sea-trade, and the large number of expatriates. These included exiles who were victims of the vagaries of politics, mercenaries in active service or seeking employment, royal officials, traders, a variety of travelers. In the last class were categories of itinerants already known in the Archaic period: artists, sculptors, painters, or architects looking for orders; musicians and poets invited to participate in religious festivals or compose epigrams; soothsayers, whose oracular science people would readily consult. Among them, as in the Classical age, were teachers of rhetoric or philosophy, lecturers and scholars of all kinds, besides the physicians who have been mentioned above (p. 190). Among these occasional visitors were athletes, whom the ever-increasing number of competitions lured out of their city of origin, and who wanted to add to the number of wreaths they had already won, in the local games held by so many cities. The more able ones were especially attracted by the traditional Panhellenic games, or those that sovereigns or rich cities had instituted to rival them. A new category of travelers appeared: Dionysiac artists, that is, actors as-

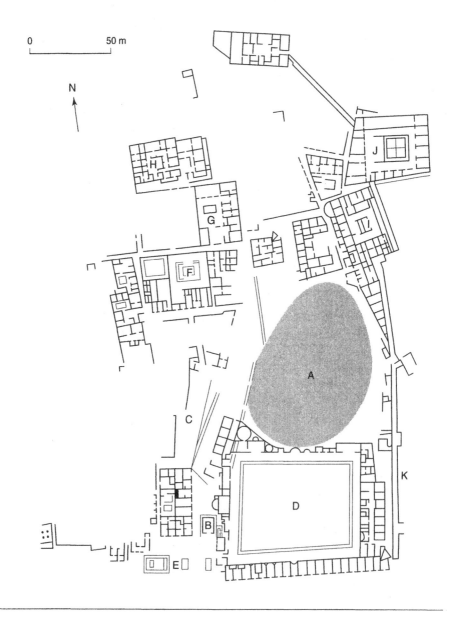

sembled in fraternities, who traveled in groups to give recitals or performances in towns, at shrines, or before royal courts. Such a varied population moved across Greece and over the length and breadth of the Mediterranean. They went to distant lands, wherever Hellenic communities had settled. This human traffic was a potent factor in fostering a sense of cultural community and ethnic solidarity among cities. With very few exceptions, to be mentioned later, such a feeling in no way erased people's fundamental devotion to a much smaller fatherland. It was superimposed on individual patriotism, as had already been the case in previous ages. By this time there was probably a deeper awareness of it than had been the case before. At any rate, the large number of honors that cities awarded to such visitors, as witnessed by honor-granting decrees and the inscribed bases prepared for their statues, demonstrates the recognition accorded by Greek cities to the contribution they made to these cities' wellbeing or prestige.

In addition to transient foreigners, there were in all important cities a sometimes considerable number of resident ones, who, without having citizenship, would sometimes enjoy a special status allowing them to practice their profession or play a role that might be important in the life of the city. They had various designations: *metoikoi* in Athens, *paroikoi* in Rhodes, *katoikoi* at Ephesus. These terms, which are close to each other in meaning – "those who live with," "beside," or "at/in" – allowed some distinction between transient guests and permanent ones. The latter paid a special tax, served in the armed forces, and had their own place in cultic ceremonies. They were craftsmen, traders, or bankers. Some made their fortunes in their new place of residence: this had been the case with Athenian *metoikoi* in the fifth and fourth centuries. Their number increased at Delos when the small island, having become an Athenian colony in 166, attracted merchant vessels traveling the Aegean, and, thanks to its privilege as a free port, served as a

Figure 1 Delos: the area of the Lake (from Bruneau-Ducat, *Guide de Délos*, plan II).

Around the sacred lake (A), now dried up, this district occupied the area neighboring Apollo's shrine on the north. Except for the small temple of Leto (B) and the "Lions' Terrace" (C), belonging to the sixth and seventh centuries respectively, all buildings in the district are Hellenistic. The large Italian agora (D), built in the late second century, is a good example of a closed agora: a large rectangular court surrounded by a Doric peristyle, beneath which open a number of exedrae and of niches for statues. Storehouses and shops open on the exterior. On the opposite side of the wide north–south street, the sanctuary of the Twelve Gods (E), built early in the third century, is provided with its altar fronting the façade. On the western hill is the establishment of the Poseidoniasts from Berytos (F). Further north, the substantial houses of the Diadoumenos (G: "House of the Young Man wearing a diadem," a statue now on display in Athens' National Museum) and of the Actors (H). North of the lake are two palaestrae: the palaestra of the Lake (I), in an advanced state of ruin, and the granite one (J), in better state of preservation. The whole district is bordered on the east by a makeshift fortification, Triarius' Wall. It was hastily built by a Roman of that name, legate to the proconsul Lucullus, in 69 BC, after a dreadful attack by pirates had ravaged the city.

center of exchange and redistribution. These foreigners congregated in associations having their own premises, their administrators, and their cults. Those best known to us brought together Hellenized Orientals and Greeks of Asia. To quote a few examples, the *Poseidoniastai* from Berytus (Beirut) were "traders, shipbuilders, wholesalers" placed under the sponsorship of Poseidon, god of the sea. The *Heracleistai* from Tyre derived their name from Heracles, the Greek hero, to whom the Phoenician Melkart was considered equivalent. Other associations grouped traders from Alexandria, who stocked imported goods in their warehouses before selling them to places abroad. Italians were grouped in a prosperous community that carried on its transactions in a vast complex of buildings, the Italians' agora, built in the late second century, adorned with statues and mosaics, and containing shops and *thermae*. All those groups were allowed to honor their own divinities – Syrian gods, Egyptian gods, and others – to whom they would raise temples. They made up partly autonomous cells within the Delian State.

Of course, such de facto recognition of organized foreign groups did not exist in every city in such an obvious way as in Delos: far from it. Yet these visitors or residents, wherever they were, could not feel safe unless formal juridical guarantees protected them from any form of abusive treatment or violence directed at their property or their persons. Such guarantees had long been in existence, thanks to the institutions of *prostatai* and *proxenoi*. The *prostates* or patron was a citizen who stood surety for a resident foreigner and was his representative in court for the defense of his interests. The *proxenos* was a citizen appointed by a city foreign to his own to receive and help travelers coming from the one that had made him its *proxenos*. His role was somewhat like that of a modern consul, with the difference that he did not belong to the city whose citizens he was to protect, but to the one in which he lived. These two institutions survived in the Hellenistic age. But the *proxenia* (meaning the office of *proxenos*) underwent a particular development, in an apparently secondary aspect of that institution, to the advantage of the *proxenos*. He received that title on the foreign city's initiative: other privileges, to be exercised in the city awarding *proxenia*, were often joined to the honor conferred by this appointment. These included exemption from taxes, the rights to appear personally in court and to acquire real estate, a guarantee against seizure in execution of a right to reprisal (see the next paragraph); and sometimes even citizenship rights, with all their juridical implications. Now, these were considerable advantages for somebody whose duties as a *proxenos* might require his presence in that city. One can thus appreciate what an important step it was to confer *proxenia*, an institution attested in the Hellenistic period by hundreds of decrees carved in stone. It did not award a purely honorary distinction, but very real privileges, allowing their beneficiary to feel safe and at ease when he was among those who had honored him in this fashion.

Apart from that type of guarantee, which could apply only to a restricted number of individuals, the Greeks thought out other juridical instruments for

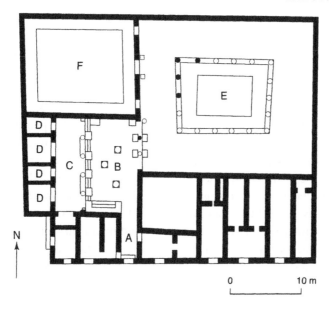

Figure 2 Delos: the building complex of the Poseidoniasts from Berytus (from Bruneau-Ducat, *Guide de Délos*, fig. 20).

The association of Poseidoniast "traders, shipbuilders, and warehousemen" from Berytus (modern Beirut) brought together under the protection of Poseidon, god of the sea, Syrian merchants doing business at Delos. Toward the end of the second century they built a fine edifice used at the same time as a club, a hostelry, and a warehouse, with a series of small shrines dedicated to their "ancestral gods." Through an entrance and a small vestibule (A), opening onto the street on the south side of the establishment, one entered a forecourt (B), framed on the east and west by two colonnades. The western one acted as a portico (C), fronting four chapels dedicated to three divinities worshiped by Syrian Greeks (Poseidon being one of them) and to the goddess Rome. The eastern colonnade separated the forecourt from the Great Court (E), surrounded by a large peristyle, as was done in private houses. Beneath the court, in its center, a large cistern had been inserted that was roofed with a vault, above which was a mosaic floor. A second court (F) filled the northwest corner of the building. South of the peristyle were living quarters and storehouses.

the protection of foreigners; these were bilateral agreements between cities, called *symbola* (the plural of *symbolon*). They were meant to impose limitations on a right to seizure by way of reprisal (pledges thus seized were called *syla*) that was widely admitted in the Greek world. This authorized the creditors of a foreigner who had placed himself out of their reach to recover debts owed to them by the seizure of goods in their own city belonging to a compatriot of the debtor. The rationale for such an action was felt to lie in the juridical solidarity binding members of the same city together, and allowing anybody to hold each of them answerable for the personal default of one of their fellow-citizens. That put somebody going abroad on business at serious risk. The purpose of the *symbola* was to offer a guarantee against such a threat. These agreements enshrined the modalities of settlement for disputes, in a spirit of reciprocity. Their increasing number in the Hellenistic age was to lead to a degree of uniformity in juridical practice, which varied widely from city to city in Archaic and Classical Greece.

There was a connection between these arrangements and an innovation in intercity cooperation in the judicial area, which was quite frequently employed in the third and second centuries. It consisted in resorting to the services of foreign judges in an attempt to lighten the burden of local courts. The judicial process was one of the main tasks of the State. In the case of Athens, Aristotle described in detail (*Constitution of Athens*, 63ff.) the manner in which the popular tribunal was constituted. Pausanias (I, 28) lists the various courts which, in the second century of our era, still rendered judgment on many cases referred to them, each according to its own competence. As there were no professionally trained magistrates, citizens were chosen to sit on these tribunals, and make awards in the people's name. That was why one of a citizen's first duties was "to demonstrate his equity as a judge," to use the wording of an inscription from Cos dating back to the third century. In spite of the zeal shown by these popular juries, it sometimes happened that tribunals had too heavy a caseload, or that litigants waited in vain for judgment, or serious civic discord cast doubt on the integrity of those called on to adjudicate on their fellow-citizens' disputes. A remedy was found for such crises in the working of the judicial system. It consisted in requesting a foreign city to despatch to the one facing this problem a commission made up of some of its own citizens: for instance, three judges and a secretary, constituting a tribunal that would decide on the lawsuits in abeyance. Immune from local passions and intrigues, they could not be suspected of partiality. Judges from a number of different cities were called upon to adjudicate on specially intricate cases.

According to the documentary evidence that we have, such foreign judges, as a general rule, seem to have discharged their duties in a manner that gave satisfaction to their hosts. Complying with ancestral Greek custom, they first tried to conciliate the views of the opposing parties and reach an amicable settlement; in case of failure they made an award: their standing as foreigners was a guarantee of impartiality and it was considered equitable. To record its gratitude for the service they had rendered, the host city would pass a decree conferring honors on them, as well as privileges like the *proxenia*, citizenship, various exemptions or pledges in the event of attempted seizure, the right to acquire land, and a number of other benefits. These decrees were engraved on stelae erected in public places, where they have been found in large numbers. They allow us to appreciate the widespread application of a typically Hellenistic usage, which, by these exchanges indicating mutual trust, must have gone a long way toward fostering friendly relations between cities in the same area.

■ *Relations between cities* ■ *Diverse forms of association:* synoecism,
sympoliteia, isopoliteia ■ *Confederacies or Leagues* ■ *The
Achaean League and its organization* ■ *A new-born country,
Aetolia* ■ *The Aetolian League and its organization* ■ *The
Aetolian League's extension outside mainland Greece* ■ *Its prestige
in the Greek world: the example of the embassy from Cytenium
to Xanthus* ■ *Mythical intercity blood relationships: the example
of Heraclea on Latmos* ■ *The other Confederacies: their role in
safeguarding cults (the Acarnanian example) and in protecting
public order (the Lycian Confederacy's example)*

Friendly relations created in this way might take the concrete shape of accords,
no longer just those linking a city with foreign individuals or groups of foreign
individuals, but those designed to unite one city with another or many other
cities. More than ever before there was a widespread feeling that union was
strength, as a result of the growing threat that the rise of the large empires meant
for the autonomy of Greek states. Aware of their individual weakness, groups of
small states would unite. That process, called *synoecism*, had secured the birth of
Athens in the Archaic period, and the foundation of Rhodes or Megalopolis in
the Classical age. It was sometimes used in Hellenistic times, on occasion under
pressure from a sovereign who imposed the regrouping of a large number of
neighboring towns into one. That was what Lysimachus did, according to
Pausanias' report (I, 9, 7; see also VII, 3, 4–5): "He resorted to synoecism when
he extended to the seaboard the town of Ephesus, such as it presents itself nowa-
days: he brought in to people it the inhabitants of Lebedos and Colophon, after
destroying these two cities. The poet Phoenix grieved in iambic verse over *The
Capture of Colophon*." A less brutal process was for two cities to conclude an
agreement establishing a common citizenship between them: this was called a
sympoliteia. To quote examples, this was what the two small neighboring cities
of Stiris and Medeon, in Phocis, did in the second century; or in Asia Minor,
Miletus or the Carian cities of Mylasa and Heraclea on Latmos, which enlarged
their territories by annexing small frontier-cities. For such unions the term
homopoliteia (which has a closely related sense) was also employed – rarely, as a
matter of fact – as in the agreement between the island of Cos in the Dodecanese
and the neighboring island of Calymna in the days of Ptolemy Sôter. In the last
case, it seems apparent that Calymna became a sort of dependency of the island
of Cos, in whose favor it renounced any initiative in political matters. The inscription does not reproduce the text of the agreement, but says on what terms

the solemn oath committing the two communities was to be sworn, and transcribes the formulaic phrases of the oath, thus allowing us to know the content of the agreement. Here again, it is clear that the gods' sanction served to guarantee compliance with a contract.

Isopoliteia accords were rife in those days. They had been known in Classical times, but from now on they became much more frequent. They contained the provision that citizens from the cities concerned, when living in a city other than their own, were to enjoy the same rights as citizens of the host city. Thus was established "civic equality," to use the expression referring to those rights: in other words a "virtual right to citizenship" (as it has been called in a felicitous formula), becoming effective only whenever a citizen of one city settled in another city that was party to the agreement. There could be isopolity between two or more cities, even between a city and a confederacy. In the latter case citizenship in the confederacy, not in its various component cities, was conferred on its partners. Treaties of isopolity are often attested. Thus Athens joined hands with Rhodes or Priene, Miletus with many cities of Asia Minor, Cyrene with the island of Tenos in the Cyclades. Such agreements could happen not only between neighboring cities, but also between states far removed geographically from each other.

These bilateral agreements established close ties between individual cities, but, with the exception of cases of synoecism and sympolity, left the Greek states' tradition of independence essentially untouched. But the Hellenistic age saw the efflorescence, side by side with the great monarchies and as it were to provide a counterweight to them, of confederacies or leagues (two terms used to translate the same Greek word). These united, in one organic whole, cities of one particular region that were linked by common traditions and interests. No doubt such confederacies were already in existence, especially in fringe or remote areas: in Thessaly among the Magnesians (on the Gulf of Volos), in Chalcidice, in Epirus, in Arcadia, the kind of structure called a *koinon*, that is a "community," was known. These communities regrouped either urban conglomerations, or "peoples" or tribes that preserved the same traditions and had lived through the same history. A certain form of institutional structure, varying with region and period, already existed in each *koinon*, identified by a geographical term: it was applicable to all its participants. There were thus the Thessalians' *koinon*, the respective *koina* (to use the plural of *koinon*) of the Arcadians, the Chalcidians, the Molossi (a branch of the Epirotes) – or that of the Magnesians. Boeotia, under the city of Thebes' dominant influence, had in its turn formed the Boeotian confederacy, with federal institutions controlled by the Thebans: it survived the defeat of Chaeronea and Thebes' disappearance after its rebellion against Alexander. On the other hand, powerful cities like Sparta or Athens, starting with a system of military alliances, had put in place some sort of control over the allied cities. "The Lacedaemonians and their allies," as the Peloponnesian League was named, found themselves together only in times of war, under Sparta's authority. Their only ties were bilateral accords between Sparta and other interested cities; no federal institutions had been set up. Athens had formed the maritime League of Delos after the Persian Wars, but had very soon made it the tool of her domination over the allied cities. After the collapse of 404, she made another attempt with the maritime Confederacy of 377, endowed with an embryonic federal organization. This turned out to be another failure after a few decades. The League of Corinth, a creation of Philip II of Macedon, lasted only as long as it helped the Macedonian sovereigns to accomplish their political designs. Later Antigonus Doson's Hellenic League did not call on cities for membership, but rather on confederacies of cities, which had in the meantime become important: those of the Boeotians, Phocians, Locrians, Epirotes, Acarnanians, Achaeans, Euboeans, Thessalians. The effective role of that League seems to have been short-lived. It disappeared just before Philip V's defeat at Cynoscephalae (197).

The major leagues of Achaea and Aetolia were very different. They played a first-class role in Hellenistic history. These were federal organizations in the true sense of the word, with their political institutions, their armed forces, a type of common citizenship, their own finances, and, of course, federal shrines whose religious authority was a guarantee of solidarity among the member cities of these Leagues. They were constructed in such a way that they could plan and follow a coherent and autonomous foreign policy, direct important military operations, and inspire respect or fear. They alone could face the great monarchies on an equal footing. It was not from these that they received a fatal blow, but from Roman power. In the history of Hellenistic Greece, they present the only serious attempt to solve, by means of a new political structure, the acute problem of survival that confronted the Greek cities as independent units. For they each had a restricted territory and a far from numerous population; they were torn apart from each other by rivalry, and were threatened by the ambitions of the kings.

Let us look more closely at these two confederacies. The Achaean League was the older of the two. Originally it regrouped twelve cities, later reduced to ten, all situated in the northwestern part of the Peloponnese, along the Gulf of Patras, and on the south coast of the Gulf of Corinth. Legends that Pausanias reports in minute detail at the start of Book VII, devoted to Achaea, of his *Periegesis*, told of the Achaean people expelling the Ionians, though they were said to be of the same stock. The exiles (so the story went on to say) took refuge in Attica, then in Asia Minor, and the Achaeans occupied their land. Such traditional accounts, no doubt a reflection of an original ethnic association, were of prime importance for the inhabitants of Achaea, as they were bound to be anywhere in the Greek world. The same can be said of the cult they all shared of Zeus *homagyrios* ("who assembles") in his shrine neighboring the town of Aegium, as well as that of Demeter *Panachaia*. The historian Polybius, on the one hand, and Plutarch in his *Life of Aratus* on the other provide us with plenty of information on the most brilliant period of Achaean history, in the third and second centuries BC. Aratus' role between 251 and 214 was decisive. His various initiatives, his energetic actions, his political sense transformed the confederacy, which had undergone renewal in 280 after a long period of dormancy, into a powerful federal State with an extended territory. Sicyon, Corinth, Epidaurus in the Argolid, and Megara beyond the Isthmus were joined to the League, which finally extended its authority over the major part of the Peloponnese. Its ambition was to use that united strength against Sparta, the Antigonids of Macedon and the Aetolian League. Sparta was always suspected of wanting to recapture its ancient hegemony over the Peninsula; the Antigonids cherished a policy aiming to control the whole of Greece proper; the Aetolian League was a rival confederacy dominating western and central Greece.

The Achaean League was by this time equipped with a real federal constitution, conferring on the inhabitants of member cities a common citizenship that overarched their original citizenship without superseding it. The League's institutions resembled those of the Classical city, and included an Assembly open to all male citizens aged 30 and over. It met until 188 at Aegium, which served as federal capital. There were fixed dates for ordinary meetings: the magistrates

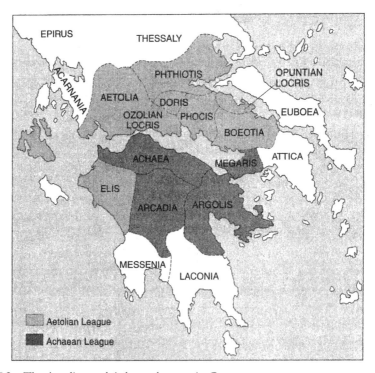

Map 10 The Aetolian and Achaean leagues in Greece.

convened extraordinary ones when questions of foreign policy demanded it. Resolutions of the Assembly were prepared by a Council (*Boulé*) and put into practice by federal magistrates elected by the Assembly. The most important of these magistrates was the *strategos*. Starting in 255, only one such officer was elected every year. He was the real leader of the League, directing its policies and commanding the armed forces. With a one-year term, he could be reelected after a single year's interruption: an arrangement that allowed Aratus to be reelected seventeen times in his long career, which lasted over thirty years, and thus exert a decisive influence on the League's destiny. The principles of the constitution were democratic in form: Polybius constantly praises it – see especially II, 37–8 – for guaranteeing freedom, equality, and harmony in relations between cities as well as between individuals. It nevertheless allowed continuity in the exercise of power and favored the implementation of long-term plans: that allowed the Achaeans to be evenly matched with contemporary monarchies. It is true that Aratus' personal convictions, and the political inclination shown by the civic group electing the Assembly, steered the League's policy in a firmly conservative direction. That became evident in the struggle with Cleomenes and his attempt at social reform. There is no doubt that, in the Achaean system, the leaders acted in accordance with their electors' wishes. This would be another proof, if one is needed, that the idea of democracy did not represent the same social reality in Antiquity as it does in our own day. The civic group mentioned above actually represented, as in all Greek cities, only a minority of the inhabitants.

The Aetolian League had already been set up by the time the Hellenistic age started. Between Ozolian Locris in the east and the river Achelous separating them in the west from Acarnania, the Aetolian tribes occupied, north of the Gulf of Patras, a very mountainous territory, arable only in the valleys and the lowland around Lake Trichonis. The marshy coast, where the town of Missolonghi is now situated, had no harbor, but there were lagoons along the seaboard. From the Tymphrestus to Mount Oeta, a high and rugged mountain barrier cut off access to the valley of the Spercheus toward the Aegean. That confined region, shut off from any passage except in the northwest, across Acarnania, toward the Gulf of Arta, was definitely beyond the fringe of the Hellenic world. Yet it had been from its very origins a land of legends known to the whole of Greece. The Achelous, the mightiest river of Greece, is the most illustrious of the river gods, the very symbol of water in the language of poets. The eponymous heroes of the Aetolian towns of Pleuron and Calydon were reputedly related to the family of Dorus, himself the eponymous ancestor of the Dorians: a relationship confirmed by dialectal kinship. The famous hero Meleager, already a celebrity in Homeric times, was the son of a king of Calydon. With the most celebrated heroic figures and demi-gods, Theseus, Atalanta, Jason, Pirithoos, Peleus, Castor and Pollux, and others who had come from the whole of Hellas, he organized the hunt for the Calydonian boar. The remains of that beast were deposited in the shrine of

Alea Athena at Tegea in Arcadia, where Pausanias saw it, in a moth-eaten state. The Aetolian region, cut off from continental Greece, was populated by mountaineers who were mostly shepherds and (to a minor degree) given to banditry. They lived in rural groups and were organized in tribes: these and some rare small towns made up a federal state. The center of that state was Apollo's shrine at Thermus, close to Lake Trichonis. Thucydides (III, 94) paints a picture of the Aetolian people as "numerous and warlike, living in villages devoid of fortifications and sparsely peopled, using only light weapons," for the most part "speaking an unintelligible dialect, and said to consume only raw foods." Those coarse and uncultured men had none the less, in 426, inflicted a heavy defeat on the Athenian general Demosthenes, who had attacked them without due precautions. Their skill in warfare was confirmed in later events, and allowed the Aetolian League to play a prominent role in the third century BC.

We hear about the League only in the Hellenistic age. Its organization was rather similar to that of the Achaean League; its institutions at the federal level were a reflection of those typical of a city. An assembly was held regularly twice a year – without counting occasional extraordinary meetings – and was open to all citizens. It dealt only with matters of foreign policy. A council made up of delegates from various cities or tribes, the number of each contingent varying with that of their population, bore the name of *synedrion* (*synedroi* are "those who sit together"). It elected from among its members a more restricted council, the *apokletoi*, who steered the policies of the League, and the magistrates, who made up its executive. At the head of these was the *strategos*, the supreme eponymous authority, head of the army, elected for one year, who could not be reelected before a certain period had gone by. Seconding him were the head of cavalry (the *hipparchus*), an *agonothete* whose duty it was to supervise the organization of religious ceremonies and federal games, a secretary in charge of the archives, and financial magistrates. The Aetolian *koinon* had its federal citizenship, without the cities renouncing their individual civic rights. Federal citizenship was convenient in that it allowed new states that did not share a border with its territory to be admitted to the League. When that occurred, the League entered into a treaty of *isopolity* that granted Aetolian citizenship to the inhabitants of the new member state, with the guarantees it brought, though not citizenship rights in any of the Aetolian cities. It was necessary to obtain citizenship in one of the cities, besides federal citizenship, for any of these external allies to become an Aetolian with full rights. On the other hand, cities or confederations on the borders of Aetolia might enter the League on the basis of *sympolity*, which created a closer juridical and constitutional link. These included certain cities in Acarnania, Ozolian (also called Western) Locris, Doris (or the Dorians of the Metropolis: see the next paragraph), the Aenianians and Dolopes, and, extending from one to the next, the cities of Thessaly and Phocis, and Opuntian Locris.

One of the major benefits of membership of the Achaean League was *asylia*, a privilege that was usually conferred (see above p. 201), with *proxenia* and citizenship, of which it was really a part. We have noted that *asylia* guaranteed individuals against the exercise of rights of reprisal (*syla*). But it also protected its holder against seizure of goods and persons in piratical operations. Now, remember that the Aetolians had taken to piracy on a large scale, not only on the coasts of the Ionian Sea, but also far away from their original base, right up to the Aegean. Thus it happened that a large number of maritime cities requested and obtained admission to the Aetolian League. These included Ambracia on the Gulf of Arta, the island of Cephallenia at the opening of the Gulf of Patras, the island of Ceos in the Cyclades, Axus in Crete, Lysimacheia in Thrace, Cius on the Propontis, Chalcedon on the Bosporus. Anatolia included Magnesia on the Maeander and Heraclea on Latmos. The League extended in this way outside continental Greece, far from its native frontiers.

A document (discovered not long ago) demonstrates the undisputed authority with which the Aetolian League took in hand the interest of members not situated on Aetolian territory. In the year 206 BC or thereabouts, the small town of Cytenium in Minor Doris (also called the Metropolis), north of Mount Parnassus, was faced with a dramatic situation. An earthquake first destroyed part of its walls. Then, twenty years earlier than the date of the document, the king of Macedon, Antigonus Doson, who had quarreled with the Aetolians and their allies, had taken advantage of Cytenium's troops being away to protect the Delphic shrine on the other side of the Parnassus massif. He had captured Cytenium, razed to the ground what was left of its walls, and set the town on fire. To rebuild their humble city, which they call in the document "the most significant in the Metropolis," the Cytenians had first to restore their walls, a means of defense that no Greek city could do without in those troubled times. But that meant a heavy outlay, while the small state, with a diminutive mountainous territory, was devoid of any resources. It was therefore appealing for solidarity from the Dorian cities outside Metropolitan Doris, and actually sending an embassy overseas, as far as Xanthus, an important city of Asia Minor, whose inhabitants looked upon themselves as Dorians.

A magnificent marble stele found at Xanthus in Leto's sanctuary, the most revered in the city, acquaints us with the main texts relating to that episode. We shall describe each of them. A decree passed by the Xanthians apologizes with some embarrassment for the relatively modest size of the contribution they feel able to offer the Cytenians. An Aetolian decree vouchsafes, in the League's name, accreditation for a delegation sent by the Dorians to the cities related to them by kinship, and to kings Ptolemy (IV) and Antiochus (III). A letter from the magistrates and *synedroi* of the Aetolian League commends the Cytenian ambassadors to the Xanthians' benevolent attention, urging a generous response to their request. Finally, a long letter from the people of Cytenium explains the situation to the Xanthians and entreats them to help. We have here a well-preserved set of texts, totaling 200 lines of Greek, providing us with new information on the history, institutions, beliefs, and dialects of the cities concerned, and their relationships with the Lagid sovereigns and the Seleucid ruler. Here it is enough to underline the Aetolians' involvement in that episode: the role they play in it is decisive. The ambassadors from Cytenium come to Xanthus as their spokesmen, for they sponsor the Cytenian plan in compliance with a decree of the Aetolian *koinon*, authorizing every such delegation sent to cities and kings to speak in its name. To this they join a letter of personal accreditation, introducing the three members of the embassy to the Council and the People of Xanthus. Their final argument in support of their request is that kings Ptolemy and Antiochus, whose names (especially Ptolemy's) carry weight in Lycia, are interested in the project. The inhabitants of Xanthus lived in Asia, far away from western Greece, in a world untouched by the disputes that the peoples of Aetolia and Doris had with the Macedonian sovereign. Still the renown and authority of the Aetolian League were impressive enough for them to feel duty-bound, in spite of heavy financial difficulties that the decree spells out in detail, to make a substantial effort in favor of Cytenium. No other circumstance allows us better to appreciate the prestige that the Aetolians had secured in the third century over the whole of Greece, thanks to the efficient manner in which they had organized their League.

A specially interesting feature of this inscription from Xanthus is the frequent mention, in the documents it transcribes, of mythical links of ancestral relationship among Dorian cities, as well as between the Ptolemaic and Seleucid dynasties, both of these claiming descent from Heracles. It would be wrong to find in such references only a stylistic turn of phrase, an unfounded and frivolous assertion, invented as a means of special pleading. Were that only a rhetorical *topos*, the allusion to a blood relationship between peoples would not be used so often as a justification for very precise requests – for gifts of money, or for diplomatic and military support. Nor would they be so readily taken up by those who, of their own volition, granted those requests. That is the case in the Cytenium–Xanthus exchange, where the three parties – Aetolians, Metropolitan Dorians, and Xanthians – recall in a detailed manner the family relationship that binds them together and links them with Ptolemy and Antiochus. The Xanthian people's decree is particularly explicit in this regard, as it clarifies and develops at great length the briefer details contained in the letter from Cytenium and in the Aetolian decree. Whoever wrote the Xanthian decree has inserted in it a veritable mythological discourse, in which a number of heroic or divine legends are evoked. He traces Xanthus' history to Apollo, Artemis, and their mother Leto, who, according to Xanthus' own tradition, running counter to the one that was current, gave birth to her two children, not on the island of Delos, but on the very site of Xanthus. Hence its choice of Leto as its major divinity and guardian. The Lycian City obviously regarded such myths as historical truth, lost as it was in a distant past. Likewise the Cytenians and their Metropolitan compatriots had unswerving faith in the historical value of genealogies tracing their descent back to an eponymous Dorus, something in which the other Greek peoples were firm believers. In the Delphic Amphictyonic Council, diminutive and pitiable Metropolitan Doris held in its own name one of the two votes imparted to the whole Dorian tribe. Powerful Lacedaemon, on the other hand, had no vote, and obtained representation in the Council only from time to time, whenever the Metropolitan Dorians agreed to allow her to use their own privileged vote. Nothing demonstrates better that both myth and history were arguments of great weight in Hellenistic times, and were sometimes decisive in intercity relationships.

We may add another instance involving the Aetolians. When the Carian city of Heraclea on Latmos requested and obtained the favor of isopolity from the Aetolian League, as we learn from a Delphic inscription, its ambassadors emphasized the kinship between Aetolia and their faraway city, recalling that Heraclea on Latmos was an Aetolian colony. It was proved not long ago that the colony–metropolis link is based on no other historical text or inscription, but was founded on a myth in which a blood relationship existed between two heroes. The eponymous ancestor of the Aetolians, Aetolus, was son of Endymion, lover of Selene, the Moon. According to the tradition of the Heracleots as reported by Pausanias (V, 1), Endymion retired in old age to Mount Latmos, which overlooks the site of Heraclea. The sacred cave where his tomb lay, an *adyton* to which the public had no access (for such is the meaning of the word), was shown there. That legend allowed Heraclea to be seen as having been founded by Endymion, and thus as being linked to Aetolia through his son Aitolus. The Heracleots made use of their opportunity (see p. 320).

In comparison with the two powerful Achaean and Aetolian Leagues, the other confederacies of Greek cities appear unimpressive. Yet these organizations, which did not overflow the limits of a region, were a help in avoiding the risk of fragmentation that faced the Hellenic world again and again. They offered a whole range of benefits to their member cities. These included the preservation of local peace, defense against external dangers (provided they were not too great for the *koinon* to cope with), maintenance of common shrines, celebration of religious festivals of special significance when the cities entrusted with that task proved no longer equal to it. We shall quote two instances out of many. Toward the end of the third century the Acarnanian Confederacy decided to transform into a common shrine Apollo's sanctuary at Actium, which the small city of Anactorium no longer had the means to keep in a good state of repair. It was to celebrate there the traditional Games every year, while relinquishing to Anactorium half the dues paid by visitors on that occasion. That was an equitable arrangement, allowing the shrine to continue playing its part in the Acarnanian community, without depriving Anactorium of the resources brought to it by the crowd of pilgrims that the Games attracted. The text of the decree was to be displayed simultaneously at Actium and at Olympia (the latter copy has survived), so that the pledges could be widely publicized. This agreement saved Apollo's shrine at Actium from the threat of being abandoned. Later, in the year 31 before our era, Augustus was to bestow great honor on it in remembrance of his victory, won under the god's own eyes.

The other example is drawn from the Lycian Confederacy, to which Xanthus belonged. A decree from the small city of Araxa in Lycia, dating from about 180 BC, honors one of its citizens, Orthagoras. It is a very long text, quite typical of this kind of document. It lists the services of a citizen who was both a diplomatist and a soldier, and who had given of his best in the federal forces as well as in those of Araxa. His *curriculum vitae* illustrates the frequency of military operations in those remote mountains of Anatolia, where conflicts were always flaring up between neighboring towns, and where the intervention of the Confederacy's army was often needed, both on the frontiers of Lycia and between member cities. The Confederacy's main role in that region seems to have been to act as an arbiter in conflicts, punish aggressors, and even repress brigands. Furthermore, it set up relations with Rome's envoys, who were to make an entry everywhere in the Greek Orient.

■ *The historical importance of the Greek city in the Hellenistic world* ■ *Its essential role in the preservation of a definite style of life and culture, though it had to fit in with wider political organizations better suited to contemporary needs*

This is the picture that can be drawn of Greek cities in the Hellenistic age from abundant evidence provided by a civilization speaking to us through its written and engraved documents. In a period of great unrest, where the ambitions of the powerful introduced a climate of violence and permanent insecurity, the civic institutions managed, after all, to survive. They provided their citizens with means to live and sometimes to live well when circumstances were favorable. They proved flexible enough to adapt to social evolution, and to a sharing of roles between those on whom fortune smiled, and destitute or less well-endowed citizens. It fell to the first to shoulder public responsibilities, with the burdens that these brought with them. The others only expected the State to ensure public order and protect its territory, provide against eventual penury, and see that the city's divinities were honored in their cult. These institutions prolonged the life of local traditions, loyalty to the heritage of a common history, the memory of illustrious ancestors; they provided literature and the arts with a receptive public and many opportunities for asserting their presence. Yet they never knew any thorough renewal. Even when they were placed in the wider context of a confederacy, they remained essentially in agreement with age-old patterns of thought, which Archaic and Classical Greece had worked out in the light of experience. For all the long-drawn-out debate it has aroused in modern times, the political system of the Leagues does not appear ever to have known a genuine form of representative government, in which delegates elected or appointed by the grass roots would have controlled the executive. It never went beyond the machinery of an Assembly open to all citizens, with a Council (*boulé* or *synedrion*) and magistrates. Even in the Aetolian League, where the *synedrion* was made up of representatives from the various cities, the retention of regular or extraordinary assemblies did not allow a representative system to be set up or even considered. Yet the territorial expansion of the federal states had made such a system indispensable. Political imagination did not belong in those days to the cities, but to the monarchy.

7/THE MONARCHICAL SYSTEM

Alexander the Great's figure and his destiny literally fascinated the ancient world and served as a model his many imitators could never really equal. This essential fact, however, should not make us forget that the Greeks, attached as they were to the political system of the city and (at least some of them) to what they called "democracy," were in no way ignorant of the monarchical system. They had all known it in the first centuries of their history and were reminded of it on many occasions. They had all learned by heart the songs of Homer, and admired those far-off heroes, each of whom was a king among his own people. The two majestic figures of Agamemnon, king of kings, and Priam, the patriarchal king, gave royal status its full dimensions in the listener's imagination. When Athenians crowded the theater on the occasion of dramatic competitions, they would again see kings appearing on the stage. In Classical Greece the two royal families of Sparta continued to occupy concurrently, from father to son, the supreme position of a dual kingship. On the northern frontier, another of Heracles' descendants, who governed it as king, led Macedon: he had an ongoing relationship with Athens. In Cyrenaica, an African region closely connected with Athens and Sparta, the dynasty of the Battiads had reigned until 440 – up to the time of Pericles. Pindar sang in sumptuous verse of Arcesilaus IV, its last descendant. He also showered praise on other powerful Greek sovereigns: the tyrants of Sicily, Hiero of Syracuse, Theron of Agrigentum, to whom he was pleased to grant the title of king. After all, the primary sense of the word *tyrannos* had been nothing but that of *king*. It was only the Sophists and their competitors, the philosophers, who gave it a pejorative connotation that it never shook off.

Those de jure or de facto monarchs had magnificently upheld, within the actual framework of a Greek city or by regrouping many of these within their government, as happened in Cyrenaica or Sicily, the visibility of statesmen who, alone, wielded supreme power. They enjoyed to the full the prestige that power and wealth could bring. In Cyprus, princes like Evagoras and his son Nicocles won admiration from the rhetorician Isocrates, who was also an eloquent advocate of Athenian democracy. The Athenians would shower honors on Dionysius, tyrant of Sicily, a harsh and cruel man who nevertheless saved the western Hellenic world from the Carthaginian menace. Geographically nearer to them, and at a time just preceding Philip II of Macedon's domination of the whole of Greece, Jason, tyrant of Pherae in Thessaly, had presented to his contemporaries the image of a dynamic leader who managed to bring the entire Thessalian League under his authority.

Indeed, age-old rivalry with the Achaemenid empire – its ruler called in the Greek tongue the king *(par excellence)* – and the fact that barbarian peoples were for the most part under monarchical rule, had developed a certain mindset among the Greeks. Such a regime seemed to them to be at variance with Hellenic tradition and with the institutions of the city. Philip's repeated victories, however, then Alexander's triumphant expedition, created an element of doubt in the minds of many Greeks. In any case, daily experience gave them obvious proof of the efficiency of one-man rule when confronted with "democratic" cities in an activity on which their very existence depended: warfare. In the smaller Greek states preparation for war, and the best fighting method, had become very important, for their very survival was at stake in a world where open conflict might break out at any moment and periods of peace were exceptions. Everybody was aware of that, even though many individuals tried to shirk the civic obligations imposed on them as a result. Now, the fourth century saw a considerable change in fighting methods, and the means required for winning a war. Military technique had made remarkable advances, and was becoming more and more complex. Weaponry, particularly war-engines, had become more intricate and diverse. The size of seagoing vessels had increased, as had that of their manpower and equipment. On the subject of land armies, problems grew more and more difficult to analyze and solve in the fields of manning and provisioning, in strategy as well as in tactics. In these circumstances the Greek cities' armed forces, essentially made up of citizens who were not professional soldiers, would now be in a state of inferiority when faced with mercenary troops. These were soldiers hardened in the practice of warfare, experienced in maneuver. They were under orders, not from fellow-citizens temporarily entrusted with military command, but from experienced officers, subject to a single leader's unchallenged authority. In such conflicts the parties were not evenly matched. No doubt cities having the requisite funds at their disposal could have recourse to the help of mercenaries and capable *condottieri*. Nor did they fail to do so. But in the final analysis the monarchical states confirmed their superiority. As will soon be demonstrated, war was their main concern, and their rapid territorial expansion provided them with powerful means of action. If the cities wished to survive, they had to organize (which is what they did in setting up leagues), compromise, or submit, according to circumstances. Monarchy gradually became a fact of life. Greece, which had in the first place been generally reluctant to acknowledge that reality, was forced to do so after being defeated by Philip and conquered by Alexander.

■ *The complex nature of Hellenistic monarchy* ■ *The diversity of the environment within which it was exercised* ■ *One definition of monarchy: Eupolemus' epigram at Cyrene* ■ *Commentary on that text*

The phenomenon of monarchy extended over three centuries to the major part of the Hellenistic world, only disappearing as a result of intervention by Rome, which in the end made it her own. This phenomenon is a complex one, not easily grasped. It showed itself at various times and in several places. Factors relating to circumstances and personality played a major role in its emergence and history. Its study is difficult if one wishes to avoid the dual risk of over-simplification, and a detailed but unfocused presentation of facts. Let us try to concentrate on the main features of the system, after bringing out, as we should, the extreme complexity they display on the practical level.

That complexity is due to the varied nature of the circumstances in which the monarchical phenomenon showed itself or developed in a world the conquest of the Orient had extended and diversified to an amazing degree. Obviously, one cannot compare exactly the great monarchies which garnered Alexander's legacy as a result of action by the Diadochi, and the countless principalities or local tyrannies which arose almost everywhere, either among Greek cities or in occupied territory. The size of these states – in some cases immense, in others modest and sometimes diminutive – presented widely disparate problems, though the solutions to these were everywhere the result of power being concentrated in the hands of a single ruler. There is likewise a difference between kingdoms, large or small, in which peoples of varying ethnic origin, language, and historical background were brought together under the sovereign's authority, and those whose king ruled over one nation, Greek or thoroughly Hellenized, like Macedon or Epirus. The second category, however, often comprised, as result of conquest, external possessions whose population was of different stock. This was the case in the mountainous districts of Thrace and Illyria, which gave so much trouble to the Argeads (see pp. 7, 50), to Cassander, Lysimachus, and the Antigonids, as well as to the Epirote dynasty of the Aeacids. Finally, historical circumstances fostering the advent of personal power were quite varied. The traditional monarchies of Sparta, Macedon, or Epirus were established regimes. Every tyranny of Greece proper, Asia Minor, or Sicily had resulted from a coup; the rise of the Seleucid and Lagid kingdoms, and their imitators in Anatolia or Bactria, was directly inspired by the example of Alexander. Nevertheless, shifts or transitions occurred from one type to another. To quote an example, Pyrrhus was king of the Molossi and leader of the Epirote community, thus a sovereign of the traditional kind. Yet he never ceased to hanker after a large empire, grouping under his authority not only Macedon and a number of Greek states, but Italy as well, with Sicily and even Libya. His famous conversation with his friend, the philosopher Cineas, in the version given by Plutarch (*Life of Pyrrhus*, 14), is an adequate reflection of his lust for a variety of conquests. Similarly Mithridates VI Eupator (see pp. 142–52), not content with his ancestral inheritance, the kingdom of Pontus, nursed the ambition of dominating the whole of the Greco-Anatolian Near East. He devoted a long fighting career to pursuing, in spite of Fortune's fickleness, a grand design that constantly eluded his grasp. Already in the fourth century, Agathocles had refused to be satisfied with a kingship that did not come with a crown, and which he had seized, tyrant-like, at Syracuse. He had attempted to add to it a great African empire at the expense of Carthage (see p. 56).

Caution is needed in trying to determine which characteristics are common, amid the diversity of individual destinies, lands, and periods, to those figures who, in such large numbers and such dissimilar contexts, wished to shoulder alone the responsibilities of power. To provide our analysis with a factual and well-defined base, we shall start with the text chosen as an epigraph to the present work. It is a dedicatory epigram found about half a century ago among the ruins of the port of Cyrene in Libya. In that fertile region where, as early as the late seventh century, Greek civilization had found an area favorable to its agricultural activities, many Greek cities in the vicinity of Cyrene, the most important among them, shared the arable lands close to Lybian tribes, which had to a certain degree evolved into a settled and Hellenized population. Ptolemy Sôter had since 322 controlled the whole of Cyrenaica. After various turns of fortune – among which was the tragic end of Ophellas, its governor, murdered on orders from Agathocles, tyrant of Syracuse, in the course of a military expedition against Carthage – he felt compelled to send an army against Cyrene, which had revolted. Ptolemy entrusted command of that army to his stepson Magas, son by a first marriage of the beautiful Berenice, whom Ptolemy Sôter had later made his mistress, then his wife. The young man, brought up in the sound Macedonian military tradition, had acquitted himself brilliantly in his task, and had subdued Cyrene and Libya, restoring Lagid authority (300 BC). To show his satisfaction,

Ptolemy asked him to govern in his name that remote section of his empire, separated from Alexandria and Egypt by 800 kilometers of desert or inhospitable coast. As long as Sôter was alive (until 283), Magas cooperated with him faithfully: witness the coinage he ordered to be struck at Cyrene, bronze pieces displaying his stepfather Ptolemy I's powerful features. The situation changed with the king's death. Following a procedure common to Hellenistic monarchies, Sôter had taken as his associate in royal power the son he had by Berenice. Born on the island of Cos in 308, he was to become Ptolemy II. A half-brother to Magas, born of the same mother, he was much younger (by twelve years) than Cyrene's governor. It seems that Magas, aware of the prestige which was his both by seniority and by the long exercise of nearly independent power, was unwilling to submit to Ptolemy II's authority. He actually took the royal title, which is solidly attested by three epigraphic texts and by coinage, in addition to evidence from the historian Agatharchides of Cnidus (second century BC) and from Pompeius Trogus (belonging to the Augustan age), later summarized by Justin (see pp. 2–3). After these events Magas ruled Cyrenaica until 250, the probable year of his death. For that lovely region, heavily stricken in the stressful years following Alexander's death, his reign was a period of peace and prosperity.

It seemed necessary to give the above information and place in its historical context the document that is of interest for our purposes. It is a short poem in four lines (two elegiac distichs, the usual metrical form usual for epigrams), engraved on a grey marble block that had served as a base for an offering. We shall translate the text literally, in a manner keeping more closely to the original than the rhythmic adaptation of our epigraph. "To Enyalius" (it runs) " it is meet to dedicate my shield, and my horses' *phalara* with their gleaming ornament. As for Victory, Eupolemus proclaims that he dedicates her to King Magas – a noble privilege! So may he under her patronage keep safe his scepters, his peoples and his cities!" The text deals with an offering made in the shrine of Enyalius (or Ares), god of war, by Eupolemus, an officer in the royal army returning from a campaign. Eupolemus dedicates to the god part of his weapons, thus conforming to a frequent usage: the shield that protected him from the enemy's blows, and the head-harness of the horses that drew his war chariot. *Phalara* were small bronze discs inlaid with silver; they were fitted on the reverse side with a loop that allowed the harness belts to pass through, and adorned the horse's forehead and the sides of its head. These fittings and the shield were hung on the wall of the temple where the dedication had taken place. Close by on the inscribed base stood the statue of Victory, *Niké*, an allegory long deified among the Greeks, the companion of Zeus, Athena, and, of course, Ares. The dedicatory epigram, conforming to the rule, lists the various components of the act of dedication, and gives the name of its author – for the god and those who visit his shrine should know who has done this pious deed.

If this were all it was doing, the text would be no more informative than hundreds of other analogous dedications, in prose or verse, that have been preserved in inscriptions and in such collections as the Palatine Anthology. But it goes further. More than half the epigram, everything concerning the statue of Niké, is devoted to a second theme, no longer related to the god Ares, but to king Magas, to whom Eupolemus dedicates the effigy of Victory, as though the king were also a god. This in fact he proclaims loud and clear, giving more than a hint that the sovereign is the *Savior* (just as his stepfather, Ptolemy I, was *Sôter*) of his kingdom and all its inhabitants, its *peoples*. This last term refers to the Libyan tribes, who still lived in a large part of Cyrenaica between the territories belonging *in proprio* to the Greek cities and the cities themselves. The Greek text calls these cities *ptoliethra*, a noble Archaic name belonging to the language of epic.

This short poem – the quality of the original text strikes the reader as exceptional in every way – is no ordinary dedication. It goes beyond the pious gesture of an offering to a god in his shrine, a routine and traditional demonstration bearing witness to the vitality of a belief and a cult. The author of this particular dedication wished to signify that beside the god stands the living king, the reigning sovereign, the favorite of Victory, who has taken him under her wing and accompanies him – "a noble privilege!" – in his role as protector of his peoples. The very term *privilege* is important. It is the term that ancient texts, first in line the poems of Homer, use to designate the choice portion that is reserved for the gods, the king, or the foremost nobles, in the produce of the soil, sacred offerings, or war booty. An exchange of sorts takes place, not without a certain ambiguity, between Victory and the king. The statue of Niké is dedicated to the king, as the offering due to his person. Simultaneously Victory, a divine entity, grants her patronage to Magas to help him accomplish his task as a savior of the heritage placed in his care. With admirable terseness the last verse defines that heritage: the *scepters*, the *peoples*, the *city*. The *scepters* are symbols of power (the plural no doubt gives expression to an implicit claim to the Egyptian throne, "usurped" by his younger half-brother Ptolemy II, beyond that of Cyrenaica, which Magas already holds). The term *peoples* is the same as the one designating the Egyptian fellahin in the papyri. Finally, the *cities* are the Greek states of Libya, Cyrene, Barce, Euhesperides, dominating vast territories and having an ambiguous relationship with the sovereign, implying obedience but not subject status. In the four lines of Eupolemus' epigram one can recognize the dense and brilliant style of Callimachus, the great Cyrenaean poet who flourished around 280 BC. They provide us, in a succinct and singularly striking way, with a definition, by one of his closest servants, of what goes into the making of a Hellenistic sovereign, at a time when a persona of that kind was imposing itself on the contemporary Greek world.

■ *Victory as the king's privilege* ■ *Agonistic notions of divine favor* ■ *Justifications based on genealogy* ■ *Alliances by marriage* ■ *The succession problem* ■ *Co-regency of father and son* ■ *Marriages between blood relations* ■ *Superhuman nature of the king* ■ *The royal cult: its various forms, municipal and dynastic*

The main feature of such an image of the king is his association with Victory. Victory is the king's privilege, his distinguishing characteristic among all mortals, the sign that allows us to recognize the favorite of the gods. This is an idea of great antiquity; it is already found in Homer, who gives it a leading role. A human being, however deserving, can do nothing unless granted divine support. One must indeed be brave, but one's bravery must also and above all be pleasing to the gods and in accord with destiny. The Greeks' profound wisdom thus expressed a feeling founded on experience: that in every human venture, however justified by the laws of reason, chance always has a part to play that is inescapable. Success, which can never be assured, appeared to them, when it actually occurred, to put the stamp of divine benevolence on an endeavor and its author. This is why they gave such importance to athletic competitions, for victory in them was not so much the recognition of exceptional physical talent as dazzling proof of the gods' favor. It honored not only the victor, who justly won glory for benefiting from such a privilege, but at the same time his city, which was happy to receive such distinction from Fortune in the person of one of her sons.

The very idea of victory is therefore deeply embedded in the Hellenic soul; it is fundamentally an *agonistic* notion. Now, the Hellenistic king, first and foremost his army's leader, appears above all as a victor. Alexander the Great had stirred human imagination, and enthroned in our world the image of a new Achilles. Failure, on the other hand, is a cause of personal devaluation. It is interpreted as a sign from the gods: those who witness it feel authorized to act accordingly. This explains how, in 321, Perdiccas' generals did not shrink from murdering their leader (see p. 44), who had failed to force a crossing over the Nile, and going over to Ptolemy's side. Similarly, Eumenes' failure in 316 led the elite corps of the Argyraspids, though they were attached to the child king Alexander IV and to Argead legitimacy, to change sides and rally round Antigonus. These Macedonian veterans could see that in spite of his deeds of valor against their adversaries, Eumenes had lost the cavalry engagement and allowed their baggage train to be plundered: the gods had made their choice, one that they had to follow. The long blow-by-blow account that Diodorus (XIX, 40–3) devotes to the various turns of that decisive encounter, makes sense only in that perspective. The Argyraspids, loyal until then, resolved that henceforth they should not resist Fate (see p. 48).

In this episode can be seen the rapid evolution that, at the start of the Hellenistic age, substituted the image of the victorious leader for that of the hereditary king. Alexander's personality was a fusion of both. But afterwards, all through the stormy period of the Diadochi, the prestige of victory prevailed over the notion of dynastic legitimacy, which could only reassert itself, when needed and after the event, by recourse to various subterfuges, political marriage, or alleged lineage. The one essential asset was in future to be the aura that a successful general won through his victory, and his victory alone, which was clear evidence of his capability as a ruler. More than anyone else, the king himself was aware of the privileged position of his person. A quip from Antigonus Gonatas, reported by Plutarch (*Life of Pelopidas*, 2), illustrates the haughty confidence that such a feeling fostered. "He was about to engage in naval battle at Andros, when someone came and told him that the enemy's fleet was more numerous than his. 'What about me?' he asked. 'How many vessels is my valour worth?' "

It is therefore the old Greek idea of victory, laden with religious meaning, that was from the outset the hallmark of Hellenistic monarchy: the notion of hereditary sovereignty, wherever that was alive, stayed in the background. It seems to have resuscitated the reverence that the illustrious tyrants of old had once inspired. Cypselus, Periander, Polycrates, Pisistratus himself appeared legitimized by success. Following these were the Sicilian tyrants Gelo, Hiero, Theron, whom the poets had celebrated, vying with each other, and Dionysius, on whom the Athenian people showered flattery. As long as they were in power, public opinion, except for a few implacable, unforgiving exiles, challenged none of them. It was posterity that gave an unflattering picture of those men, preserving only the condemnation and anathema hurled at them by their successors. In the Hellenistic age, on the other hand, for reasons given here and after a half-century of varied fortunes, the monarchical phenomenon proved an enduring one. By his prolonged stay in power the victorious sovereign revived the notion of a dynasty, or created it for his family's benefit. The overriding assertion of his personal charisma remained alive: yet he was pleased to add to it credentials borrowed from myth and history (which in Greek eyes were one and the same). Someone like Pyrrhus had no difficulty in finding these. Being of Aeacid stock he traced his descent straight back to Neoptolemus, son of Achilles and conqueror of Troy. The Ptolemies claimed descent from Heracles, using a genealogical contrivance making Ptolemy Sôter, their dynasty's founder, a bastard of Philip II of Macedon, hence Alexander's brother, born of adultery. That is how, in the long inscription from Xanthus concerning the Cytenium Dorians' embassy (mentioned in the previous chapter: see p. 209), Ptolemy IV is called "a Dorian by origin through the lineage of the Argead kings, descendants of Heracles." The same document, in the Aetolian decree transcribed in it, speaks of "the kings descended from Heracles, Ptolemy and Antiochus": which implies that the Seleucid king Antiochus III claimed like Ptolemy, or allowed others to believe, that he belonged to the same heroic lineage. Another tradition, for which evidence is first found at an earlier date (281), made a direct connection between the Seleucids' origin and Apollo. The mother of Seleucus, founder of the dynasty, was the wife of one of Philip II's lieutenants, called Antiochus. Justin (XV, 4) tells her story.

> She dreamed that she had conceived after sleeping with Apollo, that when she was pregnant she had received from him, as a present for having slept with him, a ring with a stone on which an anchor was carved, with instructions to give this to the son she was to bear. Two things made this dream astounding. The first was a ring that was found in her bed the following day bearing that very motif, and the second a birthmark in the shape of an anchor on the infant Seleucus' thigh. Laodice gave this ring to Seleucus when he went off with Alexander the Great on the Persian campaign, explaining to him how he had been born. . . . The emblem of his birth persisted in the succeeding generations, since his sons and grandsons had an anchor on the thigh as a congenital mark of their ancestry. (trans. J. C. Yardley)

That is why we occasionally find the picture of an anchor on Seleucid coinage, to serve as an extra symbol.

Plate 5   Coin of Seleucus I (Paris, Cabinet des Médailles, Bibliothèque Nationale).

The reverse of this coin, minted in the royal workshop at Pergamum, displays one of the Indian elephants (note the typical ears) that Sandracottus gave to Seleucus. The inscription reads Basileôs Seleukou, *"Of King Seleucus." It is enhanced by two symbols: a star, and an anchor pointing to Seleucus' divine origin (see Justin's text above).*

A relationship by marriage used to be sought to make up for the absence of a direct line of ancestry. Cassander, son of Antipater, entered the family of the Argeads by marrying Philip's daughter, Thessalonice. Perdiccas had already, at the instigation of Olympias, married Alexander's sister, Cleopatra. These were really political arrangements, the purpose of which was to bolster in the eyes of the Macedonians, and theirs alone, the prestige of these aspirants to supreme power by providing them with access to the royal family. But the significance of blood ties is evident above all in the most challenging of all operations in a monarchical regime: the succession process. In conformity with ancient Macedonian as well as Greek usage, accession by right of primogeniture, from male to male, was the rule. Yet the younger sons felt as suited for royalty as the eldest one, being of the same blood. Hellenistic history is full of cases of fierce rivalry between brothers, usually ending with the disappearance of one of the rivals. More than one example of this has been cited, so there is no need to recall them here, but let us quote from Plutarch (*Life of Demetrius*, 3) a text full of unsparing irony. He praises the Antigonids' immunity from family homicide, if one ignores the single case of Philip V, who felt bound to have one of his sons executed. "Contrary to them," (he writes) "nearly all other royal families have been frequent practitioners of murder on their sons, as well as their mothers and wives. As geometricians admit postulates, so for the slaughter of one's brothers: it was held as a sort of postulate granted by custom to kings, so that they could ensure their safety."

It was also to guarantee due process in succession that, as noted in many cases, the future king was made an associate in the exercise of power during the reigning king's lifetime. The practice of co-regency, of which a number of examples were already known (like those of Demetrius Poliorcetes beside his father Antigonus, or Antiochus I as an associate of Seleucus, and many others), is now seen as having been more frequent than was formerly believed. We now know that Antigonus Gonatas shared his royal power with his son Demetrius II from early days. Demetrius reigned alone for only ten years, from 239 to 229, but a deed of emancipation found at Verria in Macedonia bears the date of the twenty-seventh year of his reign, which must therefore have started long before Gonatas, his father, died. This illustrates how a humble document, apparently of limited significance, as is the case with a deed of emancipation, can unexpectedly throw light on political history. The same is true of the Cytenians' impressive stele at Xanthus. It gives us information hitherto unknown: that Ptolemy V Epiphanes was from early childhood associated with his father Ptolemy IV Philopator in the exercise of Lagid royalty. As new epigraphic texts are discovered, the chronology of sovereigns, on which the calendar of states used to be based, is gradually put into sharper focus.

The pursuit of dynastic prestige and a belief in the special virtues of royal blood account for the strange custom, so common among the Lagids, of brother–

sister marriages, which in the eyes of the Greeks were a scandalous practice, amounting to incest. The most illustrious case of such marriages in Hellenistic history was the first. Setting an example for his successors, Ptolemy II married his elder sister Arsinoe: hence their title of *Philadelphi* ("Love-bonded Sibling") Divinities. It appears that we have here a case of passionate love rather than political calculation. But subsequent analogous cases – those of Ptolemies VI, VIII, IX, XIII, and XIV – were obviously consonant with a wish to preserve dynastic privilege through inbreeding. After all, Zeus and his sister Hera seemed to give divine sanction to that departure from the directives of Greek law. As for marriages between princes and princesses of royal blood, which were common, they reflected a definite political purpose (as was seen in the period of the Diadochi), and aimed at setting up links at the personal level between states. The hope that guided these arrangements rarely became reality. But the persistence of such a matrimonial policy is an apt illustration of a widespread feeling among princely families, as well as among the people, that kings were a class apart, essentially different from common mortals.

There was only one step to take before they were elevated to divine rank. It was soon taken, since Alexander, who seems to have been persuaded of his divine ancestry by his visit to the Oasis of Ammon, demanded of Greek cities in 324 that they institute his cult as an "invincible god." A hostile reaction, from someone like Hyperides, or a contemptuous one, from Demosthenes, for example, greeted that claim. It nevertheless benefited from widespread agreement, since it did not really shock the Hellenic conscience, accustomed as that people was to bestow a cult on past heroes and even, sometimes, on living ones. Popular credulity turned an attentive ear to fabulous tales and marveled at prodigies. Was it not already being said that Olympias conceived Alexander not from Philip her husband, but from the god who approached her in the shape of a serpent? Plutarch is not above reporting these tales (*Life of Alexander*, 2–3). He then gives some curious information about the king, which he has gathered from Aristoxenus of Tarentum, a contemporary of the Conqueror: "Alexander's skin exhaled a sweet scent. A perfumed breath came from his lips, bathing his whole body, actually permeating his tunics." No doubt Plutarch attempts to explain the phenomenon he quotes by physico-physiological arguments borrowed from the learned Theophrastus, Aristotle's pupil. Yet the people saw in what was reported the sign of a superhuman nature. Similarly Pyrrhus, the most remarkable imitator of the Conqueror, according to the same Plutarch (*Life of Pyrrhus*, 3), possessed miraculous powers of healing.

> He was reputed to cure people who suffered from a diseased spleen: he would sacrifice a white cock, then lay the patients down on their back, and gently massage their spleen with his left foot . . . In the big toe of that foot, it was said, lay a supernatural power: so much so that at Pyrrhus' death, when all the rest of his body had been consumed on the funeral pyre, that toe was discovered, intact and untouched by fire.

Nations of Greek descent were encouraged by their own instinct and their up-bringing to revere countless manifestations of divine presence. No wonder that, faced with such prodigies, they placed these generous and formidable monarchs in the ranks of higher powers, whose kindness they sought, whose anger they feared. For these too could help or destroy them at will. Certain modern critics would like to fit the mental behavior of the ancient world into our logical categories. They have introduced subtle distinctions between the institution of a cult and deification, between the respective meanings of a municipal and a dynastic cult, between a king's association with another divinity and a genuine personal apotheosis. I find such niceties unfounded. In Greek religion, as surely in any other, what is of prime importance is the existence of a cult, which is after all the only remaining element of information to which the historian usually has access. Wherever the rites performed in a cult are attested, even if there was no supporting belief previous to the proven existence of that ritual, it is certain that subsequently belief grew in support of it. At the time of Alexander and the Diadochi, the people's state of mind was ripe for such changes. Let us not be too hasty in deriding the Athenians for awarding honors that were beyond any common measure to Demetrius Poliorcetes and his father Antigonus when their troops captured the city in 307. It is once again Plutarch (*Life of Demetrius*, 10) who lists them. Father and son were proclaimed Savior Gods, and a cult was instituted in their honor, the citizens electing every year the holder of its priesthood. Athena's famous *peplos*, offered to the goddess at the Great Panathenaea, was to bear, woven amid those of the other divinities, the likenesses of Antigonus and Demetrius. An altar was to be raised at the spot now pronounced sacred, where Demetrius had alighted from his chariot, and a sacrifice offered to "Demetrius Alighting," *Kataibates*, an epithet already given to Zeus at the spot where he had struck the ground with his thunderbolt. The city created two new tribes, Demetrias and Antigonis, putting their namesakes on a level with the tutelary heroes of Attica, whom the Pythian priestess had in time past chosen as *eponyms* of the other ten tribes. An addition was made to the Athenian calendar: this was the new festival of the *Demetria*. Later, in 291, the Athenians caused to be sung at the Great Eleusinia, the major festival of Demeter, a hymn in honor of Demetrius, the text of which the compiler Athenaeus (VI, 253d) has preserved for us. In it the sovereign is hailed as Demeter's companion, the son of Poseidon and Aphrodite, the only one able to protect the city against external danger and preserve its peace. While the other gods (so it continues) do exist, but stay away or are indifferent, Demetrius, present and visible, is not a statue of wood or stone, but a living, very real god. Commentators vie with each other in branding such a tribute a scandalous piece of flattery. In so doing they subscribe to Plutarch's homespun condemnation of the Athenians, when he cites such a gesture as belying the tradition of a free people, so particular in time past about safeguarding its independence and dignity. This is tantamount to discounting the spirit of the times, which allows us to understand that kind of behavior. These were times fertile in wonders, in unexpected changes of fortune, in which the people discerned, or believed it discerned, the determining action of a heaven-sent human being. Philosophers, following Epicurus' example, taught that the traditional gods were totally uninterested in the fate of common mortals, while Euhemerus propounded a doctrine tracing the origin of the gods to the cult given to outstanding men. The Athenians were doing nothing exceptional when they hailed Demetrius Poliorcetes as a god.

A quarter of a century later, the dedication made by the Cyrenaean officer Eupolemus drew a parallel between his leader, king Magas, and the god Ares. He dedicated a statue of Victory to Magas, while he gave his shield and his horses' *phalara* to Enyalius. In so doing he was only sharing in a widely held belief, a readiness among the people to render divine honors to the powerful of the day. No doubt, there was still some lack of clarity in a sentiment that first expressed itself in such gestures as sacrifices and offerings. There was no precise awareness of it, nor did it lead to a solidly constructed theological doctrine. Faith feeds on primary sentiment, on obscure and ambiguous notions, on attitudes that obtain greater clarity and forcefulness from being expressed in public. The task of translating it into coherent discourse or rhythmic language was left to philosophers and poets. What was important and novel was that widespread urge to devote a cult to the person holding power, whether that power had been gained by force of arms or received by hereditary succession from a father who was already held to be a god. Indeed, from one kingdom to another, from one sovereign to another (sometimes, in addition, within the same dynasty), from city to city in the vast Hellenistic world, all manner of nuances, differences in formulaic style and in ceremonial, told royal cults apart from each other. Altars were raised and special temples built in honor of some sovereigns, while others were simply introduced as new occupants of a shrine they shared with an already established divinity. That was probably Magas' case in the port of Cyrene, in relation to the god Enyalius. Cities often instituted royal cults on their own initiative, as Athens did in favor of Demetrius Poliorcetes. At the time of receiving the Dorians from Cytenium, Lycian Xanthus had its cult of the *Euergetai* Divinities (Ptolemy III and Queen Berenice), with whom the reigning king, Ptolemy IV Philopator, had already been coopted. The holder of their priesthood was eponymous to the city, as was the priest of the tutelary goddess Leto. On other occasions, as in the case of dynastic cults, the order came from above, resulting in a unification of the rites. A fine example is provided by the cult in honor of Queen Laodice, which the Seleucid king Antiochus III instituted for her in her own lifetime, in 193 BC. Two epigraphic texts, one from Dodurga in Anatolia, the other from Nehavend in Media, have preserved the edict instituting that cult. It was to be celebrated in the whole of the empire in the same places as the king's cult. High priestesses were to officiate, wearing gold crowns adorned with a medallion bearing the

Queen's effigy. It was also prescribed that in every administrative constituency, the high priestess's name was to serve for dating documents having legal force, as was already the case for the names of high priests in the king's cult. Such provisions clearly illustrate the official standing of these dynastic cults in the totality of the Seleucid states. On the other hand, municipal cults, or those founded by individuals or associations of private citizens, did not fit into any established format, but preserved their originality and local character, as did all Greek cults. That gives them further significance, as they allow us to measure the scope and the territorial distribution of this phenomenon. It is true that in Macedon the Antigonids, anxious to preserve the tradition of the national monarchy in their country, refrained from instituting an official cult. But they endorsed those in which the cities had taken the initiative. Eager to preserve, in their relationship with their faithful subjects, the image of the chief bound by an unwritten law, *primus inter pares*, they were still determined not to be deprived of the charisma that the Hellenistic world as a whole associated with its idea of kingship. The acclamation of the assembled people, for whom the army on campaign acted as representative and deputy, was evidence of the public acknowledgment of supreme authority. That authority, however, it did not confer. It remained the king's privilege, deriving from his royal blood and the benevolence of the gods, among whom he already had or was one day to have his place.

■ *The insignia of royalty* ■ *The royal title* ■ *Epithets added to it* ■ *The diadem, the scepter, the ring* ■ *The throne of Alexander* ■ *The weapons of Pyrrhus* ■ *Monetary effigies of sovereigns*

The titular holder of so rare a privilege had to be brought to humanity's attention by obvious signs that made him recognizable and allowed tokens to be given of the deference due to him. First was his title, the simple one of king, which went with his personal name, and proclaimed by itself his superhuman character: King Alexander, King Antiochus, King Magas. In the traditional monarchies of earlier times, the title did not come without the addition of an identifying limitation: king of the Macedonians, king of the Molossi, king of Cyrene, king of Syracuse. Often the sovereign's name was not accompanied by any title. It appears that Philip II, Alexander's father, never had himself simply called King Philip. In Hellenistic Macedon Cassander and the Antigonids seem to have kept the use of the traditional formula "king of the Macedonians," without making it a rule, and occasionally employed a term that was akin to it, "the king and the Macedonians." But everywhere else, unless the wish to avoid confusion led to the addition of a geographical detail ("who reigns over Cyprus" or "who reigns at Cyrene"), the expression "King So-and-so" is constant. The royal title expressed the sovereign's own nature, distinguishing him from the common mortal.

To that title, the essential definition of his person, an epithet was often added, following the king's name and designating one particular quality he wished to emphasize or that public opinion associated with his person. Ptolemy I was Saviour (*Sôter*), because the Rhodians gave him that added name; Ptolemy II was "His Sister's Lover" (*Philadelphus*), after his marriage with Arsinoe II; Ptolemy III was Benefactor (*Euergetes*) for having restored to the Egyptians statues of their gods that Cambyses had once taken away. Seleucus I was the Victor (*Nicator*), Seleucus II the king "of fair victory" (*Kallinikos*. see p. 77). Others were "He who Loves his Father" (*Philopator*), like Ptolemy IV, Seleucus IV, and Ptolemy VII, or "He who Loves his Mother" (*Philometor*), like Ptolemy VI. Many such appellations have the nature of a divine epithet (*epiklesis*) that used to be added to names of divinities: *Epiphanes* ("he who makes his apparition" or "manifests himself"), or simply *Theos* ("God"). Actually, *Sôter* was already an *epiklesis* of Zeus, *Kallinikos* one of Heracles. These laudatory epithets, which might appear in the official list of a sovereign's titles, should not be confused with depreciatory nicknames like *Physkon* ("the bloated one"), *Lathyros* ("chick-pea") or *Auletes* ("the flute-player"), which are found only in the writings of historians. With the passage of time, such epithets increased in number, keeping pace with the lowering of the sovereign's actual prestige: this happened as though the new epithet redeemed the sovereign. This phenomenon of compensation appears nowhere more clearly than in the list of titles belonging to the petty king of Commagene, who caused Nimrud Dagh's enormous statues to be erected. Inscriptions have preserved his complete list: "The great king Antiochus, God, Just, Epiphanes, Romanophile, and Philhellene." These high-sounding epithets did not protect him from submitting to the authority of the proconsul Lucullus.

The king's insignia of power also distinguished him. Most important among these was the diadem, a narrow band of cloth, usually white, tied round his hair above the forehead and ears, its ends being knotted at the back of the neck, usually hanging as two ribbons down his back or over his shoulders. Its origin can be traced directly to the headband that was awarded to victors in athletic competitions, like the one worn by the Delphic charioteer. It was therefore an emblem of victory, appropriately distinguishing the sovereign. With it came the scepter, already a royal attribute in Homer, and keeping in the Hellenistic age its significance as the rod of command, the symbol of the king's authority, as we see in the last line of Eupolemus' epigram. The royal ring completed this set of symbols. Its engraved stone was used to seal and authenticate the sovereign's official deeds. These insignia had a sacred character. Whoever got hold of them and used them as personal ornaments committed an act of sacrilege. The following text of Diodorus (XVII, 96) adequately conveys this principle.

> One day, while Alexander was rubbing himself with oil, the royal trappings and his diadem were lying on a throne. An Asian prisoner had freed himself from his fetters and, eluding the guards' vigilance, entered the palace without difficulty. He reached the throne, put on the royal robe and placed the diadem round his head. Seating himself on the throne, he remained motionless in that position. The king, learning this and being astonished at such extraordinary behavior, approached the throne. Keeping his composure, he calmly asked the man who he was and why he behaved in that manner. The man replied that he did not know. Alexander then consulted the soothsayers on how to interpret that event. On their advice, he had the man executed, so as to redirect onto him the disturbing omens that some were inferring from this incident.

Soon after, while he was crossing the marsh surrounding Babylon in a small boat, the king, sailing under some branches, dropped his diadem, which fell into the water. Although it was soon retrieved by some of the boatmen, the mishap was nonetheless looked on as a bad omen. Historiographers were reminded of that when, a few days later, Alexander passed away in a violent spell of malaria. Further on, Diodorus notes that one of the dying king's last gestures was to remove the royal ring from his finger and give it to Perdiccas, thus presenting him with royal power. Perdiccas was accordingly considered by his peers, at least for a time, to have received a royal investiture.

Another passage from Diodorus (XVIII, 61) makes evident the consecrating role attributed to these insignia. In 318 Eumenes, appointed *strategos* of Asia in the name of the kings, wished to make it clear to the military leaders placed under his orders that he was invested with the supreme authority, Alexander's legacy. He pretended he had had a dream instructing him to institute an impressive ceremony.

> He had a golden throne made, as well as ordering a magnificent tent to be erected, in which the throne was placed. On it were laid the diadem, the scepter and the weapons that Alexander usually bore. In addition a burning altar was raised there. All the army chiefs would approach, and offer on it a sacrifice, burning incense and the most precious herbs, which they took out of a gold casket, while venerating Alexander as a god.

It is to be noted in this text that beside the diadem, the scepter and the throne were the royal weapons. A favorite of Victory and above all a war leader, the sovereign had to be made prominent by the magnificence of his weapons. Plutarch relates (*Life of Pyrrhus*, 16) that at the battle of Heraclea against the Roman legions, Pyrrhus, who led the cavalry charge, "instantly compelled recognition by the splendour of his sumptuously adorned weapons." Being far too easily recognizable, eventually he had to exchange them for those of a companion, who lost his life as a result.

Not only in cultic ceremonies was a monarch who stood so far above the rest of humanity made the equal of the gods. On coins he was given the place reserved for divinity: his effigy would usually appear on the obverse, where the god's image had appeared until then. Thanks to this, we have in our coin and medal collections the richest and most lifelike portrait gallery of Hellenistic sovereigns, ranging from Alexander, whose features seem fixed for ever in their ideal nobility, to the facies, clothed in powerful ugliness, of Philetaerus, deified after his death, or Euthydemus of Bactria. So it was until the end of that age. Cleopatra's long, hooked nose on Antioch's coinage confirms Pascal's remark that the face of the world would have changed had her nose been shorter, and allows us to understand how seduction went hand in hand with majesty in that exceptional woman. Caesar and the Roman emperors, also placed in the ranks of the gods, were to prolong a custom demonstrating so aptly the foundation of apotheosis in the realities of life.

■ *The territories depending on the king* ■ *The right of conquest*
■ *The kingdom, being the king's inheritance, might be*
bequeathed: Ptolemy the Younger's will ■ *The royal domain*
■ *The king and the Greek cities: their ambiguous relationship*
■ *Territorial complexity of the monarchical State*

Victory's favored hero, the king reigned over territories that he or his ancestors had conquered. Even in traditional monarchies, prestige as a warrior remained the right on which power rested. An old Homeric term to designate the sovereign's dominion is revived in certain texts on that subject: "conquered by the spear," *doriktetos*. The allusion here is to Alexander's gesture when he drove his spear into Asian soil as he landed on it for the first time. The Conqueror had instructed Lysippus to portray him spear in hand: that spear which (as Plutarch writes, in *Isis and Osiris*, 24), "Time shall not rob (it) of the genuine glory that it possesses in its own right." This statue inspired an epigrammatist with a distich:

> He seems, that man of bronze, to turn his eyes up to Heaven, and say to Zeus:
> "I hold the Earth in my power, Zeus. Keep Olympus for you."

Alexander had dedicated that same spear, no doubt in Artemis' temple at Ephesus, which was burnt down on the very night of his birth, but rebuilt, thanks to his generous aid. As late as Augustan times, a fictitious dedication was written in its honor (*Palatine Anthology*, VI, 97):

Spear of Alexander! The inscription says that he consecrated you to Artemis after the war, as a complement to the shield that had covered his invincible arm. Noble spear, when he brandished you, Sea and Earth yielded to him. Be favorable to us, fearless spear. For ever will everyone be fearful at your sight, recalling the hero who handled you.

Thus was the right of conquest the foundation of royal authority, which was exercised on territories as diverse in status as they were in extent. In the great monarchies most of those territories consisted of barbarian land conquered from non-Greek states or peoples: Achaemenid Asia, principalities of the Near East, Thracian or Illyrian tribes, various populations of Sicily, Libyans, Egyptian fellahin. These were "royal domains" proper, in which the sovereign held in principle every power. Wherever Roman authority took it over, that *chora basilike* was to become *ager publicus*, the property of the Roman people. The king did as he pleased with it, and also with the inhabitants cultivating it. He would allow anyone he pleased, as a gesture of goodwill, to make use of it, and take back one day what he had granted. He could, of course, also hand it over to another prince. In a word, the monarch's states were in practical terms a heritage, over which its owner had discretionary power. Hence the importance of sovereigns' wills, when they planned to bequeath their possessions to others rather than to their legitimate successor, or, for want of an heir by blood, to appoint some beneficiary from outside their family. A famous example is the will that Ptolemy VIII (the Younger) wrote in 155, after his elder brother, Ptolemy VI Philometor, had attempted to murder him. The text runs as follows:

> May I, by the will of the gods, pursue, according to their deserts, those responsible for the impious plot hatched against me, when they planned to rob me not only of my kingdom, but of life itself. Should I experience the common fate of mortals before I can leave heirs to my kingdom, I bequeath the states that are mine to the Romans, to whose friendship and alliance I have been faithful since the start. I entrust them with the task of looking after those states' safety. I entreat them, in the name of all the gods and for the sake of their own glory, in case any attempt were to be made on the cities or the territory, to intervene in conformity with the pledges of friendship and alliance we have exchanged. I ask them to safeguard the rule of right to the utmost of their power. As guarantors of the present I designate Zeus Capitoline and the Great Gods, Helios and Apollo Archegetes, in whose shrine the text of this testament has been consecrated. With Good Fortune's help!

This is an astonishing document, which no historian had mentioned and archaeological excavation has now unearthed. It is an admirably preserved marble stele, found in the shrine of Apollo, tutelary deity and founder of Cyrene, at the very place where the text says that the inscription was to be put up – another example of the help that epigraphy gives to history.

The testament makes a clear distinction between the cities, to which a more or less extensive territory was annexed, and the royal domain, which was separate and under the sovereign's direct control. He saw to its profitable exploitation by the populations living there. In the large empires, the Lagid, the Seleucid, and the Attalid, the status of the soil was more complex: the king did not possess all the land, even when his personal domain was immense. It seems that there was also private property: more important, in regions peopled by barbarians, vast spaces were immune from straight annexation by the king. These included the possessions of the native princes, great or small, of the priests and local shrines, of tribes preserving a partial state of independence. Indeed, they were all formally dependent on the king and were part of the monarchical State, but their relations with him were of quite a varied kind, often loose, and, to our way of thinking at least, rather vague. Such a relationship, normal in so vast and complex a world, was a reflection of practical realities.

The situation was the same for Greek cities. Wherever they were ancient and powerful, the sovereign pretended to treat them with the deference due to independent states, even when his own territories enclosed them. He was less considerate with other territorial entities: there he would send a representative – a public servant, often an officer of his army – who had control *in situ* of administrative and political matters. With varying titles, these public figures were commissioners of the king, entrusted with supervision of the city. Their presence was no hindrance to the proper functioning of civic institutions; on the contrary, they saw to these, playing their traditional role in the management of city affairs, provided this did not run counter to the king's designs. They also saw to the proper administration of justice. The king would sometimes help a city to find foreign judges in another city. He could act as arbiter in serious cases, and adjudicate on disagreements between cities, or ask another city, not a party to the dispute, to make an award. Examples of such arbitration are numerous, and it is clear that in many cases the authority of the king, who possessed prestige in the area and had military power nearby at his disposal, contributed to the resolution of a conflict. Starting in the second century, Rome's presence became generalized in the East; it often happened that her representative took over the task of arbiter, if not of guardian, that had once belonged to the king.

There too the striking feature was the extreme diversity of particular cases. Relations between cities and sovereigns were in fact determined by their comparative strengths. They changed radically according to whether or not the city was under military occupation, that is, subjected to the presence on its territory of a permanent garrison, consisting of a mercenary corps. These bilateral relations were as a rule embodied in an alliance with the king, a juridical fiction that appeared to respect the citizens' susceptibilities, and gave them the illusion of having personally decided on their fate. But had the situation been different in the Classical age, in the days of the great hegemonic leagues headed by Sparta, Athens, or Thebes? This was an ambiguous relationship, where the two parties' interests, sometimes shared and sometimes at variance, were the deciding factor.

The city needed the king, who brought protection as well as subjection, and the king needed the city. He might, according to circumstances, obtain from the city tribute money, military contingents, supplies, strategic advantages, the use of a harbor, control of a sea or land passage from a stronghold. In exchange he gave the city guarantees, exemptions, and privileges; he shouldered a number of public expenses, granted aid toward restoring the walls, had porticoes and temples built, enriched the shrines, offered gifts to the population in times of penury. Like the local god, he might take up the eponymous magistracy in case of default by the citizens, owing to the cost that such a function entailed. It was all a matter of circumstances, and these could change, sometimes quite rapidly, depending on whether a particular monarch's area of influence was growing or shrinking. The city might deal with the king on an equal footing, as was often the case with Rhodes, and of course with the great leagues of the third century. It found itself more often in the situation of a protectorate. It sometimes swung between alliances, having to choose between one dynasty and another, or between a dynasty and Rome. The case of cities isolated in the midst of a large empire was different. This was the situation of the three Greek cities of Egypt, Alexandria the Great, the ancient colonial city of Naucratis (whose role had been sorely diminished), and the new foundation of Ptolemais, a duplicate of Thebes, the Pharaonic capital of Upper Egypt. The Asian cities that the Seleucids founded or developed were in a similar position: relying entirely on royal goodwill, they could not dream of an independent policy. Their role was an economic and cultural one, and their administrative context, formally comparable to that of the cities of the old Hellenic world, gave them nothing but the trappings of autonomy. Many of them, after all, provided a seat for sovereign power. This was the case with Alexandria for the Lagids, and Antioch on the Orontes for the Seleucids (who also had other capitals, Seleucia on the Tigris, for instance). Pergamum served as a seat for the Attalids; Nicomedia for the kings of Bithynia, Sinope for those of Pontus, Syracuse for Agathocles or Hiero II, Cyrene for Magas or Physcon. This role brought them prestige. They became centers of economic and administrative activity, and benefited from sizable public works, the building of sumptuous monuments. But their royal guest kept them in a marginal position. In Macedon as well, as research demonstrated not long ago, cities endowed with a Council and an Assembly, institutions that were usual in the Greek world – like Pella, Cassandreia, Amphipolis, or Philippi – remained under the king's tight control.

This was therefore the face shown by the State in the Hellenistic age (it would be more strictly accurate to say the States) when placed under a king's authority. It was a complex, heterogeneous aggregate, devoid of ethnic unity, whose frontiers were always ebbing and flowing at the mercy of wars, ambitions, and conquests. It grouped under one scepter "the dynasts, cities, and peoples" (to use a frequent expression, found in the work of ancient historians and in inscriptions). It was a conglomerate put together amid the varied turns of a troubled history, and always challenged over the years by the fortunes of internal disputes or the appetites of neighbors. The primary model of that type of monarchical State was certainly not Greek. It was the Achaemenid State, whose growth, whose dreams of a universal empire, had filled the Hellenic people with a mixture of admiration and fear: witness writers like Herodotus or Xenophon, who have described its organization and sketched its history. Its conqueror, Alexander, had made his the principle on which it was based, one that was in agreement with his vision. According to that principle, the only link able to keep such diverse components within one group was allegiance to the sovereign, the exclusive holder of power, the fountainhead and ultimate consummation of all: for he was the State's sole incarnation. Such an idea of political authority, personalized in the extreme, went to the very heart of an anxious preoccupation, shared by philosophers and states-men, in the second half of the fourth century. For they wondered how the world of Greek cities was to prevail against the ever-recurring threats of division that imperilled the survival of this world, as it stood at the time. For want of a univer-sal monarchy, the Conqueror's grand dream, which he did not have the time to turn into a reality, the Diadochi and their heirs put structured parts of it in place, with the help of flexible and efficient institutions. Now we shall analyze these.

■ *The king as the unique source of power* ■ *Reckoning of time by the years of a king's reign* ■ *Dynastic eras* ■ *The king and the law: a law based on practice* ■ *Royal correspondence* ■ *The king's advisors: the court and the Friends*

As military might was the foundation of power in a Hellenistic monarchy, the king exercised authority in his capacity as the army's leader. He was the source of every decision, whether he made it in person, or his representative did so in his name. That rule held both in time of peace and in time of war. Of course, proce-dures and methods of action that had produced results in peace could be simi-larly applied in war, and vice versa. The king's person was the ultimate reference in administrative life, and in daily life as well. The kingdom reckoned time by the years of the king's reign, a custom of very ancient origin in all monarchical states. The Seleucids were the exception, the only Greek dynasty in the Hellenistic world to have adopted a real measurement of time independent of the length of every reign. Their reckoning started with Seleucus' reconquest of Babylon in the sum-mer of 312; the beginning of each year, allowing for slight variations depending on local custom (the empire being so extensive), was in early October. The Seleucid era remained for a long time the chronological reference of the Near East, and it was still in use among Arab astronomers, who called it, wrongly, the Era of Alexander. That was an element of civilization with far-reaching consequences. The Seleucid example was followed by barbarian dynasties: by the Arsacids among the Parthians, whose era was reckoned from the spring of 247; and by the kings of Pontus and Bithynia, who used the same method of calculation, starting in the year 297/6 BC. The other monarchies, on the other hand, continued to reckon by years of individual reigns, and the cities by their own eponyms. That went on even when the custom had been established (around the third century) among ancient historians, who then referred, for the convenience of synchronized dating, to the numerical succession of Olympiads.

The king was the incarnation of the State, and the whole administration was centered in his person. The royal will was the law, though it did not displace the traditions of private law. On the contrary, these remained in force, with noticeable continuity (as far as we can judge), among Greek as well as among native communities, especially in Egypt. In that land, *demotic* contracts (that is, those drawn up in a mode of writing derived from greatly simplified hieroglyphics), which have been discovered in large numbers, are abundant proof of that fact. Babylonian contracts provide further evidence of the enduring life of local legislation in Mesopotamia. Greek cities continued to administer justice in accordance with their own laws. They did have recourse to foreign judges (see p. 202). That probably did no more than help to bring into existence, side by side with juridical traditions particular to each city, a Hellenistic common law of sorts. This was applied, in Egypt, for example, when disputes between Greeks living outside a city's territory had to be settled. This is called in the papyri "the law customary to cities," *politikoi nomoi*, the joint heritage of a variety of municipal bodies of law. The sovereign, however, had to adjudicate, in person or through his government officials, on a number of disputes, with due regard to the State's needs and interests. He was thus led to lay down or modify rules: these were usually concerned with public affairs, but they were also liable to have some impact on civil law. The king did this by means of written texts, letters to high-ranking officials or cities, ordinances set out in due form (*prostagmata*, plural of *prostagma*), or detailed regulations, generally on several matters (*diagrammata*). There was no absolutely rigorous distinction among these different kinds of royal decision: here as elsewhere, the monarch's concern was not so much juridical craftsmanship as an attempt to solve particular problems. The principles on which such solutions were based gradually became clear with practice, rather than being expressed in general, theoretical terms. It is remarkable that the word "law" (*nomos*), so much revered and so meaningful in traditional Greek vocabulary, does not appear in the royal texts, though it played such an important role in the life of cities.

These administrative texts are well known among documents surviving from the Seleucid monarchy and (especially) from Ptolemaic rule. Most are in the form of a letter, in which usage prescribes a set of formulae analogous to that of private relationships: the salutation, wishes of good health, set terms of courtesy, the date, all very simple and direct. The king's most obvious departure from that style is his frequent use of the royal plural in writing to his correspondent (not an absolute rule, however). This royal correspondence, these edicts (which modern scholars have put together in collections) took a heavy toll on the sovereign's time, requiring attention, thought, and careful study. That was public knowledge. Some instructive sayings on the subject were common currency. Thus Seleucus I's remark, as reported in Plutarch's *Moralia* (790a): "Anyone knowing the amount of work required of kings by all those letters they must read or write, would not even wish to bend down and pick up a diadem." It was the thought of that daily burden, rather than the perils of war, that prompted Antigonus Gonatas (according to Aelian, *Variae historiae* II, 20) to say to his son Demetrius that the business of kingship was "a glorious state of slavery" (see p. 89).

The sovereign was unable to shoulder so heavy a burden alone, and needed help and advice. The State establishment, an indispensable aid to the fulfillment of the king's duty, was made up of the court and the administrative machinery. Both were as a rule more concerned with efficiency than with etiquette or strict adherence to hierarchy. The court brought together the king's companions, inheriting the role of those gathered around Alexander, whom the Macedonian tradition used to call *hetairoi*. That name tended to be replaced by *philoi* (friends), a term that Alexander had already used. They were often actual friends. Comradeship in childhood or in battle, or mutual esteem, had created a bond with the sovereign; or their desire to help was motivated by a feeling of gratitude, or simply by ambition. The king enjoyed their company and conversation. He found entertainment in their wit. He requested their advice, drew on their experience, and took their criticism into account. He valued their friendship. Freedom of speech in that circle sometimes went quite far. This was the case at the court of the Antigonids, where there was a natural inclination, especially at Antigonus Gonatas' court, to display the Macedonian soldier's somewhat blunt frankness. Nor was flattery absent. Some advisors were evil. Polybius severely condemns, among many others, Sosibius and the Carian Hermias. Sosibius' ascendancy over Ptolemy IV Philopator led the monarch to commit more than one crime. As the dominant influence on Antiochus III in the first years of his reign, Hermias showed himself to be cruel, hypocritical, and prone to jealousy. In later times one could add to the list Potheinos the eunuch and Achillas the *strategos*, inciting Ptolemy XIII to have Pompey murdered. But other advisors deserved the trust that their sovereign had placed in them, though he sometimes failed, at his own cost, to heed their advice. Examples are Cineas the rhetor by the side of Pyrrhus; or the great Hannibal, to whom Antiochus III extended a generous welcome, but whose advice he failed to heed, disastrously, in his operations against

Rome. Some kings, aware of the great help they might receive from the advice of men of wisdom and experience, took pains to attract to their court philosophers, statesmen, and men practiced in warfare. Ptolemy I thus invited to Alexandria Demetrius of Phalerum, the philosopher and rhetor who had governed Athens for ten years, at the time when Cassander led Macedon and held Greece under his domination. Antigonus Gonatas valued the advice of Menedemus of Eretria, his former teacher. He was said to have invited the celebrated founder of Stoicism, Zeno of Citium, to reside at his court. The aged man, so the story goes, declined the honor, but asked two of his pupils to be his representatives at the side of Gonatas.

A custom began to use different titles for "the people associating with the sovereign," to use the term current at the time. The variety of these, at least among the Lagids, may allow us to take for granted a sort of hierarchy. Side by side with the "Friends," there appears the appellation of "Relatives" of the king, a title that does not in any way imply a blood tie or relationship by marriage, but simply a close personal link. There were the ranks of "First Friends," "Members of the Bodyguard" (*somatophylakes*), "Members of the Upper Bodyguard" (who were no longer, as under Alexander, real armed guards, but beneficiaries of a title). There were even "Successors" (*diadochi*) – a term interpreted as designating a reserve list that the king could draw upon. This set of titular positions created a privileged circle round the king: a sort of personal, lifetime nobility (for these titles were not hereditary) among whom the king chose, at its various levels, the civil or military colleagues he needed. But it is unlikely that any actual court etiquette was imposed, with rigid rules that would have made of the sovereign a lone figure. For Greek as well as Macedonian tradition kept alive the notion that the leader must remain approachable. The essentially personal nature of kingship pointed in the same direction.

■ *The central administration* ■ *The archives* ■ *Language of the Chancery* ■ *Local administration* ■ *The* strategoi

The administrative machinery of the monarchical system was fundamentally different from that of a city. The aim was no longer to manage public affairs in the name of the community, which would have meant sharing responsibility in a spirit of collegiality and the yearly renewal of magistracies. Now it was the king's business that had to be looked after, in his name and by delegation of his personal authority. There were no magistrates but ministers, though duties of such a novel kind were not given a generic designation in common parlance. That detail is significant in itself. These ministers were not part of a college. They were appointed on an individual basis, each to attend to a particular task, without such a duty having a time limit, except at the sovereign's pleasure. They received diverse appellations, differing from one monarchy to another and not corresponding to any strict definition, which highlights the individual and precarious nature of the responsibilities involved. Under the Seleucids in the second century, there was a "business superintendent," who seems to have played, at least in a temporary capacity, a very important coordinating role. The same title is found at Pergamum under the Attalids, but not in Lagid Egypt. The latter country, on the other hand, starting in Ptolemy II Philadelphus' reign, had a minister named the *dioiketes*, the "administrator" or otherwise the "income superintendent," who managed the king's treasury. The discovery, in the Fayyum oasis, of the papyrus records left by one Zeno, a businessman in the employ of the *dioecetes* Apollonius, between around 260 and 250 BC, has allowed us to see this minister of Ptolemy II at work in a well-defined sector of his activity. This extended to all areas of exploitation of a large farming domain, as well as external trade in a number of foodstuffs. We shall consider later that astonishing body of documentation on the economic and social life of Greek Egypt. It will suffice here to note, from his regular correspondence with Zeno, that the *dioecetes* Apollonius appears to have held considerable powers that he exercises in the sovereign's name. "The king and Apollonius have ordered . . .": such is the formula he uses when he settles business matters. It demonstrates that all authority derives in the final analysis, by his agency, from the sovereign in person.

The management of an extensive state demanded that an archival system be set up. Hellenistic monarchs therefore had a chancery that registered official documents, keeping a copy of them. These offices, where scribes were at work, were no novelty. The Greek cities and shrines already had their archival services, usually entrusted to public slaves, serious-minded and competent men. The Athenian archives, housed in the sanctuary of the Mother of the Gods, in the Agora, were an essential element of state administration. Hellenistic kingdoms had a similar specialized service, its role being a somewhat extended one. It registered the abundant correspondence that the king exchanged with his subordinates and other states. Hence the name of "Letter Writer" (*epistolographos*) that was given under the Ptolemies to the head of this service. It also recorded the Acts of the king, noted in a day-by-day register, the *Ephemerides*, on which the history of the reign was to be based. Alexander had started this practice: Eumenes of Cardia was the head of his chancery. His choice was significant: by choosing a Greek, not a Macedonian, for the position of archivist, the Conqueror had given a clear directive that the official Acts of his empire were to be written and transcribed in the Greek language, not in the Macedonian dialect. The Hellenistic kings did the same. They needed to make themselves understood both inside and outside large states with varied populations, having relations of every description with cities using a great diversity of dialects. That, as Alexander had realized, required the use of one language. It was to be the Attic tongue, minus a few orthographic and dialectical particularities: the language of Aristotle and the Academy, of the orators and historians. The chancery's vehicle of communication thus became the "common" language, the *koiné*, which royal servants and officers were to use in the whole of the Hellenistic world. Although quite a few cities with a Dorian tradition continued to compose their official documents in their own dialect (as was the case in Delphi, Aetolia, Boeotia, Argos, Crete, Rhodes, or Cyrenaica), use of the *koiné* soon became the rule. The Achaean Polybius used it when he wrote his history. All Hellenistic prose-writers did the same, if they aimed at a wide readership. This was the tongue that allowed the Romans, from the early second century, to convey their meaning to their Greek audience as their career of conquest progressed. Here we are faced with a linguistic phenomenon that was to have a prolonged influence on the eastern Mediterranean basin, extending to Byzantine and modern Greek. It was a major element in the march of civilization. Credit for this goes, to a large extent, to the bureaucracy of the Hellenistic monarchies.

The favored position granted to Greek, at the expense of the Macedonian dialect, shows how far the process of Hellenization had gone amid the dynasty of the Argeads, and, following them, the Macedonian dynasties. Nowhere did the Macedonian tongue survive as the usual medium of communication. The result is that our knowledge of it is very imperfect, for lack of evidence. Just as the kings claimed descent from Greek divinities, so were the language and culture that they propagated exclusively Hellenic, so much so that the very use of the Macedonian dialect tended to disappear among those princely families who boasted of preserving Alexander's heritage. Plutarch (*Life of Antony*, 27) notes that some of the great Cleopatra's ancestors had stopped speaking Macedonian. The Attic tongue's prestige and convenience had played a decisive role in this: a role made easier by the probable kinship (although there are still some scholars who doubt it) between the Greek language and the tongue spoken in Macedonia. But that situation also reflects the numerical imbalance between the Macedonian conquerors and the Greeks. The first group, relatively small from the start, was decimated by incessant wars, and many of its survivors were keen to return to their native land. The numbers of the Greeks, on the other hand, continued to increase at the royal courts, in the armies and administrations of the various kingdoms. The towns, ancient and new, where the activity of the great states was concentrated, were Greek cities. Very soon the term "Macedonian," in so far as it stayed in common usage, lost its primary ethnic content, and became merely a military technical term used to identify a category of officer or soldier. History presents us with a paradox. The victories of Philip and Alexander had impressed contemporaries as being fatal events for the greatness of Greece, and are still shown in such a light in our own day. Yet, in the final analysis, they fostered an unprecedented expansion of Hellenism.

Local administration was an extension *in situ* of action initiated at the administrative center of the kingdom. The vast spaces constituting the Seleucids' and the Ptolemies' dominion had, of course, to be subdivided into smaller territorial units to allow easier government control. Alexander had shown wisdom in preserving the division of the lands he had conquered into the satrapies of the Achaemenid system. The Seleucids respected that precedent, which had proved its efficiency, while introducing into these provinces more restricted administrative constituencies, allowing responsibility to be decentralized. The extreme diversity of the component populations and lands, soon driving a number of them to secession, complicated their task to a remarkable degree and imposed greater flexibility on the system. In Ptolemaic Egypt, less extensive and more cohesive in its geography and its traditions, the old division into provinces or nomes, subdivided into cantons (*topoi*) and villages (*komai*), was preserved. Each of these territorial units was headed by a royal official: a nomarch, a toparch, and a komarch respectively. In addition to these, the Ptolemies appointed in each nome, side by side with the nomarch, an official who had the military title of *strategos*. The *strategoi* of the nomes gained increasing importance, and became the real administrators of the provinces. A crowd of officials of middle or modest rank helped them. These had in their midst, by the very nature of things, an ever-growing number of men who, Egyptian by their origin and native tongue, had become bilingual.

Lagid Egypt was the most centralized and the best administered of Hellenistic monarchies. The important role played in it by its *strategoi*, officials whose background and title were military, is a further illustration of the fundamental connection of royal authority with the business of war. This explains why the sovereigns used the title of *strategos*, traditionally given to officers with the rank of general, to designate a number of their assistants at various levels. This was done both in their home territory and in possessions elsewhere, if there was a need to appoint a representative of the king who was to be at the same time in command of a permanent garrison of troops provisionally quartered nearby, or of a naval force. The king's military power safeguarded the allied or subject cities' loyalty. The logical consequence of this was to entrust control of that power to a general who had been given adequate means near at hand to fulfill that duty of protection. It was also to be expected that his decision-making powers would gradually extend to other matters. The *strategia* became a generalized tool of Hellenistic government. It shared nothing more than its name with what *strategia* had been – a collegial annual magistracy – in the cities of the Classical age. Now the *strategos* became an official who was first and foremost a military man, but one empowered to deal with a wide range of issues. The king appointed him to keep under his authority a territory situated within the empire or an important location outside it. There he wielded the sovereign's power by delegation. This was a flexible and many-faceted institution, so widespread that it has been called "the spine, the symbol of the Hellenistic State." The Greeks witnessed the arrival in the East of Roman generals who, leading their troops, made political or economic decisions in the Senate's name in the lands that their armies had conquered. No wonder that they called those consuls or praetors *strategoi*, the name given to generals acting as deputies of the Hellenistic monarchs.

■ *The prerogatives of a monarchical state* ■ *The king as war leader* ■ *His personal involvement*

Thus organized, the monarchical state had to attend to a number of duties. For a long time the dynasties that had inherited Alexander's empire, as well as other royal families that sprang up or developed on their pattern, administered the major part of the Near East. Their fortunes were diverse, but the principle of monarchy was not challenged, except by Rome, which displaced those sovereigns. What was their method of management? Its efficiency and longevity surprise us, when we consider the extent and variety of the territories governed by it.

The king's main objective was to protect and extend his states. War had been endemic to the Greece of cities. It was no less frequent in the Hellenistic period. The monarchical state (leaving out traditional kingdoms like Macedon) existed because of it. Threatened by countless perils, ranging from external attacks to risks of rebellion within its boundaries, it used war as its tool of survival. Here again we find a close link (often noted in our account so far) between war and the phenomenon of monarchy. Plutarch, who took a moralist's view of events, attributes the unceasing rebirth of conflicts to the insatiable lust of monarchs. As he wrote (in his *Life of Pyrrhus*, 12),

> Oceans, mountains, desert solitudes, set no bounds on the ambition of princes, when their appetite for power disregards the frontiers separating Europe and Asia. How could they, when their respective territories share a boundary, renounce all attempt on each other for the sake of peace in their own land? No! They continue fighting, because it is inborn in them to be jealous of their rivals and concoct plans against them.

The judgment of history is by and large on the side of the philosopher. Yet no one should ignore the fatality inherent in a system that, beyond individual temptations, was centered on the demands of war and its inevitability. Born of war, it perished as a result of war.

It would be wrong to find in war nothing but the normal process of an economy based on pillage. Indeed, the harvest of plunder and booty that victory brought was in no way negligible, and allowed the victor, at no cost to himself, to satisfy his mercenary troops, the backbone of contemporary armies, who fought only for gain. Such a windfall was also an advantage to the royal treasury. But it is simplistic to explain the frequent recurrence of war by an urge to redistribute the accumulated wealth of kings, cities, and individuals, on the grounds that the way in which the economy was managed led to hoarding. What really caused conflict to breed on itself was the absence of an international authority, able to impose a negotiated settlement in disputes that were bound to arise between states. Next, the built-in instability of states made up of a heterogeneous set of components was a source of internal tension that invited intervention from outside. There was finally the presence in the Near East of barbarian populations, dedicated to raiding and conquest, as the Galatians were, or engaged, like the Parthians, in a process of expansion that would transform them into powerful independent states. A power might assert itself in the area, with the required stability and strength to impose a law on cities and princes. The Romans did just that, and the Near East, in spite of some convulsions like the Jewish revolts, knew a long period of peace which ended only with the barbarian invasions.

The king's main business, therefore, was to wage war. Even a philosopher-king like Antigonus Gonatas had to devote a large part of his long reign to military operations, in which his struggles with the barbarians amid the Balkan Mountains alternated with those he had with rival kings or the states of Greece. His defense of the Hellenic world against the barbarians was one of the monarch's beneficent activities, one of those in any case that earned him the grateful remembrance of Greek-speaking communities. The major shrines harbored monuments raised in testimony to that feeling of gratitude, or commemorating the pride sovereigns took in having repelled such external threats. On the island of Delos, on the Athenian Acropolis, at Pergamum, bronze statuary groups recalled the Attalids' victories over the Galatian hordes that ravaged Anatolia. It was gratifying to compare these struggles with illustrious precedents in myth and history: the battles of the gods with the Giants, of the Greek heroes with the Amazons, or of the Hellenes with the Persians at the time of the Persian Wars. Artists and poets perpetuated these memories, a good example being the epigram in honor of Philetaerus, discovered at Delos (see p. 77).

The king had to be personally involved in these warlike adventures, as the leader and even, occasionally, as a combatant. There too Alexander had set an example, followed by the Diadochi. Craterus, Antigonus the One-eyed, Lysimachus had fallen on the field of battle, as Demetrius II did later. Pyrrhus, however, for all his outstanding valour in battle, died an unseemly death. It has been calculated that out of fourteen Seleucid sovereigns, ten died fighting. The Lagids, with the exception of the first three, showed less taste for danger. Yet Ptolemy IV had to appear in the midst of his troops to revive their spirits at the battle of Raphia; while Ptolemy VI died of his wounds after having defeated Alexander Balas. Faint-heartedness did not become a king: historians have shown withering contempt for Perseus, who fled after Pydna and allowed himself to be captured at Samothrace, thus failing to escape the shame of appearing in Aemilius Paullus' triumphal procession, and dying wretchedly in a Roman jail.

The prestige that went with courage was made all the more necessary by the expectations of the armies of mercenaries on whom the outcome of battles now depended. They were actuated only by their desire for gain and a personal attachment to their leader, their paymaster. He would benefit from such a feeling if he impressed them with his leadership and his qualities as a warrior. Personal command of his troops was the first duty of a king, one that he could not shirk without encountering failure. He thus had to take on himself responsibility for defeat, just as he deservedly reaped the rewards of victory. Preparation for war was his duty, as was the conduct of operations. Forecasts relating to manpower and material means, alliances to be secured, bases for the fleet, every aspect of strategy and tactics: all these were the king's business and required his constant attention. It should be acknowledged that many of the Hellenistic sovereigns proved to be endowed with a gift for these essential concerns. Thanks to Plutarch's writings, the lives of the Diadochi reveal again and again how the leader's personal intervention transformed the course of events. Even a muddle-headed *condottiere* like Demetrius Poliorcetes excelled in creating an army or a naval squadron out of nothing – as he did in his Greek and Macedonian ventures between 296 and 291. Antiochus III's "Anabasis," during which (between 212 and 205) he restored Seleucid authority over the eastern provinces of his empire, looked like an apt throwback to Alexander's precedent, and full justification for the title of *Great King* that he gave himself on his return.

■ *Financial resources of a monarchy: the tribute, levies, and taxes* ■ *Issues of coinage and income obtained from banking* ■ *The management of royal domains* ■ *The king's proverbial wealth* ■ *Luxury and festivities* ■ *Gifts to shrines and cities* ■ *Generosity toward individuals:* dôreai *and cleruchies*

Money was needed in the preparation and conduct of war. The Hellenistic monarchies' remarkable ability to extract income from the people and fill the king's coffers answered such a need. In parallel with the organization of the armed forces, and relying of course on their support, the fiscal machinery of these kingdoms proved extremely efficient for the times. In contrast with the cities, which were often unable to face their communities' expenses, the kings seem never to have known any financial difficulties. Their wealth was proverbial, even astonishing the Romans, just as the treasures of the Achaemenids had filled Alexander's companions with admiration. It was fed by a variety of regular sources, in addition to booty obtained by armed conquest. There was first of all tribute received from subject cities or principalities annexed to the empire. Such payments in money or kind were a legacy from the Achaemenid administration. But the Greeks also had recourse to the tribute system within the first Athenian maritime Confederacy: this was therefore no innovation. The Seleucids and Attalids exacted tribute in their realms: exemption from it, sometimes granted as an exceptional favor and subject to amendment, was a precious privilege for a city. Every satrapy was expected to pay a predetermined amount into the royal treasury, which was thus relieved of collection at source (that was the local administration's duty). To that basic tax were added a large number of indirect taxes and levies, the variety of which mirrored that of the Greek cities' corresponding impositions. Levies on the produce of the soil, taxes on crafts, harbor dues and customs duties, levies on pastureland or fisheries, tolls, transfer dues belonged to that elaborate fiscal apparatus.

The king also made a profit out of his right to issue currency. That had always been a profitable practice, as the striking of coinage in itself added value to the raw material employed for that purpose; furthermore, local currency always benefits from an exchange premium in relation to foreign currency. The Seleucids had one major mint in each satrapy, and issued a wide range of silver currency, especially in the second half of the second century, when their empire was decadent. In earlier times their States had been wide open to free circulation of coinage struck outside their realm. To authenticate these foreign coins, they limited themselves to gracing them with an "anchor" countermark (the eloquent symbol of their dynasty's Apollonian origin: see p. 222) that granted those coins the same exchange premium as that obtained by their own coinage. This was a convenient process, allowing them to cash this premium without delay, at the lowest possible cost to themselves. The Ptolemies, on the contrary, required all internal transactions to be made in Ptolemaic currency, and caused all foreign coins to be minted anew in their own workshops. A letter written in 258, in the reign of Ptolemy II Philadelphus, by the Master of the Mint at Alexandria to the *dioecetes* Apollonius (see p. 238 above) mentions that operation and reveals its size:

> In compliance with written instructions which you gave me, I received 57,000 gold coins, and returned them after a new minting . . . Foreigners landing here, traders and brokers bring their own genuine currency and our *trichyta* [gold coins issued in Egypt under the previous reign] from their lands to obtain new currency in exchange. This conforms to the regulation bidding us to take these coins and mint them anew . . . It is important that as much gold as possible be imported from abroad, and that the King's coinage be always fine and new, at no cost to him.

The king's money yielded income in the banks, which, in Egypt at least, were farmed out and held the privilege of providing and exchanging currency. As trustees of important funds, they received the product of taxes and levies, in their capacity as the king's receiving agents. They were also entrusted with deposits from private individuals. They lent money at a rate fixed by Lagid law at 24 percent. That was an extremely high rate, more than double what was current in the rest of the Greek world, where it was 10 percent (as at Delos, for instance).

Finally, a large portion of the sovereign's resources came from the exploitation of the landed domain belonging to him in person. This was the King's Land, the management of which is well known in Egypt. But it also existed in the Seleucid Empire. Such landed property was immense; its yield was considerable. It was as a rule farmed out to peasants who kept it under cultivation, paying a rent that could reach 40 to 50 percent of the produce of the soil. That was the case with wheat, for example, one of the main crops of Egypt. The wheat produced by royal farmland was transported, on the canals and on the Nile, by barges belonging to private carriers, the *naucleroi*. The owner of a barge undertook to deliver the goods to one of the royal warehouses, from which they were marketed, either in Egypt or abroad. Export was by sea, in ships of large tonnage, specially built for the transport of cereals, like the one later described by Lucian (in the second century of our era) in his dialogue *The Ship, or The Wishes* (see p. 309). In a world in which the main source of wealth was landed property, the produce of the royal domain was a significant component of the king's income.

Such revenue was enormous. An often quoted text from St Jerome, in his *Commentary on Daniel* (XI, 5), estimates Ptolemy II Philadelphus' annual income at 14,800 silver talents – approximately fifteen times Athens' annual resources at the time of Pericles. The political decadence of Ptolemaic Egypt had not reduced that revenue in any significant manner, since, according to Strabo (XVII, 798), Ptolemy XII Auletes still had at his disposal, in the middle of the first century before our era, an annual income of 12,500 talents. The treasures belonging to the Attalids of Pergamum are still treated as a standard reference in Horace (*Odes* I, 12), a century after the dynasty's disappearance. Since all income received in the name of the State belonged to the king, such accumulated wealth had a value far out of proportion to the income of cities, even the most prosperous among them. Contemporaries were especially aware of this because the kings made no secret of their wealth. On the contrary, they flaunted it, wishing to impress popular imagination by their luxurious lifestyle, a dazzling reflection of their power. Were they not entitled, like the gods, to the best and finest of whatever the world had to offer? Hence those pageants and festivals, descriptions of which are enshrined in various texts. Diodorus relates in great detail the funeral procession in honor of Hephaestion (XVII, 115), and further on (XVIII,

26–7) describes Alexander's hearse. Theocritus recalls the festival of Adonis in Alexandria (*Idyll* XV: see p. 269), in the reign of Ptolemy II and Arsinoe Philadelphi. The great Dionysiac procession is revived for us by the compiler Athenaeus (V, 197c–203b), quoting from contemporary testimony by Callixenus of Rhodes, who had seen the program of that celebration. Polybius (XXX, 25–7) describes the great pageant in honor of Daphne that Antiochus III gave in 166/5, inaugurating a whole month of festivities and athletic games. In the last case, it pleased the sovereign to demonstrate that the heavy indemnity exacted by the Romans from his father, Antiochus III, had not prevented him from rebuilding his treasure – eloquent testimony to the size of the Seleucids' regular income. We may see in the same perspective the provocative displays of luxury that some Lagids made in the last phases of their dynasty. Witness the dream vessel on which Cleopatra sailed to meet Antony on the river Cydnus, in her wish to assuage his anger and seduce him; and later, the astonishing episodes of the "Inimitable Life" that the two lovers continued to share, even after all was lost at the battle of Actium. There was in such behavior an element of Dionysiac exultation, as there already had been in the systematic exploration of elaborate pleasures, *tryphe*, in which their ancestor, Ptolemy IV Philopator, had reveled. Yet this was also, in the actors' eyes, to a large degree the normal lifestyle suitable for princes: one radically different from what was appropriate to the rest of humanity.

Generosity was, from their point of view, another fitting aspect of their conduct. It conformed to the earlier Greek tradition, well attested from Homer to Pindar, and taken over without a break by the Hellenistic poets. According to that tradition, the king could make no better use of his riches than to shower sanctuaries, cities, communities, and individuals with his open-handed donations. First and foremost came the sanctuaries, as the gods always had the first claim to service. In the third century, Attalus I of Pergamum endowed Delphic Apollo with a noble portico, for the sake of which a breach was made in the eastern side of the surrounding wall. This was to be an imposing rectangular building (32 by 9 meters), opening south on to a terrace, through a Doric colonnade. The terrace topped a vaulted hall, and accommodated a long votive base that filled the facade of the edifice and bore groups of bronze statuary. In addition, the inside of the portico was adorned with paintings on wooden panels fixed to the walls, after the manner of the famous Athenian portico of the Poikile. In those days, apart from Apollo's own temple, no monumental construction on Delphi's hallowed territory was comparable in splendor to the sovereign of Pergamum's offering. Delian Apollo was no less well treated. In the third century, Antigonus Gonatas set the northern limit of the sanctuary's sacred area by raising there a superb portico, 120 meters long, with colonnades outside and inside the building: one Doric, the other Ionic. Toward the end of the same century, Philip V, grandson of Gonatas, followed his ancestor's generous example by having another Doric portico, 70 meters long, built along the access road to the shrine's southern propylaea. Its dedication is well preserved: "Philip, king of the Macedonians, son of King Demetrius, to Apollo." Many similar consecrations were made in Panhellenic sanctuaries, a fortiori of course in those that were directly dependent on the sovereigns – at Alexandria, Pergamum, Antioch, and elsewhere. Finally, the treasuries of those holy places overflowed with royal offerings (in particular, vases made of precious metals) the source of which was identified in inscriptions. In certain privileged cases (at Delos, for instance) their fate can be traced through inventories engraved every year under the supervision of the curators of such sacred property.

Greek cities were the beneficiaries of similar generous gifts. Many of these were in the shape of religious monuments that monarchs raised at their own expense. One example was the temple of Olympian Zeus at Athens. Its exceptional measurements (108 by 41 meters) and its architectural magnificence (it was the first large temple to have an exterior colonnade with Corinthian capitals) demonstrate the generosity of Antiochus IV Epiphanes, who financed its construction in 174. But the size of the undertaking was such that it could not be completed in the Seleucid king's lifetime. The works were abandoned for more than a century, before being restarted, in part, at the time of Augustus. At long last the temple was finished and dedicated by the emperor Hadrian in the second century of our era. There were also donations of buildings to serve as public facilities. Ptolemy III had a gymnasium built near the Athenian Agora. To mark the eastern limit of the Agora, Attalus II donated the large portico that still dominates it today, restored by American archaeologists. Attalus' predecessor, Eumenes II, built a no less monumental portico on the southern slope west of the theater, to serve as a promenade gallery for spectators at the Dionysiac celebrations. Its rear wall, with its wide vaulted niches, still stands. The Greeks of the Hellenistic period, like their predecessors, regarded the old city of Athens as the metropolis of culture. She continued to attract visitors, and her citizens now lived surrounded by monuments that they owed to the generosity of Lagid, Seleucid, or Attalid sovereigns, before benefiting from the bounty of Roman emperors like Augustus or Hadrian.

Apart from buildings, enduring reminders of royal largesse, cities would receive gifts of considerable size from kings on various occasions: in times of penury or famine, for instance, shipments of cereals, or subsidies for their purchase, would be offered. A disastrous natural calamity could turn into an opportunity for generous gestures. One example is the response to the Rhodians' appeal after an earthquake ravaged the town of Rhodes in 227, laying low the famed Colossus. Polybius (V, 88) relates that "they visited cities, and especially princely courts, pleading for help in such a noble and dignified manner that not only were they granted huge donations, but their benefactors felt honored to have been the recipients of their appeal." Princes vied with each other in their response. Hiero II of Syracuse and his son sent a large number of vases made of precious metal and an enormous sum in silver coinage: to these they added a gift of machines of war, and exemption from harbor dues in Syracuse for Rhodian vessels. Ptolemy III offered three times as much money, materials and workers for the reconstruction of their fleet and the restoration of the Colossus, and nearly half a million hectoliters of wheat. Antigonus Doson provided timber from Macedonian forests to help them rebuild their fleet, together with iron, pitch, and a large sum of money. Seleucus III donated ten large warships, exempted Rhodian vessels from paying duties in his kingdom, and sent raw material for shipbuilding, as well as a supply of wheat. Prusias I of Bithynia, Mithridates III of Pontus, and various other princes of Asia Minor also made their own contributions toward raising Rhodes from its ruins. It is true that Polybius, after listing such abundant and generous help, gets a certain satisfaction from emphasizing by contrast the miserliness of contemporary sovereigns (he was writing around the middle of the second century). But this is a minor blemish frequent enough in any historian, easily transformed by familiarity with the past into a eulogist of it (*laudator temporis acti*, to quote Horace's phrase).

Finally, monarchs had to be generous toward individuals, for they wished to earn gratitude and devotion from those closest to them or working under their direction. Polybius does not forget that trait in Eumenes II of Pergamum when he praises that monarch's qualities. "He was so eager for glory," he writes (XXXII, 8), "that he showered benefits on more cities, and bestowed financial favors on more individuals, than any contemporary ruler." The king could, of course, draw on his privy purse to confer bounty on whoever he wished. It might please him to show liberality to a degree that astonished its beneficiaries: this was indeed kingly behavior. Ptolemy VIII Euergetes II relates in his *Memoirs* how he acquitted himself in an onerous duty. While he was ruler of Cyrene, in the middle of the second century, he had one year to take over the city's eponymous magistracy, the priesthood of Apollo. Usage prescribed that, on the occasion of the annual feast of Artemis, that priest was to invite the former holders of his office to a great banquet. Toward the end he would offer each of them, in remembrance of the ceremony, a large jar filled with delicacies – venison, poultry, salt fish imported from afar. In a text that Athenaeus (XII, 73) has preserved, the king writes:

> As for us, we have acted differently. We had cups of solid silver made, the value of which equalled the expense that the usual gift would have entailed. In addition, each guest was to receive a fully harnessed horse, with a groom and gold-incrusted *phalara* [for this word see p. 218]. We asked them to jump into the saddle and return home thus arrayed.

Was it possible, when faced with such magnificent and unexpected bounty, for the foremost citizens of Cyrene not to believe, in their enchanted astonishment, that a king was of a calibre different from that of common mortals?

The sovereign could also grant his principal assistants the enjoyment of a domain situated on the King's Land. That was called a "gift" (*dôrea*), not a surprising practice when the main source of wealth was landed property. In Lagid Egypt, papyri allow us to learn about many such concessions made by the king to his friends, particularly the one that Ptolemy II Philadelphus granted his minister of economic affairs and finance, the *dioecetes* Apollonius (see pp. 238, 244). Situated on the edge of the Fayyum oasis at Philadelphia, it had an area of 2,500 hectares. Its exploitation is described in the 2,000 papyri from the records of Zeno, its steward. In Ptolemy's deed, we are not dealing with a definitive cession of property, but with the usufruct, granted as a precarious tenure, of a portion of the Royal Land. Nevertheless, as long as he held that tenure, the beneficiary drew a substantial income from it. This was precisely the case of Apollonius, aided by his employee Zeno.

The king used a similar process to keep mercenary soldiers in his service. He would endow them with land, granted in principle as a precarious tenure – with the reservation that the tenant would at all times be ready to serve in the army if needed. The allotment involved was called a *kleros*: hence the name of a *klerouchos* (literally, "the occupant of a *kleros*"). The size of the *kleros* varied with the tenant's rank. At a minimum, it allowed a cleruch to make a living without needing to till the soil, by leasing it to peasants. There again, the system is best known in Egypt, thanks to papyri. A trend is noticeable over the centuries toward transforming tenure, granted in the first place for the tenant's lifetime, into a hereditary concession, and finally into full ownership. The migration of Greek and Macedonian veterans up-country, both in the Asiatic East and in the Nile Valley, favored the penetration of the Greek way of life into the conquered territories. Cleruchs did not actually live on their lands. Relying on native farmers to cultivate them, they lived in the neighboring town or village, where they gathered in Greek-speaking communities, in direct contact with the local population. Thus there reappeared, with a new slant, an ancient tradition of Greek colonization, for its main objective had always been to look abroad for arable land that was not adequately provided by their motherland's far too restricted or arid spaces.

■ A Hellenistic monarchy had no citizens ■ It was a state founded on strength and factual reality ■ Absence of any ideology to justify power ■ Flexibility and realism ■ The sovereign's personal stamp on his kingdom ■ Dynastic names for cities ■ Metonomasia: *the instance of Cyrenaica under Ptolemy Euergetes ■ The coexistence of monarchy and city*

The analysis above has highlighted the essential characteristics of the monarchical state, such as they emerged in the Hellenistic age. That state strikes the observer as being radically at variance with the concept, until then traditional among the Greeks, of the state viewed as a city. In the Hellenistic monarchy there was no "citizen" of the kingdom, any more than the king could be considered a "magistrate," even the supreme one. This implied no erasure of the Greek city by the monarchical state, which was instead situated on another plane. It might, in case of need, encompass the city: not negating what the city stood for, but subordinating it to its own ends. It was a system of government intended for large territorial aggregates, complex, heterogeneous, multiethnic ones, where barbarians had a place side by side with Greeks, where cities, dynasts, and peoples coexisted, where a variety of traditions and beliefs persisted. In a political framework that was both flexible and efficient, the sovereign's person was the permanent and sole reference. His was the only authority to assert itself, founded on an undeniable reality, the *Right of the Spear*, military might, evidence of a power that none dreamed of challenging, as it asserted its supremacy convincingly by victory or by displaying the power to win.

It was a species of monarchy born of experience, not of theoretical speculation. Alexander's prodigious adventure had shown a stunned Greek world what one man's genius could build in a few years, with a relatively small number of soldiers. That was a decisive demonstration, a lesson that the Diadochi soon translated into practice, with varied results. Experience showed that the method was good, provided that men of adequate worth applied it, for everything rested on the leader's merit. Those who won in the end could assert, as Seleucus Nicator did, as reported by the historian Appian (*Syriaca*, 61), that "a king's decisions are always just, and this is a rule that applies to all mankind."

There were undoubtedly, as the years went by, political philosophers to take up and systematize attempts that had been made in the fourth century to vindicate the monarchical regime. The historian Xenophon had tried to do so in his *Cyropaedia*; so had the rhetorician Isocrates, in his praise of the Cypriot sovereigns Evagoras and Nicocles. But a reference to the public good and the practice of virtue by the sovereign had always been nothing more than an oratorical *topos* for Hellenistic princes, a justification after the event of a de facto situation. Supreme power was an end in itself: its usefulness did not need to be demonstrated. It simply had to work efficiently, in order to establish his divine right. That was, at least, the Greeks' perception of the matter. Ideas had a strong appeal for them, but they always displayed a remarkable readiness to yield to facts.

The king, therefore, made no pretence of governing for the good of his subjects, or for the sake of bringing prosperity to his states. Whenever he spoke of the freedom of the Greeks, he was resorting to propaganda, not propounding a doctrine. His aim was to remain in power, to shine, to expand if possible: at any rate, having conquered or inherited the role of leader, to play it to the full. There was not a trace of ideology in the prince's behavior, except in so far as it involved total belief in the legitimacy of his power: that was the purpose of the cult that his person received. But there was no question of his being dedicated to the wellbeing of his kingdom, or of fathering any grand designs other than political ones. The Hellenistic king's administration aimed at keeping his authority intact, ensuring the rule of order conducive to sound management, and extracting the best possible income from the royal domain. Such an administration was first and foremost a pragmatic one. Strict devotion to justice, philanthropy, and benevolence – qualities to which kings were eager to lay claim – were means of keeping peace among his people. A display of such qualities alternated with measures marked by severity, according to circumstances. No other state model was ever less eager for pretence, less keen on any attempt to justify the power it held.

The kings treated Greeks as Greeks and barbarians as barbarians, addressing them in their own tongues. Greeks by culture, they found it normal and convenient to spread their civilization and language, but in no way tried to impose them. Under the Seleucids, side by side with the Greek *koiné*, Aramaic, a Semitic language in common use, spread unhindered. Ptolemaic Egypt never forbade the use of Egyptian, even though official documents were written in Greek. No sovereign tried to stifle or eradicate native beliefs, except when they appeared to be linked with political intrigue challenging the king's authority, as was the case of traditionalist Jewry at the time of the revolt of the Maccabees. Greeks were by nature inclined to welcome foreign divinities; they had no trouble finding in them a similarity to their own gods. Their kings never practiced cultural imperialism.

Aware on the other hand that their states belonged to them in person, the kings were none too willing to put their own stamp on them. Since Greek civilization had an urban tradition and spread its roots round urban areas, it was by founding, conquering, or developing towns that the king consolidated his hold on his territory. To make this more strongly felt, he acted upon an ancient Greek belief, attributing to a name (whether a god's or a human being's) a deeply rooted significance, if not a magic power. Thus they frequently gave foundations or conquests dynastic names, modeled on the sovereign's own name or on those belonging to close members of his family. Nothing is more indicative of the personal character of the Hellenistic state than the extraordinary spread of this new toponymy, a reflection of territorial expansion and of the power of a monarch's personal aura. The human group that he was about to establish, over which he asserted his control, was henceforth to bear witness to the sovereign's greatness.

In this as in other aspects, Alexander had been a trend-setter when he founded Alexandria in Egypt and many other cities bearing that name, including the most remote one, Alexandria the Furthest (*Eschate*), in the middle of central Asia, beyond Samarkand. They were to be landmarks for posterity of his progress from one end to the other of his empire. The Diadochi did the same. Ptolemy founded Ptolemais in Upper Egypt, Antigonus the One-eyed Antigoneia in Bithynia.

Demetrius founded Demetrias on the Gulf of Volos. In Macedon Cassander founded Cassandreia and Thessalonica, Lysimachus Lysimacheia in the Thracian Chersonese. The same Lysimachus renamed Antigoneia in Bithynia after his wife: it became Nicaea. He also changed Smyrna's illustrious name to Eurydiceia, after Eurydice, his daughter – an innovation that did not last long. It is said that Seleucus founded nine cities bearing the name Seleucia and sixteen that he called Antioch, after his father Antiochus. His successors followed his example by adding to the list of names based on those of the kings themselves, others belonging to figures of the dynasty. Numerous cities named Stratoniceia, Laodicea, Apamea recall the memory of Stratonice, Laodice, or Apame, wives or daughters of the Seleucids. The Lagids did the same by calling certain cities Berenice or Arsinoe, besides the new cities of Ptolemais in Cyrenaica, Palestine, or Ionia. Nor did the Attalids lag behind: Phrygia had its Eumeneia, Mysia its Philetaereia (after the dynasty's founder). There were cities named Attaleia in Mysia, in Lydia, and especially in Pamphylia (today's Adalia). Monarchs of Asian origin followed these examples: in Bithynia Prusias I founded Prusa (Broussa) and Nicomedes I the lovely city of Nicomedia. In Pontus Pharnaces I founded Pharnaceia on the Black Sea coast (around 180) and Mithridates had his Eupatoria, while his *strategos* Diophantes settled another in the Crimea, in the Sebastopol area. Even the sovereigns of Armenia followed the trend. Around 185, Artaxias, perhaps on Hannibal's advice, founded Artaxata on the river Araxes, flowing into the Caspian Sea. A century later, Tigranes the Great gathered the population of twelve localities at Tigranocerta, in Upper Mesopotamia, which he made his new capital. Before that ambitious Hellenistic city could be completed it was conquered in 69 by Lucullus' troops: even its actual site cannot be determined with certainty.

Such a widespread custom is evidently laden with meaning. By giving a dynastic name to a city, the king proclaimed that it was his. That portion of land was to bear the imprint of his seal. He thus shared in the aura with which founders – gods and heroes – were invested in Hellenic tradition. The first historical works, in Archaic Greece, had been poems recounting the tale (a mythical one from our point of view) of the foundation of cities. This was a theme to which Hellenistic scholarship liked to return, as we shall soon see when we speak of Callimachus. That is why a king's decision not to found a new city, but to change an existing city's name so as to give it a dynastic one, was no gratuitous gesture, no mere substitution of one name for another, in public documents and on a map. This kind of administrative operation, which the ancients called a *metonomasia* (a change of name), had religious significance. A ritual accompanied it, and it sometimes meant a transfer of the civic center from one location to another, although the new one was sometimes right beside the one it replaced. It was an occasion for urban renewal that could substantially improve the lifestyle of a city. Thus, when Lysimachus built a new city of Ephesus, he placed it at quite a distance from its predecessor, where the harbor had become silted up with alluvium from the Cayster. He gave the city a new port and new fortified walls, then called it Arsinoeia, after his wife Arsinoe, daughter of Ptolemy Sôter, and future queen of Egypt. The new name did not last long, but the new city soon became the most prosperous in Asia Minor.

The most striking and significant example of metonomasia occurred in Cyrenaica under Ptolemy III Euergetes. The marriage of the young prince, heir presumptive of his father Philadelphus, to Berenice, daughter of King Magas, had brought about reconciliation between the two kingdoms. Yet nothing less than a military campaign against Cyrenaica proved necessary after Euergetes' accession to the throne in 246, to reduce to submission the cities of that region, which refused to recognize Ptolemaic authority. Barce, Taucheira, Euhesperides, the whole of Greek western Libya had to be conquered. An epigram by Callimachus (*Epigram* 37) recalls these operations. It is the dedication, engraved in a shrine of the Lagid divinity Serapis, of the offering made by a mercenary, originating from the Cretan town of Lyttus, who had served among Ptolemy's troops during that campaign. "The Lyttian Menitas has consecrated these weapons, saying, 'Behold, Serapis, my bow and quiver! I donate them unto thee. As for my arrows, the Hesperitans have kept them in their bodies.'" To punish the rebels, Ptolemy III degraded the ancient cities, except Cyrene, where loyalty had not failed. The others suffered metonomasia, and in each case a Lagid dynastic name replaced the original name. Barce, an ancient city in the interior, a rival of Cyrene on its frontier, lost its civic identity in favor of its harbor, 25 kilometers away, which henceforth, under the name of Ptolemais (see pp. 252, 268), replaced its metropolis and administered her wealthy territory. Taucheira, an old seaboard urban area whose origin went back to the very first days of colonization, was in future to be called Arsinoe. Euhesperides, the westernmost Greek city of Africa, famous for the ancient myth of the Hesperides connected with the memory of Heracles' trip to Libya, lost its traditional name to be given that of Berenice, queen by title, daughter of Magas. Furthermore, the town was relocated slightly further west, to benefit from a more convenient harbor between the seaboard of the Syrtes and the lagoon, which had until then provided harbor facilities. In that new environment it was to prosper again (see pp. 73, 252).

This is an example of the way in which Hellenistic sovereigns reshaped the world over which they held power. Consider the material conditions in which they governed the ancient world, a world that was divided to such a degree, so difficult to travel across, so heterogeneous. That the monarchical states survived for such a long time and have left deep traces in such diverse countries is cause for utter amazement. The monarchs relied for transport on horses and boats called caïques, yet they managed to travel over their territories, transmit their orders, receive news and reports. Indeed, they fought many wars, since that was the iron law to which the Greek as well as the barbarian world was inexorably subjected. Yet they constructed and kept in place complex political groups, acted as the driving force behind bold projects and helped humanity to live its daily life. That was what they were expected to do, or so they believed, each in his own jurisdiction, and they obtained public recognition for doing just that. Rarely has a society endowed with such lucidity and refinement been so ready to agree to supreme authority being vested in one person. There was perhaps a vague feeling that personalizing power to such an extreme degree answered a real need. The efficiency that the system attained, and its longevity, may have turned that into a belief. This historical phenomenon, at any rate, coexisted for a long period with the Greek cities' social, political, or mental parameters. It did not destroy them, but allowed them to preserve their vitality. Such an achievement gives an astonishing originality to the Hellenistic age.

8/THE HELLENISTIC LIFESTYLE: ITS ENVIRONMENT

■ *Change and continuity* ■ *The need to describe reality in the context of its diversity*

Within the vastness and diversity of the Hellenistic world, two widely different kinds of state coexisted, the monarchy and the city, both being genuine Greek creations and having a complex and ambiguous relationship with each other. What was human life like in such a context? What changes had the framework of daily life undergone since Classical times? What innovations did Alexander's grand design, and the developments brought to it by his successors, introduce into the customs and conduct of the Hellenes? We shall try to find answers to these questions by stressing the most original aspects of Greek civilization in that three-century period.

No doubt on many points, especially in Greece proper, popular mentality underwent no significant change. But an evolution did occur, as was to be expected, in relation to the Classical age. There had already been premonitory signs of it since the fourth century: so much so that certain modern scholars place the start of the Hellenistic age as early as the middle of that century. The aim of my book, on *The Civilization of Greece*, was to sketch a picture of Greek Archaic and Classical civilization that would be relatively as simple and coherent as that civilization had been at its peak. The plan of the present work will be to bring to that first picture any modifications that seem necessary, wherever the situation changed. The information that follows does not try to offer a synthesis of the life of a period so complex, and so rich in varied content, that any attempt at simplification would be misleading. The factual elements of the information are given in an order that does not conform to any underlying system. They are meant to stimulate an unprejudiced meditation on a theme I shall formulate right now. That theme is the Hellenic people's ability to adapt to new circumstances, and extract from their experiences and ordeals a discipline of behavior and thought enabling them to overcome some of these and make the best of others. In short, this chapter is an "essay on mores". Its purpose is to describe reality, not to make a point.

■ *An economy that remained essentially agrarian* ■ *Capital role of the* chôra ■ *Self-sufficiency: everything rested on the peasant's activity* ■ *The peasant in Greece proper: Menander's* Dyskolos ■ *The concentration of landed property, a phenomenon that should not be overestimated* ■ *Tenant farming; farms on the island of Delos* ■ *Animal husbandry and its importance* ■ *The genuine testimony provided by the bucolic theme* ■ *Soil use* ■ *The cadastral survey* ■ *Towered houses* ■ *The Nilotic landscape and rural habitation in Lagid Egypt* ■ *Zeno at Philadelphia in the Fayyum* ■ *The landholders of Psenemphaia*

The economy of the Hellenistic world remained in its essence what it had been before, an agrarian economy. Wealth was centered in landed property, as has often been said, and human sustenance was directly dependent on husbandry. That was evident in the large kingdoms, but no less true in the cities. No city (*polis*) could survive without having at its disposal a territory (*chôra*) that provided it with its livelihood. The ancient combination of an urban built-up area and a hinterland exploited by tillers of the soil and shepherds remained the norm among the Greeks. Hence the importance that frontier disputes had in their eyes, even when these were about some acres of poor grazing land, or, in the case of islands close to the coast, land that they possessed on the continent and from which they derived a substantial part of their resources. Such an extension of their territory beyond a strait bore the name of *peraea* (literally, "land situated across" the strait). We know of their expansion and the vital importance they had for many islands of the Aegean, for instance, Thasos in the north along the Thracian coast, Samos facing Ionia, or Rhodes off Caria. After the battle of Pydna in 168 (see p. 116), Rome deprived Rhodes of the major part of the Anatolian peraea. That was a harder blow, and one with more immediate effect for that wealthy city, than the competition faced by their trade through the creation of the tax-free port of Delos.

In spite of the development of sea-trade, almost all cities were actually self-sufficient, living from the resources of their own territory. This explains the continuing importance of the population's peasant component, and the attention paid, even among town-dwellers, to the countryside and country life. There was undoubtedly nothing new in that. From Hesiod to Xenophon via Aristophanes, Greek interest in the land, in the use that was made of it, in the beauty of its landscapes, remained constant. But with the advent of the Hellenistic age, what was a self-evident interest became something more conscious and systematic. A bucolic strain appeared in art and literature, not by chance, but as a source of inspiration in its own right, something drawn upon in a conscious manner. Thanks to literary or artistic documents, we can imagine the rural life of the times with greater precision.

The text containing the most vivid evocation of country life has been known to us for little more than half a century. It is the play, performed in 317/16, by the Athenian comedy writer Menander; the essential part of it was discovered in a papyrus exercise book. The title of the play is *The Bilious Man* (Greek *Dyskolos*), or *The Misanthrope* (courtesy of Molière). Its hero is a small country landowner in Attica, named Cnemon. He runs a modest farmstead on the Parnes foothills, north of the plain of Eleusis, near the village of Phyle. The comedy is built round an adventure on which we need not dwell. On the other hand, it provides us with a lively picture of the environment and of its rustic way of life. In that remote and hardly fertile rural settlement, landed property has its price. Cnemon's scarcely productive field, "stones on which only thyme and sage will grow," is valued at a handsome 2 talents. The owner, a miserly and surly fellow, tills it in person, turning it over with his hoe, without even the help of a slave or a day-laborer, as was then the custom. An old woman servant looks after his home, which is situated in the same place. It is furnished in the plainest way imaginable, a shock for visitors, used to finding, even in country dwellings, a higher degree of comfort. Though Cnemon's misanthropy has persuaded him to choose this forlorn corner of a mountain glen, there is no shortage of passers-by. The inhabitants of the village come and pay their respects to rustic divinities like Pan and the Nymphs. These have a shrine in a neighbouring grotto, a shelter for ritual banquets, while townsfolk come on hunting parties in these parts of Attica, where game must be plentiful. This is Menander's picture. It is all the more evocative because it is not his purpose to paint it for its own sake; he uses it only as a setting for his play and its characters. There is no evidence here of a systematic exploitation of the soil, not a thought of productivity, no hint of a growing concentration of land in the hands of a relatively small propertied class.

Now, Menander's picture is an apt one for the larger part of continental Greece and the Greek islands, in the Hellenistic period as well as in earlier times. It is a mosaic of smallholdings, with their owners, who are helped by a group of workers, made up almost equally of free men and slaves, living with them on the land. These free smallholders of the countryside made up, as before, the most numerous element in the States of ancient Greece, although some of them, crushed under a load of debt, were tempted to sell off their land to wealthy citizens, who put together such acquisitions into large estates or *latifundia* (to use the Latin term). This social phenomenon appeared for the first time in the second century (it seems), while wars following Roman intervention devastated the open country. Polybius noticed at first hand, and deplored, the depopulation that they brought to the rural areas. Yet it is hard to follow precisely the changes that occurred. One should avoid exaggerating their importance. The same Polybius considers the richest Greek of his time to be an Aetolian named Alexander, whose fortune was valued at 200 talents, only a hundred times the going price for the wretched landholding in the Attic countryside on which Cnemon the misanthrope lived. The ratio of one evaluation to the other allows a fairer understanding (without exaggeration) of the result of that concentration of arable land into the hands of a few, which some modern historians, anxious to extrapolate, think they can see in Hellenistic Greece. While there was indeed at times a demand from the poorest for the abolition of debt and a redistribution of land, it does not seem to have secured a response anywhere except Sparta, where Agis IV, Cleomenes III, and Nabis tried to satisfy it. It was precisely in the Lacedaemonian state that a concentration of landed property in fewer hands had known by far the highest degree of expansion. This had started in an earlier period, while a particular type of serfdom unknown elsewhere, the one imposed on the Helots, kept a tense situation alive in Laconia. The social reforms that these kings managed to carry out, though only for a time, found no imitators in the rest of Greece, with its variety of political regimes. A deeply felt and widespread desire for land redistribution might have persuaded one or other among the cities to try such an experiment. In spite of the disturbance caused by wars and the activity of brigands, the existing regime of landed property remained stable. This bears witness to a relatively balanced situation with respect to land ownership.

Furthermore, it was common for landowners to make use of tenant farming. Peasants whose land had been expropriated could continue to cultivate their fields after these had been sold. The system allowed town-dwellers to obtain an income from their landed property. This was also a means for shrines to extract revenue from domains that had been theirs for a long time, or those that devotees had bequeathed, usually with precise instructions on the use of funds contributed by such donations to the god's treasury. The management of sacred possessions was subject to a financial report by the magistrates who had been put in charge of them. Some documents of this kind have survived, thanks to the inscriptions on which they were engraved for public inspection of the accounts. They provide us with some indirect indication of the material set-up of Hellenistic farms. Inscriptions from Delos are the most copious source of information. There Apollo's lands were divided between the southern half of the island of Delos, not occupied by sanctuaries or urban districts, and the much more extensive territory of the island of Rhenea, situated next to western Delos and separated by a narrow strait that was easy to cross. The managers of the sacred treasury, called the *hieropes*, provided a yearly statement of account, and divided the sanctuary's landed property among tenant farmers. Their records contain details of the various components of the sacred fund: fields, orchards, dwellings, and buildings connected with running the property. For instance, a domain on Rhenea consisted in 279 of "a house having two rooms (one provided with a door), a stable with no door, a sheep-pen with no door, a roofless building, a tower fitted with its door, and a door intended for the enclosure." The attention paid to the state of the doors and the roofs is explained by the rarity in the Cyclades of wood for construction or cabinet-making. The same concern is apparent in the Egyptian papyri, for palm trees cannot provide material for rafters or boards. These documents, therefore, allow one to visualize the organization of those rural domains. They also give some indication of the value in actual figures of the rent obtained. But such information is too scarce, too poor in complementary details (like the extent and nature of the lands under exploitation) to allow any worthwhile conclusions to be drawn about economic history.

In addition to arable land, Hellenistic peasants would use pasture, which was extensive in mountainous areas. Unsuitable for cultivation, offering no adequate sustenance to horses or cattle, it was fit for grazing sheep, donkeys, and mules. Herdsmen were therefore numerous in the peasant population: some were employed as cattlemen on the richer soil, others (the majority) looked after sheep, goats, and pigs. These herds supplied not only milk or meat, but also leather and wool, essential material for various crafts. Animal breeding was not only important for the economy, but played its part in the area of religion, in which public interest remained constant. A sacrifice involving one or more animals was an essential cultic act, and in the herds the finest heads were reserved for the gods. Birds were also bred, doves especially, intended for sacrifice. The life of these herdsmen, whom a traveler would come across at every turn in the countryside, was now to arouse curiosity for its own sake. Feelings which formerly had no other outlet than traditional displays of popular piety, like the "songs of the goat," satyr choruses at the origin of tragedy, were to find new modes of expression in the future. Bucolic poetry was born, one of the most remarkable novelties of the times. The Syracusan Theocritus is its first representative. A man of great refinement and culture, he is no less an attentive observer of the way of life and language of these bucolic characters that he skillfully integrates in his verse. One example is the familiar discourse of his *Reapers*: "What a grand life, friends, is a frog's! It does not take the trouble to have a drink served: it can by itself drink to its heart's content. Hey, niggardly steward! Better have our lentils cooked. You will cut your fingers by trying to plane the caraway seed!" The tone of his rustic idylls is reminiscent of the speech that epigrammatic poets put in the mouths of the supposed authors of offerings made to sanctuaries dotting the woods and fields, for whom they wrote dedications in verse, products of their fancy. Similarly the theme of the hunt, a town-dweller's diversion but a countryman's gainful activity, frequently appears in poetry. It no longer wears the mask of mythological developments, for rustic realism is enough as a source of inspiration, without any need to enlist the help of Meleager, Heracles, or Theseus. What is sought now is no longer the material satisfaction of capturing the game, but the exhilaration of tracking and pursuing it in the wilderness: witness Callimachus' picture (*Epigram* 31) of those who, in the countryside where he was born, haunt the wooded and solitary heights of Cyrenaica. "The hunter roams over the mountain slope, with a watchful eye for the tracks of the hares and stags on the white frost or the newly fallen snow. Someone may say, 'Look, here is game laid low!' but he will not bend down for it." It would be wrong to find here an erudite man's *divertimento*: such evocations reflect a deep-seated feeling, which, even in a town-dweller, is not at all artificial. Here we are dealing with a civilization in which urban centers are rarely of an unmanageable size, and where the usual means of human transport is walking. The town-dweller is thus permanently in contact with the nearby countryside. There is a note of sincerity in such texts that is evident as we read them today.

The work done in recent decades by archaeologists and historians has gradually given us a better idea of the use to which the land was put. Thanks to aerial photography, verified by ground surveys, field boundaries can be ascertained, thus revealing the existence of a cadastral survey, established from the outset in new territory and in every case placed under the control of an official authority. Such research has been particularly active in southern Italy and Sicily, as well as in southern Russia in the Olbia region, around the Bug-Dnieper estuary, and in the Crimea (see p. 178). In recent times it has taken place in Cyrenaica. These enquiries reveal that the density of land use by Greek cultivators was more extensive than originally believed. A considerable number of farmsteads were built in the countryside. They had as a rule escaped the attention of archaeologists, as they were built of coarse material, not intended to last – unbaked bricks for instance – traditionally used for buildings like these with a utilitarian purpose. But improved methods have now been found, enabling them to be located, and specialized studies have been devoted to certain types of structure. Among these are "towered houses," large farmsteads with at least one corner taken up by a square thick-walled tower, providing their residents with better protection from eventual attack. This was the case of the building on Rhenea described above (p. 259). Similar buildings are to be found from one end of the Hellenic world to the other, and the very name that our texts give them, *towers*, shows that such an original feature appeared striking to its onlookers. A rural residence endowed with one would take on a more monumental aspect, that of a stronghold, with an elevated profile that would be eye-catching in the country landscape. Hellenistic painters noted such a picture: it appears in frescoes, the coloured stucco work or mosaics of Italian villas at Pompeii and Herculaneum, and even in Rome. This was as it were a preliminary sketch of what the castles of the early Middle Ages were to look like.

In Ptolemaic Egypt, where papyri provide abundant information on rural habitats, the same concept of rustic architecture was prevalent. "Nilotic" landscapes include houses provided with towers. Taking into account the constraints of climate and local technical traditions, we find in these written documents the same terms applied to the same sections of that sort of dwelling as are found in other texts of the Greek-speaking world. Yet the Greeks, Macedonians, or Hellenized Asians settling in the Egyptian countryside had to make allowances for conditions peculiar to the Nile Valley, for there human habitation was concentrated on knolls (often artificial ones) that were safe from the river's annual flooding. Bricks made of mud mixed with thatch and baked in the sun were systematically employed. These dwellings were enclosed in wood (for lack of stone in the valley), had their reserves of water upstairs (replacing cisterns hollowed out in the soil), and, of course, terraced roofs. Numbers of peasants of European origin lived in this manner in Valley or Delta villages, owning an allotment that they cultivated or leased out to a native farmer. Their lifestyle is apparent from the records of Zeno, the steward of Apollonius the *dioecetes* (see p. 238), who managed in his master's name the vast domain of Philadelphia, at the edge of the Fayyum oasis. From his correspondence and his business papers, it can be seen that, burdened with weighty responsibilities at a local level, Zeno had nevertheless the same lifestyle as the Greeks of Caunus, a Carian town that was his motherland, facing the island of Rhodes. Wealthy in his own right, and managing his employer's considerable income, Zeno contented himself with the simple diet traditional among the Hellenic people: bread and salt, fish, oil, vegetables, and fruit were the purchases he usually brought to his table. On the other hand, he would include more refined foods on festive days, in honor of his guests: meat, chicken, game, pâtés, imported vintage wines, as well as honey and rare fruit – Black Sea nuts, for instance. Silver plate, flowers, perfumes enhanced the banquet. Religion and social relationships prescribed such expensive luxury. Zeno was an indefatigable worker: witness his bookkeeping, his notes and drafts, his varied business projects. Yet now and then he found time for relaxation and leisure. He was fond of the hunt, as was his employer: wild buffaloes, goats, gazelles, even boars haunted the marshes bordering on the Fayyum. A boar, as fearful a monster as the Calydonian one in the myth of Meleager, attacked Zeno in the course of a hunting party. The daring intervention of a young dog of Indian breed, a mastiff named Tauron, saved him. The dog jumped on the boar, and though wounded by a thrust from its snout, did not loosen the grip of his jaws until his enemy lay dead at his feet. Tauron died of his wound. The grateful Zeno had a tomb raised in his honor, for which a talented poet wrote two epitaphs, one in elegiac distichs, the other in iambic trimeters: a copy was found in Zeno's files. This unique and touching episode illustrates the high level of culture among Greek colonists settled right in the middle of the Egyptian countryside, far away from urban areas.

Other documents give some insight into the daily life of the rural communities that the colonists, long-time dwellers in the villages of the Delta, had set up so as to preserve their Hellenic tradition in spite of their distance from larger towns. As in Greece, they were grouped in associations around a sacred cult. They had their own leaders and benefactors, whose generosity perpetuated their bond of friendship, at ceremonies that brought together on fixed dates the members of these colleges, real clubs in the style of local conservatories of Hellenism. There is an outstanding example of their activity in an inscription found at Psenemphaia, a village on the edge of the Nile Delta, almost midway between Naucratis and Alexandria. It is a stele provided with a pediment, of a type that is known all over the Greek world, on which is engraved the text of a decree passed by the assembly of the "landowners" of Psenemphaia, in the year 5 BC, under Augustus' principate. The change in the political regime following the Roman conquest had in no way altered the demography or lifestyle of Hellenized Egypt. These owners of landed property were grouped in a college that met in a building called the *Cleopatreion*, which someone called Aristion had ordered, in the days of Ptolemaic rule, to be built in honor of one of the queens named Cleopatra.

The leader of the community was a distinguished citizen called Theon, acting simultaneously as priest, club president, and village mayor (*komarch*). He had just died when the association's premises and its furnishings suffered serious damage as a result of unusually heavy Nile flooding. Arrangements had to be made for repairs; a new leader had to be found. As was often the case in Greek communities of the Hellenistic age, potential candidates for such positions of responsibility, a source of great honor but also of great expense for their holders, shied away from approaches made to them. In the end only Theon's son, Apollonius, gave a generous, positive response, and succeeded his father in his various responsibilities. The decree passed by an assembly of landowners recalls his deeds, prompted by an exemplary devotion to the interest of the community, among others the restoration of the ruined facility and its furnishings. It then lists the honors granted by a unanimous vote to an outstanding benefactor. These include two bust effigies of himself, painted or sculpted in the shape of circular medallions; another bust for his son, who, though still an adolescent, is to be admitted, in spite of his youth but by an exceptional privilege, to the association's banquets. Apollonius is to be entitled to a garland at each banquet, with a double helping at table. He is given the right to commemorate, by an engraving on the lintel of the building, its restoration at his own expense. Finally, a stele is to be erected, on which the decree shall be engraved: the very one discovered in our own day. Various complementary measures are described, with the intent of placing the new president's authority over the farmers' entire group above any challenge. Opposition to his decisions is forbidden under threat of a heavy fine, the amount of which is stated to be 3,000 drachmas – half a talent.

This epigraphic text, found in a perfect state of preservation, is a very revealing one. It demonstrates the permanence of tradition in these small Hellenistic communities, even when they were almost lost amid a teeming population of fellahin. After an existence spanning three centuries in a dense and well-structured native milieu, these groups of Greek peasants, owners of their holdings, treasured their beliefs, customs, and language. Neither their mode of expression nor their lifestyle shows any trace of native influence. In the midst of a Nilotic environment, and coping with the demands of the local climate and the constraints of yearly flooding, these Greeks still lived as Greeks. They attended to their cults, and met at banquets; they kept alive their traditional modes of human relationships by preserving their ancestral rites of social life and a terminology handed down from generation to generation. On that African soil, so different from the one their forebears had left, such strong bonds were imperative if they were to preserve their ethnic identity. Their consciousness of mutual solidarity survived, thanks to these associations meeting at fixed dates and complying with a ceremonial that never varied. The Psenemphaia landowners were especially grateful to Apollonius, as their president, for having held their common banquets at the prescribed dates and punctually. They were well aware of the importance of ritual for a community's survival. Their decree also reveals the foremost role that notabilities played in their group, as it did in all cities of the Hellenistic world. Their devotion was the key to the proper working of institutions; the maintenance of the community's property, whether it consisted of movable goods or real estate, depended on their generosity. Community organizations were finding such help increasingly difficult to obtain. If they disappeared for want of financial means, the very existence of Hellenism would be endangered. That was the reason for the very few among the wealthy who did not shirk their duty of solidarity being showered with honors. By emphasizing the continuity of a family tradition, the community appealed to their personal pride. It also developed two themes, among others. One was attachment to the examples set by forebears dead or living (in the present case, Apollonius the father). The other was encouragement given to the young to commit themselves, early in life, to public service (in this same case, by the unwonted privilege granted to a young lad to share in honors reserved for adults). The Psenemphaia landowners' decree sends a message similar to one given on the other side of the Mediterranean. At about the same time, the Greeks of Thasos passed decrees honoring Epié, a woman who had restored their sacred buildings and kept alive her city's cults at her own cost (see pp. 194–5), from which we see that the same cause had the same effect everywhere.

■ *The towns* ■ *Urban planning* ■ *Miletus* ■ *Priene*
■ *Alexandria: the harbor and the town* ■ *Theocritus'* Syracusan
Women ■ *The urban house at Priene and Delos* ■ *Interior
decoration and the luxury of the human habitat* ■ *Collective
facilities* ■ *Porticoes* ■ *The Athenian Agora* ■ *The citadel of
Pergamum* ■ *The peristyle court* ■ *The "Ionian"-type agora: the
example of Messene* ■ *Assembly buildings*

Though the Hellenistic economy was based on agriculture, and in spite of the
emergence of a more conscious and more sensitive feeling for nature, Greek
civilization preserved in this period of time the close link it had with urban life in
former times. The city – in both senses of the term, political and geographical –
remained the privileged framework of individual and collective life, the focal
point of activity and culture. Speaking generally, cities developed and were em-
bellished, in Greece proper as well as in the colonies and kingdoms. By constantly founding new cities, sovereigns inserted in their faraway Asian possessions
lively nuclei of Hellenic populations. In these three centuries the urban phenomenon, which had already been the distinctive trait of the Greek world in the
Archaic and Classical ages, adopted novel forms that were transmitted to the
imperial Roman world. These stand out in strong enough contrast to the previous reality to prompt an attempt at defining them. In various ways they had an
impact on urban planning, on individual habitats, on collective facilities, and on
monumental ensembles.

A Hellenistic model of urban planning can of course be applied only to new
cities: the older cities had taken shape in the course of a slow process of growth.
They kept their age-old aspect, with narrow winding streets, pathways which, to
use Le Corbusier's phrase about Agrigentum, had had a donkey as their architect
– since they were adapted to the progress of beasts of burden, which is still the
case in most Greek villages. As a counterpart, in a world that had expanded
prodigiously, especially in Asia, many cities were created in new territory. Political or geographical circumstances had also, as we have seen (pp. 203, 268–9),
caused the transfer of urban cities to neighboring sites: new towns were thus
founded. Finally, certain cities had to be more or less rebuilt after their destruction by man or by a natural cataclysm. In this area, therefore, it appears that the
Hellenistic age was one strongly marked by creative activity. The few data provided by texts and excavations (still far too limited, for the thorough exploration
of an urban site is extremely costly) disclose at least one major tendency, evident
in the whole of the Greek world. This is the frequent use of the chessboard plan,

also called the Milesian plan, for it seems that architects and political theorists originating from Miletus had advocated it since the fifth century. One of these was the famous Hippodamus, a contemporary of Pericles, whose thinking inspired the plan of the Piraeus. The concept in question amounted to a simple and rational process for drawing up the plan of a new city, dividing a right-angled network of streets and avenues into a series of rectangular blocks of uniform dimensions. Clearly delimited lots of comparable value could thus be distributed among its inhabitants, while the required spaces reserved for public buildings and facilities, civic and religious, corresponded to one or a number of blocks. It was normal for those who founded cities to make use of such a convenient method, which in addition allowed them to make long-term provision for the development of the urban area in the distant future. They could thus reserve entire zones, the planning of which was already done, for future construction. This is the way town-planners of our own day work in countries or regions starting from scratch – as happened in Brasilia, for example. This was the case at Miletus. A vast city that the Persians had completely destroyed in 494, at the time of the Ionian revolt, it knew a gradual rebirth over the centuries, in conformity with a grand design thought out by Milesian architects soon after the end of the Persian Wars. Its case is exemplary. It illustrates brilliantly the way in which a city, among the most densely populated of the ancient world, handled its development. This was adapted to the resources that commercial prosperity or princely generosity put at its disposal, without ever outgrowing the framework originally assigned to it, which proves how realistic and clear-headed those planners had been in analyzing their data and the concomitant problems, and how persistent in their effort the citizens were in the following centuries.

Although Hellenistic architects did not innovate in this area, they made more systematic use of a preexisting rational mode of town-planning, which was conveniently applied in virgin territory. The most curious instance of such a use is certainly that of Priene, a small city in the lower Maeander valley, a short distance north of Miletus. This town was settled on its present site in the third quarter of the fourth century, in other words, at the very start of the Hellenistic period. The inhabited districts climbed up a steep south-facing cliff, conforming to the dividing lines of a regular chessboard plan, providing blocks with unvarying dimensions of 160 by 120 feet (about 47 by 35 meters). Roadways, crossing at right angles, were designed along two axes, running north–south and east–west. They climbed the hills without winding; the result was that the north–south streets, following the rise of the steeper slope, were actually stairways. Streets were more or less on even ground only in the upper section of the city: they included the street on which the theater was situated, and the terrace of Athena's sanctuary. Public monuments fitted into that plan. These were the theater, the Council building (*Bouleuterion*), the temple of Athena Polias (built in Alexander's time by Pytheus, the architect of Halicarnassus' famous Mausoleum), the agora with its shrine of Olympian Zeus, and finally the gymnasium at the foot of the hill. Only the training track and the stadium, which prolonged the palaestra eastward, were exempt from following the orthogonal plan; they ran diagonally across it. The need to have a perfectly level ground for a distance of 200 meters justified such an exception. An extensive fortified enclosure stretched round the town. Its circuit was determined by strictly military considerations, taking no account of the orthogonal plan. Its wall climbed uphill much higher than the area of human habitation, beyond the rocky cliff overhanging the town, and reaching, at an altitude of 380 meters, on an outcrop of the mountain, a secluded hideout serving as the acropolis. It was mostly independent of the built-up section of the city, surrounding a much larger area that could eventually afford shelter to country-dwellers. Hellenistic cities often presented this feature, but precedents going further back in time were not lacking.

The case of Priene is of particular significance, as it was a settlement of modest size, probably having 4,000 or 5,000 inhabitants. It has been possible to study the plan of the city thoroughly, since the major part of the built-up area has been excavated. On the other hand, when we turn to Alexandria, the largest city of the Hellenistic world, we find very different material conditions to study. The modern town covers the whole surface of the ancient one, the detailed plan of which cannot be ascertained because of sporadic excavation. However, we learn enough from the texts at our disposal to be certain that, as at Priene, the principles of rectangular planning had been applied to that immense capital. Alexander had entrusted the Rhodian architect Deinocrates with the task of drawing up the plan of the new town that the Conqueror wished to be named after him. Plutarch (*Alexander*, 26) and Strabo (XVII, 1, 6 = 792) describe the circumstances of its foundation in some detail. Plutarch attributes the choice of the site to supernatural inspiration: the king had dreamed of the aged Homer reciting two verses of the *Odyssey* (IV, 354–5), mentioning the island of Pharos lying off the Egyptian coast. Alexander, steeped in Homeric poetry since childhood, went there, and realizing how much the geography of the area favored his project, decided that it would provide the site of what was to be Alexandria. According to Plutarch, the story goes back to a second century BC Alexandrian scholar, Heraclides Lembus: a fact that gives it a certain degree of authenticity. It demonstrates in any case the value that the brightest minds of the political world attributed to heaven-sent omens in making essentially practical decisions.

As a matter of fact, the coast of the Delta is flat, sandy, inhospitable, lying open to surf from the high sea. The island of Pharos, more than three kilometers long, and situated slightly more than one kilometer offshore, offered ships a shelter that was most welcome. Its position created a channel accessible from east and west that could easily be transformed into a harbor if the island and the continent were linked by a dyke. A causeway was therefore built, interrupted by two bridges allowing ships to sail from the east port (the Great Harbor) to the

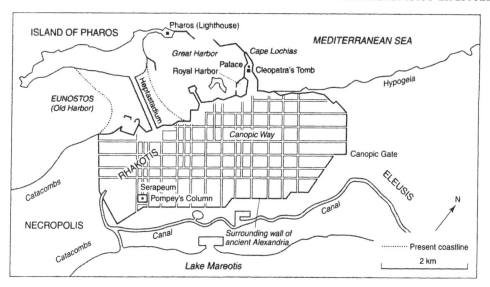

Figure 3 Ancient Alexandria (drawn by Neroutsos Bey).

Between the sea and Lake Mareotis the city extended from the old native township of Rhakotis in the west to the Canopic Gate in the east, beyond which was suburban Eleusis. The chessboard plan has only been reconstructed notionally, as the modern city covers the ancient one in its entirety. The island of Pharos, at the eastern extremity of which stood the Lighthouse, was linked to the continent by the artificial wharf of the Heptastadium. In the east the Great Harbor, protected by two breakwaters, was bordered on the west and south by the royal district, with its palaces, the Museum, and the Library. Toward the west the harbor of Eunostos communicated with the Great Harbor by means of two passages cut into the Heptastadium, and spanned by bridges. The necropolises were situated outside the city, following the usual practice.

western *Eunostos* (Good Return) port. The total length of the work with its two bridges was 7 stadia (slightly more than 1,200 meters): hence its name *Heptastadium*. Jetties protected the eastern port by exploiting the slim headland bearing the name of Cape Lochias. The town could thus provide a haven for sea traffic. The famous lighthouse, soon erected on the eastern tip of the island, made it even safer for mariners.

That dual harbor answered a need frequently felt among the Greeks to secure easy access to a safe mooring for their ships, whatever the direction of the winds or the waves happened to be. The location of the town was the nearly flat isthmus separating the sea from the extensive lagoon of Lake Mareotis, into which flowed canals starting from the Canopic branch of the Nile. It was thus protected by water on its southern and northern sides. The lake and the canals allowed communication with the interior of Egypt, the harbors with the rest of the world. The town was situated on the edge of the Delta, but in contact with its cultures

267

and, thanks to sea breezes and trade winds, benefited from less torrid summers than those of the rest of Egypt. This was indeed a favored site, which its inhabitants have appreciated right down to our own times. According to Strabo and Plutarch, Deinocrates and his team drew up the plan of the town on the terrain of the Isthmus, giving it the configuration of a chlamys, that is, a rectangular coat that was broader than it was high, with rounded lower corners. The line of the ramparts, starting from the coast, turned southward at right angles, and curving on each side, went down to the edge of the lake. A grid system of streets and avenues, wide enough to accommodate chariot and horse traffic, covered the town. The main axes, one 5 kilometers in length and running east and west, the other 2 kilometers long, running north and south, intersected more or less in the center of the city. Their exceptional width exceeded one plethrum, that is, 100 feet or 30 meters. These two magnificent avenues gave the urban landscape a grandiose and truly monumental aspect, to a degree not reached by any other Greek city up to that time. Even a great colonial city like Cyrene, with its wide paved street and its vast perspective, which had made such an impression on Pindar, fell far short of Alexandria's dimensions. The lesson was not lost and found applications in diverse places: Ptolemais of Cyrenaica, which Ptolemy III founded in the second half of the third century (see p. 253), actually a hundred years later, is an impressive instance of Alexandrian town-planning.

Though excavation in modern times has not allowed the plan of this metropolis to be verified in great detail, we have texts bearing explicit witness to the impression it made on its inhabitants and visitors. The little play entitled *The Syracusan Women*, inserted in Theocritus' *Idyll XV*, conjures up in a marvelous manner the atmosphere of that very large city around the year 275 BC. The two ladies of Alexandria's bourgeois class that appear in it originate from Syracuse and still use their native city's Dorian dialect. One of them lives "at the other end of the world" in an outlying district. To come and meet her, her friend has had to face the hustle and bustle of the town centre: "I had no small task extricating myself alive from that huge crowd, from all those four-horse chariots! Boots everywhere, everywhere soldiers wearing the chlamys. An endless journey!" As a matter of fact, this day is a holiday, the king's army is everywhere in the streets, with the combat chariots once donated to Alexander by the Cyrenaeans, and kept in use under the Ptolemies. These impress the public all the more as no such chariots are seen any longer elsewhere. The two women are on an outing to the palace where Queen Arsinoe is celebrating the feast of Adonis: "My goodness, what a throng! When and how shall we get across such a massed crowd? A veritable ants' nest, countless and without end!" They are very nearly knocked down by a squadron of horsemen riding in procession, and finally manage to make their way to the palace amid the bustling crowd.

Nothing is more vivid than these street scenes painted from life, including the hit-and-run thieves who used to take advantage of these gatherings and do their pilfering "Egyptian style" – at least, until Ptolemy put an end to such practices with his police. We see, conjured up before our mind's eye, the picture of a major cosmopolitan city, in which Hellenes of various backgrounds rubbed shoulders in a colorful medley. The presence among them of a native population gave a colonial look to these Greek cities, which had quite a different aspect from the one the cities of mainland Greece had preserved.

For want of any archaeological data extracted from the ground, we have no knowledge of the exterior appearance of Alexandria's private houses. Theocritus' *Idyll XV* alludes only to a courtyard through which one had access to a street-door: nothing new from the point of view of a Greek house. At Priene and Delos, on the other hand, the clearing of whole blocks of human habitation has revealed the ground plan and exterior aspect of houses in towns of small or middle size, in other words, the immense majority of Hellenistic cities. There are few many-storied buildings (*synoikiai*: also called *pyrgoi*, "towers"), such as certainly existed in densely populated major towns. The usual dwelling was a single house, not an isolated one, situated as it was within one of the blocks of buildings bounded by the streets. At Priene an individual house would have a court on which the owners' living quarters opened, usually on its north side, for the sake of exposure to the sun in the south. An antechamber shaped like a porch, often with two columns standing between the lateral walls, preceded the large hall round which smaller adjoining rooms were placed. Service rooms could fill one or more sides of the court. Along a corridor that opened on that court, one entered the house from the street. This was a simple plan, well suited to the climate, and fostering the sense of family life centered on its own habitat and insulated from inquisitive glances and the bustle of life outside. The only remarkable difference from the Classical house was the antechamber preceding the main hall: the wide open porch, especially when it was provided with columns, gave a monumental look to the building.

At Delos the theater district, as well as other urban areas that have been excavated, has a rather different aspect: no chessboard plan there, but a network of small winding streets, occasionally intersected by very narrow alleys. Terraced houses, built on the slopes, rarely followed a regular plan. Some were of very modest size, but a number of others were quite generous. They were always built round a court, which was surrounded in wealthy residences by a four-sided portico: this was the *peristyle* court arrangement (see p. 274), which had already made a rare appearance at Priene. At Delos, where most construction dates back to the second century, the architects used marble from the Cyclades, conveniently close at hand, in those porticoes. The court floor was paved or adorned with a mosaic, under which a cistern had often been placed, to collect water from the roof. Water could be drawn from a well placed in a corner. Sometimes one side of the portico – usually opening on the south – was higher in relation to the others. This created a "Rhodian" peristyle. Quite a few houses had an upper floor, accessible by a flight of stairs. Some, like the *House of the Hermes*, had up to three stories, an arrangement favored by the steep rise of the hill against which the house rested.

Interior decoration, amply documented at Delos, was more abundant and more cheerful than had been the case in the houses of the Classical age. Walls made of stone, or of unbaked bricks on a stone base, had a covering of colored stucco, either plain or showing a series of strips. They often looked like a wall of dressed stone, with simulated joints drawn on them, incisions outlining the stone base, even light relief shaped as bosses. Red and yellow were the most frequently used colors. The painter would sometimes create courses of imitation stone, simulating a variety of materials – stone conglomerate, alabaster, or veined marble. The decoration could also represent architectural friezes, with their usual motifs: ova, "hearts-and-darts" (*rais de cœur*), fretwork, strapwork, sometimes brought out by a slight relief in the stuccoed band. Exceptionally, there might be a figured frieze, for instance, in the "House of the Tritons," a race of chariots ridden by little Cupids. Such elements of decoration are similarly attested in many other Hellenistic towns, though less profusely than at Delos, and can be seen as belonging to a widespread practice. They are, to a great extent, those found in the most ancient decorative ensembles of Pompeii and Herculaneum – what specialists call those "of the first style." Hellenistic taste had reached by a direct road the towns of southern Italy, to which wealthy customers used to attract Greek artists.

In the Hellenistic towns, therefore, private houses contrasted with those of the previous age, in which luxury on an individual scale had been very rare and marked by discretion. It is evident that a desire for comfort, for noble materials and refined ornament, was by then widespread. There were still modest homes in the towns as well as in the country. But the number of those who enjoyed houses that were spacious and, by the standard of the time, convenient and comfortable, must have increased considerably, if one relies on proof provided by excavation. Other evidence supports that conclusion, demonstrating the growth of prosperity in a large number of Greek cities, in spite of all the trials imposed by war and natural catastrophes.

That prosperity also showed itself in the emphasis placed on community facilities. We tend to forget, dazzled as we are by the noble buildings that were erected in the age of Pericles, to what extent the Hellenistic age favored the many-faceted activity of builders in cities as well as sanctuaries. It was a most important period for every department of architecture. It was characterized by astonishing inventiveness and remarkable initiative in responding to the varied needs of society, in providing for the demands of daily life, making human relationships easier, fostering the celebration of cults. Some examples will throw light on the functional nature and the diversified use of these many types of public buildings. They will bring out, here and there, the originality of the solution chosen and the aesthetic quality of its realization.

Among civic buildings, special notice must be taken of porticoes (or *stoai*, plural of *stoa*), which played a considerable role in Hellenistic town planning. They were found everywhere, as an essential element of architectural composition, in sanctuaries as well as in public squares. They were built wherever a shelter was needed for strollers, traders, the audience of a rhetor or a philosopher, even judges sitting on a tribunal. These courtyards, opening to the exterior by a colonnade occupying the whole length of a building, had existed in earlier times, but were then smaller and more restricted. Porticoes were now used to structure the vast monumental groups of buildings that grew fast in the Greek world with the development of cities, thanks to the generosity of the kings. The most striking example of this phenomenon is certainly the transformation that the Athenian Agora underwent in the second century BC. The great portico bearing the name of Attalus of Pergamum was built there at his expense, serving as the eastern boundary of the quadrangle occupied by this public square. The building, which has now been magnificently restored by American archaeologists, set the tone for the character of the whole site. Placed on a terrace commanding its environment, it unrolled the two superimposed stories of its exterior colonnade. It exposed to the public eye the vast covered spaces that a row of inner, widely spaced columns allowed to be seen as they extended in front of the back wall, in which the doors of twenty-one high-ceilinged and spacious shops opened. Staircases provided access to the upper story at either end. As it appears in its meticulous reconstruction, this is surely the monument, among all those remaining from the ancient world, that best conveys today the grandiose inspiration and the technical know-how of architects belonging to this period. A whole side of the Agora was from that time on to be occupied by that noble portico, which served both as boundary and as backdrop for the square with its statues, its altars, its small sanctuaries, and the stalls made of light material that stood in it.

Concern for the organization of the whole in a clear and majestic arrangement of its parts is evident in the fact that, about the same time, a portico of even greater dimensions, called the Middle Portico, was built. It rose at right angles to that of Attalus on the southern side of the Agora. Nearly 150 meters long, but not storied, it was a large hall without walls, whose exterior colonnade opened, on all four sides, around a row of median columns supporting the roof. Like the previous one, it was a building with a utilitarian purpose, with its northern side turned toward the center of the Agora. It marked the southern limit of an area that was the kernel of the city's political and cultural life, while its long southern side faced another portico, the Southern Portico, occupying the foot of the slopes leading up to the Areopagus. Between those two parallel porticoes, an oblong space running east and west was used as a market: thanks to the Middle Portico or Stoa, which one could easily cross, that space reserved for commercial activities remained in convenient communication with the rest of the Agora. What was left was to complete on the west the rearrangement of monuments in the old public square that was still the heart of Athens. There, at the foot of the hill where the temple of Hephaestus, also called the Theseion today, had stood since Periclean times, the shrine of the Mother of the Gods was built, in front of the meeting hall of the Council (*Bouleuterion*). The archives of the city were kept there. The façade of the new edifice, almost at right angles to the northern side of the Middle Portico, was adorned with a colonnade that was nearly 40 meters in length.

The area of the Agora, in the center of the city, was thus clearly delimited in the east by the Portico of Attalus, in the south by the Middle Portico, in the west by the series of buildings aligned beneath the temple of Hephaestus. It thus offered the visitor arriving on the Sacred Way the prospect of a magnificent array, with long porticoes spreading out in their horizontal development, their colonnades standing out, thanks to the regular disposition of their pillars, against the shade of the inner courtyards serving as a background. Dominating the whole were the bare cliff of the Areopagus and the high, imposing mass of the Acropolis. The town-planners of Hellenistic Athens had no doubt received training from the architects Attalus II had sent from Pergamum. They proved worthy of their illustrious predecessors, Ictinus and Mnesicles, who had deployed their skill, on instructions received from Pericles and Phidias, three centuries earlier on the sacred plateau. They gave to the hallowed civic heart of their city a monumental framework with noble and simple lines, conceived as a unified whole. That was in keeping with the new spirit of Hellenistic town-planning, anxious to organize coherent townscapes. Such a preoccupation, unknown to the Archaic and Classical ages, showed the way to the future.

The citadel of Pergamum, with its rugged slopes and its difficult terrain, had served as a testing ground for the architects and engineers of Eumenes II and Attalus II in giving its ultimate shape to their conception of impressive ensembles modulated by magnificent porticoes. Powerful terraces, fitted with buttressed retaining walls, coped with the problem of sloping ground, and offered scope for long colonnades. On the terrace that was to be a promenade gallery for theatergoers, an immense portico more than 200 meters long was built on three levels. Seen from the surrounding countryside, it appeared to serve as a foundation for the totality of the buildings – temples, altars and libraries, palaces and barracks, occupying the summit of the acropolis in apparent disorder. The outline of the town filled the viewer with wonder, perched as it was on its own trachyte peak overhanging the Caicus valley, between two tributaries flowing down the mountain. The chronology of its monuments still presents a number of obscure points of detail. What is certain is that those two great Attalid kings made of Pergamum a real focal point of inventive activity for the world of builders. The lesson they gave, through the buildings erected at their expense in Athens and at Delphi, had a wide and receptive audience. It would, however, be

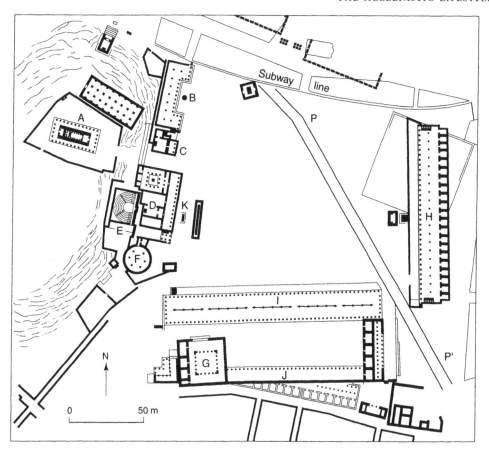

Figure 4 The Athenian Agora toward the end of the Hellenistic period (from *The Athenian Agora: A Guide to the Excavations*, American School at Athens, fig. 5).

Overlooked since the fifth century BC by the temple of Hephaestus (A), still standing west on the hill called Colonos Agorios, the Athenian Agora was crossed in an oblique line from the northwest to the southeast by the way leading to the Acropolis (P-P'), that was used by the Panathenaic procession. In the Classical period only the western side of the Agora was still bordered by buildings. From north to south stood the Portico of Zeus (B), the temple of Apollo Patróos (C), the temple of the Mother of the Gods (D), where the State archives were deposited, the Council Hall or Bouleuterion (E), the Tholos (F), a circular edifice where the prytanes met. In the south a large square building no doubt housed the people's tribunal, the Heliaea (G). In the north, the trench made in modern times for the underground railway marks the northern limit of the excavations. The essential contribution of the Hellenistic age is made up of the two monumental porticoes framing the Agora on the east and south. On the east is the two-storied portico built at the expense of Attalus II of Pergamum (H). South are the Middle Portico (I), a long hall open on all sides, and the South Portico (J), which covered a previous building and ends west at the Heliaea, thus setting the limit for the market, separated by the Middle Portico from the rest of the Agora. Finally, on the west, a more modest portico (K), raised as a façade for the temple of the Mother of the Gods (rebuilt on that occasion), gave more unity to that side of the Agora. The desire is evident here to organize the civic center of the city by giving it an architectural framework characterized by grandeur and coherence. Such an outlook was foreign to the Athenians of the Classical age.

wrong to attribute a "Pergamene" character to all ensembles with porticoes of that period. To deal with analogous problems raised elsewhere by sheer sloping ground, various architects, analyzing them independently, found and applied parallel solutions. At Cyrene, for instance, we have no reason to imagine any exchanges with Pergamum. It was local builders who erected there in the second century the great portico north of the agora, with its impressive walls and its two levels demanded by the gradient of the hill. They had always proved able to overcome such difficulties.

The construction of a set of porticoes around an open or rectangular space led to the birth of the peristyle court (see p. 289), an architectural style that was soon in great vogue. It was enough to join together the four porticoes framing a square to obtain an enclosed area. Entrance was by a porch, to which a monumental aspect could be given if required. This model of a closed agora, fitting easily into the urban grid of a chessboard plan, was considered typical of the Ionian cities, where indeed it was often found. Pausanias confirmed this when he remarked on the agora of Elis in the Peloponnese (VI, 24, 2), "This public square is not structured on the model of Ionian towns or of the Greek cities close to Ionia. It is built on the old model, with porticoes that are not joined end to end and between which room has been left for streets." On the other hand Messene, another town in the Peloponnese, was endowed with a very typical closed agora, which has been cleared as a result of excavation. A 50-meter-square court was enclosed within a continuous set of four porticoes, with a colonnade in the middle, serving as a wide pedestrian avenue on which neighboring buildings opened. Most of these were dedicated to various cults. Pausanias mentions many of them, but they cannot be located. They were the shrines of the Mother of the Gods, of Eilithyia, who presided over childbirth, of the Couretai, of Demeter, of the Dioscuri; as well as that of the heroine Messene, bearing the same name as the city. In the center of the court was a temple of Asclepius and his daughter Hygieia (Health), with a high altar on its façade, turned eastward: excavation has cleared its ruins. In the same temple, says Pausanias, were also a number of other divine statues: those of Apollo, father of Asclepius, the Muses, Heracles, Tyché (Fortune), Artemis bearing a torch. The effigy of Epaminondas, whose victories had freed Messene from the Lacedaemonian yoke, was also on show, as well as the allegorical figure of Thebes, his motherland.

This list illustrates the richness and diversity of religious life in Hellenistic cities, even the smallest ones, and the urge to build that resulted from it. Yet Pausanias does not tell the full story. The large hall occupying the northwestern corner of the set of four porticoes has been identified as a shrine of Artemis, bearing the *epiclesis* Orthia, as she did at Sparta, and also called the Virgin. As evidence, there is a metrical dedication on the base of a statue found there of a young priestess named Mego. It runs as follows:

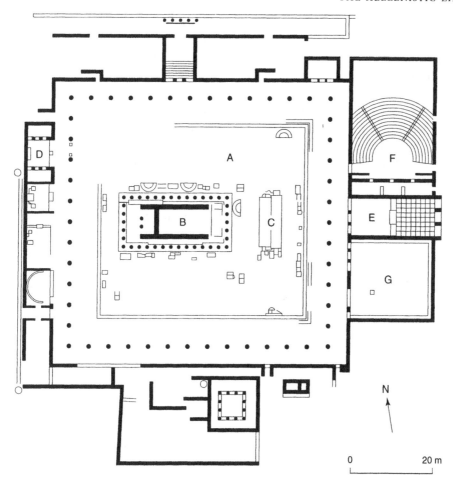

Figure 5 Messene: plan of the agora (from *Bulletin de correspondance hellénique*, 1972, p. 665, fig. 179. Plan drawn by A. K. Orlandos).

This is a typical example of a closed Hellenistic agora. The square court (A) is framed by a set of porticoes in quadrilateral formation, fitted with an intervening colonnade. In the center of the court is the temple of Asclepius and Hygieia (B), in front of which is the altar (C). In the northwest corner, opening under the portico, is the sanctuary of Artemis (D), an oblong chapel where the base of Mego's statue was found. On the east, framing the vestibule (E) that gives access to the agora, are two buildings: an auditorium (F) with tiers in a semicircle and a Council Hall (G) with benches along the walls.

Unto you, Virgin, venerable Orthia, Damonicus and his wife Timarchis have con-secrated me, their daughter Mego, born of a noble father. In my hand I hold your effigy, Artemis, and the torch I swung over your altars. Be it granted that I repay the debt of gratitude I owe my parents. For it is just that children honor, as repay-ment, those who gave them life.

Not only does that short poem disclose the existence at Messene of a cult to Artemis Orthia, and help to identify the sanctuary consecrated to her. It also shows what close links bound public cults with the institution of the family, the cellular unit on which the city's future depended. The parents' gesture in consecrating the effigy of their daughter, the priestess, is just one of an ever-increasing number of family monuments that were erected during this period. While illustrating the strong bond of mutual love that kept the family group together, these bear witness to the need felt by such groups for public recognition. We also find here further evidence of the first-rate role that notabilities played in Hellenistic cities (see pp. 262–3, inscription from Psenemphaia).

The agora of Messene was entered through a vestibule situated in the middle of the eastern side of the rectangle and facing the temple of Asclepius. On each side of the vestibule was a sizable building. To the north was a sort of auditorium, with tiers in a semicircle, which no doubt served for performances by itinerant rhetoricians or musicians, a practice that was frequent at the time. On the south side a large square building, with a bench along the lower part of the walls and windows on the upper story, sheltered a large room, the roof of which rested on four interior supports. It was meant to serve for meetings of the Council, the main political instrument of the city. Such buildings, specially designed for assemblies, are well known in Hellenistic architecture, at Priene or Miletus, for instance. They are proof of the vitality that civic institutions had preserved, and the care taken to provide them with appropriate meeting-places.

The peristyle court of the Greek agora was to provide a model for the Roman forum, as is well demonstrated at Pompeii. It also found a place in many buildings of a utilitarian nature, like gymnasia and caravanserais, as well as palaces. Finally it inspired the *atria* of Christian basilicas, convent cloisters, and the inner courtyards of mosques. There too the spirit of innovation displayed by Hellenistic architects had an abundant and enduring aftermath.

■ *The Hellenistic palace* ■ *The progress of architectural technique* ■ *The Pharos of Alexandria* ■ *The first vaults and arcades*

Now for another totally new kind of building: the palace. The Homeric age had known large royal residences, an inheritance from Mycenaean times, with a court surrounded by walls, porches, a vast antechamber, a huge *megaron* with a central hearth, and a complex of rooms reserved for private use. Homer's descriptions, for want of concrete evidence that has completely vanished, allow readers to

Plate 6   Pella: a mosaic signed by Gnosis (Archaeological Museum, Pella; photo ©
Archaeological Receipts Fund, Athens).

*This is undoubtedly the finest mosaic from Pella, for the quality of both the central scene (a
stag hunt) and its generous framework of luxuriant acanthus foliage, with tendrils, florets,
and palmettes in which the artist displays exceptional ingenuity and decorative skill. The
work is bordered by a series of straight lines. The technique employed does not use tesserae,
but small, colored, bright or dark pebbles embedded in some sort of bonding cement. The
central motif, bearing the artist's signature at the top and on the right – "Gnosis made
[it]" – displays very demanding technical standards. The striking athletic appearance of
the huntsmen's naked bodies, their tense facial expressions, the artistic skill with which the
space available has been filled (chlamydes blown around, hat flying off in mid-air) bear
the imprint of a master. These give an idea of what the great achievements of painting
must have been like at the start of the third century, after Apelles' or Protogenes' masterpieces (see p. 375 for more comment).*

visualize them pretty well. However, the Greek city of the Classical age, from
which monarchy was excluded, had more or less forgotten that tradition. The
rebirth and prodigious development of the monarchical system revived it. Archaeology is of little help in allowing us to work out the exact physical form of
this revival. The royal residences of Alexandria and their legendary magnificence
remain entombed beneath the modern city (like the remainder of the ancient
city). Those of Pergamum, in the uppermost part of the citadel, were short of the
space that would have allowed them unconstrained development: they were more

like private mansions with peristyles than palaces. In Macedonia the excavations at Pella, the capital of the last Argeads and the Antigonids, on the plain west of the Vardar, have brought to light some luxurious private houses. They are adorned with splendid mosaics dating back to the end of the fourth century and the beginning of the third. But they do not form the sovereign's residence. On the other hand, this is certainly the case at Palatitsa-Vergina, also in Macedonia, where a vast building has been discovered that was laid out around a peristyle court 40 meters square. Mosaics covered the floors of the rooms, and the exterior walls were painted. Its plan is reminiscent of Apollonius of Rhodes' description in the *Argonautica* (I, see 215ff.) of the palace of Aeetes, king of Colchis and custodian of the Golden Fleece. In this text, Jason and his companions arrive at the gates, they stop at the entrance and admire the colonnades aligned around the perimeter, which means that a portico surrounded the palace. The building opens to the outside; here the poet inserts a precise detail: its marble cornice overhangs a Doric frieze with bronze triglyphs (obviously, a facing attached to a stone base). A columned porch must precede the monumental door. Anyone going through the vestibule would reach a vast court where verdant groves, with bowers of climbing vines, shelter freshwater springs. This is a feature born of the poet's imagination: it brings into the myth the pools and grottoes of later times, the purpose of which was to maintain an atmosphere of natural freshness in these indoor gardens. They were a constant element of wealthy Roman establishments, and are well attested in Greece, in the Leonidaeum at Olympia, for instance. In the court at the heart of the palace, the two buildings at the entrance and at the back, facing each other, have more than one story and serve as a residence for King Aeetes and his son. A peristyle surrounds the court. On to it open through wide doorways the rooms where the king's daughters live, attended by their maids. In such a sheltered atmosphere, they blossom free from care.

It would appear that in painting this picture Apollonius, whose sole aim was to create an ambience for the action of his poem, was recalling for his listeners a monument of a type familiar to them. Similarly the two Syracusan ladies in Theocritus' *Idyll* XV (see p. 268) visit the gardens where they can admire the sacred *tableau vivant* that Queen Arsinoe has ordered for the feast of Adonis (see pp. 245–6). There in the verdant arbors are the modeled or painted images of the divine couple, Aphrodite and her lover, stretched on their ceremonial couch. The texts of the two poets are mutually complementary, and throw light on each other by recalling actual reality, as established by archaeology. The peristyle court, now an essential feature of Hellenistic architecture, plays a full part here. It provides an environment, appropriate to the climate, in which the closed world of the monarch is situated, a sanctum cut off from the outside world, where, in the company of his family and friends, he leads the privileged life befitting his position. In the same way a Greek living in a traditional city finds in a home safe from the noise and anonymous bustle of the street, the retreat where his rest, his family bonds, and his thoughts find peace and shelter. In this case too, the parallel between a citizen's behavior in his city and a king's in his royal domain is clearly expressed. Nothing in these customs entailed a break with the unvarying, age-old tradition of those Hellenic populations, nothing that could derive from a conscious imitation of civilizations of Oriental origin or their widespread influence. The Hellenistic civilization was unreservedly receptive to evolution in its way of life and the technical progress that the passage of time, Greek inventive ability, and the prodigious widening of its political environment had fostered. It remained nonetheless in the mainstream of Greek civilization, as it had been in previous ages. Far from renouncing or distorting that heritage, it embraced its implications without any mental reservation.

Technical progress was also evident in the advent of an original style of building, responding to better-defined practical needs. Here the outstanding example is the Pharos (Lighthouse) of Alexandria (see pp. 266–7). For a long time the ancient world had recognized the usefulness of bringing to the attention of navigators certain landmarks on the coast, by erecting typical buildings, usually towers, on which fires could be lit when needed. One instance is the tower which, on a cape on the eastern coast of Thasos, a certain Aceratus had had erected to serve as his tomb: the dedicatory inscription, which has been retraced, indicates its intended role as a signpost for mariners. On the low coast of Alexandria, no seamark allowed the coast to be distinguished from the high seas: that made for difficult and dangerous navigation. Strabo expresses the situation clearly (XVII, 791): "As the coast was inaccessible on both sides of the town and on a level with the waves, it was imperative to erect a high and clearly visible signpost, so that ships arriving from the high seas might sail straight into the harbor entrance." As early as the start of the third century, works were undertaken to raise in front of the harbor of Alexandria a very high tower, made of masonry and more than 100 meters high, which would guide mariners in their approach. A wide base laid on the actual rock, at the eastern extremity of the island of Pharos, commanded the waves by its height of 6 to 7 meters. The first story, the tallest, undoubtedly with a square perimeter, rose to about 60 meters. Its terrace was not reached by a stairway, but by a ramp that wound inside, climbing up the four inner surfaces of the construction, in which many windows opened onto the outside. Four bronze tritons were placed at the corners of the terrace, each blowing into a conch. The second story, clearly set back, was octagonal and 30 meters high. Inside was a stair leading to a second terrace on which rose the third story, a cylindrical one, more than 7 meters high. At the top a colossal bronze statue of Zeus the Savior watched over the navigators' safety: Zeus "who surveys the harbor" (Limenoskopos), as Callimachus calls him. On one of the upper terraces a fire could be lit at night. The inside ramp was intended to allow a passage up to the first terrace for beasts of burden to bring the fuel required.

Figure 6   The Pharos of Alexandria (from the frontispiece to Thiersch's *Pharos*).

This drawing is a reconstruction giving a good idea of this extraordinary monument, one that was made the more impressive by its height (it rose about 100 meters above sea level) as it had been erected on a low coast. The mass of the first section was arresting, at the expense of the second and third levels, which appeared, for those who took a close look at the monument, only as an elevated pedestal for the statue of Zeus Limenoskopos ("He who surveys the harbor"). A quadrangular structure (represented here in a slightly fanciful manner) probably enclosed the area in which the tower rose on the island of Pharos. The bridge on the right, stretching over a row of arcades, is notional. The Heptastadium wharf (nearly 1,200 meters long) linked the island with the coast. On the left is the entrance to the main harbor. It was called the Bull's Horn, *and is mentioned in the epigram by Posidippus of Pella translated below.*

The lighthouse was built of "white stone," probably the fine limestone that Egypt provides in abundance, rather than marble that would have to be imported by sea. A dedication from a famous epigrammatic poet, the Macedonian Posidippus of Pella, was engraved on the monument. It defined its utility as well as its religious significance. A papyrus has preserved the text:

> Lord Proteus, this safeguard of the Greeks, this watcher placed on Pharos, Sostratus son of Dexiphanes, from Cnidus, has caused to be erected. For Egypt does not offer you mountainous islands to serve as watch-posts. No, the bay that receives the ships stretches level with the waters. Wherefore a tower stands erect, outlined on the sky's background, visible far away in the daytime. And at night the sailor shall soon notice amidst the waves the mighty fire burning on top of it. Sailing straight toward the Bull's Horn, he will unfailingly reach Zeus the Savior, oh Proteus, whoever sails these waters.

Pharos had therefore been dedicated to the ancient local divinity, Proteus, the "Old Man from the Sea," a seal herdsman whom Homer had already mentioned as lord of the island of Pharos. There, together with Zeus, who had in other places (at the

Piraeus, for instance) the epithet of Savior, Proteus took pleasure in helping mariners in distress. The tower standing high above a flat landscape would attract attention from the furthest limit of the horizon, and serve as a seamark during the day. At night the fire kept alight on the upper terrace allowed ships arriving late to head straight for the passage giving access to Alexandria's eastern harbor – the passage called "above the Bull's Horn." Posidippus' poem, written between 280 and 260, gives the impression of an eyewitness account. It mentions, as expected, the name of the patron who had had the monument erected and ordered the dedicatory epigram. Sostratus, a Greek from Anatolia like the *dioecetes* Apollonius (see pp. 238, 244) was a man of considerable attainments, one of the "Friends of the King." We also know him from honors granted to him at Delos and Delphi for services rendered.

The monument's exceptional height, comparable to that of the Pyramids, the enormous mass of its lower story (which engravers emphasized by reproducing its profile on their coins), the boldness of its design, and the workmanship of its execution: all these created a profound impression. It became the quintessential symbol of Alexandria, just as in modern times the Eiffel Tower became in the minds of visitors the symbol of Paris. The name of the lighthouse, borrowed from the island of Pharos, became a common name for various similar fire-towers that Hellenistic and Roman architects later raised in other ports or on the coast of the Mediterranean. On the small island of Delos alone, scholars have claimed to identify as many as four of them. The Pharos won admiration above all for its colossal size and the technical prowess it embodied. The skill of the engineer who, making light of difficulties, handled the heaviest stones and placed them so high up in the sky, earned widespread admiration mixed with amazement

A few centuries later, a similar feeling is expressed in an epitaph of the Imperial age that has been found at Hermoupolis in Middle Egypt, on the tomb of a Greek architect named Harpalus. As often happens, it is in the form of a dialogue between a passer-by and the tomb:

"I am the tomb of Harpalus."
"Which Harpalus?"
"Listen: *the* Harpalus who by his ingenious science proved the most resourceful of men."
"Oh Fates, I have understood! The engineer's art has died! Who among the living can equal him?"
"It was he who built the enormous walls of temples, he who raised lofty columns for porticoes. How often did he move mountain peaks that he had made responsive to traction by thin cables, as though they were light wisps of straw!"
"So did Amphion once, so did Orpheus effortlessly move boulders enchanted by their music."
"Know that Achilles lies here as well, Harpalus' son; the same coffin received them both."
"I am not surprised: too strong is the web that the Fates weave. No scholar ever devised an engine that would overcome death."

Among technical innovations in architecture, the use of the vault and the arch should be included. They had not been unknown before in construction using dressed stone, but they were very rarely used before the end of the fourth century. In the Hellenistic age, however, arches and barrel vaults became frequent. The tombs of Macedonia, the underground hall of the sanctuary of the dead at Ephyra in Epirus, the basement of Attalus I's portico at Delphi, the two vaulted corridors of Apollo's temple at Didyma were examples of their use. Many more were found in Pergamum, in the basement of the Acropolis buildings. The large cisterns at Delos (those of the theater for example) and the oracular crypt of the temple of Clarus in Anatolia may be added. All these are dated from various times between the end of the fourth century BC and the first of our era. In those days engineers obviously preferred to use vaults and arches in the course of underground building, so that pressure from the sides could be absorbed by the neighboring land mass, thus doing away with the need for buttresses. But they had also discovered the superiority of such devices on horizontal lintels or flat architraves, for they continued to use these in open-air construction. They were, however, quite willing to build arches over doors opening through thick walls, the mass of which had no difficulty in counteracting any pressure, as in the theater of Dodona, the Ephyra shrine, or the theater in Leto's shrine at Xanthus. But in the last case, dating from the second century, the arcade was inserted in an arrangement of pilasters and Doric entablature surmounted by a pediment. This was a purely artificial device, attached to the surface of the wall; it had no more than a decorative value. Such an association of an arch and a triangular pediment, with cornerstones appearing between the arcade and architrave, produced such a good impression that architects in succeeding centuries made most generous use of it, particularly in Roman triumphal arches. The whole of western architecture in later times was to bear the mark of such Hellenistic research and its inventions.

■ *Hellenistic sanctuaries* ■ *Colossal temples: the example of the* Didymeion ■ *Hermogenes' Ionic temples* ■ *Circular monuments* ■ *Monumental altars* ■ *The wealth and power of Hellenistic architecture* ■ *Variety of offerings* ■ *Statues of sacrificial animals*

The Greek world had never known such an urge to build. How can anyone talk of decadence, as still happens too often in our day, when in reality so many monuments, of such richness and size, were raised in so many sanctuaries? There is the case of the oracular temple of Didyma. It rivaled in size and originality the largest temples of the Archaic and Classical ages, like Hera's temple at Samos, that of Artemis at Ephesus, or of Olympian Zeus at Agrigentum. Its construction took into account the lessons inherited from these buildings, while adapting them in an original fashion. The architects Paeonius of Ephesus and Damis of Miletus, at the start of the third century, were entrusted with the construction of Apollo's shrine, in territory dependent on the latter city. It was to be a colossal edifice that would house the statue of the god, the sacred laurel tree, and the oracular spring. In conformity with such a program, the central portion of the temple was left exposed to the outside; it was a vast open court enclosed by a wall 25 meters high adorned with pilasters bearing a frieze running beneath a cornice. At its far end an open chapel housed the cultic statue. Framing that carefully preserved enclosure, a double colonnade of mighty dimensions, with Ionic pillars 20 meters high, rose from a seven-stepped base, creating the illusion of a peristyle temple. Such a forest of immense pillars was particularly impressive on the façade, where the antechamber (*pronaos*) prolonged it by means of twelve similar pillars placed between the ends of the lateral walls. Such a majestic porch was in reality a dead end. It was ended by a wall, in which an immense bay had been opened – an inaccessible opening, as its threshold was about a meter and a half above the antechamber's floor. Only two vaulted corridors on the sides allowed a sloping access to the interior court. On the other side, a monumental stairway rose eastward from that court and occupied its whole breadth between the ends of the two corridors. It gave access to a high covered hall, opening on to the court by three large doors, and to the *pronaos* by the wide bay mentioned above.

The building was therefore made up of three distinct elements. One was the peristyle, which was no more than an exterior decoration, with its deep porch-antechamber, freely accessible to pilgrims. Next was the inner court, placed at a distinctly lower level, accessible only through two lateral corridors, obviously intended for the purpose of screening visitors, who could go in only one at a time. The third element was a monumental stairway, dominating the court like the tiers of a theater, and the large covered hall, communicating with the antechamber only through a false door allowing people to see but providing no way in. This was a disconcerting arrangement, the purpose of which has not been explained; but it undoubtedly complied with some requirement connected with the ritual. One can imagine ceremonies taking place in the courtyard, around the chapel and the spring, while spectators looked on from the steps. Or they might have happened in the large roofed hall, in the shape of apparitions that could be seen from the eastern bay by pilgrims crowded into the *pronaos*, or through the three doors at the top of the monumental stairway for privileged spectators who were admitted to the inner courtyard. However this was arranged, the whole building appears to have been conceived as an immense setting for ritual performances of a cult that fired the popular imagination. The powerful architecture, the rich sculptured motifs that breathed life into it, the sharply contrasting effects of light and shade were intended to move and surprise by means of studied effects. This was done in a style that can be called baroque, in any case one quite at variance with Classical restraint.

Many instances of such bold and original architecture could be mentioned: Pytheus (see p. 265) at Priene, or Hermogenes at Magnesia on the Maeander raised magnificent temples, in which new directions were evident. There the Ionic order was in favor. At the time, there were admirable developments of it in Anatolia. Hermogenes modified the tradition of a double colonnade (as he did at Didyma) in the peristyle of large temples. He obtained an extensive airy courtyard by eliminating the interior row of columns, while keeping for the peristyle the dimensions required by double intercolumniation. The temple of Artemis Leucophryene at Magnesia, built in the first half of the second century, exemplifies his theories. The Roman Vitruvius, a writer of the Augustan age, collated these in his treatise *On architecture*, which inspired the western Renaissance as long as it lasted. Original designs began to appear. One is the circular monument, like the heroic sanctuary of Macedonian kings, Olympia's Philippeum. Another was the first example of a large round building (20 meters in diameter) without an interior support, the Arsinoeum in Samothrace (see pp. 333–4 and figure 11). Elegant as well as functional, it was the result of a complex and sophisticated system of carpentry.

A taste for grandeur and monumentality expressed itself in the construction of altars. Some illustrated a change in size, like the colossal altar that Hiero II raised at Syracuse. It had the length (192 meters) of an Olympic stadium. It was an immense table of masonry (which still remains visible today) along which, on the western side, ran an equally long platform for the sacrificing priests. Other altars had a more splendid architectural environment. They were placed on a high rostrum, to which access was obtained by a monumental stairway: colonnades and walls were built round them. This was the case of the altars of Artemis Leucophryene at Magnesia on the Maeander, or of Asclepius at Cos. It applied above all to the famous altar of Zeus at Pergamum, the base of which was decorated with a frieze in high relief depicting the Gigantomachy, a masterpiece of expressionist sculpture and a triumph of Hellenistic baroque. On the wall that enclosed the altar, another frieze, in a less exuberant style, depicted episodes of the legend of Telephus, son of Heracles and revered hero of the Caicus valley.

Sculpture and architecture were used together to honor the gods in an abundance of decoration, to which lively colors (now vanished) applied to moldings and reliefs gave more distinctiveness, as well as an added sparkle. It has been said correctly that the long Ionic friezes dealing with a repetitive theme, like the Amazonomachy of the temple of Artemis at Magnesia on the Maeander, played an essentially ornamental role in a building, like that of luxuriant foliation. We should therefore notice without surprise, among the decorative motifs that enliven the architecture of the Didymeum, the emergence of human elements, for instance busts of divinities, or animal ones, griffins for example. Faces of Gorgons,

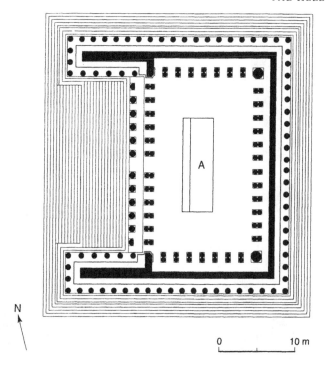

N

0   10 m

Figure 7   The altar of Zeus, Pergamum (from A. W. Lawrence, *Greek Architecture*, fig. 117).

This monumental altar, standing out in the midst of a vast esplanade, was typical of the religious architecture of the Hellenistic age. It exemplified a complex composition displaying itself as it rose, a systematic use of colonnades, and lavish representational art. On a high, nearly square base (about 36 meters by 34 meters), the altar proper (A) occupied the center of a platform enclosed on three sides by a wall. On the fourth side, a flight of twenty-seven steps allowed access to the altar. Two extensions of the platform framed it, the wall advancing further west. Around that wall an elegant gallery of Ionic columns crowned the platform, the external face of which bore a long frieze representing the Gigantomachy in high relief. On the internal face of the wall, all round the platform, another frieze illustrated in bas-relief the story of Telephus, beneath a portico held up by pilasters. The altar was turned toward the east, following traditional usage.

bulls' heads, *Boukranoi*, theater masks, phials, rosettes appear on friezes and often serve as a support for garlands. *Putti* would soon be added to the list: small child Cupids, with impish gestures – a theme that was to be used on sarcophagi. They can already be seen on the reliefs of the Saint-Rémy Mausoleum in Provence, dating from the time of Augustus – a product of genuine Hellenistic ancestry. Trophies that the Attalid generals erected after their victories over the Galatians led to the appearance of the weapons of barbarians as an ornamental motif in balustrades and friezes, for example in the propylaea to Athena's sanctuary at Pergamum. The Romans were later to make great use of such a theme.

Plate 7 Pergamum: the Gigantomachy (Staatliche Museen Berlin, Bildarchiv Preussischer Kulturbesitz, Antikensammlung).

The frieze (see the description of figure 7) is a genuine timepiece of baroque art, the work of an artist whose imagination delighted in shapes depicting extreme tension, violent gestures, and strong feelings. It unfurled a series of simultaneous episodes of the Gigantomachy, the fight of the Gods with the Giants, monsters born of Earth (Gé), who had human bodies and legs in the shape of serpents. This was a traditional theme, celebrating the victory of the Olympians over their adversaries, and of Order (Cosmos) over Chaos. The piece illustrated here shows the unequal duel between Athena and her winged adversary Alcyoneus, whom she seizes by the hair while he collapses. Niké (Victory) crowns the triumphant goddess, while Gé rises out of the soil, making a gesture of supplication to Athena – in vain. The Gigantomachy stands in striking contrast to the Telepheia, bathed in an atmosphere of serenity.

The moldings set on walls were decked with a rich sculptured or painted decoration – interlacing, interwoven laurel leaves, foliage of all descriptions, various palmetti – were now added to the ova and "heart-and-dart" patterns (*rais-de-cœur*, see A. W. Lawrence, *Greek Architecture*, p. 134: see plate 1) of the traditional repertory. Imagination was given wide scope: in the *pronaos* of the Didymeum, the bases of the twelve Ionic columns belong to diverse (sometimes hardly canonical) types. Instances are to be found in those in which a dodecagonal element with sculptured panels is inserted under a torus with interwoven leaves, a different model adorning each panel. Similarly, Ionic capitals became more intricate; the Corinthian capital was more frequent until it finally came into in general use in the Roman Imperial period. All that belonged to a growing trend toward lavishness, welcome in an age when a taste for luxury was spreading and the restraint of Classical buildings no longer satisfied it.

Memorials became more and more prominent on public squares and in sanctuaries. Some were offerings made by cities or princes. Others, more and more numerous, came from individuals: we have seen, from the example of Mego's statue at Messene (pp. 274–5), that these monuments were raised as tokens of affection or family devotion. They added their presence to that of traditional ex-votos. New ways appeared of setting up those offerings. Statues were raised at the back of public benches, or *exedrae*, built in rectangular (with two lateral armrests) or semicircular shapes, which had been placed for the convenience of passers-by. They could be put at a higher level than previous monuments by being erected on a base borne by two columns or at the top of a high quadrangular pillar. Both of these methods were applied at Delphi, a sanctuary particularly crowded with memorials of this kind. Roman triumphal arches, which were actually enormous bases for groups of statuary placed above an archway across a passage, were to a large degree derived from such Hellenistic experiments.

Among these offerings, special attention will be paid here to statues of animals. Already known in former times, they occurred from now on in greater numbers, a reflection of the general spread of wealth among the faithful. An offering of this kind served a very special purpose. By erecting in a sanctuary the bronze or marble likeness of an animal that had been sacrificed in honor of the divinity, the dedicator perpetuated the memory of the sacrifice, hoping to make a more lasting impression on the gods and humanity. Accounts of monuments in this category, to which Pausanias often refers in his *Periegesis*, convey clearly the meaning of a widespread custom that brought a large clientele to sculptors of animal figures. These had to reproduce as faithfully as possible the features in actual life of the sacrificed victim, since they were expected to perpetuate by their art a precise yet transient reality. Hence the surprisingly lifelike appearance of these animal reproductions from the days of Archaic art to the Hellenistic period, when a taste for expressive detail, well served by the craftsmen's versatility, gave a special impetus to this form of art. A certain appetite for showing off generosity and power, which sovereigns and even mere notables were apt to display, led to strange deeds. One remarkable example concerns a priest of Apollo at Cyrene who, around the middle of the third century, caused many bovine statues to be erected in commemoration of the hecatomb he had funded. Two copies of the epigram that he ordered to be engraved on the base of these statues have been found. The epigram runs as follows: "This monument Hermesander, son of Philo, has consecrated over the fountain, after sacrificing to the goddess by bringing to her sanctuary one hundred and twenty head of cattle on the occasion of Artemis' feast. Hence these offerings: ornament, memorial, noble title to glory." The bronze effigies of Hermesander's cattle, arranged on the slope above the esplanade before the shrine, were to be a permanent reminder of the generosity of the donor, one of the major landowners at the head of the city of Cyrene. They recalled that he had levied from his own herds that hecatomb of fatted victims. Propertius the Latin poet, writing (II, 31, 7–8) in the reign of Augustus, saw at Rome, near Apollo's temple on the Palatine, a group of similar bovine statues in bronze, which a victorious general must have brought back from the east. "There stood around the altar," he says, "a mighty herd, four bulls, statues breathing life, the work of Myron the sculptor."

After his victory at Raphia in 217 BC (see pp. 102–3), which saved Egypt from a Seleucid invasion, Ptolemy IV Philopator sacrificed four war elephants to Helios. It is known that the Lagids had by then organized elephant hunts in their southern territories, which they had entrusted to specialized groups designated for the task. The king dedicated to the god four bronze elephants that would keep their memory alive forever. In those days religious statuary had the possibility of treating other exotic themes. Pausanias notes the presence in the shrine of the Muses, on Mount Helicon in Boeotia, of a portrait statue of Queen Arsinoe II, the sister–spouse of Ptolemy II Philadelphus, "borne," he says (IX, 31), "on a bronze ostrich". That seems a strange pedestal for the effigy of an illustrious sovereign who, as a patron of the world of letters, had been rewarded with her statue being raised near Hippocrene in the valley of Ascra. However it was made, the choice of an ostrich to serve as a base for her statue shows what interest artists and the public took in curiosities from abroad. The Hellenistic age loved all that was unusual, everything that came from foreign parts. It was made of whatever was picturesque, fantastic, or bizarre, of surprising tales and unexpected dénouements: of all that in later days the Romans would place under the general term of *mirabilia*. The collections of extraordinary stories that proliferated in those days satisfied a taste for the exotic that was evident in representational art.

- *The Hellenistic theater; its often unrecognized importance*
- *Technical innovations: the stage* ■ *The theater in civic life*

Perhaps the prodigious development of theatrical production in the Greek world of this period should also be attributed to this eager curiosity, this attraction toward whatever was out of the ordinary. The reality is that the very fact of this development escaped the notice of historians far too long. The prestige of the great Athenian tragedians of the fifth century and Aristophanes' genius, and the total disappearance of later dramatic works, have led to a mistaken belief concerning an essential area of ancient literature. According to this belief, the Greeks of succeeding centuries no longer demonstrated a creative spirit and turned away from a form of art that had by then become obsolete. The discovery, half a century ago, of entire plays and substantial fragments of Menander's comedies hardly drew general attention to the vitality of New Comedy. Nor has the social importance of Hellenistic theatrical activity really been acknowledged, except among specialists. Yet in actual fact nearly all theaters left as majestic ruins of themselves for modern eyes to see, in cities or sanctuaries, go back to the Hellenistic age, although they underwent important modifications later, in the Roman Imperial period. Even in Athens, the cradle of dramatic art, it was only under the administration of Lycurgus, a contemporary of Alexander the Great, that the theater of Dionysus was for the first time built entirely of stone. The theater of Epidaurus probably came later. Its construction proceeded until the third century. In the great sanctuaries all theaters date back to Hellenistic times: at Dodona, Delos, and Delphi. In those days every city wished to have its own theater, and those of the great cities of Anatolia – Miletus, Ephesus, Pergamum – were built at this time. Such a large number of very costly constructions dedicated to this one special purpose bears witness to the contribution of dramatic performances to the lifestyle of the period. Far from being a mere survival, and limiting itself to reviving the works of the Classical dramatists, the theater of that age had an exceptional vitality.

This was due above all to the great popularity and widespread implantation of the cult of Dionysus, to which theatrical performance traces its origin. The Dionysia, as the cycle of the god's festive events was called, were celebrated everywhere, and were the occasion for competitions in the areas of the dithyramb (a sort of oratorio belonging *in proprio* to his cult), tragedy and comedy, even satyric drama, for which there is abundant epigraphic evidence. The custom also spread of introducing dramatic choruses into many other festivals: those of Apollo, patron god of singers and poets, but also other gods, and as a rule into most of the major festivals, where such performances gave special pleasure to the people. From then on, a tradition originally reserved for Athens and a small number of other cities (in Sicily, for instance) became current everywhere. The spread of the practice received an impetus from actors, and those working with them. They organized themselves into fraternities of Dionysiac artists (*technitai*, plural of *technités*) which, under the god's patronage, grouped together these practitioners of sacred presentations (see pp. 198–9). As they traveled from one city to another, responding to demand, their presence allowed organizers of festivals and competitions to offer performances of a definitely higher quality than had been the case with choruses of the Classical age, made up of volunteers recruited among fellow-citizens for each occasion. These competitions had a category reserved for the actors, who could now receive prizes just as poets and musicians did. The respect and admiration that the texts of the great Classical authors had won led to repeat performances being allowed in the fourth century: something unthinkable in the past. These occasions did not require a prize to be bestowed on the play in question; on the other hand, they were a venue for competitions open to actors. Yet the practice continued, as it was still prescribed, of offering new plays to the god. In this the Dionysiac cult was no different from others, for which it was considered normal to have new hymns or paeans composed each time a festival was celebrated. The ensuing constant demand incited poets and musicians to produce hitherto unheard pieces. Religious festivals increased in number, and thanks to the generosity of sovereigns, were celebrated more magnificently than before. The Hellenistic age was thus one of intense productivity, in which writers and artists found a clientele willing to reward them properly for their work.

Contrary to widespread opinion, we are not dealing here only with a closet literature, intended for appreciation by no one but scholars. It was, as before, occasional literature, a response to society's needs, that is, to the exigencies inherent in the practice of cults and the celebration of sacred festivals. Playwrights flourished in large numbers. Only some of their names have emerged from oblivion. Among the tragedians are Alexander of Aetolia, Lycophron of Chalcis (whose poem *Alexandra* has been preserved), Philicus of Corcyra, Homer of Byzantium. Among the writers of comedy, coming after the better-known Menander, are Philemon of Syracuse, who obtained citizenship at Athens, Diphilus of Sinope, Apollodorus of Carystus, Posidippus of Cassandreia, and a long list of other authors (at least sixty names have reached us). The whole of that enormous production intended for the stage has disappeared. Only some honorary inscriptions and isolated quotations found in papyri provide any indication of the renown that these poets enjoyed in their lifetime. Their works were certainly not handed down to posterity among those that were studied at school. This allowed them to disappear, to the advantage of some plays by Aeschylus, Sophocles, Euripides, and Aristophanes, which provided, with the poems of Homer and Hesiod, spiritual nourishment for young Greeks. It would be wrong to infer from this that these Hellenistic dramatists were worthless. They cast their spell on audiences that were more demanding and enlightened than fifth-century Athenians. Scholars appreciated them as refined writers, with a keen sense of nuance. In an epigram in which he commits himself without reservation, Callimachus, the supreme authority on literature, comforts his friend Theaetetus of Cyrene, who was denied the prize in a Dionysiac competition: "Theaetetus has launched himself on an untrodden path. If it does not lead to your garland of ivy, Bacchus, the names of other poets will, for a short while, be proclaimed by the voice of heralds. As for Theaetetus' genius, Greece will never cease proclaiming it." Alas! Evidence of his genius, which captivated a connoisseur like Callimachus, no longer exists for us to appreciate it.

For these plays of a new kind, the material arrangements of the theater underwent some important changes. We know that, in the tragedies and comedies of the Classical period, actors and members of the chorus were assembled on the circular platform called the *orchestra* (meaning literally "the dance floor"). Facing it were the tiers accommodating the spectators, arranged in a semicircle, on a natural slope that had been adapted for the purpose. In the centre of the *orchestra* was the altar of Dionysus. Around it the chorus went through its rhythmic motions. It often engaged in dialogue with two or three of the actors in the course of a tragedy. In a comedy it would occasionally be involved with them in confrontation or even pursuit – something that is imaginable only if the chorus and the actors moved at the same level. There was, it is true, a structure called the *skéné*, a "tent" (since at first it had been a light assembly of wood and canvas), a low wooden stage reached by a short flight of stairs. At best it would allow the actors, at the moment judged appropriate, to distance themselves from the chorus by occupying a slightly raised position. The *skéné* was not yet a stage (the sense of the French *scène*), but simply the backstage structure that served only as a decoration and backdrop during the performance. Hellenistic theaters abandoned that arrangement, usual until the fourth century, and adopted a totally different one, foreshadowing that of modern theaters, in other words, a real stage for actors.

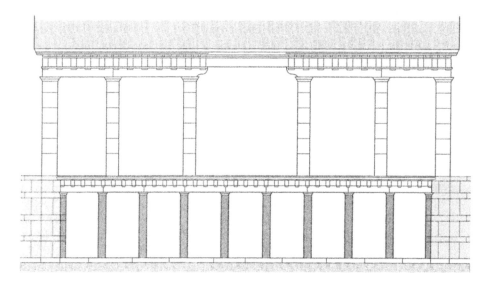

Figure 8   Theater of Oropus: the stage (from E. Fiechter, *Die baugeschichtliche Entwicklung des antiken Theaters*).

The Oropus theater was part of the sanctuary of the hero Amphiraus, seer and healer, on the northern coast of Attica, in a small valley not far from the sea, on the Euboean strait. It was built in the third century, and, in spite of its modest scale, is a good illustration of arrangements special to Hellenistic theaters. The stage was four meters deep and opened generously in the upper story through five large bays; on the platform of the proscenium that was prolonged into the orchestra. That platform was held up by a Doric colonnade made up of eight pillars, to each of which a half-column was added to serve as a façade. Painted panels could be inserted in the space between the columns to serve as a background for the movements of the chorus in the orchestra. Other panels could be placed on the upper story within the bays of the skéné *to serve as scenery for the action on the proscenium.*

The essential elements of this novelty begin to be clearly visible, at the start of the third century, in the theater of Priene. The stone-built *skéné* was at that time a building provided with a rather high upper floor. In front of the ground floor, opposite the *orchestra*, was a Doric portico, supported by a row of pillars against which half-columns rested as a façade. The portico was covered by a wooden floor serving as a roof, to which access was obtained through a door from the high floor of the *skéné*. This floor accommodated the actors, and from that time on served as a stage, in the modern sense of the word. The chorus remained in the *orchestra*, nearly 3 meters lower, and had no direct contact with the stage. Finally, an inner stairway allowed access to an opening at the level of the roof of the *skéné*, at the height, therefore, of an upper story. This area was used for divine apparitions. The portico in front of the *skéné* was called the *proskénion* (proscenium). It is likely that such porticoes had already been erected in the fourth century, but they served only as an ornament in front of the backstage structure, not as a stage for the actors. A piece of banter from the comic poet Antiphanes is a good illustration of this: speaking of Nannion, an aged courtesan living at the time of Alexander the Great, he gives her the nickname of *Proskénion*. She looked attractive when she was wearing a magnificent dress, but once that had been taken off, she was hideous to behold: just as the *proskénion* of a theatre, when stripped of its painted canvas, revealed its plain, bare skeleton. The novelty with the *proskénion* consisted in its being used to hold up the platform on which the actors appeared. From that time on, their raised location made them more conspicuous, and quite distinct from the chorus, whose role became definitely a secondary one. For in Menander's comedies, it no longer played a vocal part; its appearance was indicated only to remind its members of occasions when they were to execute some dance movements between episodes of the play.

Such a major transformation in the method of production obviously reflected a decisive evolution in the current idea of drama. Emphasis was now placed on individuals, on their behavior and psychology, rather than on the global tragic or comic action, the chorus's reaction to which had found some resonance in the collective soul. Interest was now transferred from the terrifying intervention of destiny and divinity, crushing humanity under their impact, to the character of the tragic hero, his own individual adventure, his human personality. This is where the actor's skill came into play. On the elevated stage, alone and in full view, he was the center of attention, and could make full use of his vocal and mimetic potential. He resorted to various devices so as to heighten the effect. Tragic masks were not intended to serve as amplifiers of voices (as has mistakenly been stated), but allowed the same actor to play more than one part in the same drama. Simple implements originally, they were given considerably increased dimensions when topped with a high tuft of hair that gave them a strange, very characteristic look. In the middle of the second century came in addition the use of sandals with very thick soles, meant to increase even more the height of the actor's silhouette: these were later to be called *kothornoi* (plural of *kothornos*). The essential features of the Hellenistic theater were thus gradually defined. It was to be a theater for actors rather than a dramatic chorus, a theater-spectacle rather than a drama constantly demanding the audience's emotional involvement. Rome was eventually to pass on to the world of the Renaissance such an idea of dramatic composition: it was to be predominant in later centuries right down to the nineteenth. Our contemporary society, tired of this tradition as of so many others, is trying to return, by various methods and with varying fortunes, to the antique ritual of participation.

These theaters, which were often vast constructions in which the population of each city gathered, allowed the civic community to cultivate its sense of unity. This actually happened in all religious festivals requiring the involvement of a large gathering. But such a feeling of togetherness was better demonstrated in a building planned to receive a large audience that was comfortably seated and benefited from a clear view and proper acoustics. The custom was thus established of using theatrical performances, especially those of the Dionysia, to proclaim honors awarded to Euergetai (see p. 195). We have seen this in the case of the decree from Apollonia Pontica (see pp. 168–73). There Hegesagoras was to be "crowned with a gold crown at the Dionysia," while in his native city of Istrus he was to be awarded similar honors in the course of games that his fellow-citizens were to celebrate. In both cases, advantage was taken of an occasion when the population was gathered to give maximum exposure to decisions made by the Council and Assembly. It often happened that the theater was used for political gatherings; for example, at Megalopolis, capital of the League of Arcadian cities, the theater, a vast one, was the venue for the sittings of the Federal Assemblies.

■ *The gymnasium* ■ *Athletic Games* ■ *Physical exercise and military preparation* ■ *The gymnasium as a place of teaching and a symbol of culture*

Another essential element of civic life was the gymnasium. It was a complex outfit, the main purpose of which, as the name implies, was the practice of physical exercise. It housed first and foremost a palaestra, a specialized building that grouped around a large quadrangular court changing rooms, training rooms, sanitary installations, as well as exedras, open courtyards providing benches for relaxation and conversation, even lecture halls. Close to the palaestra was an open-air running track, twinned with a covered one for use in bad weather: both

Plate 8   Scene from a comedy (Museo Nazionale, Naples; photo SCALA).

In the so-called "House of Cicero" at Pompeii, two small panels of floor mosaic have been found, conspicuous for their technical perfection, signed by the Greek mosaicist Dioscourides of Samos. The lettering of the inscription points to the second century BC, i.e., the period of the fine mosaics from Delos. The scenes depicted are drawn from two comedies by Menander. Here we have a scene from Possessed (Theophoroumenè). *It shows musicians performing in honor of Cybele, Mother of the Gods. In front of the wall and doorway of a house, a "double flute" (aulos) woman player is accompanied by a child blowing a sort of horn. Meanwhile, in the front part of the stage, two men in Asiatic clothes (wearing under their tunics close-fitting leotards) give the beat, one of them with a pair of small cymbals, the other with a large dulcimer, while performing a ritual dance. The décor is evidently that of a theatre proscenium; the artist gives an exact depiction of comic masks worn by actors.*

were one *stadion* (about 190 meters) long. Depending on circumstances, a stadium for competitions was provided near the gymnasium. Finally, it happened occasionally that, as at Delphi, an open-air swimming pool was added to these facilities; but scarcity of water did not allow such a facility to be offered in many locations, in Greece proper at least. On the other hand, bathrooms were found as a rule in every gymnasium, often provided with troughs for washing one's feet. It seems proper to note here that attention to bodily cleanliness became widespread in the Hellenistic age. Every house had its own area for personal hygiene, sometimes a real bathroom fitted with a bath. Public baths became a common feature. These had rotunda-shaped structures (more common than rectangular rooms), with several tubs fitted with sitz baths, with a niche in the wall above each bath, serving as a shelf for toiletries that were used in the absence of soap, unknown in Greek Antiquity. Such public establishments, like the baths in gymnasiums prefigure the therms of Roman civilization.

The part that the gymnasium played in the life of Hellenic cities cannot be overestimated. Young men and men of mature age would gather there, first of all to practice athletic disciplines. These were notably running, jumping, throwing the javelin, boxing, wrestling, or the pancratium (which combined the last two). Some of them were grouped in the five events of the pentathlon, which went into global ranking at the games. Many competitions were set up, fostering rivalry in excellence. The previous Greek age had been steeped in the *agonistic* (from *agón*, "contest") spirit. This did not abate – far from it. The vast majority of competitions were of interest only to the city holding them, even though foreigners might be allowed to participate. Others were renowned throughout the Greek world, and attracted the best athletes from everywhere, provided these were acknowledged as Greeks. They were called *sacred* or *stephanite* games, for they brought no money prizes, but only a crown of leaves. Taking place every four years at Olympia and Delphi, every two at the Isthmus of Corinth and at Nemea, those competitions, which traced their origin to very ancient times, still brought together the elite of sportsmanship in the Hellenic world. The Romans were soon to gain admission to them. Their facilities were carefully maintained, at great expense. A statement of account dated 247/6 from Delphi gives the breakdown of expenses incurred in that year for the Pythian Games: these bear on the gymnasium, in connection with the training of competitors, as well as on the stadium and the hippodrome, where the events were held. The stadium that was the venue for the Nemean Games was excavated in the 1970s by an American team: as a result, one can visualize the splendid environment in which the games took place. The renown of these Panhellenic competitions did not wane in Hellenistic times. They were looked upon as being in a class apart, called the *period*. There could be no more glorious feat for an athlete than to be victorious in these four great games: then he bore the envied title of *periodonikos*, "victor in the period."

On the model of those renowned stephanite games, many Hellenistic sovereigns or cities wished to initiate other "sacred" competitions, which were to be held every two or four years. Other cities were requested to grant these games a status analogous to the one enjoyed by the games of the period. Such recognition was to have an official stamp, because the new games were always linked, like their predecessors, with the holding of a religious festival. Ambassadors, called *theôroi*, went around canvassing cities, which granted their consent by decree. Numerous sets of epigraphic documents have survived, relating to these negotiations. Examples are decrees of seventy Greek towns recognizing the institution of festivals at Magnesia on the Maeander in honor of Artemis Leucophryene, or those concerning the festivals of Asclepius on the island of Cos. A similar status was granted to the *Sôteria* that the Aetolians instituted at Delphi, in commemoration of the defeat of the Gauls, who had threatened the sanctuary in 278. Such a harvest of sacred games is shining testimony to the vitality of religious and civic traditions in the Hellenistic age. They were a powerful encouragement to contacts between cities. Prior to the periodic celebration of a set of sacred competitions, the organizing city would invite foreign ones to take part in the festival by sending official delegations. A whole network of personal relationships was thus created between one city and another. The same hosts, called *theôrodokoi*, "those giving hospitality to *theôroi*," would receive these on the occasion of each visit. The lists of their names were kept with great care. Such a list, engraved at the beginning of the second century, has been found at Delphi. It gives the names of cities that the Delphians' sacred envoys were to visit prior to the Pythian Games, dividing among themselves the major sectors of the Greek world. It constitutes a document of first-rate importance concerning the political geography of the time.

In the exercises of the gymnasium, athletes were divided into age groups: usually *boys* or *beardless ones* (corresponding to our juniors), young men, and men of mature age. These last two categories were not set apart from each other for the purposes of competition: there was only one distinction, between "boys" (sometimes "beardless ones") and "adults". Such demarcations were not meant only to weight the performance of competitors according to age. They also reflected the military origin of athletic training, the purpose of which was to afford practice to the citizen in his duties as a soldier. Even when such an obligation, while never disappearing entirely, was considerably relieved by the widespread use of mercenaries, the link between gymnasium and army was not completely severed. In cities where the institution of the *ephebeia* existed (see *The Civilization of Greece*, p. 173), young men (*ephebes*) who submitted for one or two years to a regime of compulsory or voluntary service, frequented the gymnasium. There they received training both in physical exercise and in the handling of weapons. Among salaried employees of the State whose names appear in inscriptions are found instructors in various skills. They gave training in shooting with the bow, throwing the javelin, fencing with the hoplite's weapons (spear, sword, and shield) or those of the light infantryman, even in using the catapult. Every age group went through such training. Young men who had received it could be enlisted in war operations. Explicit mention of the fact appears in some texts. An inscription from Berenice in Libya, published not long ago, praises a citizen of that town for having, in the first half of the first century BC, led a troop of young men in defense of the countryside, which brigands and pirates had been devastating.

Finally, the gymnasium was a privileged center for human relationships and the spread of culture. Among youths and adults, who often had no regular professional activity, being a habitué of the gymnasium was a privileged pastime. Under the patronage of Hermes and Heracles, traditionally presiding over unpaid physical activity, citizens and foreigners (though not slaves, except when providing their services) were happy to meet in such spacious surroundings. These were situated either in the suburbs, where all the necessary space could be found, or in the urban center, where Hellenistic architects contrived to integrate gymnasiums in the city plan. In that era, Athens had five gymnasiums at its disposal. Among them were three ancient ones, the Lyceum in the east, the Academy in the northwest, the Cynosarges in the south: all situated outside the city. To these two new ones were added. The Gymnasium of Ptolemy (no doubt built at Ptolemy III Euergetes' expense: see p. 91) was in the actual Agora, at the very heart of the city. That of Diogenes was also in town, probably built at the end of the third century in honor of the commander of the Macedonian garrison who in 229/8 had agreed, in return for a sum of money, to withdraw from Athens. For this gesture he was looked upon as a benefactor of the city (see p. 74).

Now, these five installations were not limited to the practice of athletics, their original purpose. The Lyceum, where Protagoras the Sophist had lectured in the fifth century, became in the next the setting for the teaching of Aristotle and his successors. The name of their *Peripatetic* school is derived from the word *peripatoi*, meaning the strolls that the philosopher and his disciples took in the annexes to the gymnasium. In the Academy, which owed its name to the hero Academus, Plato had taught from the age of 40. After his death in 347, the faithful Xenocrates, then the successive heads of the school, called the Academy, continued the practice of lecturing there. The philosopher Antisthenes took up his quarters in the Cynosarges, in the heyday of the Classical age, and spread his doctrine from there: hence the name of Cynic for the school that grew from it. These three gymnasiums were thus each the birthplace of a great philosophical tradition. As for the Gymnasium of Ptolemy (see p. 91), where, according to Pausanias (I, 17), a statue of Chrysippus the Stoic was set up beside that of the founding Lagid, it housed an important library mentioned in inscriptions. The Academic school, then headed by Antiochus of Ascalon, transferred its seat there when Sulla's troops, devastating the Attic countryside during the siege of Athens in 87/6, destroyed the gymnasium of the Academy. Finally, the Gymnasium of Diogenes, which remained active until the end of the third century AD, was also a center of literary and scientific studies. This is where, at the start of the second century of our era, Plutarch witnessed the *strategos* Ammonius "subjecting ephebes who studied there to tests in literature, geometry, rhetoric, and music" (*Moralia*, 736d).

The gymnasium was thus a teaching institution, a place for relaxation and human contact, and a group of buildings and facilities intended for the practice of physical exercise. It was the physical expression of an institution placed under the protection both of the traditional divinities, who continued to be honored with a cult till the end of Antiquity, and of the deified sovereigns to whom reverence was given as benefactors. Free citizens enjoyed meeting in such an environment. On the walls or monuments that excavation has brought to light numbers of graffiti appear, a playful way for the gymnasium regulars to immortalize their names, with the occasional addition of a date (as happens in our own day). Like the theater, the gymnasium was a throbbing center of the Hellenic way of life, not only in the Greece of earlier days, but wherever Macedonian conquerors and their soldiers went and founded cities. Sharing the life of the gymnasium, being one of "those rubbing their bodies with oil," as users of such a facility called themselves, was part of keeping alive the Greek lifestyle, or, from the foreigner's point of view, of gaining access to it. The introduction, by the Hellenizing priest Jason, of a gymnasium into Jewish society was one of the main causes of the orthodox Jews' revolt in 167, under the leadership of the Hasmonean chiefs and Judas Maccabeus (see pp. 121–3). Nothing represents better than the gymnasium the ideal of Hellenistic education, widely acknowledged by the Greeks of the time: the close link of bodily development through physical exercise with enrichment of the mind by the teaching of literature, rhetoric, and philosophy. This was an ideal meant for an honorable person, entrusted with a tradition and culture, yet made entirely immune from unforeseen pressures in daily life by not being forced to ply a trade. Hellenistic man, like the Greek of the Classical age, was a free man, with free use of his time, and an idle one. Thanks to the work of others, to city institutions, to benevolent sovereigns, he could devote his time, following his inclination, to mental speculation, to social life, or to public office. He was one of a privileged group. In this respect we are faced with the fundamental notion that Ancient society as a whole relied for its survival on the institution of slavery, which freed the citizen from the daily bondage of material tasks and provided him with access to culture.

■ *The defense of cities* ■ *Fortified walls* ■ *Philo the Mechanic*
■ *Armies: a majority of mercenaries, Greek or barbarian* ■ *New methods of warfare* ■ *The Macedonian phalanx* ■ *Light troops*
■ *The cavalry* ■ *Elephants* ■ *The navy*

These Hellenistic cities, whose prestige as lively centers of civilization shone far and wide, nevertheless felt threatened by ever-recurring conflicts opposing cities or princes, or by barbarian attempts on their safety. To protect themselves, they

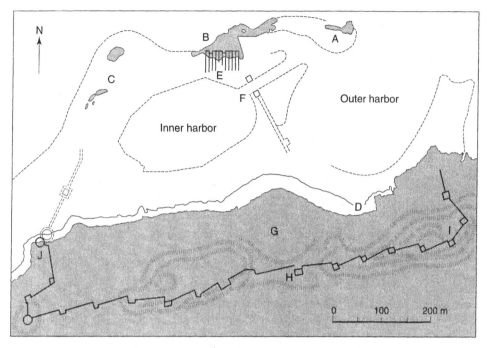

Figure 9 Apollonia in Cyrenaica: its surrounding wall and harbor (from the plan drawn up by the archaeological mission of the University of Michigan).

The city was built on the coast, abutting a line of hills (fortified dunes) and the basins of the harbor, which was protected by two small islands (A, B) and shoals (C), the mainstays of an artificial dyke. The port opened toward the east. It was made up of an exterior basin, used as a trading harbor and lined with docks and warehouses cut in the rock (D), and an interior basin, where ten docking berths are still visible (E), built for the accommodation of triremes, Cyrene's war fleet. The entrance to the military harbor was a narrow channel between two towers (F). A lowering of the coastline due to subsidence led in Antiquity to part of the town being submerged. The agora (G) was in a depression west of the acropolis near one of the gates of the surrounding wall (H). That wall, with an indented outline, ran over the hilltops, the highest of which, in the east, served as acropolis (I). West was a second gate (J) protected by a large round tower.

felt obliged to engage in a huge defensive effort: both by a single long-term investment endowing them with fortified enclosures, and by constantly striving to keep their armed forces in fighting condition. War had been a permanent feature of the Greek world since its origins. It was the very foundation of the Hellenistic monarchy. It never ceased to weigh heavily on the fate of urban communities, until Roman authority imposed its law and put an end to a tradition of conflict extending over many centuries. The divide between the Hellenistic and Imperial periods is more evident in this respect than in any other. The Hellenistic age was always dominated by concern for self-protection, the *sine qua non* of survival for every kingdom and city. The Imperial age relieved cities of a fear that the Empire and its legions were to take over, heralding an enduring period of peace for the peoples of the Hellenized East. There is no better illustration of this fact than the case of Apollonia in Cyrenaica. This port had long been a dependency of Cyrene, as it was its natural outlet toward the sea. Rome made it an independent city. Its theater, built after that event, backed directly on to the wall of the acropolis, but on the outer side, which considerably reduced the protective value of the surrounding fortification, a very strong one elsewhere. A dedicatory inscription in front of the stage mentions the emperor Domitian, who belongs to the first century of our era, and thus provides a precise chronological reference. In the very first century of the Empire, therefore, the magistrates and people of Apollonia decided to raise there a splendid edifice that was to nullify the protection afforded to their town by the surrounding wall, built in the second century BC. They now considered such protection unnecessary, being given the guarantee of safety that the Roman army provided to the countryside of Cyrenaica and the adjoining sea.

The path followed by that surrounding wall, well preserved over a full half of its course (the whole northern half having been destroyed by the sea as a result of subsidence of the coastline) is quite typical of urban fortifications in the Hellenistic age. It consisted of a cohesive line, without in any way seeking to fit in with the grid pattern of the streets: the wall was adapted to the major features of the terrain, making the best possible use of them for purposes of defense. On that seaboard site, hills of modest height running parallel to the coast allowed a view of the plain extending south toward the mountain, while providing a convenient vantage point over the sea and the harbor. The surrounding wall, following the ridges, had the solid support of the rock that quarry men had cut to obtain building material. They had done their work in a direction leading away from the town, cutting trenches, the depth of which added to the height of the wall.

The plan was a combination of two types of wall: the indented type and the one dotted with towers. The first type offered the advantage of economy. A number of rectangular notches measuring a few meters were made in the line of the wall, each such projection allowing the shooting range of missile weapons to cover the next curtain. The length of these curtain walls corresponded to the shooting range of the weapons. In the case of javelins and arrows, each portion of the wall they covered was no more than 20 to 30 meters long. Now, the length of curtains at Apollonia was normally 50 to 60 meters. The reason was that the fortified wall had been planned for the use of war-engines, catapults that shot powerful projectiles, capable of hitting many men at the same time. The extended target range meant effective protection at a much greater distance than would have been achieved with arrows. The use of these engines for attack as well as defense spread in the fourth century, and became generalized in the Hellenistic age. Apollonia's surrounding wall illustrates it. Each projection was meant to accommodate catapults, shooting parallel to the curtain stretching further to the right (from the defenders' point of view). The attacking party attempting to approach that curtain exposed their right flank, unprotected by their shields, to the covering artillery. Catapults were thus placed in the projection of the wall, which was for that purpose set up like a square tower serving as an extension of the left curtain, with which it was totally integrated, forming a corner at its end. Such towers could have a number of floors, each of them a casemate, with a window-recess for shooting covering the next curtain. These recesses could be protected by wooden shutters swinging vertically on two lateral swivel-pins mounted on the upright frame of the recess. The defense available for strongholds was perfected in this way, with a technical finesse that the Middle Ages were to resurrect.

Occasionally in the Apollonia plan, whenever the terrain demanded such a change, a line dotted with quadrangular or circular towers, which jutted out in front of the wall, would replace the indented line. This was especially the case with the two carriage gateways 4 meters wide that allowed entrance through the surrounding wall. One, situated in the west, had the protection of a large round tower. The other one, servicing the agora, harbor and acropolis quarter, opened southward on the countryside and was protected by a strong square tower. Neither of these gateways opened at right angles to the line of the wall, but parallel to it, through the piece of wall that linked the protective tower, resolutely jutting forth, and the curtain. This was a contrivance ensuring better defense of the gate by making it necessary for the assailant to advance sideways when attempting to force a passage.

Hellenistic surrounding walls were henceforth often built entirely of cut stone, no longer of unbaked bricks laid on a stone foundation, as was formerly the case. The overall appearance of these strong walls, bristling with elevated towers, was impressive. The regular lines of their foundations had occasional projections meant to steady the blocks of stone, sizable bondstones displaying strong bosses as a rule. These gave added resistance to the exterior dressing of the wall while enhancing its aesthetic appeal through a lively interplay of its moving shadows. One is reminded of Stendhal's remark, "Beauty is no more than the outward projection of the useful." On other occasions architects treated these walls in an even more elaborate fashion. Each stone would receive, in the area of the joints, a beveled edge around the boss: a process usually reserved for the noblest style of building. Corner grooves were meticulously executed; or the stonemason would finish the bosses with his point, using that tool to trace parallel oblique scores, in a herringbone pattern, in one direction or the other. The fortification with which the city had to surround itself for its survival became at the same time its exterior ornament: the Greek craftsman's ingenuity delighted in extracting an aesthetic effect from what had been originally an imposition of necessity.

Such works of fortification were very expensive. We have seen the case of the small city of Cytenium in Doris (see pp. 209–11), which had had to collect offerings around the Hellenic world in order to restore its walls. But how could a city prevail without such protection against an attempted invasion by foreigners or pirates? The Hellenistic age saw a proliferation of urban fortifications and fortresses. Famous examples are the "Fetters of Greece" (see p. 60) – Demetrias on the Gulf of Volos, Chalcis in Euboea mounting guard on the Euripus, Acrocorinth dominating the Isthmus. This was also the case in the Piraeus of the fortress of Munychia, the Macedonian occupation of which was enough, as long as it lasted, to keep Athens in bondage (see p. 297, on the Gymnasium of Diogenes). Defended by hardened troops, these strongholds were almost impregnable, discounting, of course, the factor of surprise or treason. The history of the times is full of anecdotal evidence about the success or failure of attempts to capture one or other of them. Undoubtedly the most famous story is that of Aratus' success in capturing Corinth and its citadel on a summer night in 243 (see p. 88). The overriding factor in every case was the abiding anxiety of leaders and populations, to which, at the end of the third century, a military engineer's book bears witness. His name is Philo of Byzantium, also called *the Mechanic*, and his preoccupation is both technical and tactical. His work deals with war-engines (catapults in particular) and the siege operations of an army on campaign. But he is also especially concerned with means of defense for a besieged position. Philo gives advice on the benefit that its defenders can extract from extra-urban facilities. In a necropolis, storied mausoleums can be used as small forts. Within the town, he recommends that the population be organized into districts that can be isolated if necessary through the closure of its streets should the enemy burst into the town. He advocates the storing of reserves of food, weapons, and machines; and the recruitment of experienced doctors to attend to the wounded. Such very carefully thought out treatises, devoid of any pretensions to literary effect, were a response to public demand. They give us a vivid picture of the realities of war, the context of life for the people of this time.

The armies that fought each other in those days had two sources of recruitment. One conformed to civic tradition, and drew in each city on the category of citizens who still owed military service for the defense of the community. In theory, the purpose of preserving the institution of the *ephebeia* was to prepare them for such a task – even in cases like that of Athens, where the compulsory nature of that service had been abolished and its duration shortened. The young men concerned, the ephebes (see p. 296), continued to be garrisoned at frontier posts and went through their practice under the guidance of specialized instructors. They appeared at religious and civic ceremonies, carrying their weapons. The people would show recognition of their role by granting them honors for their piety, their good bearing, their zeal in the service of the State, and their compliance with orders from the *kosmétés*, their commanding officer. Attic inscriptions inform us of this aspect of civic life, which has been mentioned in the previous section on the gymnasium. But the transformation of military technique, added to the evolution in social mores, brought about a sizable decrease in civic recruitment into Hellenistic armies, to the advantage of the mercenary intake. This fact prolonged and strengthened a phenomenon that had been apparent since the beginning of the fourth century. From then on, owing to the enormous need (kept up by endless wars) for manpower in the armies of princes, a considerable market developed in the Greek world for professional soldiers. Some privileged locations became meeting-places for aspiring recruits. Cape Taenarum, at the southern end of Mount Taygetus, attracted the largest crowds. Arcadian mountaineers, shepherds from the Maina in Laconia, hardy warriors from Aetolia or Macedonia, Cretan archers supplied numerous and much sought-after contingents, to which were added adventurers and drifters from other regions of Greece.

Barbarian troops now began to be recruited into Greek armies. They became more and more numerous. The Antigonids had Illyrians, tribes from the Balkans, and Thracians in their service; the Seleucids had Asiatics; the Lagids Semites and native-born Egyptians. The case of the Galatians is interesting. War was their industry. Now they would cause dynasts and Greek cities of Thrace or Anatolia to shudder, now they would put themselves at their service. They were fearful allies, since at the start of his reign Ptolemy II had to quell by a massacre a mutiny among his Gallic mercenaries – an exploit that Callimachus celebrated in verse. After all, those barbarians became perfectly Hellenized as a result of contact with their Greek neighbors and paymasters. A demonstration of this is to be found in the metrical epitaph of a Galatian officer found at Maroneia on the Thracian coast and dating from the second century: "Under this earth I lie, I Briccon son of Ateuristos. From Apamea my fatherland, I came heading a troop of Galatians. Alone in the first rank, leading a merciless combat in the fray, I fell. But I shall gain admittance to the great city of the Just, at least if in Hades too honor is due to the merit of mortals." This Gaul came to Thrace to fight at the head of a troop of Galatian mercenaries, probably in the service of King Antiochus III, who conducted operations in that area at the start of the second century. He hailed from a Greek city founded by the Seleucids, most likely Apamea in Phrygia. He had recruited his regiment among the warlike Galatians, his compatriots, settled in the heart of Anatolia, beyond Phrygian territory. Yet his epitaph, composed by an epigrammatist who was well acquainted with the themes and the usual verse-form of poems of that kind, shows that he had adopted to perfection his Greek employers' customs and beliefs – eloquent testimony to the assimilating power of Hellenism.

Fighting methods evolved in step with the transformations of armies and military technique. The phalanx was a massive battalion in which heavily armed hoplites, closing ranks behind their long spears, had fearful destabilizing power. It remained, until the Roman victories of the second century, the major formation of troops engaged in battle. The Macedonian method of equipment had

strengthened its impact by the use of the *sarissa*, a pike 6½ to 7 meters long, which the soldier held with both hands at the moment of attack. The phalanx was usually sixteen rows deep, the first five holding their pikes horizontally, and presenting to their enemy a formation bristling with murderous points, pushed forward in the fray by the whole of that compact, iron-wrapped, human mass. The bulging Macedonian shield was circular, like the Classical hoplite's. It sometimes had bright silver plating, like that of the *Argyraspids* ("Silver Shields": see p. 48), those veterans of Alexander who played such an important part in confrontations among the Diadochi. The shape of their helmets had changed: they became wider, enclosing the forehead and the back of the neck, thus ensuring better protection. Occasionally, they were topped with horns instead of being plumed. These elite troops distinguished themselves not only by the glitter of their weapons, but also by the magnificence of their garb: Plutarch notes that at Pydna Perseus' Macedonian battalions dazzled the eyes with their golden armor and the brand-new chlamys that they wore. A head-on clash between such battle formations was a terrible trial of strength, in which the more cohesive and hardened body crushed its foe, the moment he showed the slightest weakness. For the essential tactical advantage hung on the preservation of a closed formation, in spite of all losses. That meant, however, that the phalanx could be deployed only on flat ground presenting no break or obstacle. Nor did it have the capacity for rapid conversion, since it needed cover on its flanks and rear from light troops and cavalry, without which it ran a great risk of dislocation. Such shortcomings explain how that formidable tool of warfare, inherited from Greek tradition and perfected by the Macedonian monarchy, finally succumbed before the Roman infantry, no less obstinate in combat but capable of greater flexibility in its movements. In his account of the battle of Cynoscephalae (XVIII, 28–32: see here p. 108), Polybius makes a remarkable analysis of the tactical differences between the foes, and demonstrates the causes of the legions' victory.

There were numerous light troops of varied description around the phalanx: archers, slingers, foot-soldiers wearing no armor but holding a small shield, barbarian soldiers with their own traditional weaponry. The Galatians kept to their characteristic mode of combat. Their warriors were almost naked, had shaggy hair, wore a stiff twisted neck-chain (*torques*), were armed with a long sword and

Plate 9 The soldier Epithetos (Musée du Louvre, Paris; photo RMN, Hervé Lewandowski).

A funerary stele from western Crete. The style of engraving dates from the second or the first century BC: "Epiphila, daughter of Sosos, to Epithetos, son of Tharsagoras: from his wife this memorial" (the text is in Doric dialect). The man wears the outfit of a light trooper: a tunic and a chlamys, buskins, no helmet, a small round shield standing on the ground, and a lance held in his left hand. Crete provided the armies of the Hellenistic period with a large supply of mercenaries, especially light infantry and archers.

an elongated shield of ellipsoidal or hexagonal shape, fitted with a strengthening piece in the middle. Their trumpets had a funnel shaped like the mouth of an animal. Pergamene artists reproduced these exotic traits in sculptures recalling the victories their sovereigns had won over such troublesome neighbors. These picturesque representations won their place in the repertory current in art workshops, so much so that in later times sculptors in the service of Rome's glory adopted them when they commemorated the conquest of Celtic Gaul. Indeed, the Gauls depicted in the Roman triumphal arch at Orange in southern France, dating from the first century BC, are actually the Galatians whom the Attalid princes had seen in Anatolia two centuries earlier, not Julius Caesar's historical adversaries.

Cavalry had become a shock weapon since the time of Philip and Alexander. Though stirrups were then unknown, the cavalry was trained to charge, and some squadrons were supplied with cuirasses. Horsemen worked wonders when engaged in combat with light troops. Sometimes, as at the battles of the Granicus and Arbela, they determined the ultimate outcome. A momentous innovation was put in place to second them: the use of war elephants. Alexander had become acquainted with that means of combat while confronted by Indian princes, King Porus in particular. Among the booty he brought back from that expedition were many elephants, with their mahouts. These hitherto unknown animals had fired his contemporaries' imagination. Diodorus notes (XVIII, 27) that one of the pictures painted on wood panels and adorning Alexander's funeral chariot, as his embalmed body was being convoyed from Babylon to Memphis (see p. 44), showed a procession of war elephants. An Indian mahout and an armed Macedonian soldier rode on each of them. In recounting the great battles that took place among the Diadochi, historians (notably Diodorus, always very attentive to the unfolding of operations from a tactical point of view) mention the role of these animals as massive numbers of them, in tens if not hundreds, were brought into action. Seleucus I received 500 elephants from Sandracottus, the king of the Mauryas (see p. 51). He learned how to make effective use of them, and their role was decisive at the battle of Ipsus in 301(see p. 54), according to Plutarch's testimony (*Demetrius,* 28–9). For they prevented Demetrius and his cavalry, who had the upper hand for a while, from joining Antigonus' phalanx, which was thus isolated and outflanked, and ultimately forced to surrender. In a later development, the elephant was made to carry a rectangular crenellated tower, from which two or three soldiers could shoot arrows or throw javelins. Such a tower was already fitted on the elephants that Pyrrhus used in his Italian expedition and on those of Antiochus I when he beat the Galatians in 275/4. From that time on the war elephant, bearing his tower and protected by some pieces of armor, played a role like that of a war tank, based both on the power of its bodily impact and the shooting activity of its riders. The Ptolemies replaced Indian elephants with African ones. Their men, commanded by officers who specialized in the task, would hunt for these in the southern desert between the Nile and the Red Sea. But their mahouts were still designated as Indians. The Carthaginians also adopted that style of combat. In the Punic Wars the Romans were confronted by their elephants as they had been by those of Pyrrhus. Nevertheless, they soon devised effective methods to counter those monstrous adversaries. Neither against Hannibal at Zama, nor against Antiochus III at Magnesia, did they have to suffer excessive damage from their enemies' elephants. As a result the use of these animals in Hellenistic armies was soon on its way out except in faraway eastern states, where this legacy of Indian customs lasted longer.

Naval warfare had its innovations too. These were in two opposite directions: the introduction of large vessels, more powerful than the triremes of the Classical age, and that of light ones, which piratical operations demanded. The trireme was certainly not abandoned as a model of warship. But this fast and manageable craft was not fit to carry war-engines, and its crew, essentially made up of rowers, had only a small number of soldiers, hoplites, or archers. As early as 330, the Athenian fleet had, besides its 300 triremes, 18 *tetraremes*, five years later it had 50 ships of this new type. It is not known if these galleys had four superimposed ranks of rowers, or two banks of oars, but with two rowers for each oar. The latter arrangement is more likely, for several superimposed ranks of oarsmen would create insoluble problems. The ship would be too high to maintain stability on rough seas, and the length of the oars at the higher levels would be such as to make it impossible for one man to handle each one. It seems preferable to conclude that, beyond the trireme stage, heavy galleys were equipped with oars, each requiring a number of oarsmen, as were those of modern times in the Mediterranean. These vessels were, of course, wider than slim-line triremes, allowing room for long rowing-benches. *Quinqueremes* (with five banks of oars) are mentioned in some texts, then galleys with 6, 7, 8, up to 15, 20, or 30 rows in third-century BC squadrons. In the final analysis, the arrangement of oars on such enormous ships remains entirely a matter of conjecture, since no exact description, no illustrative document gives any information on the subject. What is certain is that their bulk allowed them to accommodate catapults, capable of hurling heavy missiles or boulders, on superstructures built fore and aft and on their upper deck. Sailing artillery of this type was a major modification of naval tactics. Ptolemy IV Philopator's monstrous vessel (*c*.220–210) represented the very summit of gigantic shipbuilding. Plutarch (*Demetrius*, 43) gives a number of details. It had 40 banks of oars, a length of more than 125 meters and a breadth of over 20 meters at the stern (always, it must be said, built much higher than the prow in ancient ships), 4,000 oarsmen, and 400 sailors, as well as room for 3,000 soldiers. But, as he notes,

That was only a ship built for show ... not for use, as it was so dangerous and difficult to steer. By contrast, the beauty of Demetrius' ships was no hindrance to steering, nor did the refinement of their equipment [with 15 or 16 banks of oars, as Plutarch says earlier] deprive them of their usefulness. For they were as worthy of admiration for their speed and power as for their superior size.

The princes thus introduced these bulky units, which became the backbone of their fleets. This was thanks to their enormous resources, while less well-endowed cities like Rhodes were content with more modest vessels, triremes or tetraremes, meant for the defense of their coast and their channels of communication. But, as noticed before (see pp. 90, 100, 146, 149) the second and first centuries BC witnessed the development of naval piracy, mainly based in Illyria, Aetolia, Caria, and Crete. The devastation that buccaneers caused extended over all coastal regions of the central and eastern parts of the Mediterranean. They supplied the slave markets, as illustrated by Caesar's adventure in his youthful days. Taken prisoner by Cilician bandits in the Aegean, he bought back his freedom at a high price. Then, putting together a small squadron at Miletus, he soon returned and took his former captors by surprise. After recovering his ransom, he had them crucified, as promised in the course of his captivity. These pirates did not as a rule make use of large ships for their operations. They employed a great number of light and fast vessels that were easy to handle, fitted with sails as well as oars, and could without difficulty lie hidden in inlets in wait for the passage of merchant ships. Sovereigns and cities paid attention to the help that could be obtained from such small craft, for they could be steered more easily than their heavy warships. At the battle of Actium in 31, they contributed to Mark Antony's defeat (see p. 162). In conclusion, the war fleets of Hellenistic times differed from those of the preceding age because of both the size and the wide range of their vessels. That contrasted with the uniformity of Classical squadrons, of which the trireme was the essential component.

■ *The merchant navy* ■ *The seaports: the example of Apollonia in Cyrenaica* ■ *Sea-trade* ■ *Stamps on amphoras: the wine trade* ■ *The perils of the sea: epitaphs in memory of shipwrecked sailors*

Merchant vessels, the usual target of pirates, had also benefited from advances made in shipbuilding. Their size and capacity were notably increased, sometimes reaching the maximum dimensions possible for wooden naval craft, which were not surpassed until the nineteenth century of our era. These large cargo ships were more than 40 meters long, like the one that sank off Mahdia in Tunisia at the start of the first century BC, carrying a cargo of fully sculptured pillars and of works of art. Their width at the midship beam (about 12 meters on the Mahdia wreck) was more than a quarter of their length. An approximate calculation of the tonnage of such cargoes has been made. This was 400 to 500 metric tonnes: at least twice, if not three times, the capacity of caïques used in the fourth century. The transport of goods, first and foremost of cereals, without which Rome could not have survived in the Imperial period, was thus made possible thanks to the skill of Hellenistic engineers. Two texts commemorate for us exceptional vessels that aroused wondering admiration in Antiquity. One is a small work, *The Ship, or The Wishes*, by Lucian of Samosata, a Greek from upper Anatolia who was the Voltaire of the century of the Antonines. It describes an enormous cargo ship loaded with wheat that had been blown off course by a storm between Alexandria and the Italian coast, and had unexpectedly put in at the Piraeus, where all the Athenian people had come down to behold it. It was 120 cubits long (over 53 meters), and more than 13 meters wide, which translates into a dead weight capacity of 1200 tonnes. The greatest distance from the upper deck to the bottom of the keel was 13 meters. Between the prow and the stern, both built very high, were anchors, capstans, winches intended for the working of the derricks. The mainmast, solidly stayed, and the mainsail, topped with a fiery triangular identification mark, had no less impressive dimensions than the hull. The name of the ship was *Isis*, the effigy of that Greek divinity, borrowed from the Egyptians and the patron goddess of mariners, appearing on each side of the high prow. Characters in Lucian's story are depicted chatting with members of the crew, "so numerous that one would have said it was an army." The ship-owner tells of the adventure he had. The carpenter takes pleasure in giving every kind of detail of the building of the ship. There are also the pilot, whose advanced age is no impediment to his handling the two enormous rudders, and a swarthy young ship's boy whose hair, knotted at the back of his neck, and exotic features have aroused a lively interest in one of the visitors. If the scene, as Lucian so vividly describes it, took place in the year 165 of our era or thereabouts, one can believe that nothing essential had changed since Ptolemaic times, when a vessel of that kind was first designed and built – a prodigious feat for the times. For Hiero II, sovereign of Syracuse, had ordered a colossal craft to be built (Athenaeus V, 206c ff.), which must have had a transport capacity of about 2,000 tonnes. That ship actually sailed only once, between Syracuse and Alexandria, the only port of a size to accommodate it. It never went to sea any more, fated to grow old in idleness, a curious sight relegated to the furthest end of a wet dock. Such are the limitations imposed on a craze for the gigantic.

To receive these ever bigger and more numerous merchant ships, and the products they carried, the harbors of the main maritime cities were equipped with basins protected by breakwaters, quays, docks, and warehouses. We have already noted the impressive works that were carried out at Alexandria. We know very little about them, as is the case for those of the Piraeus and of Rhodes, because more recently built facilities have destroyed them or covered them over. Elsewhere, as at Ephesus or Miletus, the accumulation of silt has modified the appearance of the place. Scant study has been devoted to the port of Delos: one is, after all, struck by the fact that its likely dimensions are so modest, considering the intense activity that took place in it. Yet Cyrene's harbor, later named Apollonia when it became an independent city, is happily an exception to the rule. Owing to subsidence of the coastline and destruction wrought by the ocean, a large portion of the ancient remains has disappeared. Enough, however, has remained, for underwater exploration has allowed us to trace the inner basin on the west side, with its dry-docks for warships, and the outer harbor on the east, separated from the western basin by a dyke, at the middle point of which was a passage controlled by two square towers. The two islands that served as supporting bases for the protective breakwater in the north were used for quarrying, but also for warehousing in artificial caverns cut in the rock. It seems that there was a lighthouse at the eastern limit, signaling the entrance to the port. On the seaboard and below the acropolis were quays, high-capacity store pits dug in the rock, docks, underground halls cut in the cliffs, or warehouses with vaulted ceilings made of masonry. These served as accommodation for goods that were imported or that Cyrene's luxuriant countryside provided for export. From the nearby agora, one could easily reach that countryside through one of the two gates (obviously set up for traffic) in the surrounding wall. These facilities remained in use until the end of Antiquity and the time of the first emperors of Byzantium. But they had essentially been planned and set up at the time when the fortified wall was built, in the third century BC (see pp. 299–301, with plan). They give us an accurate picture of a major Hellenistic port.

Apart from wheat, sea-trade handled the same products as before. There were first of all such indispensable primary materials as were not found everywhere in the Hellenic world, like wood or marble (the latter conveniently serving as ballast for the ships that carried them). Among metals were the usual ones, like copper and tin, needed for making bronze, or lead, used for ducts and funerary urns; and precious metals, silver (in ingots or currency) and gold, in much greater demand with the spread of luxury. Manufactured goods ranged from cloths and carpets, through jewelry and ceramics, to spices and perfume. Finally there were slaves, for trading in this commodity extended to the whole of the Mediterranean, starting from major marts. We have very little information about these exchanges. Documentation yielded by excavation does not allow us to determine the size or frequency of commercial trends. It provides evidence at best of relations that came into existence between Greek cities, as well as between the Hellenistic world and its neighbors. In respect of the latter, there is no doubt that Alexander's conquests had opened new routes, thereby creating new needs. There were caravan tracks across the mountains of central Asia, the Arabian deserts, or the Libyan portion of the Sahara; use was made of the Nile and the Euphrates waterways, of the Indian sea-route via the Persian Gulf or the Red Sea. Exotic products would thus be transported to the markets in the cities of Seleucid Mesopotamia, of Anatolia, Syria, Cyrenaica, or Egypt, and spread later to the Aegean Sea and further. Such exchanges, apart from consignments of cereals, supplied no vital need for the vast majority of the Hellenistic world, since most cities still had a self-contained economy. Yet trade on the high seas, certainly more highly developed than in previous centuries, introduced new trends in lifestyles, at least among the affluent and, as a consequence, into Greek society as a whole. It is not irrelevant to quote an example from evidence found in a papyrus from the Fayyum. We find there that around the middle of the third century, an ordinary Greek person, who kept an account of his daily purchases, bought among other food items fresh nuts from the Pontus, that is, from the Black Sea, and others imported from Chalcis in Euboea. Such exotic delicacies reached an Egyptian village in the same way as oranges or bananas reach people of all continents in our day. They evidently enhanced daily life with the flavor they brought to it.

There is one product, however, for which the number of archaeological documents allows us to appreciate the quantitative importance of some exports: this is wine. In many producing areas (but certainly not all of them, far from it), it had become customary since the Classical period to insert a mark on earthen amphoras used for transporting wine. A stamp identifying their place of origin and the potter's name was pressed on the handles before the firing process. These stamps in relief were almost indelible once the amphora had been baked, and as the handle was thick and sturdy, it often survived the broken amphora, along with the lower, pointed end of the vessel. This is how thousands of stamped fragments have been found in the course of excavation, particularly in the heaps of litter where the Greeks got rid of their refuse and unwanted objects. The study of these fragments constitutes a special branch of archaeology in its own right. The shapes and characteristics of the stamps are quite varied. They range from a mere symbol, devoid of title, to elaborate compositions in which, together with a diversity of motifs, the names of the country of origin, of a magistrate or civil servant, of the producer, and even the month of production are inscribed. These stamps changed with the times and were much more numerous in the Hellenistic period. They are believed to have aimed less at guaranteeing the origin of the produce that the amphora contained (as our labels of certified content do these days) than the volume of the vessel, therefore the quantity of wine exported or sold, for ease of fiscal imposition. There are still areas of uncertainty in such an interpretation, and dating often remains tentative. Yet the information we have at our disposal is solid enough to warrant some interesting conclusions.

The areas where amphoras were stamped were first of all the island of Rhodes and the nearby territory of Cnidus on the coast of Asia Minor. It seems that wine from both regions, exported in large quantities, was commonly drunk: this is explained by the supposition that it was intended for consumption by mercenary troops. A collection of such stamped handles put together, because of his personal interest in them, by an inhabitant of Alexandria numbers over 66,000, five-sixths being Rhodian and about one-tenth Cnidian. Among the rest, the most numerous are from the island of Cos. These figures bear witness to economic links, well attested by other sources, between Lagid Egypt and the southwest Anatolian coast, which has Rhodes and Cos for neighbors. The same collection also contains amphora handles from Pamphylia, where a wine that was much appreciated was produced round the Gulf of Adalia. The finds made in the Fayyum are less numerous, but the breakdown of their provenance displays similar proportions. In Athens, on the other hand, where about 40,000 stamped handles have been listed, those from Cnidus are three times more numerous than the ones from Rhodes. Other areas of production, like Thasos or Chios, appear to have exported only quality wine. A map of their clientele can be tentatively drawn. Chios has Athens and Delos as its main customers; Thasos also has the custom of these two cities, with Pergamum, the Greek cities on the west coast of the Black Sea, and Ptolemaic Egypt. Amphora handles reveal the fame that some vintages had won, which are not mentioned in the texts we possess, examples being the wines from Sinope on the Black Sea, or those from the Crimea. They also give evidence of the widespread trade in Greek wines that took place not only in the eastern basin of the Mediterranean, but in Cyrenaica (itself, however, a producing area), at Carthage, in Sicily, in Italy, at Marseille, even at Ampurias on the Catalan coast. The chronological study of these documents still continues, and will allow their interpretation to gain in precision. It is already acknowledged that, in an archaeological site, amphora stamps constitute a category of artifact as important as coins.

Wine provides a good illustration of sea-trade in the Hellenistic age. The substantial profit that it brought was an incentive for businessmen eager to amass a fortune rapidly. Such are those whom we have seen setting up their cultural associations at Delos, where they erected impressive building complexes, like that of the Poseidoniasts at Berytus (see pp. 200, 201). They were men who, blinded by their appetite for gain, did not fear to face the perils of the sea – perils, however, that were very real: witness the large number of funerary epigrams written in memory of the shipwrecked. One of these, attributed in the past to Theocritus (*Palatine Anthology* VII, 534) reads as follows:

> Man, be sparing of your life: beware of going to sea out of season! Unhappy Cleonicus, you longed to put in to opulent Thasos, coming from Coele-Syria to ply your trade. Your trade, Cleonicus! Sailing at the time of the setting of the Pleiades, you disappeared with them in the deep.

Another, from the poet Theaetetus, friend of Callimachus, says (ibid., VII, 499):

> Mariners sailing along this coast, Ariston of Cyrene entreats you, in the name of Zeus the Hospitable, to go and say to his father Menon that he lies by the cliffs of Icaria, having lost his life in the Aegean Sea.

The wrath of the waves sometimes found an ally in the malice of wreckers, who pitilessly put to death those who had accidentally been stranded on their shores. This is the tale of an epitaph engraved in the second century BC on a cenotaph on the island of Delos:

> This grave deserves your tears, though a mere cenotaph raised in memory both of Pharnaces and of his brother Myron, luckless posterity of Papos their father. They came from Amisus, strangers, and were shipwrecked, surprised by a squall from the North Wind. They found death on the island of Seriphus, murdered by louts, the end of a cruel and jealous fate. In a creek of Rhenea Protos has raised this funerary monument to the memory of his companions, weeping over their sad destiny.

These texts, whether they have reached us through the *Anthology*, where they are counted by the dozen, or have been found carved in stone, convey the age-old apprehension, more than fully justified by such tragic adventures, that the Greeks felt when thinking of the ocean's terrible risks. Horace, the Latin poet, writing at the time of Augustus, echoes that feeling when he evokes the boldness shown by traders in the Aegean Sea (*Odes* I, 1, 15–18): "When the African blast wrestles with the waves around Icaria, the merchant, a prey to fear, praises the quiet countryside by his native town. But he soon repairs his damaged skiffs, he who has not learned to endure a modest livelihood." In a famous ode recalling one of Callimachus' poems, he addresses in superb style the vessel taking Vergil to Greece (I, 3, 9–13). "He had a breast fortified by oak and triple bronze, who was the first to entrust his frail boat to the wild ocean, nor feared the headlong African wind battling the Boreal blasts." From Hellenistic tradition to Latin poetry, the inspiration remains the same. Nor has the theme changed.

■ *The love of travel in the Hellenistic world* ■ *The phenomenon of curiosity: travel-guide literature* ■ *Tourism: Athens and Ilium as examples* ■ *Ethnographic literature and "paradoxography"* ■ *Catilius, son of Nicanor, at Philae*

We have had a rapid overview of the material conditions of life in the vast Hellenistic world, and noted some significant examples of it. These have illustrated the continuity of certain traditions and customs, as well as the developments, even the innovations, that the passage of time and the great extension of the geographical framework led the Greek people to introduce into their usual lifestyle. Some Greeks, the large majority no doubt, remained faithful to their centuries-old mode of life, limiting their field of vision to the boundaries of their civic territory or the small surrounding states. They tilled the land inherited from their family, preserved piously their ancestral cults. They felt busy enough with local problems, their only concern being to maintain, by negotiation and in case of need by recourse to arms, their city's autonomy, which was always precarious. Others, far fewer, but increasingly numerous with the evolution in mores, were willing to face the risks incurred in traveling or even in being uprooted. Indeed, in the faraway days of colonization, whole groups had left their land to try their luck in barbarian territory and had founded thriving settlements, lively transplants of the Hellenism of much earlier times. Now, however, individual adventure replaced collective action. What is striking in the Hellenistic age is the frequency and diversity of travel (see pp. 197–9). Numbers of people would go to distant places for a prolonged stay, in spite of the uncertainties of sea travel. These were not only traders or soldiers, on whom the needs of their calling had always imposed travel. Artists as well, following the example of the masters of the Classical age, showed a willingness to migrate from their country if their clientele so wished. Signatures of sculptors preserved in large numbers testify to the mobility of these craftsmen, and it is not surprising to find at Delos many works by Polianthes of Cyrene, or at Cyrene the signature of a sculptor who hailed from Miletus. We have already noted how actors, musicians, and fraternities of Dionysiac artists responded to foreign demand and moved easily from one festival to another (see pp. 200, 289–90). The same applied to poets and philosophers. Posidippus of Pella came to Alexandria and composed the Pharos dedicatory inscription (see p. 280). Antigonus Gonatas attracted a number of such men to his court (see p. 89). These included the philosophers Menedemus of Eretria and Persaeus of Citium in Cyprus, the poets Aratus of Soli in Cilicia and Antagoras of Rhodes, the historian Hieronymus of Cardia, and even, from his native southern Russia, the aggressively self-assertive Cynic wanderer Bion of Borysthenes. The needs of cities fostered human mobility. Doctors, foreign judges (see p. 202), ambassadors sent to negotiate (sometimes very far away, like those who came to Rome, requesting the Senate's benevolence: see p. 129), delegations of theôroi (see pp. 295–6), official envoys sent to consult an oracle. Sovereigns used their influence to foster such contacts, for they recruited their friends, their administrators, their war captains from every possible source, and extended their network of representatives over a vast area. All this migrant population traveled as individuals or in groups, in every direction; but mercenaries moved in properly constituted units, and their recruitment was quite varied. The result was an ever-increasing trend to develop personal contacts, and a rapid dissemination of techniques, tastes, and ideas, an even stronger belief than before in belonging to the great family of Hellenes that had spread across the entire inhabited world. One can see at that juncture many signs of the strengthening of a feature of the Greek persona that goes back to its origins, since it already shows itself in Homer, but which circumstances were going to stimulate from then on. This is curiosity. It was indeed a major aspect of Ulysses' character, for he is the exemplar of all adventurers. With the passage of time, travelers and ethnographers, from Aristeas of Proconnesus to Hecataeus of Miletus and Herodotus, had responded generously to encouragement from their public in that respect. But the Hellenistic age witnessed a real explosion of curiosity. All readers were eager to learn, as Ulysses had been, about "so many diverse peoples, their cities and their ways" (*Odyssey* I, 3). A love of travel for its own sake became widespread, encouraged by an abundant "periegetic" or guidebook literature, a distant posterity of Herodotus' writings. It flourished in the third and second centuries, to a degree that is surprising in its volume, richness, and variety. Only one complete piece of evidence concerning it has survived, produced indeed at a much later time, in the midst of the second century of our era, under the emperors Antoninus and Marcus Aurelius. This is the famous *Periegesis of Greece*, a detailed tourist guidebook for mainland Greece, written by Pausanias. It gives us a good enough idea of treatises compiled by his predecessors, which had been of use to our author. Diodorus the Periegete (late fourth to third century BC), for instance, had written a work *On the Demes of Attica*, a survey of the townships of that district, their shrines and curiosities. Another work by the same author was *On Funerary Monuments*, of the same area, no doubt. As tombs stood by the roadside, outside inhabited areas, and were often adorned with sculptures and inscriptions, passers-by, especially foreigners, liked to know who was buried there and what that person's life story had been. Heliodorus the Periegete (middle of the second century?) wrote a *Guidebook of the Athenian Acropolis*, a highly detailed work, as it was made up of fifteen books. He also wrote a monograph *On the Tripods of Athens*, in which he studied that particular category of offerings, so common in Dionysus' cult that a street neighboring the Acropolis and the theater was called Tripod Street. He had also, it seems, written a comprehensive book *On Athenian Votive Offerings*. A few years earlier another specialized author, Polemo of Ilium, from whom Pausanias seems to have borrowed heavily, had devoted a treatise in four books to the *Votive Offerings of the Athenian Acropolis*. One fact is worthy of note: this kind of literature paid particular attention to the curiosities of Attica and its capital. The reason was that Athens, despite its decadence in the area of high-level politics, retained an undiminished prestige in those of art and culture. Strangers came to that city in crowds, visitors who were eager to admire the monuments of an illustrious past, and to meet the great masters of philosophy and rhetoric who taught there. We find a description of Athens that one Heraclides wrote in the third century, in his work *On the Towns of Greece*. He makes no secret of certain antiquated aspects of the old city, like the insufficient number of public fountains or the discomfort of urban dwellings. Yet he pays a deserved tribute to the exceptional beauty of such monuments as the theater of Dionysus and the Parthenon, "which dominates the theater and makes an extraordinary impression on those who behold it." He speaks of the three gymnasiums, the Academy, the Lyceum, and the Cynosarges, with their groves and lawns. He mentions the frequent festivals, the intellectual exchanges, and the quality of life (a costly one, though!) that the visitor can enjoy in this city: hence the crowds of tourists, to which Athenians have grown accustomed.

We are better informed about Athens than we are about other Greek cities. Yet the strong appeal that this city had for the outside world should not obscure the fact that many others exerted a strong attraction as well. There were such beautiful and richly endowed cities as Alexandria, Antioch, Rhodes, Ephesus, Byzantium, Tarentum, or Syracuse; renowned sanctuaries like those of Olympia, Delphi, the Isthmus, Nemea, Epidaurus, Delos, Clarus (near Ephesus), Daphne (near Antioch). These attracted large numbers of pilgrims and visitors. Even the shrine of Dodona, lost in the mountains of Epirus, knew a spell of renewed activity, attested by the building of a vast and handsome theater.

Ilium was a special destination, where visitors could evoke the presence of Homer on the actual site of Troy. The example of Alexander (see p. 14), whom Caesar was to imitate later, had by then already been followed by thousands of tourists, who dreamed of a glorious past among those ruins that the local population did not hesitate to identify as memorials of Homeric heroes. At Ilium, as Lucan was to say, *nullum est sine nomine saxum,* "there is not one stone without its name." People admired the tombs of Achilles, Patroclus, and Ajax, the site of the Achaean camp, Paris' grotto on Mount Ida, various more or less genuine traces of Priam's city, and physical embodiments of the countless legends that had grown around it. Strabo's *Geography* is not short of allusions to these. For the benefit of visitors, Demetrius of Scepsis, a son of the soil, had in the second century written a *periegesis* of the Troad. This was in the shape of a commentary on the text in which Homer, having given the "Catalogue of the Ships" of the Greeks, lists the Trojan forces (*Iliad* II, 811ff.).

Other authors were interested in the barbarian peoples, as Herodotus had been in earlier times. But they were motivated by a taste for the picturesque and a desire to discover the existence among those foreigners of traditions of wisdom that could be of benefit to the Greeks. A contemporary of Ptolemy I, Hecataeus of Abdera, is one of these. His book *On Egypt* seems to have been very well received. He also dealt, turning to the opposite end of the known world, with the Hyperboreans. Alexander's companions had written a great deal about Asia in their memoirs of his conquests. Geographers and ethnographers developed such testimony, giving it greater precision in works of a more technical nature. In the middle of the second century Agatharchides of Cnidus, who had written a

Figure 10   Dodona: Zeus' sanctuary at the end of the third century (from *Antike Kunst*, 15, 1972, p. 68, fig. 2. Restoration by S. I. Dakaris, B. Charisis and Chr. Rongotis).

View taken from the south. The tiers of the theater, which was slightly larger than the one at Epidaurus, rose on the southern slope of the acropolis. Fronting the location (orchestra) *reserved for the chorus was the* skéné *building. On the left was the end of the stadium, the venue for the games. Close to the retaining wall, east of the theatre, was the large building (Bouleuterion) where the federal Council of the Epirotes took place: there was a portico in front of the façade. Further to the right were two small temples of Aphrodite and Themis, then, close to the tall venerable oak that gave the oracles, the building consecrated to Zeus. Still further to the right, near the surrounding wall, was the temple of Heracles. At the top of the hill were the fortifications of the acropolis. A fortified wall surrounded the sanctuary proper. One entered through a turret-flanked gate seen in the foreground, on the right. It opened onto a large square shaped like an irregular quadrilateral with a portico onto each of two sides, intended for use during ceremonies and celebrations. The surrounding area is a mountainous one with verdant vegetation in the valley.*

History of Asia, published a *Description of the Erythrean Sea* (which literally means the Red Sea: but the term then designated the sum total of the seas surrounding Arabia, including the Indian Ocean and the Persian Gulf). We have some extracts from the latter work, thanks to the Byzantine scholar Photius. Later, around 100 BC, Artemidorus of Ephesus drew on the experience of his many travels to compose eleven books of *Geographical Studies*, in which Asia had pride of place. These two authors provided material for Diodorus Siculus and Strabo, who sometimes used their very words. Such an abundant production was evidently a response to the demands of a public anxious to learn about these faraway regions toward which mercenaries and traders put to sea. Like Ulysses' accounts of his travels, these works were not wanting in fabulous details, mingled with descriptions of things actually seen and of modes of life reported from direct observation. The Greeks have always had a taste for the marvelous. Hellenistic authors catered for it by relating strange facts, weird and unexpected ones, *paradoxa*, whence the generic name of such writings, *paradoxography*. The same trend showed, in a parallel fashion, in a number of historical accounts. This genre was highly successful, and collections of *Extraordinary Stories* kept appearing right up to the end of Antiquity. One of the first among these, a *Collection of Extraordinary Stories* to be precise, was produced in the middle of the third century. It was due to Antigonus of Carystus, who lived at the court of Attalus I of Pergamum, and also wrote biographies of the philosophers he had known and a theoretical treatise on painting. It is not incongruous that a mind immersed both in art and in philosophy showed such interest in the exotic and the uncanny, for this happens to be one of the original aspects of the Hellenistic turn of mind.

A passion for travel thus developed, with the sole aim of satisfying curiosity about far-off lands, a wish to see with their own eyes people and monuments described in books. In other words, there was a widespread appetite for tourism (to use a modern term that seems appropriate). This was a major novelty of the time. It naturally came with the temptation to tell of things one had seen. Hence the proliferation of memoirs and accounts in which the authors mentioned above found their material. It is worth citing a last example of these, a curious one belonging to the end of the period in question. Its exact date is March 8 of the seventh year of our era, during Augustus' reign. On that day a Greek from Alexandria, a man with a cultured mind and a Latin name, Catilius, son of Nicanor, was on the island of Philae on the Upper Nile, near Aswan above the first cataract. He had come out of curiosity, as he had heard of the outstanding beauty of the site. He was a skilled writer and poet, and, to commemorate his visit, he left us two rather elegant epigrams that are engraved on a pylon of the temple of Isis, where they were found in the last quarter of the twentieth century. The first of these gives due praise to the emperor and to the prefect of Egypt, for Philae "is Egypt's lovely frontier and the limit of the land of the Ethiopians." The other is of a more special kind in its style and inspiration. Its ten lines make up an acrostic: their first syllables form the name and surname of the author. Catilius invites the reader to play that little game. He then goes on to say: "Farewell, Philae, farewell! The sight of these rocks and mountains overwhelms me, oh cataracts! I too shall be able to write a genuine account of my travels, after my return, when I have seen again Nicanor and the rest of my family." This text reveals the literary taste of a lover of the genre, who takes pleasure in giving a witty turn to a short piece of verse, the meaning of which will be apparent to none but the perceptive reader. But above all it sheds light on the inner urge that had brought our traveler to Egypt's furthest frontier, at such a distance from his Alexandrian home. He wished to feel the tremor of sharing in a sight filled with grandeur – the cataract, the mighty river, the rugged cliffs – a source of inspiration, on his return to his home town, for a written account that would fill his friends with enchantment. There is nothing more modern than this manner of linking action with feeling.

■ *Cosmopolitanism* ■ *The attachment to cultural tradition: mythography* ■ *The vitality of Hellenism implanted in barbarian territory: Aï Khanum in Bactria, and its inscriptions by Clearchus of Soli* ■ *The fundamental importance of the spiritual content of Hellenism*

The end product of such diverse and manifold experiences might have been cosmopolitanism. For by dint of seeing lands and peoples that were so different from each other, did the Greeks not risk losing the notion of their own identity? Abstract reflection rather than experience had led certain schools of philosophy to such a concept. These were the Stoics, the Epicureans, and the Cynics, who made varying analyses resulting in the same conclusion, the assertion of the sameness of the human condition, no matter where humanity lived. This view is echoed in commonly held opinion, for example in the plays of Menander. Terence, a Latinized African playwright, borrowed from him (in a play, *The Self-tormentor*, written *c.*165 BC) the famous line, *Homo sum: humani nil a me alienum puto*, "I am a man: nothing in a human being's condition appears foreign to me." The most forceful assertion of cosmopolitanism is to be found in the epitaph of the poet Meleager of Gadara, a Syrian Greek, the author of many epigrams, who lived in the first half of the first century before our era. "I am a Syrian," it says. "Why are you astonished? Stranger, we live in the same motherland, the world, and the same Chaos begot all mortals." Such an attitude actually belonged to a minority of enlightened human beings. As for other mortals, they might have the comfortable feeling of regarding the rest of the world with sympathy and generosity. But that in no way lessened their attachment to tradition and custom. No other period paid so much attention to myths – a fact to which literary texts, inscriptions, and figurative monuments bear ample testimony. Reference is made there, again and again, to the most ancient local legends, which have a historical value even in the eyes of cultured people. We have seen (see pp. 209–11), when dealing with the Cytenian embassy to Xanthus, how myths, even when they diverged from the widely agreed version, were an object of reverence both for the politically powerful and those with responsibilities for cults. Many handbooks of mythology were published, like the one by Dionysius of Mytilene, called "Leather Arm" (*Skytobrachion*): Diodorus Siculus made great use of it. A hundred years earlier, in the reign of Ptolemy Philadelphus, Callimachus had written the "Causes" (*Aitia*). In this, his most ambitious work, the poet brilliantly evoked a large number of legends explaining rites that were still in use in many Greek shrines. It would be wrong to look upon poems of this type as no more than erudite *divertimenti*, meant to delight the minds of closet scholars. For they are based on a thorough acquaintance with actual cult, which was always founded in myth. This was illustrated not long ago as a result of research on the city of Heraclea on Latmos, in Caria. It was then shown that what made the area famous was a cave on the wild mountain of Latmos. There the shepherd Endymion, lover of Selene (the Moon), had fallen into an endless sleep, of which the goddess took advantage to stay by him without his knowledge. This legend, dear to the hearts of the people of Heraclea, was used, as we saw above (p. 211), to prove the "family ties" linking that city with the Aetolians, whose eponymous hero Aetolos was Endymion's own son. Hellenistic cities would piously preserve the ancestral treasury of their myths, the foundation of their civic, religious, and cultural identity.

Thus it can be said that, in spite of the allure of cosmopolitanism, the Hellenistic Greeks still placed all their trust in the outstanding merit of their secular civilization, in their own mode of life, and in their gods. Whenever the vagaries of fortune in their own lives or the political situation forced them to settle abroad, they took with them the essence of Hellenism. Even when isolated as a small minority on foreign soil, in the midst of unfamiliar populations, they remained true to their customs and mores, apparently impervious to their environment. We have some illustration of this in the Greco-Macedonian communities settled in the countryside of Ptolemaic Egypt, far from the cities. The same may be said of the Greek cities on the Euxine, surrounded by Thracian or Scythian tribes who derived profit from the cultural impact of these cities without providing much in exchange beside food supplies. But the most striking testimony to the vitality of Hellenism was provided in the 1970s by excavations that a French mission started in 1964 on the northern frontier of Afghanistan, at a place named Aï Khanum on the river Oxus (Amu Darya today) in ancient Bactria. A Hellenistic city, whose ancient name is unknown, had been established there – one of the foundations made by Alexander and his successors in that faraway satrapy. Exploration of the ruins has brought to light the street grid, conforming to the right-angled plan of new cities, the line of the fortified surrounding wall, and administrative buildings. These included a public bath with mosaic paving, after the ancient technique of cobblestone mosaics, as evidenced at Olynthus and Pella. There was in addition a gymnasium with a large court 90 meters square, provided with exedras, and a dedication to Hermes and Heracles, divine protectors of the gymnasium. The ceramic work displays a genuinely Greek inspiration; the stamps on the amphoras are proof that Mediterranean

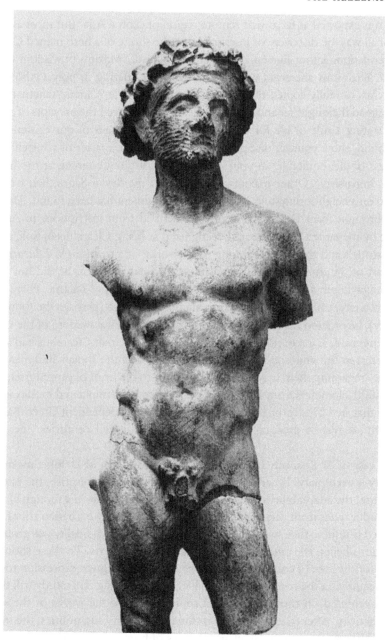

Plate 10 Statuette of an ephebe from Aï Khanum.

Apart from the obvious quality of its composition, which gives it an honorable place in Hellenistic sculpture, this work is of particular interest because of its unfinished state. The face is simply rough-hewn, and the garland of foliage bears no sign of detailed execution. Even the shape of the body, already well thought out, needed polishing. It provides evidence that there were sculpture workshops at Aï Khanum, employing talented artists.

wine was exported as far as that remote region of central Asia. But most astonishing of all was the discovery of inscriptions in the shrine of a hero named Cineas: a real revelation. A four-line epigram reads as follows: "Maxims of wisdom worded by our illustrious ancestors were engraved on an offering in holy Pythô. There Clearchus carefully copied them, so that, on this stele in Cineas' sanctuary, they may spread their light far and wide." Beneath are engraved the precepts of a moral code stating a rule of life for each of the successive stages of our existence: "In childhood, show yourself disciplined; as a young man, master of yourself; in the ripeness of life, equitable; in your old age, one of good counsel; at the hour of death, impassive." Other maxims, attributed to the Seven Sages, had been engraved on a neighboring stele, of which only a fragment has been found. They had been brought from Delphi, diligently transcribed from inscriptions in Apollo's shrine by the same Clearchus, now recognized as being Clearchus of Soli, a pupil of Aristotle's and the author, among other works, of a treatise *On Education*. At the start of the third century, therefore, in Seleucus I's reign, he did not shrink from engaging in a long trip that was to take him to Upper Bactria. There, in an unknown city, and in a shrine raised in memory of a hero (perhaps the founder of the city), he ordered the maxims summing up the ancestral wisdom of the Greeks to be engraved, as a reminder of his visit. We also know that Clearchus had shown an interest in the philosophy of the eastern Magi and the Indian Brahmans. His curiosity regarding them may explain his journey to the heart of central Asia, more than 5,000 kilometers from Delphi. Hellenism had been implanted in Alexander's time in that area. Under the Seleucids, then within the independent Greco-Bactrian kingdom, it was to prosper for a further one-and-a-half centuries (see p. 75 above).

The case of Aï Khanum and of Clearchus' importation of Delphic maxims to that city is exemplary. It certainly illustrates the spirit of enterprise, the taste for adventure, the adaptability of the Greeks. It also shows how in a foreign clime, a thousand leagues from their own land, and surrounded by barbarian tribes, they remained faithful to their way of life. It shows finally that such fidelity was grounded in religious belief, the practice of letters, reflection on texts. To these should be added, for the sake of completeness, a love of art, which gives expression to faith while beautifying the context of human life. In its final stage this study will therefore be centered on these interrelated topics: religion, the works of the spirit, artistic activity. After examining the machinery of society and politics, the framework of daily life and the main characteristics of human behavior, we must now focus on the inner life of the people of that age. We must now try to gauge, if at all possible, not their aptness for life and survival, but their ability to respond to spiritual or aesthetic urges by the practice of traditional disciplines or the discovery of innovative solutions. Faced with such an ambitious and complex task, we must be content with no more than a bold outline.

9/THE NEEDS OF THE SOUL

No more than the Greeks of previous ages could those of the Hellenistic age do without their gods. They felt the same need for divinity in their inner selves. Like their predecessors, they were faced with the uncertainties and sufferings of life, and asked themselves the same questions when confronted with the enigmas of the universe and the decrees of fate: nor could they elude the prospect of an inevitable death. Only a few philosophers found, or believed they found, a response to such questionings and anxieties in the exercise of rational thought. But most people did not care for such reasoning. They found far more reassurance and a much easier remedy by putting their trust in some superior power that would listen to their prayers and respond to their veneration and their offerings – an approach to which age-old custom, handed down through generations, gave testimony as being effective. Hellenic polytheism put at the disposal of humanity's weakness a prodigious variety of divine personalities, with which the inexhaustible resources of that people's imagination had filled their world. Some of these were illustrious ones, endowed with definite characteristics, as were the principal members of the traditional Pantheon. Even so, thanks to a proliferation of sacred epithets (*epikleseis*, plural of *epiklesis*), each of these deities could be given diverse attributes; their special relationship with each of an abundant number of cultic sites could thus be identified. Other divinities had less rich personalities, which were not so precisely defined. These were the minor ones, belonging to an agrarian location, to a modest local shrine. They abounded under generic appellations: Nymph, Hero, Heroine, Daemon, sometimes with a name to identify them, but often staying anonymous and no less revered. Both in Greece and beyond, the Hellenistic world was no less peopled with gods than previous ages had been. The Hellenic soul remained attentive to the sacred, which was perceived as being present everywhere in nature, even in a hostile one. In the desert regions east of Egypt, between the Nile and the Red Sea, caravan traders, hunters, soldiers, gold-mine workers have left dedications to Pan of the Desert engraved on burning rocks, along the tracks or beside a spot used as an encampment for a single night. They are in honor of "Him who haunts the mountain," "who shows the right way," or "provides gold." In the midst of such dismal solitude, a devotion to the old pastoral god of the Greeks, who was assimilated without difficulty to the Egyptian Min, brought confidence and comfort.

Religious faith was no less necessary to the group than to the individual. Every human community needs to become conscious of its unity if it is to survive. To stay free from internal dissension and remain united in the face of an external menace, it requires something different from abstract reasoning or calculation based on self-interest – exercises hardly apt to urge citizens to make sacrifices when these are unavoidable. The survival of the social group is conditional on the unreasoning acceptance of its higher value compared with that of the individual. The Greeks knew this from experience. They had for centuries linked the city's existence with the cult of tutelary deities, the civic (*poliades,* plural of *polias,* e.g. Athena Polias) divinities that were associated in perpetuity with every deed of the State. There was nothing more important in such circumstances than the exact observance of ritual, the holding of traditional festivals at fixed dates, public prayers, processions, sacrifices, the maintenance of sacred buildings and their appointments, the consultation of oracles. Leaving the altars of the city's divinities unattended was the equivalent of bringing ruin on the city itself. Since the city, as we have seen, remained the obvious frame of civic life for the vast majority of Greeks of the time, they were in no way likely to allow civic cults to founder, unless material means were utterly lacking. As a matter of fact, excavations and inscriptions provide the same evidence: religious life lost none of its vitality in Hellenistic cities.

The intervention of sovereigns – even that of Rome at a later stage – certainly did it no harm, and was actually a factor in its development. The royal cult was instituted on the initiative of cities before being officially organized in the kingdoms concerned. It was an innovation that enriched a tradition welcoming newly introduced divinities, provided these had the familiar look of Greek deities. Self-interest was no stranger to such recognition. But this was a reaction that had not been without precedent since the very origins of Greek religion, with cults of heroes like that of Heracles (so often hardly distinguishable from a divine cult), or the widespread veneration granted to the heroic founders of cities. In addition, the assimilation of the sovereign with a divinity already known made things easier. Thus, when Lysimachus the Diadoch struck coins portraying Alexander the Great with a ram's horns, a specific attribute of

Zeus-Ammon, he secured a place for the Conqueror, to whose heritage he was laying claim, in the restricted circle of the Olympian gods. He solemnly proclaimed him son of Zeus. The city of Cyrene had done likewise for Hermes in the preceding century. It had struck coinage portraying the beardless, short-haired profile of the god of the gymnasium, wearing ram's horns: these were a visual translation of the local epithet of Parammon. Nearly three centuries later, the Alexandrian Catilius, son of Nicanor (see pp. 318–19), urged by a similar feeling, composed a poem to the glory of Augustus, which he ordered to be engraved on a pylon at Philae. He hailed the prince in these words: "To Caesar, master of the seas and sovereign over the continents, Zeus the Liberator having Zeus for father, master of Europe and Asia, star that has risen in all its majesty over the whole of Greece as Zeus the Savior: on sacred stone Catilius has offered this pious epigram." The *Imperator's* omnipotence takes over, in a logical sequence, from that of the Lagid king, and confers upon him the same rank among the gods.

Contrary to what is often written on the subject, the introduction of a cult in honor of sovereigns was no indication of a weakening of traditional religion, but actually gave it renewed vitality. In 274 Callicrates, an admiral in the service of Ptolemy II Philadelphus, founded the sanctuary of Zephyrion on the Egyptian coast east of Alexandria. It was consecrated to Queen Arsinoe, who had been assimilated to Aphrodite during her lifetime. Pilgrims came in eager crowds, bringing their offerings. Callimachus wrote a dainty epigram (*Epigram 5*) for one of these, a nautilus shell that Selenaia, a woman from Smyrna in whose name the dedication was made, had picked up on the beach of Ioulis on the island of Ceus. Posidippus of Pella was invited by Callicrates to write the sanctuary's dedicatory epigram. This text was transcribed on the same papyrus that has preserved for us the Pharos dedication (see p. 280). It is as precise as it is evocative:

> Midway between the promontory of Pharos and the mouth of Canopus I have found my station in the midst of the waves, prominent on this windy coast of Libya rich in lambs, facing the Zephyr blowing from Italy. Here Callicrates has laid my foundation and given me my name: Sanctuary of Queen Arsinoe Cypris. Come, daughters of the Hellenes, you pure of heart, hasten to the shrine of Aphrodite, who shall henceforth be called Zephyritis! Come, you too, workers of the sea! For our admiral has ordered this shrine to be built in a secure harbor, allowing access at all times.

Devotion to the queen links up with the very ancient veneration of sailors for Aphrodite *Euploia*, "the goddess of safe navigation," patroness of mariners, and gives it even greater validity.

■ *The prestige of the major sanctuaries* ■ *The example of Delos*
■ *Callimachus'* Hymn IV ■ *Evidential value of his* Hymns
■ *The case of Delphi* ■ *The Athenian Pythais* ■ *The survival
of ancient cults*

The traditional gods therefore kept their devotees, and their service was not neglected. Actually, circumstances arose that favored the development of their shrines. Such was the case of Dodona, no doubt thanks to Pyrrhus and the sovereigns of Epirus, then to the confederacy of the Epirotes. Pilgrims would come to the old oracle of Zeus and consult it, writing their questions on leaden tablets, many of which have surfaced as a result of excavation. New buildings were erected to serve the city and the cults (for this and what follows, see pp. 315–16). New accommodation was built for the Panhellenic sanctuaries of Delphi and Olympia. These continued to be showered with a variety of offerings. At Delos, at the time of independence (in the years 314–166, see p. 49), then under Athenian domination reinstated by Rome (see p. 117), the temple of Apollo regained its prestige as a religious center in the Aegean. There the Antigonid, Ptolemaic, and Attalid sovereigns, eager to honor the god, vied with each other in generosity. They had porticoes built, sent precious offerings (duly recorded in inventories), instituted foundation festivals, and raised votive monuments. One of these, perhaps due to Demetrius Poliorcetes, is of an absolutely exceptional type. It is a narrow and elevated gallery 67 meters long, which sheltered an entire warship, and was dedicated to the god as a votive offering in memory of a naval victory. Two inner pillars each had its capital decorated with the forepart of a bull's body, hence the appellation of "Monument of the Bulls" that is given to this strange building. The temple of the Twelve Gods was also built in the third century, perhaps at a sovereign's expense. The League of the Islanders (*Nesiotai*: see p. 49, as above, concerning Delos) did not fail to institute its own festivals. Finally, the Roman generals and their great adversary, Mithridates Eupator, showed their piety toward the Delian deity. What motivated them was not the thought of the political gain that such a gesture would bring. It was an obvious urge to give concrete expression to widespread interest in a shrine whose renown went far beyond the Cyclades. Those whose action had an impact on that area found it normal to honor Delian Apollo.

An admirable evocation of such devotion and the celebrations associated with it is to be found in Callimachus' *Hymn IV*, written in about 275 BC at the request of Ptolemy II Philadelphus. Its elevated inspiration and rich imagery are served by an extraordinary verbal virtuosity. It sings of the island that unshaken withstands the blast of the winds and the shock of the waves, and, more welcoming to the flight of seagulls than to the trampling of horses' hooves, remains erect in the midst of a sea that unceasingly unrolls its surf on the shoreline, wiping away all the foam borne by the Icarian waves.

The poet then narrates the myth of Apollo's birth: how Leto, bearing the child whose delivery was thwarted by Hera's jealousy, found in tiny Delos the only haven that agreed to welcome her. He describes the miracle that, as soon as Apollo was born, changed for a while all places, everything that made up the divine child's environment, into gold, the gods' own metal. The final part of the poem recounts the never-ending succession of rites and sacred festivals that took place in the sanctuary:

> Island of a thousand altars, island of a thousand prayers, what mariner, what trader sailing the Aegean Sea, ever shunned your coast? No, never do the winds drive his ship on so forcefully, never does necessity so hasten its progress that his sailors forget to furl their sails immediately. Nor will they put out to sea again before having circled your mighty altar, lustily flogging it, and having bitten, hands tied behind their back, the olive tree's sacred trunk. These are the rites that the Delian nymph invented to amuse the child, and provoke Apollo's laughter.

These ritual gestures – lashing the sides of the altar, and leaving the imprint of a bite on the bark of the sacred tree near which the god was born – were evidently prescribed by a tradition centuries old. Their original meaning had faded into oblivion, but they were still preserved, kept alive by popular piety.

An unfortunate error of interpretation is current, relating to Callimachus' six *Hymns*. They are looked upon as closet exercises, the result of a laborious effort of bookish scholarship by an author whose sole purpose was to provide entertainment for a restricted circle of connoisseurs and literati. Recent research has shown that these *Hymns*, like their models the *Homeric Hymns*, were occasional pieces, each intended for recitation at the particular festival for which it had been written. They should be read as genuine documents, qualifying for parity with numerous sacred poems composed after being commissioned, which are mentioned in contemporary inscriptions, sometimes containing a transcription of the text. Every important festival was a setting for this traditional type of literature. It was heard in intoned recitation, the lyre providing a musical accompaniment; or in choral singing, as was the case with paeans and dithyrambs. When he wrote his *Hymns*, Callimachus was responding to a specific request. It might have come from the Lagid sovereign, like *Hymn IV* on the occasion of a Ptolemaic feast at Delos. Or it came from Cyrene, his native city, for the festival of Apollo (*Hymn II*), for a celebration in honor of Zeus in King Magas' time (*Hymn I*), or again for the feast of the Thesmophoria in honor of Demeter (*Hymn VI*). The text was closely adapted to the ceremony, with precise allusions to the ritual as it unfolded, and to the topographical and architectural environment of the festival, which architectural data allow us to verify. We thus possess texts of great brilliance and density, providing important evidence about Hellenistic religion.

Civic piety and frequent intervention by sovereigns managed between them to preserve the prosperous situation of traditional cult. New cities (see pp. 282–8) rivaled each other, especially in Asia Minor, in erecting splendid temples. Many buildings of various kinds, together with offerings, found their place in the great sanctuaries, thanks to the generosity of monarchs or the gratitude of devotees. In the third century, under Aetolian domination, Delphi knew a period of great prosperity that extended into the next century, only to fade away, it is true, in the course of the first century before our era. The *Sôteria*, a great festival that was instituted in memory of the sanctuary's miraculous preservation (thanks in no small measure to the Aetolians) during the Gallic invasion in the year 279, were celebrated with brilliance for a long time, on a par with the Pythian Games (also held at Delphi). Flamininus, then Aemilius Paullus, both of them Roman victors, did not fail to honor Apollo. But the wars against Mithridates and the depredations of Sulla (who demanded the surrender of the sacred treasures, which he had melted down into coinage) marked the start of the oracle's decadence. Yet Delphi had known happier days before these times of sore trial. In the second century Athens had financed the restoration of the Pythais, a rite that had fallen into obsolescence in the fourth century. Four times in 138/7 and 98/7 the city sent an official deputation named the Pythais to Delphi. It processed from the shrine of Pythian Apollo at the foot of the Acropolis, walking all the way to the seat of the oracle, via Eleusis, the saddle of the Cithaeron, and Boeotia. The signal prescribed for the expedition to start was to be heaven-sent, a flash of lightning over a peak on Mount Parnes, northwest of Athens, the shape of which, resembling a chariot-cab, had earned it the name of the Chariot, *Harma*. Lightning illuminated the Harma very rarely, since watching for the prodigy to happen was prescribed for only nine days in the year. When the event did occur, a procession of magistrates, priests, and the faithful assembled and started the journey, with an escort of armed ephebes proceeding on foot as well as on horseback. Arriving at Delphi, they were received in great pomp. The Pythaists acquitted themselves in their duties toward the god. They sang paeans and solemnly consecrated a tripod, the traditional offering to Delphic Apollo. Returning to Athens, the Pythais brought back on a chariot, in another tripod intended for the purpose, the sacred flame that had been obtained from Hestia's altar in the Delphic temple. It was an enviable honor to have taken part in a Pythais. We have a dedicatory inscription commemorating the fact that two Athenians, a brother and sister who had settled at Delos (where their statues were erected), participated in the Pythais of 106/5. The brother had been a Pythaist, and his sister a *kanephoros* (or bearer of an offering-basket), a role normally reserved for females in a sacred ceremony.

As can be seen, there is an abundance of documents testifying to the vitality of religious faith in the Hellenistic period. Why is there so much talk of its decadence or degradation? It may well happen that people allow their judgment to be clouded by an undeniable phenomenon, the rise of critical thought among philosophers and certain representative spirits of the intelligentsia, while an immense amount of evidence regarding the actual conduct of individuals and social groups is neglected. But what do we actually see? We notice communities preserving ancient rites at a heavy cost, or even establishing new ones. Particular care was taken to lay down the rules of cultic ceremonial in detail, and to ensure that they were engraved and displayed in public, so that no one would be unaware of them. Personal effort did not lag behind. Individuals emulated each other in their generosity toward the gods. Can one really believe that such expense and effort were meant only for show, and should be rated as attachment to empty formality, a survival from the outdated institutions of the past? It seems more appropriate to admit candidly that here we are faced with manifestations of a sincere piety that had lost none of the fervor of previous ages.

■ *The popularity of oracles: the case of Apollo* Koropaios
■ *Apollo's oracles in Anatolia: Clarus and Didyma* ■ *The oracle of Daphne in Syria* ■ *The mystery cults* ■ *The influence of Eleusis* ■ *Mysteries in Arcadia and Messenia* ■ *The Andania inscription* ■ *Dionysiac mysteries* ■ *The popularity of Dionysos* ■ Phallophoriai ■ *The mysteries of Samothrace*

To adapt Racine's rhetorical question about *miracles*, "What age was ever more fertile in *oracles*?" These flourished everywhere, first of all those of Apollo, the oracular god *par excellence*. Apart from Delphi, a number of sanctuaries specializing in prophecy were thriving in Greece proper. An example is the one at Corope in Magnesia, on the coast of the Gulf of Volos. Two sets of rules relating to its cult have been preserved, both very detailed, and dating from the end of the second century. They are two decrees passed by the city of Demetrias, to which the sanctuary of Apollo Koropaios was attached. In one of them the civic authorities, in agreement with the Confederacy of the Magnesians, take measures to ensure proper consultation of the oracle, following a ceremonial procedure deemed worthy of the god. It is specifically mentioned that such a rule is needed "because of the large number of strangers coming to the oracle for consultation." The intent of the other text, passed in the same year as the first, is to protect the trees and greenery growing on sacred property, forbidding woodcutting or cattle grazing on that land, under pain of a penalty. This is an edifying example, among many others, of the concern felt in the ancient world for preserving from any interference the natural state of sites that had been placed under divine protection.

The major Anatolian sanctuaries of Apollo were those of Clarus, not far from Ephesus, and Didyma, near Miletus. At Clarus, where excavation by the French has brought the temple to light, consultation took place underground. The rites happened at night, by lamplight, in a labyrinth of underground corridors and paved surfaces, vaulted by powerful arcades erected in the first century before our era. At Didyma, as was seen earlier (pp. 282–4), the immense and deep inner court was intended to accommodate pilgrims and people coming for a consultation. Such grandiose buildings had obviously been erected with large crowds of worshipers in mind. The Seleucids were well known for their devotion to Apollo. Seleucus I had founded in Syria the sanctuary of Daphne, near Antioch. Its renown was sufficiently widespread to merit the sarcasm of Christian polemicists like Clement of Alexandria and Gregory Nazianzus, who heaped on it the same scorn as they did on the sanctuaries of Delphi and Dodona. At Daphne, divination was dispensed as a direct result of the bubbling of sacred water, to which the name of Castalia had been given, after Delphi's illustrious fountain. Priests observed the movement and gurgling of the water, which they interpreted for visitors coming for a consultation. Nothing in this process was essentially different from ancient Greek practice: according to its tradition, any sign could be a manifestation of divine will and the lesson it wished to transmit. This could be the rustle of leaves caused by the wind, the flame and smoke on an altar, a bird's flight, the noise made by a spring, a victim's entrails, an inspired person's incoherent speech. There was still belief in the meaning of such signs, which soothsayers and prophets understood. Oracular shrines still attracted crowds. Pausanias mentions many of them in his *Periegesis*.

The popularity of mysteries developed alongside that of oracles. They did not constitute a novelty. Those of Demeter and Koré ("The Maiden," her daughter Persephone) at Eleusis had been in existence for a long while. An attempt to imitate them was possibly made at Alexandria. A district of that city was given the name of Eleusis, where coins have been found (admittedly dating from the period of the Antonines) showing the effigy of Triptolemus riding a serpent-drawn chariot, and bringing to the world the seed of wheat, Demeter's gift. A mistaken belief has for a long time taken Callimachus' *Hymn VI* to refer to Alexandrian festivals connected with Demeter. The occasion for which it was written is actually the Thesmophoria at Cyrene. Yet the existence at Alexandria of mysteries of Demeter and Koré remains a distinct possibility. Ptolemy I Sôter had invited from Eleusis Timotheus, a member of the ancient family of the Eumolpidae, to whom tradition assigned one of the two main priesthoods in the cult of the two goddesses. He was to act as advisor (*exegetés*) to Sôter in religious matters, and may have played a part in organizing ceremonies in honor of Alexandrian Demeter. It seems that at Pergamum also mysteries were part of the cult of Demeter and Koré. Pausanias (VIII, 31) notes the direct influence of the Eleusinian mysteries on those that were celebrated in honor of the Great Goddesses at Megalopolis in Arcadia. This probably occurred in the third century. Arcadia had another shrine in which mysteries were performed, at Lycosura, southwest of Megalopolis. It belonged to a divinity that was simply called *Despoina*, "The Mistress." She was reputed to be the daughter of Demeter and Poseidon. "Arcadians revered her more than any other divinity," says Pausanias. The text of a sacred law passed in the third century has been found there, with fragments of the marble cult statue erected in the second century by the Messenian sculptor Damophon. Not far from there in Messenia, at Andania, a township among the mountains, other mysteries were celebrated, on which a curious document provides information. This is a long inscription dating from 92/1 BC, which throws light on many allusions that Pausanias makes to ceremonies of this category in Book IV of his *Periegesis*. It lists a large number of meticulous prescriptions. Measures relating to public order, such as rules on the right of asylum in the sanctuary or on the supply of drinking water, are described side by side with precise instructions concerning the practice of cult. These include the wording of oaths, the description of sacrificial victims, the order of procession, the part played by priests and priestesses, vestments and ornaments to be worn – everything down to the smallest detail. One need look for no clearer demonstration of the importance that such ceremonies had for the fervent pilgrims who came in crowds to participate in the celebrations taking place in that remote valley.

Apart from that of Demeter, Dionysus' cult too had its mysteries. They were rare in mainland Greece in our period, but appear frequently on the islands and in Anatolia. Arrangements for their festivals and ceremonies were often made by fraternities or sororities (see below) called *thiasoi* (plural of *thiasos*). Membership of these often borrowed their appellation from Bacchus, one of the epithets of the god: they were then called Bacchants. Their rites had an orgiastic character, tracing its origin to an ancient tradition. Female *thiasoi* might celebrate these mysteries, and their reputation could very well suffer as a result: hence the famous senatorial edict of the year 186, forbidding the celebration of Bacchanalia, its avowed purpose being to protect the Roman people's morality. Dionysus' popularity, however, did not stop growing in the Hellenistic age. We have seen how a taste for the theater increased at that time, thanks to groups of Dionysiac artists. Ptolemy IV Philopator showed special interest in this cult. In an ordinance, the text of which has been preserved in a papyrus, he ordered those in charge of Dionysiac initiation in Egypt to bring to him the sacred documents they possessed, so that he might be acquainted with them. His grandfather, Ptolemy II Philadelphus, had already given a Dionysiac flavor to the great procession that he organized in Alexandria on the occasion of the *Ptolemaia* (in 271/0: see p. 72). Popular imagination had been fired by the example of Alex-

Plate 11   The Derveni Crater (Archaeological Museum, Thessaloniki).

Nothing gives a better idea of the wealth of the Hellenistic princes than the huge vase of gilded bronze that was found in the first half of the last century in a tomb north of Salonica. It has luxuriant decoration of fine quality, arranged with such art that it gives no impression of overabundance. Its themes are Dionysiac, appropriate for an urn (crater) *in which wine was mixed with water for distribution at banquets. Dionysus and Ariadne are shown on the bulging part of the vase, the nonchalant god stretching, with his right leg on the lap of his beloved. Maenads dance around them. Figures in the round, a satyr and a maenad, are seated on the shoulders of the urn. The friezes are made up of beasts and vine and ivy leaves. On the handles are lush palm-leaves and medallions of bearded masks. The structural limits of the ensemble are defined by the use of moldings taken from architectural decorations: hearts-and-darts, boss beading, ova, or vertical strips. This is a masterpiece in a really exceptional state of preservation. It is 90 centimeters tall and weighs 40 kilograms. An inscription on the ova along the edge reads: "I belong to Astion son of Anaxagoras, of Larissa." The owner, who lived at the end of the fourth century, was a Thessalian.*

ander, who thought that in the Orient, at Nysa in an Afghan valley (see p. 27), he had found a living recollection of the god's passage. Diodorus Siculus gives the essence of a whole body of literature that evoked Dionysus' path of conquest as far as India and his triumphal return journey toward Europe, amid an exotic and noisy procession. Southern Italy had, in addition, witnessed for a long period the association of Dionysus' cult with that of Demeter and Koré. This seems to have taken on an eschatological tinge in that environment: like Eleusinian initiation, it offered to its own devotees certain assurances regarding their fate after death. All of the above remains, on the whole, clouded in obscurity. Yet it allows us to understand the development of a sort of Dionysiac mysticism. The god of wine, who offered solace for humanity's trials in his banquets and drinking bouts, held out hope for the afterlife. Hence the great popularity of Dionysus, attested by the frequency of proper names deriving from the god's name: it has given us the first name Denis (or Dennis), for example. This explains as well the abundance of Dionysiac iconography, with its surfeit of depictions of the god. He appears in it as a young man with effeminate features, naked or wearing a long robe, long hair streaming down his shoulders, with an ivy-decorated band around his forehead. In one hand he holds the thyrsus, a long beribboned scepter topped with a pine cone, in the other a drinking vessel with a distinctive shape, a *cantharus*. He willingly accepts support from a young satyr, as his state of drunkenness has unsteadied his step. A panther accompanies him, a symbol of the retinue of wild beasts he brought back from his Asian expedition. Greek art was tireless in producing this ambiguous figure and his familiar companions: Ariadne his beloved, Sileni and Satyrs, Maenads and Bacchants, who were later to be joined by Cupids. His traditional festivals continued to be celebrated at the same time, with choruses singing the dithyramb, and performances of tragedies and comedies. Documentary evidence found at Delos is explicit enough. We learn from it that a strange rite, the *phallophoria*, was part of the Dionysiac solemn procession. It consisted in parading, on a chariot across the town, an enormous lifeless figure, made of wood and fabric stuffed with straw. This was a symbol of the god in the shape of a bird's body, whose neck and head had been replaced by a huge phallus. In this the old peasant belief asserted itself, which considered Dionysus to be a god of vegetation and renewal, preserving the fertility of the soil and the fecundity of flocks: hence the sexual symbolism of the phallus. Traditional aspects and new features thus combined in the complex cult of a divinity that satisfied the requirements of the great civic ceremonies and gave fulfillment to the aspirations of personal mysticism. Its popularity in a society with yearnings of such diversity can easily be understood.

The attraction that mysteries exerted on people of the time also serves to explain the appeal of another cult, that of the Cabiri of Samothrace. Already known in the fifth century, it enjoyed a considerable expansion in the Hellenistic age. In honor of those "Great Gods," whose precise nature is unknown, a sanctuary was set up in a narrow valley opening on the north coast of the island. On the steep-faced bank of a deep, narrow valley, buildings arose that were intended for initiation ceremonies. There was also a large rotunda, the Arsinoeum, which Queen Arsinoe (see pp. 58, 64), the wife of Lysimachus and

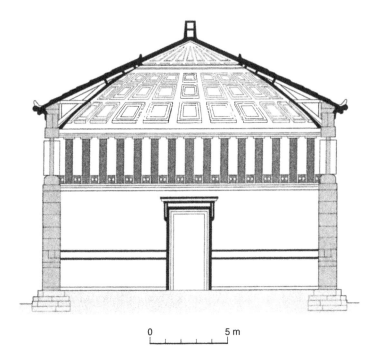

0   5 m

Figure 11 Samothrace: section of the Arsinoeum (from A. W. Lawrence, *Greek Architecture*, fig. 103).

This graphic restoration allows one to imagine what the inside of this vast circular building (nearly 17 meters in diameter) looked like. High above a wall that had no other opening than a door, a set of pilasters serving as intervals in a row of high bay windows supported a timber roof in the shape of a low paneled dome. The pilasters were Doric outside, Corinthian inside. The style of construction provided aeration as well as diffusion of light, which suited the purpose of an edifice housing altars. Substantial painted stucco decoration enhanced its appearance.

future wife of Ptolemy II Philadelphus, ordered to be built between 289 and 281. It was meant to afford shelter for altars. On the opposite side of the ravine was a long storied portico, a theater, and a quadrangular niche hollowed out in the ground on the slope leading to the bank. There stood on a ship's prow, in the middle of a water-filled basin representing the sea, the famous monument of Victory, which was erected in the second century. The sanctuary, judging from the state to which excavation has restored it, belongs entirely to the Hellenistic period. It illustrates the prosperity of the cult of the Cabiri, which flourished especially in the second century. People would come from far away to be initiated, from the islands of the Aegean, from Asia Minor, Alexandria, Cyrene, even from Italy. In 168 Perseus, king of Macedon, wished to take refuge there after his defeat at Pydna (see p. 116). The Cabiri were also looked upon as giving protection to sailors. As they shared this role with the Dioscuri, Castor and Pollux, the Great Gods ended up being confused with Helen's brothers, so much so that a temple was consecrated at Delos in 101 BC to "the Great Gods Dioscuri Cabiri of Samothrace." This was a case of contamination, of *syncretism* (to use a more recent term), of which there are many instances in this period, and which was to be a marked characteristic of the evolution of paganism under the Roman Empire.

■ *The gods of healing* ■ *Asclepius* ■ *His sanctuary at Cos*

As the mystery cults comforted the soul, the gods of healing brought help to the body. They too were in great favor in the Hellenistic age. The renown of the cult of Asclepius radiated from his major shrine at Epidaurus, which continued to attract devotees and produced a multitude of miraculous cures. Yet the god demanded something more than ritual purity of his visitors: a higher requirement, moral integrity. This is expressed in an epigram engraved on the temple (*Palatine Anthology*, XIV, 71): "Let him be pure, who enters the temple where incense burns. Purity is to have none but holy thoughts." In fact, while medical practice in the Hippocratic tradition was not foreign to the kind of healing that Asclepius provided, it is certain that psychical methods, like autosuggestion, also played a major part in it. The cult had spread from Epidaurus to other places, like Balagrae in Libya, near Cyrene, or Lebena in Crete. An epigram by Callimachus (*Epigram 54*) was to appear on a votive picture that a doctor named Aceson had consecrated in the sanctuary at Balagrae. He had promised the god that he would pay into the shrine's treasury a gift of 100 drachmae (1 mina) if his ailing wife was cured. He had discharged his obligation, something of which he reminds the god on the small painted panel that he caused to be hung in the shrine as an *ex-voto*. His brisk and playful tone is typical of the relationship of confident familiarity that the Greeks had with their gods: "You are receiving, Asclepius, the amount of the debt that Aceson contracted in terms of a vow on behalf of his wife Demodicé: make a note of it. However it may be, were you perchance to forget and to claim a mina from him, let it be known that this picture will attest payment."

At that time the most prestigious sanctuary of Asclepius was the one at Cos, Hippocrates' birthplace. His disciples and descendants ran a school there that prospered and attracted crowds. At some distance from the city, on a hill's gentle slope, where a beneficent spring gushed forth (an indispensable element in a center of healthcare), a terrace had been set up on which a temple and its monumental altar were erected at the end of the fourth century. The poet Herondas has described the setting humorously, in a short comedy entitled *Women visiting Asclepius*. Two housewives of modest standing arrive at the sanctuary to sacrifice a cock and consecrate a votive picture as a token of gratitude for someone's recovery. They admire the marble statues of Asclepius and Hygieia (Health), his daughter, standing by the altar, which the sons of the great Praxiteles had carved twenty or thirty years before. They are ecstatic at the sight of other works of art: a group showing a child clasping the neck of a goose, a Coan woman's picture whose closeness to the real-life original overwhelms them. They enter the temple, as a consecrated servant, a *neokoros*, has just opened its door. There they behold a marvelous painting by Apelles, depicting the preparation of a sacrifice: its realism, creating the illusion of life, fills them with enthusiasm. They finally leave their money offering "in the mouth of the serpent" made of bronze that serves as a cover for the alms-box, and depart highly satisfied. They will feast at home on the cock whose throat they have just cut, without forgetting to donate one of its legs to the *neokoros*, who thus obtains his wage in kind. Nothing is more realistic than this pen picture, in dialogue form, of a customary scene of popular religion!

The sanctuary at Cos was enlarged considerably in the second century to accommodate more comfortably the increasing crowd of pilgrims: two extensive terraces were added to the first. This meant a complete change in the overall plan. At the lower level was a vast rectangular terrace measuring 100

Figure 12 Cos: plan of the sanctuary of Asclepius (from Schatzmann-Herzog, *Kos I*, plan 37).

The sanctuary, facing north, occupied three terraces placed at three superimposed levels and dominating the coastal plain, some distance from the city. There had been at the start, on the middle terrace, an open-air cult, having an altar (A) turned toward the east, following tradition. In the third century a small temple was built for the cult statue, west of the altar. Herondas' two housewives, featured in the text above, visit that temple (B). A colonnade was raised at that time round the altar. In the second century, a monumental design added the other two terraces. The lower one featured a vast rectangular esplanade (C) surrounded on three sides by a chambered portico. In the middle of the north wall a long porch (D) served as an entrance for visitors. In the axis, more or less, of that entrance a stairway, built through the retaining wall of the middle terrace, gave access to the temple and altar. Further south the uppermost terrace (E), buttressed by a powerful retaining wall, was also framed on three sides by a portico, this one simply an ambulatory. Its fourth side gave an unencumbered view of the sanctuary, the plain, and the sea. In the middle of the esplanade, crowning the overall perspective, a new temple of Asclepius (F) was built. Larger and more richly endowed than the first one, and preceded by a peristyle, it faced the north and the monumental stairway giving access to the upper terrace in the axis of the ground plan. The wish to organize a grandiose ensemble is evident. The design was based on symmetry and the distribution of architectural mass at three levels on the slopes; but out of respect for ritual tradition, the primitive altar of Asclepius preserved its original eastern orientation. At a later date, a third temple (G) was raised east of the altar.

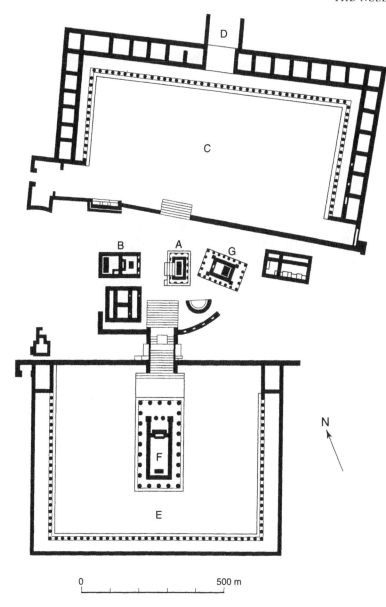

0   500 m

meters by 50. Its limits were a retaining wall buttressing the original terrace, and a large portico extending over the three remaining sides. This was the reception area, reached by a ramp and an entrance within the portico. From there a wide stairway in the entrance axis led to the area of the altar and temple. Finally, at a still higher level, a third terrace, dominating the whole complex, was the counterpart of the first, inverting the arrangement of its components.

Plate 12 Sacrifice of a bull (Musée du Louvre, Paris; photo RMN, Hervé Lewandowski).

In the presence of the seated Asclepius and his daughter Hygieia (who is standing) is a family that has arrived to sacrifice a bull, the head of which is seen in the background – a servant holds it. The father lays on the altar offerings (grain or cakes) that he has taken from a flat basket held out to him by a naked assistant. The rest of the family is further to the right: two women with a little girl, and a baby in the arms of a nurse.

It had a portico on three sides, the fourth opening onto the sanctuary and the countryside, above a sturdily built retaining wall. In the center of the topmost terrace a new temple was built, larger than the older one; it had a fine Doric peristyle. It was oriented toward the original altar, situated on the middle terrace, to which it was linked by a monumental stairway, its upper steps forming a façade for the new temple. This ample architectural composition was a response to a new trend, with its three successive terraces, the framework of each of the two porticoes, and an attempt at symmetry brought out by the axial position of the stairways and the upper temple. It was a prelude to the majestic distribution of components that the Romans favored in Imperial times, and of which the shrine of Fortuna at Praeneste, built in Sulla's time (see the description of plate 3 on p. 137), was to be the first impressive illustration on Italian soil.

■ *Foreign gods: the example of Serapis* ■ *The statue of the god*
■ *His cult: epigrams by Callimachus* ■ *Serapis' shrines at Delos*
■ *The cult of Isis* ■ *Aretalogies* ■ *The Great Mother and Attis*
■ *The Syrian cults: Adonis* ■ *Local nature of cults*

Asclepius was not the only god of healing. Many other divinities, gods or heroes, also played this part. Such was the case of Serapis (or Sarapis), an original creation of this period. It deserves special attention, being an excellent example of the manner in which the Greeks, making the acquaintance of barbarian peoples whom they had conquered, occasionally borrowed divinities from them that they placed in the Hellenic Pantheon. This enrichment of Greek religion by foreign imports is considered, with good reason, one of the major achievements of the Hellenistic age. Yet it is necessary to examine the individual modalities of these borrowings. The annexation of Serapis is revealing in this regard. The origin of the new cult is the subject of contradictory traditions, making one or other of the first three Lagid sovereigns responsible for introducing it. But reliable evidence demonstrates that it had been established as early as Ptolemy I Sôter's time (see pp. 67–9). A curious text in Tacitus' *Histories* (IV, 83–4) tells us that the king had a dream urging him to have the statue of the god removed from Sinope on the Black Sea. It was to be found in a temple in this town. Having consulted the Delphic oracle, Ptolemy persuaded (with some difficulty) the inhabitants of Sinope to grant him possession of the divine effigy. For them it portrayed Zeus, but a "Chthonian" Zeus, like Hades master of the underworld and conjoined with Persephone. The statue was brought to Alexandria and placed in the old Egyptian quarter of Rhacotis, where a temple was built for it on the site of a small native shrine of Serapis and Isis. The name Serapis, Egyptian *Osor-Hapis*, belonged to a native divinity combining two originally quite distinct divine figures. These were Osiris, Isis' famous husband, and the celebrated bull Apis, a living animal-god that the Egyptians worshiped at Memphis and whose mummies they kept in the immense underground necropolis of the Serapeum.

The name of Serapis was therefore given to the new god who had been imported from Sinope to Alexandria. This was the only Egyptian feature he had in his changed environment: in every other respect he was Greek. Various documents tell us what his statue looked like. It resembled those of Zeus, Hades, or Asclepius. It had a majestic head, long-haired and heavily bearded, with lush vertical locks streaming down his forehead. A sort of high, more or less cylindrical basket sat on it by way of a headdress. This was the *calathos*, also known by the Latin term *modius* (bushel), with a decoration of olive branches or ears of wheat. The god was dressed in Greek fashion. He was seated on a throne, near which was Cerberus, the monstrous dog of the Underworld. Other depictions, on Imperial coins, show Serapis standing half-naked, a scepter in his hand and a *modius* on his head, Cerberus crouching at his feet: a representation looking like those of Jupiter without the *modius* and Cerberus. The original statue was reputed to be by Bryaxis, a famous fourth-century sculptor who had (around 350) worked on the Mausoleum of Halicarnassus. He may very well have created for Sinope, in the second half of the fourth century, the effigy of Zeus-Hades (*Jupiter-Dis*) to which Tacitus refers. At any rate, though renamed Serapis in Egypt, his appearance did not seem strange to Greek eyes in any respect.

We have two ancient pieces of evidence concerning Serapis' cult. These are dedicatory epigrams by Callimachus on the occasion of two separate offerings made to the god. One of the offerings was a twenty-burner lamp. This means that it produced a light of exceptional brightness which, in the poet's words, outshone the evening star. The other epigram is about a Cretan mercenary's consecration of his bow and quiver after the military campaign that Ptolemy III Euergetes waged on the city of Euhesperides in Cyrenaica at the start of his reign (see p. 73). Neither of these offerings had an exotic character; they could just as well have been made to any Greek god. The cult in honor of Serapis, in spite of the god's name, is therefore a Greek cult that was originally intended for the Greeks settled on Egyptian soil. In earlier times the Greeks of Libya had instituted the cult of Zeus-Ammon, a Greek cult belonging *in proprio* to Cyrenaica. The Libyan cult does not reveal any weakening of Hellenic religious tradition, or a dilution of that tradition as a result of foreign contact. Nor does the later cult. It was not the result of fusion or, to employ a much-used term, of "syncretism" between Greek and Egyptian elements. All it demonstrates is the strong power of assimilation inherent in Hellenism, then as in previous ages.

Sanctuaries of Serapis were very numerous. They were found at the very start in Egypt, in the city of Alexandria and its suburban area, as in the township of Canopus, near the mouth of the Nile that was nearest to the city; next in lands outside Egypt, where the new god met with quite a degree of success. The case of Delos is especially significant, as the remains of three sanctuaries have been found on that island. Two

Plate 13 Isis standing, with the baby Horus on one arm (Cyrene Museum).

This statue, found at Cyrene, is in a Greek style. The model chosen for the goddess's body, as well as the head, conforms to the taste of the high Hellenistic period. A ringlet on each side of the neck is the only exotic feature. The ornament on top of the head belongs to the Isaic repertory. The baby Horus on his mother's arm is like the small Dionysus on the arm of Praxiteles' Hermes holding Dionysus.

were private, the older one having been founded as early as the first half of the third century. The third, founded in the second century, was a public sanctuary, where the city was responsible for the activities connected with the cult of the god. In it Serapis was associated with other Egyptian divinities: Isis, Anubis, or Harpocrates. We have little information on the last two: their role was quite minor. Isis, on the contrary, enjoyed great popularity, like Serapis, in the Hellenistic world.

By rights an Egyptian divinity, she too was adopted, dressed in Greek clothes, by the Greeks. Yet her statues sometimes preserved a number of features borrowed from Pharaonic representations of her. There was her headdress with two long vertical plumes, rising above a cow's horns enclosing a medallion. She was draped in a tight-fitting dress with an "Isiac" knot, foreign to Hellenic style, on the breast. But features of this kind were not exempt from variation. For example, an iconographic pattern like that of Isis *Euploia* (cf. Aphrodite *Euploia*, p. 325) or *Pelagia* ("of the high sea"), protectress of mariners, shows no trace of an Egyptian origin and is apt to portray any female divinity among the Greeks. The texts at our disposal repay careful study. They are either hymns or texts in prose listing (and extolling) the various powers or virtues (*aretai*) of the goddess: hence the name of *aretalogies* given to these documents. They belong to a diversity of periods, ranging from the second century before our era to the late Imperial age. They are found in Egypt as well as in the most varied areas of the ancient world: in the Cyclades (at Ios and Andros), in Thrace (at Maroneia), in Asia Minor, or in Cyrenaica. There are reminiscences of them in authors like Diodorus Siculus and Apuleius. Such texts mention Isis as a patroness of humanity, on which she has bestowed the benefits of civilization. These include language, the invention of writing, law, justice, reverence for one's parents, the unveiling of the mysteries, alleviation of sickness. She also appears as a cosmic divinity, ruling the movement of the stars and the march of the universe. Few elements in these lists of divine benefactions give evidence of any borrowing from Egyptian tradition. We are dealing here with a commonplace of Hellenic sacred literature, applied on such occasions to a new divinity. What is without precedent, however, is the care taken to attribute to Isis all manifestations of divine power by acknowledging her full authority over the whole universe. This reveals, no doubt, a trend toward monotheism that will become more evident under the Empire.

A number of other foreign gods were similarly given a cult in Hellenistic cities. Such a god would receive either a private cult, tended by an individual or an association, or a public one. Some had been instituted for a very long time, like that of the Mother of the Gods, Cybele (also called the Great Mother), whose temple in Athens had been used since the Classical age as the official repository of State records. This Anatolian divinity had been fully integrated in the ranks of the Greek gods. Little by little, she brought in her wake other personalities belonging to her legend, like Attis, the young man wearing a Phrygian cap who castrated himself, or the strange Agdistis. But their audience remained for a long time very limited. That story of castration did not appeal to the Greeks, and her eunuch priests, the Galli, were always looked upon with mistrust. Yet specialists in religious problems showed interest in this cult: thus Ptolemy I's advisor, the Athenian Timotheus (see p. 330), devoted a study to it, which is referred to, many centuries later, by Arnobius, the Christian apologist. The Syrian goddess Atargatis also stayed on the fringe. She was honored at Delos, a port frequented by Phoenician merchants and Syrian Greeks. But it is clear that she was almost totally confused with Aphrodite, whose name appears in dedications side by side with the original Oriental name, and even ends up replacing it sometimes. The cult of Adonis, originally a Syrian divinity, was introduced to Alexandria, where Queen Arsinoe II celebrated in the royal palace (around the year 272) the feast of the *Adonia*, described in Theocritus' *Idyll XV* (see p. 268). Theocritus' account illustrates the high degree to which the Oriental cult had been Hellenized. The people saw the statues of Aphrodite and Adonis on an embowered banquet couch, surrounded by abundant offerings of flowers and delicacies, after the manner of the *Theoxenia*, the traditional sacred banquets. A female narrator would chant a hymn, in conformity with ancient usage. In short, whenever foreign divinities were admitted into the circle of Hellenic polytheism, they arrived under the usual appearance of Greek divinities. Their ritual was adapted to the requirements of an age-old tradition: for the people would not agree without unease to any formal modification of it. It had always had a welcoming attitude toward newcomers, but would attire them in its own style, essentially depriving them in this way of whatever might be a source of surprise or scandal.

Neither should one forget the predominantly local nature of cults in Greek religion: a fact that makes generalization rather futile. The piety of the faithful always found expression in the restricted environment of thousands of public and private sanctuaries, where centuries-old rites were carefully preserved. Every occasion prompted such zealous piety to create new shrines. There was a proliferation of heroic and rustic cults. The landscape paintings of Pompeii give a good idea of this. The Roman villas of this town are full of stucco decorations recalling the surrounding countryside. Their so-called "picturesque" reliefs (sometimes wrongly termed "Alexandrian") depict rural scenes. They portray the natural environment of the Mediterranean (never the landscapes of the Egyptian Delta), within which one always finds altars, statues of divinities, or small shrines. These appear in bucolic poems as well, or in the countless dedications to the gods of the woodland and the fields that figure in the *Anthology*. For the Greek psyche, nature remained peopled with divinities whose presence it would notice on foreign soil as well as in its own land. That was why the Greeks had no difficulty showing reverence for a barbarian divinity in an environment that was unfamiliar to them, provided they found a way of equating that foreign god with one of their own. This explains how Alexander and his companions had no difficulty recognizing Dionysus in the local god at Nysa (see p. 27), a township nestled in the valley of the Himalayas. A host of legends flourished as a result of this episode. The same explanation applies to Greeks who traveled in Upper Egypt finding it natural to engrave their laudatory epigrams or their *proskynemata* (formulas of worship, plural of *proskynema*: cf. pp. 26–7, the question of *proskynesis*) on the pylons of Egyptian temples. This was common at Philae (cf. Catilius' inscription, p. 318). The Greeks' readiness to assimilate exotic divinities to their own gods made the Hellenization of regions like Thrace or Anatolia much easier. It was enough to dress up local gods in Greek or Hellenized garb, to give them an anthropomorphic look, for the Greeks to join the ranks of native worshipers, thus helping these cults to survive in their infinite variety.

■ *The criticism of traditional religion* ■ *Euhemerus* ■ *Limits to his influence* ■ *The part played by mythographers* ■ *Epicurus' teaching* ■ *The religion of the Stoics* ■ *The cult of* Tyché, *Fortune* ■ *Superstition and magic* ■ *The cult of the dead* ■ *Salutations to the dead* ■ *The evidence of epigrams for eschatological beliefs* ■ *"Passports for the world beyond"* ■ *The architecture of tombs* ■ *Funeral rites and offerings* ■ *The sincerity of belief in the afterlife*

One can best comprehend the reality of religious beliefs by referring to their concrete manifestations: offerings, sacrifices, festivals, cultic buildings, and sacred laws. For the Hellenistic age our evidence is so plentiful and precise that one cannot doubt the permanence and vitality of faith among the vast majority of Greeks living at that time. Some enlightened minds, however, had been led by the teaching of philosophers to ask themselves questions on every kind of subject, including belief in the existence of the gods. Various forms of criticism emerged, ranging from a rationalistic interpretation of myths to skepticism and radical atheism. The influence of such views remained restricted to a narrow circle of cultured minds, bringing no noteworthy change in the behavior of the popular masses: but had it been otherwise in the case of Anaxagoras or Heraclitus? Let us survey briefly the main features of that intellectual movement.

The most striking one is no doubt Euhemerism, which had a great resonance, direct or indirect. Euhemerus, who lived at the end of the fourth century and the beginning of the third, had written a strange work, a sort of philosophical novel, entitled *A Sacred Story*. It gave an account of an imaginary journey among islands of the Indian Ocean, the main one among them being named Panchaea. Its inhabitants were a composite population, where native people lived side by side with immigrants coming from India, Scythia, and even Crete. It had Cretan priests for leaders. In the splendid temple of Zeus Triphylius, an inscription engraved on a gold stele recounted the history of the ancient kings of the land, who were none other than the traditional gods of Greece, Uranus, Cronus, Zeus, whose myths were presented as historical fact, devoid of any marvelous element. Zeus in particular appeared in the inscription as a wise and benevolent sovereign, who had journeyed all over the world and spread his benefactions amid humanity, before going to Crete and dying there. Grateful populations had then raised temples and altars in his honor and had made a god of him. Euhemerus thus propounded a historical explanation of the religious phenomenon. Gods were simply mortals of ancient times, whose power and prestige caused them to be looked upon as superior beings after their death, worthy of being honored with a cult. This simply meant secularizing a fundamental idea of Greek religion, whereby the Immortals were of a kind distinct from human beings. Euhemerus was therefore considered an atheist in ancient times. But few of his readers understood all the implications of his historical interpretation. Most of them were content to place the current myths in a historical framework, without questioning the existence or power of the gods whose terrestrial adventures were now presented as those of kings who had actually lived in our world. The reality of the times, after all, with the institution of a royal cult that was very much alive, was no incentive for a skepticism that was based on a hypothetical memory of the past. This is why we may say that mythographers like Dionysius Skytobrachion (see p. 320), who recounted Dionysius' adventures all over the Orient and Africa, contributed in no way to the obliteration of traditional religion. This is evident in the case of Diodorus Siculus. He offers an abundant compilation of mythographic literature in the first books of his *Historical Library*. The essential part of what is now known about Euhemerus is due to the evidence he gives on such writers. Far from behaving like a freethinker, Diodorus is careful to emphasize in his history whatever can be interpreted as a reward for piety or as chastisement for sacrilege. Two centuries later Pausanias, who was an avid reader of the mythographers, was no less pious a man, showing great attachment to the rites inherited from ancestral times, and in no way doubting the existence of the gods.

Nor should one overestimate the destructive role that philosophers may have played in this respect, for their speculations reached a restricted number of people. Their reasoning led to a great variety of conclusions, with little impact on popular beliefs. Of the two major schools of thought that arose and developed in Hellenistic times, only the Epicurean was of a kind that could encourage unbelief. This can be seen from Lucretius' fiery outbursts against religion. For, to use his words, before Epicurus, "It used to oppress humanity, showing its horror-striking and menacing face from the heights of heaven". . . But now it is "in its turn laid low and trodden under foot: a victory that uplifts us to the skies," as a result of Epicurus' victorious assault. Such eloquent appeals had in fact no effect on the masses. In Rome, as in the Greek East, they kept faith in their old superstitions and the comforting hopes that these held out to them. Lucretius, after all, went beyond the genuine teachings of Epicurus, who never thought of denying the existence of the gods, but declared them uninterested in the fate of mortals. Why then should mortals show any concern for gods? This was the conclusion that could obviously be drawn from such views, and the disciples of the master did not fail to do so. But a certain moral strength was needed to renounce the help that religion could give, at the same time as ridding oneself of the fear that it inspired. This explains why Epicurus' flock was never very large.

Quite different was the viewpoint of the other school, that of the Stoa, or Stoicism. Its successive leaders, Zeno of Citium, Cleanthes of Assus, Chrysippus of Soli (in Cilicia), then Panaetius of Rhodes, each introduced his own particular nuance into the school's doctrine. But all propound a global and rational explanation of the universe, which they show obeying the rule of Providence extending over everything. According to Cleanthes, whose *Hymn to Zeus* has survived, this supreme divinity presides over a coherent order of things within which good and evil have their place, justified in both cases. Hence the moral principle that is the glory of Stoicism: a lucid distinction between "what depends on us" and what is beyond our control, and as a result, an uncomplaining acceptance of what we cannot prevent. This was a challenging morality, paired with a sublimated theology, totally in conflict with Hellenic anthropomorphism, and leading in the final analysis to monotheism. For, in the words of Servius, the Latin compiler, commenting on a text of Vergil's *Georgics* (I, 5), "The Stoics say that there is only one god, one and the same divine power, to which various names are given, according to the role that it plays."

In this case too, these were views held by intellectuals, and unlikely to captivate the crowd. Yet they contributed to widespread acceptance of the idea that a superior power rules the march of the universe, favoring or frustrating human designs. The name usually given to this power was not Providence, but Fortune, *Tyché*. There was nothing new in this. Homer had bequeathed the notion that Fate is inescapable, and even prevails against divine wishes. But from that time on the human mind became accustomed to taking Fortune into account, whether individual destinies or those of cities and empires were concerned. This abstract entity became a principle of explanation that history placed above the role of human causes, which it favored or thwarted in an unforeseeable manner. Already in the second century this point of view can be seen in the historian Polybius, but more clearly a century later in Diodorus Siculus, who, to stimulate his reader's interest, emphasizes on every occasion the *paradoxical* (that is, contrary to expectation) nature of the events he recounts. The ancient Greek propensity to deify allegories did not fail to assert itself in the case of Fortune, as it had done before in that of Victory, *Niké*. Temples were built in her honor. Pausanias mentions many of these in the Peloponnese: at Hermione, Argos, Megalopolis, Elis.

He also saw the one at Thebes, showing Tyché holding her child Plutus (Wealth) in her arms. Among new cities Antioch, soon after its foundation by Seleucus I, ordered from one of Lysippus' pupils, Eutychides of Sicyon, a statue of the city's Tyché. Surviving copies allow us to imagine the impression it made on the beholder. A maiden with a queenly air, draped in a cloak, is seen seated on a rock, her legs crossed. She appears nonchalant and relaxed, holding in one hand a sheaf of ears of grain, a token of wealth, and wearing on her head a wreath of towers, symbolizing the city ringed with fortifications. At her feet, half of his body emerging from the water, is the allegorical figure of the river Orontes, arms outstretched like those of a swimmer. This work of art was conceived as a set of symbols, without its variety of implied meanings causing it to appear contrived. In the same manner, philosophical abstractions sometimes appear in the midst of temples, the work of the artist's hand – the result of a mind-set peculiar to the Greek tradition.

In a direction opposite to that of such speculations, ordinary people, in many cases cultured minds as well, continued to have recourse to superstitious practices and magic. There was nothing new in this, but evidence of such occurrences proliferates in the period under study. People would place symbols on their doors or houses that were supposed to bring good luck or turn away misfortune (hence, in the latter case, the term *apotropaia*, "things that turn away"). One of the most widespread was the phallus, sometimes provided with wings, as is seen at Delos. The caps and star of the Dioscuri are also found, as well as Heracles' club. Again at Delos, the mosaic bearing the "Symbol of Tanit," in the vestibule of the House of the Dolphins, plays the part of an *apotropaion*: contact with barbarian civilizations could lead to reverence for one or another of their specific traits, as something endowed with a mysterious power. Sometimes an inscription conspicuous for its serious tone would be added, like this one, attested in various places: "Zeus' son, Heracles *Kallinikos* ['The Victorious One': cf. Seleucus II, p. 78] lives here: into this place Evil cannot penetrate." Charms, carriers of magic words or symbols, were supposed to have a protective power, especially if they were cut in precious or semiprecious stone, endowed with its own virtue. Egyptian influence is evident here. Bronze, lead, or terracotta figurines, pierced with pins or nails, were used to cast a spell; a number of these have been found in the course of excavations. Tablets made of marble or metal (particularly lead, which lent itself more readily to engraving), were used for curses. A famous literary text introduces us to a magic scene. This is Theocritus' *Idyll II*, *The Female Magicians*, in which a love-sick young woman tries to bring back her unfaithful lover by means of incantations and philters. She invokes Selene (the Moon) and Hecate, a fearful divinity who was also the patroness of Medea the magician. In Book III of Apollonius of Rhodes' *Argonautica*, Medea is depicted preparing her spells for Jason. On her advice, Jason sacrifices to Hecate before facing the ordeals against which Medea's magical powers will successfully arm him. Such dramatic adventures did not arouse skepticism among readers who were accustomed to the superstitious practices that were current in their environment.

Simnilar practices also occurred, as can be expected, in the cult of the departed. Thus, to quote one example, in an epigram from the area of Alexandria, dating from the second or first century, the deceased woman addresses the passer-by in these words: "Stop, and say in a loud voice, 'This is the tomb of Aliné,' then wish me goodbye." The simple fact of uttering a name in a loud voice was supposed to have a magical power, literally to recall the deceased one, to whom it would, as it were, restore a degree of presence. This is why the text goes on to say, "May you in your turn obtain a twofold benefit from a similar tribute!" Another epigram from Egypt, coming from the upper valley of the Nile and belonging to the same period, ends with a conversation between the passer-by and the deceased man, an officer named Ptolemy, buried with his son Menodorus.

"Well! Hail to you, valiant Ptolemy, even among the dead!"
"Invoke my son's name as well, traveler, and proceed on your way."

This ancient belief (already attested in the *Odyssey*, Book XI) in the evocative power of the human voice explains why so many funerary epigrams are in dialogue form. By addressing the passer-by they encouraged him to give a courteous response, uttering in a loud voice the name of the deceased person.

Appearing in such large numbers, these texts, whether preserved in the *Anthology* (Book VII being entirely devoted to them) or engraved on stone, provide instruction on Greek beliefs relating to the afterlife. Some are a reflection of the skeptical attitude of certain philosophers in religious matters, like *Epigram 13* by Callimachus. The passer-by engages in a dialogue with the tomb:

"Do you shelter Charidas' repose?"
"If it is the son of Arimmas the Cyrenaean that you mean, I do shelter him."
"Charidas, what is the Underworld like?"
"Very deep darkness."
"How does one ascend back to earth from it?"
"This is a lie."
"How about Pluto?"
"A fable."
"Woe to humanity!"
"I have nothing else that is true to tell you."

One feels like discerning in this a resonance of the negative teaching of Theodorus, called the Atheist, a philosopher then living at Alexandria. A similar tone is found in a formulaic utterance in the vein of the Epicurean tradition. Often repeated in the Imperial period, it conveys perfect detachment, a total indifference to life and death: "I was not, I was born; I was, I am not any more: that is all. Anyone who says the contrary is a liar: never again shall I be." But the large majority of epigrams demonstrate real confidence in a form of afterlife, imagined in various ways. Some believe that the soul flies away in the air, far from its terrestrial remains, as in this text from Hermione in Argolis (late third to early second century): "Ether received your soul, Lysixenus; the earth holds your body here, now consumed." The soul's departure for the world of the dead is more often mentioned, whether that lies in the underground realm of Hades, or in some imprecise location. Thus the myth of the Islands of the Blest, already known to Pindar, was often to reappear in funerary iconography in the Roman period. The epitaph of Sosibius, an Egyptian Greek, goes further, since it promises him admittance to a seat by the side of the Judge of the Lower World: "I shall enter the dim halls of Pluto and Persephone, to take my seat by Minos, among the Blest. As for you, passer-by, after greeting me in a loud voice, proceed on your way, your heart at peace, your safety assured."

The bas-relief adorning the tomb of the Rhodian philosopher Hieronymus attempts to illustrate that underground world, with Hades and Persephone as its central figures. Many in their anxiety wished to be reassured by a guide's company or help provided by a talisman as they tried to find their way in it after death. To respond to such a yearning was the objective of the mysteries, of which we spoke earlier (see pp. 330–4), as well as certain teachings that are hypothetically linked with Orphism, and had already been known in the Classical age. The gold leaves found in Hellenistic tombs at Petelia in southern Italy, or at Eleuthernae in Crete, are "passports for the Great Beyond," with the same mysterious text engraved on them as the Pharsalus gold leaf featured in the fourth century. In other texts, the help of some Underworld divinity was expected. They received prayers requesting protection for the deceased person. The effigy of a draped woman, sculptured in marble, up to half of its height, stood on the tombs of Cyrene, as though she was emerging from the soil in which she remained up to her hips. Although there is no inscription to enlighten us, it is likely that we have here a representation of Persephone, Queen of the Shadows, sovereign of the underground realm, unveiling her face to the person who arrives to join her. Sometimes the gesture of revelation is merely sketched, and the goddess's features are only transparent. Sometimes again, instead of a face, a rounded surface, devoid of features, emerges from the torso: it wears a veil and has hair, as though to keep the mystery of the world beyond in view of the living. This strange rite survived for centuries at Cyrene, with remarkable continuity.

No less care than in previous ages was shown in providing the remains of the dead with a shelter. People in exalted positions followed the example of Mausolus, the dynast of Halicarnassus (see p. 340), and caused storied tombs that would be their own to be erected, with rich architectural ornamentation.

Thus we have near Ephesus the quadrangular mausoleum of Belevi (third century), or near Agrigentum the monument of Theron (as it is wrongly called) dating from the first century before our era. The Agrigentum tomb heralds a style of building similar in height to that of the mausoleum that a Gallic family was to erect in Augustus' time at Glanum near Saint-Rémy-de-Provence (see p. 285). It is no surprise to recognize favourite themes of Hellenistic art in the various reliefs decorating the Saint-Rémy mausoleum. They had reached the Rhone valley via Rome and Marseille. These storied funerary constructions must have been a common sight, since Philo of Byzantium, as we have seen (p. 302), advised the defenders of a besieged city to use them as secondary fortresses outside the city walls. Many examples of another type of sumptuous tomb have been found in Macedonia: this is the tumulus, a vast earthen mound covering a funerary chamber, with an antechamber and an exterior court. Though the intention had been to place it below ground level, out of the sight of passers-by, the façade visible from the court was sometimes richly adorned with stone or stucco architectural motifs and paintings, as in the lordly tombs of Vergina or Langada. Frescoes might also be painted inside the chamber, as at Kazanlak in Thrace. Elsewhere tombs were built in the shape of chapels, with stone doors protecting the compartments in which the remains of the deceased had been laid to rest. This was the case at Cyrene, where such collective monuments were found in great numbers in the necropolises extending around the city. At Cyrene again, tombs were hollowed out in a rocky cliff or in the vertical walls of a quarry. A succession of chambers sometimes went deep underground, while the exterior façade, remaining visible, could certainly be adorned with a pediment, an entablature, columns or pilasters, cut straight into the rock. The same arrangement is found in certain necropolises of Alexandria.

Inside the funerary monuments the corpses were placed on couches that were often cut in bedrock, or in sarcophagi sometimes ornamented with relief work, like the famous so-called "Sarcophagus of Alexander" (see plate 1), which was actually sculpted at Sidon in the late fourth century for a local prince. Cremation was, however, a widespread practice: the ashes were collected in a metal or earthenware vase or in a leaden urn not supported by a base. Offerings were often left in the tombs. These would be furniture, weapons, jewels, vases, or terracotta statuettes. The quality of such appointments varied with the deceased person's means. They accompanied the dead in their last abode. This was both a tribute from their survivors and testimony to the prolongation (in a manner of speaking) of their way of life on earth. This constant feature of Hellenistic behavior demonstrates an opinion of the afterlife that was quite widespread in that period, and recognition of the dignity of the dead. The idea had been expressed by Aristotle in his dialogue *Eudemus*, as reported by Plutarch, quoting the following text from it in his *Consolation to Apollonius* (ch. 27):

Not only do we consider the dead happy and blessed, but we believe it is impious to lie or utter slanderous words about them. For they have become better and more powerful beings. This is such a firmly established belief among us, and comes from such far-off Antiquity, that none is able to say when it started or who was the first to institute it. This is because it has existed without interruption throughout countless ages.

There was no more solid foundation for that period's religious faith.

■ *The marginal character of innovations in the area of religion during the Hellenistic period* ■ *Evolution but not revolution: an unbroken continuity with the previous age*

The account above has been able to describe Hellenistic religion only in very broad outline. Documents on the subject are overabundant, and each cult has to be considered in its own particular configuration, which makes synthesis extremely hard. A large number of interesting facts, nuances that deserve careful attention, have had to be left out. The aim has been to stress, in this area as in that of the political life of cities, the phenomenon of continuity with previous periods, explained by the permanence of the city as an institution. What remained constant was, as before, the opinion of the large majority. People remained faithful to their gods, just as they stayed attached to the environment of their daily life, to the town where they were born. Their civic institutions were still invested, after Alexander, with the very same aura they had had before him. The anthropomorphic character of ancestral religion was remarkably well adapted to a restricted framework commensurate with humanity, whose essential needs it met. It was not devoid of a potentiality for renewal and enrichment: this included an ability to give a concrete personality to abstractions, to endow them with life and make them accessible. The case of Fortune (*Tyché*: see pp. 346, 347) is a significant one, but there are many others: a number of Hellenistic cities instituted a cult for *Demos* (the People) and for *Polis* (the City), even a cult for Rome and the Roman people. These were additions to cults rendered to traditional civic divinities, and did not appear superfluous or embarrassing. The deification of human beings, building on the legacy left by the advent of hero-worship in earlier times, was another enriching factor. Side by side with the cult of sovereigns, which did not strike people as scandalous, was the cult of *euergetai*, a form of apotheosis that honored the benefactors of cities. These were innovations that were quite superficial, for they were a logical sequel to a very ancient tradition that had disposed people to admit all sorts of new cults, provided their ritual was modeled on customary form. We are faced here with the fundamental idea that for the Greeks ritual was more important in a cult than theological content. Religion was in their eyes an essentially social phenomenon, manifesting itself in exterior deeds. If these conformed to custom, society would feel no urge to react to new forms of religion intruding on its life by rejecting them.

This does not mean that the Hellenistic age did not witness the emergence of new modes of thought in the realm of religion. Three centuries is a very long period of time, within which minds and institutions are expected to evolve, the more so in an age so rife in dramatic events and amid trials of every kind for the various populations concerned. But real innovations were actually of a marginal nature, and their effect was not fully felt until later. They related first of all to the contribution made by the Epicurean and Stoic philosophers, to a modification of the traditional idea of the world. Its impact radiated in wide circles, but only after the Roman conquest, particularly in Imperial times: even so, it was at all times restricted to the intelligentsia, with no appreciable consequences for the masses' way of thinking. Another new trend, influenced by a greater mastery of astronomical knowledge and in part by the spread of a number of Oriental cults, consisted in granting a privileged status among the gods to those that were traditionally associated with the stars, or that theological speculation tended to link with them. A discreet form of astral religion had in fact emerged at the beginning of the Hellenistic age, as we have seen in the case of Isis. Other symptoms of this phenomenon can be noted. In one of Serapis' shrines, at Delos, a stele has been found with an epigram inscribed on it, starting with the words, "Thus did the poet Menedemus, son of Apollonius, sing of the Immortals of the celestial universe." The pediment of the stele is adorned with symbols of obvious meaning: a star, a solar disc, or a lunar crescent. It is clear that the poet in question, who is said later in the text to have been born in the valley of the Cayster, near Ephesus, had written an astronomical poem bestowing divine honors on the heavenly bodies. But a real solar theology was not to assert itself until the Empire (especially at the time of the emperor Julian). Finally, the massive invasion of the Mediterranean world by eastern monotheistic religions like Christianity, or with monotheistic tendencies like Mithraism, could occur only as a result of the widespread interpenetration of populations that Roman policy and administration fostered. One can indeed sense in the Hellenistic world premonitory signs of these radical changes, for it paved the way to their advent. The fact remains, however, that it was essentially a world in which the religious life of Classical Greece was prolonged without a break.

10/THE LIFE OF THE SPIRIT AND THE FLOWERING OF ART

■ *The blossoming of thought, literature, and art in the Hellenistic age*

The Hellenistic Greeks' way of life, as we have tried to describe it so far, demonstrated no urge to break with the past. The same remark cannot apply to the realm of speculative thought, literary creation, and taste, for in these areas momentous innovations took place that blazed a trail for future developments. The truth of this statement makes it all the more surprising that their contribution to history goes unrecognized as a rule. Only specialists show an interest in the achievements of a period that suffers, in the eyes of later generations, from being wedged in, as it were, between the golden age of Greek literature and art and that of Latin literature and Roman Imperial art. In works of a general scope, Hellenistic literature and art usually receive short shrift. They are treated as an appendix to the Classical era. The glory of Sophocles, Thucydides, Plato, or Demosthenes is considered to outshine that of Aristotle, Menander, Callimachus, or Polybius. Similarly, the names of Phidias, Polyclitus, Scopas, or Praxiteles overshadow the prestige of the great Hellenistic painters or the unknown creators of Pergamene expressionism. We should shake off such conventional ideas. In doing so we would certainly not detract in any way from the admiration that is due to the great pre-Alexandrian masters of the fifth and fourth centuries. Yet we have to place in a proper historical perspective our debt to the thinkers, writers, and artists of the three centuries that witnessed so many radical changes in the Mediterranean basin. We shall attempt to do just this. Our objective here will not be to sketch a history of the literature and art of the time: that would lead us into developments of an excessive length. We shall be content with stressing the main features, underlining their originality and bringing to light the fertilizing role they played in the history of civilization.

■ *Aristotle and scientific method: the system of the sciences*
■ *Mathematics* ■ *Technique* ■ *Medicine* ■ *Erasistratus: the tale
of Antiochus and Stratonice* ■ *Pharmacy: Nicander of Colophon*
■ *Geography and astronomy* ■ *Eratosthenes of Cyrene* ■ *The
development of history*

Giving credit where it is due, let us mention first of all Aristotle of Stagira, who died in 322, one year after Alexander, whose tutor he had been. Like his pupil, he towers above the whole later period, to which he gave new intellectual directions. Endowed with a mind of outstanding caliber, he is truly the first of the Moderns. A disciple of Plato, he stayed at the Master's side until his death. But he managed, while benefiting from the essence of his teaching, to avoid the Academy's (see p. 297) indulgence in the style of verbal battles, steer his thinking away from the futile clash of warring ideas, and concentrate on hard fact. Those works of his that have come down to us are predominantly lecture notes, devoid of charm or literary polish. What is important anyhow is their content – and the methodology that it illustrates. This is in actual fact the methodology of science, as it has been practiced since Aristotle by all the scholars who have structured European sciences. Instead of appealing to unfounded speculation and myth, a pretext for dazzling feats of verbal acrobatics or wanderings in the realm of poetic fancy, Aristotle lays down the principle that acquaintance with concrete fact is the prerequisite for interpretative thought. One should therefore collect documentary evidence before stating a theory. Analysis should precede synthesis; enquiry is the precondition for any sort of systematization, the acquisition of knowledge to philosophical thinking. This principle has never been improved upon. The search for information implies group work, the moment the subject of enquiry has a certain degree of amplitude. Aristotle organized such group work, distributing its various aspects and sectors among his pupils. He was thus the first director of group research in intellectual history.

His study of political science provides a good example of this. Before writing the major work of synthesis that has come down to us under the title of the *Politics*, the Stagirite wrote or caused to be written 158 monographs on the constitutions of as many Greek cities. Only one of these, *The Athenian Constitution*, has survived nearly in its entirety, the others being lost. One can imagine what an undertaking such an enquiry implied from the point of view of gathering information. Since no prior works were available for use, information had to be gathered *in situ*, records consulted, assistance obtained from those qualified to give it. Judging from the *Athenian Constitution*, the plan adopted for every report was clear and simple. The first part, the historical one, retraced the constitutional evolution of the city. The second part was descriptive: it gave a meticulous and highly detailed account of contemporary institutions. Such was the plentiful and instructive material gathered for use by those specializing in public law and social history. It constitutes the underpinning of the *Politics*. The acuity of its analysis, marked by uncommonly close reasoning, would not have been so often on target had their author not been enabled by that preparatory work to make a comparative evaluation of such a large number of concrete cases.

Aristotle's thirst for knowledge was limitless. It had an encyclopedic dimension. From the teaching he had received from Plato (whom one could call, in a playful manner, the last of the Presocratics), he had conceived the ambition of finding an overall explanation of the universe. Besides political science, he concerned himself with ethics, logic, rhetoric, poetics, biology, physics, and metaphysics. His disciples of the Lyceum (see p. 297) surveyed the whole system of the natural and human sciences. After his departure from Athens in 323, his pupil Theophrastus succeeded him at the head of the school, and continued with his master's life work, showing the same breadth of outlook and the same energy. However, the treatises on natural history that have reached us under his name reveal a shortcoming in the application of Aristotle's method, which was rendered inevitable by the working conditions prevailing in those days. Too often, when the object of research is remote or difficult of access, we are given information that is secondhand or extracted from books. On the one hand that leads to errors. On the other, a process of analysis that is not based on facts established by personal enquiry is apt to lead to a species of formal classification that turns out to be far from enlightening. However it may be, such blemishes, such occasional lack of precision, did not in the final analysis prevent Aristotle's wonderful intellectual instrument from achieving prodigious results over the centuries. Even in our own day we are beholden to him in this regard, more so than to any other intellectual mentor among the Greeks.

Mathematics, however, being concerned with abstractions, did not need Aristotle, for the great mathematicians of the fourth century, Theodorus of Cyrene for example, had already taken their analytic work quite far. Yet the task of bringing together all acquired data into a coherent whole, which would serve as a basis for new enquiries, remained unaccomplished. That was the service that Euclid rendered to humanity at the start of the third century, when he wrote the thirteen books of his *Elements*, a masterpiece of didactic method that was to be used as the textbook of mathematicians until modern times. His successors in our day, having asserted their freedom from the principles governing Euclidean geometry, feel bold enough to give free rein to their creative speculations. The fact remains that we humble mortals move in a three-dimensional space, and the *Elements* have preserved their rational and functional value intact in the reality of our world. Not long after his time, Archimedes of Syracuse, who has been justly called "Antiquity's greatest mathematician," shone both as a mathematical theoretician and an engineer. Applied science was never separate in his mind from pure science. His treatises on conical figures, on the sphere and the cylinder, examined challenging problems of geometry in space. These found their prolongation, toward the end of the same century, in Apollonius of Pergé's treatise on conic sections. The same Archimedes' studies on the principle of the lever, on the center of gravity in bodies, on hydrostatics (with the famous principle of Archimedes) were of use to him in practical applications, especially military ones, which won high praise from his contemporaries. Thus the devices used in the defense of Syracuse managed to destroy ships and war-engines and filled the Roman assailants with terror. Unfortunately, as is well known, Archimedes perished when the city was captured (see pp. 96–7). Absorbed in deep thought on a geometrical problem, he neglected to reply to urgent questioning by a brutal trooper, but simply asked him not to spoil the diagrams he had drawn on the sand. The man was enraged and killed him.

Warfare and civil engineering techniques made notable progress in these times. The handling of the heaviest weights by means of gins, cranes, and derricks, using a complicated array of levers, ropes, and pulleys, was then fully mastered. Those engaged in maritime trade had the means to ensure the safe transport of cargoes of considerable weight, for example blocks of marble weighing many tonnes, monolithic columns, or consignments that were both heavy and fragile, like statues ready to be put in place. Groundwork structures of major size and requiring great skill were realized to facilitate communication by land. In the later part of the twentieth century the track of the road joining Cyrene with its harbor was identified, alongside a deep, long ravine. The works that had been carried out on the cliff side, to accommodate the roadway and protect it against seepage, were so extensive that in Imperial times the Romans no longer maintained them. They chose another layout, less convenient for heavy vehicles, but requiring less laborious maintenance. In short, Hellenistic engineers provided their Roman colleagues with the technique they needed to endow the ancient world with roads and other channels of communication, aqueducts, and impressive constructions of every kind.

One can pay a similar tribute to medicine, which then knew its first golden age. We have seen what store the cities set by the availability of renowned practitioners of the art, and how sovereigns were keen to keep near them trusted doctors, whom they honored with their friendship. The famous School of Cos, tracing its origin back to Hippocrates, and that of Cnidus, its neighbor, had been rivals for many generations. Distancing itself from their more ancient and conservative professional tradition, and their rivalry, rose a more demanding school of medicine. It benefited from the interest that the Peripatetic school – Aristotle, Theophrastus, and their followers – had shown in biology (especially the study of animals) and botany. We should not forget that Aristotle himself was the son of a doctor, Nicomachus, and that he had asked one of his pupils, Meno, to gather material for a history of medicine, a fragment of which has been preserved in a papyrus at our disposal. In Alexander's time the doctor Diocles of Carystus attended the Lyceum. Aristotle's own daughter, Pythias, married Metrodorus, a doctor belonging to the Cnidian School. It was from Metrodorus that the famous Erasistratus, who had first belonged to the Coan School, eventually received his training. He was said to have miraculously healed the young king Antiochus I, who had been pining away with consumption. This is perhaps an apocryphal anecdote, which nevertheless has some significance, and deserves to be told in its entirety. Antiochus' father, Seleucus I, had married Demetrius Poliorcetes' daughter Stratonice (see pp. 00–0), a woman much younger than he was. Let us turn to Plutarch's account (*Demetrius,* 38):

> Antiochus had fallen in love with Stratonice, who was very young, though already the mother of a child by Seleucus. He was distraught, and made every effort to prevail against his feelings. He finally realized that he was prey to a sinful passion, and beset with an incurable disease against which reason was helpless. He sought a way to put an end to his own life, gradually undermining his own health by ceasing to attend to his bodily needs and abstaining from all food, under pretext of illness. The physician Erasistratus had no difficulty discovering that Antiochus was in love. Wishing to know (something that was hard to guess) who was the object of his love, he took up his quarters in his patient's room. Whenever a young man or woman entered, Erasistratus would observe with great attention Antiochus' face, watching at the same time the parts of the body most closely connected with the emotions, and the reactions attendant on these. Now, while Antiochus remained impassive when other people came, yet whenever Stratonice visited him (alone or in Seleucus' company), behold! Just at that moment those very symptoms that Sappho [frag. 31 Lobel-Page] describes were evident: speechlessness, intense blushing, disturbed vision, sudden perspiration, an irregular and fast-beating pulse; finally, as though the soul succumbed under its trials, distress, stupor and pallor.

Having observed these phenomena, Erasistratus resorted to a stratagem. He told Seleucus that his son was hopelessly in love with his own (Erasistratus') wife.

> "Well," said Seleucus, "if you are my friend, surrender your spouse to him, as this is the only available remedy." "But," replied the doctor, "you would not do this if he was in love with your wife." Seleucus then exclaimed, "Would it were Heaven's pleasure that such was the solution! I would then do without delay what you suggest."

Erasistratus then told him the truth, and Seleucus soon decided to unite Antiochus and Stratonice in wedlock, appointing his son on the same occasion king of the Upper satrapies (see p. 75).

This is a touching and romantic story which, told by Plutarch, has for centuries cast its spell on the imagination of readers: Phaedra's love affair, with roles interchanged between the main actors, and with a happy ending in this particular case. It gives at any rate, as recounted by Plutarch, an accurate picture of the part played by a doctor in those days. He is an acute observer, attentive to the physical signs of disease, and capable of giving a shrewd diagnosis, even if sickness of the soul is involved. The primacy granted to observation, leading to a conjectural hypothesis on the cause of the disease, is characteristic of Hellenistic medicine, pointing to its kinship with Aristotelian methodology. A contemporary and rival of Erasistratus, Herophilus of Chalcedon, used a similar approach to the etiology of disease. Both were invited to teach at Alexandria during the reign of Ptolemy II Philadelphus. Their research led to great progress in anatomy, owing to the use of dissection, even of vivisection occasionally – for the purposes of which royal authority put at their disposal people condemned to death.

Pharmacy progressed at a similar pace. Theophrastus had shown a particular interest in botany. His system was indeed marked by purely formal and oversubjective preoccupations: for example, the distinction between plants that could be cultivated and those that could not. But it allowed a large amount of information to be collected that proved useful to medicine. No other period witnessed greater activity in the study of poisons and venoms, of counter-poisons and antidotes. Comparative tests were made on methods of healing where traditional old remedies, with their magic components, had a place side by side with innovative experiments. Sovereigns showed an interest in them. For example, Attalus III, last king of Pergamum, developed a passion for *iology*, the science of poisons. A contemporary doctor, Nicander of Colophon, who had written a hymn in honor of the king, produced two important didactic poems on these specialized subjects. One was the *Theriaka* (or "Of Venomous Beasts," on remedies for venomous bites and stings), the other was the *Alexipharmaka* ("Preventive Pharmacy," on counter-poisons or antidotes). These works have been preserved, which is proof of the esteem in which later generations continued to hold this kind of technical literature. They are indeed noted both for the refinement and brilliance of their expression and for their scientific content. Nicander transmitted to posterity, in a verse form that encouraged memorization, a corpus of empirical knowledge that amounted to a *summa* in pharmacopoeia. We can thus appreciate the fact that, not long after Nicander's time, Mithridates VI Eupator managed to protect himself by preventive medicine against every sort of poison: hence the terms *Mithridatism* (immunity from poison), *to Mithridatize* (oneself or others).

The Hellenistic age progressed in a decisive manner in another area, in the two closely linked disciplines of geography and astronomy. Eudoxus of Cnidus, Plato's contemporary, had, in the fourth century, blazed a trail in the study of astronomy. The main problem had been to account for the seemingly puzzling movements of stars in the heavens. The challenge was to combine the regular rotation of the "sphere of fixed stars," carrying the nocturnal stars, with the apparent daily movement of the sun, and its successive apparitions among the twelve signs of the zodiac in the ecliptic. This had also to be reconciled with the lunar month and its phases and, finally, the movements of the planets, "wandering stars" (the literal meaning of *planets*), as they seemed to be. Attempts were made to account for all this by geometrical constructions that inspired three-dimensional models combining metal circles and meant to give a material picture of the astral movements. The two most ancient Greek scientific texts that have survived, the *Sphere in Movement* and the *Heliacal Risings and Settings*, were written by Autolycus of Pitane (a town of Aeolis in Asia Minor), who lived in the second half of the fourth century. These works attempted to improve on Eudoxus' theory of homocentric spheres. In the same period, in about 330–325, a great mariner, Pytheas of Massilia (Marseille), ventured into the Atlantic and reconnoitered the western and northwestern coasts of Europe, reaching up to the Baltic and to the islands north of Scotland. His purpose was to verify by exploration the theoretical views that geographers had propounded on the various latitudes and on the Arctic Circle. Similarly Callisthenes (see pp. 27, 36), Aristotle's nephew, who accompanied Alexander on his expedition to Asia, had been entrusted with the task of sending detailed information to his uncle on observations that Chaldean astronomers had recorded over the centuries. Here too experience and practice were put to use as a means of verifying theory. Such an intellectual procedure had full relevance to an era of progress.

The great name among geographers of the age is Eratosthenes of Cyrene. His curiosity was universal, and so were his natural gifts, which meant that the range of his interests was very wide indeed. A pupil and friend of his compatriot Callimachus, he wrote poems and was the author of treatises on mythography and philology, of works on chronology and mathematics. Such variety in his production aroused jealousy in the milieu of Alexandrian scholars in which he lived. It is related that he was sometimes nicknamed *Beta*, because (so it was said) like that Greek letter, the second in the alphabet, he was always second in every discipline he practiced. Whatever may have been said from envy, his geographical production was first-rate. He managed to calculate the total length of the terrestrial meridian, reaching a quite respectable approximate figure. To measure the portion of the meridian's curve that lay between Alexandria and Syene (Aswan), he had recourse to comparative observations of the shadows that a vertical control fixture cast at the Sun's passage at its zenith over those two localities. As royal land surveyors had measured the distance between them, Eratosthenes was able to evaluate the earth's circumference at 250,000 stadia. Taking into account the margin of uncertainty concerning the length of the referential stadium, on which we have no precise information, the figure he reached is quite close to the actual one of 40,000 kilometers. He thus secured a piece of information essential to our knowledge of the world.

The same Eratosthenes also established the framework of world chronology on trustworthy data. Until his time chronological systems varied with cities or empires. Making use of the elements of information he had at his disposal, he assembled the essential facts of Greek history in a coherent whole, from the Trojan War (1194–1184 BC) down to the death of Alexander the Great. As a complement to this work, entitled *Chronographies*, he drew up a list of *Olympic Victors*, in which appeared in chronological order the names of all those who had won athletic competitions at the Olympic Games. The order of succession among the Olympiads being independent of the particular calendars of various cities, later historians adopted it as a convenient reference: Polybius did so, and after him Diodorus Siculus. The essentials of our chronology of Classical Antiquity thus go back to Eratosthenes' scholarly work, the purview of which was extended in the second century by Apollodorus of Athens, who added occasional corrections. The Christian historian Eusebius' *Chronicle* has transmitted this series of dates to posterity, which continues to quote from it.

The interest shown in chronology is only one aspect of the passion that the Hellenistic Age had for history. At no other period before modern times, without doubt, have such a number of researchers devoted their effort to the study of the past. It has been calculated that from that span of three centuries the names of nearly 600 Greek historians have come down to us. Some limited their enquiries to the history of one city. The writing of monographs flourished, these being concerned both with hard fact and with myths: the latter were held to be no different from genuine events, belonging like them to the civic community's heritage. Others were more ambitious, striving after an all-embracing view, going as far as universal history, which they attempted to explain by analyzing causes. Some aimed at delighting their readers or showed an inclination for the romantic, turning an attentive ear to fable. The best writers tried to verify facts and evaluate the available evidence, using the criteria of reason and verisimilitude. This method bore the name of *pragmatic* history, dealing mainly with recent times when documentation is surer and more plentiful. When historians could claim a personal knowledge of war or public affairs, and had witnessed, or participated in, the events they recounted, they obtained results with the explanatory approach, which allowed one to understand human actions. This was demonstrative (*apodeictic*) history, of which Polybius is the best exponent. A number of writers, however, were content to report what they saw, even what they did: accounts of such a nature, as well as memoirs, were produced in abundance, right from the time of Alexander. As often occurs in such literature, the need for personal self-justification or mere romancing often colored these accounts. Even sovereigns occasionally allowed themselves to be tempted and wrote down their reminiscences: one example is Ptolemy Sôter on Alexander's expedition; another is Ptolemy VIII Euergetes II Physcon (see p. 137). Major libraries were full of these incomplete pieces of evidence that few people were in a position to consult, and that compilers, abridgers, and the creators of a wide range of tales drew upon in a later age, sharing their discoveries with their readers. Under the Empire this abundant material proved of use to biographers like Plutarch, historians like Arrian or Appian, and even an itinerant travel writer (a *periegetés*) like Pausanias.

■ *Libraries* ■ *The Library of Alexandria*

Such curiosity, extending to all areas of knowledge, could not develop without finding constant support in earlier conquests of the mind. A striking feature of the Hellenistic age is the part played by written documents, especially books. This was the time of the first great libraries. First came those that Aristotle and after him Theophrastus set up at Athens for purposes of teaching and research. Next, and above all, came the famous Library of Alexandria, which Ptolemy I started in the first years of the third century, with help from Demetrius of Phalerum (after he left Athens for exile, see p. 51). It was an annex to the Mouseion, or Sanctuary of the Muses, which the Lagid monarch had set up close to his palace. He assembled there a number of writers and scholars, who thus belonged to his entourage and were enabled by his generosity to devote their lives, with undivided atttention, to scientific and literary pursuits. A policy of systematic purchase rapidly increased the collections of the Library, which actually acquired part of Aristotle's library in 286. Illustrious scholars were appointed to head the Library. The first to be chosen was Zenodotus of Ephesus, a distinguished Homeric scholar. The poet Apollonius of Rhodes (cf. pp. 347–8 on Medea), the learned Erastosthenes (see above, pp. 359–60), the philologist Aristophanes of Byzantium held this position of trust after him. They saw to the continued enrichment of Alexandria's Great Library. Its holdings and those of the one situated in Serapis' shrine in the same city soon totaled half a million volumes. The Great Library had 700,000 volumes when a fire destroyed it, in the course of the revolt against Caesar (see p. 158). No other institution ever boasted such a wealth of learned works until the end of Antiquity. The *volumes*, or papyrus rolls, were carefully classified and deposited in sets of pigeonholes or wall cupboards, arranged in both logical (according to their discipline) and then alphabetical order (by name of author). Descriptive catalogues helped readers in their search. Among other services that he rendered to scholarship, the poet Callimachus was essentially the author of these catalogues. They were called *Pinakes* (*Tables*). They listed works under headings, according to literary genre or scientific discipline, and under authors' names (each name accompanied by a biographical note). As the repertory embraced "the world of writers who have shone in all areas of culture, and the list of their works," one can imagine the size of the task that its author had assigned himself. Callimachus drew up a complete inventory of Greek literature and thought. There is no better illustration of the fundamental role that scholarship was to play, from then on, in Hellenistic civilization.

Other sovereigns, imitating the Ptolemies, took measures for public libraries to be opened in their States. Such was the case at Pergamum, where the Attalids proved to be generous patrons, particularly in the second century. It was there that, under Eumenes II, the manufacture of parchment (a word derived from the name of Pergamum) was developed with the aim of competing with papyrus, Lagid Egypt's monopoly. But the great success of this new writing material, reminiscent of the *diphtherae* (tanned goatskins) that the Greeks of the early Archaic period used before being acquainted with papyrus, was not confirmed until the later Empire. One can include among court libraries those at Antioch, under the Seleucids, and at Pella in the Macedonian kingdom. Even Mithridates VI Eupator, who certainly had preoccupations of another kind, was careful to provide a form of patronage that was close to the heart of sovereigns. But libraries could also be found in cities of modest size. Nysa in Caria had one, counting Strabo among its readers. Tauromenium (Taormina) in Sicily had one too, from which a fragmentary catalogue has survived.

■ *Hellenistic scholarship* ■ *Learned poetry* ■ *Callimachus: his career as a poet and his works of scholarship* ■ *Literary polemic* ■ *The epigrammatic genre*

The increasing availability of libraries and the ever-widening dissemination of books had a decisive influence on the literature of the times. We have seen this phenomenon happening in the case of history (see above, pp. 360–1). It was the same in other disciplines. Scholarship asserted itself everywhere. The weight of tradition was felt in every area of literary creation, supported by the patient work of philologists. In Alexandria's Mouseion and similar institutions, they worked diligently on ancient texts, striving to establish them by applying stringent criteria, ridding them of interpolations, restoring their original form, which copyists might have modified in earlier times, and resolving difficulties of interpretation. Zenodotus led the way. He was the master of all scholars. After him came the great Homeric specialists, Aristophanes of Byzantium and Aristarchus of Samothrace (his name became a byword for a particularly demanding critic). These have been mentioned earlier (see above, p. 361). There were also Apollodorus of Athens, commentator on the famous *Catalogue of Ships* in the

Plate 14   The apotheosis of Homer (British Museum, London).

This famous bas-relief is signed, beneath the picture of Zeus, by the sculptor Archelaus of Priene. The lettering points to the second century, while stylistic analysis leans toward the second half of that period. The composition is complex, with groups in tiers, in a way much used by painters. Zeus is seated at the peak of a mountain, with a sacred eagle at his feet. Not far from him stands Mnemosyne (Memory), the mother of the Muses; all nine of these, with their distinctive attributes, are shown on two of the groups. In their midst, beneath a rocky arcade, is Apollo with his lyre, near the Delphic omphalos. On the right, standing on a pedestal, is a statue of a poet holding a papyrus scroll. In the lowest band, in front of a curtained background, the apotheosis of Homer is taking place. He is enthroned, holding a scepter and flanked by the two allegorical figures of the Iliad *and the* Odyssey. Time *(Chronos) and* Inhabited Earth *(Oikoumene), standing behind the poet, crown him. A sacrifice is taking place on a cylindrical altar facing him, the sacrificers being allegories of literary genres and various virtues.*

second book of the *Iliad*, and, at Pergamum, Crates of Mallus, who propounded a Stoic-inspired interpretation of Homeric poetry. The work of these philologists, which has been handed down to us by later grammarians, serves as the foundation, in the essentials, of present-day knowledge of Homeric texts. They stated in clear terms most of the problems raised by their study. The reasoning of much modern research limits itself to reasserting arguments that were developed by Alexandrian scholars.

The achievements of Hellenistic research on Homeric poetry, the very foundation of any culture in Greek eyes, give us a good idea of what the scholarship of that age consisted in, and how painstaking its work was in the area of literature. Lexicons and grammars were produced. Collections were compiled of rare and difficult terms (these were called "expressions," *glossae*), their selection being made with the utmost care. The diverse literary languages, with their important dialectal variations, provided plentiful material for such research. Poets made it their preserve, and found delight in enshrining in their verses such *glossae* as had won the favor of the learned world. These appealed to the reader's fancy, and gave a nobler tone to the work of poets. Nurtured in the Classical texts, these authors could escape the risk of repetition only by subtle modifications of their exact recollections, which their reader, having had contact with the same source, relished with the sensitivity of a true connoisseur. Poetry became a refined game between accomplices, author and reader: a mere hint created mutual understanding. It had been acknowledged since its origins as a challenging art. The first authors of hymns and epics had invariably claimed an equal possession of knowledge and professional skill. But now the public was no longer content naively to admire an inspired singer's strains. Well aware of the refinements of the art, it was to grant no respite to the poet. Untiring precision was the prerequisite for any work of high quality; it was to be at every turn a feat of technical ability. Hence an inner tension that surprises and often wearies us, since it knows no relaxation. This explains how Hellenistic poetry favored the short poem with its striking effects, as contrasted with the long poem, which by necessity would grant its hearer restful moments of transition from one episode to another. The only epic of any major dimension that has survived, Apollonius of Rhodes' *Argonautica* (see pp. 278, 347–8), adds up to 5,833 lines in its four books: half the length of the *Odyssey*, which in its turn, with its 12,110 lines, is shorter than the *Iliad*. But every one of its lines, one might say every word in it, constitutes a conscious appeal for the reader's attention.

This was obviously poetry of the learned kind, a fact which, however, did not alienate the reading public. For, after an earlier unfortunate experience at Alexandria, Apollonius, having retired to Rhodes, won great applause in his native city when he presented his poem in its definitive form, "having polished and reshaped it." His master Callimachus, the most illustrious writer of the age and judged by later generations to be the equal of the greatest, has provided us with models of this refined literary genre. A prodigious craftsman of verse form, more given to self-criticism than anyone before him had ever been, he attained a density of expression that can only be compared to that of Pindar – the exemplar that he always looked up to. One is too often apt to forget that his *Hymns*, so rich in erudite allusions, and so meticulously elaborate in form, are not closet exercises, meant to delight a small number of privileged spirits. They are occasional pieces ordered for recitation in the presence of people attending a particular religious festival (see pp. 326–8): an eloquent testimony to the intellectual and cultural level of a popular audience at Cyrene, Delos, Argos, or Alexandria.

In addition to these poetic contributions to contemporary public life, Callimachus took delight in composing works that were intended solely for the world of scholars. Thus in the four books of the "Origins" (*Aitia*) he recalled in a series of short poems a large number of legendary accounts that were still presented, in various shrines of the Hellenic world, as the explanation, based on myth, of rites still practiced in his day. The ancients held the *Aitia* to be Callimachus' masterpiece, and undoubtedly the prime achievement of Hellenistic poetry. For one finds in it the quintessential charm and meaningfulness of that poetry: the richness and originality of its themes, the brevity of preliminaries, a feeling for life and psychological insight in the act of resurrecting the past, a refined and dense expression. It is a great loss for us that texts which won such admiration have almost all disappeared. Yet papyrologists have managed, with great perspicacity, to retrieve enough elements for us to have an unprejudiced idea of a work that fully justifies its author's celebrity. Three centuries later Ovid (*Tristia* 2, 367) was to write, *Battiades semper toto cantabitur orbe*: "The glory of Battus' descendant" (Battus was the reputed founder of Cyrene) "will always be sung all over the world." The Greeks and Latins were nurtured in such learned and exquisite poetry, and have looked to it for inspiration and models to imitate. From the second half of the third century (following the poet's death) onward, commentaries were written to render his work accessible to the public. That was a consecration that put him on a level with the great Classical authors. From what is left of his work, we cannot doubt that his renown was deserved.

What is astonishing is that such a conscientious craftsman, so anxious for the perfect form of expression, gifted with such sensitivity, has to his credit immense and varied achievements in the realm of pure scholarship. The *Pinakes* have already been mentioned (see p. 361) – bio-bibliographical catalogues of firstrate importance. But many other learned collections are mentioned, bearing testimony to Callimachus' multifarious appetite for knowledge and his extraordinary capacity for work. Only their titles survive, but they are suggestive enough by themselves. We shall mention a few. *Foundations of Island States and of Cities, with their name-changes, Barbarian Customs, Ethnic Denominations* were three studies of history and ethnology, the last being devoted to a survey of vocabulary in various languages or dialects. *The Diverse Names of Fishes* and *The Names of the Months, grouped according to Peoples and Cities using them* were two other lexicographical works. *Of Winds, Of Birds, Of Rivers of the Inhabited World* were treatises on geography or natural history, starting, it would appear, from vocabulary and proper names. *Of the Nymphs* was a study in mythology. *Marvels of the Whole World, presented in geographical order* seems to have been a foundation work for "paradoxography," a branch of history whose remarkable development in the Hellenistic age has been mentioned (see p. 318). *Against Praxiphanes* was a small polemical work aimed at a Peripatetic philosopher bearing this name, a native of Mytilene and collaborator of Theophrastus, who had written a dialogue on poetry and style. This list of titles gives us the picture of a rigorous scholar, a lover of books, devoting his days to taking notes that would be material for his lexicons – and a man with a passion for literature.

The last-named trait is something new and of great significance. Literary polemic figures in many of Callimachus' works. We find him defending or attacking one theory or another at the expense of his rivals and adversaries. Before his time, authors like Pindar or Simonides had certainly expressed their feelings on similar subjects. From the early Archaic age onward, poetic competitions had taken place between professional bards, just as in later times competitions of tragedy or comedy took place on the occasion of Dionysiac celebrations. Such rivalries were a normal outlet for a spirit of emulation, the "agonistic" spirit that was so much alive in Greek cities. But something else was to occur from this time on. This was internal conflict within the particular world of literary creation. Now the literary phenomenon appeared on the scene with its own specific features. One can surmise that schools were emerging, each with its own doctrine, headed by a master in the field, and ready to take part in controversies in which the public was to be the ultimate judge, as was the case for philosophical schools. Literature, especially poetry, without forsaking its role in the city, which continued to solicit its cooperation, became in addition an autonomous activity in its own right, deserving total dedication on the part of the individual practitioner. This is a landmark in the history of civilization, for Latin poets of the Augustan age (Horace in the first place) were to be conscious of an example that they were to hand down to the whole of Western Europe, from the Renaissance to our own day.

One does not tire of studying the many-faceted personality of Callimachus of Cyrene. It is fully representative of the persona of the Hellenistic man of letters. Another aspect of it has to be mentioned here, since it is the one that makes our contemporary world most aware of his exceptional poetic gifts. It concerns his work as a writer of epigrams. The genre was a very ancient one, for once writing had been invented, the idea came to inscribe brief dedications on offerings or tombs, often in verse form. Poets like Simonides had shone in an exercise that required simplicity and sobriety on the part of the versifier. As is evidenced by inscriptions that have come down to us, epigrams increased in number with the spread in Greek society of a taste for literary expression. This poetic genre reached its golden age in Hellenistic times. The demand for epitaphs or dedications in verse became a general phenomenon, so much so that talented poets like Posidippus of Pella (see pp. 280–1, 325) described themselves as "composers of epigrams." A good number of such texts have been quoted in the preceding chapters. They are closely linked with contemporary life, with people's beliefs and hopes, and provide us with direct testimony that is often moving and always enlightening. Like so many other writers of his time, Callimachus would be called upon to compose epigrams. Such a task was remunerated according to the author's repute and talent, as was the writing of a hymn, an ode, a dithyramb, or a tragedy. That was one aspect of the poet's place in society, which the evolution in mores had in no way reduced – far from it! The epigrammatic genre was submitted to certain constraints. These were in perfect agreement with Callimachus' genius and literary theories: brevity, density, an effort to concentrate much meaning into a few words, a search for originality by means of subtle variations within a framework well defined by tradition. Within such parameters the Cyrenaean poet could fully express his meaning, being a virtuoso of litotes, a verbal magician, and a master of verse craftsmanship. No one could better enshrine sincerity and delicacy of feeling in an epitaph, or display in a dedication the cheerful piety and good-humored wit indicative of the dedicator's familiarity with the god. Thanks to him, the engraved epigram rose to the dignity of the most elevated poetry.

He made a notable addition to the epigrammatic genre. With unequaled felicity he developed a use for it that had been known before his time, but had remained a very minor one. It consisted in composing poems that had the brevity and condensed form of the dedication or the epitaph, but were not meant to be engraved on a monument, while affording a new outlet for the author's emotions and ideas. We quote below an example of these, coming from Philetas of Cos, a contemporary of Alexander and Ptolemy I, who showed the way to Callimachus, his junior by a few years, and certainly influenced the first Alexandrian poets. In this epigram he formulates his conception of a type of poetry that draws on the poet's scholarly training. "He who shall wrest victory from me is not some uncultured peasant coming down the mountainside flourishing his rustic hoe, but one learned in the art of verse, trained by years of study, skillful in scenting the track of the most diverse myths."

This short piece in no way sounds like an epitaph or a dedication. Nor did Philetas compose it with an inscription in mind. It is the equivalent of a brief manifesto stating his doctrine, and proclaiming his legitimate pride. Quite a few of Callimachus' epigrams follow this model. They express the author's personal feeling – friendship, mourning, love, his literary tastes, even a philosophical opinion or a moral thought. Some are brief epistles, delicately worded missives to his friends. Others are veritable elegies, written in a condensed form that enhances their pathos: a lament on the death of a loved one, or the complaint of disappointed love. Still others set out a subject for one's meditation, or consist in a brief sentence, a maxim for life. These epigrams include every manifestation of what we call personal lyricism, side by side with traditional themes of the genre, which thus extends its scope to a large variety of new topics. Those who emulated Callimachus' example, or came after him, were to tread the same path, Latins as well as Greeks. They were not to attain, however, the sovereign, yet effortless, verbal intensity of the Cyrenaean poet's shorter poems.

■ *Hellenistic education* ■ *The philosophical schools: the Academy and the Lyceum* ■ *The criticism of idealism: the Cyrenaics; Skepticism; the Cynics* ■ *Stoicism* ■ *Epicurus and his disciples*

Callimachus' work provides an excellent illustration of Hellenistic literature, considered in its most favorable light. It is a literature that is given to self-criticism. Conscious of the importance of a tradition that it has no thought of abandoning, it nevertheless tries to explore new paths by asking scholarly research for out-of-the-way themes, and by imposing on itself strict rules and extreme refinements in matters relating to form. It is a literature reserved for learned practitioners. It plays to the full the role that is its own in the city, whose needs in the area of its competence have in no way disappeared. Besides, and for the first time in history, it targets another public in addition to the usual one of civic assemblies and religious festivals. That other public consists of learned people. The literature of the day complies with its preferences, more exacting ones than those of the multitude. This fact presupposes the existence of a reasonably large group of educated hearers and readers capable of grasping understated allusions and appreciating stylistic excellence. Such a new conception of the world of letters can only have arisen and asserted itself as a result of the impulse given to a liberal education, which was becoming the norm for the population of a Hellenistic city. Schools flourished nearly everywhere, for parents wanted their children to acquire a culture that had a solid foundation. Varied evidence is available for this phenomenon. Terracotta figurines have survived, depicting children going to their classes accompanied by a trusted slave, the *pedagogue*, who is in charge of them, as well as papyrus copy-books, their pages covered with copies of literary texts or exercises. Inscriptions have been found commemorating donations by rich citizens, occasionally by generous kings, endowing the city with capital intended for the payment of teachers "for the education of all free-born children." These come, for instance, from Miletus or Teos in Ionia, or from Delphi, in the last case being gifts from Attalus II of Pergamum. The role that the gymnasium played in the realm of culture, under the patronage "of Hermes, Heracles, and the Muses," has already been noted (see pp. 296–8). The first school textbooks appeared, the most ancient being a handbook of grammar, a very brief and very arid one, written in the second half of the second century by a pupil of Aristarchus,

Dionysius the Thracian. The success of such an education is not in doubt, judging from the number, the variety, and the wide topographical range of evidence provided by papyri in Lagid Egypt, and from the audience that renowned masters attracted almost everywhere.

The teaching of philosophy was the culmination of the educational process. In the hands of their numerous disciples, the enduring legacy left by Plato, then Aristotle, played a seminal role in the progress of Greek thought, which, under the leadership of various masters, was steered into a number of different paths. Some strove to preserve the doctrine of these illustrious founders. In the Academy Xenocrates and his successors (notably Arcesilas of Pitané in the third century, Carneades of Cyrene – see p. 129 – in the second, and Antiochus of Ascalon in the first) prolonged the teaching of Plato in its essentials. They initiated some original variations, however. In the Lyceum, the Peripatetic disciples of Aristotle pursued his endeavors under the leadership of Theophrastus (see above, pp. 355, 358), in the spirit of multidisciplinary studies and paying attention to scientific objectivity, as defined by the Stagirite. Strato of Lampsacus, then Critolaus of Phaselis (see p. 129) were the inheritors of that tradition, though reshaping it to suit the inclination of their own thought. In the late fourth century, a branch of the Peripatetic school took up its quarters at Rhodes, where it flourished independently of the Lyceum.

In a parallel fashion, claiming that they took their inspiration directly from Plato – or even further back than Plato, from Socrates – other schools of thought vigorously questioned the very basis of idealism, submitting it to a radical critique. The most ancient among these traced its roots back to Aristippus of Cyrene, a pupil of Socrates, flourishing in Libya in the first instance. This was a philosophy based on pleasure, suiting the inclination of people living in a wealthy and prosperous environment. But when, soon after Alexander's death, Theodorus of Cyrene, called Theodorus the Atheist, went so far as to deny openly the existence of the gods, his fellow-citizens, fearing that they would bring divine wrath on themselves, condemned him to exile. He took refuge in Athens at the time when Demetrius of Phalerum was at the head of affairs in that city (see p. 46). But there he was prosecuted for impiety; he went to Alexandria, where Ptolemy I made him welcome. Toward the end of his life he managed to return to Cyrene, to the court of Magas, a liberal and enlightened sovereign (see p. 57, esp. pp. 218–19). Some resonance of his teaching can be seen in the poetry of Callimachus, his compatriot.

The skepticism of Pyrrho of Elis was no less destructive of any theoretical certainty. Like Socrates before him, this philosopher left nothing in writing. But, unlike Socrates, he traveled a great deal, following Alexander's expedition to Asia before returning to his native town, where, esteemed by his fellow-citizens, he led a withdrawn life in modest circumstances. Four centuries later Pausanias saw his tomb in suburban Elis, and in the town's agora the statue of a philosopher "who had never believed in any affirmation whatsoever." Montaigne, after many others, was to quote Pyrrho's example in suspending judgment on the most serious matters, conscious as he was of a human being's limitations and weaknesses.

Cynicism was just as thoroughgoing in its theoretical conclusions, and more blunt in the implications of these in practical life. It was originally derived from the teaching of Antisthenes, one of Socrates' pupils, but was really developed by Diogenes of Sinope, a contemporary of Alexander. The name of the school came at the outset from that of the Athenian gymnasium, the Cynosarges, where Antisthenes had lectured. But later a relationship was perceived with the nickname of "Dog" (*kyôn: kynikos*, dog-like) given to Diogenes, as a result of the state of extreme neglect in which he had elected to live. His philosophy aimed at removing all artificial needs, every external constraint, from a human being's mode of life. The Cynic's lifestyle was characterized by poverty, detachment, indifference to social links, and total freedom of speech. It bore some analogy with the lifestyle of today's hippies, and could attract only a small number of people living on the fringe, as it implied a complete break with family and city. But the ascetic aspect of such a way of life appealed to people's imagination, and the picturesque portrait of the Cynic philosopher, a scoffing and ragged vagrant, inspired writers and artists. A number of anecdotes made the rounds concerning Diogenes, especially the apocryphal one about his reply to Alexander asking what he could do for him, "Get out of my light!" These stories and his typical "panoply" – a coarsely made overcoat, a stick, a beggar's pouch holding all his worldly goods – were just so many stereotypes that were all the more likely to please people with cultured minds as none of them was attracted to such a life of renunciation. Yet a few rare adherents of the Cynic doctrine, who chose a wandering life and total destitution, impressed their contemporaries by the sincerity, the uncompromising severity, and the acerbic vitality of their utterances. Among these were Crates of Thebes and his wife Hipparchia, who were for a time the hosts of Lysimachus, king of Thrace (one of the Diadochi, see chapter 3, esp. pp. 61–3). Bion of Borysthenes won favor from Antigonus Gonatas (see p. 89). In the third century Menippus of Gadara created a new literary genre, mixing prose and verse, which made fun of myths, poets, and philosophers. This kind of composition inspired the Roman Varro, a contemporary of Caesar and Pompey, who wrote 150 books of *Menippean Satires*, of which only fragments remain. Later, in the second century of our era, the prolific Lucian made Menippus the main participant in his famous *Dialogues of the Dead*. The history of Cynicism illustrates the phenomenon of an aberrant doctrine that was scant in elaborate exposition and short on formal attractiveness, with few disciples and no influence on the evolution of society, nevertheless attaining enduring notoriety among the intelligentsia. All it needed was to be adopted by a few colorful personalities and to be a source of diversion for people's imagination. There will always be some characters who stay on the fringe of any civilization: they help it to exorcise its phantasms, without deflecting it from fundamental problems.

The latter, on the other hand, were demonstrated in their fullness and in a new perspective by Stoicism and Epicureanism. They were schools in which speculative thought had as an end product an ethical doctrine that, in both cases, proved more important than the theoretical reflections of which it was a tributary. They gave definition to two fundamental conceptions of the practice of life. In spite of changes in our mores extending over at least twenty centuries, they continue, long after they penetrated the ancient world, to provide material for moral thought in the society of our own time. They stand out as an essential contribution of the Hellenistic age to our culture.

Both schools were born in Athens at about the same time, between the end of the fourth century and the start of the third. Zeno, the founder of Stoicism, came from Citium in Cyprus. After being trained in philosophy for more than ten years, listening to various masters, he started (in 301/0 BC) teaching under a portico on the north side of the Agora – the *Poikilé* (Painted Portico), famous for the paintings with which it was adorned. The name of Stoicism or philosophy of the Portico (*Stoa*), given to his school, came from the location of its teaching activities. Zeno's two immediate successors built solidly on his intellectual heritage. Cleanthes of Assus' *Hymn to Zeus* has been preserved. The religious feeling to which it gives expression is of an elevated spiritual quality. After him came Chrysippus of Soli (in Cilicia). He organized the Stoic doctrine in a strongly structured system. The school branched out into various cities: Rhodes, Tarsus, Seleucia on the Tigris in the Seleucid Empire, even Rome. Stoicism attracted a universal audience, to a degree that no other philosophical school ever attained. The names of a few of its great teachers can be listed. In the second century Panaetius of Rhodes established an intellectual relationship with Scipio Aemilianus (see pp. 117, 129, 135) and the enlightened circle that gathered around him at Rome. Blossius of Cumae became one of the intimates of Tiberius Gracchus before going to Pergamum, where he participated in Aristonicus' rebellion (see p. 127). He committed suicide after Aristonicus' death. Finally, we shall single out Posidonius of Apamea (a town of Syria, on the Orontes). He was not only a philosopher, but also a historian, a geographer, a philologist, learned in all subjects after the manner of an Aristotle or a Theophrastus. He taught at Rhodes, where he was awarded civic rights, and counted among his audience Cicero, on whose thought he exerted a profound influence, and Pompey, to whose personality he devoted a historical study. Each of the philosophers named made his contribution to Stoic doctrine, one of the most cohesive in Antiquity. It was a unitary and rationalistic theory, propounding a synthetic view of the world: in it the gods played their part, and Providence held overriding power. Theology, physics, logic, and of course ethics fitted into each other as an articulated whole. The absurdities apparently inherent in the myths were interpreted as a set of allegories. Since the cosmic aggregate was so well organized by a supreme Logos, humanity needed only to rely on a power surpassing its own, a human being wise enough to comprehend that power was capable of liberation from the passions obscuring our reason, and thus attain the happiness provided by virtue. Sufferings and trials were not the individual's responsibility, according to this philosophy. It was therefore appropriate to face them with constancy, knowing that one was powerless against them. "Fortitude and abstinence (or self-control)" was the school's motto. This was an austere morality that appealed to the Romans, traditionally inclined to self-sacrifice. It is no wonder that Romans like the philosopher Seneca, under Nero's rule, and later the emperor Marcus Aurelius (writing in Greek) passed on to us the essence of Stoic ethics.

In contrast with the Stoa, to the fame of which a succession of original thinkers have contributed, Epicureanism reflects exclusively the thought of its founder, whose name it legitimately bears. A contemporary of Zeno, Epicurus was an Athenian born at Samos, then an Athenian possession. After having taught at Mytilene, then at Lampsacus, he took up residence at Athens in 306, and gathered around him a few disciples, who lived together on a small estate that was called the *Garden*: the name survived to designate the school. Among his companions, he held particularly dear Metrodorus of Lampsacus, ten years his junior. The master had a high regard for the bond of friendship. Among the members of the Garden, he fostered a spirit of harmony that extended to women. Many courtesans, forsaking their dissolute life, joined this band of philosophers, developing with them a spirit of mutual understanding. One of them married Metrodorus.

Epicurus' doctrine (see pp. 345–6), which he propounded in a large number of works that have almost all been lost, is derived from Democritus. It is based on an almost undiluted materialism, giving a predominant role to Chance, *Tyché*, or Fortune (see pp. 346–7), which holds a prominent place in Hellenistic thought. While not denying the existence of the gods, Epicurus considers them totally uninterested in humanity. He complies with the demands of ritual, which, however, he deprives of its meaning through his conviction that divinity does not intervene in human affairs. Hence a total freedom vis-à-vis any sort of superstition: an attitude that can easily turn into atheism, but at the same time causes the disappearance of both the myths relating to the afterlife and some of the terrors that death inspires. The result of all this is an individualistic morality, advocating the search for happiness, which is not to be confused with pleasure: for pleasure, when excessive, is a cause of disturbance within one's own self, and hence of suffering. Epicurus recommends moderation in our needs and desires, inner serenity or *ataraxia* ("absence of disturbance"), the ideal of the wise. Such a morality is not compatible with the demands of public life: hence the maxim "live without attracting notice," which suited those who dwelt in the Garden.

It can easily be seen that such views appealed to sensitive souls aspiring to a life of peaceful happiness with no worries about the afterlife. Yet they exerted no less influence on a mentality lacking in refinement, which found in them justification for its hankering after pleasure. Epicurus' philosophy met simultaneously with a remarkable degree of success, in particular among cultured minds, and spirited opposition, especially from Stoics upset by such a seemingly facile morality. His writings reached out to a wide public. Papyrological finds at Herculaneum have yielded fragments of Epicurean texts that Philodemus of Gadara wrote around the middle of the first century BC. Later, around AD 200, one Diogenes had other extracts from Epicurus inscribed in his native city of Oenoanda in Lycia, for the instruction of his fellow-citizens. Lucretius' great poem *On the Nature of Things* is the high-water mark in the commemoration of Epicurean thought. Its powerful verse conveys the enthusiasm with which that philosophy, nullifying the terrors of superstition, filled a mind anxious to comprehend the cosmic system and allay the anguish felt over the human predicament. Lucretius' majestic power and Horace's elegant art illustrate the fertilizing role that Epicureanism – like Stoicism – played in the evolution of Roman thought and literature.

■ *Representational art* ■ *A strong increase in demand* ■ *Rome takes over from the Hellenic clientele* ■ *The progress of applied art* ■ *Mural painting* ■ *Floor mosaics*

The Hellenistic age was no less important in the field of art than it was in those of thought and literature. It is difficult, however, to evaluate precisely its contribution, since the relevant archaeological evidence is still imperfectly classified, the chronological sequence is uncertain, and attempts at synthesis by modern historians remain largely burdened by arbitrariness. This makes it all-important to state clearly the limits of our knowledge, while bringing out as we proceed the main features of an art whose vitality never flagged, while its complexity is not easy to grasp. We shall not concern ourselves any more with architecture in the following pages, for it has been given sufficient emphasis in the chapter on the framework of Hellenistic life. Only representational art in its various forms will be considered here.

A major increase in demand for works of art, and for luxury articles in general, is a fact that deserves to be underlined in the first place. A number of factors contributed to this phenomenon. Immense territories endowed with unlimited resources were conquered. That meant a concentration of enormous wealth in the hands of princes and their entourage. The movement of goods developed, cities grew in Greece proper and outside the ancient Aegean world. Overall economic prosperity was the rule and, in spite of wars, persisted nearly everywhere until the great crises of the first century before our era. In cities where life remained buoyant, the class of the well-endowed, no doubt more numerous than in the Classical age and eager for good living and visibility, provided craftsmen and artists with a larger and more varied group of customers than before. Even in the first century, in spite of the insecurity born of Mithridates' activities, civil discord, and piracy, it appears that there was no decrease in demand, owing to material transfers that were to Rome's advantage. Wealthy Romans, for whom their conquests and bouts of plunder had been an avenue to Greek tastes and customs, took over from the Hellenic clientele. They became an abundant source of customers for the Greek workshops, which moved, in part, to Italy – as is vividly illustrated at Pompeii and Herculaneum. Cicero's *Letters* and his *Verrine* orations supply ample evidence of this. Horace and Vergil say exactly the same thing in two texts that deserve to be quoted. *Graecia capta ferum victorem cepit et artes intulit agresti Latio*, says Horace in his *Epistles* (II, 1, 156): "Conquered Greece prevailed against her fierce victor, and brought the arts to rustic Latium." These words are addressed to Augustus, and refer above all to Greek influence on Latin literature. But the term "arts" does not have a restrictive sense. This is indicated by a famous passage in which Vergil claims for Rome the privilege of ruling the world, while leaving to "others," meaning the Greeks, the task of developing the plastic arts, rhetoric, or astronomy. "Others will know better how to give breath to bronze and carve living faces out of marble," he says in the *Aeneid* (VI, 847f.) . . . "Thou, Roman, remember how to rule the nations with thy imperial command (such arts will be thy own), to establish the ways of peace, to spare the vanquished and crush the arrogant." This candid statement is an important one, as it comes from a poet well known for his elevated conception of his country's greatness. It only reflects, however, a situation that existed in those days in the city of Rome and in Latin Italy, which had for a century welcomed the arrival – first as booty, later in execution of commercial orders – of works produced by Greek workshops. The abundance of that production finds support in a passage from Pliny the Elder's *Natural History* (XXXIV, 36). This text, written in about AD 70, quotes a figure of 73,000 statues "still found today" at Rhodes, and similar numbers for Athens, Olympia, and Delphi. As Rhodes' prosperity dates from the Hellenistic age in particular, this enormous number of works of art (or at least a very large one, as the text makes clear, even if the figures handed down by tradition may be questioned) belonged to that period of time.

Bronze or marble statues, votive reliefs, or figurative decoration of architectural buildings were produced in response to demand from cities and shrines. Their needs in respect of monuments connected with cult or honors granted to individuals and communities were considerable, as we have seen. But artists received assignments in those days that hardly ever came their way in former times. The sole purpose of these was to create a pleasant environment for daily life, and transform objects in current use into luxury artifacts. Applied art then knew an extraordinary development. Painting was no longer confined to adorning the walls of porticoes or temples. It reached into private homes: first on a modest scale, as witnessed at Delos, then in a sumptuous manner, as it did at Pompeii with the art belonging to the so-called "Second Style." The frescoes of the Villa of the Mysteries at Pompeii, or of Fannius Synistor's villa at Boscoreale, or the *Aldobrandini Nuptials* at Rome, are admirable examples of this phenomenon. They reflect the tradition of Hellenistic workshops, and allow us to appreciate their inspiration and their virtuosity, if we look, for purposes of comparison, at the works of their immediate successors. Similarly floor mosaics, which were just beginning to spread in the fourth century, without great technical finesse, underwent an amazing development from the time of the Diadochi. Mosaics found at Pella in Macedonia illustrate the know-how of the first skilled workers in mosaic to appear in the history of Greco-Roman art. Still using limited means, and exploiting only moderately the possibilities of color, they composed amazingly vigorous and elegant pictures, set in decorative foliated scrolls conspicuous for inventiveness and magnificence. A short time later the use of tesserae of varied colors created a multiplicity of possible applications for an art that found its way into individual dwellings, as it had already done into palaces. The Delos mosaics, in the second half of the second century BC, are its high-water mark. The fashion was to survive until the end of Antiquity. Proceeding from the floor, where they played the role of a carpet, mosaics spread to walls and vaults. A legacy of the Hellenistic age, mosaic was to remain one of the major arts of the Middle Ages, in the east as well as the west.

■ *Decoration and imagery* ■ *Household furnishings: beds, tableware, torch-holders* ■ *Copies and* pasticcio ■ *From the Derveni crater to the Sakha Dionysus*

Such works enhanced the environment of daily life for those who were fortunate enough to be able to afford them. Apart from their intrinsic quality, they have evidential value for us: they are a faithful enough reflection of the masterpieces of major Greek painting, which have entirely disappeared, but were, as long as they survived, no less admired than the productions of the best sculptors of the time. On the walls of villas at Pompeii or Herculaneum, a mythological composition or a landscape painting fills the center of a panel, just as a representational scene can be the central motif of a mosaic. For such subjects, mural painters or workers in mosaic could allow themselves to be inspired by the work of illustrious masters, which they reproduced with more or less fidelity. It can easily be imagined that collections were circulated in workshops, displaying such models. Hence the recurrence of the same motifs, similarly illustrated (except for a few variations in detail) in many different copies.

This allows us to grasp an important aspect of Hellenistic art in its final phase, and in its immediate extension to Imperial art. This is the influence of past masters, whose works were reproduced without any scruple, though not in a slavish manner. The authority of the past was evident in all areas of art, in sculpture or in intaglio engraving, as well as in painting or mosaic. From the last century before our era, new creations by artists endowed with originality – they were not in short supply – appear side by side with frequently repeated clichés, inspired by artists of the Classical period. These were recreated with meticulous precision, more often than not showing slight variations in matters of detail. As the price of such work depended on attention to craftsmanship, the search for originality was not a prime consideration. A need might even be felt to bring together in one work contributory elements of varied origin. The result was then a *pasticcio*, an eclectic (in some cases heteroclite) combination of motifs borrowed from Classical works belonging to diverse periods. Such a device found favor at the start of the last century before our era, when the workshop of the sculptor Pasiteles and his pupils Stephanus and Menelaus employed it at Rome. The famous *Extractor of Thorns (Spinario)* and *Venus on the Esquiline* are good examples of this new formula.

In addition to the faithful copy and the *pasticcio*, public interest in ancient art showed itself in the rise of the "archaizing" style, which had already shown signs of emergence in the second century BC. The idea here was not to reproduce a well-known model. It was to imitate, for the purpose of new creations, both reliefs and figures in the round, modeling practices that masters of Archaic sculpture and of the Severe Style had applied in the sixth and early fifth centuries. The *Korai* of the Athenian Acropolis and the funerary reliefs preceding the Persian Wars had long since disappeared. They had been piously interred under the floor of the sanctuary after the destruction caused by the Persian invader, or reused as construction material for the new wall surrounding the Acropolis. Yet, elsewhere in Greece proper, there remained enough monuments dating back to that famous creative period to encourage artists to revive its spirit by the use of *pasticcio*. A widespread yearning for the past encouraged this new trend, which may be considered akin to Mannerism, as it was given to certain systematic diversions from naturalness. These consisted in adding length to the body's proportions, stressing thinness in the facial area or, contrariwise, heaviness in the chin. Attitudes and gestures would be given an artificial elegance, the arrangement of clothing an unreal look, aiming at a merely diagrammatic effect. There is disagreement among modern critics as to when this school, often called Neo-Attic, began and how it came into existence. What is certain is that it represents an original aspect of Hellenistic art, and met with enough success to survive under the Empire until the second century of our era.

It is significant that in certain "bucolic" landscapes decorating residences in Hellenistic Italy, the statues of divinities placed in countryside shrines are of the archaizing type. For wealthy Hellenized Romans of the first century, such conscious references to the artistic past of Greece satisfied the thirst for a change in environment. That had been the aim and achievement of the exotic setting of Nilotic landscapes, the fairytale atmosphere of Ulysses' wanderings, or heroic scenes borrowed from tragedy. The architecture of theatrical settings seen on the walls of the villas of Pompeii opens up a perspective on a mysterious and fantastic dream world that extended *ad infinitum* the scope of imagination. This was nothing more than a decorative setting in which one would look in vain for a precise religious or philosophical message. Its purpose was to enrich, with the display of these beautiful pictures and objects, the daily life of an enlightened public that had inherited an old tradition of civilization and culture. It would provide a delightful reminder of their education and their readings, allowing them to engage in a fruitful, intimate conversation with themselves, filled with references to a past that stayed alive in its complexity and boundless wealth. Pompeian paintings supplied this sort of environment. The "apartment" sculptures of Delian houses had already, for some time, served the same purpose by putting a touch of life into their decoration. The numerous naked Aphrodites that have been found in the ruins of these houses obviously had no definite cultic significance. With other pleasing sights, they were part of a traditional imagery (at best overlaid with an undefined religious coloring), similar to the one found on painted vases or embossed terracottas, on metal plate, rings, or jewels.

The opening of a considerable market for such goods was a strong stimulus to creativity among craftsmen and artists. Luxury furniture was in great demand, especially couches adorned with bronze fittings, on which those participating in banquets stretched themselves. The silver and vermilion treasures that have been found in Macedonian tombs give an idea of the magnificence spread on the tables of the mighty in the age of the Diadochi. Vases made of bronze, sometimes plated with gold, were even more numerous and no less impressive for their elegance of shape and beauty of ornament. The Derveni Crater, 90 centimeters high, discovered near Salonica, is a prodigious illustration of the versatility of Greek workers in bronze in the late fourth century. It is completely covered with shapes and figures, some done in repoussé work, others inlaid separately after being melted: all deriving from the Dionysiac repertory (as was fitting for an essential accessory to a banquet). Far from creating an impression of excess, this superabundance of detail is organized into a harmonious whole, resulting from perfect execution, precision in draftsmanship, and a well-planned distribution of various elements. At the end of the Hellenistic period, monumental marble vases, like the famous Borghese Vase in the Louvre, are proof that such a tradition had continued unimpaired. At about the same time, bronze torch-bearing statues would light the banquet halls. Many of these, representing Dionysus or companions of his Bacchic procession, with the physique of handsome ephebes (see p. 296), have survived to our day. They provide testimony to the spread of their use from one end of the ancient world to the other: in Attica, at Pompeii, at Volubilis in Morocco, at Sakha and Zifteh in Egypt. Lucretius (cf. p. 373) is a witness to the vogue for metal torch-bearers in the first half of the last century BC. Nature's own delights, he says, can do without "golden statues of young men holding in their right hands fire-bearing torches providing light for nocturnal feasts" (II, 23f.). For these three centuries Greek workshops continued to provide luxury articles to a society anxious to make the most of its wealth and eager to dazzle. These ranged from the Derveni Crater, which was used in the drinking bouts of Macedonian nobles at the time of Alexander, to the Sakha Dionysus, which may have provided light to the banquets of Antony and Cleopatra when they led the "Inimitable Life" (see p. 160). When such a clientele ran short of means, Roman society, having learned from it, inherited the same thirst for such products, as is shown in the case of Verres, the notorious governor of Sicily (cf. Cicero's *Verrines,* mentioned on p. 374), and allowed artists to add to their production. The silver vases of Boscoreale (in the Louvre Museum), of Berthouville (in the Cabinet des Médailles, Paris), or of Hildesheim (in Berlin), which are reputed to date from the time of Augustus or Tiberius, are a direct extension of Hellenistic tradition.

■ *The diversity of styles* ■ *Chronological uncertainty* ■ *The difficulty of defining local schools* ■ *The phantom of an "Alexandrian" art* ■ *The uncertainty of present classifications*

The size of the market for works of art in those days explains in a way the extreme diversity in trends and styles that makes the study and chronological arrangement of production very difficult. To respond to such heavy demands scattered over a very wide area, artists were prepared to travel, as they had already done in previous times. Surviving signatures are testimony to their mobility, which fostered contact among workshop traditions and disseminated tendencies and fashions, with their resulting interaction. Variety in customers' tastes, and the retroactive prestige of the great Classical masters, forestalled an evolution of style in the Greek world, marked by continuous linear development. Already in the fourth century BC, during the second Classical age, which witnessed the rise of Scopas (see p. 353) and Praxiteles (see *The Civilization of Greece,* p. 359, plates 196, 226), the complexity of that evolution is notable. The result is that even when sculptures are well preserved and display a typical style, archaeologists find it impossible to date them within half a century. Starting with the age of Alexander, classification becomes even harder and relies in a large measure on arbitrary and subjective criteria. To quote only one instance, a portrait of which we have many copies and in which the comic poet Menander has been identified (no doubt rightly), was for a long time considered by prominent specialists to be that of Vergil. Now, there is a three-century interval between the late fourth century BC and the Augustan age, which gives a proper measure of our ignorance and uncertainty. For this reason we shall, without any reservation, shun a beguiling temptation to which art historians have yielded and still yield too easily, and which consists in dividing Hellenistic art into three periods – high, middle, and late. This is a fallacious, purely nominal solution to an extremely complicated problem: it is more candid to recognize the labyrinthine difficulties it presents.

The truth of the matter is that the starting point of any serious study of the question is not sufficiently established. Solidly identified and dated works are rare. The consensus of sorts that appears in a few cases to have been reached among scholars conceals, more often than not, the precariousness of its underlying reasons, resting as it does on an argument of authority or an abdication of one's own critical spirit. Neither the Victory of Samothrace nor the Venus of Milo has been dated beyond reasonable doubt. The Vatican Laocoon, which the astonishing discoveries made not long ago in the Sperlonga Grotto now allow us to place with certainty in the Flavian period, c. 80–70 BC, was for a long time considered, and is still held by some, to be a Hellenistic work. The magnificent Aphrodite of Cyrene, whose plinth encased in molding compels us to consider it a work of the second century of our era, is readily stated by some to be a typical sculpture of the "Alexandrian" period. Reliable critics consider (rightly in our view) the Hermes of Olympia to be a marble copy, dating from the Augustan age, of a now lost original. Yet many admire it as an authentic masterpiece from the hands of Praxiteles. The definitive history of Hellenistic sculpture has still to be written, starting from monuments whose dating rests on external and objective criteria that will exclude every abusive simplification that has hampered research for far too long.

By the same argument, any systematic classification based on the existence of a local school, be it Athenian, Rhodian, Pergamene, or Alexandrian, should be avoided. These various centers maintained or hosted very productive workshops, but one cannot define with precision their characteristic styles. For example, the monumental Altar of Zeus was built, with its prodigious sculptured decoration, at Pergamum under Eumenes II, in the first half of the second century. One could not imagine any greater difference than the one between the two friezes adorning the same monument. The frieze on the base is in high relief, depicting in a continuous movement the fearful struggle between gods and giants. Savage violence is portrayed here, in a series of merciless duels involving monsters, beasts, male and female divinities. Looking at this, one might believe that the baroque imagination that was to be let loose in the works of Michelangelo or Giulio Romano was already at work. The interior frieze, on the other hand, is done in less striking relief. It unfurls the successive episodes of the myth of the hero Telephus, by means of varied compositions in which the figures' Classical lines are inserted in an exquisitely picturesque framework in which the portrayal of landscape finds its place. One is at a loss to decide which of the two finished works is specifically "Pergamene." Each of them is representative of a well-defined vision of plastic art, each was brought to completion by a homogeneous team of professionals, masters of every resource of their craft. Modern criticism tends to opt for the Gigantomachy – erroneously, it would seem.

It is necessary to exorcise the long-lived phantom of an "Alexandrian" art. Three-quarters of a century ago an eminent scholar cast doubt on its existence. His questioning nearly caused a scandal. There is still a considerable degree of willingness to take for granted an art born in the capital of Ptolemaic Egypt, and spreading from there to the whole of the Mediterranean world. Ancient Alexandria's immense prestige in science and literature dazzles the world of archaeology, which would like to bestow on that city the same dominant role in the realm of art. A wealthy city like Alexandria did indeed, together with its residents the Lagid monarchs, offer a choice clientele to artists. Its palaces, sanctuaries, public buildings, and necropolises were full of paintings and statues. Numerous workshops and their craftsmen catered for the needs of a prosperous population, encouraged by the sovereigns' example to cultivate a taste for luxury. Outside Egypt the Ptolemies made numerous foundations and donations, which can sometimes be traced over the years, in the Delian inventories, for example. There is therefore no doubt that Ptolemaic Egypt, its metropolis in particular, responded abundantly to the demand for works of art in the Hellenistic age. Unfortunately, no significant body of documentation allows us to know precisely in what direction that demand manifested itself. Too few artists are mentioned in our texts or in inscriptions as originating from Alexandria or Greek Egypt. No evidence is found of a local school of sculpture or painting. Excavation has yielded few sculptured artifacts, and these are hardly distinctive. The only ones to impress the viewer as the outcome of a rather special inspiration are bronze and terracotta figurines. Human features with a local typology, for example, regional facial types or grotesque caricatures, have a place apart among these, beside religious objects in which Egyptian influence is evident (Isis, Harpocrates, Isiac priests). But, generally speaking, these purely Alexandrian productions do not stand out for their quality, which is inferior to that of other workshops of the Hellenistic world and does not reveal an original style. Barring a few portrayals, typically indigenous ones, the same themes are found elsewhere, at Tanagra, Smyrna, Myrina, or in Syria, where they are treated with more competence and vigor than in Egypt. The theory of Alexandria's determining influence on the representational art of our period has therefore no foundation in fact. The city was certainly a prosperous marketing center that must have attracted artists, but it was not the seat of an original production that left a deep imprint on contemporary art history. This is no matter for surprise. Was it not the case of London between the seventeenth and nineteenth centuries? In conclusion, we shall avoid mentioning an Alexandrian artistic style, since the works that really deserve that label have no more than a minor place in the whole spectrum of Hellenistic art.

It seems wise therefore, in the present state of our knowledge, to steer clear both of a geographical distinction among local schools and a chronological division into major periods – ancient, middle, and late Hellenistic – explaining a general evolution in style. The complex nature of reality does not agree with such simplistic classifications. Analysis proves, on the contrary, that in the same period and sometimes in the same place quite divergent trends coexisted. We find fidelity to Classical norms as well as a mania for archaizing; reliance on models by the great masters of the fourth century – Scopas, Praxiteles, Lysippus – as well as a baroque expressionism. A species of Mannerism striving after elegance in long-lined profiles (cf. p. 376) is present side by side with a sensual depiction of plump and well-filled shapes. Composition of scenes with a multiplicity of figures was sometimes approached from a purely frontal and linear viewpoint, sometimes in depth, with a suggestion, through a variety of devices, of a series of successive planes. A number of solutions would be found; style and inspiration would be modified to suit the clientele's taste or the workshop's own tradition. Definitive conclusions as to how such an abundance of conflicting activities and mutually contradictory approaches organized itself will be the culmination of prolonged and arduous research.

■ *Distinct features of Hellenistic art* ■ *An interest in powerful shapes and violent movements* ■ *Complex groupings and pyramidal compositions* ■ *Realism, naturalism, exoticism* ■ *The lifelike portrait*

These reservations having been duly expressed, it still remains possible, when one considers Hellenistic art as a whole, to analyze the main elements of its contribution to history, which is in itself considerable and of major significance for later times. While many artists in that age had no further ambition than to apply the methods perfected by their famous predecessors of the Classical age, others explored new approaches, thus creating works of profound originality. This was the case with sculptors who tried to express physical power or violent movement with a suggestive strength that had never before been attained. The celebrated Lysippus initiated the trend. He was a virtuoso of bronze work, a highly productive artist if ever there was one, since he was credited with 1,500 statues. Many copyists reproduced his standing *Heracles*, leaning on his cudgel, in particular Glycon, the sculptor of the Farnese Hercules at Naples. A stunning mountain of bone and muscle in temporary rest, it seethes with repressed energy, though a sort of melancholy fatigue, brought on by so many demanding labors, is reflected in its bearing and visual expression. The same impression of formidable power is found in the seated *Boxer*, a work in bronze in Rome's National Museum. The same can be said of the famous *Belvedere Torso* in the Vatican, signed by the Athenian Apollonius son of Nestor, which was admired by Michelangelo and suggested his allegory of *The Day* on Julius II's tomb. Again, Lysippus provided models of instantaneous effects and violent movements: one is the allegory of *Kairos* ("The Propitious Moment"), capturing the fleeting apparition of a winged youth as he strides in a race. An equestrian statue retrieved from the sea near Cape Artemisium, and now in Athens' National Museum, provides the best illustration of such bold experiments. It does not show the victorious steed standing or pacing slowly, after its victory in the games, which the statue is meant to commemorate. Rather, the Hellenistic sculptor portrays it galloping, legs outstretched as it provides its most vigorous effort, while on its back the little jockey, still a child but already a professional in such races, looks back, half-turned, over his shoulder at his outdistanced competitors. What a contrast with the Delphic Charioteer (*The Civilization of Greece*, p. 366, plate 191), motionless on his chariot after his triumph! The Charioteer had been the idea of a master of the Severe Style, three centuries earlier. The fashion of attitudes translating movement reappears in statues of fighters like the Borghese Gladiator in the Louvre, signed by Agasias of Ephesus in *c*.80 BC. Sculpture in the round vies with relief or painting in attempting to secure such effects.

We notice the same boldness in compositions grouping many figures in a coherent whole. Until then these had been conceived as an alignment of figures facing the viewer, in the manner of pedimental decorations in which statues are placed side by side, fronting a flat-surfaced wall, joined in an action that the eye can take in at one glance. Now pyramidal groups appear, like *Menelaus holding Patroclus' corpse* or *Achilles and Penthesilea*. To grasp their meaning and appreciate their plastic quality, it is no longer enough to consider them from only one privileged angle. We may look at the work while going all round it, blending its varying aspects in our own minds. A dynamic vision replaces one that is static. This is an innovation of great significance. The same remark applies to the *Ludovisi Gaul* committing suicide after killing his wife. The original of that work is (no doubt rightly) considered to have been one of the monuments that Attalus I caused to be erected (*c*.230 BC) in his capital Pergamum (see pp. 78–80, including plate 2). Another example is the *Child with a Goose*, which the poet Herondas

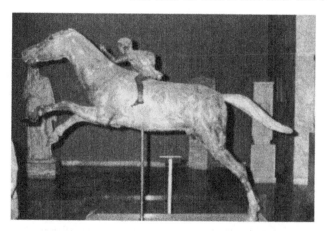

Plate 15 The Artemisium Jockey (National Museum, Athens; photo Ancient Art and Architecture Collection).

This amazing artifact has been rescued twice by modern techniques, first by hauling it from the seabed near Cape Artemisium, north of Euboea, then (at a more recent date in the second half of the last century) by a skillful restoration of the very fragmentary body of the horse. Now we can see the bronze equestrian statue that the owner of this horse dedicated as a memorial of its victory. It is shown at full gallop, at the very moment it was flying toward success, spurred on by its young jockey. He is a child, for several texts tell us that very young boys, with the advantage of being lighter, were trained for racing. He is probably a barbarian slave, whose features the artist has faithfully brought out – in any case, a professional, for he is wearing spurs. Here is an outstanding achievement of realism and a signal success in seizing the defining moment – two prime aspirations of Hellenistic art.

saw, in the third century, in Asclepius' shrine at Cos (see p. 336). Even the *Drunken Old Woman*, the work of one Myron of Thebes, had been designed by its sculptor to be seen successively from a variety of angles as a really multidimensional work of art.

These last three works illustrate another original feature of Hellenistic art: an interest in realism that had not been shown before. The very small child, the decrepit old person, the barbarian – Celt, Persian, or Negro – a grotesque or misshapen figure, are themes now treated without any need to justify them by a myth. Their value as picturesque figures is enough. Naturalism stakes its claim, together with exoticism, beside the traditionally idealized human model. This is a response to a taste already noted in literature for character-sketches or *mimes* drawn from daily life (see p. 336, as above), for stories of travel and *mirabilia* (see pp. 286, 313–19). A magnificent high-relief discovered at Athens shows a groom with distinctly African features restraining a saddle-horse: a striking, no doubt intentional, contrast is displayed here by the powerful liveliness of the steed and the guiding slave's less expressive silhouette. For Hellenistic sculptors wished to illustrate the first-rate vitality of their workmanship by these portrayals of animals. Their naturalism showed in such works, which were often meant to provide for the needs of cult (as we saw earlier, pp. 287–8). The awe-inspiring bull made of marble that was found a few decades ago in the necropolis at Oreus, in the north of Euboea, is an outstanding example of this. Realism and naturalism gave impetus to the portrait genre. Contrary to what is commonly believed, the Greeks had shown their ability to reproduce accurately an individual's features since the years of the Severe Style, as evidenced by the masterly portrait of Themistocles which has survived. There was, however, no widespread desire to preserve a faithful likeness of great historical figures until the fourth century, when, starting with Alexander the Great, the prestige of monarchs imposed itself worldwide. The proliferation of statues raised in honor of sovereigns, generals, or public benefactors (*Euergetai*: see pp. 191–2) developed interest among artists in works of that kind – not busts, but sculptures in the round. It was only toward the end of the Hellenistic age, in response to demand from a Roman clientele wishing to adorn its villas and gardens, that sculptors began to fashion busts or herms, placed on a stand on which the name of the honored person could conveniently be inscribed. Coinage stamps, revealing in very recognizable form the profiles of sovereigns, together with their names, contributed to an innovation that gave pride of place to facial traits.

Apart from the military and those who were active in political life, it was to thinkers and poets above all that people wished to erect statues. We are acquainted with the features of the most prominent philosophers, Plato, Aristotle, Epicurus, Zeno, Chrysippus, or Posidonius, through copies of their original portraits. Similarly, Demosthenes' effigies are copies deriving, it seems, from a posthumous bronze statue erected in 280 BC, the work of the sculptor Polyeuctus. Menander's likeness, too, was widely copied from an original. The usage improved in quality with widespread practice. It responded so well to the taste of the times that even purely imaginary depictions, like those of Homer, were then endowed with personalized features: a small terracotta head found at Chios is a curious example of this custom. Having received such training, Greek sculptors had no difficulty complying with their Roman customers' specifications when they ordered *imagines*, true-to-life representations of their ancestors, near or far removed in time, which every family kept piously in its home. At the start of the second century the consul Flamininus (see pp. 107–9) had caused his marble statue, whose head has been preserved until our time, to be consecrated at Delphi. When the need came to portray Pompey, Mark Antony, Caesar, then Augustus and the princes of the Imperial family, Hellenistic workshops were ready: it is from them that what we call the Roman portrait originated.

■ *Historical subjects* ■ *Scenes of daily life, and paintings representing battle scenes* ■ *Pictures enshrining the memory of Alexander* ■ *The mosaic of the House of the Faun at Pompeii* ■ *Treatises on art written by artists* ■ *A significant example: the* Aldobrandini Nuptials ■ *Analysis of this work: its inherent meaning, its influence, the idea it gives of the ambitions and resources of Hellenistic art*

Realism and a new grasp of complex compositions led artists in this period to widen the range of their activity to areas in which their predecessors had worked only occasionally. Without implying a complete break with the past, a notable evolution occurred, reflecting a change in ideas and mores. Art became more oriented toward contemporary reality, which meant the development of "historical" painting and relief, with, as its corollary, a greater scope in such works for the architectural environment and for landscape. Artists strove to focus on, and immortalize, events to which they were close in time, something they had witnessed, or an instantaneous phenomenon. This would sometimes supersede the traditional thinking of artists living in the Classical age, who had been more attached to the timeless than to the transitory, more naturally inclined to transpose history into the realm of myth. Direct observation had no doubt never ceased to provide Hellenic artists with the necessary material basis that would become the embodiment of their inspiration. But they had tended to stylize or sublimate their factual data, leaving it to craftsmen of the minor arts, terracotta modelers or vase painters, to produce a straight reproduction of daily life. That life was from then on introduced – of course, with due caution – into major art.

The painting of battle scenes bears witness to this. Starting from the fourth century, renowned painters no longer opted to celebrate ancient feats of arms in their works, like the battles of Marathon or Plataea, which could have been treated in the manner of the episodes of the Trojan War. They were to extoll contemporary events instead, like the battle of Mantinea (362), where Epaminondas met his death, and which the painter Euphranor soon after portrayed on a wall of the Stoa of Zeus, in the Athenian Agora. His contemporary Pausias expressed this judgment, according to Demetrius of Phalerum (see p. 361) writing at the end of the fourth century:

A painter's talent should not allow itself to be debased by being minted into small coinage – meaning, for example, bouquets or small birds. It should rather portray naval battles or cavalry engagements, with horses galloping, others rearing, others again collapsing, horsemen brandishing their javelins or falling off their horses.

The admonition was not in vain: for the epic tale of Alexander and the struggles among the Diadochi provided Hellenistic painters with magnificent material, which they put to excellent use. Diodorus tells us (XVIII, 27) that the funeral chariot that transported Alexander's body from Babylon to Memphis in 323 (see p. 44), was adorned with four painted panels recalling the conqueror's glory:

> The first depicted him seated on a splendidly decorated chariot. He held a magnificent scepter, surrounded by the King's House made up of armed Macedonians and Persian guards and equerries. The next one showed accompanying elephants in war outfits, mounted in front by Indian mahouts, and behind by Macedonians in traditional apparel. On the third one, cavalry squadrons went through their maneuvers as in a pitched battle, while on the fourth warships were displayed, ready for action.

The practice that became current in later times, of Roman generals having paintings carried in their triumphal processions to make known their exploits, was a reenactment of a celebratory usage that had survived over the centuries in the works of Greek artists. The consul Aemilius Paullus caused an episode of the battle of Pydna (168: see p. 116) to be sculpted in relief on an elevated pillar bearing his statue at Delphi. This proves that sculptors were no less ready than painters to depict contemporary events. There too, Hellenistic art blazed a trail for Imperial art.

The large mosaic depicting *Alexander's Battle* that was discovered at Pompeii is enough to give us a good idea of these ambitious compositions. A conjecture that seems probable judges it to have been inspired by a painting that Philoxenus of Eretria did for Cassander (see pp. 45–7), king of Macedon, toward the end of the fourth century. It is an evocation of the clash between two empires and two peoples. In the middle of the fray the young Macedonian hero is engaged in an irresistible charge across the Persian battalions, and meets the Great King at his wits' end, about to flee and making a gesture of distress from his raised station in his chariot. The human mass bristling with spears contrasts with the two protagonists, who appear in the foreground. The horsemen's steeds and those drawing the chariot are shown in a wide variety of positions of the utmost mobility, foreshortened in astonishing ways. The picturesque exoticism of carefully represented styles of clothing is a striking sight that does not distract from the dramatic nature of the action. Every possible asset of composition, design, and color is called into service in the fulfillment of a grand design. It can be said that the mosaicist, in spite of occasional clumsiness on points of detail, was not unequal to his model. Historical painting has not achieved anything in the modern western world to surpass this effort. One can appreciate Cicero's verdict (*Brutus* 18, 70), according to which, with Protogenes and Apelles, the great painters of Alexander's time, *perfecta sunt omnia*, "perfection was attained down to the last detail."

Technical perfection having been achieved in all areas of art, it was now partnered by theoretical thinking, for which practicing artists were responsible. The example of Polyclitus writing his *Canon* was not forgotten. Texts mention many treatises on sculpture or painting. Toward the end of the fourth century the painter Protogenes wrote on his branch of artistic creation. Xenocrates of Athens, a sculptor connected with Lysippus' school, wrote many books on sculpture, while Antigonus of Carystus, also known for other writings, dealt with works in bronze. Finally, at the start of the last century BC, the sculptor Pasiteles (see p. 376), whose teaching propagated a distinct species of academic taste in Rome, produced five books on the main masterpieces known in the Greek world. A form of art criticism was born, originating from artists. This was in conformity with Hellenic tradition, which from its beginnings stipulated that a work of art, while demanding full technical mastery and every skill of eye or hand, was to remain in a sense bathed in an intellectual ambience. When he uttered his famous aphorism, *La pittura è cosa mentale*, "Painting is a matter of intelligence," Leonardo da Vinci reasserted a crucial principle of Greek art.

A celebrated mural painting has survived as a memorial to the ambitious program that this statement formulates. It illustrates the intimate link that Hellenistic artists achieved between the human world and their contemporary lifestyle, the human world and the divine. It is named the *Aldobrandini Nuptials* (see p. 375) because, after it was discovered at Rome at the end of the sixteenth century, it first belonged to Cardinal Aldobrandini before becoming part of the Vatican collection. It was painted at the time of Augustus toward the end of the last century before our era to adorn a Roman villa, and has a certain kinship with compositions of the "Second Style" that adorned the walls of houses in Pompeii at about the same time. Like them, it is not the production of a first-rate artist, but of a conscientious craftsman working closely on models dating from earlier days. It supplies us with testimony that can be regarded as genuine, for there is no evidence in any of its components of intrusion from foreign elements. Everything in its inspiration and composition, and in the details of clothing, is Greek. The work is fortunately complete and on the whole well preserved. It therefore lends itself all the better to detailed analysis, and can be considered fully representative of the aspirations and achievements of Hellenistic art.

Its theme is a wedding, a solemn event above all others, since the survival of the City is dependent on it. For a citizen is by definition a legitimate child born of a legally recognized partnership. An elaborate ceremonial, involving the family as well as the City and its religion, brings out the importance of the occasion. At the same time, a wedding unites two human beings, two individual destinies, a man and a woman, for better or for worse. It is looked upon as a personal venture, a landmark in one's life. This is especially the case for the bride, who has stayed, in compliance with Greek custom, in the section of the house reserved for women (the *gynaikeion* or gynaeceum: see p. 194), and who, before the ceremony, hardly knows the man her parents have chosen to be her husband. Now, the Hellenistic age, as shown by its literature from Menander to Apollonius of Rhodes, or by its art (consider the statues honoring women benefactors – see pp. 194–5 – or the terracottas from Tanagra), was interested in woman as a social being, in emotions that were specifically hers. The painter of the *Aldobrandini Nuptials*, or rather the great artist from whom he drew his inspiration, is from this point of view a man of his times: portraying a wedding, he keeps in mind the bride, and the bride alone. The moment he chooses is the most moving of all: the bride-to-be, who has recently been taken to the nuptial chamber, waits for the bridegroom to join her. The artist employs the means specific to his art to convey the feelings that are hers at this moment.

His portrayal of the scene, into which he brings ten participants, is characterized by clarity and extreme refinement. His frieze-type composition is structured into three groups that he diversifies skillfully so as to avoid excessive symmetry. The two groups placed at the ends, each made up of three women, belong to the real world, that of daily life. On the right are three friends of the bride, performing the nuptial ritual. One of these young women burns aromatic spices in a large, splendidly engraved censer. The other two sing the wedding song to the accompaniment of their lyre; *Hymen, O Hymenaeus!*, the choral song that traditionally greeted the arrival of the bride-to-be at her conjugal home. On the left side, the bride's mother, draped in her ceremonial dress and holding a fan in her left hand, checks with her right hand the temperature of the lukewarm water that two maids have poured into a basin for the young bride's ritual ablutions. In conformity with a canon of Greek art, as verified in funerary and votive stelae, the two slave maidens appear smaller than their mistress: this introduces an element of divergence into the symmetry between the three-person lateral groups. Both of these are skillfully arranged in depth around a pivotal appointment, the censer on the right, the hand-basin on its pedestal on the left. The lighting comes from the right, which makes it obvious that the singers have taken their stand out of doors, while the mother and the maids are by now at the very center of the house. These arrangements are discreetly indicated, with a most sparing use of material aids. The viewer, being accustomed to such ritual, has no difficulty recognizing it.

The essential role belongs to the central group, whose arrangement conforms to a carefully thought-out strategy. We are now in the nuptial chamber, as indicated by the large state bed, laid out diagonally. One of the legs of the bed, made of carved wood, supports its head, and is conspicuous as the median axis of the whole composition. The architectural framework is reduced to a minimum. A plain cornice-topped wall shows that the event takes place inside a house. A bend in the wall on the left suggests that the nuptial chamber is separated from the room in which the mother and the maids are getting the lustral water ready for use. A pilaster behind the head of the bed indicates that the house stops there

Plate 16 The Aldobrandini Nuptials (Biblioteca Vaticano, Rome; photo SCALA).

An overall view of the mural painting given this name. From left to right are the bride's mother and two maidservants. In the center is a group made up of Aphrodite, seated by the bride on the nuptial couch and clasping her, with Aphrodite's maid on the left and Hymenaeus sitting on a step on the right. Finally comes a group of friends of the bride, outside the house.

and that the group at the right is in the open air. Such a summary representation of the environment remains intentionally elliptical: the aim is to avoid distracting the viewer's attention towards an accessory detail. Similarly, in the famous painting entitled *Alexander's Battle* in Naples' National Museum (see p. 386), a denuded tree-trunk is enough to conjure up the natural frame in which the action takes place: a compressed indication of the landscape, equivalent to an intelligible hint. In the Hellenistic age Greek art did not forget to use the artistic equivalent of litotes whenever it appeared useful or necessary.

Two women, one having her arm round the other, are seated on the bed. The second woman, heavily veiled, so that one has only a glimpse of her face, is the young bride, still wearing her wedding gown. She has recently been taken to the nuptial chamber, where she stays waiting for her spouse, who is due to arrive soon. At this solemn moment her head is bowed with emotion and maidenly modesty. The woman seated by her is no mortal but a divinity, as shown by her half-nakedness. This is Aphrodite, goddess of love, who has descended from Olympus to comfort the new bride and help her to overcome her fears and modest reserve. Intervening as a nuptial divinity, she has drawn back her veil over her laurel-decked head, revealing the splendour of her radiant beauty. With her left arm round the young maiden's neck, she directs toward her a look of tender friendship, and makes a gesture of encouragement with her right hand. The pairing of these two women, one the senior and stronger one, the other younger and more fragile, is in conformity with an ancient tradition of Greek art, which often rendered the tender affection bonding a mother–daughter pair or two friends. The significance of this pair is heightened in the present case by the fact that it is made up of a goddess and a mortal. One has come to help the other, in the familiar spirit of trust and total devotion that links the Greek soul with its divinities. The warm and compassionate presence of the goddess brings to the young bride, at a time of emotional stress, the relief that will dispel her fears and lay open to her the path toward happiness. Nobility and dignity in deportment, discretion in gesture, earnestness in facial expression create a feeling of religious solemnity with which the scene is infused, and convey the elevated idea that the Greeks had of the sacred act of matrimony.

Left of Aphrodite a half-naked woman, supported by a low pillar, pours into a large conch the contents of a small vase of perfume. Her dress indicates that she is no mortal but a divine being. She is a maid in Aphrodite's retinue, one of the Graces, who is to help in getting the bride ready, thus cooperating at the material level with the comfort the goddess is providing in the moral sphere. The painter has given this divinity a posture that is typically Hellenistic: nonchalance in the way she leans on a stand coming just above her waist, an emphasized projection of the hips, crossed legs, arms half-outstretched, are features found in sculptures of this age. In the painting under discussion, she marks the transition to the group on the far left. We notice, however, that two women neighboring each other, the mother in austere ceremonial dress and Aphrodite's gracious bare-breasted companion, have their backs turned to each other, as though each of the women were unaware of the other's presence. The representatives of the world of divinities, whose purpose in coming into our world is to break the young bride's solitude, are visible to her alone, not to other mortals.

The tenth person in the picture is its only man. He is the counterpart of the two women sitting on the bed. He is seated on a low step, close to the bed-head. His face is turned toward the bride and the goddess as he gazes intently at them, while they, engrossed in their intimate dialogue, do not heed his presence. His gaze, resting on the two women, is his only link with them, but a strong one, bringing into a coherent whole these three central figures of the picture. The almost naked young man, his head wreathed with foliage, is not a mortal but a god. He is the god Hymenaeus (see p. 388), personifying marriage, in accord-

ance with a propensity highly developed among the Greeks, representing allegories in human shape. He presides over nuptial union: the hymn sung by the bride's
young friends at the right of the stage is a ritual invocation of the god. His presence is therefore necessary. The place he occupies is the very threshold of the
house, the step on which he is seated – in a natural and relaxed pose, well known
to Hellenistic sculptors, the invention of which dates back to Lysippus. The mode
of his presentation is an admirable element in the picture, writ large, a touch of
great professional confidence. Intent on observing the conversation between the
two women, Hymenaeus watches for its outcome. As soon as the bride, reassured
by Aphrodite, feels ready to welcome her husband, the god will go and bring
him: for he is waiting outside the nuptial chamber, though the painter has chosen
not to include him in his picture. The role of this allegorical personality is to
evoke discreetly the love and impatience of the absent spouse. His anxious glance
denotes his expectation of the *kairos*, the propitious moment (see above, p. 382,
and below about Lysippus' statue of *Kairos*), and his unsteady posture hints that
he will bound forward to accomplish his mission. An empty space separates him
from the two women, with the foot of the bed paradoxically occupying alone the
centre of the pyramidal composition represented by the middle group. It is full of
symbolic meaning: still kept apart by a remnant of apprehensive modesty, the
couple will soon be united in love triumphant, by a divine will which, through the
matrimonial rite, ensures the continuity of humankind.

The *Aldobrandini Nuptials* reveals itself on analysis as laden with allusions and
symbols. The painter excels in expressing, by strictly plastic processes, feelings,
moods, every nuance of psychological sensitivity. He brings out at the same time
the fundamental nature of the marriage rite for the society that he depicts. In so
doing he draws upon the usual repertory of divine figures that stand surety for
the permanence of the civic bond and have always been trusted witnesses of the
hopes and fears of Greek humanity. Divinities and anthropomorphic allegories
help him to make intelligible the inherent meaning of his painting. He makes
them part of the world of mortals with the same ease with which Phidias, in his
organization of the Parthenon frieze, depicted the Athenian people processing
toward the assembled Olympians. The scene of the *Nuptials*, however, does not
occur within the environment of shrines and public spaces. It takes place in the
intimate atmosphere of a bedroom. Its aim is not to make evident the harmony
of the community of citizens: rather, the hesitant reserve of a young maiden in
the presence of the mystery of love and the bridegroom's impatient desire. The
help the bride receives from family and society, represented by the two lateral
groups, including the mother and the two friends, is not enough to prevail against
the scruples of a sensitive soul. Only the benevolence of divine intervention will
bring the support that the situation requires.

In the work there is a subtle interplay of signs, an abundance of moral purpose, a skillful organization of the whole design, a perfect plastic application of

the artist's recollection of his model (evident in the portrayal of the various participants). This leads us to believe the *Nuptials* to be a faithful reproduction of a masterpiece by a great Hellenistic painter. It has preserved for us an important share in what was best in the art of that age – a perfect mastery of technique in the service of a lofty ambition. In those days the artist had a message to convey. He meant to instruct with his brush or his chisel. The lesson he taught was intended for the mind as well as for the eye. One could apply to his method the answer that Posidippus of Pella (see pp. 366–7) puts on the lips of Lysippus' *Kairos*, a brilliant allegory of the Propitious Moment, whom a curious passer-by interrogates on the hidden message he bears:

> "What purpose did the artist have in fashioning you?"
> "Stranger, he had in mind visitors to this place. He consecrated me in the vestibule to make people think."

Doing exactly the same, with the resources and the shades of meaning appropriate to the age, the work of art we have examined showed fidelity to the Hellenic tradition. It responded in anticipation to the demands that, many centuries later, painters of the Renaissance and of modern times were to elaborate in their minds and formulate. This explains how fascinated they were when it became accessible to them. Rubens was fired with enthusiasm, Van Dyck produced a drawing of it, Pietro da Cortona and Poussin copied it lovingly. For over four centuries the decoration of a bedroom painted by a Greek workshop in Augustus' time has stayed in our judgment as one of the most enthralling vestiges of Hellenistic art. It allows us to measure the greatness of the bequest which that art entrusted to Rome and which we were to enjoy so many centuries later.

CONCLUSION

■ *The wealth and dynamism of the Hellenistic age* ■ *An age of startling contrasts, with a sense of continuity and capacity for innovation* ■ *Its heritage, handed down and modeled by Rome, is of prime importance for Western civilization*

At the end of what has been a summary account of the Hellenistic world in the immense diversity of its aspects, what overall picture of that age should we recall? It was, first of all, not an age of decadence, as those are inclined to think who reserve admiration for none but the dazzling beauty of the masterpieces of Archaic and Classical Greece and who are still in mourning for Alexander's defeat of the rest of Greece at Chaeronea. Nor was it a period of transition which saw the glory of arms, the dignity of law, the prestige of art and intellect gradually passing, at the conclusion of a chaotic and bloody history, from the Aegean to Italy, from the Greek East to the Latin West, from Athens to Rome. Historic reality is far more complex than school textbooks show, subjected as they are to the abusive demands of simplification. We have become aware of this complexity in the course of the preceding chapters, discovering at every turn, on every subject, innovation paired with continuity, adherence to tradition with the appearance of new interests, human beings hankering for the past with others gazing passionately into the future.

The existence side by side of these conflicting tendencies, sometimes inhabiting the same minds, was consistently typical of the Greek community in the Hellenistic age. Holding in trust a cultural heritage of exceptional quality, they had at the same time to face vital problems of an entirely new character, which their astounding expansion in the footsteps of the Macedonian conqueror brought them, far from their motherland. They proved to be the creators both of scholarship, the revered guardian of the ancients' precious legacy, and of scientific method, our guide to knowledge of the contemporary world. They certainly did not destroy the foundations of the City, whose inhabitants knew each other and shared each other's concerns. But they thought out and put into practice the procedures, the administrative instruments, and the ideology which made it possible, in a far wider environment, to organize and manage large States, the only administrative units compatible with the new dimension of their universe. They showed a receptive attitude toward foreign beliefs without breaking with their traditional cults, which they preserved faithfully and zealously. They gave splendor to their cities, while preserving a taste for nature in the open countryside. Competent as town-planners, they also showed a bucolic instinct (see pp. 256–9). Their artists explored every approach to their craft without forgetting the teaching of the great masters. Their philosophers revered Plato, but, disregarding his example, worked out an ethic centered on the individual, referring only occasionally to the City. In those times of sharp contrasts and conflicting experiences, the sovereigns flaunted their luxury unscrupulously within sight of the Cynics' voluntary state of destitution.

It was an age that shimmered with a varied light. It had its sombre aspects: unbridled ambition, palace intrigue, plunder, and carnage. It also had many zones of light: progress in housing and in collective amenities, the bounty of *euergetai*, the ever-increasing number of festivals as witnessed by the proliferation of theaters, the impulse given to art and craftsmanship, the creation of libraries. So many bold speculations, so many endeavors crowned with success! It was the age of Aristotle, father of modern science; of Menander, founder of character comedy. Euclid was to be the oracle of mathematicians for twenty centuries. Callimachus was the first in time of men of letters, the emblematic figure of scholarship. Eratosthenes was the quintessential chronologist and geographer. Archimedes was both skillful as an engineer and an inspired researcher. Polybius was a marvelous analyst of the laws of history: no longer (like Thucydides) within the microcosm of Aegean Greece, but on the scale of the whole Mediterranean world. Finally, there was the long Stoic lineage, from Zeno to Epictetus and Marcus Aurelius. Such was the Hellenistic world's contribution in the realm of the spirit, briefly reviewed here to include only its stellar names. Without these we would not be what we are, and our Greek heritage would suffer from serious shortcomings. For the role that they played in it was one of decisive importance, and remains in many respects what is most alive in this legacy.

It is therefore proper to acknowledge our debt to those three centuries that extend from Alexander the Great to Augustus. Fortune often changed sides during that period between sovereigns or states, while by and by, in a slow and difficult process, a new Mediterranean order was emerging, which Rome was ultimately to control, after playing a major role in working out its defining characteristics. The benefit bestowed on Rome through close and prolonged contact with Hellenistic culture is a theme that will never be exhausted. Her scholars were nurtured in that culture. Cicero's higher education took place as he listened to the lectures of the Rhodian rhetors and the philosophers of the Academy. Lucretius' doctrine in its entirety is indebted to Epicurus. To express their feelings and emotions Catullus, Vergil, and Horace used a vocabulary, a mythology, and an imagery that were borrowed from the Alexandrians, so much so that the paradoxical view has been held that to know about the great Hellenistic poets one should turn to Latin poetry. The magnificent decoration provided by the paintings, sculptures, and mosaics with which the Emperors decked their capital and other cities of the empire was thought out, and often accomplished, by artists trained in Greek workshops. They placed themselves in the service of Rome, and found a felicitous response to the specific needs and tastes of the new masters of the world. Finally, in the area of politics, the principate's efficient system, to which Augustus, with the benefit of experience, gradually gave a definitive shape that endured for centuries, owes its essential inspiration to Hellenistic monarchy. Such borrowings Rome assimilated to perfection. She made them hers by enlivening them with her own genius. Thanks to Rome, the whole of the Western world, and everyone in it, reaped the benefits of Hellenistic civilization.

LEXICON OF TERMS

A term is not usually listed here if its meaning is given in the text.

ACADEMY   Name given to Plato's philosophical school, which originally met in the shrine of the Attic hero Academus, in the northwestern suburb of Athens.

ACHAEMENIDS   Royal dynasty of Persia, thus named after its founder Achaemenes (7th century BC).

ACROCORINTH   Fortress built on an enormous rocky peak (*akron*) that served as acropolis (*top of the city*) in Corinth.

ADYTON   Term employed to designate a sacred building or a part of it to which the public was not allowed access (the word means "inaccessible"). Lat. *penetrale*.

AEACIDS   Descendants of Aeacus, son of Zeus and the nymph Aegina, eponymous (see the term) to the island of that name. His son was Peleus, father of Achilles, whose descendants (real or supposed) called themselves Aeacids: thus Pyrrhus and Alexander the Great.

AGER PUBLICUS   "Public land": made up of landed property belonging to Rome in conquered territory.

AGON   Public competition, especially in athletic prowess, sport, or cultural accomplishment. Term used for the well-known Games – the Olympic and other Games.

AGONISTIC   Agonistic spirit: urge to compete in an *agon,* in a manner respectful of the rules.

AGONOTHETE   Magistrate in charge of the organization and supervision of a competition.

AMIXIA   Savagery, the vice of someone who has no connection (literally, does not mix) with humanity's feelings: typical of Ptolemy Physcon ordering the murder of his nephew and stepson.

AMPHICTYONY (Also spelled *Amphictiony*).   A politico-religious organization of Greek States or cities, centered round a common sanctuary. The Delphic one was the best known.

ANABASIS   Expedition "up from the sea" into the interior: the best known being

333

that of Xenophon. In Hellenistic history Antiochus III's great expedition to the eastern satrapies of the Seleucid Empire was called his *Anabasis*.

ANTHOLOGY see PALATINE ANTHOLOGY.

APOIKIA "A home, or homeland, abroad": a colony.

APOKLETOI In the Aetolian League, "those called from the ranks (of the SYNEDROI), chosen ones": members of a restricted council, elected to steer the policies of the League.

APOTROPAION (pl. APOTROPAIA) A term designating an object or an artifact, even a magical formula, supposed to be able to turn away (Gk. *apotrepein*) bad luck and protect against evil. Hence the adj. apotropaic.

ARCHEGETES (in Anglicized form, ARCHEGETE) A Greek epithet, meaning the "arch-leader" or founder of a new city, which was added to the name of a god or hero. Thus Apollo was Cyrene's ARCHEGETES.

ARCHON A term designating in various Greek cities the magistrate(s) entrusted with its government.

ARETALOGY Enumeration of the powers and virtues of a god: a common theme in hymns in honor of divinity.

ARETÉ The fullness of one's powers, excellence: virtue, especially military valor or courage in combat.

ARGYRASPIDS The term means "Silver Shields." It designated the elite corps of the veterans from Alexander's Asian campaigns. The encrusted silver on their large round shields distinguished them. They played a decisive role in the defeat of Eumenes of Cardia in 316.

ASYLIA Juridical guarantee of inviolability (freedom from SYLA, see below) for one's person or goods: it could be called legal immunity. Granted by a city either to a foreign individual, or to the citizens of a friendly or allied city.

ATARAXIA State of the soul that is "immune from disturbance": the Epicurean's goal in life.

ATRIUM Latin word denoting a large open space at the heart of the Roman household.

AUTOKRATOR Added to the title of a magistrate or officer, the term means that his authority is unlimited. A *strategos* (see below) who was *autokrator* was invested with every decision-making power: thus Antiochus III leading in 192–191, at the request of the Aetolians, the war against Rome.

BACCHANALIA Festivities in honor of Bacchus at Rome. As a result of some scandalous happenings in 186, the Senate placed severe restrictions on their celebration.

BOULÉ The Council of the city.

BOULEUTERION   The building in which the *Boulé* met.

BRANCHIDAE   Milesian family, descendants of the soothsayer Branchos. They administered the oracular shrine of Apollo at Didyma (about 20 km from Miletus).

CABEIRI or CABIRI (KABEIROI if transliterated from Greek)   Divinities of the Samothrace sanctuary.

CALATHOS   see KALATHOS.

CHILIARCH   Literally "Commander of the Thousand": head of the Royal Guard of Achaemenid monarchs. Alexander made Hephaestion his Chiliarch, then Perdiccas after Hephaestion's death.

CHLAMYS   Military cloak. It was relatively short, and consisted of a rectangle of cloth held on the right shoulder by a brooch or fibula.

CHORA (in Greek CHÔRA, with the omega)   The territory of the city, its "countryside," as distinguished from the urban area. The *chôra basilike* belonged *in proprio* to the king.

CHORUS   A group of men, women, or children singing a choral hymn in a religious festival. In the theatre the chorus would stand and move around in the ORCHESTRA (see below).

CHTHONIAN   Adjective formed from *chthôn*, meaning earth. It designates the divinities of the Lower World, as distinct from the Uranian (heavenly) divinities.

COELE-SYRIA   Literally "Hollow Syria": the conventional designation of the southern half of the region of Syria and Palestine, from the Egyptian frontier to the north of Byblos. Egyptian monarchs treated it as their kingdom's glacis: a cause of recurrent conflict.

CORÉ (plural CORAE: KORÉ, KORAI in transliterated Greek) see KORÉ.

CORYBANTS   Priests of Cybele, the Mother of the Gods, whose worship consisted of noisy music and wild armed dances; later interchanged with the Curetes (Gk. Kouretes), Cretan daemons of vegetation, who protected Zeus, newly born in Crete, from being devoured by Kronos his father.

CYNICISM   The teaching of this philosophy started with Antisthenes and, especially, his pupil Diogenes of Sinope (nicknamed *Kyôn*, Dog). Antisthenes taught in the Cynosarges, a gymnasium in the southern suburb of Athens.

DEMOS   This Greek word means "the people." A number of cities instituted a cult in honor of Demos.

DEMOTIC   This term (meaning "popular") applies to a hieroglyphic, but highly simplified, mode of writing that was in current usage in Lagid Egypt, particularly for the transcription of contracts between individuals. It was a cursive script, distinct from the hieroglyphic in the strict sense, which was reserved for the engraving of texts on monuments.

DESPOINA   Meaning "Mistress," this term designated among the Arcadians the main divinity of the shrine of Lycosoura. She was assimilated to Koré-Persephone, daughter of Demeter.

DIADEM (Gk. *diadema*)   A white headband that served as the distinguishing mark of Hellenistic kingship.

DIADOCHI (pl. of *Diadochus*; Gk. *Diadochoi*, pl. of *Diadochos*)   Term meaning "Successors," used by historians to designate the immediate heirs of Alexander the Great. Also used under the Ptolemies to mean a pool of potential successors for holders of higher office.

DIAGRAMMA   A detailed rule written and promulgated by royal authority.

DIOIKÉTÉS (in Anglicized form, DIOECETES)   A term meaning "administrator." Under the Ptolemies this term was applied in particular to the minister of finance.

DIONYSIAC ARTISTS   At the beginning of the 3rd century, associations of artists – actors, musicians, dancers, singers – and poets (grouped under the name of *technitai* in semi-religious, semi-professional associations) traveled around the Greek world for celebrations in honor of Dionysus. They fostered a considerable development of the Hellenistic theatre.

DIPHTHERAE (Gk. *–ai*)   In Archaic Greece, goatskins that had been tanned for writing on (see *The Civilization of Greece*, p. 332). The technique was later adopted for the fabrication of parchment.

DITHYRAMB   A choral poem in honor of Dionysus (see *The Civilization of Greece*, pp. 237, 338).

DOREA   Meaning "gift": especially landed property granted by the king to one of his friends.

DORIKTÉTOS   Meaning "conquered by the spear": term applied to territories conquered by Alexander and the Hellenistic monarchs.

DOSON (Gk. *Dôsôn*)   "He who intends to hand over" the throne, e.g. Antigonus Doson.

DRACHMA   A unit of weight (the Attic drachma being equivalent to 4 grams) as well as of currency: the latter was subdivided into 6 obols.

DYNAST   A general term designating any prince or ruler holding absolute power.

ELEGIAC DISTICH   A couplet made up of a dactylic hexameter and a dactylic pentameter, often employed in EPIGRAMS.

ENYALIUS   Epithet of Ares, god of war: perhaps originally the name of another divinity, taken over by Ares.

EPHEBEIA   A widespread institution in Greek cities especially well known at Athens (see *The Civilization of Greece*, p.173). Its purpose was to ensure the moral formation and physical training of young men aged between 18 and 20, called ephebes, and prepare them for military life. The training of ephebes took place mainly in the gymnasium.

EPHEMERIDES A (literally *day-by-day*) record of the king's actions, kept by a permanent archivist under certain Hellenistic sovereigns. The man responsible under Alexander the Great for that chronicle of daily events was Eumenes of Cardia.

EPIGONI (Gk. *Epigonoi*) A term applied to the immediate descendants of the Diadochi. Originally used in the epic of the Theban Cycle, the tale of the capture of Thebes by the sons or Epigoni (literally "those born after") of the Seven Chiefs who had failed to do so.

EPIGRAM The word properly means "inscription," particularly a metrical inscription, a poem that was to be engraved: a verse dedication or an epitaph. This genre knew considerable development in Hellenistic poetry.

EPIKLESIS The ritual epithet given to a divinity in a local cult, designating an essential part of the divine personality (the word means "additional appellation").

EPIMELETES (Gk. *Epimeletés*) Literally "he who looks after," a magistrate or public servant entrusted with a particular task. A vague term used to designate a large variety of responsibilities. Perdiccas was *epimeletes*, a *de facto* regent, after the death of Alexander; Demetrius of Phalerum was chosen, in agreement with Cassander, the Macedonian conqueror, *epimeletes* of Athens, a position that he occupied for ten years until 307.

EPISTOLOGRAPHER Literally "he who writes letters," the head of correspondence under the Ptolemies.

EPONYMOUS Literally "who gives his name to a city, a sanctuary, a social group or a year" (in a few cases *her* name, as happened at Thasos and Cyzicus – see chapter 6). This applied in particular in Greek cities to the one (magistrate or divinity) whose name was used to designate that particular year in the local calendar.

EUERGETES Meaning "Benefactor," the term designates individuals (citizens or foreigners) who have served the city well and to whom honors are awarded. This laudatory epithet was attached to the names of Ptolemy III and Ptolemy VIII (Euergetes II Physcon).

EUHEMERISM An explanation of the origin of god-worship given by Euhemerus, a mythographer who lived in the 4th and 3rd centuries BC and wrote a *Sacred Tale* that was a powerful influence on later historians and mythographers. According to it the gods had been mortals who proved great benefactors of humanity.

EXEDRA Semicircular or *pi*-shaped stone bench, the back of which could serve as a base for statues. By extension, a semicircular or rectangular room open on one side and provided with benches: found especially in gymnasiums.

FORTUNA   Roman divinity corresponding to the Greek TYCHÉ. The famous Nilotic mosaic of the Barberini Palace (see plate 3) was found in the shrine of Fortuna at Praeneste (modern Palestrina).

GLOSSAE (Gk. *Glossai*)   Literally " tongues." Grammarians used this term to designate rare words, borrowed from Archaic Greek or Greek dialects, which erudite poets took pleasure in using in their ancient or dialectal meaning.

GYMNASIARCH   A magistrate or the holder of a LITURGY, who supervised the operation of a gymnasium, and met various expenses connected with it.

GYMNASIUM   See *The Civilization of Greece*, p. 307, and chapter 8 here. See also EPHEBEIA.

GYNAECEUM (Gk. *gynaikeion*)   The women's quarters in a Greek house.

GYNAIKONOMOS   A magistrate whose duty was to monitor the conduct of women in a Greek city.

HASIDIM   Hebrew word meaning "pious people," used to designate traditionalists among Jews of the 2nd century BC.

HASMONEANS   Name of the Jewish family to which the Maccabees belonged.

HELIAEA (Gk. *Heliaia*)   A popular court in Athens, the members of which were chosen from the whole citizen body.

HELOTS   A category of serfs, particular to Sparta, confined to the tilling of the soil (see *The Civilization of Greece*, pp. 98, 124, 140, 302–3).

HERM   A quadrangular pillar on which was placed a representation of the head of the god Hermes. Later, a bust replaced the head. In the Roman Imperial period it was common to place such busts of famous men in public gardens or libraries.

HESTIA   The fireplace, and the name of the goddess of the hearth. From Hestia's altar at Delphi, the Athenian PYTHAIS would bring back the sacred flame to Athens.

HETAIROI   Literally "Companions." Name given to the Macedonian cavalry corps fighting next to the king. See PHILOI.

HIEROGLYPHIC see DEMOTIC.

HIPPARCH (Gk. *Hipparchos*)   Commander of the cavalry. There is a particular case at Cyzicus (see chapter 6) where a woman who is the EPONYMOUS magistrate is called the Hipparch.

HOMAGYRIOS   An EPIKLESIS of Zeus, "he who assembles."

HOMOPOLITEIA (if Anglicized, HOMOPOLITY)   Political union between two cities.

HYGIEIA   Meaning "health"; its deified allegory, represented by a young woman, daughter of Asclepius (see plate 12).

HYPOGAIA   Plural of hypogaion (-EION), underground chamber.

IOLOGY   The science pertaining to poisons (Gk. *ioi*, pl. of *ios*) and their anti-dotes, in which a high degree of research was developed in the Hellenistic period.

ISOPOLITEIA (if Anglicized, ISOPOLITY)   Equality of civic rights agreed upon by treaty between two cities, and applying to citizens of one of them settling in the other.

KABEIROI see CABEIRI.

KALATHOS   Greek word meaning "basket." In such wicker baskets the implements of cult would be carried in procession. The term applies also to the high basket-shaped headdress worn by Serapis.

KALLINIKOS   An epithet meaning "he of the fair victory," usually given to Heracles; Seleucus II attributed it to himself.

KATAIBATÉS   "He who hurls down" the thunderbolt: epithet given by the Athenians, in imitation of Zeus' EPIKLESIS, to Demetrius Poliorcetes after he had freed them from Cassander.

KATOIKOI   Ephesian equivalent for METOIKOI.

KERAUNOS   Meaning "Thunder," an appellation given to Ptolemy (son of Ptolemy I Sôter), the murderer of Seleucus I: *Ptolemaios Keraunos* or Ptolemy Ceraunus.

KLEROS   The term means an allotment, the beneficiary often being a soldier, who was called a *clerouchos* (cleruch), holder of an allotment. Hellenistic monarchs, especially those of Egypt, used the system for the resettlement of their mercenaries.

KOINÉ   The "common" tongue widely used in the Hellenistic world, and based on the classical Attic dialect.

KOINON   Literally "a community": a confederacy of cities, usually based on proximity or ethnic connection (SYNGENEIA: see chapter 6).

KORÉ (also CORÉ), pl. KORAI   Signifying "maiden." Persephone, Demeter's daughter, was commonly called Koré, the maiden *par excellence*. An important element of Greek sculpture (see *The Civilization of Greece*, pp. 256–7).

KOSMETES (literally "he who adorns, arranges in proper order")   Athenian magistrate, whose duty it was to supervise the training of the ephebes (see EPHEBEIA).

LAMPADEPHOROI   Literally "bearers of lamps": bronze candelabra, sometimes in the shape of the statue of an ephebe or a divinity.

LATIFUNDIA   A Latin word designating vast landed property in Italy farmed with the help of a large slave population. Greece also experienced the phenomenon of concentration of land in the hands of a few landowners, at the expense of the free peasantry.

LEGATE   An envoy of the Roman Senate, with full powers. Also the second-in-command of a general.

LEMBOS (pl. *lemboi*)   A light war vessel used by pirates as well as by Hellenistic war fleets.

LEUKOPHRYENE   An EPIKLESIS of Artemis, worshiped in a temple at Leucophrys, near Magnesia on the Maeander.

LITURGY   A direct obligation incumbent on rich individual citizens, e.g. financing the fitting out of a trireme, or a gymnasiarchy.

LYCEUM   A gymnasium in the western suburb of Athens, where Aristotle taught. His school is thus known as the Lyceum, or the PERIPATOS.

MEDIMNOS   A measure equivalent to 52 liters in the Attic system of weights and measures.

MERIS   A territorial and administrative division of Macedonia after the fall of the Macedonian king Perseus in 168.

METOIKOI   Literally, "people having changed their abode." Resident aliens.

METONOMASIA   Replacement of the name of a city by another.

MILESIAN PLAN   The orthogonal plan used by the planners of the new cities. According to tradition, the invention of that plan, or rather its systematic use, was due to Hippodamus of Miletus.

MIRABILIA   The Hellenistic mind was eager to know about the marvels of the world. Hence a number of writings on them, e.g. *On the Seven Marvels* by Philo of Byzantium. An epigram of the PALATINE ANTHOLOGY (IX, 58) enumerates these.

MOUSEION   Strictly speaking, sanctuary of the Muses, divine patrons of the arts. Scholars and philosophers would often congregate in the precinct of these sanctuaries. The most notable case was the foundation of the Mouseion of Alexandria by Ptolemy I on the advice of Demetrius of Phalerum.

NAUKLEROS   A private carrier owning a ship that he uses for the transport of merchandise. *Naukleroi* were specially active in Ptolemaic Egypt, some owning large ships for transporting cereals belonging to the king to warehouses and to foreign lands.

NAVARCH   The commander of a naval squadron. His rank was equivalent to that of an admiral.

NEOKOROS   An official who plays a role in the administration of a sanctuary. His duties and prerogatives are not well ascertained.

NEISOTES (Anglicized form of *Nesiotai*, pl. of *Nesiotés*)   Meaning "Islanders." Those of the Cyclades formed a confederacy under the leadership of Delos.

NICAEA   The name of many Hellenistic cities, particularly Nicaea in Bithynia, that Lysimachus founded in 300 and named after his wife *Nikaia*.

NIKÉ   Greek name of Victory. An allegory personified by a young winged woman (see fig. 7). The monarchical system would use Niké as the foundation of its authority (see chapter 7).

NOME   A territorial and administrative division in Ptolemaic Egypt.

NOMOPHYLAKES   Literally "guardians of the laws." Magistrates entrusted with a controlling role in Hellenistic cities: e.g., supervision of compliance with laws and regulations, the safety and integrity of public records.

NOMOS, NOMOI   Singular and plural of the Greek word for "law."

NUMISMATICS   The science pertaining to coinage that is legal tender (Gk. *nomismata*, lit. "things of recognized value," from which Lat. *numismata*).

OLYMPIAD   A period of four years at the end of which the Olympic Games were celebrated, the first Olympiad beginning in 776/5. It was the essential reference for Greek chronology, which was consolidated by Eratosthenes of Cyrene.

ORCHESTRA   An esplanade placed in the Greek theater lower than the spectators' tiers in front of the building constituting the stage. In Hellenistic times it was semicircular, instead of circular (as it was originally), because of space taken by the PROSCENIUM. The Chorus was in the Orchestra, while the actors would be higher up, on the stage that was above the Proscenium (see fig. 8).

ORPHISM   A mystic and arcane doctrine connected with the legendary figure of Orpheus. The "sacred texts" of Orphism contained a cosmogony, a theogony, and a system of eschatology.

PAEAN   A choral song in honor of a divinity, especially of Apollo, whose epithet Paean stresses his role as a healing god. Many Hellenistic paeans are preserved in inscriptions, which demonstrates the vitality of the genre in that age.

PALATINE ANTHOLOGY   A collection of Greek EPIGRAMS put together in the Middle Ages by Byzantine scholars, and preserved in the library at Heidelberg, in the Palatinate (hence the name).

PANACHAIA   An EPIKLESIS of Demeter: "She whom all Achaeans revere."

PANATHENAIC FESTIVAL   The great religious festival celebrated each year in June and July in honor of the goddess Athena (see *The Civilization of Greece*, pp. 214, 222, 232, 357).

PARADOXOGRAPHY   A literary genre that collated extraordinary or surprising facts (*paradoxa*).

PAROIKOI   Rhodian equivalent of METOIKOI.

PASTICCIO   An Italian word denoting a hybrid work of art made up of previous works which may be widely different in style: see the index entry for Pasiteles.

PATRÉ   This Greek word denoted a subdivision of the city, at both the religious and the political levels, that corresponded, in some Ionian cities like Thasos, to what was elsewhere the *phratria* (see *The Civilization of Greece*, pp. 71, 231,

306, 311). To become a citizen one had to be registered in a *patré*.

PEDAGOGUE (Gk. *paidagôgos*)   A trusted, usually aged, slave who accompanied a child to school.

PENTATHLON   A competition for all-round athletes in the Great Games. In the Hellenistic period it involved five contests: jumping, racing, throwing the discus and the javelin, wrestling.

PERAEA (Gk. *Peraia*, derived from *peras*, "beyond")   "The land beyond (or across) the sea": territory occupied by an island city (e.g. Rhodes) on nearby continental land.

PERIEGESIS   Description in the form of a guidebook, like Pausanias' *Periegesis* of Greece. Periegetic literature responded to a demand for information on historical sites and the accompanying wish to visit them.

PERIOD   The aggregate of the four Great Games: the Olympian, the Pythian, the Isthmian, and the Nemean. The winner of the same competition in all four Games was a *periodonic* athlete.

PERIPATOS   "A walk about, or back and forth," while teaching or engaged in discourse. Such strolls in the area of the Lyceum gave the Aristotelian school the name of "the Peripatos," hence the Peripatetic school.

PERISTYLE   A colonnade surrounding a building (e.g. a temple) or an open space, like the court of a house or a palace, an agora.

PHALANX   Greek or Macedonian hoplites (heavy infantry) in close formation.

PHALARA (plural word)   Metal disk-shaped ornaments, usually decked with incrustations, for a horse's harness.

PHILOI   Plural of *Philos*. The Friends of the Ptolemaic king. The term tended to replace HETAIROI.

PINAKES   Plural of *Pinax*. These "tablets" or "tables" designated the systematized catalogues of Greek literature that Callimachus composed.

PISTIS   The relationship of mutual trust between states (Latin *fides*), considered the foundation of the friendly relationship established by treaty between Rome and a subject community.

POIKILE (sc. *Stoa*)   The Painted Stoa or Portico: a name given because of the paintings that adorned it. It was situated north of the Athenian agora (see STOICISM).

POLIS   The city: the name designated both the town as opposed to the countryside (CHORA), and the community of citizens.

PRAETOR   Roman magistrate ranking immediately after the consul. Praetors had a judicial function, as well as administrative and military responsibilities.

PROSCENIUM (Gk. *Proskenion*)   A one-story high platform supported by pillars or columns, in front of the building on top of which was the stage in a Hellenistic theatre; see ORCHESTRA.

PROSKYNEMA   Form of worship before a god.

PROSKYNESIS   A Persian fashion of prostrating oneself before the king, which Alexander wished to introduce into court protocol and which met with hostility among his Macedonian Companions.

PROSTAGMA   A royal ordinance.

PROSTATÉS   A citizen representing a resident alien vis-à-vis the authorities of his own city.

PROXENIA   A widespread Hellenistic institution. The *Proxenus* looked after the interests of another city in his own city.

PYLON   Monumental entrance of an Egyptian temple: the gate being framed by two imposing rectangular towers with slightly inclined walls.

PYTHAIS   A delegation sent to the Delphic sanctuary when lightning appeared on a peak on Mount Parnes called the *Harma* ("Chariot," because of its shape).

SATRAPY   A territorial subdivision of the Achaemenid empire that was preserved by Alexander. It was administered by a satrap.

SEPTUAGINT   The Old Testament (actually only the Pentateuch) translated into Greek. According to a controversial tradition, Ptolemy II Philadelphus appointed 72 (hence the term *Septuagint*, Greek for 70) Jews in Alexandria to do the work of translation.

SITOPHYLAX   Plural SITOPHYLAKES, magistrates supervising the cereal trade.

SKÉNÉ   The building on which the stage was set: see ORCHESTRA and PROSCENIUM.

SOMATOPHYLAKES   Literally "bodyguard." Originally an elite military unit in Hellenistic armies; later an honorary title given to certain dignitaries of the court.

SÔTER   Epithet meaning "Savior," given to some divinities (Zeus among others) and certain sovereigns (like Ptolemy I, Antiochus I).

SÔTERIA   A Delphic festival in honor of Apollo and Zeus Sôter, in remembrance of the preservation of the sanctuary from the Gallic invasion of 279.

STADION   A length equal to 600 ft, the equivalent at Olympia (since the actual length of the foot varied) being 192.27 meters. Also, the running track.

STATER   The term designates the coin on which the monetary system was based (the *didrachm* in gold coinage; the *didrachm*, sometimes the *tetradrachm*, in silver coinage).

STEPHANITE   "Endowed with a crown." Name given to athletic competitions for which the prize was a crown of foliage, no money reward being added.

STOICISM   Philosophical school founded by Zeno, who taught in the portico called Stoa poikile.

STRATEGOS   1. A magistrate elected in Greek cities to command the troops: an office the nature of which changed in Athens in the Hellenistic period. 2.The name given by a Hellenistic king to an officer entrusted with the administration and military control of a territory.

SYLA   1. As a feminine word (= *Sylé*; or = the neuter *Sylon*): mostly used in the plural. Meaning the right of seizure. 2. As the plural of *Sylon*, goods taken in virtue of a right of seizure; see ASYLIA.

SYMBOLA (pl. of SYMBOLON)   Agreements made between cities giving mutual guarantees against SYLA (1).

SYMPOLITEIA (if Anglicized, SYMPOLITY)   Agreement between two cities establishing common citizenship.

SYNCRETISM   A combination of cults or divine figures into one divinity.

SYNEDROI   A college of magistrates, or a board appointed by the Assembly, in various Greek cities.

SYNGENEIA   Kinship, as invoked e.g. by the Cytenians requesting help from Xanthus (chapter 6); see KOINON.

SYNOECISM   A regrouping of various localities into one political unit.

SYNOIKIA   A multistoried building housing rental units.

THEORODOKOI   Citizens listed by a city as granting hospitality to THEOROI.

THEOROI   Envoys sent by a city or a shrine to announce the holding of an important festival.

THEOXENIA   A sacred banquet offered to one or many divinities, considered as partaking personally in it.

TOPOS   1. A common rhetorical or philosophical theme. 2. A territorial division of a province (NOME) in Ptolemaic Egypt.

TORQUES   Metal necklaces worn by some barbarian peoples, the Celts in particular.

TRYPHÉ   Greek word designating the life of luxury and extravagance led by certain sovereigns.

TYCHÉ   Allegory of Fortune, deified by the Greeks: cf. FORTUNA.

TYRANNOKTONOI   "Killers of the tyrant": the Athenians Harmodius and Aristogeiton who killed Pisistratus' son in 514. The Athenians assimilated Demetrius Poliorcetes and his father Antigonus to them when those princes freed Athens in 307.

CHRONOLOGICAL TABLES

The aim of these tables is to help the reader use the book by providing a synopsis of the main historical facts, spread over four geographical areas: Greece proper (including its immediate northern neighbors, Macedonia and Thrace) with the islands of the Aegean Sea; Asia; Africa (from Egypt to the Maghreb); the West (Italy, Spain, Gaul). The last column is devoted to events pertaining to civilization. Synchronism has been indicated in the most important cases, in Roman history especially. One should, however, not forget that a number of dates in ancient history lie astride two "Julian" years because of local modes of chronological reckoning. As a result some events can only be dated within a margin of error of a few months. A time-swing of one year is often evident (end of a Julian year or start of the next one): a very approximate method in many cases. The main ones among these are indicated by a question mark. In the literary and (especially) artistic areas, events that have been reliably dated have as a rule been chosen. This has avoided interference by chronological hypotheses based only on stylistic criteria. The reduced number of data that have been inserted gives an idea of the extent of our ignorance in this respect.

DATES	GREECE AND ISLANDS	ASIA	AFRICA	THE WESTERN WORLD	ART AND THOUGHT
338	Battle of Chaeronea			338–335 Rome subdues Latium	Aristotle (384–322) Death of Isocrates Lysippus' *Agias*
336	Death of Philip II Alexander III his successor	Accession of Darius III Codomannus			
335	Capture and destruction of Thebes				335–323 Aristotle at Athens Monument erected by the *choregus* Lysicrates
334		Battle of the Granicus		334–330 Alexander the Molossian in southern Italy	
333		October: Battle of Issus			
332		Capture of Tyre	Alexander occupies Egypt; founds Alexandria; journeys to the oasis of Ammon		
331	Revolt and defeat of Agis III	October 1: battle of Arbela Capture of Babylon and Susa Conflagration at Persepolis Philotas' plot			Lycurgus' *Against Leocrates*
330	330–326 Dearth of cereals				The lawsuit "concerning the Crown"
329		Conquest of Bactria			
328		Alexander in Sogdiana			
327	End of Lycurgus' administration at Athens	The marriage of Alexander and Roxane Execution of Callisthenes			
326		Alexander on the Indus			c.335–323 Portraits of Alexander by Lysippus, Leochares, and Apelles

Year					
325		Return of the expeditionary force December: Alexander in Carmania			
324	Edict on the return of the banished	Difficulties with Harpalus The Nuptials at Susa Death of Hephaestion June 13: death of Alexander			
323	The Lamian War				
322	September: battle of Crannon		Ptolemy occupies Cyrene		
321	Death of Antipater	Death of Craterus The Agreement of Triparadisus Polyperchon *epimeletes* of the kings	Death of Perdiccas		Theophrastus' *Characters* (?)
319				Agathocles seizes power at Syracuse	
318	Death of Phocion				
317	317–307 Athens governed by Demetrius of Phalerum				Menander's *Dyskolos*
316	Cassander restores Thebes	Eumenes' defeat and death			
314	Delos becomes independent				
312		Battle of Gaza	Revolt and repression at Cyrene		
311		Seleucus at Babylon 312/11: start of the Seleucid era Agreements among the Diadochi			
310			Agathocles lands in Africa		*c*.310: birth of Callimachus

DATES	GREECE AND ISLANDS	ASIA	AFRICA	THE WESTERN WORLD	ART AND THOUGHT
309	Foundation of Lysimacheia				
308			The expedition and death of Ophellas	Agathocles returns to Syracuse	Epicurus (b. 341) settles at Athens
307	Demetrius Poliorcetes captures Athens				
306		Demetrius' victories in Cyprus	306/5: Cyrene revolts		
305	Demetrius besieges Rhodes				
304	Demetrius raises the siege of Rhodes				c.304–300: Chares of Lindos' *Rhodian Colossus* Zeno of Citium arrives at Athens
303		Seleucus abandons the provinces of the Indus			
301		Battle of Ipsus			c.300: Eurychides of Sicyon's *Tyche* at Antioch
300			Magas reconquers Cyrene		
298	Death of Cassander				c.295: Athens stops minting its "owls" Death of Menander
294	Demetrius Poliorcetes king of Macedon				
291	Demetrius takes Thebes				
288	Demetrius suffers defeat in Macedonia				
287			Building of the Pharos of Alexandria Ptolemy II shares power with his father		Death of Theophrastus
285		Demetrius surrenders	Death of Ptolemy I Soter		Between 289 and 281: the Samothrace *Arsinoeum*
283		Death of Demetrius	283–246: Ptolemy II		

Year					
220	"Social" War				c.220: Attalus I's ex voto for his victories over the Galatians
219		219–217: Fourth Syrian War			
218				Hannibal captures Saguntum; 218–202: Second Punic War	
217	Peace of Naupactus	Battle of Raphia		Battle of Trasimene	
216	216–205: First Macedonian War			Battle of Cannae	
215	Alliance of Philip V and Hannibal				
212	Alliance of Rome and the Aetolians	212–205: Antiochus III's "Anabasis"		Capture of Syracuse	Death of Archimedes
208					c.208–204: death of Chrysippus
207			207–186: secession in Upper Egypt	Battle of the Metaurus	
206				Roman province of Spain	
205	Treaty of Phoenice				
204			204–180: Ptolemy V	Attalus I sends Cybele's Black Stone to Rome	
202		202–200: Fifth Syrian War	Battle of Zama		
201	Philip V's operations in the Aegean Sea	Philip V in Anatolia			
200	200–197: Second Macedonian War	Battle of Pannium			
197	Battle of Cynoscephalae	197–159: Eumenes II of Pergamum		The province of Spain divided into two parts	Flamininus' statue at Delphi
196	Flamininus at the Olympic Games				

DATES	GREECE AND ISLANDS	ASIA	AFRICA	THE WESTERN WORLD	ART AND THOUGHT
261		261(?)–253: Second Syrian War			
251	Aratus frees Sicyon				
250					c.250: Stoa of Antigonus at Delos
248			Death of Magas	New treaty between Rome and Hiero II	
247		Start of the era of the Parthian Arsacids			
246		246–241(?): Third Syrian War; 246–226: Seleucus I	246–221: Ptolemy III Euergetes		
243	Aratus captures Corinth				
242	Agis IV's reforms				
241	Death of Agis IV	241–197: Attalus I king of Pergamum		Battle of the Aegates Islands	
240	240/39: death of Antigonus Gonatas				
239	239–229: Demetrius II				
235	235–222: Cleomenes III				
232					Death of Cleanthes of Assus
229	229–221: Antigonus Doson			229/8: Roman expedition to Illyria	
227	Earthquake at Rhodes				
226		226–223: Seleucus III			
223	Cleomenes captures Megalopolis	223–187: Antiochus III			
222	Battle of Sellasia				
221	221–179: Philip V		221–204: Ptolemy IV		

Year					
220					c.220: Attalus I's ex-voto for his victories over the Galatians
219	"Social" War	219–217: Fourth Syrian War		Hannibal captures Saguntum	
218				218–202: Second Punic War	
217	Peace of Naupactus	Battle of Raphia		Battle of Trasimene	
216	216–205: First Macedonian War			Battle of Cannae	
215	Alliance of Philip V and Hannibal				
212	Alliance of Rome and the Aetolians	212–205: Antiochus III's "Anabasis"		Capture of Syracuse	Death of Archimedes
208					c.208–204: death of Chrysippus
207			207–186: secession in Upper Egypt	Battle of the Metaurus	
206				Roman province of Spain	
205	Treaty of Phoenice				
204			204–180: Ptolemy V	Attalus I sends Cybele's Black Stone to Rome	
202		202–200: Fifth Syrian War	Battle of Zama		
201	Philip V's operations in the Aegean Sea	Philip V in Anatolia			
200	200–197: Second Macedonian War	Battle of Pannium			
197	Battle of Cynoscephalae	197–159: Eumenes II of Pergamum		The province of Spain divided into two parts	Flamininus' statue at Delphi
196	Flamininus at the Olympic Games				

DATES	GREECE AND ISLANDS	ASIA	AFRICA	THE WESTERN WORLD	ART AND THOUGHT
192	Death of Nabis War between Rome and Antiochus III				First half of second century: the Great Altar of Zeus at Pergamum First half of second century: the architect Hermagenes active at Magnesia on the Macander
189		Battle of Magnesia on the Sipylus		Roman colony founded at Bononia	
188	Philopoemen takes Sparta	Peace of Apamea			
187		187–175: Seleucus IV			
186				Senatorial decree on the Bacchanalia	
183	Death of Philopoemen	Death of Hannibal		The Elder Cato Censor	Death of Plautus
180			180–145: Ptolemy VI		
179	179–168: Perseus				
175		175–164: Antiochus IV			
171	171–168: Third Macedonian War				
170		170–168: Sixth Syrian War			c.170: New Style Athenian coinage c.170–160: work begins on the Olympieum at Athens Post 168: Aemilius Paullus' pillar at Delphi
168	Battle of Pydna Young Polybius exiled to Italy		"Popilius' Circle"		
164		End of the revolt of the Maccabees			
163			Ptolemy the Younger king of Cyrene		
159		159–139: Attalus II of Pergamum			Death of Terence

Year					
155			Testament of Ptolemy the Younger	Carneades takes part in embassy to Rome	Mid-second century: Stoa of Attalus at Athens
150	Polybius returns to Greece	Parthian progress in Mesopotamia			
148	Roman province of Macedon				
146	Corinth destroyed		Carthage destroyed		
145		145–126: Demetrius II	145–116: Ptolemy the Younger reigns as Ptolemy VIII		Second half of second century: Damophon of Messene
143		Start of the Hasmonean era			
140			Scipio Aemilianus visits Egypt		
139		139–133: Attalus III of Pergamum			
138					138/7: Dioscorides and Cleopatra, statues at Delos
135					c.135: Nicander of Colophon's *Theriaka* and *Alexipharmaka*; c.135–51: Posidonius
133		Rome designated as heir of Attalus III		133–121: Reforms by the Gracchi	
129		Roman province of Asia			
121		121–63: Mithridates VI Eupator, king of Pontus			
118				The Roman colony of Narbonne founded	
111			111–105: wars with Jugurtha		
102				102/01: Marius defeats the Cimbri and Teutons	

DATES	GREECE AND ISLANDS	ASIA	AFRICA	THE WESTERN WORLD	ART AND THOUGHT
309	Foundation of Lysimacheia				
308			The expedition and death of Ophellas	Agathocles returns to Syracuse	
307	Demetrius Poliorcetes captures Athens				Epicurus (b. 341) settles at Athens
306		Demetrius' victories in Cyprus	306/5: Cyrene revolts		
305	Demetrius besieges Rhodes				
304	Demetrius raises the siege of Rhodes				
303		Seleucus abandons the provinces of the Indus			c.304–300: Chares of Lindos' *Rhodian Colossus* Zeno of Citium arrives at Athens
301		Battle of Ipsus			
300			Magas reconquers Cyrene		c.300: Eutychides of Sicyon's *Tychē* at Antioch
298	Death of Cassander				
294	Demetrius Poliorcetes king of Macedon				c.295: Athens stops minting its "owls" Death of Menander
291	Demetrius takes Thebes				
288	Demetrius suffers defeat in Macedonia				
287			Building of the Pharos of Alexandria Ptolemy II shares power with his father		Death of Theophrastus
285		Demetrius surrenders	Death of Ptolemy I Sōter		
283		Death of Demetrius	283–246: Ptolemy II		Between 289 and 281: the Samothrace *Arsinoeum*

BIBLIOGRAPHY AND
SUGGESTIONS FOR
FURTHER READING

Year					
55	Death of Lucretius				
54	c.54: death of Catullus				
53				Battle of Carrhae and death of Crassus	
51			Ptolemy XIII and Cleopatra VII become sovereigns of Egypt		
49		Caesar crosses the Rubicon / Capture of Marseille			
48			Death of Pompey / Caesar in Egypt / The Library of Alexandria destroyed by fire		Battle of Pharsalus
47				Defeat and death of Pharnaces	
46	Arccesilaus' *Venus Genitrix*				
44		March 15: death of Caesar			
43		Second triumvirate			
42					Battle of Philippi
41				Antony and Cleopatra at Tarsus	
39	Vergil's *Bucolics*				
37				Antony reorganizes the East	
34			The "Donations" of Alexandria		
31					September 2: Battle of Actium
30			Death of Antony and Cleopatra		

BIBLIOGRAPHY AND SUGGESTIONS FOR FURTHER READING

The following is a revision, prepared by the author with the cooperation of the translator, of the bibliography provided in the original French editions (1981 hardback – the *editio maior* – and 1985 paperback), mainly with an English-speaking readership in mind. Thanks have been expressed in the foreword to the present edition for help received in composing it. Many of the works mentioned below have detailed bibliographies. A special mention should be made of two surveys on Hellenistic scholarship, which have proved invaluable. These are nos. 1 and 5 in the Publications of the Association of Ancient Historians (1987 and 1997, Claremont, CA). Chester G. Starr authored *Past and Future in Ancient History* (vol. II, pp. 19–32 on the Hellenistic age); Stanley M. Burstein edited *Ancient History: recent work and new directions,* himself surveying the Hellenistic age (vol. II, pp. 37–54).

Titles are provided under headings approximately following the order of the chapters of the present work. Indications relative to general works surveyed under that heading (section X of bibliography) in *The Civilization of Greece in the Archaic and Classical Age* by the same author (translated by W. S. Maguinness, London and New York, 1965) are not repeated here. They are, however, valid for the Hellenistic period. As specialized works are extremely numerous, only a starting point for further reading has been provided. Occasional reference is made to detailed studies of texts examined in the body of the work. Consultation of the *Oxford Classical Dictionary* (3rd edn, 1996, ed. S. Hornblower and A. Spawforth) will of course be found helpful.

I. GENERAL WORKS ON HELLENISTIC CIVILIZATION

An ample synthesis will be found in C. Schneider, *Kulturgeschichte des Hellenismus* Munich, 2 vols, 1967–9 (very abundant references, no illustrations or maps). A less analytical but admirably informed overview is found in C. Préaux, *Le monde hellénistique, la Grèce et l'Orient, 323–146 av. J.-C.* (2 vols, Paris, 1978); the work begins, pp. 13–76, with a very rich, well classified bibliography. W. Tarn's memorable *Hellenistic Civilisation,* first published in 1927, was revised in a 3rd edition by the author and G. T. Griffith (London, 1952: numerous reprints since). On M. Hadas' *Hellenistic civilization: fusion and diffusion,* see section V below. F. W. Walbank's *The Hellenistic World* (London, 1981) now appears in a revised edition (Cambridge, MA, 1993). Peter Green authored *Alexander to Actium: the historical evolution of the Hellenistic Age* (Berkeley, CA, 1990), and edited *Hellenistic History and Culture* (Berkeley, CA, 1993). P. Cartledge, P. Garnsey, and E. Gruen edited *Hellenistic Constructs: essays in culture, history and historiography* (Berkeley, CA, 1997). A recent publication is G. Shipley, *The Greek World after Alexander: 323–30 BC* (London, 2000).

II   HISTORY

Comprehensive works on ancient history will be mentioned first. Second editions, provided with extensive bibliographies, of parts of the Cambridge Ancient History (*CAH* henceforth), vol. VII. 1 (with a companion volume of plates), *The Hellenistic World to the Coming of the Romans*, vol. VII. 2, *The Rise of Rome from 220 BC*, vol. VIII, *Rome and the Mediterranean, 218–133 BC*, and vol. VI, *The Fourth Century BC*, appeared in 1984, 1989, 1989, and 1994 respectively. The 4th edition (1969) of H. Bengtson's *Griechische Geschichte* appeared in 1988 in an English translation by E. F. Bloedow (University of Ottawa Press), as *History of Greece: from the beginnings to the Byzantine era*; it provides substantial bibliographical surveys and updates. *A History of Ancient Greece*, by C. Orrieux and P. Schmitt Pantel (translated from the French by J. Lloyd: Oxford, 1999) has a bibliography, pp. 410–12, on the Hellenistic period.

Literary sources remain fundamental, and the Loeb Classical Library is a convenient source for original texts and translations (note in particular P. Brunt's edition and translation of Arrian). Fragments from minor historians are collated in F. Jacoby's *Die Fragmente der griechischen Historiker* (Leiden, 1952–4, 15 vols, with later reprints); texts relating to Alexander with notes and translations, are in J. Auberger, *Historiens d'Alexandre* (Paris, 2001). W. Spoerri provides excellent articles on most of the Hellenistic historians in *Lexicon der alten Welt* (Bern, 1965).

Translations (or translations of edited texts) include M. Austin, *The Hellenistic World from Alexander to the Roman Conquest* (Cambridge, 1981); in the series Translated Documents of Greece and Rome (Cambridge, 1985, 1985, 1984): P. Harding, *From the end of the Peloponnesian War to the battle of Ipsus*, S. M. Burstein, *The Hellenistic Age, from the battle of Ipsos to the reign of Cleopatra VII*, and R. K. Sherk, *Rome and the Greek East to the Death of Augustus*; Y. Garlan, *L'esclavage dans le monde grec: traduction de textes grecs et latins* (Paris, 1984); J. Rowlandson (ed.), *Women and Society in Greek and Roman Egypt: a sourcebook* (Cambridge, 1998): 289 translated texts (mostly Greek papyri, occasionally Demotic, Latin, and Coptic texts) ranging from the Ptolemies to the Byzantine period.

Among commentaries see: F. W. Walbank, *A Historical Commentary on Polybius*, I–III (Oxford, 1957–74); J. Briscoe, *A Commentary on Livy:* books XXXI–XXXIII, XXXIV–XXXVII (Oxford, 1973, 1981); A. B. Bosworth, *A Historical Commentary on Arrian's History of Alexander* (2 vols, Oxford, 1980 and 1995: these cover four-fifths of the History); J. R. Bartlett, *Jews in the Hellenistic World: Josephus Aristeas, the Sibylline Oracles, Eupolemus* (Cambridge, 1985); J. E. Atkinson, *A Commentary on Q. Curtius Rufus' Historiae Alexandri Magni, Books 3–4, 5–7.2* (Amsterdam, 1980). Add: *Quintus Curtius Rufus, The History of Alexander,* translated by J. Yardley, with an introduction and notes by W. Heckel (Harmondsworth, 1994: revised edition, 2001); J. Yardley and R. Develin (translation and commentary): *Justin, Epitome of the Philippic History of Pompeius Trogus* (Atlanta, GA, 1994); J. Yardley and W. Heckel, translation and commentary, *Justin's Epitome of the Philippic History of Pompeius Trogus, Vol. I: Books 11–12, Alexander the Great* (Oxford, 1997). S. M. Burstein has translated and edited (London, 1989) Agatharcides of Cnidus, *On the Erythrean Sea* (cf. in the present work ch. 8, p. 317 on Hellenistic travel literature).

Scientific texts: M. R. Cohen and I. E. Drabkin, *Source Book in Greek Science* (Cambridge, MA, *c*.1948, 1958); A. J. Sachs and H. Hunger, *Astronomical Diaries and Related Texts from Babylonia* (2 vols, Vienna, 1988–9). Finally, in *Die Staatsverträge des Altertums*, directed by H. Bengtson, vol. III, by H. H. Schmitt, *Die Verträge der griechisch-römischen Welt von 338 bis 200 v. Chr.* (Munich, 1969): see Hiero II of Syracuse, later in this section.

For chronology, a compendious and convenient account of the main problems will be found in E. J. Bickerman, *Chronology of the Ancient World* (2nd edn, London, 1968). For more details see A. E. Samuel, *Greek and Roman Chronology*, in *Handbuch der Altertumswissenschaft*, I, 7 (Munich, 1972) and E. Manni, *Fasti ellenistici e romani, 323–31 a.C.* (Palermo, 1961).

The basic modern historical work on the Hellenistic period is É. Will, *Histoire politique du monde hellénistique* (2 vols, 2nd edn, Nancy, 1982). It provides a detailed and critical account of events starting with the death of Alexander, and "cites virtually all relevant literature" (C. G. Starr, *Past and Future*, p. 19, n. 1): more briefly in *CAH* VII.1, "The succession to Alexander," pp. 23–61, and "The formation of the Hellenistic kingdoms," pp. 101–17. Will writes vigorously and suggestively on the Hellenistic world from 323 to 187 in É. Will, C. Mossé, P. Goukowsky, *Le monde grec et l'Orient: II. Le IVe siècle et l'époque hellénistique* (Paris, 1975).

The following works have appeared in recent years: A. M. Eckstein, *Senate and General: Individual Decision-making and Roman Foreign Relations, 264–194 BC* (Berkeley, CA, 1987), and *The Moral Vision of the Histories of Polybius* (Berkeley, CA, 1995); A. B. Bosworth, *From Arrian to Alexander: Studies in Historical Interpretation* (Oxford, 1988); N. G. Hammond and F. W. Walbank, *A History of Macedonia. III, 336–167 BC* (Oxford, 1988); E. Gruen, *The Hellenistic World and the Coming of Rome*, I, II (Berkeley, CA, 1988); P. Cabanes, *Le monde hellénistique de la mort d'Alexandre à la paix d'Apamée* (Paris, 1995); C. Vial, *Les Grecs de la paix d'Apamée à la bataille d'Actium* (Paris, 1995); T. Duff, *Plutarch's Lives: Exploring Virtue and Vice* (Oxford, 1999).

Epigraphic sources are of primary importance, but difficult of access for the uninitiated. L. Robert's essay in the collective work *L'histoire et ses méthodes* (Paris, 1961), pp. 453–97, will serve as an introduction. Citations of L. Robert's epigraphic commentaries appear below. K. Sokolowski's collections of epigraphic texts relating to various cults will be listed in section VI, Religion. Starting in 1938, J. and L. Robert published every year (for almost 60 years) a *Bulletin épigraphique* in the *Revue des études grecques* (henceforth *REG*), giving an account of the bulk of epigraphic publication in the scholarly world. Note also L. Moretti, *Iscrizioni storiche ellenistiche*, I. II (Florence, 1967–75). The series Texts and Documents of Greece and Rome, a term including epigraphic texts, has been mentioned above. On the evolution in styles of engraving: S. V. Tracy, *Athenian Letter Cutters of 229 to 86 BC* (Berkeley, CA, 1990), *Athenian Democracy in Transition: Attic Letter Cutters of 340 to 290 BC* (Berkeley, CA, 1995).

For papyrology: E. G. Turner, *Greek Papyri: an introduction* (2nd edn, Oxford, 1980), *Elephantine Papyri in English* (Leiden, 1996); C. Préaux, *Le monde hellénistique*, I, pp. 24–7 (for bibliography).

For numismatic sources: bibliography in C. Préaux, *Le monde hellénistique*, pp. 27–31; G. K. Jenkins, *Monnaies grecques* (Fribourg and Paris, 1972: abundantly illustrated); C. M. Kraay, *Greek Coins* (London, 1966); N. Davis and C. M. Kraay, *The Hellenistic Kingdoms: portrait coins and history* (London, 1973); R. R. R. Smith, *Hellenistic Royal Portraits* (Oxford, 1988); M. J. Price, *The Coinage in the Name of Alexander the Great and Philip Arrhidaeus: a British Museum catalogue* (2 vols, Zurich and London, 1991); A. Stewart, *Faces of Power: Alexander's image and Hellenistic politics* (Berkeley, CA,

1993) on the iconography of Alexander and its social effects; O. Mørkholm, *Early Hellenistic Coinage: from the accession of Alexander to the peace of Apamea* (edited by P. Grierson and U. Westermark, Cambridge, 1991). The standard reference is G. M. A. Richter, *The Portraits of the Greeks* (3 vols, London, 1965), of which vols 2 and 3 are on the Hellenistic age.

We now turn to bibliographical details concerning Alexander, the Diadochi, Macedonia, kingdoms and principalities of the Hellenistic age.

On Alexander, a remarkable synthesis is to be found in P. Goukowsky's *Essai sur les origines du mythe d'Alexandre* (2 vols, Nancy, 1978–81); his edition and translation of Books XVII and XVIII of Diodorus Siculus in the Budé Collection will repay attention. Among works on the *Alexander Romance*, cf. W. Heckel, *The Last Days and Testament of Alexander the Great* (Stuttgart, 1988). Conflicting views on the proper assessment of Alexander are reviewed in G. T. Griffith, *Alexander the Great: the main problems* (Cambridge and New York, 1966). Their disparity is represented by the wide gap in outlook between N. G. L. Hammond, *The Genius of Alexander the Great* (Chapel Hill, NC,1997) and A. B. Bosworth, *Conquest and Empire: the reign of Alexander the Great* (Cambridge, 1988), *Alexander and the East: The Tragedy of Triumph* (Oxford, 1996).

On the Diadochi: W. Heckel, *The Marshals of Alexander's Empire* (London, 1992). The following biographies have appeared: R. A. Billows, *Antigonos the One-Eyed and the Creation of the Hellenistic State* (Berkeley, CA, 1990); W. M. Ellis, *Ptolemy (I) of Egypt* (London, 1994); J. Longega, *Arsinoe II* (Padua, 1965); J. D. Grainger, *Seleucos Nikator: Constructing a Hellenistic Kingdom* (London, 1990). H. S. Lund's *Lysimachus* is mentioned at the end of section IV, Monarchy. On descendants of Antigonus: J. Gabbert, *Antigonus II Gonatas: A Political Biography* (London, 1997); S. Le Bohec, *Antigonos Dóson, roi de Macédoine* (Nancy, 1993). (Note: see also the first lines on p. 426.)

On the Ptolemies: G. Hölbl, *History of the Ptolemaic Empire* (trans. from the German by T. Saavedra: London, 2000). C. Préaux's view of separate coexisting Greek and Egyptian societies is a source of controversy in recent historiography: see A. E. Samuel's Survey (Publications of the Association of Ancient Historians, no. 2: Lanham, MD, 1989), *The Shifting Sands of Interpretation: Interpretations of Ptolemaic Egypt*.

On the Seleucids: see especially S. Sherwin-White and A. Kuhrt, *From Samarkhand to Sardis* (Berkeley, CA, 1993); J. D. Grainger, *Hellenistic Phoenicia* (Oxford, 1991), *A Seleukid Prosopography and Gazetteer* (Leiden, 1997); on the last years of Seleucid rule: R. D. Sullivan, *Near Eastern Royalty and Rome, 100–30 BC* (Toronto, 1990); J. Ma, *Antiochus III and the Cities of Western Asia Minor* (Oxford, 1999). Note also P. C. Hammond, *The Nabataeans* (Lund, 1973).

More on settlements, colonies, and local dynasts will be found in section III, The City. Note also D. T. Potts, *The Arabian Gulf in Antiquity* (Oxford, 1990).

On Hiero II's change of sides in the Second Punic War see H. H. Scullard in *CAH* VII. 2, pp. 546, 547, 564; J. Briscoe in *CAH* VIII 1989, ch. III and in *OCD* (3rd edn, Hiero); A. M. Eckstein in *Moral Vision in the Histories of Polybius* (cited above), pp. 207–9; H. H. Schmitt, vol. III of *Die Staatsverträge*, pp.137–9, no. 479 entitled "Friede und Bündnis zwischen Rom und Hieron II von Syrakus," which quotes all texts pertaining to the arrangement between Rome and Hiero, and the variety of appellations given to the new relationship.

III The City

For a global view of the political and social organization of the Hellenistic States (cities and kingdoms): V. Ehrenberg, *The Greek State* (2nd edn, London, 1969: many reprints, the French version providing bibliographical addenda by É. Will), pp. 135–237. On the economy of Greek cities, L. Migeotte, *L'économie des cités grecques. De l'archaïsme au Haut Empire romain* (Paris, 2001). On slavery: Y. Garlan's book was mentioned among editions, translations, and commentaries in section II, History. On society and the economy: bibliography in C. Préaux, *Le monde hellénistique*, pp. 57–69; É. Will, *Le monde grec et l'Orient*, II, pp. 524–6. On doctors in public employment: L. Cohn-Haft, *The Public Physicians of Ancient Greece* (Northampton, MA, 1956). The apparently paradoxical view (quoted here, pp. 166–7 at the start of ch. 6) of the Hellenistic period as the Golden Age of the Greek city, is in a stimulating contribution, "The Greek city," by C. Bradford-Welles in *Studi in onore di A. Calderini e R. Paribeni*, I (Rome, 1956), pp. 81–96.

On bilateral conventions between cities: P. Gautier, *Symbola. Les étrangers et la justice dans les cités grecques* (Nancy, 1972). On foreign judges: L. Robert in *Xenion, Festschrift für P. Zepos*, I (Athens, Freiburg, and Cologne, 1973), pp. 780ff. On *asylia*: K. J. Rigsby, *Asylia: territorial inviolability in the Hellenistic world* (Berkeley, CA, 1996). On interstate arbitration: S. A. Ager, *Interstate Arbitration in the Greek World 337–90 BC* (Berkeley, CA, 1996). On the role of kinship in relations between cities and States: O. Curty, *Les parentés légendaires des cités grecques. Catalogue raisonné. Analyse critique* (Geneva, 1995) and C. P. Jones, *Kinship Diplomacy in the Ancient World* (Cambridge, MA, 1999).

On the engraved stele honoring Hegesagoras, found on the site of Istrus (ch. 6, pp. 169–72 in the present work), see L. Robert, no. 419 of the *Bulletin Épigraphique* (*REG* 74, 1961, 187–201), a commentary on and rectification of an article by D. M. Pippidi and E. Popescu in *Dacia*, 1959. The Xanthus stele concerning Cytenium (ch. 6, pp. 209–13) was published with commentary by J. Bousquet in *REG* 101, 1988, pp. 12–53. On the (mythical) foundation by the Aetolians of Heraclea on Latmos (Delphic inscription, ch. 6, p. 211), see L. Robert in *Bulletin de Correspondance hellénistique (BCH)* 102, 1978, 477–90.

On marriage: A.-M. Vérilhac and C. Vial, *Le mariage grec du VIe siècle av. J.-C. à l'époque d'Auguste* (Athens, 1998). On the decrees honoring Épié at Thasos for her devotion to the city, see F. Salviat, *BCH* 83, 1959, 362–97. On the position of women: S. Pomeroy, *Women in Hellenistic Egypt: from Alexander to Cleopatra* (New York, 1984); on dynastic politics and royal marriages see below under section IV, Monarchy. On *euergetai*: P. Gautier, *Les cités grecques et leurs bienfaiteurs (IVe–Ier s. av. J.-C.): BCH*, Supplément 10, 1984. On the place of *euergesia* in Hellenistic citizenship ideology: P. Veyne, *Bread and Circuses: historical sociology and political pluralism* (translated from the French by B. Pearce, London, 1992), pp. 70–200.

On the foundation of cities: P. M. Fraser, *The Cities of Alexander the Great* (Oxford, 1996); G. M. Cohen, *The Seleucid Colonies* (Wiesbaden, 1978), *The Hellenistic Settlements in Europe, the Islands, and Asia Minor* (Berkeley, CA, 1995); J. D. Grainger, *The Cities of Seleukid Syria* (Oxford, 1990); R. Billows, *Kings and Colonists: aspects of Macedonian imperialism* (Leiden, 1995); see also J. Ma (p. 423). On individual cities: P. M. Fraser, *Ptolemaic Alexandria*, I–III (Oxford, 1972); G. Barker, J. Lloyd, J. Reynolds (eds), *Cyrenaica in Antiquity* (Oxford, 1985), and A. Laronde, *Cyrène et la Libye hellénistique* (Paris, 1987); D. J. Thompson, *Memphis under the Ptolemies* (Princeton, NJ,1988); C. Vial, *Délos indépendante* (*BCH*, Suppl. 12, Paris, 1985); C. Habicht, *Athens from Alexander to Antony* (translated from the German by D. Lucas Scheneder, Cambridge, MA, 1997): the same work with revisions, *Athènes hellénistique* (translated by M. and D. Knoepfler, Paris, 2000); P. Cartledge and A. Spawforth, *Hellenistic and Roman Sparta: a tale of two cities* (London, 1989). On social reforms at Sparta: B. Shimron, *Late Sparta: The Spartan Revolution, 243–146 BC* (Buffalo, NY, 1972).

On Olbia and the cities on the northern Black Sea: A. Wasowicz, *Olbia Pontique et son territoire: l'aménagement de l'espace* (Paris, 1971); S. D. Kryzhitskii et al. (in Russian, 1999), *Olbia: An Ancient City North of the Black Sea*: a bibliographical summary of works published over a span of 20 years; S. D. Kryzitskii, "The Chôra of Olbia Poetica: the main problems," *Echos du Monde Classique Classical Views*, NS 19, 2000, 167–78; on Olbia and Chersonesus: A. Sceglov (translated from the Russian by Y. and J. Garlan: no. 118 in *Annales de l'Université de Besançon*, Paris, 1992) *Polis et chôra. Cités et territoires dans le Pont.*

On the Greeks in India: A. K. Narain, *The Indo-Greeks* (2nd edition, Oxford, 1962), "The Greeks in Bactria and India," *CAH* VIII, 1989, pp. 388–421; K. Karttunen, *India and the Hellenistic World* (Helsinki, 1997); F. L. Holt, *Thundering Zeus: the making of Hellenistic Bactria* (Berkeley, CA,1998). A series of studies of the Aï Khanoum excavations appear in the "Mémoires de la Délégation archéologique française en Afghanistan," starting with P. Bernard, *Fouilles d'Aï Khanoum I* (Paris, 1973); the series reached vol. VIII in 1983: cf. P. Bernard, "Aï Khanum on the Oxus: A Hellenistic City in Central Asia," *Proceedings of the British Academy*, 53, 1967, 71–95. Events in Afghanistan have hampered progress, but vol. IX is expected to appear in 2002. For the maxims of Clearchus of Soli: L. Robert in *CRAI* 1968, pp. 416–57.

On Leagues: J. A. O. Larsen, *Greek Federal States, their Institutions and History* (Oxford, 1968); J. D. Grainger, *The League of the Aitolians and Aitolian Prosopographical Studies* (Leiden, 1999 and 2000); J. Scholten, *The Politics of Plunder: Aitolians and their Koinon in the early Hellenistic era, 279–217 BC* (Berkeley, CA,1997). On a related subject: P. De Souza, *Piracy in the Greco-Roman world* (Cambridge, 1999).

IV MONARCHY

V. Ehrenberg, *The Greek State* (see section III), provides an overall view, C. Préaux a more detailed analysis: *Le monde hellénistique* (see section I), I, pp. 181–388 (bibliography pp. 54–7): as mentioned in section II, Préaux's view of the parallel development of the Greek and native populations has been challenged. On strategy, an essential instrument of royal administration: H. Bengston, *Die Strategie in der hellenistischen Zeit* (3 vols., 2nd edn, Munich, 1964–7). On war in the Hellenistic age: Y. Garlan, *La guerre dans l'Antiquité* (Paris, 1972); M. Launey, *Recherches sur les armées hellénistiques* (2 vols., Paris, 1949–50); also, see below under war in section V.

On royal income: C. Préaux, *Le monde hellénistique*, I, pp. 358–88, the same author's *L'économie royale des Lagides* (Brussels, 1939) is fundamental. Add R. S. Bagnall, *The Administration of the Ptolemaic Possessions outside Egypt* (Leiden, 1976); R. Bogaert, *Banques et banquiers dans les cités grecques* (Leiden, 1968). On *metonomasia*: L. Robert, *Hellenica* XI–XII (Paris, 1960), pp. 155–65.

On institutions, dynastic politics, and royal marriages: R. E. Allen, *The Attalids' Kingdom: a constitutional history* (Oxford, 1983); M. B. Hatzopoulos, *Macedonian Institu-*

tions under the Kings (2 vols, Meletemeta 22, Athens, 1996); R. M. Errington, *A History of Macedonia* (translated by C. Errington: Berkeley, CA, 1990), a deconstruction of the current notion of the Macedonian *Staatsrecht* (see S. M. Burstein's Survey (above, p. 420), p. 45); J. Whitehorne, *Cleopatras* (London, 1994); D. Ogden, *Polygamy, Prostitutes and Death: the Hellenistic dynasties* (London and Swansea, 1999); E. D. Carney, *Women and Monarchy in Macedonia* (Norman, OK, 2000).

Finally, a work that has attracted deserved attention: S. Sherwin-White and A. Kuhrt, *From Samarkhand to Sardis: A New Approach to the Seleucid Empire* (Berkeley, CA,1993).

V THE ENVIRONMENT OF LIFE AND MORES

See above, section III, on society and economy. On houses fitted with towers: M. Nowicka, *Les maisons à tours dans le monde grec* (Wroclaw, 1975); C. Préaux presents a brief and lively synthesis in *The Greeks in Egypt according to the Archives of Zeno* (Brussels, 1947). R. Martin writes on Hellenistic civic and religious architecture in J. Charbonneaux, R. Martin, F. Villard in *Hellenistic Art, 330–50 BC* (translated from the French by Peter Green) (London and New York, 1973). On Alexandria: P. M. Fraser's fundamental work, *Ptolemaic Alexandria* (see above under section III). The Leonideum at Olympia (thus named after Leonidas of Naxos), built in the second half of the 4th century, is described by Pausanias, V, 15: commentary by A. Jacquemin in the 1999 Budé edition (cf. p. 278 in the present work).

The stele erected by the Psenemphaia landowners was published by A. Bernard in *Le Delta égyptien d'après les textes grecs,* vol. I (Cairo, 1970), pp. 899–913. On the dedicatory epigram by Posidippus on the Pharos of Alexandria: F. Chamoux in *Hommages à Claire Préaux* (Brussels, 1975), pp. 214–22. On the epitaph for the architect Harpalus: E. Bernand, *Inscriptions métriques de l'Égypte gréco-romaine* (Paris, 1969), pp. 128–33. On the Rhenea epigram in memory of Pharnaces and Myron of Amisos (see ch. 8, p. 313): L. Robert, *BCH*, Suppl I, *Études déliennes*, 1973, pp. 468–72. Catilius' inscription at Philae: E. Bernard, *Les inscriptions grecques et latines de Philae*, vol. II (Paris, 1969), pp. 85–91.

On the Hellenistic theater: G. M. Sifakis, *Studies in the History of Hellenistic Drama* (London, 1967); T. B. L. Webster, *Greek Theatre Production* (2nd edn, London, 1970); M. Bieber, *History of the Greek and Roman Theater* (2nd edn, Princeton, NJ, and London, 1961); D. Wiles, *Greek Theatre Performance: An Introduction* (Cambridge, 2000).

On gymnasiums: J. Delorme, *Gymnasion* (Paris, 1960), "with the corrections in *Journal of Egyptian Archaeology*, 47 (1961), p. 144" (C. G. Starr, *Past and Future*, p. 29, n. 49). On baths: R. Ginouvès, *Balaneutiké* (Paris, 1962). On fortified walls: Y. Garlan, *Recherches de poliorcétique grecque* (Paris, 1974); F. E. Winter, *Greek Fortifications* (Toronto, 1971). On Philo the Mechanic: Y. Garlan in *Historia*, 22, 1973, 16–33.

On war: see above in section IV. Add: A. M. Snodgrass, *Arms and Armour of the Greeks* (London, 1967); B. Bar-Kochva, *The Seleucid Army* (Cambridge, 1967); G. T. Griffith, *The Mercenaries of the Hellenistic world* (Cambridge, 1935); E. W. Marsden, *Greek and Roman Artillery*, I–II (Oxford, 1969–71); D .W. Engels, *Alexander the Great and the Logistics of the Macedonian Army* (Berkeley, CA, 1978); G. R. Bugh, *The Horsemen of Athens* (Princeton, NJ, 1988); W. K. Pritchett, *Greek States at War*, I–V (Berkeley, 1971–1991). On warships: J. S. Morrison (with J. F. Coates), *Greek and Roman Oared Warships* (Oxford, 1996: see *Classical Review*, 51, 2001, 103–5).

On shipping and seamanship for purposes of war or trade: J. Rougé, *La marine dans l'Antiquité* (Paris, 1975); L. Casson, *Ships and Seamanship in the Ancient World* (3rd edn, Princeton, NJ, 1992). On wine amphoras and their stamps in relief: Y. Garlan, *Amphores et timbres amphoriques grecs* (Paris, 2000).

On Hellenization and local response to it: V. Tcherikover, *Hellenistic Civilization and the Jews* (New York, 1970); M. Hadas, *Hellenistic Civilization: fusion and diffusion* has been mentioned in section I; it illustrates "the ambiguities in Jewish attitudes" (C. G. Starr, *Past and Future*, p. 29, n. 48); A. Momigliano, *Alien Wisdom: The Limits of Hellenisation* (London, 1975); A. Kuhrt and S. Sherwin-White, *Hellenism in the East: the interaction of Greek and non-Greek civilisations from Syria to central Asia after Alexander* (London, 1987); E. J. Bickerman, *The Jews in the Greek Age* (Cambridge, MA, 1988); J. L. Ferrary, *Philhellénisme et impérialisme. Aspects idéologiques de la conquête romaine du monde hellénistique* (Paris, 1988). On the Greeks in India, see section III, The City.

VI RELIGION

To the works of general interest listed in *The Civilization of Greece in the Archaic and Classical Age*, pp. 380–81, add W. Burkert, *Greek Religion* (translated from the German by J. Raffan, Cambridge, MA, 1985). Though this work deals with the pre-Hellenistic age, it helps one to appreciate, by comparison, the degree to which traditional religion was preserved in the Hellenistic period. Add G. Zuntz, *Persephone: Three Essays on Religion and Thought in Magna Graecia* (Oxford, 1971); E. E. Rice, *The Grand Procession of Ptolemy Philadelphus* (Oxford, 1983); S. Cole, *Theoi megaloi: the cult of the Great Gods at Samothrace* (Leiden, 1984); L. H. Martin, *Hellenistic Religions* (Oxford, 1987); J. D. Mikalson, *Religion in Hellenistic Athens* (Berkeley, CA, 1998). M. P. Nilsson's *Geschichte der grieschichen Religion*, II (Munich, 1961) remains the fundamental handbook on Hellenistic Greek (including religion); cf., by the same author, *The Dionysiac Mysteries of the Hellenistic and Roman Age* (Lund, 1957).

Epigraphic texts relating to various cults are conveniently gathered in F. Sokolowski, *Lois sacrées de l'Asie Mineure*; *Lois sacrées des cités grecques, Supplément; Lois sacrées des cités grecques* (Paris, 1955, 1962, 1969 respectively). These works provide the Greek texts without translation, with some commentary: the inscription on the mysteries of Andania (see ch. 9, p. 331) appears in the last volume, pp. 120–34. On Delphi: G. Roux, *Delphes, son oracle et ses dieux* (Paris, 1976). On Delos: P. Bruneau, *Recherches sur les cultes de Délos à l'époque hellénistique et à l'époque impériale* (Paris, 1970) gives a complete picture marked by precision, sensitivity, and great critical integrity. On the Monument of the Bulls (p. 326) see J. Tréheux in *CRAI* 1987, 168-84.

On the cult of Isis: V. Tran Tam Tinh, *Essai sur le culte d'Isis à Pompéi* (Paris, 1964), *Isis lactans. Corpus des monuments gréco-romains d'Isis allaitant Harpocrate* (Leiden, 1973); F. Dunand, *Le culte d'Isis dans le bassin oriental de la Méditerranée* (Leiden, 1973); Y. Grandjean, *Une nouvelle arétologie d'Isis à Maronée* (Leiden, 1975). On the cult of Serapis: J. E. Stambaugh, *Sarapis under the Early Ptolemies* (Leiden, 1972).

Funerary epigrams are collected in W. Peek, *Griechische Grab-Gedichte, griechisch und deutsch* (Berlin, 1960); cf. R. Lattimore, *Themes in Greek and Latin Epitaphs* (reprinted, Urbana, IL, 1962). The metrical epitaph on the poet Menedemus (p. 352) has a commentary in L. Robert, *Études déliennes* (see above, section V), pp. 472–8.

VII Literature and Art

In the areas of philosophy, science, and literature, cf. the general works mentioned on pp. 383–4 of *The Civilization of Greece*. Add C. J. de Vogel, *Greek Philosophy: A Collection of Texts*. III, *The Hellenistic and Roman Period* (2nd edn, Leiden, 1964 and reprints); A. A. Long and D. N. Sedley, *The Hellenistic Philosophers*, I–II (Cambridge, 1987); M. Schofield and G. Striker (eds), *The Norms of Nature. Studies in Hellenistic Ethics* (Cambridge, 1985); A. Laks and M. Schofield, eds, *Justice and Generosity: Studies in Hellenistic Political Philosophy* (Symposium Hellenisticum 6: Cambridge, 1994); J. E. Annas, *The Hellenistic Philosophy of Mind* (Berkeley, CA, 1992); K. Algra, J. Barnes, J. Mansfeld and M. Schofield, *The Cambridge History of Hellenistic Philosophy* (Cambridge, 1999). An outstanding source of information is H. Lloyd-Jones and A. E. Parsons, *Supplementum Hellenisticum* (Berlin and New York, 1983).

On science: G. E. R. Lloyd, *Greek Science after Aristotle* (London, 1973): cf. the same author in *CAH* VII.1, pp. 321–52 (bibliography pp. 591–8); on Hellenistic science: G. Aujac, *Strabon et la science de son temps* (Paris, 1966); P. Pédech, *La géographie des Grecs* (Paris, 1976). D. T. Potts, *The Arabian Gulf in Antiquity* is mentioned at the end of section II. On technology: B. Gille, *Les mécaniciens grecs. La naissance de la technologie* (Paris, 1980). M. R. Cohen and I. E. Drabkin's *Source Book in Greek Science* was mentioned under scientific texts in section II, History.

On the Library of Alexandria: A. E. Parsons, *The Alexandrian Library, Glory of the Hellenistic world* (2nd edn, Amsterdam, 1967); L. Canfora, *The Vanished Library* (Berkeley, CA, 1990). On other libraries: Burzachechi, *Ricerche epigrafiche sulle antiche biblioteche del mondo greco* (in *Rendiconti dell'Accademia dei Lincei*, 1963, pp. 75–96). On the method of fabrication of papyrus, and the part that material played in the Greek world: N. Lewis, *Papyrus in Classical Antiquity* (Oxford, 1974). On Hellenistic scholarship: R. Pfeiffer, *History of Classical Scholarship from the Beginnings to the End of the Hellenistic Age* (Oxford, 1968). On Callimachus: C. Meillier, *Callimaque et son temps* (Lille, 1979). On the epigrammatic genre: K. I. Gurtzwiller, *Poetic Garlands: Hellenistic Epigrams in context* (Berkeley, CA, 1998).

On education and culture: H. I. Marrou, *History of Education in Antiquity* (translated from the French by G. Lamb, Toronto, 1964). On *ephebeia*: C. Pélékidis, *Histoire de l'éphébie attique* (Paris, 1962).

Hellenistic Art, 330–50 bc has been mentioned above in section V, The Monarchy: it is generously illustrated and provides an abundant bibliography. Add J. J. Pollitt, *Art in the Hellenistic Age* (Cambridge, 1986), illustrating and describing in detail a large number of the works mentioned here; S. B. Downey, *Hellenistic Religious Architecture: Alexander through the Parthians* (Princeton, NJ, 1988). The Vergina finds have been published in M. Andronikos, *Vergina: The Royal Tombs* (Athens, 1984). On the famous Alexander Mosaic in the National Museum of Naples (pp. 17, 386, 389) see A. Cohen, *The Alexander Mosaic: Stories of Victory and Defeat* (Cambridge, 1997). On the relationship between literature and art: T. B. L. Webster, *Hellenistic Poetry and Art* (London, 1964).

INDEX

food commodities 189, 261, 311
food distribution 189, 190
foreigners, Greek cities 197–202
fortifications 298–302
Fortuna 338, 346; *see also* Tyché
forum 276
frescoes 350, 375
friendship 119, 126, 168
friezes 284, 379–80, 391
funerary epigrams 348
furniture 377

Galatia 160
Galatians: Antiochus I 306; Asia Minor 76;
   Attalids 242; Eumenes II 115, 126;
   expansion of territory 242; Lysimacheia
   battle 82; mercenaries 82, 303, 305–6;
   Mithridates VI Eupator 147; ornamental
   motifs 285–6; Philetaerus 77; Romans 152
Galli, eunuch priests 343
Gallic mercenaries 78, 303; *see also* Gauls
Gangaridae kingdom 28
Ganges river 28
Gaugamela, battle of 22
Gauls 64, 76, 84–5; *see also* Gallic mercenaries
Gaza, siege of 18, 50
Gedrosia 30, 75
Gela, battle of 56
Gelo the tyrant 221
genealogies 211
generals 241; *see also strategos*
generosity 246–7, 248
geographers 316–17
geography 358–9, 365
Gerrha 104
Gigantomachy 284, *286*
glossae 364
Glucon 382
gods 224, 345, 372; *see also* divinities
goodwill 168
Gordion knot 15
Goukowsky, P. *21*
Gracchus, Tiberius 127, 371
graffiti 298
grammarians 363–4
grammars 364, 368–9
Granicus, battle of 14, 32, 306
gratitude 168
Great Cameo of France 37
Great Eleusinia 225
Greco-Macedonian communities 320–2
Greco-Roman world 154
Greece *43*, 130–1; guidebooks 315;
   Macedonians 5, 9, 86, 173–4; map *118*
Greek cities 165–6; after Alexander's death
   41; alliances 41–2, 66–7, 76, 167–8;
   Anatolia 180; Antigonus Gonatas 85;
   Antigonus the One-eyed 49; autonomy
   314; barbarians 168–9; bilateral agreements
   201–2, 203–5; Black Sea 114, *143*; civic life
   182; confederacy 179, 211–12; Council
   171–2; cults 190, 226, 227, 324; cultural
   community 199; Cyprus 181; Demetrius

Poliorcetes 53; democracy 214; Diadochi
   46, 49, 50, 188, 251–2; epigraphy 166–7;
   Euxine 320; Flamininus 129; foreigners
   197–202; fortifications 298–302; gifts from
   kings 247; guidebooks 316; Hellenism
   165–7; Ionia 14; justice 202, 235; kingship
   165–6, 214–16, 232–3, 247; Lagids 210;
   Libya 56, 141, 219; military expenditure
   190–1; political organization 187;
   Polyperchon 46; on the Pontus 141–2;
   Romans 131, 141; royal domain 231–2;
   Russia 143; Seleucids 210; statues 172–3;
   Syria 153; temples 328; Tigranes 140;
   urban planning 264–8
Greek colonies 9, 97, 262
Greek language 238, 239
Gregory Nazianzus 330
guidebooks 315–16
gymnasiarchy 191, 197
gymnasium 293–5; agonistic spirit 295–6;
   Amu Darya 320, 322; Athens 74, 247,
   297, 316; Jason 298; Jews 298; Lyceum
   297; Priene 266; teaching institution 296,
   297–8, 368
Gymnasium of Diogenes 297, 302
Gymnasium of Ptolemy 297
gynaeceum 194, 387
gynaeconomoi (guardians of women's conduct)
   197

Hades 349
Hadrian 247
Haliartus, Boeotia 117
Halicarnassus 15, 179, 349–50; mausoleum
   340
Hannibal: Antiochus III 110, 236–7; Philip V
   100, 106, 114, 149; Scipio 111; Zama 307
harbors 309–10
Harpalus 19, 28, 30, 32, 41
Harpalus, architect 281
Harpocrates 342
harvest failure 32
hasidim 121
Hasmoneans 124, 298
healing cults 335–8
Hecataeus of Abdera 316
Hecataeus of Miletus 8, 27, 315
Hecate 179, 347
Heckel, W. 3
Hegesagoras 169, 170–1, 172, 293
Helenus 89
Helice 174
Heliodorus 119, 121
Heliodorus the Periegete 315
Heliopolis 189
Hellenic Congress 109
Hellenic League 58, 93, 99, 101, 107, 205
Hellenism 1–6; Argeads 239; Asia 75, 125;
   barbarians 303; Commagene 151;
   cosmopolitanism 320; Greek cities 165–7;
   Jews 121, 180; kingship 215–16, 221,
   249–51; Macedonia 239; Mithridates VI
   Eupator 146; polytheism 33, 323; Pontus

CPSIA information can be obtained at www.ICGtesting.com
Printed in the USA
LVOW03s0002131213

365078LV00003B/12/P